Spring Framework

A Step by Step Approach for Learning Spring Framework™

Prepared by

Srinivas Mudunuri

Trademarks

Cover Design & Images By: Richard Castillo (http://www.digitizedchaos.com)

Printing History:

Feb 2013   First Print

ISBN-10: 1482395983

ISBN-13: 978-1482395983

Dedicated

To

My Mother
&
Son Abhishek

Table of Contents

Preface

This document provides a step-by-step approach for developing applications using Spring framework. It is specially designed to help the individuals who want to learn Spring framework. This book can be used as a reference table guide for Spring and Java developers.

The Audience for this book is:

- Individuals who want to do more practice and read less theory.
- Individuals who want to learn the complete use of Spring framework supported technologies.
- Individuals who want to learn various view, service and database layer technologies.
- Individuals who are looking for step-by-step approach for developing applications using Spring framework.
- Individuals who want to learn REST-based and SOAP-based web services using Spring framework.
- Individuals who want to learn application development using Apache-CXF, Drools Expert and Spring-Web Service frameworks.
- Individuals who want to design and implement Spring-based technologies in their projects.
- Individuals who want to design and implement Spring-messaging technologies in their projects.
- Individuals who want to learn Spring-Web and Security supported features.
- Individuals who want to learn Spring-Core, Batch, AOP and JMX supported features.
- Architects who want to compare the technical capabilities of various Spring-based technology frameworks available in the market.

A prior knowledge of Java programming and web application development is required. It is good to have some XML knowledge but an XML novice can understand without much difficulty. It is also good to have enterprise application development knowledge but it is not mandatory. The chapters are arranged based on the increasing order of their complexity and its dependency. Inline code snippets are provided while explaining each topic and a complete working example is provided at the end of the each topic. A step-by-step approach is followed for developing code examples, so it is easy for a beginner to understand the application development.

The topics covered in this book are given below:

- Spring Core
- SpEL and Spring Resources
- Spring-Web
- Spring Data Access
- Spring Transactions
- Spring with JMX
- Spring AOP
- Spring Security
- Spring Batch
- Spring Remoting
- Spring Messaging

- Spring with REST
- Spring Web Services (SOAP-based)
- Spring with Apache-CXF
- Spring with Drools Expert
- Spring Mail
- Annotations, Namespaces and Templates.

This book contains 100 diagrams and approximately 200 Java programs used for developing the Spring framework tutorials. I ran these examples several times on my laptop before including them into this book.

Structure of the Book

This book contains 17 chapters. The structure of the book is given below.

Chapter 1 (Spring Core) covers the dependency injection, inversion of control, the use of application context files, wiring beans, XML, annotation and Java-based container configurations, the use of bean metadata and required configurations. It also covers the method injection and auto-scanning of the spring components.

Chapter 2 (SpEL and Spring Resources) covers the spring support for accessing resources, the spring support for resource bundles. It also covers the use of Spring Expression Language.

Chapter 3 (Spring-Web) covers the spring integration with Velocity, Freemarker, JSP and JSF. It also covers the complete use of spring-MVC controller framework, integrating spring with Ajax frameworks, the use of annotations for developing web applications using spring framework.

Chapter 4 (Spring Data Access) provides the details about database integration, the complete use of Spring-JDBC, Hibernate and MyBatis frameworks.

Chapter 5 (Spring Transactions) covers the Spring support for declarative and programmatic transaction management, annotation and AOP-based transaction management using Spring.

Chapter 6 (Spring with JMX) will help you to understand the spring integration with JMX infrastructure.

Chapter 7 (Spring-AOP) covers the Spring-AOP fundamentals, it provides the details about AspectJ annotations, integrating Spring with AspectJ, schema and annotation-based implementation approaches using Spring-AOP framework.

Chapter 8 (Spring Security) covers the http and form-based authentication, Spring security configurations for authentication, authorization and access-control, Spring security annotations for authorization and access-control, the use of custom expression evaluators, providing authorization and access-control for object and methods using spring security framework.

Chapter 9 (Spring Batch) covers the batch scheduler, task execution provided features, the use of annotations for batch scheduling and task execution. It also covers the spring batch integration framework.

Chapter 10 (Spring Remoting) covers the RMI, EJB, Hessian, Burlap and http-based services development using spring framework.

Chapter 11 (Spring Messaging) covers the Spring support for messaging, message-driven POJO's, Spring-provided message listener containers and its use.

Chapter 12 (Sprint with REST) provides the details about REST fundaments, REST principles, terminology, its advantages, using REST with Spring and CXF, REST URL design, client design and use of REST annotations for developing web services.

Chapter 13 (Spring Web Services) covers the web services development using Spring-WS. It provides the details about web services development using Spring framework, web services development methodologies, Web Service client and service endpoint design scenarios, details of SOAP message handlers and its use with Spring-WS and logging SOAP messages using Spring-WS.

Chapter 14 (Spring with Apache-CXF) covers the web services development using Apache-CXF. It provides the details about web services development using CXF framework, integrating CXF with Spring, web services development methodologies, JAX-WS message handler framework and logging SOAP messages using CXF.

Chapter 15 (Spring with Drools Expert) covers the business rules development using Drools rule engine, various forms of rules and Spring integration with Drools.

Chapter 16 (Spring Mail) covers the spring-provided mail API classes and their use, support for sending email messages with and without attachments.

Chapter 17 (Annotations, namespaces and Templates) covers the commonly used Spring annotations, namespaces and template classes.

Acknowledgements

This book could not have been written without the encouragements, support and contributions from many people.

The primary references to this book are various Spring framework articles, white papers, tutorials available on the web and my own experience with Spring framework. I would like to thank everyone who contributed to the Spring community which I used to gain the knowledge of Spring and Java technologies.

First of all, I would like to thank my friend Uday Thota who helped me to build my career in USA. The sad part is he is no more with us; may Almighty God grant him eternal rest and may his soul rest in peace.

I would like to thank my friend Kishori Sharan; who trained me in Oracle and Power Builder technologies. This book would not have completed without Kishori's help and guidance. He is there to help me all the time, time after time and every time.

I would like to thank Richard Castillo who designed the cover page for this book.

I would like to thank Weidong Zhang who was my lead Architect in my previous job; he gave me an opportunity to implement Spring framework for a student learning application.

I would like to thank my colleagues Darr Moore, Himanshu Mandalia, Suk Fung, Venkata Tripasuri and Vivek Sharma. Thanks to everyone who helps me at work place every day and it is a great team.

I would like thank my friends Rama Raju Saripella, Prabhakar Kandikonda, Gopi Krishnam Raju Sangaraju, Vijay Polasani, Madhava Rao, Ramesh Masa, Raghavendra Swamy, Ravi Nallakukkala, Suresh Pattipati, Neeraj Oberai, Rakesh Jaiswal, Tej Kalidindi, Rama Chitirala, Madhan Retnaswamy, Ramesh Kondru, Bala Talagadadeevi, Mallik Somepalli, Phani Narem and Phani Tangirala. I would say simple thanks are not enough for their help and support. A special thanks to Madhan who helped me during my initial days of stay in Phoenix, Arizona.

I would like to thank all my students who provided me an opportunity to teach Java and Spring framework.

A special thanks to Sylburn Peterkin and Narayan Sithemsetti who helped me to review this book in spite of their busy schedules.

I would like to thank my childhood class mates Tulasi Narayana Rao, Venkata Appa Rao, Srinivas Baratam and Siva Kumar. I have spent so much time with them and I do carry lot of childhood memories. Once in a while, I go to my home town they are always there to give a helping hand and warm reception.

Finally I want to thank my wife Radha Mudunuri, my mother, father, brothers and in-laws who provide me great support and help all the time. I would like to thank my three year old son Aayush Mudunuri and six months old daughter Akshara Mudunuri and her cousin sister Aakankhsa.

Errata

The errata for this volume may be downloaded from http://www.raju.jdojo.com.

Source Code, Questions and Comments

Please direct all your queries to mudunuri1234@yahoo.com or sraju@jdojo.com

Chapter 1. Spring-Core

The phrase "Spring Framework" has been a box office hit for several years. Enterprise applications have been using the spring framework for more than a decade. It is an open-source application framework and Inversion of Control (IOC) container for the Java platform. *Rod Johnson* invented this framework in 2002, and it was released under the Apache license in 2003.

The spring framework provides several modules for developing enterprise applications. Spring framework modules can also be integrated with other software components. The services provided by each module can be used at various layers for developing enterprise applications. Applications can take advantage of these services for developing Java-based enterprise applications. The spring framework is very popular in the Java community and has become an integral part of the application development for Java-based applications.

The various spring framework modules covered in this book are listed below.

- Spring Core: This module provides Dependency Injection (DI) and Inversion of Control (IOC) functionality.
- View Layer: Spring provides support for integration with various view layer technologies such as Velocity, Freemarker, JSP, JSTL, and JSF.
- Controller Layer: The spring HTTP-based servlet framework can be used for developing web applications and HTTP-based web services. This framework is used in the controller layer for developing HTTP-based web controllers.
- Service Layer: The spring web services framework can be used to develop web services.
- Data Layer: The spring database framework can be used to communicate with relational databases.
- Transaction Management: Spring provides a consistent transaction management framework that can be used with any data access framework.
- Aspect Oriented Programming (AOP): Spring provides an AOP framework that can be used to implement custom aspects.
- Java Management Extensions (JMX): Spring provides a high-level API to integrate your application with the JMX infrastructure.
- Spring Web Services: The spring web services framework can be used for developing Simple Object Access Protocol (SOAP)-based web services.
- Spring Remoting: Spring remoting is used for developing, integrating, and accessing remote applications. This framework simplifies the application-to-application integration.
- Spring Messaging: The spring messaging framework provides a simplified higher-level API for synchronous and asynchronous message processing.
- Spring Security: The spring security framework provides security services to Java EE-based applications. This framework provides authentication, authorization, and access-control functionality to the enterprise applications.
- Spring Mail: The spring mail framework is used to send and receive email messages. Spring provides utility classes to enable email functionality within your application.
- Spring Batch (core): The spring batch framework is used for the batch processing of large volumes of data, providing the abstractions for batch scheduling and asynchronous task execution.
- Spring Batch Integration: The spring batch integration framework can be used for application-to-application data integration. This framework provides utilities for reading, transforming, and writing large volumes of data.
- Spring Resources: Spring provides an abstraction to access the low-level resources.

- Spring Expression Language (SpEL): Spring provides powerful expression language that can be used to wire values into beans properties.
- Testing: The spring testing framework can be used for unit and integration testing.

The commonly used layers in the n-tier architecture are listed below. Spring framework modules can be used in all these layers for developing Java-based applications.

- View layer
- Controller layer
- Service layer
- Data layer

Similarly, the spring framework can be integrated with many other open-source frameworks, such as Drools to process business rules, Apache-CXF to develop web services, and so forth. This book illustrates the above-listed spring modules in greater detail. Let us start this chapter with spring-core module fundamentals.

In this chapter will discuss the following topics:

- Spring-core fundamentals and supported annotations.
- Spring dependency injection and IOC container
- The structure of spring application context files
- The use of bean metadata configurations to manage spring beans
- The XML-based approach for configuring spring beans
- The Annotation-based approach for configuring spring beans
- The Java-based approach for configuring spring beans
- Auto-detection of spring beans and component scanning

Prerequisites/Setting Up the Environment

- The complete spring distribution is available in the form of JAR files. Download the spring JAR files from the spring website. The following table has the complete list of JAR files, with the name of the JAR file representing the module name.

org.springframework.aop-RELEASE.jar	org.springframework.jdbc-RELEASE.jar
org.springframework.aspects-RELEASE.jar	org.springframework.jms-RELEASE.jar
org.springframework.asm-RELEASE.jar	org.springframework.orm-RELEASE.jar
org.springframework.beans-RELEASE.jar	org.springframework.test-RELEASE.jar
org.springframework.context-RELEASE.jar	org.springframework.transaction-RELEASE.jar
org.springframework.context.support.RELEASE.jar	org.springframework.web.servlet-RELEASE.jar
org.springframework.core-RELEASE.jar	org.springframework.web-RELEASE.jar
org.springframework.expression-RELEASE.jar	spring-ws.RELEASE-all.jar
spring-ws-core-RELEASE.jar	spring-ws-support-RELEASE.jar

Spring Core Terminology

This section explains the terminology commonly used in the core spring framework while developing spring-based Java applications. The core spring framework terminology is defined below.

Spring Beans: The application-specific Plain Old Java Objects (POJO) is called spring beans. These beans are loaded into the spring container during startup and are configured in the application context file.

Application Context XML File: This is the XML file used to configure application-specific POJO classes.

ApplicationContext Interface: This is the primary interface that represents the spring container.

Spring Container: The spring container is responsible for configuring and instantiating the configured spring beans. The spring container reads the metadata defined in the application context xml file to configure, load, and instantiate the bean classes.

Structure of the Spring Application Context Configuration File

The spring application context XML file is used to configure the application-specific POJO classes and their dependent object references. Each configured POJO class is called a spring bean During startup, the spring container loads the configured spring beans and their dependent object references into the spring container. The following points illustrate the XML file structure.

- Declare the various spring-supported namespaces. The root element name should be `<beans/>`. All other elements are child elements to the `<beans/>` element.
- The root element `<beans/>` can contain any number of `<bean/>` elements.
- Each `<bean/>` element represents a single POJO class and has a unique "id" attribute.
- The "id" attribute of the `<bean/>` element can be used to refer to the other dependent beans. The "class" attribute of the `<bean/>` element represents the fully qualified POJO class.

A simple spring application context configuration is provided below. The `Employee` and `Department` classes are configured in the spring application context as spring beans. The configured spring beans are loaded into the spring container.

```
<?xml version="1.0" encoding="UTF-8"?>
<beans xmlns="http://www.springframework.org/schema/beans"
    xmlns:xsi="http://www.w3.org/2001/XMLSchema-instance"
    xsi:schemaLocation="http://www.springframework.org/schema/beans
    http://www.springframework.org/schema/beans/spring-beans-3.0.xsd">

    <!-- Employee class configured in Spring -->
    <bean id="employee" class="com.learning.spring.core.Employee">
        ...
    </bean>

    <!-- Department class configured in Spring -->
    <bean> id="dept" class="com.learning.spring.core.Department">
        ...
```

```
        </bean>

</beans>
```

Bean Scopes

There are five possible ways for a bean scope to be configured in the spring framework. The following bean scopes are supported.

- Singleton: The spring container creates a single object instance per bean definition per single IOC container. This is the default bean scope if you don't specify the scope. An example "singleton" scope configuration is provided below.

```
<bean id="stockDataManager"
        class="com.learning.spring.core.StockDataManager"
        scope="singleton">
```

Use of `scope="singleton"` is optional. This is the default configuration if you don't specify one. The following bean configuration is equivalent to the above.

```
<bean id="stockDataManager"
        class="com.learning.spring.core.StockDataManager">
```

- Prototype: This scope is used for non-singleton beans. Every time a fresh new bean instance is created to serve the request. An example "prototype" scope configuration is provided below.

```
<bean id="stockData"
        class="com.learning.spring.core.StockData"
        scope="protoype">
```

- Request: The spring container creates a new bean instance for each HTTP request. An example "request" scope configuration is provided below.

```
<bean id="stockData"
        class="com.learning.spring.core.StockData"
        scope="request">
```

- Session: The spring container creates a new bean instance per single HTTP session. An example "session" scope configuration is provided below.

```
<bean id="stockData"
        class="com.learning.spring.core.StockData"
        scope="session">
```

- Global Session: This scope is similar to HTTP session and is used only for portlet-based web applications. An example "globalSession" scope configuration is provided below.

```
<bean id="stockData"
        class="com.learning.spring.core.StockData"
        scope="globalSession">
```

Spring IOC and Dependency Injection

Let us review the following simple scenario before illustrating the spring container features. We have three classes: A, B, and C. The structure of class A is provided below.

```
public class A {
    public void printName() {
        B b = new B();
        String name = b.getName();
        System.out.println(name);
    }
}
```

The `printName()` method of class A invokes the `getName()` method of class B. The structure of class B is provided below.

```
public class B {
    public String getName() {
        C c = new C();
        return c.getName();
    }
}
```

The `getName()` method of class B invokes the `getName()` method of class C. The structure of class C is provided below.

```
public class C {
    public String getName() {
        return " John Smith ";
    }
}
```

Use the following `Main` class to print the name.

```
public class Main {

    public static void main(String[] args) {
        A a = new A();
        a.printName();
    }
}
```

Thus far, none of this is new; this is what we do in traditional Java programming. Class A depends on class B, and class B depends on class C to obtain the final output. The relationships between A, B, and C are shown in Figure 1-1.

Figure 1-1: Classes A, B and C

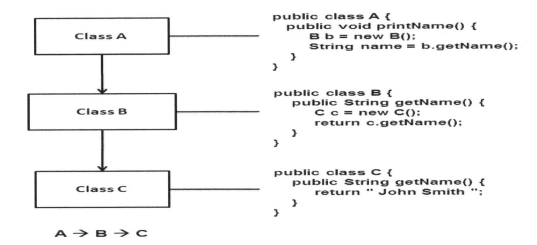

```
public class A {
   public void printName() {
      B b = new B();
      String name = b.getName();
   }
}

public class B {
   public String getName() {
      C c = new C();
      return c.getName();
   }
}

public class C {
   public String getName() {
      return " John Smith ";
   }
}
```

A → B → C

Let us review the following approach for implementing the above example. The structure of class A is provided below.

```
public class A {

    private B b;

    public void setB(B b) {
        this.b = b;
    }

    public void printName() {
        String name = b.getName();
        System.out.println("--- name ---" + name);
    }
}
```

The setter method setB() sets the instance of class B. Class A uses the instance of class B to access its methods. The printName() method invokes the getName() method of class B. The structure of class B is provided below.

```
public class B {

    public C c;

    public void setC(C c) {
        this.c = c;
    }

    public String getName() {
        return c.getName();
    }
}
```

Similarly, the setter method `setC()` sets the instance of class C. Class B uses the instance of class C to access its methods. The `getName()` method invokes the `getName()` method of class C. The structure of class C is provided below.

```
public class C {
    public String getName() {
        return " John Smith ";
    }
}
```

What will create the required bean instances of the dependent objects and set those objects using the setter methods so that you can use it in your application? The answer is the "spring container". The relationship between the Java classes, the spring container, and the resulting output is shown in Figure 1-2.

Figure 1-2: Spring container

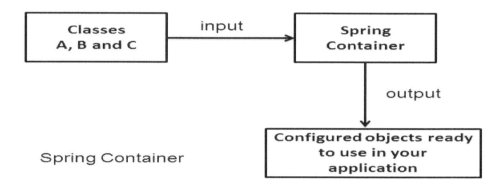

The steps required to load the configured application classes into the spring container are listed below.

- Identify the application classes to be loaded into spring container.
- Create a spring application context XML file to configure the application classes.
- Create a main class to invoke the configured class operations.

Configure classes A, B, and C in the spring application context file. The configured classes will be loaded into the spring container. The required configurations of the spring application context file are provided below; the file is named the "applicationContext.xml"

```
<?xml version="1.0" encoding="UTF-8"?>
<beans xmlns="http://www.springframework.org/schema/beans"
    xmlns:xsi="http://www.w3.org/2001/XMLSchema-instance"
    xsi:schemaLocation="http://www.springframework.org/schema/beans
    http://www.springframework.org/schema/beans/spring-beans-3.0.xsd">

    <bean id="a" class="com.learning.spring.core.A">
        <property name="b" ref="b"/>
    </bean>

    <bean id="b" class="com.learning.spring.core.B">
        <property name="c" ref="c"/>
```

```
        </bean>

        <bean id="c" class="com.learning.spring.core.C"/>

</beans>
```

Let us review each element in the above XML. In spring, the configured Java classes are called spring beans. Each bean element represents a Java class. All configured spring beans are loaded into the spring container. The following XML element configures application class C.

```
<bean id="c" class="com.learning.spring.core.C"/>
```

Similarly, the following XML element configures application class B. Class B has an object reference of the class C instance.

```
<bean id="b" class="com.learning.spring.core.B">
    <property name="c" ref="c"/>
</bean>
```

- The "name" attribute of the "property" element represents the setter-method name of class B.
- The "ref" attribute of the "property" element represents the reference to class C.

The spring container sets the class C object reference using the following setter method, so class B has an object reference of the class C instance.

```
public void setC(C c) {
    this.c = c;
}
```

Similarly, use the following XML element to load class A into the spring container. Class A has an object reference of the class B instance.

```
<bean id="a" class="com.learning.spring.core.A">
    <property name="b" ref="b"/>
</bean>
```

The spring container sets the class B object reference using the following setter method. Class A has an object reference of the class B instance.

```
public void setB(B b) {
    this.b = b;
}
```

In the traditional Java approach, the application developer creates a new class instance using the "new" operator. The spring approach configures all classes and their dependent objects in an XML file. The spring container loads and creates the object references for you to use in your application. The setter methods are used to set the object references for their dependent objects.

The following Java code instantiates the spring container and loads the objects configured in an XML file into the spring container.

```
ClassPathXmlApplicationContext context =
    new ClassPathXmlApplicationContext("applicationContext.xml");
```

The `getBean()` method of the spring application context is used to gain access to the configured bean objects. The following Java code gets the class A object reference.

```
A a = (A) context.getBean("a");
```

Listing 1-1 provides the complete Java code to print the name.

Listing 1-1: Main class.

```
// Main.java
package com.learning.spring.core;

import org.springframework.context.support.
        ClassPathXmlApplicationContext;

public class Main {

    public static void main(String[] args) {
        ClassPathXmlApplicationContext context =
            new ClassPathXmlApplicationContext
                    ("applicationContext.xml");
        A a = (A) context.getBean("a");
        a.printName();
    }
}
```

Listing 1-1 provides the following output.

```
----- name ----- John Smith
```

Let us analyze the object creation process in the preceding scenario. Class A depends on class B; class B depends on class C. The spring container creates an instance of the class C object reference, injecting (setting) that object reference using the class B setter method. Similarly, the spring container creates an instance of the class B object reference and injects that object reference using the class A setter method. The process of defining the objects, configuring the objects and their dependencies, and injecting the bean references into their dependent objects is called "dependency injection (DI)". The spring container injects those dependencies while creating the bean instances. The process of injection now happens in reverse order; C is injected into B, and B is injected into A. Hence, this process is called "inversion of control (IOC)". The spring framework implements the IOC principle. The spring-provided IOC container can be used to instantiate, configure, and assemble the collaborating bean classes.

Spring Container

The spring `ApplicationContext` is the primary interface representing the spring container. This interface provides access to the spring-managed bean classes. There are several implementations of the `ApplicationContext` interface for instantiating the spring container.

The following Java code instantiates the spring container and loads the configured spring beans into the spring container. The application context definition file is loaded from the application classpath.

```
ClassPathXmlApplicationContext context =
        new ClassPathXmlApplicationContext("applicationContext.xml");
```

The application context definition file is loaded from the file system.

```
FileSystemXmlApplicationContext context =
        new FileSystemXmlApplicationContext("applicationContext.xml");
```

The following Java code instantiates the spring container and loads the beans configured in the AppConfig class into the spring container.

```
AnnotationConfigApplicationContext context =
        new  AnnotationConfigApplicationContext(AppConfig.class);
```

The following Java code provides access to the web application context used for web-based applications.

```
WebApplicationContext webAppContext =
    WebApplicationContextUtils.getWebApplicationContext(
        request.getSession().getServletContext());
```

The getBean(...) method of the context object is used to obtain the configured spring bean reference.

Spring Dependency Injection

This section illustrates the various spring dependency injection implementation solutions. There are two ways a dependency injection can be implemented in the spring framework.

- Constructor-based dependency injection
- Setter method-based dependency injection.

Constructor-based Dependency Injection

The spring container invokes the class constructor with the required arguments. Constructor-based dependency injection is accomplished by invoking the parameterized constructor of a class and its dependencies. The four ways a constructor-based dependency injection can be implemented are listed below.

- Constructor arguments with data type
- Constructor arguments with index number
- Constructor arguments with name
- Constructor arguments with object references

CASE 1: Constructor arguments with data type

The steps required to implement this example are listed below.

1. Create an "applicationContext.xml" file to configure the spring beans.

2. Create a POJO class
3. Create a main class to test the constructor-based dependency injection.

Step 1: Create an "applicationContext.xml" file to configure the spring beans.

In this approach, the "type" attribute of the `<constructor-arg>` element is used to specify the data type of the constructor argument. An example of the "type" attribute's use is provided below.

```
<constructor-arg type="int" value="812133"/>
<constructor-arg type="java.lang.String" value="John Smith"/>
<constructor-arg type="long" value="102300"/>
```

The complete application context XML file is provided below; it is named the "applicatioContext.xml"

```
<?xml version="1.0" encoding="UTF-8"?>
<beans xmlns="http://www.springframework.org/schema/beans"
    xmlns:xsi="http://www.w3.org/2001/XMLSchema-instance"
    xsi:schemaLocation="http://www.springframework.org/schema/beans
    http://www.springframework.org/schema/beans/spring-beans-3.0.xsd">

    <bean id="employee" class="com.learning.spring.core.Employee">
        <constructor-arg type="int" value="812133"/>
        <constructor-arg type="java.lang.String" value="John Smith"/>
        <constructor-arg type="long" value="102300"/>
    </bean>

</beans>
```

Step 2: Create a POJO class.

The `Employee` class has a three argument constructor: `empId`, `adEntId`, and `salary`. The complete `Employee` class code is provided below.

```
// Employee.java
package com.learning.spring.core;

import java.beans.ConstructorProperties;

public class Employee {

    private int empId;
    private String adEntId;
    private long salary;

    public Employee(int empId, String adEntId, long salary) {
        this.empId = empId;
        this.adEntId = adEntId;
        this.salary = salary;
    }

    public void printEmpData() {
        System.out.println("Emp Id: " + empId + " AdEntId: " + adEntId
                    +" Salary: " + salary);
    }
```

```
}
```

Step 3: Create a main class to test the constructor-based dependency injection.

The following Java class loads the configured beans into the spring container. Listing 1-2 provides the complete class code.

Listing 1-2: Main class.

```
// Main.java
package com.learning.spring.core;

import org.springframework.context.support.
             ClassPathXmlApplicationContext;

public class Main {
    public static void main(String[] args) {
        ClassPathXmlApplicationContext context =
            new ClassPathXmlApplicationContext
                      ("applicationContext.xml");

        Employee employee = (Employee) context.getBean("employee");
        employee.printEmpData();
    }
}
```

Listing 1-2 provides the following output.

```
Emp Id: 812133 AdEntId: John Smith Salary: 102300
```

CASE 2: Constructor arguments with "index" number

In this approach, the "index" attribute of the `<constructor-arg>` element is used to specify the index of the constructor argument. An example of the "index" attribute's use is provided below.

```
<constructor-arg index="0" value="812133"/>
<constructor-arg index="1" value="John Smith"/>
<constructor-arg index="2" value="102300"/>
```

The complete spring bean definition is provided below. Add the following XML element to the "applicationContext.xml" file.

```
<bean id="employee1" class="com.learning.spring.core.Employee">
    <constructor-arg index="0" value="812133"/>
    <constructor-arg index="1" value="John Smith"/>
    <constructor-arg index="2" value="102300"/>
</bean>
```

Add the following Java code to the `Main.java` class to view the output.

```
Employee employee1 = (Employee) context.getBean("employee1");
employee1.printEmpData();
```

CASE 3: Constructor arguments with "name"

In this approach, the value of the "name" attribute of the `<constructor-arg>` element is used to map the constructor argument's name. An example of the "name" attribute's use is provided below.

```
<constructor-arg name="empId" value="812133"/>
<constructor-arg name="adEntId" value="John Smith"/>
<constructor-arg name="salary" value="102300"/>
```

The corresponding `Employee` constructor code is provided below. The "name" attribute value should match the following constructor argument's name.

```
public Employee(int empId, String adEntId, long salary) {
    ...
}
```

The complete spring bean definition is provided below. Add the following XML element to the "applicationContext.xml" file.

```
<bean id="employee2" class="com.learning.spring.core.Employee">
    <constructor-arg name="empId" value="812133"/>
    <constructor-arg name="adEntId" value="John Smith"/>
    <constructor-arg name="salary" value="102300"/>
</bean>
```

Add the following Java code to `Main.java` class to view the output.

```
Employee employee2 = (Employee) context.getBean("employee2");
Employee2.printEmpData();
```

CASE 4: Constructor arguments with object references

In this approach, the "ref" attribute of the `<constructor-arg>` element is used to specify the constructor argument. This approach is used to inject the complex data types as constructor arguments. An example of the "ref" attribute's use is provided below.

```
<constructor-arg ref="dept"/>
```

The complete spring bean definition is provided below. Add the following XML element to the "applicationContext.xml" file.

```
<bean id="employee3" class="com.learning.spring.core.Employee">
    <constructor-arg ref="dept"/>
</bean>

<bean id="dept" class="com.learning.spring.core.Department">
    <constructor-arg type="int" value="101"/>
    <constructor-arg type="java.lang.String"
                     value="Quality and Testing"/>
</bean>
```

The `Department` class code is provided below.

```
// Department.java
```

```
package com.learning.spring.core;

public class Department {

    public int deptId;
    public String deptName;

    public Department(int deptId, String deptName) {
        this.deptId = deptId;
        this.deptName = deptName;
    }

    // Add getter and setter methods
}
```

The `Employee` class code is provided below. The `Department` object is injected into the `Employee` class constructor.

```
// Employee.java
package com.learning.spring.core;

import java.beans.ConstructorProperties;

public class Employee {

    private Department dept;

    public Employee(Department dept) {
        this.dept = dept;
    }

    public void printDeptData() {
        System.out.println("Dept Id: " + dept.getDeptId() + " Name: " +
                dept.getDeptName());
    }
}
```

Add the following Java code to the `Main.java` class to view the output

```
Employee employee3 = (Employee) context.getBean("employee3");
employee3.printDeptData();
```

The output is provided below.

```
Dept Id: 101 Name: Quality and Testing
```

Setter Method-based Dependency Injection

The setter method-based dependency injection is accomplished by the spring container injecting the object references using the bean class setter methods. A simple example is provided below. The spring container injects the `Department` object reference into the `Employee` class using the `setDept(...)` method.

CASE 1: Injecting complex object references.

The steps required to implement this example are listed below.

1. Create POJO classes
2. Create an "applicationContext.xml" file to configure the spring beans.
3. Create a main class to test the setter method-based dependency injection.

Step 1: Create POJO classes

The following `Employee` and `Department` classes are used to demonstrate the setter-method injection.

```
public class Employee {

    public Employee() {
    }

    private Department dept;

    public void setDept(Department dept) {
        this.dept = dept;
    }
}
```

The `Department` class code is provided below.

```
public class Department {

    public int deptId;
    public String deptName;

    public Department() {
    }

    // Add getter and setter methods
}
```

Step 2: Create an "applicationContext.xml" file to configure the spring beans.

Configure the beans in an application context xml file. The complete XML configuration is provided below and is named the "applicationContext.xml"

```
<?xml version="1.0" encoding="UTF-8"?>
<beans xmlns="http://www.springframework.org/schema/beans"
    xmlns:xsi="http://www.w3.org/2001/XMLSchema-instance"
    xsi:schemaLocation="http://www.springframework.org/schema/beans
    http://www.springframework.org/schema/beans/spring-beans-3.0.xsd">

    <bean id="dept" class="com.learning.spring.core.Department">
        <constructor-arg type="int" value="101"/>
        <constructor-arg type="java.lang.String"
```

```
                    value="Quality and Testing"/>
    </bean>

    <bean id="employee4" class="com.learning.spring.core.Employee">
        <property name="dept" ref="dept"/>
    </bean>

</beans>
```

Step 3: Create a main class to test the setter method-based dependency injection.

The following Java class loads the configured beans into the spring container. Listing 1-3 provides the complete class code.

Listing 1-3: Main class.

```
// Main.java
package com.learning.spring.core;

import org.springframework.context.support.
            ClassPathXmlApplicationContext;

public class Main {

    public static void main(String[] args) {
        ClassPathXmlApplicationContext context =
            new ClassPathXmlApplicationContext
                ("applicationContext.xml");

        Employee employee4 = (Employee) context.getBean("employee4");
        employee4.printDeptData();
    }
}
```

Listing 1-3 produces the following output.

```
Dept Id: 101 Name: Quality and Testing
```

CASE 2: Injecting simple data types

The following example sets the values of "empId," "adEntId," and "salary" for the `Employee` object.

```
<bean id="employee5" class="com.learning.spring.core.Employee">
    <property name="empId" value = "812133"/>
    <property name="adEntId" value = "John Smith"/>
    <property name="salary" value = "102300"/>
</bean>
```

CASE 3: Injecting Java collection objects.

The following example injects Java collection objects such as `List`, `Set`, `Map`, and `Properties`. Here, reuse the previously created application context XML file. Add the following bean definition to the application context XML file.

```xml
<bean id="rolesAndPermissions" class="com.learning.spring.core.Employee">

    <property name="roles">
        <props>
            <prop key="ROLE_ADMIN">admin</prop>
            <prop key="ROLE_USER">user</prop>
            <prop key="ROLE_SU">su</prop>
        </props>
    </property>

    <property name="permissionsList">
        <list>
            <value>READ</value>
            <value>WRITE</value>
            <value>DELETE</value>
        </list>
    </property>

    <property name="rolesMap">
        <map>
            <entry key="ROLE_ADMIN" value="admin"/>
            <entry key="ROLE_USER" value="user"/>
        </map>
    </property>

    <property name="rolesSet">
        <set>
            <value>READ</value>
            <value>WRITE</value>
            <value>DELETE</value>
        </set>
    </property>

</bean>
```

The `Employee` bean class code is provided below.

```java
public class Employee {

    private Properties roles;
    private List permissionsList;
    private Map rolesMap;
    private Set rolesSet;

    // Add getter and setter methods.
}
```

Use the following main method to test the injected bean collections. Listing 1-4 provides the complete class code.

Listing 1-4: Main class.

```java
// Main.java
package com.learning.spring.core;

import org.springframework.context.support.
```

```
                    ClassPathXmlApplicationContext;

public static void main(String[] args) {
    ClassPathXmlApplicationContext context =
        new ClassPathXmlApplicationContext("applicationContext.xml");
    Employee employee5 = (Employee)
            context.getBean("rolesAndPermissions");

    System.out.println("Props " + employee5.getRoles());
    System.out.println("List " + employee5.getPermissionsList());
    System.out.println("Map " + employee5.getRolesMap());
    System.out.println("Set " + employee5.getRolesSet());
}
```

Lookup Method Injection

By default, the spring configured beans are singletons. In spring, a singleton bean typically uses another singleton bean, or a non-singleton bean uses another non-singleton bean, by defining one bean as a setter-property of another. What happens if the two bean scopes are different? When a singleton bean has to use the non-singleton bean (scope=prototype), the container will not provide the singleton bean with a new instance of the prototype bean each time it is invoked. The technique used to solve this scenario is called Method Injection.

The steps required to implement this example are listed below.

1. Create POJO classes
2. Create an "applicationContext.xml" file to configure the spring beans.
3. Create a main class to test the lookup method injection.

Example Scenario: There are two classes: StockDataManager and StockData. The StockDataManager class is a singleton class, and the StockData is a non-singleton class. The StockDataManager class depends on the StockData class, requiring a new instance of the StockData class every time a StockDataManager method is invoked.

Step 1: Create POJO classes

The complete StockData class code is provided below. This class is configured in spring as non-singleton bean.

```
// StockData.java
package com.learning.spring.core;

public class StockData {

    private String symbol;

    public String getLatestData() {
        System.out.println(symbol);
        if(symbol != null && symbol.equals("AAPL")) {
            return "723.55";
        }
        return "999.99";
    }
```

```
        // Add getter and setter methods
}
```

The complete `StockDataManager` class code is provided below. This class is configured in spring as a singleton bean.

```
// StockDataManager.java
package com.learning.spring.core;

public abstract class StockDataManager {

    public abstract StockData getStockData();

    public void printStockData() {
        StockData stockData = getStockData();
        System.out.println(stockData.getLatestData());
    }
}
```

Step 2: Create an "applicationContext.xml" file to configure the spring beans.

The non-singleton bean configuration is provided below.

```
<bean id="stockData" class="com.learning.spring.core.StockData"
    scope="prototype">
    <property name="symbol" value="XXXX"/>
</bean>
```

The singleton bean configuration is provided below.

```
<bean id="stockDataManager"
    class="com.learning.spring.core.StockDataManager"
    scope="singleton">
    <lookup-method name="getStockData" bean="stockData"/>
</bean>
```

The following `<lookup-method/>` element refers to the non-singleton bean.

```
<lookup-method name="getStockData" bean="stockData"/>
```

The complete application context bean configurations are provided below.

```
<?xml version="1.0" encoding="UTF-8"?>
<beans xmlns="http://www.springframework.org/schema/beans"
    xmlns:xsi="http://www.w3.org/2001/XMLSchema-instance"
    xsi:schemaLocation="http://www.springframework.org/schema/beans
    http://www.springframework.org/schema/beans/spring-beans-3.0.xsd">

    <bean id="stockData" class="com.learning.spring.core.StockData"
        scope="prototype">
        <property name="symbol" value="XXXX"/>
    </bean>

    <bean id="stockDataManager"
```

```
            class="com.learning.spring.core.StockDataManager"
            scope="singleton">
            <lookup-method name="getStockData" bean="stockData"/>
    </bean>

</beans>
```

NOTE: Add the "cglib-nodep.jar" file to your application classpath to run this example.

Step 3: Create a main class to test the lookup method injection.

Run the following `Main` class to view the output on the console. Listing 1-5 provides the complete class code.

Listing 1-5: Main class.

```
// Main.java
package com.learning.spring.core;

import org.springframework.context.support.
                    ClassPathXmlApplicationContext;
public class Main {

    public static void main(String[] args) {
        ClassPathXmlApplicationContext context =
            new ClassPathXmlApplicationContext
                    ("applicationContext.xml");

        StockDataManager dataManager = (StockDataManager)
                context.getBean("stockDataManager");
        dataManager.printStockData();

        StockData stockData = (StockData) context.getBean("stockData");
        stockData.setSymbol("AAPL");
        dataManager = (StockDataManager)
                context.getBean("stockDataManager");
        dataManager.printStockData();
    }
}
```

Note: Update the `StockData` bean scope to "singleton" and view the result.

Miscellaneous Spring Bean Configurations

How to Configure the init() and cleanup() Methods

The "init-method" attribute of the `<bean/>` element can be used for initialization-related activities. Similarly, the "destroy-method" attribute can be used to perform cleanup-related activities. This

---

destroy method is invoked just before the bean is removing from the spring application context. Add the following bean element to the "applicationContext.xml" file.

The steps required to implement this example are listed below.

1. Create POJO classes
2. Create an "applicationContext.xml" file to configure the spring beans.
3. Create a main class to test the `init()` and `cleanup()` life cycle methods.

Step 1: Create POJO classes

The `Employee` class code is provided below. The spring container manages the bean life cycle; the `init()` and `cleanupData()` methods are invoked automatically by the spring container. These methods can be used to perform initialization and clean-up activities.

```
public class Employee {

    private int empId;
    private String adEntId;
    private long salary

    // ... Add getter and setter methods

    public void init() {
        System.out.println("--- init called ---");
        this.empId = 823144;
        this.adEntId = "jsmith";
        this.salary = 10978L;
    }

    public void cleanupData() {
        System.out.println("--- cleanup called ---");
        this.empId = 0;
        this.adEntId = "";
        this.salary = 0L;
    }

    public void printEmpData() {
        System.out.println("Emp Id: " + empId + " AdEntId: " + adEntId
            + " Salary: " + salary);
    }
}
```

Step 2: Create an "applicationContext.xml" file to configure the spring beans.

```
<bean id="initAndCleanup" class="com.learning.spring.core.Employee"
    init-method="init"
    destroy-method="cleanupData">
</bean>
```

Step 3: Create a main class to test the `init()` and `cleanup()` life cycle methods.

Use the following code to invoke the bean destroy method. The `registerShutdownHook()` method invokes the destroy method of the configured spring beans.

```
context.registerShutdownHook();
```

Alternatively, use the following code to invoke the bean destroy method.

```
context.close();
```

Run the below provided `Main` class to view the output on the console. Listing 1-6 provides the complete class code.

Listing 1-6: Main class.

```java
// Main.java
package com.learning.spring.core;

import org.springframework.context.support.
                    ClassPathXmlApplicationContext;
public class Main {

    public static void main(String[] args) {
        ClassPathXmlApplicationContext context =
        new ClassPathXmlApplicationContext("applicationContext.xml");

        Employee employee6 = (Employee)
                    context.getBean("initAndCleanup");
        employee6.printEmpData();
        context.registerShutdownHook();
    }
}
```

Bean Inheritance

This section illustrates the spring support for bean inheritance. The steps required to implement this example are listed below.

1. Create POJO classes.
2. Create an "applicationContext.xml" file to configure the spring beans.
3. Create a main class to test the bean inheritance.

Step 1: Create POJO classes.

This section demonstrates the spring support for configuring parent and child object definitions. The following `DataManager` class is an abstract class. The parent class code is provided below.

```java
// DataManager.java
package com.learning.spring.core;

import java.util.List;

public abstract class DataManager {

    private String country;

    // Add getter and setter methods
```

```
        public abstract List<String> getData();
}
```

The following `LocalDataManager` class overrides the `getData()` method. The child class code is provided below.

```java
// LocalDataManager.java
package com.learning.spring.core;

import java.util.*;

public class LocalDataManager extends DataManager {

    private String language;

    // Add getter and setter methods.

    public List<String> getData() {
        List<String> dataList = new ArrayList<String>();
        dataList.add("King Kong");
        dataList.add("Spider Man");
        return dataList;
    }
}
```

Step 2: Create an "applicationContext.xml" file to configure the spring beans.

Add the following bean elements to the "applicationContext.xml" file. The "parent" attribute of the child class bean definition refers to the parent class bean definition.

```xml
<bean id="dataManager" class="com.learning.spring.core.DataManager"
    abstract="true">
    <property name="country" value="USA"/>
</bean>

<bean id="localDataManager"
    class="com.learning.spring.core.LocalDataManager"
    parent="dataManager">
    <property name="language" value="English"/>
</bean>
```

Step 3: Create a main class to test the bean inheritance.

Run the following `Main` class to view the output on the console. Listing 1-7 provides the complete class code.

Listing 1-7: Main class.

```java
// Main.java
package com.learning.spring.core;

import org.springframework.context.support.
                    ClassPathXmlApplicationContext;
```

```
public class Main {

    public static void main(String[] args) {
        ClassPathXmlApplicationContext context =
        new ClassPathXmlApplicationContext("applicationContext.xml");

        LocalDataManager localDataManager = (LocalDataManager)
                        context.getBean("localDataManager");
        System.out.println(localDataManager.getData());
        System.out.println(localDataManager.getCountry());
        System.out.println(localDataManager.getLanguage());
    }
}
```

The output contains list data, the "country" value from the parent bean definition, and "language" from the child bean definition. The output is given below.

```
[King Kong, Spider Man]
USA
English
```

Object Creating Using Factory Method Pattern

This section demonstrates the spring support for creating object instances using the factory method pattern. A simple factory method pattern is shown in Figure 1-3.

Figure 1-3: Factory method pattern.

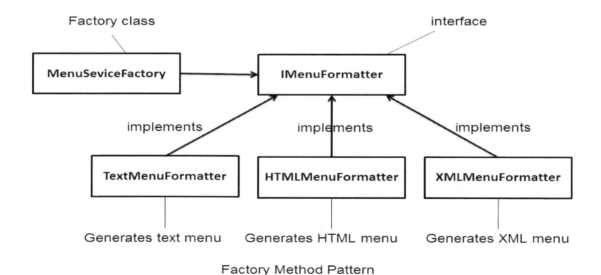

Factory Method Pattern

The IMenuFormatter interface has generateMenu(...) method. This method generates a menu in various formats; they are Text, HTML and XML. The implemented classes have a different method implementation for generating Text, HTML and XML menus.

The steps required to implement this example are listed below.

1. Create POJO classes
2. Create an "applicationContext.xml" file to configure the spring beans.
3. Create a main class to test the factory method.

Step 1: Create POJO classes

The interface definition is provided below.

```java
// IMenuFormatter.java
package com.learning.spring.core.factory;

public interface IMenuFormatter {
    public void generateMenu(String category) throws Exception;
}
```

The following `TextMenuFormatter` class implements the `IMenuFormatter` interface.

```java
public class TextMenuFormatter implements IMenuFormatter {
    ...
}
```

The complete `TextMenuFormatter` class code is provided below.

```java
// TextMenuFormatter.java
package com.learning.spring.core.factory;

import java.util.*;

/**
 * This class is used for Text menu generation.
 */
public class TextMenuFormatter implements IMenuFormatter {

    public void generateMenu(String category) throws Exception {
        List<FoodItemDVO> menuCategoryList = new
                         ArrayList<FoodItemDVO>();
        FoodItemDVO foodItemDVO = new FoodItemDVO();
        foodItemDVO.setName("Fish and Chips");
        foodItemDVO.setDescription("A smaller portion of our Dinner
                version");
        foodItemDVO.setPrice("10.99");
        foodItemDVO.setCategory(category);
        foodItemDVO.setCountry("USA");

        menuCategoryList.add(foodItemDVO);
        writeToTextFile(menuCategoryList);
    }

    public void writeToTextFile(List<FoodItemDVO> menuCategoryList)
        throws Exception {
        System.out.println("--- Generates text menu ---");

        // ... implement your logic here
```

```
        }
}
```

The following `HTMLMenuFormatter` class implements the `IMenuFormatter` interface.

```java
public class HTMLMenuFormatter implements IMenuFormatter {
    ...
}
```

The complete `HTMLMenuFormatter` class code is provided below.

```java
// HTMLMenuFormatter.java
package com.learning.spring.core.factory;

import java.util.*;

/**
 * This class is used for HTML menu generation
 */
public class HTMLMenuFormatter implements IMenuFormatter {

    public void generateMenu(String category) throws Exception {
        List<FoodItemDVO> menuCategoryList = new
                    ArrayList<FoodItemDVO>();

        // ... Get data from data source

        createHTMLFile(menuCategoryList);
    }

    private void createHTMLFile(List<FoodItemDVO> menuCategoryList)
            throws Exception {
        System.out.println("--- Generates HTML menu ---");

        // ... implement your logic here
    }
}
```

The following `XMLMenuFormatter` class implements the `IMenuFormatter` interface.

```java
public class XMLMenuFormatter implements IMenuFormatter {
    ...
}
```

The complete `XMLMenuFormatter` class code is provided below.

```java
// XMLMenuFormatter.java
package com.learning.spring.core.factory;

import java.util.*;

/**
 * This class is used for XML menu generation.
 */
public class XMLMenuFormatter implements IMenuFormatter {
```

```
public void generateMenu(String category) throws Exception {
    List<FoodItemDVO> menuCategoryList = new
                ArrayList<FoodItemDVO>();

    // ... Get data from data source

    createXMLFile(menuCategoryList);
}

private void createXMLFile(List<FoodItemDVO> menuCategoryList)
        throws Exception {
    System.out.println("--- Generates XML menu ---");

    // ... implement your logic here
    }
}
```

The complete `MenuSeviceFactory` **class code is provided below. This factory method creates an object instance for a received "menuType." Spring sets the value of "menuType" in an application context file during the context initialization.**

```
// MenuSeviceFactory.java
package com.learning.spring.core.factory;

public class MenuSeviceFactory {

    private String menuType;

    // Private constructor
    private MenuSeviceFactory() {
    }

    // Factory method
    public IMenuFormatter createServiceInstance() {
        IMenuFormatter menuFormatter = null;
        if ("XML".equalsIgnoreCase(menuType)) {
            menuFormatter = new XMLMenuFormatter();
        } else if ("HTML".equalsIgnoreCase(menuType)) {
            menuFormatter = new HTMLMenuFormatter();
        } else if ("TEXT".equalsIgnoreCase(menuType)) {
            menuFormatter = new TextMenuFormatter();
        }
        return menuFormatter;
    }

    public void setMenuType(String menuType) {
        this.menuType = menuType;
    }
}
```

Step 2: Create an "applicationContext.xml" file to configure the spring beans.

The "factory-bean" attribute of the bean element can be used to configure the factory class. The "factory-method" attribute represents the factory method. The spring application context configurations are provided below. Add the following XML to the "applicationContext.xml" file.

```xml
<bean id="menuSeviceFactory"
    class="com.learning.spring.core.factory.MenuSeviceFactory">
    <property name="menuType" value="HTML" />
</bean>

<bean id="menuFormatterService"
    factory-bean="menuSeviceFactory"
    factory-method="createServiceInstance"/>
```

Step 3: Create a main class to test the factory method.

Run the following `Main` class to view the output on the console. Listing 1-8 provides the complete class code.

Listing 1-8: Main class.

```java
// Main.java
package com.learning.spring.core;

import org.springframework.context.support.
                    ClassPathXmlApplicationContext;
public class Main {

    public static void main(String[] args) {
        ClassPathXmlApplicationContext context =
        new ClassPathXmlApplicationContext("applicationContext.xml");

        try {
            IMenuFormatter menuFormatter = (IMenuFormatter)
                    context.getBean("menuFormatterService");
            menuFormatter.generateMenu("Lunch");
        } catch (Exception ex) {
            ex.printStackTrace();
        }
    }
}
```

Bean Dependency Configuration Using Depends-on

The "depends-on" attribute of a bean element can be used to initialize all dependent beans. Let us review a simple example. There are three classes: BeanOne, BeanTwo, and BeanThree. BeanThree depends on BeanOne and BeanTwo. The BeanOne and BeanTwo classes have to be initialized before the BeanThree class can be initialized.

The steps required to implement this example are listed below.

1. Create POJO classes
2. Create an "applicationContext.xml" file to configure the spring beans.
3. Create a main class to test the depends-on feature.

Step 1: Create POJO classes

The complete `BeanThree` class code is provided below.

```java
// BeanThree.java
package com.learning.spring.core;

public class BeanThree {

    private String beanName;

    // Add getter and setter methods

    private void init() {
        System.out.println("--- BeanThree Initialized ---" + beanName);
    }

    public void printData() {
        System.out.println("--- beanName ---" + beanName);
    }
}
```

Step 2: Create an "applicationContext.xml" file to configure the spring beans

Similarly, create the `BeanTwo` and `BeanOne` classes. The "depends-on" attribute of the `BeanThree` element initializes the dependent classes before initializing this class. The spring application context configurations are provided below. Add the following XML to the "applicationContext.xml" file.

```xml
<bean id="beanOne" class="com.learning.spring.core.BeanOne"
    init-method="init">
    <property name="beanName" value="BeanOne"/>
</bean>

<bean id="beanTwo" class="com.learning.spring.core.BeanTwo"
    init-method="init">
    <property name="beanName" value="BeanTwo"/>
</bean>

<bean id="beanThree" class="com.learning.spring.core.BeanThree"
    depends-on="beanOne, beanTwo" init-method="init">
    <property name="beanName" value="BeanThree"/>
</bean>
```

Step 3: Create a main class to test the depends-on feature.

Listing 1-9 provides the complete class code. Run the following `Main` class to view the output on the console.

Listing 1-9: Main class.

```java
// Main.java
package com.learning.spring.core;

import org.springframework.context.support.
                    ClassPathXmlApplicationContext;
```

```
public class Main {

    public static void main(String[] args) {
        ClassPathXmlApplicationContext context =
        new ClassPathXmlApplicationContext("applicationContext.xml");

        BeanThree beanThree = (BeanThree) context.getBean("beanThree");
        beanThree.printData();
    }
}
```

The output is provided below.

```
--- BeanOne Initialized ---BeanOne
--- BeanTwo Initialized ---BeanTwo
--- BeanThree Initialized ---BeanThree
---- beanName BeanThree
```

Configuring Lazy-Initialized Beans

By default, all configured spring beans are pre-instantiated and loaded into the spring container. The "lazy-init" attribute of a bean element can be used to prevent the pre-instantiation of a singleton bean during start-up. This option enables the beans to be created when it is requested.

The steps required to implement this example are listed below.

1. Create POJO classes
2. Create an "applicationContext.xml" file to configure the spring beans.
3. Create a main class to test the "lazy-init" feature.

Step 1: Create POJO classes

Here, reuse the classes created in preceding example.

Step 2: Create an "applicationContext.xml" file to configure the spring beans.

The spring application context configurations are provided below. Add the following XML to the "applicationContext.xml" file.

```
<bean id="beanThreeLazy" class="com.learning.spring.core.BeanThree"
    init-method="init" lazy-init="true">
    <property name="beanName" value="BeanThree"/>
</bean>

<bean name="beanTwoNotLazy" class="com.learning.spring.core.BeanTwo"
    init-method="init">
    <property name="beanName" value="BeanTwo"/>
</bean>
```

Step 3: Create a main class to test the "lazy-init" feature.

Listing 1-10 provides the complete class code. Run the following `Main` class to view the output on the console.

Listing 1-10: Main class.

```
// Main.java
package com.learning.spring.core;

import org.springframework.context.support.
                        ClassPathXmlApplicationContext;
// Main.java
package com.learning.spring.core;

public class Main {

    public static void main(String[] args) {
        ClassPathXmlApplicationContext context =
        new ClassPathXmlApplicationContext("applicationContext.xml");
    }
}
```

Only `BeanTwo` is initialized. The output is provided below.

```
--- BeanTwo Initialized ---BeanTwo
```

Spring Core Annotations

This section illustrates the use of spring-core annotations.

- @Required
- @Autowired
- @Qualifier
- @Component

@Required

This annotation is used with the bean property setter methods. It forces you to inject the object references using setter methods during the configuration time to avoid the runtime exceptions. The following example demonstrates the use of the `@Required` annotation. In this example, the `@Required` annotation is applied to the setter method of a bean class.

```
public class StockQuoteService {

    private StockQuoteDAO stockQuoteDAO;

    @Required
    public void setStockQuoteDAO(StockQuoteDAO stockQuoteDAO) {
        this.stockQuoteDAO = stockQuoteDAO;
    }
}
```

The corresponding application context XML configuration is provided below.

```
<bean id="stockQuoteService"
    class="com.learning.spring.core.StockQuoteService">
    <property name="stockQuoteDAO" ref="stockQuoteDAO" />
</bean>

<bean id="stockQuoteDAO" class="com.learning.spring.core.StockQuoteDAO"/>
```

@Autowired

This annotation can be applied to setter methods, constructors, and fields of a bean class to inject the object references. The following example demonstrates the use of the `@Autowired` annotation. In this example, the `@Autowired` annotation is applied to the setter method of a bean class. The spring container creates a `StockQuoteDAO` object reference and injects this object into `StockQuoteService` using the setter method.

```
public class StockQuoteService {

    @Autowired
    private StockQuoteDAO stockQuoteDAO;

    @Required
    public void setStockQuoteDAO(StockQuoteDAO stockQuoteDAO) {
        this.stockQuoteDAO = stockQuoteDAO;
    }
}
```

@Qualifier

This annotation can be applied to classes, methods, fields, constructors, and parameters of a bean class to allow for greater control in using the correct reference types. The following example demonstrates the use of the `@Qualifier` annotation. In this example, the `@Qualifier` annotation is applied to the member of a class.

```
public class StockQuoteService {

    @Autowired
    @Qualifier("stockDAO")
    private StockQuoteDAO stockQuoteDAO;

    public void setStockQuoteDAO(StockQuoteDAO stockQuoteDAO) {
        this.stockQuoteDAO = stockQuoteDAO;
    }
}
```

The corresponding `StockQuoteDAO` class definition is provided below.

```
@Qualifier("stockDAO")
public class StockQuoteDAO {
    ...
}
```

@Component

This annotation applies to classes and indicates that the annotated class is a component. Spring provides specialized component-annotated classes such as `@Controller`, `@Service`, `@Repository`, and `@Endpoint`. These component-annotated classes are eligible for component scanning using the spring-provided `<context:component-scan/>` XML tag. The component-annotated classes can be auto-detected using annotation-based configurations. The following example demonstrates the use of the `@Component` annotation.

```
@Component
public class StockQuoteService {
    ...
}
```

Similarly, the following example demonstrates the use of the `@Controller` annotation for a web controller class.

```
@Controller
public class LoginController {

    @RequestMapping(value = "/demo/login.action",
                    method = RequestMethod.POST)
    public String show(HttpServletRequest request, ModelMap model) {
        ...
    }
}
```

JSR-250 Annotations with Spring Beans

JSR 250: The annotations defined in this JSR (provided below) are used for resource injection and life cycle management.

- javax.annotation.PostConstruct
- javax.annotation.PreDestroy
- javax.annotation.Resource

@javax.annotation.PostConstruct

This annotation is used at the method level to perform the required initialization. The method annotated using the `@PostConstruct` is called after the default constructor. The `@PostConstruct` annotation's definition is given below.

```
public @interface PostConstruct {
}
```

The following example demonstrates the `@PostConstruct` annotation's use. In this example, the `@PostConstruct` annotation is applied to the "init()" method of an `EmployeeServiceImpl` class to perform the required initialization.

```java
public class EmployeeServiceImpl {

    public EmployeeServiceImpl() {
        System.out.println("--- Constructor called ---");
    }

    @PostConstruct
    private void init() {
        System.out.println("--- Perform required initialization ---");
    }
}
```

@javax.annotation.PreDestroy

This annotation is used at method level to perform cleanup activities such as releasing the resources the process is holding. The method annotated with @PreDestroy is a callback method managed by the container. The definition of the @PreDestroy annotation is given below.

```java
public @interface PreDestroy {
}
```

The following example demonstrates the @PreDestroy annotation's use. In this example, the @PreDestroy annotation is applied to the "doCleanUp()" method of a bean class to perform the required cleanup activity.

```java
public class EmployeeServiceImpl {

    @PreDestroy
    private void doCleanUp() {
        System.out.println("--- Perform clean-up after you are done
        with it ---");
    }
}
```

The following example demonstrates the use of the @PostConstruct and @PreDestroy annotations. The steps required to implement this example are listed below.

1.   Create POJO classes
2.   Create an "applicationContext.xml" file to configure the spring beans.
3.   Create a main class to test the JSR 250 annotations.

Step 1: Create POJO classes

The complete EmployeeServiceImpl class code is provided below.

```java
// EmployeeServiceImpl.java
package com.learning.spring.core.java;

import javax.annotation.PostConstruct;
import javax.annotation.PreDestroy;

public class EmployeeServiceImpl {
```

```
    public EmployeeServiceImpl() {
        System.out.println("--- Constructor called ---");
    }

    @PostConstruct
    private void init() {
        System.out.println("--- Perform required initialization ---");
    }

    @PreDestroy
    private void doCleanUp() {
        System.out.println("--- Perform clean-up after you are done
        with it ---");
    }
}
```

Step 2: Create an "applicationContext.xml" file to configure the spring beans

Configure this bean with the spring application context. The complete XML configuration is provided below and is named the "applicationContext.xml."

```
<?xml version="1.0" encoding="UTF-8"?>
<beans xmlns="http://www.springframework.org/schema/beans"
    xmlns:xsi="http://www.w3.org/2001/XMLSchema-instance"
    xmlns:context="http://www.springframework.org/schema/context"
    xsi:schemaLocation="http://www.springframework.org/schema/beans
    http://www.springframework.org/schema/beans/spring-beans-3.0.xsd
    http://www.springframework.org/schema/context
    http://www.springframework.org/schema/context/
            spring-context-3.0.xsd">

    <context:annotation-config/>

    <bean id="employeeService"
        class="com.learning.spring.core.java.EmployeeServiceImpl"/>
</beans>
```

Step 3: Create a main class to test the JSR-250 annotations.

Listing 1-11 provides the complete class code. Run the following Main class to view the output on the console.

Listing 1-11: Main class.

```
// Main.java
package com.learning.spring.core.java;

import org.springframework.context.support.
        ClassPathXmlApplicationContext;

public class Main {

    public static void main(String[] args) {
        ClassPathXmlApplicationContext context =
            new ClassPathXmlApplicationContext
```

```
                   ("applicationContext.xml");

        EmployeeServiceImpl employeeServiceImpl = (EmployeeServiceImpl)
              context.getBean("employeeService");
        context.registerShutdownHook();
    }
}
```

The output is provided below.

```
--- Constructor called ---
--- Perform required initialization ---
--- Perform clean-up after you are done with it ---
```

@javax.annotation.Resource

This annotation can be applied to setter methods or fields of a spring-managed bean class. This is an annotation commonly used in Java-EE to obtain the information related to the web services context, message context, JNDI names, user principle, and role. This annotation can be used with spring-managed beans. The following example demonstrates the use of the `@Resource` annotation. In this example, the `@Resource` annotation is applied to the setter method of a spring managed bean.

The steps required to implement this example are listed below.

1. Create POJO classes.
2. Create an "applicationContext.xml" file to configure the spring beans.
3. Create a main class to test the `@Resource` annotation.

Step 1: Create POJO classes.

Here, reuse the `EmployeeServiceImpl` created in the previous example. Add the `@Resource`-annotated setter method to the `EmployeeServiceImpl` class. The spring-managed `EmployeeDAO` bean is injected using the `@Resource` annotation.

```java
// EmployeeServiceImpl.java
package com.learning.spring.core.java;

import javax.annotation.Resource;

public class EmployeeServiceImpl {

    private EmployeeDAO employeeDAO;

    @Resource
    public void setEmployeeDAO(EmployeeDAO employeeDAO) {
        this.employeeDAO = employeeDAO;
    }

    public void printData() {
        System.out.println(employeeDAO.getData());
    }
}
```

The following `EmployeeDAO` class is injected into the `EmployeeServiceImpl` class.

```java
// EmployeeDAO.java
package com.learning.spring.core.java;

import java.util.*;

public class EmployeeDAO {

    public Map<String, String> getData() {
        Map<String, String> dataMap = new HashMap<String, String>();
        dataMap.put("872323", "John Smith");
        dataMap.put("223444", "John Sims");
        return dataMap;
    }
}
```

Step 2: Create an "applicationContext.xml" file to configure the spring beans.

Configure this bean with the spring application context. The complete XML configuration is provided below and is named the "applicationContext.xml"

```xml
<context:annotation-config/>

<bean id="employeeService"
    class="com.learning.spring.core.java.EmployeeServiceImpl"/>

<bean id="employeeDAO"
    class="com.learning.spring.core.java.EmployeeDAO"/>
```

Step 3: Create a main class to test the `@Resource` annotation

Listing 1-12 provides the complete class code. Run the following `Main` class to view the output on the console.

Listing 1-12: Main class.

```java
// Main.java
package com.learning.spring.core.java;

import org.springframework.context.support.
        ClassPathXmlApplicationContext;

public class Main {

    public static void main(String[] args) {
        ClassPathXmlApplicationContext context =
            new ClassPathXmlApplicationContext
                ("applicationContext.xml");

        EmployeeServiceImpl employeeServiceImpl = (EmployeeServiceImpl)
                context.getBean("employeeService");
        employeeServiceImpl.printData();
    }
}
```

Java-based Annotations for Spring Container Configuration

The primary Java-based annotations used for spring container configuration are listed below. This section illustrates the use of these annotations.

- @Configuration
- @Bean

@Bean

This annotation is used at the method level. The @Bean-annotated method represents a spring-managed bean that can be used for injection. An example of this annotation's use is provided below. The @Bean-annotated method is equivalent to the <bean/> element in XML-based configuration.

```
public class ApplicationConfig {

    @Bean
    public StockQuoteDAO stockQuoteDAO() {
        return new StockQuoteDAO();
    }
}
```

@Configuration

This annotation is used at the class level. The @Configuration-annotated class can be used as a container to configure other spring-managed bean classes. An example of this annotation's use is provided below. The @Configuration-annotated class is equivalent to the <beans/> element in XML-based configuration.

```
@Configuration
public class ApplicationConfig {

    @Bean
    public StockQuoteDAO stockQuoteDAO() {
        return new StockQuoteDAO();
    }

    @Bean
    public StockQuoteService stockQuoteService() {
        return new StockQuoteService(stockQuoteDAO());
    }
}
```

The Java-based container configurations section provides additional details about @Configuration and @Bean annotations.

Enabling Spring Annotations

The Spring-provided `<context:annotation-config/>` XML tag is used to enable the use of annotations in your application.

The required application context XML configuration is provided below.

```xml
<?xml version="1.0" encoding="UTF-8"?>
<beans xmlns="http://www.springframework.org/schema/beans"
    xmlns:xsi="http://www.w3.org/2001/XMLSchema-instance"
    xmlns:context="http://www.springframework.org/schema/context"
    xsi:schemaLocation="http://www.springframework.org/schema/beans
    http://www.springframework.org/schema/beans/spring-beans-3.0.xsd
    http://www.springframework.org/schema/context
    http://www.springframework.org/schema/context/
            spring-context-3.0.xsd">

    <context:annotation-config/>

</beans>
```

Spring Container Configurations

In the spring framework, there are three ways in which application-specific beans and bean metadata can be configured. They are listed below.

- XML-based configurations
- Annotation-based configurations
- Java-based configurations

XML-based Configurations

So far in this chapter, we used XML-based configurations to demonstrate all code examples. In this approach, the spring-provided `<bean>` element tag is used to configure the application-specific POJO classes and bean metadata. Refer to the respective sections for details.

Annotation-based Configurations

In this approach, spring-provided annotations (instead of XML) are used to configure the bean metadata, injecting the bean references and their dependencies. These annotations can be used with classes, operations, and members of a class. It is possible to use both XML and annotation-based configurations in one application.

Use the following XML element to enable the spring annotations in same application context.

```xml
<context:annotation-config/>
```

The steps required to implement this example are listed below.

1. Create POJO classes
2. Create an "applicationContext.xml" file to configure the spring beans.
3. Create a main class to test the spring annotations.

Step 1: Create POJO classes

The following example illustrates dependency injection with spring annotations. The StockQuoteDAO class code is provided below.

```
// StockQuoteDAO.java
package com.learning.spring.core;

import org.springframework.stereotype.Component;
import org.springframework.beans.factory.annotation.Qualifier;
import java.util.*;

@Qualifier("stockDAO")
public class StockQuoteDAO {

    public Map<String, String> getStockData() {
        Map<String, String> dataMap = new HashMap<String, String>();
        dataMap.put("AAPL", "678.99");
        dataMap.put("FB", "24.99");
        return dataMap;
    }

}
```

Inject the StockQuoteDAO into the StockQuoteService class using @Autowired annotation. The complete class code is provided below.

```
// StockQuoteService.java
package com.learning.spring.core;

import org.springframework.beans.factory.annotation.Autowired;
import org.springframework.beans.factory.annotation.Qualifier;
import org.springframework.beans.factory.annotation.Required;

import java.util.*;

public class StockQuoteService {

    @Autowired
    @Qualifier("stockDAO")
    private StockQuoteDAO stockQuoteDAO;

    public void setStockQuoteDAO(StockQuoteDAO stockQuoteDAO) {
        this.stockQuoteDAO = stockQuoteDAO;
    }

    public Map<String, String> getStockData() {
        return stockQuoteDAO.getStockData();
    }
}
```

Step 2: Create an "applicationContext.xml" file to configure the spring beans.

Configure the beans and enable the annotations in the application context XML file. The following XML element enables the use of spring annotations.

```
<context:annotation-config/>
```

The complete XML file is provided below and is named the "applicationContext.xml"

```xml
<?xml version="1.0" encoding="UTF-8"?>
<beans xmlns="http://www.springframework.org/schema/beans"
    xmlns:xsi="http://www.w3.org/2001/XMLSchema-instance"
    xmlns:context="http://www.springframework.org/schema/context"
    xsi:schemaLocation="http://www.springframework.org/schema/beans
    http://www.springframework.org/schema/beans/spring-beans-3.0.xsd
    http://www.springframework.org/schema/context
    http://www.springframework.org/schema/context/
            spring-context-3.0.xsd">

    <context:annotation-config/>

    <bean id="stockQuoteService"
        class="com.learning.spring.core.StockQuoteService"/>

    <bean id="stockQuoteDAO"
        class="com.learning.spring.core.StockQuoteDAO"/>

</beans>
```

Step 3: Create a main class to test the spring annotations

Listing 1-13 provides the complete class code. Run the following `Main` class to view the output on the console.

Listing 1-13: Main class.

```java
// Main.java
package com.learning.spring.core;

import org.springframework.context.support.
                ClassPathXmlApplicationContext;
import java.util.Map;

public class Main {

    public static void main(String[] args) {
        ClassPathXmlApplicationContext context =
            new ClassPathXmlApplicationContext
                ("applicationContext.xml");

        StockQuoteService stockQuoteService = (StockQuoteService)
        context.getBean("stockQuoteService");
        Map<String, String> mapData = stockQuoteService.getStockData();
        System.out.println(mapData);
    }
}
```

Java-based configurations

In this approach, Java annotations are used to configure the bean metadata, injecting the bean references and their dependencies. These annotations can be used with classes, operations, and members of a class. No XML configurations are needed; it is possible to use both XML and Java-based annotations in one application.

The steps required to implement this example are listed below.

1. Create POJO classes
2. Use the `AppConfig` class to configure bean classes.
3. Create a main class to test the Java annotations.

Step 1: Create POJO classes

The following `StockQuoteDAO` has the `getStockData()` method which provides the stock data. The complete class code is provided below.

```java
// StockQuoteDAO.java
package com.learning.spring.core.java;

import java.util.*;

public class StockQuoteDAO {

    public Map<String, String> getStockData() {
        Map<String, String> dataMap = new HashMap<String, String>();
        dataMap.put("AAPL", "678.99");
        dataMap.put("FB", "24.99");
        return dataMap;
    }
}
```

The following `StockQuoteService` has the `stockQuoteService()` method which returns the `StockQuoteDAO` object reference.

```java
// StockQuoteService.java
package com.learning.spring.core.java;

public class StockQuoteService {

    private StockQuoteDAO stockQuoteDAO;

    public StockQuoteService(StockQuoteDAO stockQuoteDAO) {
        this.stockQuoteDAO = stockQuoteDAO;
    }

    public StockQuoteDAO stockQuoteService() {
        return stockQuoteDAO;
    }
}
```

Step 2: Use the `AppConfig` class to configure bean classes

The following method configures the `StockQuoteDAO` class.

```
@Bean
public StockQuoteDAO stockQuoteDAO() {
    return new StockQuoteDAO();
}
```

This method is equivalent to the following XML configuration.

```
<bean id="stockQuoteDAO"
    class="com.learning.spring.core.java.StockQuoteDAO"/>
```

Similarly, the following method configures the `StockQuoteService` class. The constructor-based injection is used to inject the `StockQuoteDAO` reference into the service class.

```
@Bean
public StockQuoteService stockQuoteService() {
    return new StockQuoteService(stockQuoteDAO());
}
```

This method is equivalent to the following XML configuration.

```
<bean id="stockQuoteService"
    class="com.learning.spring.core.java.StockQuoteService">
    <constructor-arg ref="stockQuoteDAO"/>
</bean>
```

The complete `AppConfig` class code is provided below. This `AppConfig` class is equivalent to the "applcationContext.xml" file in XML-based approach. This class contains bean configurations and their dependencies. The following list provides the comparison between Java and XML-based bean configurations.

- `AppConfig.java` → equivalent to "applcationContext.xml" file.
- `@Configuration` → equivalent to `<beans>` XML element.
- `@Bean` → equivalent to `<bean>` XML element.
- `AnnotationConfigApplicationContext` → equivalent to `ClassPathXmlApplicationContext` class used in XML-based approach.

```
// AppConfig.java
package com.learning.spring.core.java;

import org.springframework.context.annotation.Configuration;
import org.springframework.context.annotation.Bean;

@Configuration
public class AppConfig {

    @Bean
    public StockQuoteDAO stockQuoteDAO() {
        return new StockQuoteDAO();
    }

    @Bean
```

```
        public StockQuoteService stockQuoteService() {
            return new StockQuoteService(stockQuoteDAO());
        }
}
```

The following Java code instantiates the spring container and load the beans configured in the AppConfig class into the spring container.

```
ApplicationContext ctx = new
        AnnotationConfigApplicationContext(AppConfig.class);
```

Step 3: Create a main class to test the Java annotations

Listing 1-14 provides the complete class code. Run the following Main class to view the output on the console.

Listing 1-14: Main class.

```
// Main.java
package com.learning.spring.core.java;

import org.springframework.context.ApplicationContext;
import org.springframework.context.annotation.
        AnnotationConfigApplicationContext;
import java.util.Map;

public class Main {

    public static void main(String[] args) {
        ApplicationContext ctx = new
            AnnotationConfigApplicationContext(AppConfig.class);

        StockQuoteService stockQuoteService =
            ctx.getBean(StockQuoteService.class);
        Map<String, String> mapData =
            stockQuoteService.stockQuoteService().getStockData();
        System.out.println(mapData);
    }
}
```

Scanning Spring Components

Spring can automatically scan and auto-wire the @Component-annotated classes. This approach eliminates the configuration of many XML <bean> definitions in your application context file. Also, this approach can be used for Java-based container configurations to minimize the @Bean declarations. The spring-provided <context:component-scan> element can be used to automatically detect the @Component-annotated classes and register them as spring bean definitions with the application context. Spring also provides specialized component-based annotations such as @Controller, @Service, @Repository, and @Endpoint. These classes are eligible for component scanning using the spring-provided <context:component-scan/> XML tag.

The application context XML configuration is provided below.

```xml
<?xml version="1.0" encoding="UTF-8"?>
<beans xmlns="http://www.springframework.org/schema/beans"
    xmlns:xsi="http://www.w3.org/2001/XMLSchema-instance"
    xmlns:context="http://www.springframework.org/schema/context"
    xsi:schemaLocation="http://www.springframework.org/schema/beans
    http://www.springframework.org/schema/beans/spring-beans-3.0.xsd
    http://www.springframework.org/schema/context
    http://www.springframework.org/schema/context/
            spring-context-3.0.xsd">

    <context:component-scan base-package="com.learning.spring.service"/>

</beans>
```

The @Component-related generic and specific types are shown in Figure 1-4.

Figure 1-4 @Component generic and specific types

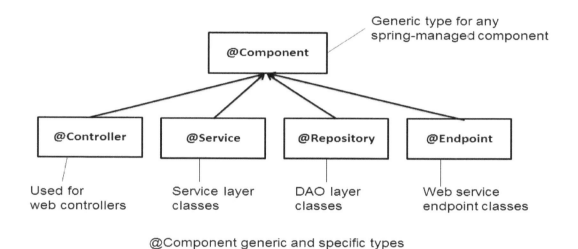

@Component generic and specific types

The characteristics of @Component-specific types are listed below.

- The @Componen annotation is a generic type can be used for any spring managed bean. This indicates the annotated class is a component.
- The @Controller-annotated class is a special type of spring component used for web application controllers.
- The @Service-annotated class is a special type of spring component used for service layer classes.
- The @Repository-annotated class is a special type of spring component used for data access objects.
- The @Endpoint-annotated class is a special type of spring component used to mark the class as a web service endpoint.

The following example illustrates the use of the @Component annotation and <context:component-scan> namespace. The steps required to implement this example are listed below.

1. Create POJO classes.
2. Enable the component scan in the application context XML file.
3. Create a main class to test the component scan feature.

Step 1: Create POJO classes

Here, reuse the previously created `StockQuoteService` class with the following change.

```java
// StockQuoteService.java
package com.learning.spring.core;

import org.springframework.stereotype.Component;

@Component
public class StockQuoteService {

    @Autowired
    private StockQuoteDAO stockQuoteDAO;

    ...
}
```

Reuse the previously created `StockQuoteDAO` class with the following change.

```java
// StockQuoteService.java
package com.learning.spring.core;

import org.springframework.stereotype.Component;

@Component
public class StockQuoteDAO {
    ...
}
```

Step 2: Enable the component scan in the application context XML file.

Use the `<context:component-scan>` configuration to auto-scan the `@Component`-annotated classes. The complete application context configuration is provided below and is named the "applicationContext.xml"

```xml
<?xml version="1.0" encoding="UTF-8"?>
<beans xmlns="http://www.springframework.org/schema/beans"
    xmlns:xsi="http://www.w3.org/2001/XMLSchema-instance"
    xmlns:context="http://www.springframework.org/schema/context"
    xsi:schemaLocation="http://www.springframework.org/schema/beans
    http://www.springframework.org/schema/beans/spring-beans-3.0.xsd
    http://www.springframework.org/schema/context
    http://www.springframework.org/schema/context/
            spring-context-3.0.xsd">

    <context:annotation-config/>

    <context:component-scan base-package="com.learning.spring.core"/>
```

```
</beans>
```

Step 3: Create a main class to test the component scan feature.

Listing 1-15 provides the complete class code. Run the following `Main` class to view the output on the console.

Listing 1-15: Main class.

```java
// Main.java
package com.learning.spring.core;

import org.springframework.context.support.
                ClassPathXmlApplicationContext;
import java.util.Map;

public class Main {

    public static void main(String[] args) {
        ClassPathXmlApplicationContext context =
            new ClassPathXmlApplicationContext
                ("applicationContext.xml");

        StockQuoteService stockQuoteService = (StockQuoteService)
        context.getBean("stockQuoteService");
        Map<String, String> mapData = stockQuoteService.getStockData();
        System.out.println(mapData);
    }
}
```

Summary

This section summarizes the core spring framework features.

- The spring `ApplicationContext` is the primary interface representing the spring container.
- The spring framework provides XML, Annotation, and Java-based solutions to configure the spring-managed beans.
- A spring-managed bean can have five valid bean scopes: singleton, prototype, request, session, and global session.
- The spring framework-provided method injection technique can be used to provide the singleton bean with a new instance of the prototype bean each time it is invoked.
- Spring can automatically scan and auto-wire the `@Component`-annotated classes. The `@Component`-annotated classes are eligible for auto detection and component scanning using the spring-provided `<context:component-scan/>` XML tag.
- The spring-provided `<context:annotation-config/>` XML tag enables the use of annotations in your application

Figure 1-5 summarizes the most important points described in this chapter.

Figure 1-5 Core spring framework features

Chapter 2. SpEL and Spring-Resources

Expression Language is a scripting language used to access Java bean components. Spring provides powerful Expression Language, called SpEL that can be used to wire values into bean properties. SpEL stands for Spring Expression Language, and it provides standard interfaces, XML, and Annotation-based configurations to access the Java bean components at runtime.

Spring provides utility classes to access low-level resources such as files, images, and so forth. Spring also provides utility classes to configure and load the locale-specific resource bundle objects; they are used for localization (l10n) and internationalization (i18n). Applications can use these locale-specific resource bundle files to customize the application for various countries.

This chapter will discuss the following topics:

- Spring support for accessing resources
- Spring support for internationalization (i18n) and localization (l10n).
- Spring Expression Language syntax and fundaments
- Accessing Java bean components using SpEL.

Spring Support for Accessing Resources

The Spring `Resource` interface provides an abstraction to access the low-level resources. All spring application contexts can be used to obtain the `Resource` interface. The possible ways of accessing the resources are illustrated below.

CASE 1: Using classpath to access the resources

In this approach, the specified file resource should be available in the classpath.

```
ApplicationContext ctx = new ClassPathXmlApplicationContext();
Resource resource = ctx.getResource("database.properties");
```

Alternatively, use the following code.

```
Resource resource = ctx.getResource("classpath:database.properties");
```

CASE 2: Using file path to access the resources

In this approach, the specified file resource should be available in the local file system.

```
ApplicationContext ctx = new FileSystemXmlApplicationContext();
Resource resource = ctx.getResource("C:/conf/database.properties");
```

Alternatively, use the following code.

```
Resource resource = ctx.getResource("file:/conf/database.properties");
```

CASE 3: Using file path to access the resources (HTTP-based)

In this approach, the specified file resource should be available in the local file system. This is used for web-based applications.

```
Resource resource = ctx.getResource("http:/conf/database.properties");
```

CASE 4: Spring XML configuration to access the resources

```
<bean id="template" class="com.learning.spring.core.spel.Pet">
    <property name="template" value="classpath:database.properties"/>
</bean>
```

This section illustrates the use of spring `Resource` interface for accessing the resources. Use the following "database.properties" file to run the examples.

```
driver_class_name=com.mysql.jdbc.Driver
url=jdbc:mysql://localhost:3306/testdatabase
username=root
password=password
```

Example 1: Spring Standalone Client for Accessing Resources

In the example below, the standalone Java program is used to access the resource files from classpath. Run the following `Main` class to view the output on the console. Listing 2-1 provides the complete class code.

Listing 2-1: Main class.

```
// Main.java
package com.learning.spring.core.resources;

import org.springframework.context.support.
            ClassPathXmlApplicationContext;
import org.springframework.core.io.Resource;

import java.io.*;

public class Main {

    public static void main(String[] args) {

        try {
            ClassPathXmlApplicationContext ctx =
                    new ClassPathXmlApplicationContext();
            Resource resource = ctx.getResource("database.properties");
            InputStream is = resource.getInputStream();
            BufferedReader br =  new BufferedReader
                        (new InputStreamReader(is));
            String line;
            while ((line = br.readLine()) != null) {
                System.out.println(line);
            }
            br.close();

        } catch (Exception ex) {
```

```
                    ex.printStackTrace();
            }
        }
}
```

The output is provided below.

```
driver_class_name=com.mysql.jdbc.Driver
url=jdbc:mysql://localhost:3306/testdatabase
username=root
password=password
```

Example 2: Spring XML Configuration for Accessing Resources

The steps required to implement this example are listed below.

1. Create a POJO class
2. Create an "applicationContext.xml" file to configure the spring beans.
3. Create a main class to test the functionality.

Step 1: Create a POJO class

Use the following Pet class to set the resource template.

```java
// Pet.java
package com.learning.spring.core.resources;

import org.springframework.core.io.Resource;

public class Pet {

    private Resource template;

    // Add getter and setter methods
}
```

Step 2: Create an "applicationContext.xml" file to configure the spring beans

In this example, the resource path is configured to a Java bean class setter method. The classpath-based approach is used to load the resource file. The complete XML configuration is provided below and is named "applicationContext-messages.xml."

```xml
<?xml version="1.0" encoding="UTF-8"?>
<beans xmlns="http://www.springframework.org/schema/beans"
    xmlns:xsi="http://www.w3.org/2001/XMLSchema-instance"
    xsi:schemaLocation="http://www.springframework.org/schema/beans
    http://www.springframework.org/schema/beans/spring-beans-3.0.xsd">

    <bean id="template" class="com.learning.spring.core.spel.Pet">
        <property name="template"
                value="classpath:database.properties"/>
    </bean>
</beans>
```

Step 3: Create a main class to test the functionality.

Run the following `Main` class to view the output on the console. Listing 2-2 provides the complete class code.

Listing 2-2: Main class.

```java
// Main.java
package com.learning.spring.core.resources;

import org.springframework.context.support.
        ClassPathXmlApplicationContext;
import org.springframework.context.ApplicationContext;
import org.springframework.core.io.Resource;

import java.util.*;
import java.io.*;

public class Main {

    public static void main(String[] args) {

        try {
            ApplicationContext ctx = new ClassPathXmlApplicationContext
                        ("applicationContext-messages.xml");
            Pet pet = (Pet) ctx.getBean("template");
            Resource resource = pet.getTemplate();

            InputStream is = resource.getInputStream();
            BufferedReader br =  new BufferedReader
                        (new InputStreamReader(is));
            String line;
            while ((line = br.readLine()) != null) {
                System.out.println(line);
            }
            br.close();

        } catch (Exception ex) {
            ex.printStackTrace();
        }
    }
}
```

The output is provided below.

```
driver_class_name=com.mysql.jdbc.Driver
url=jdbc:mysql://localhost:3306/testdatabase
username=root
password=password
```

Spring Support for Accessing Resource Bundles

The Spring `MessageSource` interface provides an abstraction to access the resource bundles. The spring `ApplicationContext` interface extends the `MessageSource` interface. The `MessageSource` interface provides the internationalization (i18n) and localization (l10n) functionality. The possible ways of accessing the resource bundles are illustrated below.

CASE 1: Using the `MessageSource.getMessage(...)` method

```
MessageSource resources = new ClassPathXmlApplicationContext
            ("applicationContext-messages.xml");
String message = resources.getMessage("field.required",
        new Object[] {"User Id", "User Id"},
        "Required", Locale.US);
```

CASE 2: Using the `ApplicationContext.getMessage(...)` method

```
ClassPathXmlApplicationContext context =
        new ClassPathXmlApplicationContext
                ("applicationContext-messages.xml");
String message = context.getMessage("field.required",
            new Object[] {"User Id", "User Id"}, Locale.UK);
```

Example 3: Spring Support for Resource Bundles (i18n & l10n)

Resource bundles contain locale-specific objects; they are used for localization (l10n) and internationalization (i18n). Applications can use locale-specific resource files to customize the application for different countries. A resource bundle file name notation is provided below.

- messages_en_US → resource bundle uses the English language for the US locale
- messages_en_GB → resource bundle uses the English language for the UK locale
- messages_FR → resource bundle uses French for the France locale
- messages_JP → resource bundle uses Japanese for the Japan locale.

The spring framework provides utility classes to resolve locale-specific messages. Messages are stored in a ".properties" file. The contents of the properties file are provided below; the file is named "messages.properties"

```
field.min.length=The field  must be at least 2 characters in length
field.required=The {0} field is required. {1} Cannot be empty
```

Similarly, you can create another properties file named "version.properties"; see below for this file's contents.

```
application_version=3.2
```

The contents of the "database.properties" file are provided below.

```
driver_class_name=com.mysql.jdbc.Driver
url=jdbc:mysql://localhost:3306/testdatabase
username=root
```

```
password=password
```

The spring application context can use the `ResourceBundleMessageSource` class to configure the resource bundles. We created three resource bundles; they are `messages.properties`, `version.properties`, and `database.properties`. Add these resource bundles to your classpath.

The steps required to implement this example are listed below.

1. Create an "applicationContext.xml" file to configure the resource bundles.
2. Create a main class to test the functionality.

Step 1: Create an "applicationContext.xml" file to configure the resource bundles.

Configure the resource bundles in the application context file. The complete XML file is provided below and is named "applicationContext-messages.xml."

```xml
<?xml version="1.0" encoding="UTF-8"?>
<beans xmlns="http://www.springframework.org/schema/beans"
    xmlns:xsi="http://www.w3.org/2001/XMLSchema-instance"
    xsi:schemaLocation="http://www.springframework.org/schema/beans
    http://www.springframework.org/schema/beans/spring-beans-3.0.xsd">

    <bean id="messageSource" class="org.springframework.context.
                    support.ResourceBundleMessageSource">
        <property name="basenames">
            <list>
                <value>messages</value>
                <value>version</value>
                <value>database</value>
            </list>
        </property>
    </bean>
</beans>
```

Step 2: Create a main class to test the functionality

Run the following `MessageTranslator` class to view the output on the console. Listing 2-3 provides the complete class code.

Listing 2-3: MessageTranslator class.

```java
// MessageTranslator.java
package com.learning.spring.core.resources;

import org.springframework.context.support.
            ClassPathXmlApplicationContext;
import org.springframework.context.MessageSource;
import java.util.*;

public class MessageTranslator {

    public static void main(String[] args) {
        MessageSource resources = new ClassPathXmlApplicationContext
                    ("applicationContext-messages.xml");
```

```
        String message = resources.getMessage("field.min.length",
                         null, "Default", null);
        System.out.println(message);
    }
}
```

The output is provided below.

```
The field must be at least 2 characters in length
```

The above example does not have any arguments. Let us review the following message, which contains two placeholders: {0} and {1}

```
field.required=The {0} field is required. {1} Cannot be empty
```

An example message with arguments is provided below. The message arguments are inserted into the placeholders during runtime.

```
String message = resources.getMessage("field.required",
        new Object[] {"User-Id", "User-Id"}, "Required", Locale.US);
System.out.println(message);
```

Run the following method to view the output on the console.

```
public static void main(String[] args) {
    MessageSource resources = new ClassPathXmlApplicationContext
                ("applicationContext-messages.xml");

    String message = resources.getMessage("field.required",
        new Object[] {"User-Id", "User-Id"},
        "Required", Locale.US);
    System.out.println(message);
}
```

The output is provided below.

```
The User-Id field is required. User-Id Cannot be empty
```

Similarly, you can use the following code to print the messages from "verison.properties" and "database.properties". The Java code is given below.

```
String version = resources.getMessage("application_version", null,
"Default", null);
String driver = resources.getMessage("driver_class_name", null,
"Default", null);
```

The output is provided below.

```
3.2
com.mysql.jdbc.Driver
```

Spring Expression Language (SpEL)

Spring SpEL supports both XML and Annotation-based configurations for defining the beans. This section illustrates the use of expressions with spring beans.

Example 4: Using Expressions with Bean Properties (XML-based)

The following XML syntax is used to access the bean properties.

```
<value>#{petMickey.name}</value>
```

The steps required to implement this example are listed below.

1. Create POJO classes
2. Create an "applicationContext.xml" file to configure the spring beans.
3. Create a main class to test the functionality.

Step 1: Create POJO classes

The `Pet` bean class code is provided below.

```
// Pet.java
package com.learning.spring.core.spel;

public class Pet {

    private String name;

    // Add getter and setter methods
}
```

The `PetStore` class code is provided below.

```
// PetStore.java
package com.learning.spring.core.spel;

import java.util.Set;

public class PetStore {

    private Set<String> pets;

    // Add getter and setter methods
}
```

Step 2: Create an "applicationContext.xml" file to configure the spring beans.

The pet names are populated into the `PetStore` object by using expressions. The complete XML configuration is provided below and is named "applicationContext-spel.xml"

```
<?xml version="1.0" encoding="UTF-8"?>
```

```xml
<beans xmlns="http://www.springframework.org/schema/beans"
    xmlns:xsi="http://www.w3.org/2001/XMLSchema-instance"
    xmlns:context="http://www.springframework.org/schema/context"
    xsi:schemaLocation="http://www.springframework.org/schema/beans
    http://www.springframework.org/schema/beans/spring-beans-3.0.xsd
    http://www.springframework.org/schema/context
    http://www.springframework.org/schema/context/
                spring-context-3.0.xsd">

    <context:annotation-config/>

    <context:component-scan base-package =
                "com.learning.spring.core.spel"/>

    <bean id="petMickey" class="com.learning.spring.core.spel.Pet">
        <property name="name" value="Mickey"/>
    </bean>

    <bean id="petDog" class="com.learning.spring.core.spel.Pet">
        <property name="name" value="Snubby"/>
    </bean>

    <bean id="petElephent" class="com.learning.spring.core.spel.Pet">
        <property name="name" value="Jumbo"/>
    </bean>

    <bean id="petStore" class="com.learning.spring.core.spel.PetStore">
        <property name="pets">
            <set>
                <value>#{petMickey.name}</value>
                <value>#{petDog.name}</value>
                <value>#{petElephent.name}</value>
            </set>
        </property>
    </bean>
</beans>
```

Step 3: Create a main class to test the functionality.

Run the following `Main` class to view the output on the console. Listing 2-4 provides the complete class code.

Listing 2-4: Main class.

```java
// Main.java
package com.learning.spring.core.spel;

import org.springframework.context.support.
            ClassPathXmlApplicationContext;

public class Main {

    public static void main(String[] args) {
        ClassPathXmlApplicationContext context =
            new ClassPathXmlApplicationContext
                ("applicationContext-spel.xml");
```

```
        PetStore petStore = (PetStore) context.getBean("petStore");
        System.out.println("--- pets ---" + petStore.getPets());
    }
}
```

Example 5: Using Expressions with Bean Properties (Annotation-based)

The steps required to implement this example are listed below.

1. Create POJO classes.
2. Create an "applicationContext.xml" file to configure the spring beans.
3. Create a main class to test the functionality.

Step 1: Create POJO classes.

The @Value annotation can be used with bean methods, fields, and constructor and method parameters to set a specified value. In this example, SpEL is used to set the data.

The following code is used to set the bean object.

```
@Value("#{subjects}")
private Subjects subjects
```

The following code is used to set the bean property value.

```
@Value("#{subjects.primary}")
private String primarySubject;
```

The complete Grade bean class code is provided below.

```
// Grade.java
package com.learning.spring.core.spel;

import org.springframework.stereotype.Component;
import org.springframework.beans.factory.annotation.Value;

@Component("grade")
public class Grade {

    private int grade;

    @Value("#{subjects}")
    private Subjects subjects;

    @Value("#{subjects.primary}")
    private String primarySubject;

    // Add getter and setter methods
}
```

The Subjects bean class code is provided below.

```java
// Subjects.java
package com.learning.spring.core.spel;

import org.springframework.stereotype.Component;

@Component("subjects")
public class Subjects {

    private String primary = "Calculus";
    private String subjectName = "Math";

    // Add getter and setter methods
}
```

Step 2: Create an "applicationContext.xml" file to configure the spring beans.

In this example, annotations are used to configure expression metadata. Enable the auto-scan and annotation configurations in the spring application context file. The complete XML configuration is provided below and is named "applicationContext-spel.xml"

```xml
<?xml version="1.0" encoding="UTF-8"?>
<beans xmlns="http://www.springframework.org/schema/beans"
    xmlns:xsi="http://www.w3.org/2001/XMLSchema-instance"
    xmlns:context="http://www.springframework.org/schema/context"
    xsi:schemaLocation="http://www.springframework.org/schema/beans
    http://www.springframework.org/schema/beans/spring-beans-3.0.xsd
    http://www.springframework.org/schema/context
    http://www.springframework.org/schema/context/
                spring-context-3.0.xsd">

    <context:annotation-config/>

    <context:component-scan base-package=
                "com.learning.spring.core.spel"/>
</beans>
```

Step 3: Create a main class to test the functionality.

Run the following `Main` class to view the output on the console. Listing 2-5 provides the complete class code.

Listing 2-5: Main class.

```java
// Main.java
package com.learning.spring.core.spel;

import org.springframework.context.support.
            ClassPathXmlApplicationContext;

public class Main {

    ClassPathXmlApplicationContext context =
            new ClassPathXmlApplicationContext
                    ("applicationContext-spel.xml");
```

```
        Grade grade = (Grade) context.getBean("grade");
        System.out.println("--- subjects ---" +
            grade.getSubjects().getSubjectName() +
            grade.getPrimarySubject());
}
```

Example 6: Standalone Client Using SpEL API

This example demonstrates the use of SpEL API for manipulating the bean property values. The `ExpressionParser` interface is used to parse the expression string. In the example below, the `Pet` object's property "name" is used for comparison. Here, reuse the `Pet` bean class created in Example-4.

```
ExpressionParser parser = new SpelExpressionParser();
Expression exp = parser.parseExpression("name");
```

The `EvaluationContext` interface is used to resolve the properties, methods and fields. An example use is provided below.

```
EvaluationContext context = new StandardEvaluationContext(pet);
String petName = (String) exp.getValue(context);
```

Run the following standalone client to view the output. In this example, SpEL API is used to manipulate bean property values. Listing 2-6 provides the complete class code.

Listing 2-6: Main class.

```
// Main.java
package com.learning.spring.core.spel;

import org.springframework.expression.spel.standard.SpelExpressionParser;
import org.springframework.expression.spel.support.
        StandardEvaluationContext;
import org.springframework.expression.Expression;
import org.springframework.expression.ExpressionParser;
import org.springframework.expression.EvaluationContext;

public class Main {
    public static void main(String[] args) {
        Pet pet = new Pet();
        pet.setName("mickey");
        pet.setAge(1);

        ExpressionParser parser = new SpelExpressionParser();
        Expression exp = parser.parseExpression("name");
        EvaluationContext context = new StandardEvaluationContext(pet);
        String petName = (String) exp.getValue(context);
        System.out.println(petName);

        parser.parseExpression("name").setValue(pet, "mickey-mouse");
        Expression exp1 = parser.parseExpression("name == 'mickey'");
        boolean result = exp1.getValue(context, Boolean.class);
        System.out.println(result);
```

```
        String newPetName = (String) exp.getValue(context);
        System.out.println(newPetName);
    }
}
```

Summary

This section summarizes the spring resources and the features of SpEL.

- The spring `Resource` interface provides an abstraction to access the low-level resources. All spring application contexts can be used to obtain the `Resource` interface.
- The spring `MessageSource` interface provides an abstraction to access the resource bundles. The spring `ApplicationContext` interface extends the `MessageSource` interface.
- Spring provides powerful Expression Language (SpEL), which can be used to wire values into beans properties.
- Spring provides `@Value`-annotation to configure the expression metadata.

Figure 2-1 summarizes the most important points described in this chapter.

Figure 2-1 Spring resources and SpEL features

Spring Resources And SpEL

Chapter 3. Spring-Web

Several open-source frameworks are available for developing web applications. There is no hard-and-fast rule regarding which framework should be used in your application; it totally depends on the application requirement and the developer's preference and prior experience. This chapter illustrates the complete use of the spring-web framework in application development. The commonly used open-source frameworks currently available in the market for web application development are listed below.

- Spring
- Struts
- Webworks
- Tapestry
- JSF

All the above-specified frameworks provide similar features and use the model-view-controller (MVC) architecture. Any of these frameworks can be used for developing web applications. The spring provided HTTP-based servlet framework can be used for developing web applications and http-based web services. This chapter illustrates the use of the spring-web controller framework for developing web applications.

This chapter will discuss the following topics:

- Spring-MVC fundamentals and supported annotations
- Velocity template language and its fundamentals
- FreeMarker markup language and its fundamentals
- Configuration of view resolvers for Velocity, Freemarker, JSP, and JSTL
- Spring integration with JSF2
- Development of web applications using the spring-MVC framework
- The use of spring MVC-provided annotations and namespaces
- Development of Ajax-based applications using the spring-MVC framework
- Prototype and JQuery integration with spring-MVC

Model-View-Controller (MVC) Architecture

MVC architecture is an adapted standard for developing web applications. The application is divided into model, view, and controller components; each component is used for a specific purpose. The primary advantages of the MVC pattern are clear separation of layers and code reusability.

- Model: Model consists of application data or business data.
- View: Displays the model information on a web page, chart, or diagram. Views are used for presenting the model data.
- Controller: Manipulates the model information to update the views. Controller manipulates the model data and updates the view with new information.

A model-view-controller architecture representation is shown in Figure 3-1.

Figure 3-1 Model-view-controller architecture

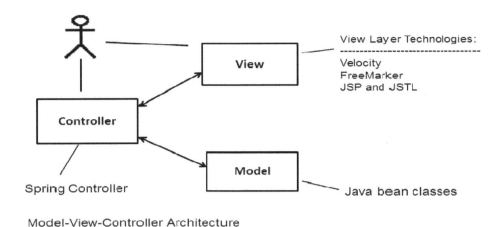

Model-View-Controller Architecture

The following list of technologies can be used to present the data in a view layer.

- Velocity
- FreeMarker
- JSP and JSTL

The spring-MVC controller can integrate with any of the above-specified view layer technologies. Plain old java bean classes are used to hold the business data.

Prerequisites/Setting Up the Environment

Before developing the code; let us discuss the configurations needed to keep the environment ready for development. The required configurations are provided below.

- The JAR files required to develop the spring-MVC examples are provided along with the spring distribution. Download the *org.springframework-xxx.jar* files from the spring website.
- Configure the spring `DispatcherServlet` in web.xml → This `DispatcherServlet` is a front controller that forwards the incoming HTTP requests to the specific controller classes.

```
<servlet>
    <servlet-name>springweb</servlet-name>
    <servlet-class>
            org.springframework.web.servlet.DispatcherServlet
    </servlet-class>
</servlet>

<servlet-mapping>
    <servlet-name>springweb</servlet-name>
    <url-pattern>*.action</url-pattern>
</servlet-mapping>
```

- Create a servlet context file → the name of the XML file follows the standard spring syntax. The suffix should be "servlet," and the prefix of the XML file should match the value of the "<servlet-name/>" tag specified in web.xml. The name used in web.xml is "springweb"; thus, the file name "springweb-servlet.xml" is used in this chapter. The prefix and suffix should be separated with a hyphen. The file name syntax is: {prefix}-{suffix}.xml, which is "springweb-servlet.xml"

The following list of JARs is required for Velocity development.

- velocity.jar
- velocity-tools.jar

The following list of JARs is required for Freemarker development.

- freemarker.jar
- Spring-provided "spring.ftl" Freemarker library.

The following list of JARs is required for JSF development.

- javax.faces-2.1.14.jar
- tomahawk-1.1.5.jar

The following list of JARs is required for JSTL development.

- jstl-api.jar
- jstl-impl.jar

There are two ways in which spring-MVC features can be enabled in web applications.

CASE 1: Using Spring-provided adapter classes.

Spring-provided adapter classes can be used to dispatch the web requests to the controllers. The required application context XML configuration is provided below.

```
<bean class="org.springframework.web.servlet.mvc.
        SimpleControllerHandlerAdapter"/>
<bean class="org.springframework.web.servlet.mvc.annotation.
        DefaultAnnotationHandlerMapping"/>
<bean class="org.springframework.web.servlet.mvc.annotation.
        AnnotationMethodHandlerAdapter"/>
```

CASE 2: Using the spring-provided `<xmlns:mvc/>` **namespace.**

The spring-provided `<mvc:annotation-driven/>` tag can be used to dispatch the web requests to the controllers. This tag will configure two beans: `DefaultAnnotationHandlerMapping` and `AnnotationMethodHandlerAdapter`. The required application context XML configuration is provided below.

```
<mvc:annotation-driven/>
```

Spring-MVC Annotations

@Controller

The `@Controller` annotation is used at the class level. The class annotated with `@Controller` is a web application controller. The `@Controller`-annotated classes are eligible for component scanning using the spring-provided "<context: component-scan/>" XML tag. This annotation is used with `@RequestMapping` annotation to handle the web requests. An example of a `@Controller`-annotation's use is provided below.

```
@Controller
public class JSPDemoController {

    public ModelAndView view() {
        . . .
    }
}
```

@RequestMapping

The `@RequestMapping` annotation can be used at the class level and method level. This annotation maps the http-requests to specific controller classes and controller class methods. `@RequestMapping`-annotated methods may have various supported method parameters and return values. The supported method parameters are `HttpServletRequest`, `HttpSession`, `@RequestParam`, `@ModelAttribute`, `ModelMap`, `BindingResult`, and so forth. The supported return values are `String`, `ModelAndView`, `Model`, and so on.

The following `updatePricing(...)` method is annotated with `@RequestMapping` annotation. An example of the use of a `@RequestMapping`-annotation is given below.

```
@RequestMapping(value = "/main/updateData.action",
            method = RequestMethod.POST)
public String updatePricing(
    @ModelAttribute("custProfile") CustomerProfile custProfile,
    @ModelAttribute("loan") Loan loan,
    @ModelAttribute("line") Line line,
    BindingResult result, ModelMap model) {

    . . .

    return "main/layout_main";
}
```

Another example of the `@RequestMapping`-annotated method signature is provided below.

```
@RequestMapping(value = "/main/showTestPage.action",
            method = RequestMethod.POST)
public String show(HttpServletRequest request, ModelMap model) {

    . . .
```

```
        return "main/layout_main";
}
```

@ModelAttribute

The `@ModelAttribute` annotation can be used for method parameters and return values. This annotation binds the method parameter and return value to a model object. An example of the use of a `@ModelAttribute`-annotation is given below.

```
public String updatePricing(
    @ModelAttribute("custProfile") CustomerProfile custProfile,
    @ModelAttribute("loan") Loan loan,
    @ModelAttribute("line") Line line,
    BindingResult result, ModelMap model) {

    ...

    return "main/layout_main";
}
```

@RequestParam

The `@RequestParam` annotation is used with method parameters. This annotation binds the HTTP-request parameter values to annotated method parameters. An example of the use of a `@RequestParam`-annotation is given below.

```
@Controller
public class SimpleDemoController {

    @RequestMapping(value = "/demo/validLogin.action",
                    method = RequestMethod.POST)
    public String show(@RequestParam("userName") String userId,
                       @RequestParam("passCode") String passCode,
                       ModelMap model) {
        ...

        return "demo/success";
    }
}
```

The various ways of receiving the HTTP-request parameters in the spring controller methods are summarized below.

CASE 1: Using a traditional `HttpServletRequest` object.

The servet-specific `HttpServletRequest` object can be used to receive the HTTP request parameters in the controller methods. An example use is provided below.

```
public String view(HttpServletRequest request, ModelMap model) {

    String userName = request.getParameter("userName");
    String passCode = request.getParameter("passCode");
```

```
        . . .
}
```

CASE 2: Using the `@RequestParam` annotation.

The `@RequestParam` annotation can be used to bind the HTTP request parameters to the controller method parameters. An example use is provided below.

```
public String show(@RequestParam("userName") String userId,
                   @RequestParam("passCode") String passCode) {
        . . .
}
```

CASE 3: Using the `@ModelAttribute` object.

The `@ModelAttribute` annotation can be used to bind the HTTP-request parameters to the controller method parameters. An example use is provided below.

```
public String updatePricing(
    @ModelAttribute("custProfile") CustomerProfile custProfile,
    @ModelAttribute("loan") Loan loan,
    @ModelAttribute("line") Line line) {

        . . .
}
```

Spring-MVC Advantages

- Provides annotations to bind the web request data to model objects.
- Provides namespace support to minimize XML bean configurations.
- Spring controller methods are flexible and can be used with various method signatures. Supports various method parameters and return values.
- Provides support for configuring various view resolvers such as Velocity, Freemarker, JSTL, JSF, and so forth. It is easy to switch from one view resolver to another.
- Spring-MVC provides a cleaner separation between views, controllers, and models.
- Spring provides integration with other web frameworks such as JSF, Struts, WebWorks, and so forth.

Spring-Web: View Layer Technologies

Several open-source frameworks are available for presenting the data in view layer. This section illustrates the complete use of view-layer technologies in web application development. The commonly used view layer open-source frameworks currently available in the market are listed below.

- Velocity
- Freemarker
- JSP with JSTL

- JSF

All of the above-specified frameworks provide similar features; spring provides view configurators for integrating with these frameworks.

Velocity Syntax and Fundamentals

Velocity is an open-source template engine that provides a scripting language to reference the Java data objects. The scripting language used in Velocity is called Velocity Template Language (VTL). The VTL scripts are embedded with HTML code. Velocity templates are used in view layer to render the controller-provided model data. Velocity can be used with any other MVC framework, such as Spring-MVC, Struts, and so forth. Velocity is an open-source framework available under the Apache license.

The commonly used extension for a Velocity template is ".vm". This section illustrates how to reference the Java objects in Velocity templates.

The Java code is:

```
model.put("heading", "Learning Spring MVC");
```

The Velocity template code is:

```
Heading: $heading
```

The Java code is:

```
List<String> namesList = new ArrayList<String>();
namesList.add("Spring");
namesList.add("Learning");
namesList.add("Vesion 3.x");
request.setAttribute("namesList", namesList);
```

The Velocity template code is:

```
#foreach($name in $namesList)
    $name <br/>
#end
```

The Java code is:

```
Map<String, String> dataHashMap = new HashMap<String, String>();
dataHashMap.put("Topic1", "Java");
dataHashMap.put("Topic2", "Spring-Security");
dataHashMap.put("Topic3", "Spring-MVC");
request.setAttribute("dataHashMap", dataHashMap);
```

The Velocity template code is:

```
#foreach($key in $dataHashMap.keySet())
    Key is: $key
```

```
            Value is: $dataHashMap.get($key) <br/>
    #end
```

The Java code is:

```
    List<Account> accountDataList = new ArrayList<Account>();
    Account account1 = new Account();
    account1.setAccountNumber("121213");
    account1.setAccountHolderName("John Smith");
    account1.setBalance(99975L);
    accountDataList.add(account1);

    Account account2 = new Account();
    account2.setAccountNumber("3434133");
    account2.setAccountHolderName("John Sims");
    account2.setBalance(45000L);
    accountDataList.add(account2);
    model.put("accountDataList", accountDataList);
```

The Velocity template code is:

```
    <table>
        #foreach($account in $accountDataList)
            <tr>
                <td> $account.getAccountNumber() </td>
                <td> $account.getAccountHolderName() </td>
                <td> $account.getBalance()   </td>
            </tr>
        #end
    </table>
```

The following example demonstrates the variable declaration in Velocity templates.

```
    #set($name = "John Smith")
```

The Java code is:

```
    Map<String, Account> accountDataMap =
                    new HashMap<String, Account>();
    accountDataMap.put("account1", account1);
    accountDataMap.put("account2", account2);
    model.put("accountDataMap", accountDataMap);
```

The Velocity template code is:

```
    <table>
        #foreach($mapKey in $accountDataMap.keySet())
            #set($accountObj = $accountDataMap.get($mapKey))
            <tr>
                <td> $accountObj.getAccountNumber() </td>
                <td> $accountObj.getAccountHolderName() </td>
                <td> $accountObj.getBalance() </td>
            </tr>
        #end
    </table>
```

The following example demonstrates the Velocity "if-else" condition syntax.

```
<div>
    #if($name.equals("Spring"))
        Spring
    #else
        Not a Spring
    #end
</div>
```

The following example demonstrates the Velocity "if-elseif" condition syntax.

```
<div>
    #if($name.equals("Spring"))
        Spring
    #elseif($name.equals("Security"))
        Security
    #else
        Java
    #end
</div>
```

The following example demonstrates the Velocity "parse" syntax. Parse is used to include a Velocity template inside another template.

```
#parse("demo/message.vm")
```

An example "message.vm" code is provided below.

```
<div id='errorMessageDiv'>
    #if($!errorMessage)
        <div style="border:1px dotted red; color:red;
                        font-weight:bold; width:70%; ">
            $!errorMessage
        </div>
    #end
</div>
```

Velocity Tools:

A Velocity tool is a simple POJO class helps for reusing commonly used functionalities such as date tool, number tool, math tool, and so forth. The Velocity tool class avoids the redundant code in your application. Common functionalities can be reused across the application. The Velocity tools are configured in the "toolbox.xml" file. A sample toolbox configuration is provided below.

```
<?xml version="1.0"?>
<toolbox>
    <tool>
        <key>math</key>
        <scope>application</scope>
        <class>org.apache.velocity.tools.generic.MathTool</class>
    </tool>

    <tool>
        <key>dateTool</key>
```

```
        <scope>application</scope>
        <class>org.apache.velocity.tools.generic.DateTool</class>
    </tool>
</toolbox>
```

The following code snippet demonstrates the Velocity toolbox example syntax. In this example, Velocity-provided built-in tools are used, and Velocity allows us to configure custom Velocity tools.

```
<div>
    Velocity Tool: <br/>
    $dateTool.format("MM/dd/yyyy", $dob) <br/>
    $math.add(100, 200) <br/>
</div>
```

Velocity Macros:

A Velocity macro is a reusable Velocity template code such as a header, footer, and so forth that can be reused in your application. The Velocity macros are configured in the "VM_global_library.vm" file. A simple Velocity macro definition is provided below.

```
#macro(commontableheader)
    <tr>
        <th width='10%'>Id</th>
        <th width='20%'>Name</th>
        <th width='10%'>Desc</th>
        <th width='10%'>Zip Code</th>
        <th width='20%'>School Type</th>
        <th width='20%'>Category</th>
    </tr>
#end
```

The following example demonstrates the use of a Velocity macro.

```
<div>
    Velocity Macro: <br/>
    #commontableheader()
</div> <br/>
```

Load the global library into the Velocity context. The "velocity.properties" file now has the reference to the global library. The complete "velocity.properties" file contents are provided below.

```
velocimacro.library=VM_global_library.vm
runtime.log.logsystem.class =
        org.apache.velocity.runtime.log.Log4JLogSystem
```

Example 1: Spring-MVC Using Velocity Templates

The steps required to implement spring-MVC using Velocity templates are listed below:

1. Configure the spring-MVC front controller in "web.xml."
2. Configure Velocity and spring MVC in the servlet context "springweb-servlet.xml" file.
3. Develop the required Velocity templates and controller classes.

4. Deploy the WAR file and test the application.

The above-specified steps are described in the following sections:

Step 1: Configure spring-MVC front controller in "web.xml"

Spring provides a front controller servlet to route incoming requests to a specific spring controller. Configure the spring-provided front controller servlet in web.xml.

```
<servlet>
    <servlet-name>springweb</servlet-name>
    <servlet-class>
        org.springframework.web.servlet.DispatcherServlet
    </servlet-class>
</servlet>

<servlet-mapping>
    <servlet-name>springweb</servlet-name>
    <url-pattern>*.action</url-pattern>
</servlet-mapping>
```

Step 2: Configure Velocity and spring-MVC in the servlet context "springweb-servlet.xml" file.

The following XML elements enable the spring controller configuration.

```
<mvc:annotation-driven/>
<context:annotation-config/>
```

The following XML element is used to configure the Velocity view resolver.

```
<bean id="viewResolver" class="com.learning.common.velocity.
                    VelocityToolboxViewResolver">
    ...
</beans>
```

The following XML element is used to load the Velocity tools configured in "toolbox.xml" into the Velocity context.

```
<property name="toolboxConfigLocation">
    <value>/WEB-INF/toolbox.xml</value>
</property>
```

The spring-provided `VelocityViewResolver` class is used to resolve the Velocity views. The `VelocityToolboxViewResolver` class extends the `VelocityViewResolver` to support the Velocity toolbox configuration.

The complete `VelocityToolboxViewResolver` class code is provided below.

```
// VelocityToolboxViewResolver.java
package com.learning.common.velocity;

import java.util.Locale;
```

```
import org.springframework.web.servlet.View;
import org.springframework.web.servlet.view.velocity.
        VelocityViewResolver;

public class VelocityToolboxViewResolver extends VelocityViewResolver {

    private String toolboxConfigLocation;

    public VelocityToolboxViewResolver() {
        setViewClass(VelocityToolboxView.class);
    }

    public void setToolboxConfigLocation(String toolboxConfigLocation) {
        this.toolboxConfigLocation = toolboxConfigLocation;
    }
    protected View loadView(String viewName, Locale locale)
                throws Exception {
        VelocityToolboxView view = (VelocityToolboxView)
                    super.loadView(viewName, locale);
        view.setToolboxConfigLocation(toolboxConfigLocation);
        return view;
    }
}
```

The following utility class is used to add extra fields into the Velocity context, such as path, context path, and so forth.

```
// VelocityToolboxView.java
package com.learning.common.velocity;

import java.util.Map;
import javax.servlet.http.HttpServletRequest;
import javax.servlet.http.HttpServletResponse;
import org.apache.velocity.context.Context;

public class VelocityToolboxView extends org.springframework.web.servlet.
        view.velocity.VelocityToolboxView {

    protected Context createVelocityContext(Map model,
                HttpServletRequest request,
                HttpServletResponse response) throws Exception {
        Context context = super.createVelocityContext(model, request,
                            response);
        context.put("base", request.getContextPath());
        return context;
    }
}
```

The complete spring servlet context configuration is provided below and is named the "springweb-servlet.xml."

```
<?xml version="1.0" encoding="UTF-8"?>
<beans xmlns="http://www.springframework.org/schema/beans"
    xmlns:xsi="http://www.w3.org/2001/XMLSchema-instance"
    mlns:context="http://www.springframework.org/schema/context"
    xmlns:mvc="http://www.springframework.org/schema/mvc"
```

```
    xsi:schemaLocation="http://www.springframework.org/schema/beans
    http://www.springframework.org/schema/beans/spring-beans-3.0.xsd
    http://www.springframework.org/schema/context
    http://www.springframework.org/schema/context/spring-context-3.0.xsd
    http://www.springframework.org/schema/mvc
    http://www.springframework.org/schema/mvc/spring-mvc-3.0.xsd">

    <context:annotation-config/>

    <context:component-scan
            base-package="com.learning.spring.controller"/>

    <mvc:annotation-driven/>

    <!-- Configure velocity view resolver -->
    <bean id="velocityConfig" class="org.springframework.web.servlet
                    .view.velocity.VelocityConfigurer">
        <property name="resourceLoaderPath"><value>/</value></property>
        <property name="configLocation">
            <value>/WEB-INF/velocity.properties</value>
        </property>
    </bean>

    <bean id="viewResolver" class="com.learning.common.velocity.
                        VelocityToolboxViewResolver">
        <property name="cache"><value>true</value></property>
        <property name="prefix"><value></value></property>
        <property name="suffix"><value>.vm</value></property>
        <property name="contentType">
            <value>text/html</value>
        </property>
        <property name="requestContextAttribute" value="rc"/>
        <property name="exposeRequestAttributes" value="true" />
        <property name="exposeSessionAttributes" value="true" />
        <property name="exposeSpringMacroHelpers" value="true" />
        <property name="toolboxConfigLocation">
            <value>/WEB-INF/toolbox.xml</value>
        </property>
    </bean>
</beans>
```

Step 3: Develop the required Velocity templates and controller classes.

The following URL is used to invoke the spring controller class.

```
http://localhost:8080/springweb/demo/velocity.action
```

The front controller routes the request to the `show(...)` method of the controller class. The URL path "`/demo/velocity.action`" should match the value attribute of the `@RequestMapping` annotation which is "`/demo/velocity.action`".

```
@RequestMapping(value="/demo/velocity.action", method=RequestMethod.GET)
public String show(HttpServletRequest request,ModelMap model) {
    ...
}
```

The following statement in the controller class is used to display the output in the Velocity template.

```
return "/demo/velocitydemo";
```

Velocity templates can reference the request and model objects data. An example is provided below.

```
model.put("heading", "Learning Spring MVC");
request.setAttribute("name", "Spring");
```

The complete controller class code is provided below.

```
// VelocityDemoController.java
package com.learning.spring.controller;

import org.springframework.stereotype.Controller;
import org.springframework.web.bind.annotation.RequestMapping;
import org.springframework.web.bind.annotation.RequestMethod;
import org.springframework.ui.ModelMap;
import javax.servlet.http.HttpServletRequest;
import java.util.*;
import com.learning.spring.security.Account;

@Controller
public class VelocityDemoController {

    @RequestMapping(value = "/demo/velocity.action",
                    method = RequestMethod.GET)
    public String show(HttpServletRequest request,ModelMap model) {

        // Adding data to a model.
        model.put("heading", "Learning Spring MVC");

        // Adding variable to request
        request.setAttribute("name", "Spring");

        // Adding variable to request
        request.setAttribute("dob", new Date());

        // Adding data to a list
        List<String> namesList = new ArrayList<String>();
        namesList.add("Spring");
        namesList.add("Learning");
        namesList.add("Vesion 3.x");
        request.setAttribute("namesList", namesList);

        // Adding data to a map
        Map<String, String> dataHashMap =
                        new HashMap<String, String>();
        dataHashMap.put("Topic1", "Java");
        dataHashMap.put("Topic2", "Spring-Security");
        dataHashMap.put("Topic3", "Spring-MVC");
        request.setAttribute("dataHashMap", dataHashMap);

        // Adding account data to a List
        List<Account> accountDataList = new ArrayList<Account>();
```

```
                Account account1 = new Account();
                account1.setAccountNumber("121213");
                account1.setAccountHolderName("John Smith");
                account1.setBalance(99975L);
                accountDataList.add(account1);

                Account account2 = new Account();
                account2.setAccountNumber("3434133");
                account2.setAccountHolderName("John Sims");
                account2.setBalance(45000L);
                accountDataList.add(account2);
                model.put("accountDataList", accountDataList);

                // Adding account data to a Map
                Map<String, Account> accountDataMap =
                                new HashMap<String, Account>();
                accountDataMap.put("account1", account1);
                accountDataMap.put("account2", account2);
                model.put("accountDataMap", accountDataMap);

                model.put("errorMessage", "Check for error messages ");

                // Display the content on velocitydemo.vm page
                return "/demo/velocitydemo";
        }
}
```

The complete Velocity template code is provided below and is named the "velocitydemo.vm". This template is used to display the model data referenced in the spring controller class.

```
<html>
<head>
     <title>Spring Velocity Demo</title>
</head>
<body>

<form id="velocityDemo" method="post">

     <div> Heading: $heading  </div><br/>
     <div> Name: $name </div> <br/>

     <div>
          If Condition: <br/>
          #if ($name.equals("Spring"))
               Spring
          #else
               Not a Spring
          #end
     </div> <br/>

     <div>
          If-elseif Condition: <br/>
          #if($name.equals("Spring"))
               Spring
          #elseif($name.equals("Security"))
               Security
          #else
```

```
            Java
      #end
</div> <br/>

<div>
      For Loop - List Data:  <br/>
      #foreach($name in $namesList)
            $name <br/>
      #end
</div> <br/>

<div>
      For Loop - Account Data List Data:  <br/>
      <table>
            #foreach($account in $accountDataList)
                  <tr>
                        <td> $account.getAccountNumber()</td>
                        <td> $account.getAccountHolderName()</td>
                        <td> $account.getBalance()</td>
                  </tr>
            #end
      </table>
</div> <br/>

<div>
      For Loop - MapData: <br/>
      #foreach($key in $dataHashMap.keySet())
            Key is: $key
            Value is: $dataHashMap.get($key) <br/>
      #end
</div> <br/>

<div>
      For Loop - Account Data Map Data:  <br/>
      <table>
            #foreach($mapKey in $accountDataMap.keySet())
                  #set($accountObj = $accountDataMap.get($mapKey))
                  <tr>
                        <td> $accountObj.getAccountNumber()</td>
                        <td> $accountObj.getAccountHolderName()</td>
                        <td> $accountObj.getBalance()</td>
                  </tr>
            #end
      </table>
</div> <br/>

<div>
      Velocity Macro: <br/>
      #commontableheader()
</div> <br/>

<div>
      Velocity Toolbox: <br/>
      $dateTool.format("MM/dd/yyyy", $dob) <br/>
      $math.add(100, 200)<br/>
</div> <br/>
```

```
#parse("demo/message.vm")

#set($firstName = "John")
#set($lastName= "Smith")
#set($fullName = "$firstName$lastName")
Full name is: $fullName
```

```
</form>

</body>
</html>
```

Step 4: Deploy the WAR file and test the application

Figure 3-1: WAR file structure

Name	Path	Type	Size	Attri
index.vm		VM File	25	
VM_global_library.vm		VM File	251	
velocitydemo.vm	demo\	VM File	2,348	
velocityhome.vm	demo\	VM File	535	
MANIFEST.MF	META-INF\	MF File	102	
springweb-servlet.xml	WEB-INF\	XML File	6,376	
toolbox.xml	WEB-INF\	XML File	1,210	
velocity.properties	WEB-INF\	PROPER..	116	A
web.xml	WEB-INF\	XML File	2,061	
VelocityToolboxView.class	WEB-INF\classes\com\learning\common\velocity\	CLASS File	1,140	
VelocityToolboxViewResolver.class	WEB-INF\classes\com\learning\common\velocity\	CLASS File	1,094	
VelocityDemoController.class	WEB-INF\classes\com\learning\spring\controller\	CLASS File	3,001	
Account.class	WEB-INF\classes\com\learning\spring\security\	CLASS File	1,055	
org.springframework.beans-3.0.7.RELEASE.jar	WEB-INF\lib\	JAR File	556,743	
org.springframework.context-3.0.7.RELEASE.jar	WEB-INF\lib\	JAR File	670,385	
org.springframework.core-3.0.7.RELEASE.jar	WEB-INF\lib\	JAR File	383,617	
org.springframework.web-3.0.7.RELEASE.jar	WEB-INF\lib\	JAR File	398,379	
velocity-1.4.jar	WEB-INF\lib\	JAR File	361,173	
velocity-tools-1.2.jar	WEB-INF\lib\	JAR File	88,194	

Selected 1 file, 25 bytes   Total 19 files, 2,420KB

This section provides step-by-step instructions for WAR file building and deployment.

- Package all of the artifacts in a WAR file. The structure of the WAR file is shown in Figure 3-1.
- Include all required JAR files in the "/WEB-INF/lib" directory.
- Copy the WAR file into the "Tomcat/webapp/" directory.
- Start the tomcat server → run "startup.bat" from command line.

After successful deployment, test the deployed application. Use the following URL to view the output.

```
http://localhost:8080/springweb/demo/velocity.action
```

Example-1 uses the HTTP-GET request operation. Now we will extend this example to handle the HTTP-POST requests. Modify the controller class request method to POST. The modified method signature is given below.

```
@RequestMapping(value = "/demo/velocity.action",
                method = RequestMethod.POST)
public String show(HttpServletRequest request, ModelMap model) {
    ...
}
```

Create a new Velocity template file to send a post request. The complete Velocity template code is provided below and is named the "velocityhome.vm."

```
<html>
<head>
<title>Spring Velocity Demo</title>
<script type="text/javascript">
    function invokeVelocityController() {
        document.forms[0].action="/springweb/demo/velocity.action";
        document.forms[0].submit();
    }
</script>
</head>
<body bgcolor="pink">
    <form action="" method="post">
        <table align="center">
            <tr>
                <td><b>
                    <a href="javascript:invokeVelocityController()">
                        Velocity Demo </a></b>
                </td>
            </tr>
        </table>
    </form>
</body>
</html>
```

The step-by-step instructions to test the POST-operation are provided below.

- Invoke the home page → http://localhost:8080/springweb/demo/velocityhome.vm
- "velocityhome.vm" page will displayed with the "Velocity Demo" hyperlink.
- Click on the "Velocity Demo" hyperlink.
- This action invokes the spring controller → velocitydemo.vm page will be displayed.

FreeMarker Syntax and Fundamentals

FreeMarker is an open-source template engine that provides a scripting language to reference the Java data objects. Freemarker templates are used in view layer to render the controller-provided data. Freemarker is an open-source framework. The commonly used extension for a Freemarker template is ".ftl". This section illustrates how to reference the Java objects in Freemarker templates.

The Java code is:

```
model.put("heading", "Learning Spring MVC");
```

The Freemarker template code is:

```
<div> Heading:  ${heading}  </div><br/>
```

The Java code is:

```
List<String> namesList = new ArrayList<String>();
namesList.add("Spring");
namesList.add("Learning");
namesList.add("Vesion 3.x");
request.setAttribute("namesList", namesList);
```

The Freemarker template code is:

```
<div>
    For Loop - List Data:  <br/>
    [#list namesList as sname]
        ${sname}  <br/>
    [/#list] <br/>
</div> <br/>
```

The Java code is:

```
Map<String, String> dataHashMap = new HashMap<String, String>();
dataHashMap.put("Topic1", "Java");
dataHashMap.put("Topic2", "Spring-Security");
dataHashMap.put("Topic3", "Spring-MVC");
request.setAttribute("dataHashMap", dataHashMap);
```

The Freemarker template code is:

```
<div>
    For Loop - MapData: <br/>
    [#list dataHashMap?keys as key]
        Key: ${key}
        Value is: ${dataHashMap[key]}<br/>
    [/#list]
</div> <br/>
```

The Java code is:

```
List<Account> accountDataList = new ArrayList<Account>();
Account account1 = new Account();
account1.setAccountNumber("121213");
account1.setAccountHolderName("John Smith");
account1.setBalance(99975L);
accountDataList.add(account1);

Account account2 = new Account();
account2.setAccountNumber("3434133");
account2.setAccountHolderName("John Sims");
account2.setBalance(45000L);
accountDataList.add(account2);
model.put("accountDataList", accountDataList);
```

The Freemarker template code is:

```
<div>
    For Loop - Account Data List Data: <br/>
    <table>
        [#list accountDataList as account]
            <tr>
                <td> ${account.getAccountNumber()} </td>
                <td> ${account.getAccountHolderName()} </td>
                <td> ${account.getBalance()} </td>
            </tr>
        [/#list]
    </table>
</div> <br/>
```

The following example demonstrates a variable declaration in Freemarker templates.

```
[#assign name = "John Smith"]
```

The Java code is:

```
Map<String, Account> accountDataMap =
                new HashMap<String, Account>();
accountDataMap.put("account1", account1);
accountDataMap.put("account2", account2);
model.put("accountDataMap", accountDataMap);
```

The Freemarker template code is:

```
<div>
    For Loop - Account Data Map Data:  <br/>
    <table>
        [#list accountDataMap?keys as key]
            <tr>
                <td>${accountDataMap[key].getAccountNumber()}
                </td>
                <td>${accountDataMap[key].getAccountHolderName()}
                </td>
                <td> ${accountDataMap[key].getBalance()}</td>
            </tr>
        [/#list]
    </table>
</div> <br/>
```

The following example demonstrates the Freemarker "if-else" condition syntax.

```
<div>
    If Condition: <br/>
    [#if name == "Spring"]
        Spring
    [#else]
        Not a Spring
    [/#if]
</div> <br/>
```

The following example demonstrates the Freemarker "if-elseif" condition syntax.

```
<div>
    If-elseif Condition: <br/>
    [#if name == "Spring"]
        Spring
    [#elseif name == "Security"]
        Security
    [#else]
        Java
    [/#if]
</div> <br/>
```

The following example demonstrates the Freemarker "include" syntax, which is used to include a Freemarker template inside another template.

```
[#include "sample.ftl"]
```

The following example demonstrates the use of a Freemarker macro.

```
<div>
    [#macro displaymessage]
    <div id="heading" style="font-weight: bold;
            text-align: left; color: red;">
        Freemarker macro displays HTML
    </div>
    [/#macro]
    [@displaymessage/]
</div> <br/>
```

Example 2: Spring-MVC Using Freemarker Templates

The steps required to implement spring-MVC using Freemarker templates are listed below:

1. Configure the spring-MVC front controller in "web.xml."
2. Configure Freemarker and spring-MVC in the servlet context "springweb-servlet.xml" file.
3. Develop the required Freemarker templates and controller classes.
4. Deploy the WAR file and test the application.

The above-specified steps are described in the following sections:

Step 1: Configure the spring-MVC front controller in "web.xml."

Here, reuse the "web.xml" provided in Example-1

Step 2: Configure Freemarker and spring-MVC in the servlet context "springweb-servlet.xml" file.

The following XML element is used to configure the Freemarker view resolver.

```
<bean id="viewResolver" class="org.springframework.web.servlet.view.
        freemarker.FreeMarkerViewResolver">
    ...
</bean>
```

The complete spring servlet context configuration is provided below and is named the "springweb-servlet.xml".

```xml
<?xml version="1.0" encoding="UTF-8"?>
<beans xmlns="http://www.springframework.org/schema/beans"
    xmlns:xsi="http://www.w3.org/2001/XMLSchema-instance"
    mlns:context="http://www.springframework.org/schema/context"
    xmlns:mvc="http://www.springframework.org/schema/mvc"
    xsi:schemaLocation="http://www.springframework.org/schema/beans
    http://www.springframework.org/schema/beans/spring-beans-3.0.xsd
    http://www.springframework.org/schema/context
    http://www.springframework.org/schema/context/spring-context-3.0.xsd
    http://www.springframework.org/schema/mvc
    http://www.springframework.org/schema/mvc/spring-mvc-3.0.xsd">

    <context:annotation-config/>

    <context:component-scan
            base-package="com.learning.spring.controller"/>

    <mvc:annotation-driven/>

    <!-- Configure FreeMarker view resolver -->
    <bean id="freemarkerConfig" class="org.springframework.web.servlet.
                    view.freemarker.FreeMarkerConfigurer">
        <property name="templateLoaderPath" value="/"/>
        <property name="defaultEncoding" value="UTF-8"/>
        <property name="freemarkerSettings">
            <props>
                <prop key="url_escaping_charset">UTF-8</prop>
            </props>
        </property>
    </bean>

    <bean id="viewResolver" class="org.springframework.web.servlet.view.
                    freemarker.FreeMarkerViewResolver">
        <property name="cache" value="true"/>
        <property name="prefix" value=""/>
        <property name="suffix" value=".ftl"/>
        <property name="contentType" value="text/html; charset=utf-8"/>
        <property name="exposeRequestAttributes" value="true"/>
        <property name="exposeSessionAttributes" value="true"/>
        <property name="exposeSpringMacroHelpers" value="true"/>
    </bean>
</beans>
```

Step 3: Develop the required Freemarker templates and controller classes.

Here, reuse the spring controller code provided in Example-1 with the following changes.

```java
@Controller
public class FreemarkerDemoController {

    @RequestMapping(value = "/demo/freemarker.action",
                    method = RequestMethod.GET)
    public String show(HttpServletRequest request,ModelMap model) {
```

```
                // ... Reuse the controller code provided in Example-1

        return "/demo/fmdemo";
    }
}
```

Include the spring-Freemarker "spring.ftl" library in "fmdemo.ftl" page. The complete Freemarker template code is provided below and is named the "fmdemo.ftl". This template is applied to the data referenced in the spring controller class.

```
[#ftl]
[#import "/spring.ftl" as spring/]
<html>
<head>
    <title>Spring Freemarker Demo</title>
</head>
<body>

<form id="freemarkerDemo" method="post">

    <div> Heading:  ${heading}  </div><br/>
    <div> Name: ${name} </div> <br/>

    <div>
        If Condition: <br/>
        [#if name == "Spring"]
            Spring
        [#else]
            Not a Spring
        [/#if]
    </div> <br/>

    <div>
        If-elseif Condition: <br/>
        [#if name == "Spring"]
            Spring
        [#elseif name == "Spring"]
            Security
        [#else]
            Java
        [/#if]
    </div> <br/>

    <div>
        For Loop - List Data:  <br/>
        [#list namesList as sname]
            ${sname} <br/>
        [/#list] <br/>
    </div> <br/>

    <div>
        For Loop - Account Data List Data:  <br/>
        <table>
            [#list accountDataList as account]
                <tr>
                    <td> ${account.getAccountNumber()}</td>
```

```
                                    <td> ${account.getAccountHolderName()}</td>
                                    <td> ${account.getBalance()}</td>
                            </tr>
                    [/#list]
            </table>
    </div> <br/>

    <div>
            [#include "sample.ftl"]
    </div> <br/>

    <div>
            [#assign firstName = "John"]
            [#assign lastName = "Smith"]
            [#assign fullName = "${firstName}${lastName}"]
            ${fullName}
    </div> <br/>

    <div>
            [#macro displaymessage]
                    <div id="heading" style="font-weight: bold; text-align:
                                    left; color: red;">
                            Freemarker macro displays HTML
                    </div>
            [/#macro]

            [@displaymessage/]
    </div> <br/>

    <div>
            For Loop - MapData: <br/>
            [#list dataHashMap?keys as key]
                    Key: ${key}
                    Value is: ${dataHashMap[key]}    <br/>
            [/#list]
    </div> <br/>

    <div>
            For Loop - Account Data Map Data: <br/>
            <table>
                    [#list accountDataMap?keys as key]
                    <tr>
                            <td> ${accountDataMap[key].getAccountNumber()}</td>
                            <td> ${accountDataMap[key].getAccountHolderName()}
                            </td>
                            <td> ${accountDataMap[key].getBalance()} </td>
                    </tr>
                    [/#list]
            </table>
    </div> <br/>

</form>

</body>
</html>
```

Step 4: Deploy the WAR file and test the application

Here, reuse the build and deployment instructions provided in Example-1. The structure of the WAR file is shown in Figure 3-3.

Figure 3-3: WAR file structure

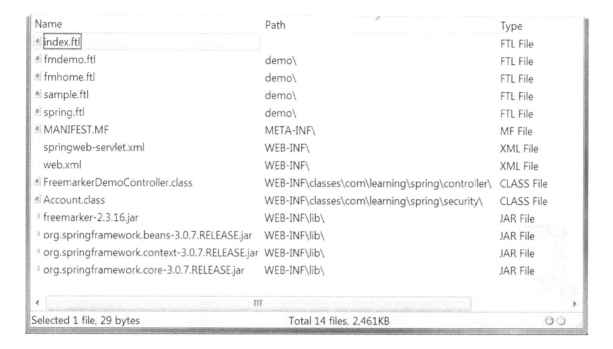

Name	Path	Type
index.ftl		FTL File
fmdemo.ftl	demo\	FTL File
fmhome.ftl	demo\	FTL File
sample.ftl	demo\	FTL File
spring.ftl	demo\	FTL File
MANIFEST.MF	META-INF\	MF File
springweb-servlet.xml	WEB-INF\	XML File
web.xml	WEB-INF\	XML File
FreemarkerDemoController.class	WEB-INF\classes\com\learning\spring\controller\	CLASS File
Account.class	WEB-INF\classes\com\learning\spring\security\	CLASS File
freemarker-2.3.16.jar	WEB-INF\lib\	JAR File
org.springframework.beans-3.0.7.RELEASE.jar	WEB-INF\lib\	JAR File
org.springframework.context-3.0.7.RELEASE.jar	WEB-INF\lib\	JAR File
org.springframework.core-3.0.7.RELEASE.jar	WEB-INF\lib\	JAR File

Selected 1 file, 29 bytes   Total 14 files, 2,461KB

After successful deployment, test the deployed application. Use the following URL to view the output.

```
http://localhost:8080/springweb/demo/freemarker.action
```

Example-2 uses the HTTP-GET request operation. Now we will extend this example to handle the HTTP-POST requests. The modified controller class method with the POST operation is provided below.

```
@RequestMapping(value = "/demo/ freemarker.action",
            method = RequestMethod.POST)
public String show(HttpServletRequest request, ModelMap model) {
    ...
}
```

Create a new Freemarker template file to send a post request; name it the "fmhome.ftl." Refer to the "velocityhome.vm" code provided in Example-1.

JSP and JSTL Syntax and Fundamentals

Java Server Pages (JSP) is used to create dynamically generated web pages that deliver HTML content. JSP is a Java-based alternative for Velocity and Freemarker. JSP is a part of the Java enterprise edition. The commonly used extension for a JSP page is ".jsp"

The Java Server Pages Standard Tag Library (JSTL) provides standard tags that can be used in the view layer for data processing. JSTL tags reference the controller-provided model data in JSP pages. These tags are used in the view layer for standard data processing such as conditional execution, looping, and so forth. The use of JSTL is illustrated in this section.

The Java code is:

```
modelMap.addAttribute("test", "JSP Test Page");
```

The JSTL code is:

```
Variable: ${test}
```

The Java code is:

```
Employee emp = new Employee();
emp.setAdEntId("jsmith");
emp.setEmpId(1233);
emp.setFirstName("John");
emp.setLastName("Smith");
emp.setMiddleName("S");
modelMap.addAttribute("employee", emp);
```

The JSTL code is:

```
<tr>
    <td>
        ${employee.adEntId}  - ${employee.empId} -
        ${employee.firstName} - ${employee.lastName} -
        ${employee.middleName}
    </td>
</tr>
```

The Java code is:

```
List<Employee> employeeList = new ArrayList<Employee>();
Employee emp1 = new Employee();
emp1.setAdEntId("jsmith");
emp1.setEmpId(1233);
emp1.setFirstName("John");
emp1.setLastName("Smith");
emp1.setMiddleName("S");

Employee emp2 = new Employee();
emp2.setAdEntId("jsims");
emp2.setEmpId(9999);
emp2.setFirstName("John");
emp2.setLastName("Sims");
emp2.setMiddleName("S");

employeeList.add(emp1);
employeeList.add(emp2);
modelMap.addAttribute("employeeList", employeeList);
```

The JSTL code is:

```
<c:forEach var="employee" items="${employeeList}">
    <tr>
        <td>
            ${employee.adEntId}  - ${employee.empId} -
            ${employee.firstName} - ${employee.lastName} -
            ${employee.middleName}
        </td>
    </tr>
</c:forEach>
```

The Java code is:

```
Map<String, List<Employee>> mapList =
            new HashMap<String, List<Employee>>();
mapList.put("employeeMapList", employeeList);
modelMap.addAttribute("employeeMapList", mapList);
```

The JSTL code is:

```
<c:forEach var="mapList" items="${employeeMapList}">
    <c:forEach var="emp" items="${mapList.value}">
        <tr>
            <td>
                ${emp.adEntId} - ${emp.empId} - ${emp.firstName}
                    - ${emp.lastName} - ${emp.middleName}
            </td>
        </tr>
    </c:forEach>
</c:forEach>
```

Example 3: Spring-MVC Using JSP and JSTL

The steps required to implement spring-MVC using JSP are listed below:

1. Configure the spring-MVC front controller in "web.xml."
2. Configure the JSP view resolver in the "springweb-servlet.xml" file.
3. Develop the required JSP pages and controller classes.
4. Deploy the WAR file and test the application.

The above-specified steps are described in the following sections:

Step 1: Configure the spring-MVC front controller in "web.xml."

Here, reuse the "web.xml" created in Example-1.

Step 2: Configure the JSP view resolver in the "springweb-servlet.xml" file.

The following xml element is used to configure the JSP view resolver. Reuse the "springweb-servlet.xml" file created in Example-1 with the following change.

```
<bean id="viewResolver" class="org.springframework.web.servlet.view.
                            InternalResourceViewResclver">
    <property name="viewClass"
```

```
                  value="org.springframework.web.servlet.view.JstlView"/>
     <property name="prefix" value=""/>
     <property name="suffix" value=".jsp"/>
     <property name="contentType"><value>text/html</value></property>
     <property name="requestContextAttribute" value="rc"/>
</bean>
```

There are two ways in which a JSP view resolver can be configured.

CASE 1: Plain old JSP without using JSTL tags.

The JSP view resolver configuration for plain old JSP is provided below.

```
<bean id="viewResolver" class="org.springframework.web.servlet.view.
                              InternalResourceViewResolver">
     <property name="prefix" value=""/>
     <property name="suffix" value=".jsp"/>
     <property name="contentType"><value>text/html</value></property>
     <property name="requestContextAttribute" value="rc"/>
</bean>
```

CASE 2: JSP with JSTL tags.

The JSP view resolver configuration for JSP with JSTL is provided below.

```
<bean id="viewResolver" class="org.springframework.web.servlet.view.
                              InternalResourceViewResolver">
     <property name="viewClass"
             value="org.springframework.web.servlet.view.JstlView"/>
     ...
</bean>
```

Case-1 also works for JSPs with JSTL, and the `JstlView` is recommended for use while working with i18N-features.

Step 3: Develop the required JSP pages and controller classes.

The complete spring controller code is provided below.

```
// JSPDemoController.java
package com.learning.spring.controller;

import org.springframework.stereotype.Controller;
import org.springframework.web.servlet.ModelAndView;
import org.springframework.web.bind.annotation.RequestMapping;
import org.springframework.web.bind.annotation.RequestMethod;
import org.springframework.ui.ModelMap;
import java.util.*;
import com.learning.spring.dvo.User;
import com.learning.spring.dvo.Employee;

@Controller
public class JSPDemoController {

     @RequestMapping(value = "/demo/jspdemo.action",
```

```
                method = RequestMethod.GET)
    public ModelAndView view() {

        User user = new User();
        user.setAdEntId("asmudun");
        user.setLanId("asmudun");
        user.setFirstName("Achyutha");

        ModelMap mm = new ModelMap();
        mm.addAttribute("user", user);

        // Simple variable
        mm.addAttribute("test", "JSP Test Page");

        // Adding values to a Map
        Map<String, String> dataMap = new HashMap<String, String>();
        dataMap.put("firstName", "John");
        dataMap.put("lastName", "Smith");
        mm.addAttribute("names", dataMap);

        // Adding java bean objects to a List
        List<Employee> employeeList = new ArrayList<Employee>();
        Employee emp1 = new Employee();
        emp1.setAdEntId("jsmith");
        emp1.setEmpId(1233);
        emp1.setFirstName("John");
        emp1.setLastName("Smith");
        emp1.setMiddleName("S");
        mm.addAttribute("employee", emp1);

        Employee emp2 = new Employee();
        emp2.setAdEntId("jsims");
        emp2.setEmpId(9999);
        emp2.setFirstName("John");
        emp2.setLastName("Sims");
        emp2.setMiddleName("S");

        // Adding java bean objects to a List
        employeeList.add(emp1);
        employeeList.add(emp2);
        mm.addAttribute("employeeList", employeeList);

        // Adding ArrayList to a HashMap
        Map<String, List<Employee>> mapList =
                    new HashMap<String, List<Employee>>();
        mapList.put("employeeMapList", employeeList);
        mm.addAttribute("employeeMapList", mapList);

        return new ModelAndView("/demo/jspdemo", mm);
    }
}
```

The complete JSP code is provided below and is named the "jspdemo.vm". This JSP displays the controller-provided model data.

```
<%@ page language="java" contentType="text/html;
                charset=UTF-8" pageEncoding="UTF-8"%>
```

```
<%@ taglib prefix="c" uri="http://java.sun.com/jsp/jstl/core" %>

<html>
<head>
    <title>Spring MVC with JSP and JSTL</title>
</head>
<body>
<form method="post">
<table>
    <tr><td>Variable: ${test} </td></tr>

    <tr><td>Iterating Map Data </td></tr>
    <c:forEach var="entry" items="${names}">
        <tr>
            <td> Key: <c:out value="${entry.key}"/> </td>
            <td> Value: <c:out value="${entry.value}"/> </td>
        </tr>
    </c:forEach>

    <tr><td>Displaying Java Bean Object Data </td></tr>
    <tr>
        <td>
            ${employee.adEntId} - ${employee.empId} -
            ${employee.firstName} - ${employee.lastName} -
            ${employee.middleName}
        </td>
    </tr>

    <tr><td>Iterating List Data </td></tr>
    <c:forEach var="employee" items="${employeeList}">
        <tr>
            <td>
                ${employee.adEntId} - ${employee.empId} -
                ${employee.firstName} - ${employee.lastName} -
                ${employee.middleName}
            </td>
        </tr>
    </c:forEach>

    <tr><td> Iterating an ArrayList inside a HashMap </td></tr>
    <c:forEach var="mapList" items="${employeeMapList}">
        <c:forEach var="emp" items="${mapList.value}">
            <tr>
                <td>
                    ${emp.adEntId} - ${emp.empId} - ${emp.firstName}
                     - ${emp.lastName} - ${emp.middleName}
                </td>
            </tr>
        </c:forEach>
    </c:forEach>
</table>
</form>
</body>
</html>
```

Step 4: Deploy the WAR file and test the application.

Here, reuse the build and deployment instructions provided in Example-1. The structure of the WAR file is shown in Figure 3-4.

After the WAR file is successfully deployed, test the deployed application. Use the following URL to view the output.

```
http://localhost:8080/springweb/demo/jspdemo.action
```

Example-3 uses the HTTP-GET request operation. Extend this example to handle the HTTP-POST requests.

Figure 3-4: WAR file structure

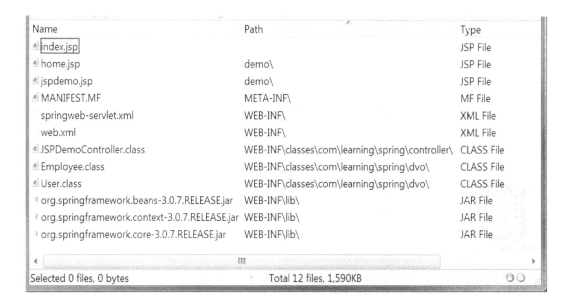

JSF Fundamentals

Java Server Faces (JSF) is a specification for developing Java-based web applications. JSF can be used with JSP and Facelets and provides a component, event-based object model for developing rich internet applications. JSF is part of Java EE, and the latest version of JSF is 2.0. This section illustrates the spring integration with JSF.

Example 4: Integrating JSF2 with Spring

JSF2 can be integrated with the spring framework. The steps required to integrate JSF with spring are listed below. In this example, spring is used for wiring the bean classes.

1. Configure the JSF front controller in "web.xml."
2. Define the bean class in the spring "applicationContext.xml."
3. Configure JSF configurations in "faces-config.xml."
4. Develop the required JSP pages, bean, and controller classes.
5. Deploy the WAR file and test the application.

The above-specified steps are described in the following sections.

Step 1: Configure the JSF front controller in "web.xml"

The complete web.xml file is provided below. Inline comments are provided to explain the purpose of each "web.xml" element configuration.

```xml
<?xml version="1.0" encoding="UTF-8"?>
<web-app version="2.4" xmlns="http://java.sun.com/xml/ns/j2ee"
    xmlns:xsi="http://www.w3.org/2001/XMLSchema-instance"
    xsi:schemaLocation="http://java.sun.com/xml/ns/j2ee
    http://java.sun.com/xml/ns/j2ee/web-app_2_4.xsd">

<display-name>Spring Web Application</display-name>

<!-- Spring listener class to load the application context files -->
<listener>
    <listener-class>
        org.springframework.web.context.ContextLoaderListener
    </listener-class>
</listener>

<listener>
    <listener-class>
        org.springframework.web.context.request.
            RequestContextListener
    </listener-class>
</listener>

<context-param>
    <param-name>contextConfigLocation</param-name>
    <param-value>
        /WEB-INF/applicationContext.xml
    </param-value>
</context-param>

<!-- Faces config listener and Servlet -->
<listener>
    <listener-class>
        com.sun.faces.config.ConfigureListener
    </listener-class>
</listener>

<servlet>
    <servlet-name>Faces Servlet</servlet-name>
    <servlet-class>javax.faces.webapp.FacesServlet</servlet-class>
    <load-on-startup>1</load-on-startup>
</servlet>

<!-- Faces Servlet Mapping -->
<servlet-mapping>
    <servlet-name>Faces Servlet</servlet-name>
    <url-pattern>*.faces</url-pattern>
</servlet-mapping>

<!-- The Welcome File -->
<welcome-file-list>
```

```
            <welcome-file>/demo/index.jsp</welcome-file>
    </welcome-file-list>

    <!-- Necessary for the Tomahawk advanced tags (e.g., inputDate) -->
    <filter>
        <filter-name>MyFacesExtensionsFilter</filter-name>
        <filter-class>
            org.apache.myfaces.webapp.filter.ExtensionsFilter
        </filter-class>
        <init-param>
            <param-name>maxFileSize</param-name>
            <param-value>20m</param-value>
        </init-param>
    </filter>

    <!-- extension mapping for adding <script/>, <link/>, and other
         resource tags to JSF-pages  -->
    <filter-mapping>
        <filter-name>MyFacesExtensionsFilter</filter-name>
        <!-- servlet-name must match the name of your
                 javax.faces.webapp.FacesServlet entry -->
        <servlet-name>Faces Servlet</servlet-name>
    </filter-mapping>

    <!-- Extension mapping for serving page-independent resources
                 (javascript, stylesheets, images, etc.)  -->
    <filter-mapping>
        <filter-name>MyFacesExtensionsFilter</filter-name>
        <url-pattern>/faces/myFacesExtensionResource/*</url-pattern>
    </filter-mapping>

</web-app>
```

Step 2: Define the bean class in the spring "applicationContext.xml."

The complete XML is provided below and is named the "applicationContext.xml." The spring-managed "userBean" reference is injected into the JSF controller class.

```
<?xml version="1.0" encoding="UTF-8"?>
<beans xmlns="http://www.springframework.org/schema/beans"
    xmlns:xsi="http://www.w3.org/2001/XMLSchema-instance"
    xmlns:context="http://www.springframework.org/schema/context"
    xsi:schemaLocation="http://www.springframework.org/schema/beans
    http://www.springframework.org/schema/beans/spring-beans-3.0.xsd
    http://www.springframework.org/schema/context
    http://www.springframework.org/schema/context/spring-context-
        3.0.xsd">

    <context:annotation-config/>

    <bean id="userBean" class="com.learning.spring.jsf.UserBean"/>

</beans>
```

Step 3: Configure JSF configurations in "faces-config.xml."

The following XML element is used to integrate JSF2 with the spring framework. This configuration allows you to access the beans configured in the spring application context file.

```xml
<application>
    <el-resolver>
        org.springframework.web.jsf.el.SpringBeanFacesELResolver
    </el-resolver>
</application>
```

The following XML configuration is used to refer to the spring bean configured in the application context file.

```xml
<managed-property>
    <property-name>user</property-name>
    <value>#{userBean}</value>
</managed-property>
```

The complete XML configuration is provided below and is named the "faces-config.xml".

```xml
<?xml version="1.0" encoding="UTF-8"?>
<faces-config xmlns="http://java.sun.com/xml/ns/javaee"
    xmlns:xsi="http://www.w3.org/2001/XMLSchema-instance"
    xsi:schemaLocation="http://java.sun.com/xml/ns/javaee
    http://java.sun.com/xml/ns/javaee/web-facesconfig_2_0.xsd"
    version="2.0">

    <application>
        <el-resolver>
            org.springframework.web.jsf.el.SpringBeanFacesELResolver
        </el-resolver>
    </application>

    <!-- User navigation -->
    <navigation-rule>
        <from-view-id>/demo/adduser.jsp</from-view-id>
        <navigation-case>
            <from-outcome>EditUser</from-outcome>
            <to-view-id>/demo/edituser.jsp</to-view-id>
        </navigation-case>
        <navigation-case>
            <from-outcome>DeleteUser</from-outcome>
            <to-view-id>/demo/deleteuser.jsp</to-view-id>
        </navigation-case>
        <navigation-case>
            <from-outcome>AddUser</from-outcome>
            <to-view-id>/demo/adduser.jsp</to-view-id>
        </navigation-case>
    </navigation-rule>

    <!-- Configuring JSF controller, injecting the spring bean class -->
    <managed-bean>
        <managed-bean-name>UserHandler</managed-bean-name>
        <managed-bean-class>
            com.learning.spring.jsf.UserHandler
        </managed-bean-class>
        <managed-bean-scope>request</managed-bean-scope>
```

```
            <managed-property>
                <property-name>user</property-name>
                <value>#{userBean}</value>
            </managed-property>
        </managed-bean>

</faces-config>
```

Step 4: Develop the required JSP pages, bean and controller classes.

The complete home JSP code is provided below and is named the "home.jsp"

```
<html>
<head>
    <title>JSF Home Page</title>
</head>
    <body>
        <a href="<%=request.getContextPath()%>/demo/adduser.faces">
            Add Users</a>  <br/>
        <a href="<%=request.getContextPath()%>/demo/edituser.faces">
            Update Users</a> <br/>
        <a href="<%=request.getContextPath()%>/demo/deleteuser.faces">
            Delete Users</a> <br/>
    </body>
</html>
```

The complete add users JSP code is provided below and is named the "addusers.jsp"

```
<%@ taglib prefix="f" uri="http://java.sun.com/jsf/core" %>
<%@ taglib prefix="h" uri="http://java.sun.com/jsf/html" %>
<%@ taglib prefix="t" uri="http://myfaces.apache.org/tomahawk" %>
<html>
<head>
<title>Add User Page</title>
</head>
<body>
<f:view>
    <h:form id="addUserForm">
        <table>
            <div> <t:outputText id="message"
                            value="#{userBean.message}"/> </div>
            <tr>
                <th align="left">First Name</th>
                <td>
                    <t:inputText id="firstName" required="true"
                            value="#{userBean.firstName}"/>
                    <t:message for="firstName" />
                </td>
            </tr>
            <tr>
                <th align="left">Last Name</th>
                <td>
                    <t:inputText id="lastName"
                            value="#{userBean.lastName}"/>
                </td>
            </tr>
```

```
            <tr>
                <th align="left">Email Id</th>
                <td><t:inputText id="emailId"
                                 value="#{userBean.emailId}"/></td>
            </tr>
            <tr>
                <th align="left">Date</th>
                <td>
                    <t:inputDate value="#{userBean.currentDate}"
                                 popupCalendar="true"/>
                </td>
            </tr>
            <tr>
                <td>
                    <t:commandButton
                    action="#{UserHandler.createUser}" value="Save"/>
                    <t:commandButton action="ReloadUser"
                                     value="Cancel"/>
                </td>
            </tr>
        </table>
    </h:form>
</f:view>
</body>
</html>
```

The following Java bean class holds the model data.

```
// UserBean.java
package com.learning.spring.jsf;

import java.util.Date;

public class UserBean {

    private String firstName;
    private String lastName;
    private String emailId;
    private Date currentDate;
    private String message;

    // Add getter and setters
}
```

The below provided UserHandler class will be invoked from the add user JSP page.

```
// UserHandler.java
package com.learning.spring.jsf;

import java.util.Date;

public class UserHandler {

    private UserBean user;

    public UserBean getUser() {
```

```
            return user;
    }

    public void setUser(UserBean user) {
        this.user = user;
    }

    public String createUser() {
        String firstName = user.getFirstName();
        String lastName = user.getLastName();
        String emailId = user.getEmailId();
        Date currentDate = user.getCurrentDate();

        System.out.println("--- Data ---" + firstName + ", " +
                lastName + " , " + emailId + "," + currentDate);
        user.setMessage("Successfully added.");

        return "AddUser";
    }
}
```

Step 5: Deploy the WAR file and test the application.

Figure 3-5: WAR file structure

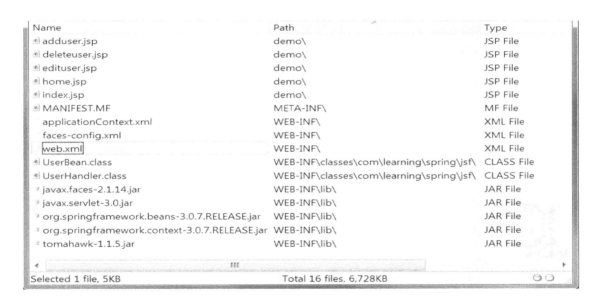

Name	Path	Type
adduser.jsp	demo\	JSP File
deleteuser.jsp	demo\	JSP File
edituser.jsp	demo\	JSP File
home.jsp	demo\	JSP File
index.jsp	demo\	JSP File
MANIFEST.MF	META-INF\	MF File
applicationContext.xml	WEB-INF\	XML File
faces-config.xml	WEB-INF\	XML File
web.xml	WEB-INF\	XML File
UserBean.class	WEB-INF\classes\com\learning\spring\jsf\	CLASS File
UserHandler.class	WEB-INF\classes\com\learning\spring\jsf\	CLASS File
javax.faces-2.1.14.jar	WEB-INF\lib\	JAR File
javax.servlet-3.0.jar	WEB-INF\lib\	JAR File
org.springframework.beans-3.0.7.RELEASE.jar	WEB-INF\lib\	JAR File
org.springframework.context-3.0.7.RELEASE.jar	WEB-INF\lib\	JAR File
tomahawk-1.1.5.jar	WEB-INF\lib\	JAR File

Selected 1 file, 5KB   Total 16 files, 6,728KB

Here, reuse the build and deployment instructions provided in Example-1. The structure of the WAR file is shown in Figure 3-5.

After you have successfully deployed the WAR file, test the deployed application. The step-by-step instructions are provided below.

- Invoke the home page → http://localhost:8080/springweb/demo/home.jsp.
- The "home.jsp" page will display three hyperlinks.
- Click on the "Add Users" hyperlink.
- This action invokes the JSF controller → "addusers.jsp" page will be displayed.

- Enter the user data → Click on Save → JSF controller will be invoked.
- A message is displayed on the add user page → successfully added.

To summarize, there are two ways a JSF-managed bean can be configured.

CASE 1: Without using spring

In this approach, the managed beans are configured in the faces servlet context. The JSF-IOC container is used to inject the managed beans.

```
<managed-bean>
     <managed-bean-name>userBean</managed-bean-name>
     <managed-bean-class>
         com.learning.spring.jsf.UserBean
     </managed-bean-class>
     <managed-bean-scope>request</managed-bean-scope>
</managed-bean>

<managed-bean>
     <managed-bean-name>UserHandler</managed-bean-name>
     <managed-bean-class>
         com.learning.spring.jsf.UserHandler
     </managed-bean-class>
     <managed-bean-scope>request</managed-bean-scope>
     <managed-property>
         <property-name>user</property-name>
             <value>#{userBean}</value>
         </managed-property>
</managed-bean>
```

CASE 2: Using spring

In this approach, the spring configured back-end bean objects are referenced using the spring expression language. The spring-IOC container is used to inject the beans.

```
<managed-bean>
     <managed-bean-name>UserHandler</managed-bean-name>
     <managed-bean-class>
         com.learning.spring.jsf.UserHandler
     </managed-bean-class>
     <managed-bean-scope>request</managed-bean-scope>
     <managed-property>
         <property-name>user</property-name>
         <value>#{userBean}</value>
     </managed-property>
</managed-bean>
```

The bean configuration in the spring application context XML is provided below.

```
<bean id="userBean" class="com.learning.spring.jsf.UserBean"/>
```

Spring-MVC Demo Examples

Example 5: Binding HTTP-Request Data to Multiple Domain Objects

Business scenario: Let us use the following business scenario to demonstrate spring-MVC with Velocity templates.

- The customer account data is mapped to three domain objects: Customer, Line, and Loan.
- The web page has three sections to view and enter customer data and line and loan information.
- Bind the user entered data to the three domain objects in the spring controller.
- Save the account information.

The steps required to implement this business scenario using the spring-MVC are listed below:

1. Configure the spring-MVC front controller in "web.xml."
2. Configure Velocity and spring MVC in the servlet context "springweb-servlet.xml" file.
3. Develop the required Velocity templates and controller classes.
4. Deploy the WAR file and test the application.

The above-specified steps are described in the following sections:

Step 1: Configure the spring-MVC front controller in "web.xml."

Here, reuse the instructions provided in Example-1

Step 2: Configure Velocity and spring MVC in the servlet context "springweb-servlet.xml" file.

Here, reuse the instructions provided in Example-1

Step 3: Develop the required Velocity templates and controller classes.

The following home page is used to view the account information and is named "accounthome.vm."

```
<html>
<head>
<title>Account Demo</title>
<script type="text/javascript">
    function showAccountHome() {
        document.forms[0].action =
            "/springweb/demo/showAccountHome.action";
        document.forms[0].submit();
    }
</script>
</head>
<body>
    <form action="" method="post">
        <table align="center">
            <tr>
                <td><b><a href="javascript:showAccountHome()">
                    View Account</a></b>
```

```
                        </td>
                    </tr>
                </table>
            </form>
        </body>
    </html>
```

The following Velocity template displays the customer account information and is named "accountdata.vm." This page has three HTML tables to provide customer, line, and loan information.

```
<html>
<head>
<title>Account Demo</title>
<script type="text/javascript">
    function updateAccoutData() {
        var accountPageForm =
                document.getElementById("accountPageForm");
        accountPageForm.submit();
    }
</script>
</head>
<body>
<form id="accountPageForm" method="post"
    action="$base/demo/updateAccountData.action">

    <div> $!message </div>

    <!-- Customer profile Information -->
    <table cellspacing="6" border="0">
        <tr>
            <td align="right"><label>Primary Borrower</label></td>
            <td>
                <input type="text" name="primaryBorrower"
                    value="$!customer.primaryBorrower" maxlength="50"
                    size="20"/>
            </td>
        </tr>
        <tr>
            <td align="right"><label style="color:red">
                Account Number:</label></td>
            <td>
                <input type="text" id="accountNumber"
                        name="accountNumber"
                        value="$!customer.accountNumber"
                        maxlength="17" size="20"/>
            </td>
        </tr>
        <tr>
            <td align="right">AU</td>
            <td>
                <input type="text" name="auCode"
                        value="$!customer.auCode"
                        maxlength="50" size="20"/>
            </td>
            <td align="left"><label>(example: 52334)</label></td>
        </tr>
```

```
    </table>

    <!-- Loan Information -->
    <table border="0">
        <tr>
            <td align="right">Original Loan Amount</td>
            <td>
                <input type="text" name="originalLoanAmount"
                    value="$!loan.originalLoanAmount" maxlength="10"
                    size="20"/>
            </td>
        </tr>
        <tr>
            <td align="right">Maturity Date</td>
            <td>
                <input type="text" name="loanMaturityDate"
                    value="$!loan.loanMaturityDate" maxlength="10"
                    size="20"/>
            </td>
            <td align="left"><label>MM/DD/YYYY</label></td>
        </tr>
        <tr>
            <td align="right">Loan Rate</td>
            <td>
                <input type="text" name="loanRate"
                    value="$!loan.loanRate" maxlength="10"
                    size="20"/>
            </td>
        </tr>
    </table>

    <!-- Line Information -->
    <table border="0">
        <tr>
            <td align="right">Line Rate</td>
            <td>
                <input type="text" name="rate" value="$!line.rate"
                    maxlength="10" size="20"/>
            </td>
        </tr>
        <tr>
            <td align="right">Available Credit</td>
            <td>
                <input type="text" name="availableCredit"
                    value="$!line.availableCredit" maxlength="10"
                    size="20"/>
            </td>
        </tr>
        <tr>
            <td align="right">Original Line Amount</td>
            <td>
                <input type="text" name="originalLineAmount"
                    value="$!line.originalLineAmount" maxlength="10"
                    size="20"/>
            </td>
        </tr>
    </table>
```

```
        <div><button onclick="updateAccountData()">Update</button></div>

</form>
</body>
</html>
```

The following `AccountDataController` class has two methods to view and update the account information. The `view(...)` method displays the "accountdata.vm" page; its method signature is provided below.

```
public String view(ModelMap model) {
    ...
}
```

The `updateAccountData(...)` updates the customer information; its method signature is provided below.

```
public String updateAccountData(
        @ModelAttribute("customer") Customer customer,
        @ModelAttribute("loan") Loan loan,
        @ModelAttribute("line") Line line, ModelMap model) {
    ...
}
```

The complete spring controller class code is provided below.

```
// AccountDataController.java
package com.learning.spring.controller;

import org.springframework.stereotype.Controller;
import org.springframework.web.bind.annotation.RequestMapping;
import org.springframework.web.bind.annotation.RequestMethod;
import org.springframework.web.bind.annotation.ModelAttribute;
import org.springframework.ui.ModelMap;
import org.springframework.validation.BindingResult;
import com.learning.spring.dvo.Customer;
import com.learning.spring.dvo.Loan;
import com.learning.spring.dvo.Line;

@Controller
public class AccountDataController {

    @RequestMapping(value = "/demo/showAccountHome.action",
                    method = RequestMethod.POST)
    public String view(ModelMap model) {
        Customer customer = new Customer();
        Loan loan = new Loan();
        Line line = new Line();

        model.put("customer", customer);
        model.put("loan", loan);
        model.put("line", line);

        return "/demo/accountdata";
```

```java
        }

        @RequestMapping(value = "/demo/updateAccountData.action",
                        method = RequestMethod.POST)
        public String updateAccountData(
            @ModelAttribute("customer") Customer customer,
            @ModelAttribute("loan") Loan loan,
            @ModelAttribute("line") Line line, ModelMap model) {

            String name = customer.getPrimaryBorrower();
            Double loanAmount = loan.getOriginalLoanAmount();
            Double rate = line.getRate();
            System.out.println("--- name ---" + name + "--- loanAmount " +
                    loanAmount + "--- rate " + rate);

            // ... Implement your business logic here.

            model.put("message", "Updated Successfully");
            return "/demo/accountdata";
        }
}
```

The following domain objects are used for data transfer.

```java
// Customer.java
package com.learning.spring.dvo;

public class Customer {

    private String primaryBorrower;
    private String accountNumber;
    private String auCode;

    // Add getter and setters
}

// Line.java
package com.learning.spring.dvo;

public class Line {

    private Double rate;
    private Double availableCredit;
    private Double originalLineAmount;

    // Add getter and setters
}
// Loan.java
package com.learning.spring.dvo;

public class Loan {

    private Double originalLoanAmount;
    private String loanMaturityDate;
    private Double loanRate;
```

```
     // Add getter and setters
}
```

Step 4: Deploy the WAR file and test the application.

The structure of the WAR file is shown in Figure 3-6.

Figure 3-6: WAR file structure

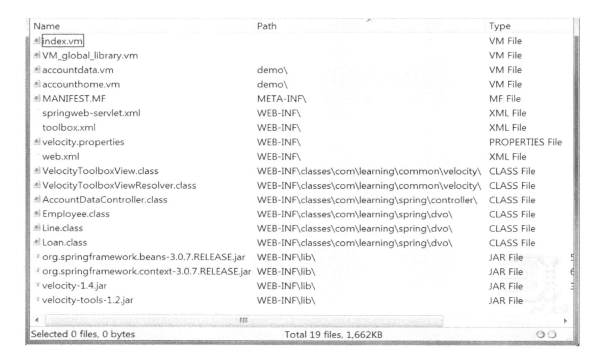

Here, reuse the build and deployment instructions provided in Example-1. The step-by-step instructions to test the deployed application are provided below.

- Invoke the home page → http://localhost:8080/springweb/demo/accounthome.vm.
- The "accounthome.vm" page will display with the "View Account" hyperlink.
- Click on the "View Account" hyperlink.
- This action invokes the spring controller → "accountdata.vm" page will be displayed.
- Enter the customer, loan, and line information → Click on Update
- Displays a message → Updated Successfully.

Spring with Ajax

Asynchronous Java Script and XML (AJAX) is a technique used for updating parts of a web page without reloading the whole page. There are more than fifty Ajax-frameworks available in the market. All of these frameworks provide similar features. This section illustrates the use of the following list of Ajax frameworks.

- Prototype
- JQuery

Let us review the spring integration with Ajax frameworks.

Prototype

Prototype is a JavaScript library used to develop dynamic web applications. This framework provides a JavaScript library for implementing Ajax-based applications. The Prototype framework is available as a single JavaScript library and is named "prototype.js." Include "prototype.js" in your web pages to start using Java script functions.

Business scenario: Display the customer demographic information without reloading the whole web page.

Example 6: Spring-MVC Integration with Prototype

The steps required to provide Ajax functionality using Prototype are listed below:

1. Develop the required Velocity templates and controller classes.
2. Deploy the WAR file and test the application,

The above-specified steps are described in the following sections:

Step 1: Develop the required Velocity templates and controller classes.

Here, reuse the `AccountDataController` class provided in Example-5. Add the following methods.

```
@RequestMapping(value = "/demo/demographics.action",
            method = RequestMethod.POST)
public String displayAddress(ModelMap model) {
    Address address = getAddress();
    model.put("address", address);

    return "/demo/demographics";
}

private Address getAddress() {
    Address address = new Address();
    address.setStreetNumber("3999");
    address.setStreetName("S. McClintock Dr");
    address.setCity("Chandler");
    address.setZipCode("85226");
    address.setState("AZ");

    return address;
}
```

Here, reuse the "accountdata.vm" created in Example-5 with the following changes.

Include the Prototype JavaScript library in "accountdata.vm" page. An example is provided below.

```
<script src="../js/prototype/prototype.js"
```

```
                    type="text/javascript"></script>
```

Use the following JavaScript function to submit the HTML form. This JavaScript function invokes the `obsubmit()` method of an HTML form.

```
<script type="text/javascript">
    function displayDemographicInfo() {
        var demographicsForm =
            document.getElementById("demographicsForm");
        demographicsForm.onsubmit();
    }
</script>
```

Update the "accountdata.vm" with the following code. The Ajax contents are displayed inside the "demographicInfoDiv" without reloading the whole page.

```
#parse("demo/demographics.vm")
<form id="demographicsForm"
    onsubmit="new Ajax.Updater('demographicInfoDiv',
        '/springweb/demo/demographics.action',
        {method:'post', asynchronous:true,
            parameters:Form.serialize(this)})">

    <input type="button"
        name="Display Demographics"
        value="Display Demographics"
        onclick="displayDemographicInfo()"/>
</form>
```

The following Velocity template contains the customer's demographic information and is named the "demographics.vm". The Ajax content is enclosed inside the "demographicInfoDiv" element.

```
<div id='demographicInfoDiv'>
    <table>
        <tr><td> $!address.streetNumber </td></tr>
        <tr><td> $!address.streetName </td></tr>
        <tr><td> $!address.city </td></tr>
        <tr><td> $!address.state </td></tr>
        <tr><td> $!address.zipCode </td></tr>
    </table>
</div>
```

Step 2: Deploy the WAR file and test the application

Here, reuse the build and deployment instructions provided in Example-1. The step-by-step instructions to test the deployed application are provided below.

- Invoke the home page → http://localhost:8080/springweb/demo/accounthome.vm.
- The "accounthome.vm" page will be displayed with the "View Account" hyperlink.
- Click on the "View Account" hyperlink.
- This action invokes the spring controller → "accountdata.vm" page will be displayed.
- Enter the customer, loan, and line information → Click on Update.
- Displays a message → Updated Successfully.
- Click on "Display Demographics" button → Customer address will be displayed without reloading the whole page.

The structure of the WAR file is shown in Figure 3-7. The JavaScript library is included inside the "/js/prototype" directory.

Figure 3-7: WAR file structure

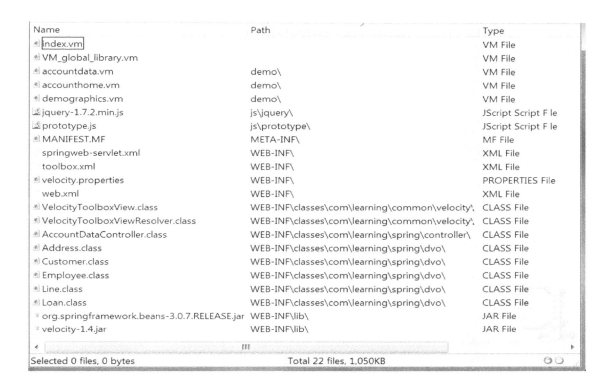

Name	Path	Type
index.vm		VM File
VM_global_library.vm		VM File
accountdata.vm	demo\	VM File
accounthome.vm	demo\	VM File
demographics.vm	demo\	VM File
jquery-1.7.2.min.js	js\jquery\	JScript Script F le
prototype.js	js\prototype\	JScript Script F le
MANIFEST.MF	META-INF\	MF File
springweb-servlet.xml	WEB-INF\	XML File
toolbox.xml	WEB-INF\	XML File
velocity.properties	WEB-INF\	PROPERTIES File
web.xml	WEB-INF\	XML File
VelocityToolboxView.class	WEB-INF\classes\com\learning\common\velocity\	CLASS File
VelocityToolboxViewResolver.class	WEB-INF\classes\com\learning\common\velocity\	CLASS File
AccountDataController.class	WEB-INF\classes\com\learning\spring\controller\	CLASS File
Address.class	WEB-INF\classes\com\learning\spring\dvo\	CLASS File
Customer.class	WEB-INF\classes\com\learning\spring\dvo\	CLASS File
Employee.class	WEB-INF\classes\com\learning\spring\dvo\	CLASS File
Line.class	WEB-INF\classes\com\learning\spring\dvo\	CLASS File
Loan.class	WEB-INF\classes\com\learning\spring\dvo\	CLASS File
org.springframework.beans-3.0.7.RELEASE.jar	WEB-INF\lib\	JAR File
velocity-1.4.jar	WEB-INF\lib\	JAR File

Selected 0 files, 0 bytes   Total 22 files, 1,050KB

JQuery

JQuery is an open-source JavaScript library used to develop Ajax-based applications. The JQuery framework is available as a single JavaScript library and is named "jquery.js". Include "jquery.js" in your web pages to start using the java script functions.

Example 7: Spring-MVC Integration with JQuery

The steps required to provide Ajax functionality using JQuery are listed below:

1. Develop the required Velocity templates and controller classes.
2. Deploy the war file and test the application.

The above-specified steps are described in the following sections:

Step 1: Develop the required Velocity templates and controller classes.

Here, reuse the "accountdata.vm" file created in Example-5 with the following changes.

Include the JQuery JavaScript library in "accountdata.vm" page. An example is provided below.

```
<script src="../js/jquery/jquery-1.7.2.min.js"
        type="text/javascript"></script>
<script type="text/javascript">
    var jq = jQuery.noConflict();
</script>
```

Use the following JavaScript function to send a POST request to the spring controller method.

```
function demographicInfoUsingJQuery() {
    jq.post("/springweb/demo/demographics.action",
        function(data, status) {
            alert("Data: " + data + "\nStatus: " + status);
            jq("#demographicInfoDiv").replaceWith(data);
        });
}
```

Update "accountdata.vm" with the following code. The Ajax contents are displayed inside the "demographicInfoDiv" without reloading the whole page.

```
#parse("demo/demographics.vm")
<form id="jQueryDataForm">
    <input type="button" name="Display Demographics (JQuery)"
           value="Display Demographics (JQuery)"
           onclick="demographicInfoUsingJQuery()"/>
</form>
```

Here, reuse the "demographics.vm" file provided in Example-6.

Step 2: Deploy the war file and test the application.

The structure of the WAR file is shown in Example-6. Follow the instructions provided in Example-6 to test the JQuery-Ajax functionality.

Summary

This section summarizes the features provided in the spring-MVC framework.

- The class with the `@Controller` annotation is a web controller. The `@Controller`-annotated classes are eligible for component scanning.
- The spring-provided `@RequestMapping` annotation can be used to map the HTTP requests to specific controller classes and controller class methods.
- The spring-provided `@ModelAttribute` annotation binds the HTTP-request parameters to a model object.
- The spring-provided `@RequestParam` annotation binds the HTTP-request parameter values to the annotated method parameters.
- Spring provides various view resolvers for integrating with Velocity, Freemarker, JSP, and JSTL.
- Ajax frameworks such as Prototype, JQuery, and so forth. can be integrated with the spring-MVC framework.
- The spring-provided `<mvc:annotation-driven/>` tag can be used to dispatch the web requests to the controllers.

Figure 3-8 summarizes the most important points described in this chapter.

Figure 3-8 Spring-web summary

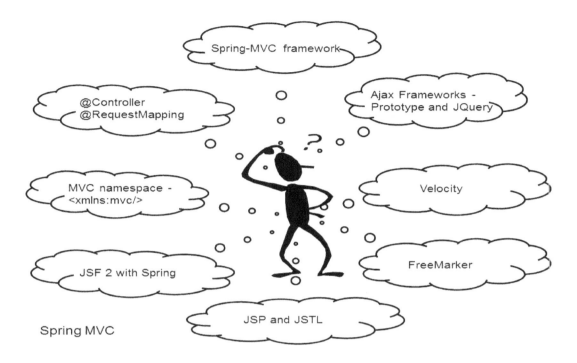

Spring MVC

Chapter 4. Spring for Data Access

Java Database Connectivity (JDBC) is a Java-based data access technology used for accessing the relational databases and is part of Java EE. JDBC is also called Core-JDBC. Sun released the first version of JDBC in 1997. Later on, several open-source and proprietary data access frameworks were developed that provide a higher-level API for data access. The commonly used open-source data access frameworks currently available in the market are listed below.

- Core-JDBC
- Spring-JDBC
- Hibernate
- MyBatis
- Java Persistence API (JPA)
- Java Data Objects (JDO)

Spring-JDBC is the technology used for accessing relational databases. Spring hides the low-level details of the Core-JDBC and provides several high-level template classes for executing SQL statements. Spring-JDBC takes care of low-level details such as opening a connection, closing a connection, closing a resultset, statements execution, exception handling, transaction management, resultset iteration, and so forth.

Hibernate is an Object-Relational (OR) mapping framework used for accessing relational databases. Hibernate maps the domain object classes to the database tables and provides a hibernate query language (HQL) for working with domain objects. Hibernate runtime converts the HQL to SQL for executing SQL statements.

MyBatis is a ResultSet-Object mapping framework used for accessing relational databases. MyBatis was formerly known as iBatis and does the opposite of what the hibernate framework does. MyBatis hides the low-level details of the Core-JDBC and provides several high-level utility classes for mapping the resultset data to the domain object classes.

All of the preceding frameworks provide the same functionality using different techniques; all are used for accessing the databases. The spring framework can be integrated with all the above-listed frameworks. This chapter illustrates the use of the Spring-JDBC, Hibernate, and MyBatis data access frameworks.

In general, the data access frameworks are categorized as follows:

- Data access frameworks that provide high level API's for accessing the resultset data (Spring-JDBC).
- Data access frameworks that use the object-relational mapping technique (Hibernate, JPA)
- Data access frameworks that use the resultset-object mapping technique (MyBatis)

This chapter will discuss the following topics:

- Spring-JDBC fundamentals and the template classes it provides
- Spring-JDBC datasource configurations
- Spring integration with Hibernate
- Spring integration with MyBatis
- Retrieval of auto-generated primary key values using Spring-JDBC, Hibernate, and MyBatis.

- Executing SQL statements in batch mode
- The various ways of executing select, insert, update, and delete statements using Spring-JDBC, Hibernate, and MyBatis
- The various ways of executing database stored procedures and functions using Spring-JDBC, Hibernate, and MyBatis

MySQL Installation and Database Setup

The MySQL database is used to demonstrate the code examples provided in this chapter. MySQL is an open-source relational database. Follow the below provided instructions to install the MySQL database.

- Download the MySQL installer from the "http://dev.mysql.com/downloads/mysql/" web-site. MySQL provides the "mysql-5.5.28-winx64.msi" installer for windows.
- Use the following credentials
  - Password = mysql
  - Default user-name = "root"
  - Default port = 3306
- After completing the installation → Go to All Programs → Open MySQL Command Line Client
- Execute the following commands from the MySQL command line client.
  - Show all available databases → SHOW DATABASES;
  - Use the test database → USE TEST;
  - Show all available tables in test database → SHOW TABLES;
- Create tables, stored procedures, and functions in the TEST database.

The following database tables are created. The "pet" table definition is provided below.

```
CREATE TABLE pet (name VARCHAR(20),
    owner VARCHAR(20),
    species VARCHAR(20),
    sex CHAR(1), birth DATE, death DATE,
    PRIMARY KEY (name)
);
```

The "USER" table definition is provided below.

```
CREATE TABLE USER (
    id MEDIUMINT NOT NULL AUTO_INCREMENT,
    first_name CHAR(30) NULL,
    last_name CHAR(30) NULL,
    PRIMARY KEY (id)
) ENGINE=MyISAM;
```

Create the following stored procedures. The "read_pet" stored procedure code is provided below.

```
DELIMITER //
CREATE PROCEDURE read_pet (
    IN in_name VARCHAR(100),
    OUT out_owner VARCHAR(100),
    OUT out_species VARCHAR(100),
    OUT out_sex VARCHAR(100),
    OUT out_birth DATE,
```

```
     OUT out_death DATE)
BEGIN
     SELECT owner, species, sex, birth, death
     INTO out_owner, out_species, out_sex, out_birth, out_death
     FROM pet where name = in_name;
END //
DELIMITER;
```

The following commands are used to execute the stored procedure.

```
CALL read_pet('Fluffy', @out_owner, @out_species, @out_sex, @out_birth,
@out_death);
```

Use the following command to view the stored procedure output.

```
SELECT @out_owner, @out_species, @out_sex, @out_birth, @out_death;
```

The "read_pet" stored procedure code is provided below. This stored procedure returns a resultset.

```
DELIMITER //
CREATE PROCEDURE read_all_pets()
BEGIN
     SELECT name, owner, species, sex, birth, death FROM pet;
END //
DELIMITER;
```

The following command is used to execute the stored procedure.

```
CALL read_all_pets();
```

Create the following stored function. The `get_pet_owner`" stored function code is provided below.

```
DELIMITER $$
CREATE FUNCTION get_pet_owner(in_name VARCHAR(200)) RETURNS VARCHAR(200)
BEGIN
     DECLARE out_owner VARCHAR(200);

     SELECT owner
     INTO out_owner
     FROM pet where name = in_name;

     RETURN out_owner;
END;
$$
```

The following command is used to execute the stored function.

```
SELECT get_pet_owner('Fluffy') AS owner; $$
```

Prerequisites/Setting Up the Environment

Download the mySQL server-specific driver class files. The JAR file name is provided below.

- mysql-connector-java-5.1.6-bin.jar

The following JAR file is required for developing Spring-JDBC code examples.

- org.springframework.jdbc-3.0.7.RELEASE.jar

The following list of JAR files is required for developing Spring-MyBatis code examples.

- mybatis-3.0.3.jar
- mybatis-spring-1.0.0-RC3.jar

The following list of JAR files is required for developing Spring-Hibernate code examples.

hibernate3.jar	javax.validation-1.0.0.GA.jar
hibernate-jpa-2.0-api-1.0.1.Final.jar	slf4j-api-1.6.1.jar
hibernate-validator-4.2.0.Final.jar	slf4j-log4j12-1.6.3.jar
hibernate-validator-annotation-processor-4.2.0.Final.jar	log4j-1.2.16.jar
joda-time-2.0.jar	javassist-3.12.0.GA.jar
joda-time-hibernate-1.3.jar	antlr-3.4-complete.jar
jta-1.1.jar	antlr-runtime.jar
jsr94.jar	Aspectjrt.jar
aspectjtools-1.5.4.jar	

Obtaining the Database Connection

There are two ways a database connection can be obtained using Spring JDBC.

- For standalone clients
- From web (Tomcat) container using JNDI-lookup

CASE 1: Getting a database connection for standalone clients

Configure the datasource in the spring application context file. This datasource encapsulates database connection parameters such as the driver class name, URL, user-name, and password needed to establish a connection with the database. The following XML element provides the required datasource XML configuration in the spring application context file.

```
<bean id="mySqlDataSource"
    class="org.springframework.jdbc.datasource.DriverManagerDataSource">
    <property name="driverClassName">
        <value>com.mysql.jdbc.Driver</value>
    </property>
```

```
        <property name="url">
            <value>jdbc:mysql://localhost:3306/test</value>
        </property>
        <property name="username">
            <value>root</value>
        </property>
        <property name="password">
            <value>mysql</value>
        </property>
</bean>
```

Configure the spring `JdbcTemplate` class. This `JdbcTemplate` class encapsulates database-specific information such as datasource, connection, statement, resultset creation, and cleanup. The following XML element provides the required XML configuration in the spring application context file.

```
<bean id="springJdbcTemplate"
    class="org.springframework.jdbc.core.JdbcTemplate">
    <property name="dataSource">
        <ref bean="mySqlDataSource"/>
    </property>
</bean>
```

Inject the `JdbcTemplate` class as configured above into your data access object (DAO) class to perform any database-specific operations. The following XML element provides the required XML configuration in the spring application context file. The `SpringDataAccessManager` class includes the methods used for executing select, insert, delete, and update statements.

```
<bean id="dataAccessManager"
    class="com.learning.spring.db.SpringDataAccessManager">
    <property name="jdbcTemplate">
        <ref local="springJdbcTemplate"/>
    </property>
</bean>
```

CASE 2: Getting a database connection from the web (Tomcat) container using JNDI-lookup

Configure the datasource in your web container. Add the following XML to the "context.xml" file. This file is available in the "\apache-tomcat-6.0.29\conf" directory.

```
<Resource name="jdbc/mysqltestdb"
    auth="Container"
    type="javax.sql.DataSource"
    username="root"
    password="mysql"
    driverClassName="com.mysql.jdbc.Driver"
    url="jdbc:mysql://localhost:3306/test"
    maxActive="50"
    maxIdle="4"/>
```

The spring-provided `<jee:jndi-lookup>` element is used to obtain the reference to the datasource, which is configured in your Tomcat server. The complete application context XML configuration is provided below.

```
<?xml version="1.0" encoding="UTF-8"?>
```

```xml
<beans xmlns="http://www.springframework.org/schema/beans"
    xmlns:xsi="http://www.w3.org/2001/XMLSchema-instance"
    xmlns:context="http://www.springframework.org/schema/context"
    xmlns:jee="http://www.springframework.org/schema/jee"
    xsi:schemaLocation="http://www.springframework.org/schema/beans
        http://www.springframework.org/schema/beans/
                    spring-beans-3.0.xsd
        http://www.springframework.org/schema/jee
        http://www.springframework.org/schema/jee/spring-jee-3.0.xsd
        http://www.springframework.org/schema/context
        http://www.springframework.org/schema/context/
                    spring-context-3.0.xsd">

    <!-- Using JNDI look-up for datasource -->
    <jee:jndi-lookup id="mySQLDataSource"
                    jndi-name="jdbc/mysqltestdb"/>

    <!-- JDBC access to the datasource -->
    <bean id=" springJdbcTemplate"
        class="org.springframework.jdbc.core.JdbcTemplate">
        <constructor-arg>
            <ref bean="mySQLDataSource"/>
        </constructor-arg>
    </bean>

    <!-- Inject the JdbcTemplate to all DAO classes -->
    <bean id="dataAccessManager"
        class="com.learning.spring.db.SpringDataAccessManager">
        <property name="jdbcTemplate">
            <ref local="springJdbcTemplate"/>
        </property>
    </bean>
</beans>
```

CASE 3: Getting the database connection from the web container using JNDI-lookup (XML-bean configuration)

In this approach, the spring-provided `JndiObjectFactoryBean` class is used to obtain the reference to the datasource, which is configured in your web container.

The following application context XML configuration is used for the Tomcat server.

```xml
<bean id="mySQLDataSource"
    class="org.springframework.jndi.JndiObjectFactoryBean">
    <!-- For Tomcat -->
    <property name="jndiName">
        <value>java:comp/env/jdbc/yodadb</value>
    </property>
</bean>
```

The following application context XML configuration is used for the Weblogic server.

```xml
<bean id="mySQLDataSource"
    class="org.springframework.jndi.JndiObjectFactoryBean">
    <!-- For Weblogic -->
    <property name="jndiName"><value>jdbc/yodadb</value></property>
```

```
</bean>
```

Spring JDBC

Spring JDBC Templates

Spring provides various template classes to execute select, insert, delete and update statements. This section illustrates the use of the following spring templates for executing the SQL statements.

- JdbcTemplate
- NamedParameterJdbcTemplate
- SimpleJdbcTemplate

JdbcTemplate: This is the core class used in spring JDBC for executing SQL statements such as select, insert, delete, and update as well as stored procedures and functions. The JdbcTemplate class is obtained by injecting a DataSource reference. An example configuration is provided below.

```
<bean id="springJdbcTemplate"
     class="org.springframework.jdbc.core.JdbcTemplate">
        <property name="dataSource">
            <ref bean="mySqlDataSource"/>
        </property>
</bean>
```

Alternatively, you can configure the DataSource as a spring bean; use this datasource reference to create a JdbcTemplate instance. An example code is provided below.

```
JdbcTemplate jdbcTemplate = new JdbcTemplate(dataSource)
```

NamedParameterJdbcTemplate: This template class is used in spring JDBC for executing the SQL statements using named parameters. The following SQL statement uses the named parameters "sex" and "name."

```
select owner from pet where sex = :sex and name = :name
```

The NamedParameterJdbcTemplate class is obtained by injecting a DataSource reference as a constructor argument. An example configuration is provided below.

```
<bean id="namedParameterJdbcTemplate"
     class="org.springframework.jdbc.core.namedparam.
            NamedParameterJdbcTemplate">
     <constructor-arg ref="mySqlDataSource"/>
</bean>
```

The NamedParameterJdbcTemplate class wraps the JdbcTemplate class. Use the getJdbcOperations() method of the NamedParameterJdbcTemplate class to get access to the operations defined in the JdbcTemplate class.

```
JdbcOperations jdbcOperations =
    namedParameterJdbcTemplate.getJdbcOperations();
```

`SimpleJdbcTemplat`: This template class is designed to use features provided in Java 5 such as generics and autoboxing. The `SimpleJdbcTemplate` class is obtained by injecting a `DataSource` reference as a constructor argument. An example configuration is provided below.

```
<bean id="simpleJdbcTemplate"
    class="org.springframework.jdbc.core.simple.SimpleJdbcTemplate">
    <constructor-arg ref="mySqlDataSource"/>
</bean>
```

This `SimpleJdbcTemplate` template class provides the subset of the operations defined in the `JdbcTemplate` class. The `SimpleJdbcTemplate` class wraps the `JdbcTemplate` class. Use the `getJdbcOperations()` method of the `SimpleJdbcTemplate` class to get access to the operations defined in the `JdbcTemplate` class.

```
JdbcOperations jdbcOperations = simpleJdbcTemplate.getJdbcOperations();
```

Similarly, use `getNamedParameterJdbcOperations()` method of the `SimpleJdbcTemplate` class to get access to the operations defined in the `NamedParameterJdbcTemplate` class.

```
NamedParameterJdbcOperations namedParameterJdbcOperations  =
simpleJdbcTemplate.getNamedParameterJdbcOperations();
```

Example 1: Select-Insert-Delete-Update Operations

This example illustrates how to execute SQL statements using the spring-provided JDBC template classes. The steps required to implement this example are listed below.

1. Create a DAO class
2. Create a data value object (DVO) class
3. Configure the datasource and spring template classes in the application context file.
4. Create a main class to test the code.

The preceding steps are described in the following sections:

Step 1: Create a DAO class

The `SpringDataAccessManager` class contains methods used for executing the SQL statements. The complete class code is provided below.

```
// SpringDataAccessManager.java
package com.learning.spring.db;

import org.springframework.jdbc.core.*;
import org.springframework.jdbc.core.simple.SimpleJdbcTemplate;
import org.springframework.jdbc.core.namedparam.*;
import org.springframework.dao.DataAccessException;

import java.sql.Types;
import java.sql.SQLException;
```

```java
import java.sql.ResultSet;
import java.util.*;

public class SpringDataAccessManager {

    private JdbcTemplate jdbcTemplate;

    private NamedParameterJdbcTemplate namedParameterJdbcTemplate;

    private SimpleJdbcTemplate simpleJdbcTemplate;

    // ... Add setter methods

    public String getPetOwnerName(String petName) throws
                                DataAccessException {
        String SQL_SELECT_PET_OWNER =
                "select owner from pet where name = ?";
        Object[] params = new Object[]{petName};
        String owner = this.jdbcTemplate.queryForObject(
                SQL_SELECT_PET_OWNER, params, String.class);
        return owner;
    }

    // Add other select-insert-delete-update methods here
}
```

Step 2: Create a data value object (DVO) class

The following data value object maps the table data. The "pet" table column values are mapped to the PetDVO class attributes.

```java
// PetDVO.java
package com.learning.spring.db;

import java.util.Date;
import java.io.Serializable;

public class PetDVO implements Serializable {

    private String name;
    private String owner;
    private String species;
    private String sex;
    private Date birth;
    private Date death;

    // Add getter and setter methods
}
```

Step 3: Configure the datasource and spring template classes in the application context file.

The spring application context file is used to configure the datasource, spring templates and data access objects. The complete application context XML file is provided below; it is named the "applicationContext-SpringJdbc.xml".

```xml
<?xml version="1.0" encoding="UTF-8"?>
```

```xml
<beans xmlns="http://www.springframework.org/schema/beans"
    xmlns:xsi="http://www.w3.org/2001/XMLSchema-instance"
    xmlns:context="http://www.springframework.org/schema/context"
    xsi:schemaLocation="http://www.springframework.org/schema/beans
    http://www.springframework.org/schema/beans/spring-beans-3.0.xsd
    http://www.springframework.org/schema/context
    http://www.springframework.org/schema/context/
            spring-context-3.0.xsd">

    <!-- Datasource configuraton -->
    <bean id="mySqlDataSource"
        class="org.springframework.jdbc.datasource.
                    DriverManagerDataSource">
        <property name="driverClassName">
            <value>com.mysql.jdbc.Driver</value>
        </property>
        <property name="url">
            <value>jdbc:mysql://localhost:3306/test</value>
        </property>
        <property name="username">
            <value>root</value>
        </property>
        <property name="password">
            <value>mysql</value>
        </property>
    </bean>

    <!-- The JdbcTemplate encapsulates connection, statement, resultset
        creation and cleanup; so the appplication code can focus on the
        SQL query and resultset processing. -->
    <bean id="springJdbcTemplate"
        class="org.springframework.jdbc.core.JdbcTemplate">
        <property name="dataSource">
            <ref bean="mySqlDataSource"/>
        </property>
    </bean>

    <!-- The NamedParameterJdbcTemplate configuration -->
    <bean id="namedParameterJdbcTemplate"
        class="org.springframework.jdbc.core.namedparam.
                    NamedParameterJdbcTemplate">
        <constructor-arg ref="mySqlDataSource"/>
    </bean>

    <!-- The SimpleJdbcTemplate configuration -->
    <bean id="simpleJdbcTemplate"
        class="org.springframework.jdbc.core.simple.
                SimpleJdbcTemplate">
        <constructor-arg ref="mySqlDataSource"/>
    </bean>

    <!-- DAO class with all three templates  -->
    <bean id="dataAccessManager"
        class="com.learning.spring.db.SpringDataAccessManager">
        <property name="jdbcTemplate">
            <ref local="springJdbcTemplate"/>
        </property>
```

```
            <property name="namedParameterJdbcTemplate">
                <ref local="namedParameterJdbcTemplate"/>
            </property>
            <property name="simpleJdbcTemplate">
                <ref local="simpleJdbcTemplate"/>
            </property>
        </bean>
</beans>
```

Step 4: Create a main class to test the code.

Listing 4-1 provides the complete class code; run the following standalone class to view the output.

Listing 4-1: Standalone class used for testing

```java
// SpringJDBCManager.java
package com.learning.spring.db;

import org.springframework.context.support.
                    ClassPathXmlApplicationContext;

import java.util.*;

public class SpringJDBCManager {

    public static void main(String[] args) {

        ClassPathXmlApplicationContext appContext =
            new ClassPathXmlApplicationContext( new String[]
                    {"applicationContext-SpringJdbc.xml"} );

        SpringDataAccessManager dataAccessManager =
                (SpringDataAccessManager)
                appContext.getBean("dataAccessManager");

        // Print the data
        String ownerName = dataAccessManager.
                        getPetOwnerName("Puffball");
        System.out.println("--- ownerName ---" + ownerName);
    }
}
```

The spring JDBC template classes provide several methods for executing the SQL statements. Let us review each method and its use.

CASE 1: Executing an SQL statement and querying a String value.

The following method executes the SQL statement and returns a string value.

```java
public String getPetOwnerName(String petName)
            throws DataAccessException {
    String SQL_SELECT_PET_OWNER="select owner from pet where name = ?";
    Object[] params = new Object[]{petName};
    return this.jdbcTemplate.queryForObject(SQL_SELECT_PET_OWNER,
            params, String.class);
}
```

CASE 2: Executing an SQL statement and populating a single domain object.

Add the following method to the `SpringDataAccessManager` class. This method executes the SQL statement and populates the resultset data into a domain object class.

```java
public PetDVO getPetObject(String petName) throws DataAccessException {

    String SQL_SELECT_PET_OBJECT = "select name, owner, species, sex,
                     birth, death from pet where name = ?";
    Object[] params = new Object[]{petName};

    PetDVO petDVO = this.jdbcTemplate.queryForObject(
        SQL_SELECT_PET_OBJECT, params, new RowMapper<PetDVO>() {
            public PetDVO mapRow(ResultSet rs, int rowNum) throws
                                 SQLException {
            PetDVO petDVO = new PetDVO();
            petDVO.setName(rs.getString(1));
            petDVO.setOwner(rs.getString(2));
            petDVO.setSpecies(rs.getString(3));
            petDVO.setSex(rs.getString(4));
            petDVO.setBirth(rs.getDate(5));
            petDVO.setDeath(rs.getDate(6));
            return petDVO;
        }
    });

    return petDVO;
}
```

CASE 3: Executing an SQL statement and querying a list of column values.

Add the following method to the `SpringDataAccessManager` class. This method executes the SQL statement and provides the list of values from a single database column.

```java
public List getListOfPetNames(String sex) throws DataAccessException {
    String query = "select name from pet where sex = ?";
    Object[] params = new Object[] {sex};
    int[] types = new int[] {Types.VARCHAR};
    return jdbcTemplate.queryForList(query, params, types);
}
```

CASE 4: Executing an SQL statement and populating a list of domain objects.

Add the following method to the `SpringDataAccessManager` class. This method executes the SQL statement and populates the list of domain objects.

```java
public List<PetDVO> getListOfPetObjects() throws DataAccessException {
    String SQL_SELECT_PET_OBJECTS = "select name, owner, species,
                  sex, birth, death from pet";

    List<PetDVO> pets = this.jdbcTemplate.query(SQL_SELECT_PET_OBJECTS,
                   new RowMapper<PetDVO>() {
        public PetDVO mapRow(ResultSet rs, int rowNum) throws
                             SQLException {
            PetDVO petDVO = new PetDVO();
            petDVO.setName(rs.getString("name"));
```

```
                petDVO.setOwner(rs.getString("owner"));
                petDVO.setSpecies(rs.getString("species"));
                petDVO.setSex(rs.getString("sex"));
                petDVO.setBirth(rs.getDate("birth"));
                petDVO.setDeath(rs.getDate("death"));
                return petDVO;
            }
        });

        return pets;
    }
```

CASE 5: Executing an SQL statement and populating a list of domain objects.

Add the following method to the `SpringDataAccessManager` class. This method executes the SQL statement and populates the list of domain objects.

```
public List<PetDVO> getListOfPets(String sex) throws DataAccessException{
    final List<PetDVO> petList = new ArrayList<PetDVO>();
    String query = "select name, owner, sex from pet where sex=?";
    Object[] params = new Object[] {sex};
    int[] types = new int[] {Types.VARCHAR};

    jdbcTemplate.query(query, params, types, new RowCallbackHandler(){
        public void processRow(ResultSet rs) throws SQLException {
            PetDVO petDVO = new PetDVO();
            petDVO.setName(rs.getString(1));
            petDVO.setOwner(rs.getString(2));
            petDVO.setSpecies(rs.getString(3));
            petList.add(petDVO);
        } });

    return petList;
}
```

CASE 6: Executing an SQL statement and populating list of domain objects.

Add the following method to the `SpringDataAccessManager` class. This method executes the SQL statement and populates the list of domain objects.

```
public List<PetDVO> getListOfPets1() throws DataAccessException {
    final List<PetDVO> petList = new ArrayList<PetDVO>();
    final String query = "SELECT * FROM pet";
    jdbcTemplate.query(query, new ResultSetExtractor() {
    public Object extractData(ResultSet rs) throws SQLException,
                        DataAccessException {
        while (rs.next()) {
            PetDVO petDVO = new PetDVO();
            petDVO.setName(rs.getString(1));
            petDVO.setOwner(rs.getString(2));
            petDVO.setSpecies(rs.getString(3));
            petDVO.setSex(rs.getString(4));
            petDVO.setBirth(rs.getDate(5));
            petDVO.setDeath(rs.getDate(6));
            petList.add(petDVO);
        }
```

```
            return null;
    }});

    return petList;
}
```

The following examples illustrate the use of the `NamedParameterJdbcTemplate` for executing SQL statements.

CASE 7: Executing an SQL statement with a named parameter for querying a list of column values.

Add the following method to the `SpringDataAccessManager` class. This method executes the SQL statement and populates the list of column values.

```
public List getPetNamesUsingNamedParameter(String sex) throws
                DataAccessException {
    String query = "select name from pet where sex = :sex";
    SqlParameterSource namedParameters = new
                    MapSqlParameterSource("sex", sex);
    return namedParameterJdbcTemplate.queryForList(query,
            namedParameters);
}
```

CASE 8: Executing an SQL statement with named parameters.

Add the following method to the `SpringDataAccessManager` class. In this example a Java `HashMap` class is used to map the named parameter values.

```
public int getCountUsingNamedParameter(String sex, String name) throws
                DataAccessException {
    String query = "select count(*) from pet where sex = :sex
                and name = :name";
    Map<String, String> namedParameters = new HashMap<String, String>();
    namedParameters.put("sex", sex);
    namedParameters.put("name", name);
    return namedParameterJdbcTemplate.queryForInt(query,
            namedParameters);
}
```

CASE 9: Executing an SQL statement with named parameters that maps to a bean class

Add the following method to the `SpringDataAccessManager` class. In this example a domain object class is used to map the named parameter values.

```
public List getOwnerList(PetDVO petDVO) throws DataAccessException {
    String query = "select owner from pet where sex = :sex
        and name = :name";
    SqlParameterSource namedParameters = new
                BeanPropertySqlParameterSource(petDVO);
    return namedParameterJdbcTemplate.queryForList(query,
            namedParameters);
}
```

CASE 10: Executing an SQL statement and populating a list of domain objects.

Add the following method to the `SpringDataAccessManager` class. In this example, the `getJdbcOperations()` method of the `NamedParameterJdbcTemplate` class is used to access the operations defined in the core `JdbcTemplate` class.

```
public List<PetDVO> getListOfPetsUsingParameterJdbcTemplate(String sex)
    throws DataAccessException {
    final List<PetDVO> petList = new ArrayList<PetDVO>();
    String query = "select name, owner, sex from pet where sex=?";
    Object[] params = new Object[]{sex};
    int[] types = new int[]{Types.VARCHAR};

    namedParameterJdbcTemplate.getJdbcOperations().
            query(query, params, types, new RowCallbackHandler() {
        public void processRow(ResultSet rs) throws SQLException {
            PetDVO petDVO = new PetDVO();
            petDVO.setName(rs.getString(1));
            petDVO.setOwner(rs.getString(2));
            petDVO.setSpecies(rs.getString(3));
            petList.add(petDVO);
        }
    });
    return petList;
}
```

The following examples illustrate the use of the `SimpleJdbcTemplate` for executing SQL statements.

CASE 11: Executing an SQL statement and populating a domain object class.

Add the following method to the `SpringDataAccessManager` class. In this example, the `SimpleJdbcTemplate` class is used to execute the SQL statements.

```
public PetDVO getPetObjectUsingSimpleJdbcTemplate(String petName,
            String sex) throws DataAccessException {
    final String SQL_SELECT_PET_OBJECT = "select name, owner, species,
            sex, birth, death from pet where name = ? and sex = ?";

    RowMapper<PetDVO> mapper = new RowMapper<PetDVO>() {
        public PetDVO mapRow(ResultSet rs, int rowNum) throws
                            SQLException {
            PetDVO petDVO = new PetDVO();
            petDVO.setName(rs.getString(1));
            petDVO.setOwner(rs.getString(2));
            petDVO.setSpecies(rs.getString(3));
            petDVO.setSex(rs.getString(4));
            petDVO.setBirth(rs.getDate(5));
            petDVO.setDeath(rs.getDate(6));
            return petDVO;
        }
    };

    return this.simpleJdbcTemplate.queryForObject(SQL_SELECT_PET_OBJECT,
        mapper, petName, sex);
}
```

The following examples illustrate the use of the `JdbcTemplate` class for executing insert statements.

CASE 1: Executing an insert statement that has placeholder values.

Add the following method to the `SpringDataAccessManager` class. In this example, the placeholder values are populated with the domain object data while an insert statement is executed.

```
public void addPet(PetDVO petDVO) throws DataAccessException {
    String SQL_INSERT_STATEMENT = "INSERT INTO pet (name, owner,
        species, sex, birth, death) VALUES (?, ?, ?, ?, ?, ?)";
    this.jdbcTemplate.update(SQL_INSERT_STATEMENT,
    petDVO.getName(), petDVO.getOwner(), petDVO.getSpecies(),
    petDVO.getSex(), petDVO.getBirth(), petDVO.getDeath());
}
```

CASE 2: Executing an insert statement that has named parameter values.

Add the following method to the `SpringDataAccessManager` class. In this example, the named parameter values are populated with the domain object data while an insert statement is executed.

```
public void addPetUsingNamedParameter(PetDVO petDVO) {
    String SQL_INSERT_STATEMENT = "INSERT INTO pet (name, owner,
        species, sex, birth, death) VALUES
        (:name, :owner, :species, :sex, :birth, :death)";

    Map<String, Object> parameters = new HashMap<String, Object>();
    parameters.put("name", petDVO.getName());
    parameters.put("owner", petDVO.getOwner());
    parameters.put("species", petDVO.getSpecies());
    parameters.put("sex", petDVO.getSex());
    parameters.put("birth", petDVO.getBirth());
    parameters.put("death", petDVO.getDeath());

    this.jdbcTemplate.update(SQL_INSERT_STATEMENT, parameters);
}
```

The following examples illustrate the use of the `JdbcTemplate` class for executing an update statement.

CASE 1: Executing an update statement

Add the following method to the `SpringDataAccessManager` class. In this example, the placeholder values are populated with parameter values while an update statement is executed.

```
public void updatePetData(String owner, String name) throws
            DataAccessException {
    String SQL_UPDATE_STATEMENT = "UPDATE pet SET owner = ?
                    WHERE name = ?";
    Object[] params = new Object[] {owner, name};
    int[] types = new int[] {Types.VARCHAR, Types.VARCHAR};
    jdbcTemplate.update(SQL_UPDATE_STATEMENT, params, types);
}
```

The following examples illustrate the use of the `JdbcTemplate` class for executing delete statements.

CASE 1: Executing a delete statement

Add the following method to the `SpringDataAccessManager` class. In this example, the placeholder values are populated with parameter values while a delete statement is executed.

```
public void deleteData(String name, String sex) throws
                DataAccessException {
    String SQL_DELETE_STATEMENT = "delete from pet where name = ?
            and sex = ?";
    Object[] params = new Object[]{name, sex};
    int[] types = new int[]{Types.VARCHAR, Types.VARCHAR};
    this.jdbcTemplate.update(SQL_DELETE_STATEMENT, params, types);
}
```

Alternatively, use the following method for executing a delete statement.

```
public void deletePetData(String name) throws DataAccessException {
    String query = "delete from pet where name = '" + name + "'";
    jdbcTemplate.update(query);
}
```

NOTE: Use the `SpringJDBCManager` standalone class to access the above specified select, insert, delete and update operations. Run each method to view the output on the console.

Batch Operations

The spring batch operations can be used to optimize performance in the execution of SQL statements. This section illustrates the execution of the SQL statements in batch mode.

CASE 1: Batch processing with the `JdbcTemplate`

In this example, batches of ten records are inserted from the "petList" instead of inserting a record each time. The `batchUpdate()` method of the `JdbcTemplate` class can be used for executing SQL statements in batch mode.

Add the following method to the `SpringDataAccessManager` class.

```
public void insertBatch(final List<PetDVO> petList) {
    final String SQL_INSERT_STATEMENT = "INSERT INTO pet (name, owner,
        species, sex, birth, death) VALUES (?, ?, ?, ?, ?, ?)";

    // Batch of 10 records are inserted
    final int batchSize = 10;

    for (int j = 0; j < petList.size(); j += batchSize) {
        final List<PetDVO> batchList = petList.subList(j, j + batchSize
                > petList.size() ? petList.size() : j + batchSize);

        jdbcTemplate.batchUpdate(SQL_INSERT_STATEMENT,
```

```
                              new BatchPreparedStatementSetter() {
            @Override
            public void setValues(PreparedStatement ps, int i) throws
                                      SQLException {
                PetDVO petDVO = batchList.get(i);
                ps.setString(1, petDVO.getName());
                ps.setString(2, petDVO.getOwner());
                ps.setString(3, petDVO.getSpecies());
                ps.setString(4, petDVO.getSex());
                ps.setDate(5, new java.sql.Date(petDVO.getBirth().
                                      getTime()));
                ps.setDate(6, null);
            }

            @Override
            public int getBatchSize() {
                return batchList.size();
            }
        });
    }
}
```

CASE 2: Batch processing with the `SimpleJdbcTemplate`

In this example, the spring `SimpleJdbcTemplate` class is used to execute an update statement. This update statement uses named parameters.

```
public int[] batchUpdate(final List<PetDVO> petList) {
    SqlParameterSource[] batch = SqlParameterSourceUtils.
            createBatch(petList.toArray());
    String sql = "update pet set death = :death,
                    sex = :sex where name = :name";
    int[] updateCounts = simpleJdbcTemplate.batchUpdate(sql, batch);
    return updateCounts;
}
```

Example 2: Executing Stored Procedures Using SimpleJdbcCall

This section illustrates the spring support for executing database stored procedures. The spring `SimpleJdbcCall` class is used to call the database's stored procedures and stored functions. The `SimpleJdbcCall` class is created using the spring `JdbcTemplate` class.

```
SimpleJdbcCall simpleJdbcCall = new SimpleJdbcCall(jdbcTemplate)
```

The steps required to implement this example are listed below.

1. Create a stored procedure in the database.
2. Create a DAO class
3. Create a data value object (DVO) class
4. Configure datasource and spring template classes in an application context file.
5. Create a main class to test the code.

The preceding steps are described in the following sections:

Step 1: Create a stored procedure in the database

Create a stored procedure in the database. This procedure provides the details for a given pet name. This procedure has one IN parameter and five OUT parameters. The complete stored procedure code is provided below.

```
DELIMITER //
CREATE PROCEDURE read_pet (
    IN in_name VARCHAR(100),
    OUT out_owner VARCHAR(100),
    OUT out_species VARCHAR(100),
    OUT out_sex VARCHAR(100),
    OUT out_birth DATE,
    OUT out_death DATE)
BEGIN
    SELECT owner, species, sex, birth, death
    INTO out_owner, out_species, out_sex, out_birth, out_death
    FROM pet where name = in_name;
END //
DELIMITER;
```

Use the following command to test the created stored procedure.

```
CALL read_pet('Fluffy', @out_owner, @out_species, @out_sex, @out_birth,
@out_death);
```

Use the following command to view the output.

```
SELECT @out_owner, @out_species, @out_sex, @out_birth, @out_death;
```

Step 2: Create a DAO class

Here, reuse the `SpringDataAccessManager` created in Example-1. Add the following `executeStoredProcedure()` method to the `SpringDataAccessManager` class.

The following code is used for specifying the stored procedure input parameters.

```
new SqlParameter("in_name", Types.VARCHAR),
```

The following code is used for specifying the stored procedure output parameters.

```
new SqlOutParameter("out_owner", Types.VARCHAR),
```

There are several ways to execute a stored procedure using the `SimpleJdbcCall` class. Let us review the various execution scenarios.

CASE 1: Explicitly specifying "in" and "out" parameters to execute a stored procedure.

The complete method code is provided below. In this example, the "in" and "out" parameters are specified explicitly using the `declareParameters()` method.

```
public void executeStoredProcedure() {
    jdbcTemplate.setResultsMapCaseInsensitive(true);
    SimpleJdbcCall simpleJdbcCall = new SimpleJdbcCall(jdbcTemplate)
```

```
        .withProcedureName("read_pet")
        .withoutProcedureColumnMetaDataAccess()
        .useInParameterNames("in_name")
        .declareParameters(
            new SqlParameter("in_name", Types.VARCHAR),
            new SqlOutParameter("out_owner", Types.VARCHAR),
            new SqlOutParameter("out_species", Types.VARCHAR),
            new SqlOutParameter("out_sex", Types.VARCHAR),
            new SqlOutParameter("out_birth", Types.DATE),
            new SqlOutParameter("out_death;", Types.DATE)
        );

    HashMap<String, String> input = new HashMap<String, String>();
    input.put("in_name", "Fluffy");
    Map<String, Object> result = simpleJdbcCall.execute(input);

    System.out.println(" owner: " + result.get("out_owner"));
    System.out.println(" species: " + result.get("out_species"));
    System.out.println(" sex: " + result.get("out_sex"));
    System.out.println(" birth: " + result.get("out_birth"));
    System.out.println(" death: " + result.get("out_death"));
}
```

CASE 2: Specifying only IN parameters to execute a stored procedure.

In this example, only the IN parameters are specified using the declareParameters() method.

```
public void executeStoredProcedure2() {
    SimpleJdbcCall readPetProc = new SimpleJdbcCall(jdbcTemplate).
                withProcedureName("read_pet");
    SqlParameterSource input = new MapSqlParameterSource().
                addValue("in_name", "Fluffy");

    Map result = readPetProc.execute(input);
    System.out.println(" owner: " + result.get("out_owner"));
    System.out.println(" species: " + result.get("out_species"));
    System.out.println(" sex: " + result.get("out_sex"));
    System.out.println(" birth: " + result.get("out_birth"));
    System.out.println(" death: " + result.get("out_death"));
}
```

CASE 3: Handling returned "ResultSets" or "Cursors" from stored procedures

Before working on this example, create the following stored procedure in your database. This procedure returns all the records from the "pet" table. In general, stored procedures return multiple records in the form of ResultSets or Cursors.

```
DELIMITER //
CREATE PROCEDURE read_all_pets()
BEGIN
    SELECT name, owner, species, sex, birth, death FROM pet;
END //
DELIMITER;
```

Use the following command to test the above stored procedure.

```
CALL read_all_pets();
```

Now, let us review how to handle the multiple records retuned from the "read_all_pets" stored procedure using the `SimpleJdbcCall` class.

```java
public void executeStoredProcedure3() {
    SimpleJdbcCall procReadAllActors = new SimpleJdbcCall(jdbcTemplate)
        .withProcedureName("read_all_pets")
        .returningResultSet("pets",
        ParameterizedBeanPropertyRowMapper.newInstance(PetDVO.class));

    HashMap<String, String> input = new HashMap<String, String>();
    input.put("in_name", "Fluffy");
    Map<String, Object> result = procReadAllActors.execute(input);

    List<PetDVO> petList = (List<PetDVO>) result.get("pets");
    for(PetDVO petDVO : petList) {
        System.out.println(" name : " + petDVO.getName() +
            "-- owner : + petDVO.getOwner());
    }
}
```

Step 3: Create a data value object (DVO) class

Here, reuse the `PetDVO` class created in Example-1

Step 4: Configure datasource and spring template classes in an application context file.

Here, reuse the "applicationContext-SpringJdbc.xml" context file created in Example-1.

Step 5: Create a main class to test the code.

Listing 4-2 provides the complete class code; run the following standalone class to view the output.

Listing 4-2: Standalone class to call the stored procedures

```java
// TestStoredProcedure.java
package com.learning.spring.db;

import org.springframework.context.support.
        ClassPathXmlApplicationContext;

public class TestStoredProcedure {

    public static void main(String[] args) {

        ClassPathXmlApplicationContext appContext =
            new ClassPathXmlApplicationContext(
                new String[]{"applicationContext-SpringJdbc.xml"});

        SpringDataAccessManager dataAccessManager =
                (SpringDataAccessManager)
                    appContext.getBean("dataAccessManager");

        // CASE 1: Executing a stored procedure with parameters
        dataAccessManager.executeStoredProcedure();
```

```
        // CASE 2: Executing a stored procedure with "in" parameters
        dataAccessManager.executeStoredProcedure2();

        // CASE 3: Processig ResultSets/Cursors
        dataAccessManager.executeStoredProcedure3();
    }
}
```

Example 3: Executing Stored Procedures Using StoredProcedure Class

In this example, the spring-provided StoredProcedure class is used to call the stored procedure. The steps required to implement this example are listed below.

1. Create a stored procedure in the database.
2. Create a DAO class
3. Create a data value object (DVO) class
4. Configure datasource and spring template classes in an application context file.
5. Create a main class to test the code.

The preceding steps are described in the following sections:

Step 1: Create a stored procedure in the database

Here, reuse the "read_pet" stored procedure created in Example-2.

Step 2: Create a DAO class.

In this example, the spring StoredProcedure class is used to call the stored procedures. The application class must extend the StoredProcedure class.

```
public class PetStoredProcedure extends StoredProcedure {
    ...
}
```

The complete class code is provided below.

```
// PetStoredProcedure.java
package com.learning.spring.db;

import org.springframework.jdbc.object.StoredProcedure;
import org.springframework.jdbc.core.SqlOutParameter;
import org.springframework.jdbc.core.SqlParameter;
import org.springframework.jdbc.core.JdbcTemplate;

import java.sql.Types;
import java.util.*;

public class PetStoredProcedure extends StoredProcedure {

    public PetStoredProcedure(JdbcTemplate jdbcTemplate) {
        super(jdbcTemplate, "read_pet");
        declareParameter(new SqlParameter("in_name", Types.VARCHAR));
```

```
        declareParameter(new SqlOutParameter("out_owner",
                                Types.VARCHAR));
        declareParameter(new SqlOutParameter("out_species",
                                Types.VARCHAR));
        declareParameter(new SqlOutParameter("out_sex",Types.VARCHAR));
        declareParameter(new SqlOutParameter("out_birth", Types.DATE));
        declareParameter(new SqlOutParameter("out_death", Types.DATE));

        compile();
    }

    public void execute() {
        Map<String, Object> sqlMap = new HashMap<String,Object>();
        sqlMap.put("in_name", "Fluffy");
        Map<String, Object> result = super.execute(sqlMap);

        System.out.println("owner: " + result.get("out_owner"));
        System.out.println("species:"+ result.get("out_species"));
        System.out.println("sex: " + result.get("out_sex"));
        System.out.println("birth: " + result.get("out_birth"));
        System.out.println("death: " + result.get("out_death"));
    }
}
```

Step 3: Create a data value object (DVO) class

Here, reuse the `PetDVO` class created in Example-1

Step 4: Configure datasource and spring template classes in an application context file.

Here, reuse the "applicationContext-SpringJdbc.xml" context file created in Example-1. Add the following `PetStoredProcedure` bean definition to the application context file.

```
<bean id="petStoredProcedure"
    class="com.learning.spring.db.PetStoredProcedure">
    <constructor-arg ref="springJdbcTemplate"/>
</bean>
```

Step 5: Create a main class to test the code.

Listing 4-3 provides the complete class code; run the following standalone class to view the output.

Listing 4-3: Standalone class to call the stored procedures

```
// TestStoredProcedure.java
package com.learning.spring.db;

import org.springframework.context.support.
        ClassPathXmlApplicationContext;

public class TestStoredProcedure {

    public static void main(String[] args) {

        ClassPathXmlApplicationContext appContext =
            new ClassPathXmlApplicationContext(
```

```
                    new String[]{"applicationContext-SpringJdbc.xml"});

        PetStoredProcedure petStoredProcedure = (PetStoredProcedure)
                appContext.getBean("petStoredProcedure");

        // Calling stored procedure
        petStoredProcedure.execute();
    }
}
```

Example 4: Executing Stored Functions

In this example, the `SimpleJdbcCall` class is used to call the stored functions. Here, reuse the classes created in previous examples. Add the following `executeStoredFunction()` method to the `SpringDataAccessManager` class.

```
public void executeStoredFunction() {
    jdbcTemplate.setResultsMapCaseInsensitive(true);
    SimpleJdbcCall petOwnerFunction = new SimpleJdbcCall(jdbcTemplate).
            withFunctionName("get_pet_owner");

    HashMap<String, String> input = new HashMap<String, String>();
    input.put("in_name", "Fluffy");
    String result =petOwnerFunction.executeFunction(String.class,input);
    System.out.println("result  : " + result);
}
```

Add the following code to the `TestStoredProcedure` class to view the stored function result.

```
dataAccessManager.executeStoredFunction();
```

Retrieving Auto-Generated Keys

Spring supports the retrieval of auto-generated primary key values. Here, use the "user" table to insert a new record. Use the following `getGeneratedKey()` method to retrieve the auto-generated primary key.

```
public void getGeneratedKey() {
    final String SQL_INSERT_QUERY =
        "INSERT INTO User (first_name, last_name) values (?, ?)";
    final String firstName = "Steven";
    final String lastName = "Day";

    KeyHolder keyHolder = new GeneratedKeyHolder();
    jdbcTemplate.update(new PreparedStatementCreator() {
        public PreparedStatement createPreparedStatement
            (Connection connection) throws SQLException {
            PreparedStatement ps = connection.prepareStatement
                    (SQL_INSERT_QUERY, new String[] {"id"});
            ps.setString(1, firstName);
            ps.setString(2, lastName);
            return ps;
```

```
                }
            },
        keyHolder);

        // Printing the auto generated key value.
        System.out.println("--- Id is ---" + keyHolder.getKey());
}
```

Spring with Hibernate

Hibernate can be used with or without spring integration. This section illustrates the Hibernate integration using the spring framework. The spring-provided `HibernateTemplate` class uses different methods to execute select, insert, delete, and update statements. This is the utility class used to access the relational databases. The `HibernateTemplate` class encapsulates the hibernate session factory, which is used to establish the database connection.

The following list of annotations is used in this section while developing the code examples.

- `@Entity`: This annotation is used to mark the class as an Entity bean.
- `@Table`: This annotation specifies the table used to persist the data.
- `@Id`: This annotation specifies the identifier used to access the entity bean and is used with the primary key column.
- `@Column`: This annotation is used to map the column name to the bean property name.
- `@GeneratedValue`: This annotation specifies the primary key generation strategy.

Spring-based Hibernate Template

`HibernateTemplate`: This is the core class used in spring-based hibernate to execute SQL statements such as select, insert, delete, and update, as well as stored procedures and functions. The `HibernateTemplate` class is obtained by injecting a `SessionFactory` reference. An example `HibernateTemplate` configuration is provided below.

```
<bean id="hibernateTemplate"
    class="org.springframework.orm.hibernate3.HibernateTemplate">
    <property name="sessionFactory">
        <ref bean="sessionFactory"/>
    </property>
</bean>
```

The datasource reference is injected into the session factory, which has database-specific details such as the server name, database name, user-name, and password. An example session factory configuration is provided below.

```
<bean id="sessionFactory" class="org.springframework.orm.hibernate3.
            annotation.AnnotationSessionFactoryBean">

    <property name="dataSource" ref="dataSource"/>

    ...

</bean>
```

Example 5: Select-Insert-Delete-Update Operations

This example illustrates how to execute SQL statements using the spring-provided `HibernateTemplate` class. The steps required to implement this example are listed below.

1. Create a DAO class
2. Create a data value object (DVO) class
3. Configure the datasource and hibernate template classes in an application context file.
4. Create a main class to test the code.

The preceding steps are described in the following sections:

Step 1: Create a DAO class

The `PetDAO` interface contains methods to execute the SQL statements. The complete class code is provided below.

```
// PetDAO.java
package com.learning.spring.db.hibernate;

import java.util.List;

public interface PetDAO {

    PetDVO getPeyByName(String name);

    List<PetDVO> findAllPets();

    void insertPetData(PetDVO pet);

    void deletePet(String name);

    void updatePet(String owner, String sex, String species,
        String name);
}
```

The `PetDAOImpl` class implements the above specified `PetDAO` interface methods. The `@Repository` annotated class is a special type of component class used for data access components. The `@Repository`-annotated classes are eligible for auto-scanning using the spring-provided `<context:component-scan>` configuration.

```
@Repository
public class PetDAOImpl implements PetDAO {
    ...
}
```

The complete class code is provided below. This class contains methods used for select-insert-delete-update operations.

```
// PetDAOImpl.java
package com.learning.spring.db.hibernate;

import org.springframework.beans.factory.annotation.Autowired;
import org.springframework.orm.hibernate3.HibernateTemplate;
```

```java
import org.springframework.orm.hibernate3.HibernateCallback;
import org.springframework.stereotype.Repository;
import org.hibernate.Session;
import org.hibernate.HibernateException;
import org.hibernate.Query;

import java.util.List;
import java.sql.SQLException;

@Repository
public class PetDAOImpl implements PetDAO {

    @Autowired
    private HibernateTemplate hibernateTemplate;

    // Gets a pet by name
    public PetDVO getPeyByName(final String name) {
        final String HQL_GET_PET_DATA_BY_NAME =
                "from PetDVO p where p.name = '" + name + "'";
        List<PetDVO> petList =
                hibernateTemplate.find(HQL_GET_PET_DATA_BY_NAME);
        return petList.get(0);
    }

    // Getting all pets
    public List<PetDVO> findAllPets() {
        String HQL_GET_PET_DATA = "from PetDVO";
        return hibernateTemplate.find(HQL_GET_PET_DATA);
    }

    // Insert a pet
    public void insertPetData(PetDVO pet) {
        hibernateTemplate.save(pet);
    }

    // Delete a pet
    public void deletePet(final String name) {
        final String delquery =
                "DELETE FROM PetDVO WHERE name = :name";
        hibernateTemplate.execute(new HibernateCallback() {
        public Object doInHibernate(Session sess) throws
                        HibernateException, SQLException {
            Query query = sess.createQuery(delquery);
            query.setParameter("name", name);
            int rows = query.executeUpdate();
            return rows;
        } });
    }

    // Update pet data
    public void updatePet(final String owner, final String sex,
                    final String species, final String name) {
    final String updquery = "UPDATE PetDVO SET owner = :cwner, sex =
                    :sex WHERE species = :species and name = :name";
    hibernateTemplate.execute(new HibernateCallback() {
        public Object doInHibernate(Session sess) throws
                            HibernateException, SQLException {
```

```
                    Query query = sess.createQuery(updquery);
                    query.setParameter("owner", owner);
                    query.setParameter("sex", sex);
                    query.setParameter("species", species);
                    query.setParameter("name", name);
                    int rows = query.executeUpdate();
                    return rows;
            }});
        }

        public void setHibernateTemplate(HibernateTemplate
                                hibernateTemplate) {
            this.hibernateTemplate = hibernateTemplate;
        }
}
```

Step 2: Create a data value object (DVO) class

The `PetDVO` class has `@Column`-annotated getter methods. The `@Column` annotation is used to map the column name to the bean property name. The `@Table` maps the object name to the table name. The `@Id` annotation maps the bean property with the table primary key column. The complete class code is provided below.

```
// PetDVO.java
package com.learning.spring.db.hibernate;

import org.hibernate.annotations.Type;
import org.joda.time.DateTime;

import javax.persistence.*;

@Entity
@Table(name = "pet")
public class PetDVO {

    private static final long serialVersionUID = -1213133L;

    private String name;
    private String owner;
    private String species;
    private String sex;
    private DateTime birth;
    private DateTime death;

    //... Add setter methods

    @Id
    @Column(name = "name")
    public String getName() {
        return name;
    }

    @Column(name = "owner")
    public String getOwner() {
        return owner;
    }
```

```java
@Column(name = "species")
public String getSpecies() {
    return species;
}

@Column(name = "sex")
public String getSex() {
    return sex;
}

@Column(name = "birth")
@Type(type = "org.joda.time.contrib.hibernate.PersistentDateTime")
public DateTime getBirth() {
    return birth;
}

@Column(name = "death")
@Type(type = "org.joda.time.contrib.hibernate.PersistentDateTime")
public DateTime getDeath() {
    return death;
}
}
```

Step 3: Configure the datasource and hibernate template classes in an application context file.

The spring application context file is used to configure the datasource, hibernate session factory, hibernate template and data access objects. The complete application context XML file is provided below and is named the "applicationContext-hibernate.xml".

```xml
<?xml version="1.0" encoding="UTF-8"?>
<beans xmlns="http://www.springframework.org/schema/beans"
    xmlns:xsi="http://www.w3.org/2001/XMLSchema-instance"
    xmlns:context="http://www.springframework.org/schema/context"
    xsi:schemaLocation="http://www.springframework.org/schema/beans
    http://www.springframework.org/schema/beans/spring-beans-3.0.xsd
    http://www.springframework.org/schema/context
    http://www.springframework.org/schema/context/
            spring-context-3.0.xsd">

    <!-- Autoscan the @Repository-annotatted classes -->
    <context:component-scan
            base-package="com.learning.spring.db.hibernate.*"/>

    <!-- Configure datasource -->
    <bean id="dataSource"
        class="org.springframework.jdbc.datasource.
                    DriverManagerDataSource">
        <property name="driverClassName">
            <value>com.mysql.jdbc.Driver</value>
        </property>
        <property name="url">
            <value>jdbc:mysql://localhost:3306/test</value>
        </property>
        <property name="username">
```

```
                    <value>root</value>
        </property>
        <property name="password">
                <value>mysql</value>
        </property>
    </bean>

    <!-- Configure hibernate and the annotated model objects.-->
    <bean id="sessionFactory" class="org.springframework.orm.hibernate3.
                    annotation.AnnotationSessionFactoryBean">
        <property name="dataSource" ref="dataSource"/>
        <property name="mappingResources">
            <list>
                <value>petsql.hbm.xml</value>
            </list>
        </property>

        <!-- Autoscan the annotated model objects -->
        <property name="packagesToScan"
                value="com.learning.spring.db.hibernate"/>

        <!-- Configure hibernate properties dialect, show sql, etc.-->
        <property name="hibernateProperties">
            <props>
                <prop key="hibernate.dialect">
                    org.hibernate.dialect.MySQLDialect
                </prop>
                <prop key="hibernate.show_sql">true</prop>
                <prop key="hibernate.hbm2ddl.auto">update</prop>
            </props>
        </property>
    </bean>

    <!-- Configure hibernate DB template -->
    <bean id="hibernateTemplate"
        class="org.springframework.orm.hibernate3.HibernateTemplate">
        <property name="sessionFactory">
            <ref bean="sessionFactory"/>
        </property>
    </bean>

    <!-- Configure the DAO class -->
    <bean id="petDAOImpl"
        class="com.learning.spring.db.hibernate.PetDAOImpl">
    </bean>
</beans>
```

Note: The "petsql.hbm.xml" file is not used in this example. This file can be used to externalize the HQL queries. An example XML file is provided below.

```
<?xml version="1.0"?>
<!DOCTYPE hibernate-mapping PUBLIC "-//Hibernate/Hibernate Mapping DTD
3.0//EN" "http://hibernate.sourceforge.net/hibernate-mapping-3.0.dtd">
<hibernate-mapping>

    <query name="PetDVO.getByName">
        from PetDVO pet where pet.name = ?
```

```
        </query>

        <query name="PetDVO.findAllPets">from PetDVO</query>

</hibernate-mapping>
```

Step 4: Create a main class to test the code.

Listing 4-4 provides the complete class code; run the following standalone class to view the output.

Listing 4-4: Standalone class to test the DAO methods.

```java
// HibernateDataAccessManager.java
package com.learning.spring.db.hibernate;

import org.springframework.context.support.
            ClassPathXmlApplicationContext;
import org.joda.time.DateTime;
import java.util.List;

public class HibernateDataAccessManager {

    public static void main(String[] args) {
        try {
            ClassPathXmlApplicationContext appContext =
                new ClassPathXmlApplicationContext(new String[]
                    {"applicationContext-hibernate.xml"});

            PetDAO petDAO = (PetDAO) appContext.getBean("petDAOImpl");

            // Calling select methods
            List users = petDAO.findAllPets();
            System.out.println("--- pets ---" + users.size());

            PetDVO pet = petDAO.getPeyByName("Fluffy");
            System.out.println("--- pet owner ---" + pet.getOwner());

            // Calling insert method
            PetDVO petDVO = new PetDVO();
            petDVO.setName("Slim1");
            petDVO.setOwner("Joe Ann");
            petDVO.setSpecies("snake");
            petDVO.setSex("m");
            petDVO.setBirth(DateTime.now());
            petDVO.setDeath(DateTime.now());
            petDAO.insertPetData(petDVO);

            // Calling update method
            petDAO.updatePet("Kris Bennet", "f", "snake", "Slim1");

            // Calling delete method
            petDAO.deletePet("Slim1");

        } catch (Exception ex) {
            ex.printStackTrace();
        }
    }
}
```

```
}
```

Batch Operations

Add the following methods to the `PetDAO` interface.

```
public interface PetDAO {
    void saveAll(List<PetDVO> petList);
    void deleteAll(List<PetDVO> petList);
}
```

The above methods are implemented in the `PetDAOImpl` class. Add the following methods to the `PetDAOImpl` class. The following `saveAll(...)` method is used to insert the records in batch mode.

```
public void saveAll(List<PetDVO> petList) {
    hibernateTemplate.saveOrUpdateAll(petList);
    hibernateTemplate.flush();
}
```

Similarly, the following `deleteAll(...)` method is used to delete the records in batch mode.

```
public void deleteAll(List<PetDVO> petList) {
    hibernateTemplate.deleteAll(petList);
}
```

Listing 4-5 provides the complete class code; run the following standalone class to view the output.

Listing 4-5: Standalone class to test the batch operations.

```
// HibernateDataAccessManager.java
package com.learning.spring.db.hibernate;

import org.springframework.context.support.
            ClassPathXmlApplicationContext;
import org.joda.time.DateTime;

import java.util.*;

public class HibernateDataAccessManager {

    public static void main(String[] args) {
        try {
            ClassPathXmlApplicationContext appContext =
                new ClassPathXmlApplicationContext(new String[]
                    {"applicationContext-hibernate.xml"});
            PetDAO petDAO = (PetDAO) appContext.getBean("petDAOImpl");

            List<PetDVO> petBatchList = new ArrayList<PetDVO>();
            for (int i = 0; i < 20; i++) {
                PetDVO petObj1 = new PetDVO();
                petObj1.setName("Slim" + i);
                petObj1.setOwner("Suk1");
                petObj1.setSpecies("snake1");
```

```
                        petObj1.setSex("m");
                        petObj1.setBirth(DateTime.now());
                        petBatchList.add(petObj1);
                    }

                    // Inserting all records
                    petDAO.saveAll(petBatchList);

                    // Deleting all records
                    petDAO.deleteAll(petBatchList);

            } catch (Exception ex) {
                ex.printStackTrace();
            }
        }
    }
}
```

Example 6: Executing Stored Procedures

The getNamedQuery(...) method of hibernate session can be used to execute a database stored procedures. Here, reuse the previously created "sp_read_all_pets" stored procedure. The complete method signature is provided below.

```
public List getPetDataUsingStoredProc() {
    return (List) hibernateTemplate.execute(new HibernateCallback() {
        public Object doInHibernate(Session session) throws
                            HibernateException, SQLException {
            Query query = session.getNamedQuery("sp_read_all_pets");
            return query.list();
        }
    });
}
```

Here, reuse the PetDVO class created in Example-5 with the following change. Use the hibernate-provided @NamedNativeQuery annotation to specify the stored procedure-related metadata. The modified domain object code is provided below.

```
@Entity
@Table(name = "pet")
@org.hibernate.annotations.NamedNativeQuery(name = "sp_read_all_pets",
    query = "call read_all_pets()",
    callable = true, readOnly = true, resultClass = PetDVO.class)
public class PetDVO {

    ...

}
```

Example 7: Executing Stored Functions

The hibernate session provides a doWork() method that gives you direct access to the java.sql.Connection. Use the conn.prepareCall() method to execute the stored function.

Here, reuse the previously created "get_pet_owner" stored function. The complete method signature is provided below.

```
public void execurteStoredFunction(final String name) {
    hibernateTemplate.getSessionFactory().openSession().
        doWork(new Work() {
            public void execute(Connection conn) throws
                    HibernateException, SQLException {
            // Syntax is same as Core-JDBC API
            CallableStatement stmt = conn.prepareCall
                    ("{ ? = call get_pet_owner(?) }");
            stmt.registerOutParameter(1, Types.VARCHAR);
            stmt.setString(2, name);
            stmt.execute();
            String owner = stmt.getString(1);

            System.out.println("--- owner ---" + owner);
            // Use this value in your application.
        }
    });
}
```

Retrieving Auto-Generated Keys

Hibernate automatically populates the auto-generated key value into the corresponding bean property. An example code is provided below.

```
@Id
@GeneratedValue
@Column(name = "ID", nullable = false)
public Long getId() {
    return Id;
}
```

Spring with MyBatis

MyBatis can be used with or without spring integration. This section illustrates the MyBatis integration using the spring framework. Spring provides the `SqlSessionTemplate` class, which uses different methods to execute select, insert, delete, and update statements. This is the utility class used to access the relational databases. The `SqlSessionTemplate` class encapsulates `SqlSessionFactory`, which is used to establish the database connection.

Spring-based MyBatis Template

`SqlSessionTemplate`: This is the core class used in spring-based MyBatis for executing SQL statements such as select, insert, delete, and update as well as stored procedures and functions. The `SqlSessionTemplate` class is obtained by injecting the `SqlSessionFactory` reference. An example of a `SqlSessionTemplate` configuration is provided below.

```
<bean id="sqlSessionTemplate"
```

```
        class="org.mybatis.spring.SqlSessionTemplate">
        <constructor-arg index="0" ref="sqlSessionFactory"/>
</bean>
```

The datasource reference is injected into the session factory, which includes database-specific details such as server name, database name, user-name, and password. An example session factory configuration is provided below.

```
<bean id="sqlSessionFactory"
        class="org.mybatis.spring.SqlSessionFactoryBean">

        <property name="dataSource" ref="dataSource"/>

        ...
</bean>
```

Example 8: Select-Insert-Delete-Update Operations

This example illustrates how to execute SQL statements using the spring-provided SqlSessionTemplate class. The steps required to implement this example are listed below.

1. Create DAO classes.
2. Create a data value object (DVO) class
3. Configure the datasource and MyBatis-specific classes in an application context file.
4. Create a MyBatis-specific "sqlMapConfig.xml" file.
5. Create a MyBatis-specific "mapper.xml" file.
6. Create a main class to test the code.

The preceding steps are described in the following sections:

Step 1: Create DAO classes.

The PetDAO interface contains methods used for executing the SQL statements. The complete class code is provided below.

```
// PetDAO.java
package com.learning.spring.db.mybatis;

import java.util.List;

public interface PetDAO {

    List<PetDVO> getAllPetsData();

}
```

The PetDAOImpl class implements the above specified methods. The complete class code is provided below. This class contains methods used for select-insert-delete-update operations.

```
// PetDAOImpl.java
package com.learning.spring.db.mybatis;

import org.mybatis.spring.SqlSessionTemplate;
```

```
import java.util.*;

public class PetDAOImpl implements PetDAO {

    private SqlSessionTemplate sqlSessionTemplate;

    public List<PetDVO> getAllPetsData() {
        return (List<PetDVO>)
            sqlSessionTemplate.selectList("getAllPets");
    }
}
```

Step 2: Create a data value object class

The following data value object maps the table data. The "pet" table column values are mapped to the PetDVO class attributes.

```
// PetDVO.java
package com.learning.spring.db;

import java.util.Date;
import java.io.Serializable;

public class PetDVO implements Serializable {

    private String name;
    private String owner;
    private String species;
    private String sex;
    private Date birth;
    private Date death;

    // Add getter and setter methods
}
```

Step 3: Configure the datasource and MyBatis-specific classes in an application context file

The spring application context file is used to configure the datasource, MyBatis session factory, MyBatis template and data access objects. The complete application context XML file is provided below and is named the "applicationContext-myBatis.xml".

```
<?xml version="1.0" encoding="UTF-8"?>
<!DOCTYPE beans PUBLIC "-//SPRING//DTD BEAN//EN"
        "http://www.springframework.org/dtd/spring-beans.dtd">
<beans>

    <!-- Configure datasource -->
    <bean id="dataSource"
        class="org.springframework.jdbc.datasource.
                              DriverManagerDataSource">
        <property name="driverClassName">
            <value>com.mysql.jdbc.Driver</value>
        </property>
        <property name="url">
            <value>jdbc:mysql://localhost:3306/test</value>
```

```
            </property>
            <property name="username">
                <value>root</value>
            </property>
            <property name="password">
                <value>mysql</value>
            </property>
        </bean>

        <!-- Configure session factory and load myBatis configurations -->
        <bean id="sqlSessionFactory"
            class="org.mybatis.spring.SqlSessionFactoryBean">
            <property name="dataSource" ref="dataSource"/>
            <property name="configLocation" value="sqlMapConfig.xml" />
        </bean>

        <!-- Configure myBatis DB template -->
        <bean id="sqlSessionTemplate"
            class="org.mybatis.spring.SqlSessionTemplate">
            <constructor-arg index="0" ref="sqlSessionFactory"/>
        </bean>

        <!-- Configure DAO classes -->
        <bean id="petDAOImpl"
            class="com.learning.spring.db.mybatis.PetDAOImpl">
            <property name="sqlSessionTemplate" ref="sqlSessionTemplate"/>
        </bean>

</beans>
```

Step 4: Create a MyBatis-specific "sqlMapConfig.xml" file

This file contains database-specific settings, domain object configurations and mapper files. The complete XML file is provided below and is named the "sqlMapConfig.xml".

```
<?xml version="1.0" encoding="UTF-8" ?>
<!DOCTYPE configuration PUBLIC "-//mybatis.org//DTD Config 3.0//EN"
"http://mybatis.org/dtd/mybatis-3-config.dtd">

<configuration>

    <settings>
        <setting name="cacheEnabled" value="true"/>
        <setting name="lazyLoadingEnabled" value="true"/>
        <setting name="multipleResultSetsEnabled" value="true"/>
        <setting name="useColumnLabel" value="true"/>
        <setting name="useGeneratedKeys" value="false"/>
        <setting name="defaultExecutorType" value="SIMPLE"/>
        <setting name="defaultStatementTimeout" value="100"/>
    </settings>

    <!-- Configure domain objects -->
    <typeAliases>
        <typeAlias alias="PetDVO"
                    type="com.learning.spring.db.mybatis.PetDVO"/>
    </typeAliases>
```

```
<!-- Configure mapper xml files -->
<mappers>
    <mapper resource="petmapper.xml"/>
</mappers>

</configuration>
```

Step 5: Create a MyBatis-specific "petmapper.xml" file

This file contains database-specific SQL statements such as select, insert, delete and update. The complete mapper XML file is provided below and is named the "petmapper.xml"

```
<?xml version="1.0" encoding="UTF-8" ?>
<!DOCTYPE mapper PUBLIC "-//mybatis.org//DTD Mapper 3.0//EN"
"http://mybatis.org/dtd/mybatis-3-mapper.dtd">

<mapper namespace="petmapper">

    <select id="getAllPets" resultType="PetDVO">
        SELECT NAME as name, OWNER as owner, SPECIES as species,
        SEX as sex, BIRTH as birth, DEATH as death
        FROM Pet
    </select>

</mapper>
```

Let us review the SQL statement.

- select → used for executing the select statements
- getAllPets → unique name used for identifying the SQL statement.
- resultType → resultset return type mapping object.
- NAME, OWNER etc. → represents the database table column names.
- name, owner, etc. (column alias names) → represents domain object properties

MyBatis maps the database's returned resultset to the domain objects. The Java code used to retrieve all pets is provided below.

```
List<PetDVO> petList = sqlSessionTemplate.selectList("getAllPets");
```

Step 6: Create a main class to test the code.

Listing 4-6 provides the complete class code; run the following standalone class to view the output.

Listing 4-6: Standalone class to test the MyBatis DAO methods.

```
// MyBatisMain.java
package com.learning.spring.db.mybatis;

import org.springframework.context.support.
                ClassPathXmlApplicationContext;

import java.util.*;
```

```
public class MyBatisMain {

    public static void main(String[] args) {
        try {
            ClassPathXmlApplicationContext appContext =
                new ClassPathXmlApplicationContext(new String[]
                    {"applicationContext-myBatis.xml"});

            PetDAO petDAOImpl = (PetDAO)
                appContext.getBean("petDAOImpl");

            // Printing pets data
            List<PetDVO> users = petDAOImpl.getAllPetsData();
            System.out.println("--- pets ---" + users.size());

        } catch (Exception ex) {
            ex.printStackTrace();
        }
    }
}
```

The MyBatis `SqlSessionTemplate` class provides several methods for executing SQL statements. Let us review each method and its use.

CASE 1: Executing an SQL statement and populating a single domain object.

The following method executes an SQL statement and returns a single domain object.

```
public PetDVO getPetObject(String petName) {
    HashMap<String, String> inputMap = new HashMap<String, String>();
    inputMap.put("name", petName);
    return (PetDVO)
        sqlSessionTemplate.selectOne("getPetObject", inputMap);
}
```

The corresponding select statement in the "mapper.xml" file is provided below.

```
<select id="getPetObject" parameterType="java.lang.String"
        resultType="PetDVO">
    SELECT NAME as name, OWNER as owner,SPECIES as species,
        SEX as sex, BIRTH as birth, DEATH as death
    FROM Pet where name = #{name}
</select>
```

CASE 2: Executing an SQL statement and populating a list of domain objects.

Add the following method to the `PetDAO` interface and its implementation class. This method executes the SQL statement and populates the resultset data into a domain object class.

```
public List<PetDVO> getAllPetsData() {
    return (List<PetDVO>) sqlSessionTemplate.selectList("getAllPets");
}
```

The corresponding select statement in the "mapper.xml" file is provided below.

```
<select id="getAllPets" resultType="PetDVO">
    SELECT NAME as name, OWNER as owner, SPECIES as species,
    SEX as sex, BIRTH as birth, DEATH as death FROM Pet
</select>
```

CASE 3: Executing an SQL statement and populating a list with column values.

Add the following method to the `PetDAO` interface and its implementation class.

```
public List<String> getAllSpecies() {
    return (List<String>)
            sqlSessionTemplate.selectList("getAllSpecies");
}
```

The corresponding select statement in the "mapper.xml" file is provided below.

```
<select id="getAllSpecies" resultType="java.lang.String">
    SELECT distinct(SPECIES) as species FROM Pet
</select>
```

CASE 4: Executing an SQL statement and populating a list based on select criteria.

Add the following method to the `PetDAO` interface and its implementation class.

```
public List<PetDVO> selectPets(String sex) {
    HashMap<String, String> inputMap = new HashMap<String, String>();
    inputMap.put("sex", sex);
    return (List<PetDVO>)
        sqlSessionTemplate.selectList("selectPets", inputMap);
}
```

The corresponding select statement in the "mapper.xml" file is provided below.

In this example, an externally defined parameter map is used to map the return type. The mapping between the column name and bean property name configuration is provided below.

```
<resultMap id="petResultMap" type="PetDVO">
    <id property="sex" column="sex"/>
    <result property="name" column="name"/>
    <result property="owner" column="owner"/>
    <result property="species" column="species"/>
    <result property="birth" column="birth"/>
    <result property="death" column="death"/>
</resultMap>
```

The "resultMap" attribute of the `<select>` element refers to the externally defined parameter map.

```
<select id="selectPets" parameterType="java.lang.String"
                    resultMap="petResultMap">
    SELECT NAME as name, OWNER as owner, SPECIES as species,
        SEX as sex, BIRTH as birth, DEATH as death
    FROM Pet where SEX = #{sex}
</select>
```

The following examples illustrate the use of the `SqlSessionTemplate` class for executing insert statements.

CASE 1: Executing an insert statement.

Add the following method to the `PetDAO` interface and its implementation class. This example is used to insert a new record into the "pet" table.

```
public void createPet(PetDVO petDVO) {
    HashMap<String, Object> inputMap = new HashMap<String, Object>();
    inputMap.put("name", petDVO.getName());
    inputMap.put("owner", petDVO.getOwner() );
    inputMap.put("species", petDVO.getSpecies() );
    inputMap.put("sex", petDVO.getSex());
    inputMap.put("birth", petDVO.getBirth());
    inputMap.put("death", petDVO.getDeath());

    sqlSessionTemplate.insert("createPet", inputMap);
}
```

The corresponding select statement in the "mapper.xml" file is provided below.

```
<insert id="createPet" parameterType="java.util.Map">
    INSERT INTO Pet (NAME, OWNER, SPECIES, SEX, BIRTH, DEATH)
    VALUES (#{name}, #{owner}, #{species}, #{sex}, #{birth}, #{death})
</insert>
```

The following examples illustrate the use of the `SqlSessionTemplate` class for executing update statements.

CASE 1: Executing an update statement.

Add the following method to the `PetDAO` interface and its implementation class. This example is used to update an existing record in the "pet" table.

```
public void updatePetData(PetDVO petDVO) {
    HashMap<String, Object> inputMap = new HashMap<String, Object>();
    inputMap.put("birth", petDVO.getBirth());
    inputMap.put("sex", petDVO.getSex());
    inputMap.put("name", petDVO.getName());

    sqlSessionTemplate.update("updatePetData", inputMap);
}
```

The corresponding select statement in the "mapper.xml" file is provided below.

```
<update id="updatePetData" parameterType="java.util.Map">
    UPDATE Pet p
    SET p.birth = #{birth}, p.sex = #{sex}
    WHERE p.name = #{name}
</update>
```

The following examples illustrate the use of the `SqlSessionTemplate` class for executing delete statements.

CASE 1: Executing a delete statement.

Add the following method to the `PetDAO` interface and its implementation class. This example is used to delete an existing record in the "pet" table.

```
public void deletePet(PetDVO petDVO) {
    HashMap<String, String> inputMap = new HashMap<String, String>();
    inputMap.put("species", petDVO.getSpecies());
    inputMap.put("name", petDVO.getName());

    sqlSessionTemplate.update("deletePet", inputMap);
}
```

The corresponding select statement in the "mapper.xml" file is provided below.

```
<delete id="deletePet" parameterType="java.util.Map">
    DELETE FROM Pet WHERE name = #{name} AND species = #{species}
</delete>
```

Building and Executing Dynamic SQL Statements

In application development, a common requirement is the building of dynamic SQL statements. MyBatis-provides the most powerful features for building dynamic SQL statements. This section illustrates the building and execution of dynamic SQL statements.

CASE 1: Conditionally including the WHERE clause.

Add the following method to the `PetDAO` interface and its implementation class. This method builds the SQL statement dynamically and populates the resultset data into a domain object class.

```
public List<PetDVO> findAllSnakes() {
    HashMap<String, String> inputMap = new HashMap<String, String>();
    inputMap.put("species", "snake");
    inputMap.put("sex", "f");
    inputMap.put("owner", "Su%");
    return (List<PetDVO>) sqlSessionTemplate.
            selectList("findAllSnakes", inputMap);
}
```

The corresponding select statement in the "mapper.xml" file is provided below. The WHERE clause is appended using the `<if>` statement.

```
<select id="findAllSnakes" parameterType="PetDVO" resultType="PetDVO">
    SELECT * FROM Pet WHERE species = #{species}
    <if test="sex != null">
        AND sex = #{sex}
    </if>
    <if test="owner != null">
        AND owner like #{owner}
    </if>
</select>
```

CASE 2: Building dynamic SQL using the switch statement.

Add the following method to the `PetDAO` interface and its implementation class. This method builds the WHERE clause dynamically and populates the resultset data into a domain object class.

```java
public List<PetDVO> findSnakePets() {
    HashMap<String, String> inputMap = new HashMap<String, String>();
    inputMap.put("species", "snake");
    inputMap.put("sex", "f");
    inputMap.put("owner", "Su%");
    return (List<PetDVO>) sqlSessionTemplate.
                    selectList("findSnakePets", inputMap);
}
```

The corresponding select statement in the "mapper.xml" file is provided below. The WHERE clause is appended using the `<choose>` statement.

```xml
<select id="findSnakePets" parameterType="PetDVO" resultType="PetDVO">
    SELECT * FROM Pet WHERE species = #{species}
    <choose>
        <when test="sex != null">
            AND sex = #{sex}
        </when>
        <when test="owner != null">
            AND owner like #{owner}
        </when>
        <otherwise>
            AND name like 'Slim%'
        </otherwise>
    </choose>
</select>
```

CASE 3: Building dynamic SQL using the "foreach" statement.

Add the following method to the `PetDAO` interface and its implementation class. This method builds the WHERE IN select statement dynamically and populates the resultset data into a domain object class.

```java
public List<PetDVO> selectPetsIn() {
    HashMap<String, Object> inputMap = new HashMap<String, Object>();
    List<String> speciesList = new ArrayList<String>();
    speciesList.add("snake");
    speciesList.add("cat");
    speciesList.add("dog");
    inputMap.put("speciesList", speciesList);
    return (List<PetDVO>) sqlSessionTemplate.
            selectList("selectPetsIn", inputMap);
}
```

The corresponding select statement in the "mapper.xml" file is provided below. The WHERE IN clause of the select statement is appended using the `<foreach>` statement.

```xml
<select id="selectPetsIn" resultType="PetDVO">
    SELECT * FROM Pet P WHERE species IN
    <foreach item="item" index="index" collection="speciesList"
            open="(" separator="," close=")">
        #{item}
```

```
        </foreach>
</select>
```

CASE 4: Building an update statement dynamically.

Add the following method to the `PetDAO` interface and its implementation class. This method dynamically builds the UPDATE statement.

```
public void updatePetDynamically(PetDVO petDVO) {
    HashMap<String, Object> inputMap = new HashMap<String, Object>();
    inputMap.put("birth", petDVO.getBirth());
    inputMap.put("death", petDVO.getDeath());
    inputMap.put("sex", petDVO.getSex());
    inputMap.put("name", petDVO.getName());

    sqlSessionTemplate.update("updatePetDynamically", inputMap);
}
```

The corresponding select statement in the "mapper.xml" file is provided below. The UPDATE clause built dynamically using the `<set>` statement.

```
<update id="updatePetDynamically" parameterType="java.util.Map">
    UPDATE Pet
        <set>
            <if test="birth != null">birth=#{birth},</if>
            <if test="death != null">death=#{death},</if>
            <if test="sex != null">sex=#{sex}</if>
        </set>
    WHERE name=#{name}
</update>
```

Example 9: Executing Stored Procedures

Here, reuse the previously created "sp_read_all_pets" stored procedure. The stored procedure execution syntax is the same as what is used in select statement execution. The complete method code is provided below.

CASE 1: Executing a stored procedure that returns a resultset.

Add the following method to the `PetDAO` interface and its implementation class. This method returns the list of records from the "pet" table.

```
public List<PetDVO> callReadAllPets() {
    return (List<PetDVO>)
        sqlSessionTemplate.selectList("callReadAllPets");
}
```

The corresponding select statement in the "mapper.xml" file is provided below. The CALL statement is used to execute a stored procedure.

```
<select id="callReadAllPets" resultType="PetDVO"
                            statementType="CALLABLE">
    { CALL read_all_pets() }
```

```
</select>
```

CASE 2: Executing a stored procedure that has IN and OUT parameters.

Add the following method to the `PetDAO` interface and its implementation class. This method prints the stored procedure OUT parameter values.

```java
public void callReadPet() {
    HashMap<String, String> inputMap = new HashMap<String, String>();
    inputMap.put("name", "Fluffy");
    inputMap.put("owner", "");
    inputMap.put("species", "");
    inputMap.put("sex", "");
    inputMap.put("birth", "");
    inputMap.put("death", "");

    sqlSessionTemplate.selectOne("callReadPet", inputMap);

    // Printing the result
    System.out.println("--- owner ---" + inputMap.get("owner"));
    System.out.println("--- species ---" + inputMap.get("species"));
}
```

The corresponding select statement in the "mapper.xml" file is provided below.

```xml
<select id="callReadPet" parameterType="java.util.Map"
        resultType="java.util.Map" statementType="CALLABLE">
    { CALL read_pet(
        #{name, mode=IN, jdbcType=VARCHAR},
        #{owner, mode=OUT, jdbcType=VARCHAR},
        #{species, mode=OUT, jdbcType=VARCHAR},
        #{sex, mode=OUT, jdbcType=VARCHAR},
        #{birth, mode=OUT, jdbcType=DATE},
        #{death, mode=OUT, jdbcType=DATE}
    )}
</select>
```

Example 10: Executing Stored Functions

Add the following method to the `PetDAO` interface and its implementation class. Here, reuse the previously created "get_pet_owner" stored function. The complete method code is provided below.

```java
public void callPetOwnerFunction() {
    HashMap<String, String> inputMap = new HashMap<String, String>();
    inputMap.put("name", "Slim");
    inputMap.put("owner", "");

    sqlSessionTemplate.selectOne("callPetOwnerFunction", inputMap);

    // Printing the function return value
    System.out.println("--- Function result owner ---" +
                inputMap.get("owner"));
}
```

The corresponding select statement in the "mapper.xml" file is provided below.

```
<select id="callPetOwnerFunction" parameterType="java.util.Map"
        resultType="java.util.Map" statementType="CALLABLE">
    { #{owner, javaType=String, jdbcType=VARCHAR, mode=OUT} =
        call get_pet_owner(#{name, javaType=String, jdbcType=VARCHAR,
                                mode=IN}) }
</select>
```

Listing 4-7 provides the complete class code; run the following standalone class to view the output.

Listing 4-7: Standalone class to test the stored procedures and functions.

```
// MyBatisTestStoredProcedures.java
package com.learning.spring.db.mybatis;

import org.springframework.context.support.
            ClassPathXmlApplicationContext;

import java.util.List;

public class MyBatisTestStoredProcedures {

    public static void main(String[] args) {
        try {
            ClassPathXmlApplicationContext appContext =
                new ClassPathXmlApplicationContext
                (new String[]{"applicationContext-myBatis.xml"});

            PetDAO petDAOImpl = (PetDAO)
                        appContext.getBean("petDAOImpl");

            // Calling stored procedure (read_all_pets)
            List<PetDVO> procResult = petDAOImpl.callReadAllPets();
            for (PetDVO petDVObj : procResult) {
                System.out.println("--- name --"+ petDVObj.getName());
            }

            // Calling stored procedure (read_pet)
            petDAOImpl.callReadPet();

            // Calling stored function (get_pet_owner)
            petDAOImpl.callPetOwnerFunction();

        } catch (Exception ex) {
            ex.printStackTrace();
        }
    }
}
```

Retrieving Auto-Generated Keys

Create the following table in your database.

```
CREATE TABLE USER (
```

```
    id MEDIUMINT NOT NULL AUTO_INCREMENT,
    first_name CHAR(30) NULL,
    last_name CHAR(30) NULL,
    PRIMARY KEY (id)
) ENGINE=MyISAM;
```

Use the following `User` object to map the resultset data.

```
public class User {

    private int id;
    private String firstNmae;
    private String lastName;

    // Add getter and setter methods
}
```

Use the following `insertUser()` method to retrieve the auto-generated key value.

```
public void insertUser() {
    HashMap<String, Object> inputMap = new HashMap<String, Object>();
    User user = new User();
    inputMap.put("id", user.getId());
    inputMap.put("firstName", "John");
    inputMap.put("lastName", "Smith");

    sqlSessionTemplate.insert("insertUser", inputMap);
    System.out.println("--- Id value ---" + inputMap.get("id"));
}
```

The corresponding insert statement in the "mapper.xml" file is provided below. If your database supports auto-generated keys, you can retrieve the generated key value as follows:

```
<insert id="insertUser" parameterType="java.util.Map"
        useGeneratedKeys="true" keyProperty="id">
    INSERT INTO User (first_name, last_name)
    VALUES (#{firstName}, #{lastName})
</insert>
```

Comparison between Hibernate and myBatis

The following table summarizes the comparison between the various technical features of Hibernate and MyBatis.

Hibernate	MyBatis
Hibernate is an Object-Relational mapping technique used to access the databases. The domain objects are mapped to database entities.	MyBatis is a Resultset-Object mapping technique used to access the databases. The resultset data maps to the domain objects. This is the reverse of what Hibernate does.
Preferable for simpler database schemas and tables that has well defined	Uses the power of SQL statements, easy to execute complex sub-queries and

relationships.	correlated sub-queries.
Requires more of a learning curve; tuning and debugging are challenging.	Simple, flexible, easy to learn, simpler in package size and provides more powerful features for building dynamic SQL statements.
Developers use HQL (Hibernate Query Language) to define relationships and join conditions. Hibernate runtime converts the HQL to SQL for database interaction. HQL is similar to SQL.	Developers use SQL statements for database operations.
HQL is database independent.	SQL is database dependent. It is the preferred solution if you need more control over SQL statements.

Summary

Figure 4-1 summarizes the most important points described in this chapter.

Figure 4-1 Spring data access features

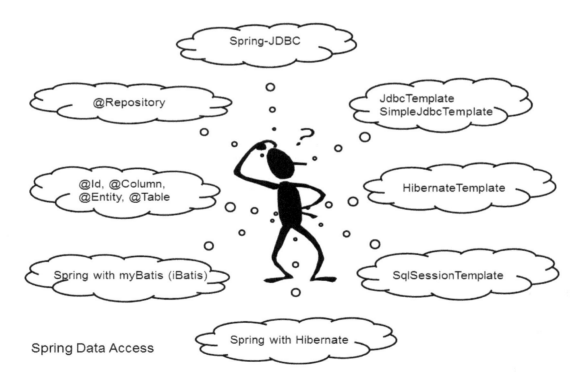

This section summarizes the features provided in the spring data access framework.

- Spring provides various template classes to execute select, insert, delete and update statements. The spring-provided JDBC template classes are listed below.
  - JdbcTemplate
  - NamedParameterJdbcTemplate

- SimpleJdbcTemplate
- The `HibernateTemplate` class is the core class used in spring-based Hibernate for executing SQL statements such as select, insert, delete, and update as well as stored procedures and functions.
- The `SqlSessionTemplate` class is the core class used in spring-based myBatis for executing SQL statements such as select, insert, delete, and update as well as stored procedures and functions.
- The following annotations are used to map the domain objects to the database tables.
    - @Table
    - @Entity
    - @Id
    - @Column
- The `@Repository`-annotated class is a special type of component class used for data access components. The `@Repository`-annotated classes are eligible for auto-scanning using the spring-provided `<context:component-scan>` configuration.

Chapter 5. Spring Transaction Management

The spring framework provides a transaction management API to manage transactions for Java-based applications. Spring provides a consistent transaction management framework that can be used with any data access framework such as Spring-JDBC, Hibernate, MyBatis, and so forth. The spring transaction framework is an alternative to the EJB-provided container managed entity bean transaction model. However, the spring transaction framework does not require an application server to manage the transactions.

This chapter will discuss the following topics:

- Spring declarative transaction management
- Spring programmatic transaction management
- Spring annotation-based transaction management
- The transaction propagation attributes and their use

Advantages of Spring Transactions

- Spring provides a simple AOP-based configuration to manage the transaction behavior of methods.
- Spring provides annotation and API-based programming models to manage transactions.
- Spring provides support for both declarative and programmatic transaction management.
- Spring provides support for standalone and JNDI-based data sources and it functions in any environment.
- It is a simple and consistent programming model that supports various data access frameworks such as Spring-JDBC, Hibernate, MyBatis, and JPA.
- An application server is not needed to manage the transactions; spring can be used in any standalone environment.

Declarative and Programmatic Transaction Management

Spring provides support for both declarative and programmatic transaction management. In the case of declarative transaction management, spring provides AOP-based XML configurations to manage the transaction behavior. The spring declarative transaction behavior can be applied to any class or interface method without modifying the application code. The benefit of this approach is that the application code does not depend on spring's API and looks cleaner.

In the case of programmatic transaction management, spring's API is used to manage the transactions. Spring also offers the annotation-based programming approach to manage transactions. This chapter illustrates the capabilities of both declarative and programmatic transaction management.

Transaction Propagation in EJB and Spring

This section illustrates the purpose of transaction attributes in EJB and spring. EJB supports the following six transaction attributes. A transaction attribute specifies how the container must manage the transaction when a client invokes a method of an EJB component.

- REQUIRED
- REQUIRESNEW
- MANDATORY
- SUPPORTS
- NOT SUPPORTED
- NEVER

The following table summarizes the significance of each transaction attribute in EJB.

Transaction Attribute	Invoking client has transaction	Invoking client does not have transaction
REQUIRED	Transaction is propagated	New transaction will be started.
REQUIRESNEW	Suspends the current transaction; starts a new transaction	Starts a new transaction
MANDATORY	Propagates the current transaction.	Throws a `TransactionRequiredException`
SUPPORTS	Propagates the current transaction.	
NOT SUPPORTED	Suspends the current transaction.	
NEVER	Throws `RemoteException`	

Similarly, the following transaction attributes are used in the spring framework to control transaction propagation.

- REQUIRED
- REQUIRESNEW
- NESTED

In spring, the REQUIRED and REQUIRESNEW transaction attributes function the same as they do in EJB. The NESTED transaction attribute is used for a single transaction that has multiple save points and allows the transaction to roll back to the specified save point.

Demo Examples

Example 1: Declarative Transaction Management

This example illustrates the configurations required to handle declarative transactions. The steps required to implement this example are listed below.

---

1. Create a DAO interface and its implementation class
2. Create a data value object (DVO) class
3. Configure the datasource and transaction manager in an application context file.
4. Create a main class to test the code.

The above-specified steps are described in the following sections.

Step 1: Create a DAO interface and its implementation class

The definition of the `PetDAO` interface is provided below. This interface has read-only, insert, and delete methods.

```
// PetDAO.java
package com.learning.spring.tx.dao;

import java.util.List;

public interface PetDAO {

    List getListOfPetNames(String sex);

    void doInsertAndUpdateInTx();

    void insertPet(PetDVO petDVO);

    void updatePetData(String owner, String name);
}
```

The above-specified interface methods are implemented in the `PetDAOImpl` class. The `doInsertAndUpdateInTx()` method is used to wrap the insert and update methods and is executed in one transaction. If an exception occurs in this method, it has to roll back both the insert and update operations. The `doInsertAndUpdateInTx()` method code is provided below.

```
public void doInsertAndUpdateInTx() {
    insertPet(petDVO);
    updatePetData("Steven Sun", "Buffy");
}
```

Let us modify the above method slightly to create an exception between insert and update. The following code throws a divide-by-zero exception. In this scenario, the insert operation will roll back autimatically.

```
public void doInsertAndUpdateInTx() {
    insertPet(petDVO);

    // create an error
    int i = 0;
    int j = 100 / i;

    updatePetData("Steven Sun", "Buffy");
}
```

The complete class code is provided below.

```java
// PetDAOImpl.java
package com.learning.spring.tx.dao;

import org.springframework.jdbc.core.JdbcTemplate;
import org.springframework.transaction.TransactionStatus;

import java.util.*;
import java.sql.Types;

public class PetDAOImpl implements PetDAO {

    private JdbcTemplate jdbcTemplate;

    public List getListOfPetNames(String sex) {
        String query = "select name from pet where sex=?";
        Object[] params = new Object[]{sex};
        int[] types = new int[]{Types.VARCHAR};
        return jdbcTemplate.queryForList(query, params, types);
    }

    public void doInsertAndUpdateInTx() {
        PetDVO petDVO = new PetDVO();
        petDVO.setName("Slim1");
        petDVO.setOwner("Steve");
        petDVO.setSpecies("Snake");
        petDVO.setSex("f");
        petDVO.setBirth(new Date());

        // Inserting a new record
        insertPet(petDVO);

        // Create an error to get the exception
        int i = 0;
        int j = 100 / i;

        // Update a record
        updatePetData("Steven Sun", "Buffy");
    }

    public void insertPet(PetDVO petDVO) {
        String SQL_INSERT_STATEMENT = "INSERT INTO pet (name, owner,
            species, sex, birth, death) VALUES (?, ?, ?, ?, ?, ?)";
        jdbcTemplate.update(SQL_INSERT_STATEMENT,
            petDVO.getName(), petDVO.getOwner(), petDVO.getSpecies(),
            petDVO.getSex(), petDVO.getBirth(), petDVO.getDeath());
    }

    public void updatePetData(String owner, String name) {
        String SQL_UPDATE_STATEMENT =
                "UPDATE pet SET owner = ? WHERE name = ?";
        Object[] params = new Object[]{owner, name};
        int[] types = new int[]{Types.VARCHAR, Types.VARCHAR};
        jdbcTemplate.update(SQL_UPDATE_STATEMENT, params, types);
    }

    public void setJdbcTemplate(JdbcTemplate jdbcTemplate) {
```

```
        this.jdbcTemplate = jdbcTemplate;
    }
}
```

Step 2: Create a data value object (DVO) class

The following domain object is used.

```java
// PetDVO.java
package com.learning.spring.tx.dao;

import java.util.Date;
import java.io.Serializable;

public class PetDVO implements Serializable {

    private String name;
    private String owner;
    private String species;
    private String sex;
    private Date birth;
    private Date death;

    // Add getter and setter methods
}
```

Step 3: Configure the datasource and transaction manager in an application context file.

The spring application context file is used to configure the datasource, transaction manager, spring JDBC template and data access objects. The complete application context XML file is provided below and is named the "applicationContext-tx.xml"

```xml
<?xml version="1.0" encoding="UTF-8"?>
<beans xmlns="http://www.springframework.org/schema/beans"
    xmlns:xsi="http://www.w3.org/2001/XMLSchema-instance"
    xmlns:context="http://www.springframework.org/schema/context"
    xmlns:aop="http://www.springframework.org/schema/aop"
    xmlns:tx="http://www.springframework.org/schema/tx"
    xsi:schemaLocation="http://www.springframework.org/schema/beans
        http://www.springframework.org/schema/beans/
                   spring-beans-3.0.xsd
        http://www.springframework.org/schema/context
        http://www.springframework.org/schema/context/
                   spring-context-3.0.xsd
        http://www.springframework.org/schema/tx
        http://www.springframework.org/schema/tx/spring-tx-3.0.xsd
        http://www.springframework.org/schema/aop
        http://www.springframework.org/schema/aop/spring-aop-3.0.xsd ">

    <!-- Configure the datasource -->
    <bean id="mySqlDataSource" class="org.springframework.jdbc.
                datasource.DriverManagerDataSource">
        <property name="driverClassName">
            <value>com.mysql.jdbc.Driver</value>
        </property>
        <property name="url">
```

```xml
            <value>jdbc:mysql://localhost:3306/test</value>
        </property>
        <property name="username">
            <value>root</value>
        </property>
        <property name="password">
            <value>mysql</value>
        </property>
    </bean>

    <!-- Transaction manager for the data source -->
    <bean id="txManager" class="org.springframework.jdbc.datasource.
              DataSourceTransactionManager">
        <property name="dataSource" ref="mySqlDataSource"/>
    </bean>

    <!-- Configure the Spring JdbcTemplate -->
    <bean id="springJdbcTemplate"
          class="org.springframework.jdbc.core.JdbcTemplate">
        <property name="dataSource">
            <ref bean="mySqlDataSource"/>
        </property>
    </bean>

    <!-- Configure the AOP pointcut expression -->
    <aop:config>
        <aop:pointcut id="petDaoOperation" expression="execution
            (* com.learning.spring.tx.dao.PetDAO.*(..))"/>
        <aop:advisor pointcut-ref="petDaoOperation"
                     advice-ref="txAdvice"/>
    </aop:config>

    <!-- Configure the advice for interface methods -->
    <tx:advice id="txAdvice" transaction-manager="txManager">
        <tx:attributes>
            <tx:method name="get*" read-only="true"/>
            <tx:method name="*"/>
        </tx:attributes>
    </tx:advice>

    <!-- Configure the DAO class -->
    <bean id="petDAOImpl"
        class="com.learning.spring.tx.dao.PetDAOImpl">
        <property name="jdbcTemplate">
            <ref local="springJdbcTemplate"/>
        </property>
    </bean>

</beans>
```

Step 4: Create a main class to test the code.

Listing 5-1 provides the complete class code; run the following standalone class to view the output.

Listing 5-1: Standalone class used for testing

```java
// TxMain.java
```

```
package com.learning.spring.tx;

import org.springframework.context.support.
            ClassPathXmlApplicationContext;
import org.springframework.context.ApplicationContext;
import com.learning.spring.tx.dao.PetDAO;

public class TxMain {

    public static void main(final String[] args) throws Exception {
        ApplicationContext ctx = new ClassPathXmlApplicationContext(new
                    String [] { "applicationContext-tx.xml" });
        PetDAO petDAO = (PetDAO) ctx.getBean("petDAOImpl");
        petDAO.doInsertAndUpdateInTx();
    }
}
```

Example 2: Programmatic Transaction Management

This example illustrates management of transactions programmatically using spring API. The steps required to implement this example are listed below.

1. Create a DAO interface and its implementation class.
2. Create a data value object (DVO) class.
3. Configure the datasource and transaction manager in an application context file.
4. Create a main class to test the code.

The above-specified steps are described in the following sections:

Step 1: Create a DAO interface and its implementation class

Here, reuse the `PetDAO` and `PetDAOImpl` classes created in Example-1. Add the following method to the `PetDAO` interface.

```
public interface PetDAO {
    void doInsertAndUpdateUsingTxTemplate();
}
```

Spring provides the `TransactionTemplate` class to execute the methods in a transaction. The `status.setRollbackOnly()` method rolls back the transaction if any exception occurs within the scope of a transaction. The complete method code is provided below.

```
public void doInsertAndUpdateUsingTxTemplate() {

    transactionTemplate.execute(new TransactionCallbackWithoutResult() {
        protected void doInTransactionWithoutResult(
                        TransactionStatus status) {
            try {
                PetDVO petDVO = new PetDVO();
                petDVO.setName("Slim1");
                petDVO.setOwner("Steve");
                petDVO.setSpecies("Snake");
                petDVO.setSex("f");
```

```
                    petDVO.setBirth(new Date());

                    // Insert a record
                    insertPet(petDVO);

                    // Create an error to get the exception
                    int i = 0;
                    int j = 100 / i;

                    // Update a record
                    updatePetData("Steven Sun", "Buffy");

                } catch (Exception ex) {
                    // Printing the transaction status
                    System.out.println(" is Completed " +
                            status.isCompleted());
                    status.setRollbackOnly();
                }
            }
        });
}
```

Step 2: Create a data value object (DVO) class.

Here, reuse the `PetDVO` class created in Example-1.

Step 3: Configure the datasource and transaction manager in an application context file.

The spring application context file is used to configure the datasource, transaction manager, spring JDBC template, transaction template and DAO classes. The complete application context XML file is provided below and is named the "applicationContext-tx-template.xml".

```
<?xml version="1.0" encoding="UTF-8"?>
<beans xmlns="http://www.springframework.org/schema/beans"
    xmlns:xsi="http://www.w3.org/2001/XMLSchema-instance"
    xmlns:context="http://www.springframework.org/schema/context"
    xsi:schemaLocation="http://www.springframework.org/schema/beans
    http://www.springframework.org/schema/beans/spring-beans-3.0.xsd
    http://www.springframework.org/schema/context
    http://www.springframework.org/schema/context/
                spring-context-3.0.xsd">

    <!-- Configure datasource -->
    <bean id="mySqlDataSource" class="org.springframework.jdbc.
                datasource.DriverManagerDataSource">
        <property name="driverClassName">
            <value>com.mysql.jdbc.Driver</value>
        </property>
        <property name="url">
            <value>jdbc:mysql://localhost:3306/test</value>
        </property>
        <property name="username">
            <value>root</value>
        </property>
        <property name="password">
            <value>mysql</value>
```

```
            </property>
        </bean>

        <!-- Transaction manager for the data source -->
        <bean id="txManager" class="org.springframework.jdbc.datasource.
                    DataSourceTransactionManager">
            <property name="dataSource" ref="mySqlDataSource"/>
        </bean>

        <bean id="springJdbcTemplate"
                class="org.springframework.jdbc.core.JdbcTemplate">
            <property name="dataSource">
                <ref local="mySqlDataSource"/>
            </property>
        </bean>

        <!-- Configure spring TransactionTemplate class -->
        <bean id="txTemplate" class="org.springframework.
                    transaction.support.TransactionTemplate">
            <property name="transactionManager" ref="txManager"/>
        </bean>

        <!-- Injecting TransactionTemplate and JdbcTemplate into DAO -->
        <bean id="petDAOImpl"
            class="com.learning.spring.tx.dao.PetDAOImpl">
            <property name="jdbcTemplate">
                <ref local="springJdbcTemplate"/>
            </property>
            <property name="transactionTemplate" ref="txTemplate"/>
        </bean>

</beans>
```

Step 4: Create a main class to test the code.

Listing 5-2 provides the complete class code; run the following standalone class to view the output.

Listing 5-2: Standalone class used for testing

```java
// TxMain.java
package com.learning.spring.tx;

import org.springframework.context.support.
            ClassPathXmlApplicationContext;
import org.springframework.context.ApplicationContext;
import com.learning.spring.tx.dao.PetDAO;

public class TxMain {

    public static void main(final String[] args) throws Exception {
        ApplicationContext ctx = new ClassPathXmlApplicationContext(new
                String [] { "applicationContext-tx-template.xml" });
        PetDAO petDAO = (PetDAO) ctx.getBean("petDAOImpl");
        petDAO.doInsertAndUpdateUsingTxTemplate();
    }
}
```

Transaction Management Using Spring Annotations

The `@Transactional` annotation with `<tx:annotation-driven>` XML configuration provides the transactional behavior to the annotated methods. The `@Transactional` annotation is used to specify the metadata required for the runtime infrastructure in managing transactions. This annotation can be used with interfaces, methods of an interface, classes, and methods of a class. The `<tx:annotation-driven>` element enables the annotation-based transactional behavior, and this tag looks for only `@Transactional`-annotated methods or classes.

The following XML element enables the annotation-based transaction behavior.

```
<tx:annotation-driven transaction-manager="txManager"/>
```

The default `@Transactional`-annotation properties are listed below.

- Transaction Propagation = REQUIRED
- Isolation level = DEFAULT
- Rollback-for = Any runtime exception triggers a transaction roll back

The following code demonstrates the use of `@Transactional`-annotation.

```
@Transactional(readOnly = false)
public void doInsertAndUpdateInTx() {

    // Insert a record
    insertPet(petDVO);

    // Update a record
    updatePetData("Steven Sun", "Buffy");
}
```

Example 3: Annotation-based Transaction Management

This example illustrates programmatic handling of transactions using spring annotations. The steps required to implement this example are listed below.

1. Create a DAO interface and its implementation class
2. Create a data value object (DVO) class
3. Configure the datasource and transaction manager in an application context file.
4. Create a main class to test the code.

The above-specified steps are described in the following sections:

Step 1: Create a DAO interface and its implementation class

Here, reuse the `PetDAO` and `PetDAOImpl` classes created in Example-1. The `@Transactional`-annotated method is executed in a transaction. The annotated method signature is provided below.

```
@Transactional(readOnly = false)
public void doInsertAndUpdateInTx() {
    PetDVO petDVO = new PetDVO();
```

```
petDVO.setName("Slim1");
petDVO.setOwner("Steve");
petDVO.setSpecies("Snake");
petDVO.setSex("f");
petDVO.setBirth(new Date());

// Insert a record
insertPet(petDVO);

// Create an error to get the exception
int i = 0;
int j = 100 / i;

// Update a record
updatePetData("Steven Sun", "Buffy");
}
```

Step 2: Create data value object (DVO) class

Here, reuse the PetDVO class created in Example-1.

Step 3: Configure the datasource and transaction manager in an application context file.

The complete application context XML file is provided below and is named the "applicationContext-tx-annotations.xml".

```xml
<?xml version="1.0" encoding="UTF-8"?>
<beans xmlns="http://www.springframework.org/schema/beans"
    xmlns:xsi="http://www.w3.org/2001/XMLSchema-instance"
    xmlns:context="http://www.springframework.org/schema/context"
    xmlns:tx="http://www.springframework.org/schema/tx"
    xsi:schemaLocation="http://www.springframework.org/schema/beans
    http://www.springframework.org/schema/beans/spring-beans-3.0.xsd
    http://www.springframework.org/schema/context
    http://www.springframework.org/schema/context/spring-context-3.0.xsd
    http://www.springframework.org/schema/tx
    http://www.springframework.org/schema/tx/spring-tx-3.0.xsd ">

    <bean id="mySqlDataSource" class="org.springframework.jdbc.
                    datasource.DriverManagerDataSource">
        <property name="driverClassName">
            <value>com.mysql.jdbc.Driver</value>
        </property>
        <property name="url">
            <value>jdbc:mysql://localhost:3306/test</value>
        </property>
        <property name="username">
            <value>root</value>
        </property>
        <property name="password">
            <value>mysql</value>
        </property>
    </bean>

    <!-- Transaction manager for the data source -->
    <bean id="txManager" class="org.springframework.jdbc.datasource.
```

```
                DataSourceTransactionManager">
        <property name="dataSource" ref="mySqlDataSource"/>
    </bean>

    <!-- Enable the annotation-based transaction behavior -->
    <tx:annotation-driven transaction-manager="txManager"/>

    <bean id="springJdbcTemplate" class="org.springframework.jdbc.core.
                        JdbcTemplate">
        <property name="dataSource">
            <ref local="mySqlDataSource"/>
        </property>
    </bean>

    <bean id="petDAOImpl" class="com.learning.spring.tx.
                annotations.PetDAOImpl">
        <property name="jdbcTemplate" ref="springJdbcTemplate"/>
    </bean>
</beans>
```

Step 4: Create a main class to test the code.

Listing 5-3 provides the complete class code; run the following standalone class to view the output.

Listing 5-3: Standalone class used for testing

```
// TxMain.java
package com.learning.spring.tx;

import org.springframework.context.support.
            ClassPathXmlApplicationContext;
import org.springframework.context.ApplicationContext;
import com.learning.spring.tx.dao.PetDAO;

public class TxMain {

    public static void main(final String[] args) throws Exception {
        ApplicationContext ctx = new ClassPathXmlApplicationContext(new
            String [] { "applicationContext-tx-annotations.xml" });
        PetDAO petDAO = (PetDAO) ctx.getBean("petDAOImpl");
        petDAO.doInsertAndUpdateInTx ();
    }
}
```

Summary

This section summarizes the features of the spring transaction framework.

- Spring provides the `TransactionTemplate` class to execute the methods in a transaction. The `status.setRollbackOnly()` method rolls back the transaction if an exception occurs within the scope of a transaction.
- The `@Transactional` annotation with `<tx:annotation-driven>` XML configuration provides the transactional behavior to the annotated methods.

- The supported spring transaction propagation attributes are REQUIRED, REQUIRESNEW and NESTED.
- The `<tx:advice>` tag is used to specify the various transaction settings.

Figure 5-1 summarizes the most important points described in this chapter.

Figure 5-1 Spring transaction management features.

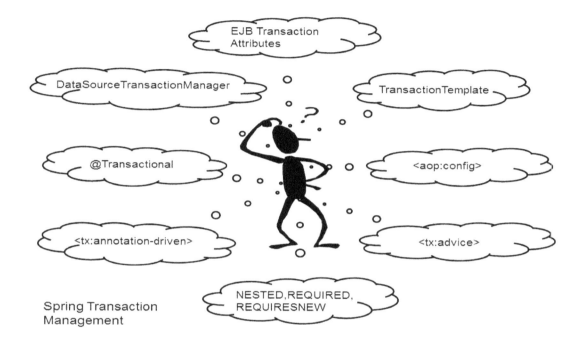

Chapter 6. Spring-JMX

Java Management Extensions (JMX) is a Java technology used to manage and monitor applications, Java components, devices, and networks. JMX-provides a standard API for managing Java applications and is part of the Java SE platform. JMX-managed resource objects are called managed beans (MBeans). The MBean is a resource running inside the Java Virtual Machine (JVM). The applications create a managed bean and register them with the MBean server. The registered beans can be managed locally or remotely using a standard JMX API. JMX can also be used to monitor JVM. The console used to monitor the managed bean instances is the JConsole. And it is part of your JDK. Spring provides a high-level API to integrate your application with the JMX infrastructure. This chapter illustrates the spring integration with the JMX infrastructure.

This chapter will discuss the following topics:

- Fundamentals of JMX monitoring
- Exposing the Java bean as a JMX-managed bean with and without using the spring framework
- Spring framework-provided JMX infrastructure components
- Monitoring local and remote services using the spring framework
- Annotation support for exposing the Java bean as a JMX-managed bean
- Spring support for publishing JMX notifications

Spring JMX Advantages

- Spring provides a simplified approach to expose the spring-managed bean as a JMX-managed bean.
- Spring supports both XML and Annotation-based approaches for exposing Java beans as JMX-managed beans.
- Spring provides support for managing bean resources locally and remotely.
- Spring provides a cleaner approach for integrating your applications with the JMX infrastructure. Loose coupling between your application components and spring JMX components.

Exposing the Java Bean as an MBean

Example 1: Exposing a Java Bean as an MBean (without Spring)

This example illustrates how to expose the Java bean properties and methods as attributes and operations of a managed bean (MBean) class. This is a standalone Java code; spring is not used in this example.

The steps required to expose a Java class as an MBean are listed below.

1. Create an interface.
2. Create an implementation class.
3. Expose the Java bean as an MBean using JMX API.

4. Use the JConsole to view and manage the attributes and operations.

The above-specified steps are described in the following sections:

Step 1: Create an interface

Create an interface with the MBean suffix; this suffix is not mandatory, but it is recommended to follow JMX-naming conventions. The `EmployeeMBean` interface definition is provided below.

```
// EmployeeMBean.java
package com.learning.spring.core.jmx.corejava;

public interface EmployeeMBean {

    int getAge();

    void setAge(int age);

    String getName();

    void setName(String name);

    int calculateTotalSalary(int base, int bonus);

    void updateName();
}
```

Step 2: Create an implementation class.

The complete implementation class code is provided below. This class implements the `EmployeeMBean` interface and has Java bean properties and methods. The Java bean properties are exposed as JMX-attributes; methods are exposed as JMX-operations.

```
// EmployeeImpl.java
package com.learning.spring.core.jmx.corejava;

public class EmployeeImpl implements EmployeeMBean {

    private int age;
    private String name;

    public EmployeeImpl(String name, int age) {
        this.name = name;
        this.age = age;
    }

    public int getAge() {
        return age;
    }

    public void setAge(int age) {
        this.age = age;
    }

    public String getName() {
```

```
        return name;
    }

    public void setName(String name) {
        this.name = name;
    }

    public int calculateTotalSalary(int base, int bonus) {
        return base + bonus;
    }

    public void updateName() {
        this.name = name + " Sims ";
    }
}
```

Step 3: Expose the Java bean as an MBean using JMX-API

Listing 6-1 provides the complete class code; JMX-API is used to expose the Java bean class as an MBean.

Listing 6-1: Main class

```
// JmxMain.java
package com.learning.spring.core.jmx.corejava;

import javax.management.StandardMBean;
import javax.management.ObjectName;
import javax.management.MBeanServer;
import java.lang.management.ManagementFactory;

public class JmxMain {

    public static void main(String[] args) throws Exception {
        MBeanServer server =
                ManagementFactory.getPlatformMBeanServer();
        ObjectName id = new ObjectName
                ("name.employee.test:type=employee1");
        EmployeeImpl employeeImpl = new EmployeeImpl("John", 40);
        StandardMBean mbean = new StandardMBean(employeeImpl,
                                EmployeeMBean.class);
        server.registerMBean(mbean, id);
        System.out.println("--- Sleeping the thread ---");
        Thread.sleep(Long.MAX_VALUE);
    }
}
```

Step 4: Use the JConsole to view and manage the attributes and operations.

In this example, the JConsole is used to view and manage the JMX attributes and operations. The JConsole is packaged along with JDK. Follow the below provided steps to run the JConsole.

- Open the command line; go to your installed "\jdk\bin" directory.
- Execute the "jconsole.exe" batch file from the "\jdk\bin" directory. The JConsole will be displayed along with the process id and package name "com.learning.spring.core.jmx.corejava" This is shown in Figure 6-1.

Figure 6-1: JConsole with process id and package name

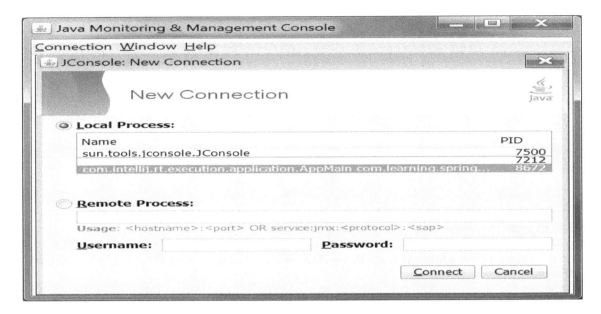

- Select your process id → click on "Connect". The following console will be displayed. The managed bean attributes and operations are shown in Figure 6-2.

Figure 6-2: JConsole showing registered Java bean as MBean

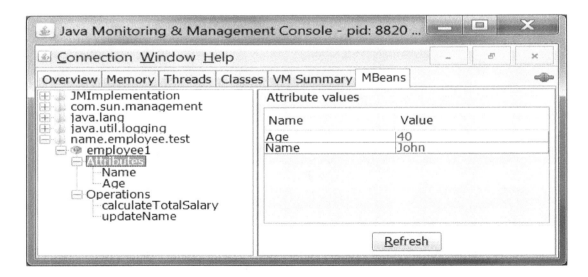

- Navigate to Operations → Select "updateName" → Click on "updateName" button.
- Navigate to Attributes → You can see the updated name.

Similarly, you can navigate to the exposed attributes and operations to update the registered Java bean properties and methods.

NOTE: If you have multiple JDK's installed on your machine; make sure you use the correct JDK-specific JConsole to view the registered MBeans.

Example 2: Exposing a Spring-managed Bean as an MBean (with Spring)

This example illustrates how to expose the spring-managed bean properties and methods as attributes and operations of a managed bean (MBean) class. Spring is used in this example.

The steps required to expose a spring-managed bean class as an MBean are listed below.

1. Create an interface.
2. Create an implementation class.
3. Expose a spring-managed bean as an MBean using the spring application context.
4. Create a main class to start the application
5. Use the JConsole to view and manage the attributes and operations.

The above-specified steps are described in the following sections:

Step 1: Create an interface

Here, reuse the `EmployeeMBean` interface created in Example-1.

Step 2: Create an implementation class

Here, reuse the `EmployeeImpl` class created in Example-1.

Step 3: Expose a Spring-managed bean as an MBean using the Spring application context.

Spring provides an `MBeanExporter` class which encapsulates the JMX-API. This class can be used to expose the spring-managed beans as MBeans. This class registers the spring-managed beans with `MBeanServer`.

The complete application context xml configuration is provided below and is named the "applicationContext-jmx-mbeans.xml".

CASE 1: Environment that has its own "MBean" server

This approach is used when your application is running in an environment that has its own `MBeanServer` instance. `MBeanExporter` detects the `MBeanServer` instance to register the managed beans.

```xml
<?xml version="1.0" encoding="UTF-8"?>
<beans xmlns="http://www.springframework.org/schema/beans"
    xmlns:xsi="http://www.w3.org/2001/XMLSchema-instance"
    xmlns:context="http://www.springframework.org/schema/context"
    xsi:schemaLocation="http://www.springframework.org/schema/beans
    http://www.springframework.org/schema/beans/spring-beans-3.0.xsd
    http://www.springframework.org/schema/context
    http://www.springframework.org/schema/context/
            spring-context-3.0.xsd">

    <bean id="mBeanExporter"
```

```
                    class="org.springframework.jmx.export.MBeanExporter"
                    lazy-init="false">

                <property name="beans">
                    <map>
                        <entry key="bean:name=springEmployeeImpl1"
                                value-ref="springEmployeeImpl"/>
                    </map>
                </property>
        </bean>

        <bean id="springEmployeeImpl"
                class="com.learning.spring.core.jmx.corejava.EmployeeImpl">
                <constructor-arg name="name" value="John" />
                <constructor-arg name="age" value="40" />
        </bean>
</beans>
```

CASE 2: Standalone environment that does not have its own MBean server

This approach is used when your environment does not have its own MBean server. In this approach `MBeanServerFactoryBean` creates the `MBeanServer` instance. `MBeanExporter` uses this `MBeanServer` instance to register the managed beans.

```
<?xml version="1.0" encoding="UTF-8"?>
<beans xmlns="http://www.springframework.org/schema/beans"
    xmlns:xsi="http://www.w3.org/2001/XMLSchema-instance"
    xmlns:context="http://www.springframework.org/schema/context"
    xsi:schemaLocation="http://www.springframework.org/schema/beans
    http://www.springframework.org/schema/beans/spring-beans-3.0.xsd
    http://www.springframework.org/schema/context
    http://www.springframework.org/schema/context/
            spring-context-3.0.xsd">

        <bean id="mbeanServer"
                class="org.springframework.jmx.support.MBeanServerFactoryBean">
                <property name="locateExistingServerIfPossible" value="true" />
        </bean>

        <bean id="mBeanExporter"
                class="org.springframework.jmx.export.MBeanExporter"
                lazy-init="false">

                <property name="beans">
                    <map>
                        <entry key="bean:name=springEmployeeImpl1"
                                value-ref="springEmployeeImpl"/>
                    </map>
                </property>

                <property name="server" ref="mbeanServer"/>
        </bean>

        <bean id="springEmployeeImpl"
                class="com.learning.spring.core.jmx.corejava.EmployeeImpl">
                <constructor-arg name="name" value="John" />
```

```
              <constructor-arg name="age" value="40" />
      </bean>
</beans>
```

Step 4: Create a main class to start the application

Listing 6-2 provides the complete class code; run the following `JmxMain` class.

Listing 6-2: Main class

```
// JmxMain.java
package com.learning.spring.core.jmx.corejava;

import org.springframework.context.support.
        ClassPathXmlApplicationContext;
import org.springframework.jmx.export.MBeanExporter;

public class JmxMain {

    public static void main(String[] args) throws Exception {
        ClassPathXmlApplicationContext context =
            new ClassPathXmlApplicationContext(
                "applicationContext-jmx-mbeans.xml");
        MBeanExporter mbeanExporter = (MBeanExporter)
                        context.getBean("mBeanExporter");

        System.out.println("--- Sleeping for some time ---");
        Thread.sleep(Long.MAX_VALUE);
    }
}
```

Step 5: Use the JConsole to view and manage the attributes and operations

Figure 6-3: JConsole showing the registered spring-managed bean as an MBean

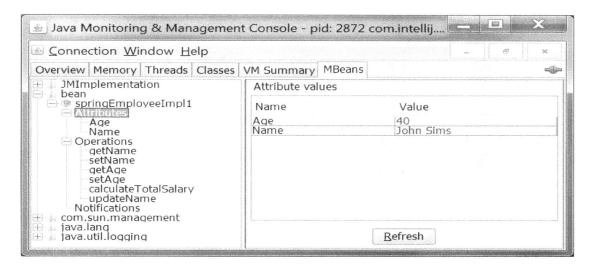

Here, follow the instructions specified in Example-1.

- Select your process id → Click on "Connect". JCconsole will be displayed as shown in Figure 6-3. The managed bean attributes and operations are shown in Figure 6-3.
- Navigate to bean → Operations → Select "updateName" → Click the "updateName" button.
- Navigate to bean → Attributes → You can see the updated name.

Similarly, you can navigate to exposed attributes and operations to update the registered spring-managed bean properties and methods.

Example 3: Spring Annotations for Exposing MBeans

This example illustrates the use of spring annotations to expose the Java bean properties and methods as attributes and operations of a managed bean (MBean) class.

The steps required to expose a Spring-managed bean class as an MBean are listed below.

1. Create an interface.
2. Create an implementation class.
3. Create a spring application context file.
4. Create a main class to start the application.
5. Use the JConsole to view and manage the attributes and operations.

The above-specified steps are described in the following sections.

Step 1: Create an interface.

Here, reuse the `EmployeeMBean` interface created in Example-1.

Step 2: Create an implementation class

The complete implementation class code is provided below. This class implements the `EmployeeMBean` interface and has Java bean properties and methods. The Java bean properties are exposed as JMX-attributes; methods are exposed as JMX-operations. In this example, the following spring annotations are used to expose the Java bean properties and operations.

- `@ManagedResource` → Registers the class instance with JMX server.
- `@ManagedAttribute` → Exposes the Java bean properties as JMX-managed bean attributes. This annotation is used only for getter-and-setter methods.
- `@ManagedOperation` → Exposes a Java bean method as JMX-managed bean operation.
- `@ManagedOperationParameters` and `@ManagedOperationParameter` → Used with method parameters to define their descriptions.

The following example demonstrates the use of the above-specified annotations. The `getAge()` method is annotated. Conversely, the `setAge()` method is not annotated, indicating that this method is used for read-only operations. The `updateName()` method is not annotated, indicating that this method does not expose as a JMX-managed operation. The complete class code is provided below.

```
// AnnotationEmployeeImpl.java
package com.learning.spring.core.jmx.corejava;

import org.springframework.jmx.export.annotation.*;
```

```java
@ManagedResource(objectName = "bean:name=annotationEmployeeImpl",
        description = "JMX Managed Bean",
        currencyTimeLimit = 15,
        persistPolicy = "OnUpdate", persistPeriod = 200,
        persistLocation = "employeeImpl", persistName = "employeeImpl")
public class AnnotationEmployeeImpl implements EmployeeMBean {

    private int age;
    private String name;

    public AnnotationEmployeeImpl(String name, int age) {
        this.name = name;
        this.age = age;
    }

    @ManagedAttribute(description = "The Age Attribute")
    public int getAge() {
        return age;
    }

    public void setAge(int age) {
        this.age = age;
    }

    @ManagedAttribute(defaultValue = "John")
    public String getName() {
        return name;
    }

    @ManagedAttribute(description = "The Name Attribute",
                      persistPolicy = "OnUpdate")
    public void setName(String name) {
        this.name = name;
    }

    @ManagedOperation(description = "Calculate Total Salary")
    @ManagedOperationParameters({
    @ManagedOperationParameter(name = "base",
                                description = "Base Amount"),
    @ManagedOperationParameter(name = "bonus",
                            description = "Bonus Amount")})
    public int calculateTotalSalary(int base, int bonus) {
        return base + bonus;
    }

    public void updateName() {
        this.name = name + " Sims ";
    }
}
```

Step 3: Create a spring application context file.

The complete spring application context configurations are provided below; named the
"applicationContext-jmx-annotations.xml".

```xml
<?xml version="1.0" encoding="UTF-8"?>
<beans xmlns="http://www.springframework.org/schema/beans"
    xmlns:xsi="http://www.w3.org/2001/XMLSchema-instance"
    xmlns:context="http://www.springframework.org/schema/context"
    xsi:schemaLocation="http://www.springframework.org/schema/beans
    http://www.springframework.org/schema/beans/spring-beans-3.0.xsd
    http://www.springframework.org/schema/context
    http://www.springframework.org/schema/context
            /spring-context-3.0.xsd">

    <bean id="mBeanExporter"
        class="org.springframework.jmx.export.MBeanExporter"
        lazy-init="false">
        <property name="assembler" ref="assembler"/>
        <property name="namingStrategy" ref="namingStrategy"/>
        <property name="autodetect" value="true"/>
    </bean>

    <bean id="jmxAttributeSource"
        class="org.springframework.jmx.export.annotation.
                    AnnotationJmxAttributeSource"/>

    <bean id="assembler"
            class="org.springframework.jmx.export.assembler.
                    MetadataMBeanInfoAssembler">
        <property name="attributeSource" ref="jmxAttributeSource"/>
    </bean>

    <bean id="namingStrategy"
        class="org.springframework.jmx.export.naming.
                    MetadataNamingStrategy">
        <property name="attributeSource" ref="jmxAttributeSource"/>
    </bean>

    <bean id="annotationEmployeeImpl"
        class="com.learning.spring.core.jmx.corejava.
                AnnotationEmployeeImpl">
        <constructor-arg name="name" value="John"/>
        <constructor-arg name="age" value="40"/>
    </bean>
</beans>
```

Step 4: Create a main class to start the application.

Listing 6-3 provides the complete class code; run the following JmxMain class.

Listing 6-3: Main class

```java
// JmxMain.java
package com.learning.spring.core.jmx.corejava;

import org.springframework.context.support.
        ClassPathXmlApplicationContext;
import org.springframework.jmx.export.MBeanExporter;

public class JmxMain {
```

```
        public static void main(String[] args) throws Exception {
            ClassPathXmlApplicationContext context =
                new ClassPathXmlApplicationContext(
                    "applicationContext-jmx-annotations.xml");
            MBeanExporter mbeanExporter = (MBeanExporter)
                            context.getBean("mBeanExporter");

            System.out.println("--- Sleeping for some time ---");
            Thread.sleep(Long.MAX_VALUE);
        }
}
```

Step 4: Use JConsole to view and manage the attributes and operations.

Here, follow the instructions specified in Example-1.

- Select your process id → Click on "Connect." The following console will be displayed. The managed bean attributes and operations are shown in Figure 6-4.
- Navigate to bean → Operations → Select "setName" → Enter new value → Click the "setName" button.
- Navigate to bean → Attributes → Click on "Refresh" → You can see the updated name.

Similarly, you can navigate to the exposed attributes and operations to update the registered Spring-managed bean properties and methods. Figure 6-4 shows the managed beans in the JConsole.

Figure 6-4: JConsole showing annotated bean as MBean

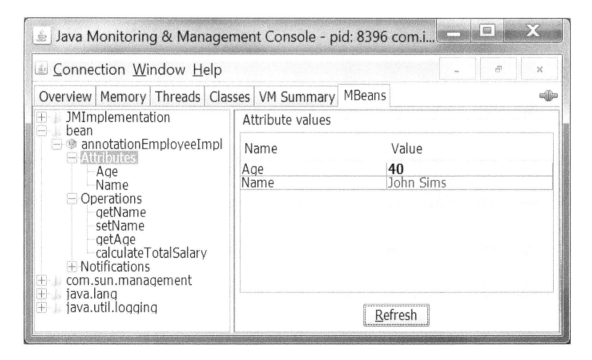

Registering Listeners and Publishing Notifications

This section illustrates the use of JMX listeners to receive notifications in case of any changes to the registered managed bean. An MBean can notify the MBeanServer of its internal changes (to the attributes) by implementing the javax.management.NotificationListener interface. Spring also supports publishing notifications. The notification publisher will send a notification to all registered listeners about any changes that occur to the managed bean.

Example 4: Spring Support for Publishing JMX Notifications

This example illustrates the spring support for publishing notifications whenever there is a change occurred to the Java bean properties-and-methods. The steps required to implement a notification-aware bean (to publish notifications) are listed below.

1. Create an interface.
2. Create an implementation class.
3. Create a spring application context file.
4. Create a main class to start the application.
5. Use the JConsole to view and manage the attributes and operations.

The above-specified steps are described in the following sections.

Step 1: Create an interface.

Here, reuse the EmployeeMBean interface created in Example-1.

Step 2: Create an implementation class

The setter methods setName() and setAge() will send a notification if there is any attribute change. The complete class code is provided below.

```java
// EmployeeNotificationImpl.java
package com.learning.spring.core.jmx.corejava;

import org.springframework.jmx.export.notification.
        NotificationPublisherAware;
import org.springframework.jmx.export.notification.NotificationPublisher;
import javax.management.Notification;

public class EmployeeNotificationImpl implements EmployeeMBean,
        NotificationPublisherAware {

    private int notificationIndex = 0;
    private NotificationPublisher notificationPublisher;
    private String name;
    private int age;

    public EmployeeNotificationImpl(String name, int age) {
        this.name = name;
        this.age = age;
    }

    public String getName() {
```

```
            return name;
        }

    public void setName(String newName) {
        System.out.println("--- newName ---" + newName);
        notificationPublisher.sendNotification(
                buildNotification(this.name, newName));
        this.name = newName;
    }

    public int getAge() {
        return age;
    }

    public void setAge(int age) {
        notificationPublisher.sendNotification(
                buildNotification(age+"", age+""));
        this.age = age;
    }

    private Notification buildNotification(final String oldName,
                    final String newName) {
        final String notificationType =
                "com.learning.spring.core.jmx.JmxManagedBean";
        final String message = "Converting " + oldName + " to " +
                                newName;
        final Notification notification = new
            Notification(notificationType, this, notificationIndex++,
                        System.currentTimeMillis(), message);
        notification.setUserData("Notification Example :" +
                            notificationIndex);
        return notification;
    }

    public void setNotificationPublisher(NotificationPublisher
            publisher) {
        this.notificationPublisher = publisher;
    }

    public int calculateTotalSalary(int base, int bonus) {
        return base + bonus;
    }

    public void updateName() {
        this.name = name + " Sims ";
    }
}
```

Step 3: Create a spring application context file.

The complete spring application context configurations are provided below; named the "applicationContext-listener.xml".

```
<?xml version="1.0" encoding="UTF-8"?>
<beans xmlns="http://www.springframework.org/schema/beans"
    xmlns:xsi="http://www.w3.org/2001/XMLSchema-instance"
```

```
xmlns:context="http://www.springframework.org/schema/context"
xsi:schemaLocation="http://www.springframework.org/schema/beans
http://www.springframework.org/schema/beans/spring-beans-3.0.xsd
http://www.springframework.org/schema/context
http://www.springframework.org/schema/context/
            spring-context-3.0.xsd">

<bean id="mBeanExporter"
     class="org.springframework.jmx.export.MBeanExporter">
     <property name="beans">
          <map>
               <entry key="bean:name=springEmployeeImpl3,
                    type=springEmployeeImpl"
                    value-ref="springEmployeeImpl"/>
          </map>
     </property>
</bean>

<bean id="springEmployeeImpl"
     class="com.learning.spring.core.jmx.corejava.
            EmployeeNotificationImpl">
     <constructor-arg name="name" value="John"/>
     <constructor-arg name="age" value="40"/>
</bean>
</beans>
```

Step 4: Create a main class to start the application

Listing 6-4 provides the complete class code; run the following JmxMain class.

Listing 6-4: Main class

```
// JmxMain.java
package com.learning.spring.core.jmx.corejava;

import org.springframework.context.support.
        ClassPathXmlApplicationContext;
import org.springframework.jmx.export.MBeanExporter;

public class JmxMain {

    public static void main(String[] args) throws Exception {
        ClassPathXmlApplicationContext context =
            new ClassPathXmlApplicationContext(
                "applicationContext-listener.xml");
        MBeanExporter mbeanExporter = (MBeanExporter)
                        context.getBean("mBeanExporter");

        System.out.println("--- Sleeping for some time ---");
        Thread.sleep(Long.MAX_VALUE);
    }
}
```

Step 5: Use the JConsole to view and manage the attributes and operations.

Here, follow the instructions specified in Example-1.

- Select your process id → Click on "Connect." The JConsole will be displayed as shown in Figure 6-5. The managed bean attributes, operations, and notifications are shown in Figure 6-5.
- Navigate to Notifications → Click on "Subscribe"
- Navigate to bean → Operations → Select "setName" → Enter new value → Click the "setName" button.
- Navigate to bean → Operations → Select "setAge" → Enter new value → Click the "setAge" button.
- Navigate to bean → Attributes → Click on "Refresh" → You can see the updated name.

Similarly, you can navigate to the exposed attributes and operations to update the registered Spring-managed bean properties and methods. The published notifications can be monitored in the JConsole as shown in Figure 6-5.

Figure 6-5: JConsole showing published notifications

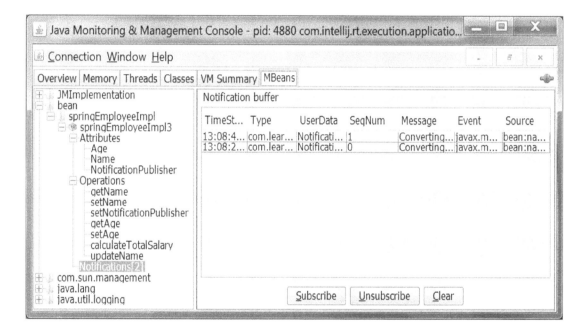

Example 5: Spring Support to Receive JMX Notifications

An `MBean` can notify the `MBeanServer` of its internal changes (for the attributes) by implementing the `javax.management.NotificationListener` interface. This example illustrates the use of notification listeners to receive JMX notifications.

The steps required to register a notification listener with MBean to receive notifications are listed below.

1. Create an interface.
2. Create an implementation class.
3. Create a notification listener class.
4. Create a spring application context file.
5. Create a main class to start the application.

6. Use the JConsole to view and manage the attributes and operations.

The above-specified steps are described in the following sections:

Step 1: Create an interface.

Here, reuse the `EmployeeMBean` interface created in Example-1.

Step 2: Create an implementation class.

Here, reuse the `EmployeeImpl` interface created in Example-1.

Step 3: Create a notification listener class.

The notification listener class must implement the `NotificationListener` interface. Register this listener class to a managed bean class. The `handleNotification(...)` method of the `NotificationListener` class will be invoked if any change occurs to the attributes of a managed bean class.

The following code is used to receive the updated attribute values.

```
Integer age = (Integer) mbeanServer.getAttribute(objectName, "Age");
String name = (String) mbeanServer.getAttribute(objectName, "Name");
```

The complete listener class code is provided below.

```
// JMXNotificationListener.java
package com.learning.spring.core.jmx;

import javax.management.*;
import java.lang.management.ManagementFactory;

public class JMXNotificationListener implements NotificationListener,
NotificationFilter {

    public JMXNotificationListener() {
    }

    public void handleNotification(Notification notification,
                                   Object handback) {
        try {
            MBeanServer mbeanServer =
                ManagementFactory.getPlatformMBeanServer();
            ObjectName objectName = new
                ObjectName("bean:name=springEmployeeImpl6");

            Integer age = (Integer)
                mbeanServer.getAttribute(objectName, "Age");
            String name = (String)
                mbeanServer.getAttribute(objectName, "Name");
            System.out.println(" --- age --- " + age +
                               "--- name ---" + name);

            // ... Implement your logic here.
```

```
        } catch (Exception ex) {
            ex.printStackTrace();
        }
    }

    public boolean isNotificationEnabled(Notification notification) {
        return AttributeChangeNotification.class.
            isAssignableFrom(notification.getClass());
    }
}
```

Step 4: Create a spring application context file.

The complete spring application context configurations are provided below; named the "applicationContext-notifications.xml".

```xml
<?xml version="1.0" encoding="UTF-8"?>
<beans>

    <bean id="mBeanExporter"
        class="org.springframework.jmx.export.MBeanExporter">
        <property name="beans">
            <map>
                <entry key="bean:name=springEmployeeImpl6"
                    value-ref="springEmployeeImpl"/>
            </map>
        </property>

        <!-- Configure notification listener -->
        <property name="notificationListenerMappings">
            <map>
                <entry key="springEmployeeImpl">
                    <bean class="com.learning.spring.core.jmx.
                        JMXNotificationListener"/>
                </entry>
            </map>
        </property>
    </bean>

    <bean id="springEmployeeImpl"
        class="com.learning.spring.core.jmx.corejava.EmployeeImpl">
        <constructor-arg name="name" value="John"/>
        <constructor-arg name="age" value="40"/>
    </bean>
</beans>
```

Step 5: Create a main class to start the application

Listing 6-5 provides the complete class code; run the following `JmxMain` class to print the managed bean attribute values.

Listing 6-5: Main class

```java
// JmxMain.java
package com.learning.spring.core.jmx.corejava;
```

```java
import org.springframework.context.support.
        ClassPathXmlApplicationContext;
import org.springframework.jmx.export.MBeanExporter;

public class JmxMain {

    public static void main(String[] args) throws Exception {
        ClassPathXmlApplicationContext context =
            new ClassPathXmlApplicationContext
                ("applicationContext-notifications.xml");
        MBeanExporter mbeanExporter = (MBeanExporter)
                    context.getBean("mBeanExporter");

        ObjectName objectName = new
                ObjectName("bean:name=springEmployeeImpl6");
        MBeanServer springMBeanServer = mbeanExporter.getServer();
        Integer age = (Integer) springMBeanServer.
                        getAttribute(objectName, "Age");
        String name = (String) springMBeanServer.
                        getAttribute(objectName, "Name");
        System.out.println(" --- age --- " + age +
                        "--- name ---" + name);

        System.out.println("---- Sleeping for some time ----");
        Thread.sleep(Long.MAX_VALUE);
    }
}
```

Step 6: Use the JConsole to view and manage the attributes and operations

Update the "Age" and "Name" attributes in the JConsole.

- Open the JConsole from the command line.
- Navigate to bean → Attributes → Update "Age" and "Name" values.

The `handleNotification(...)` method will be invoked automatically; you can see the updated values on the console. The complete output is shown below.

```
--- age --- 40--- name ---John
---- Sleeping for some time ----
--- age --- 35 --- name ---Smith
```

Monitoring Remote Services

This section illustrates the spring support for monitoring managed beans remotely. Spring `ConnectorServerFactoryBean` creates and starts a `JMXConnectorServer`. This server exposes the local `MBeanServer` to remote clients through the JMXMP protocol.

Example 6: Spring Support for Monitoring Remote Services

This example illustrates the spring support for monitoring the remote services. The steps required to implement this example are listed below.

1. Create an interface.
2. Create an implementation class.
3. Create a spring application context file.
4. Create a main class to start the application.
5. Use the JConsole to view and manage the attributes and operations.

The above-specified steps are described in the following sections.

Step 1: Create an interface.

Here, reuse the `EmployeeMBean` interface created in Example-1.

Step 2: Create an implementation class.

Here, reuse the `EmployeeNotificationImpl` interface created in Example-4.

Step 3: Create a spring application context file.

The complete spring application context configurations are provided below; named the "applicationContext-jmx-remoting.xml".

```xml
<?xml version="1.0" encoding="UTF-8"?>
<beans xmlns="http://www.springframework.org/schema/beans"
    xmlns:xsi="http://www.w3.org/2001/XMLSchema-instance"
    xmlns:context="http://www.springframework.org/schema/context"
    xsi:schemaLocation="http://www.springframework.org/schema/beans
    http://www.springframework.org/schema/beans/spring-beans-3.0.xsd
    http://www.springframework.org/schema/context
    http://www.springframework.org/schema/context/
              spring-context-3.0.xsd">

    <bean id="springEmployeeImpl" class="com.learning.spring.core.jnx.
                    corejava.EmployeeNotificationImpl">
        <constructor-arg name="name" value="John"/>
        <constructor-arg name="age" value="40"/>
    </bean>

    <bean id="mBeanExporter" class=
    "org.springframework.jmx.export.MBeanExporter">
        <property name="beans">
            <map>
                <entry key="bean:name=springEmployeeImpl4,
                    type=springEmployeeImpl"
                    value-ref="springEmployeeImpl"/>
            </map>
        </property>
    </bean>

    <!-- Configure RMI registry -->
    <bean id="registry" class="org.springframework.remoting.rmi.
```

```
                    RmiRegistryFactoryBean">
        <property name="port" value="1099"/>
    </bean>

    <bean id="serverConnector" class="org.springframework.jmx.support.
            ConnectorServerFactoryBean" depends-on="registry">
        <property name="objectName" value="connector:name=rmi"/>
        <property name="serviceUrl" value="service:jmx:rmi://localhost/
                jndi/rmi://localhost:1099/jmxrmi"/>
    </bean>
</beans>
```

Step 4: Create a main class to start the application.

Listing 6-6 provides the complete class code; run the following JmxMain class.

Listing 6-6: Main class

```
// JmxMain.java
package com.learning.spring.core.jmx.corejava;

import org.springframework.context.support.
        ClassPathXmlApplicationContext;
import org.springframework.jmx.export.MBeanExporter;

public class JmxMain {

    public static void main(String[] args) throws Exception {
        ClassPathXmlApplicationContext context =
            new ClassPathXmlApplicationContext(
                    "applicationContext-jmx-remoting.xml");
        MBeanExporter mbeanExporter = (MBeanExporter)
                        context.getBean("mBeanExporter");

        System.out.println("--- Sleeping for some time ---");
        Thread.sleep(Long.MAX_VALUE);
    }
}
```

Step 5: Use the JConsole to view and manage the attributes and operations

Follow the steps listed below to view and manage the JMX attributes and operations using the JConsole.

- Open the command line; go to your installed "\jdk\bin" directory.
- Execute the "jconsole.exe" batch file from the "\jdk\bin" directory. The JConsole will be displayed as shown in Figure 6-7.
- Select your Remote Process → Enter RMI service url =
  `service:jmx:rmi://localhost/jndi/rmi://localhost:1099/jmxrmi`
- Click the "Connect" button → The "JConsole" will be displayed with the managed bean attributes, operations, notifications and RMI-connector as shown in Figure 6-7.
- Navigate to Notifications → Click on "Subscribe"
- Navigate to bean → Operations → Select "setName" → Enter new value → Click the "setName" button.
- Navigate to bean → Operations → Select "setAge" → Enter new value → Click the "setAge" button.

- Navigate to bean → Attributes → Click on "Refresh" → You can see the updated name.

Figure 6-7: JConsole remote process

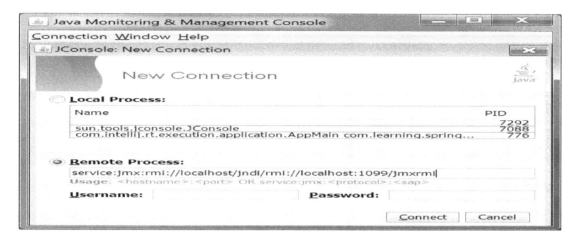

Similarly, navigate to exposed attributes-and-operations to update the registered Spring-managed bean properties-and-methods

Figure 6-8: JConsole remote process

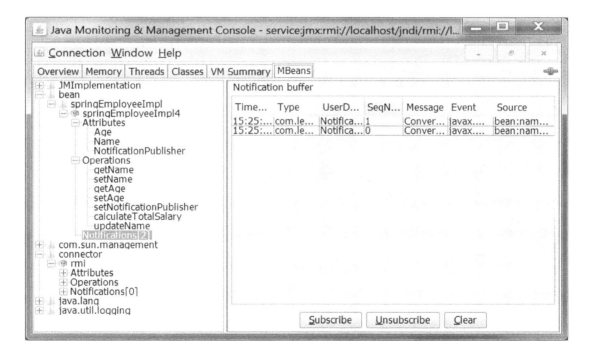

Summary

This section summarizes the features of Spring-JMX framework.

- Spring provides the `MBeanExporter` class which encapsulates the JMX-API. This class can be used to expose the spring-managed beans as MBeans. This class registers the spring-managed beans with `MBeanServer`.
- Spring provides `MBeanServerFactoryBean` to obtain the `MBeanServer` reference. By default, `MBeanServerFactoryBean` creates a new `MBeanServer` instance. This can be used for standalone environments that do not have their own `MBeanServer`.
- The following spring annotations can be used to expose the Java bean properties and methods as managed bean attributes and operations.
  - `@ManagedResource`
  - `@ManagedAttribute`
  - `@ManagedOperation`
  - `@ManagedOperationParameters` and `@ManagedOperationParameter`
- Spring `ConnectorServerFactoryBean` creates and starts a `JMXConnectorServer`. This server exposes the local `MBeanServer` to remote clients through the JMXMP protocol.
- Spring provides support for publishing notifications and registering listeners to receive notifications.

Figure 6-8 summarizes the most important points described in this chapter.

Figure 6-8 Spring-JMX features summary

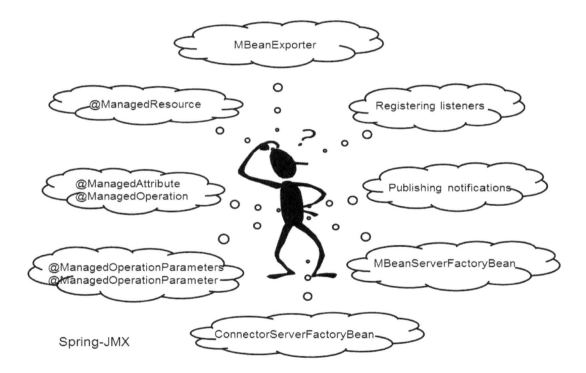

Chapter 7. Spring-AOP

Aspect Oriented Programing (AOP) is a programming technique used to modularize the application code. In AOP, a module unit is called an aspect and can be reused various places in your application without duplicating the code. Let us review a simple scenario. Whenever a method throws an exception, you want to create an audit record. You want to provide this functionality several places throughout your application without explicitly calling a method. Similarly, you may want to execute a specific functionality before and after a method execution or after a method returns a value. AOP-based frameworks provide a simplified solution for such scenarios. AspectJ is an AOP extension created for Java, and the AspectJ framework provides powerful features for implementing custom aspects. Spring-AOP can be integrated with the AspectJ framework.

Spring-AOP provides a simplified approach to implement the aspects using schema-based and AspectJ annotations. Spring-AOP also provides a powerful solution for implementing custom aspects for transaction management, auditing, logging, exception handling, and so forth.

This chapter will discuss the following topics:

- Spring-AOP terminology
- Advantages of the Spring-AOP framework
- Annotation-based approach for implementing aspects
- Schema-based approach for implementing aspects
- Commonly used AspectJ annotations
- Spring intergradation with the AspectJ framework.
- The Pointcut Expression language syntax fundamentals.

Spring AOP Terminology

This section explains the terminology commonly used in Spring-AOP while developing aspect-based applications. The AOP terminology is defined below.

Aspect: In Spring-AOP, the @Aspect-annotated classes are called aspects. The @Aspect-annotated class can be configured the way one would configure a regular Java bean. An example @Aspect-annotated class is provided below.

```
@Aspect
public class AuditAspect {
    ...
}
```

The corresponding application context configuration of the aspect bean is provided below.

```
<bean id="auditAspect" class="com.learning.spring.aop.audit.AuditAspect">
    ...
</bean>
```

The following element in an application context file enables the @AspectJ-support in spring. Using this configuration, spring automatically detects the @AspectJ-annotated classes.

```
<aop:aspectj-autoproxy/>
```

Join Point: A join point is a point of execution such as a method, field, constructor, and so forth. In Spring-AOP, the join point is always a method execution.

Advice: An advice describes a method which modifies the some other method. The commonly used Spring-AOP advices are "Before", "After", "Around", "AfterReturning" and "AfterThrowing". Advice is a method of specifying the code run at a join point; it can run after, before, and around the join points.

An example use of the before advice is given below.

```
@Before(...)
public void addBeforeAuditRecord(JoinPoint joinPoint) {
    ...
}
```

Pointcut: A pointcut is a set of join points. An advice is associated with a pointcut expression and executes the matched join points specified in the pointcut expression. A pointcut expression is represented in AspectJ expression language.

Let us review the pointcut expressions provided below, the first of which executes the addUser() method.

```
execution(* com.learning.spring.aop.dao.UserDAO.addUser(..))
```

The following pointcut expression executes any method defined in the PetService interface.

```
execution(* com.learning.spring.tx.service.PetService.*(..)
```

The following pointcut expression executes any method defined in the service package.

```
execution(* com.learning.spring.tx.service.*.*(..)
```

Let us review the following method.

```
@Before("execution(* com.learning.spring.aop.dao.UserDAO.addUser(..))")
public void addBeforeAuditRecord(JoinPoint joinPoint) {
    ...
}
```

The Advice, Pointcut and Join point of the above method is listed below.

- @Before → advice
- execution(* com.learning.spring.aop.dao.UserDAO.addUser(..)) → pointcut expression
- addUser() → method (Join point)

Prerequisites/Setting Up the Environment

The following list of JAR files is required to implement the Spring-AOP functionality. Add all other dependent JAR files.

- Aspectjrt.jar
- aspectjtools-1.5.4.jar
- aspectjweaver.jar
- cglib-nodep-2.2.2.jar
- org.springframework.aop-3.x.RELEASE.jar

Use the following SQL script to create an (optional) audit table. If you want to print the data on the console, this table is not needed.

```
CREATE TABLE AUDIT (
    id MEDIUMINT NOT NULL AUTO_INCREMENT,
    description VARCHAR(300) NULL,
    PRIMARY KEY (id)
) ENGINE=MyISAM;
```

Advantages of Spring AOP

This section illustrates the technical and non-technical benefits of the Spring-AOP framework.

- Spring-AOP provides support for implementing annotation and schema-based approaches for implanting aspects.
- Spring-AOP complements the AspectJ framework in a simplified manner.
- Existing application interfaces can be intercepted easily without any code modifications. Spring-AOP is loosely coupled with the application code.
- Spring-AOP can reuse the full advantages of the spring container-provided features.

XML Schema and Annotation-based AOP Support

Spring-AOP supports both the annotation and schema-based approaches for implementing the aspects. The approach of choice totally depends on your application needs. The minimum requirement for implementing annotation-based aspects is Java-5. The most commonly used Spring-AOP annotations are demonstrated in this section.

For the annotation-based approach, the following list of AspectJ annotations is used in Spring-AOP.

- @Aspect
- @Before
- @After
- @AfterReturning
- @AfterThrowing
- @Around

For the schema-based approach, the following lists of schema elements is used in Spring-AOP

- <aop:config>
- <aop:aspect>
- <aop:pointcut>
- <aop:before>
- <aop:after>
- <aop:after-returning>
- <aop:after-throwing>
- <aop:around>

The following section illustrates the complete use of the above-specified annotations and namespace elements for implementing the aspects.

Demo Examples: Annotation-based Approach

This section illustrates the Spring-AOP framework integration with AspectJ annotations. This framework can be used for intercepting the methods of an interface.

Before Advice

The before advice is declared in an aspect using `@Before` annotation. This advice runs before the method execution. An example of the use of such annotation is provided below. In this example, the `@Before`-annotation intercepts the `adduser()` method of a `UserDAO` class.

```
@Before("execution(* com.learning.spring.aop.dao.UserDAO.addUser(..))")
public void addBeforeAuditRecord(JoinPoint joinPoint) {
    ...
}
```

Example 1: How to Use @Before Annotation

This example illustrates the use of `@Before` annotation. The steps required to implement this example are listed below.

1. Create a DAO interface and its implementation class.
2. Create a data value object (DVO) class.
3. Create an Aspect class to intercept the DAO methods.
4. Enable the AOP-based configurations in a spring application context file.
5. Create a main class to test the code.

The above-specified steps are described in the following sections.

Step 1: Create a DAO interface and its implementation class.

The definition of the `UserDAO` interface is provided below.

```
// UserDAO.java
```

```java
package com.learning.spring.aop.dao;

public interface UserDAO {

    void addUser();

    Integer getInsertedUserId() ;

    void addUserThrowsException() throws Exception;

    void addUserAround(String firstName, String lastName);

    void validateUser(User user);
}
```

The above-specified methods are implemented in `UserDAO` interface implementation class. The complete `UserDAOImpl` class code is provided below.

```java
// UserDAOImpl.java
package com.learning.spring.aop.dao;

import org.springframework.jdbc.support.KeyHolder;
import org.springframework.jdbc.support.GeneratedKeyHolder;
import org.springframework.jdbc.core.PreparedStatementCreator;
import org.springframework.jdbc.core.JdbcTemplate;

import java.sql.*:

public class UserDAOImpl implements UserDAO {

    private JdbcTemplate jdbcTemplate;

    public void addUser() {
        // Implement your logic here
    }

    public Integer getInsertedUserId() {
        final String SQL_INSERT_QUERY =
            "INSERT INTO User (first_name, last_name) values (?, ?)";
        final String firstName = "Steven";
        final String lastName = "Day";
        KeyHolder keyHolder = new GeneratedKeyHolder();
        jdbcTemplate.update(new PreparedStatementCreator() {
            public PreparedStatement createPreparedStatement
                    (Connection connection) throws SQLException {
                PreparedStatement ps = connection.prepareStatement(
                        SQL_INSERT_QUERY, new String[] {"id"});
                ps.setString(1, firstName);
                ps.setString(2, lastName);
                return ps;
            }
        }, keyHolder);

        return keyHolder.getKey().intValue();

        // Otherwise simply return a hardcoded value
```

```
        // return 100;
    }

    public void addUserThrowsException() throws Exception {
        // Creating a divide-by-zero error
        int i = 10;
        int j = i/0;
    }

    public void addUserAround(String firstName, String lastName) {
        System.out.println("--- name ---" + firstName +
                "--- lastName ---" + lastName);

        // Implement your logic here
    }

    public void validateUser(User user) {
        System.out.println("--- id ---" + user.getId());

        // Implement your logic here
    }

    public void setJdbcTemplate(JdbcTemplate jdbcTemplate) {
        this.jdbcTemplate = jdbcTemplate;
    }
}
```

Step 2: Create a data value object (DVO) class.

Create the following User domain object.

```
// User.java
package com.learning.spring.aop.dao;

public class User {

    private int id;
    private String firstName;
    private String lastName;

    // Add getter and setter methods.
}
```

Step 3: Create an Aspect class to intercept the DAO methods.

The following AuditAspect class methods are used to intercept the DAO class methods. The addUser() method of a UserDAO interface is intercepted using the @Before annotation. The addBeforeAuditRecord(...) method is invoked before calling the addUser() method of a UserDAOImpl class.

```
@Before("execution(* com.learning.spring.aop.dao.
                        UserDAO.addUser(..))")
public void addBeforeAuditRecord(JoinPoint joinPoint) {
    ...
}
```

The complete `AuditAspect` class code is provided below. This class's method is used to add an audit record.

```java
// AuditAspect.java
package com.learning.spring.aop.audit;

import org.aspectj.lang.annotation.*;
import org.aspectj.lang.JoinPoint;
import org.aspectj.lang.ProceedingJoinPoint;
import org.springframework.jdbc.core.JdbcTemplate;

import java.util.Arrays;
import com.learning.spring.aop.dao.User;

@Aspect
public class AuditAspect {

    private JdbcTemplate jdbcTemplate;

    @Before("execution(* com.learning.spring.aop.dao.
                        UserDAO.addUser(..))")
    public void addBeforeAuditRecord(JoinPoint joinPoint) {
        String name = joinPoint.getSignature().getName();
        addAuditRecord(name);
    }

    public void addAuditRecord(String description) {
        final String SQL_INSERT_QUERY =
                "INSERT INTO AUDIT (description) VALUES (?)";
        jdbcTemplate.update(SQL_INSERT_QUERY, description);
    }

    public void setJdbcTemplate(JdbcTemplate jdbcTemplate) {
        this.jdbcTemplate = jdbcTemplate;
    }
}
```

Step 4: Enable the AOP-based configurations in a spring application context file.

The spring application context file is used to enable the AspectJ support for the spring framework. The complete application context XML file is provided below; it is named the "applicationContext-aop.xml"

```xml
<?xml version="1.0" encoding="UTF-8"?>
<beans xmlns="http://www.springframework.org/schema/beans"
    xmlns:xsi="http://www.w3.org/2001/XMLSchema-instance"
    xmlns:aop="http://www.springframework.org/schema/aop"
    xsi:schemaLocation="http://www.springframework.org/schema/beans
    http://www.springframework.org/schema/beans/spring-beans-3.0.xsd
    http://www.springframework.org/schema/aop
    http://www.springframework.org/schema/aop/spring-aop-3.0.xsd">

    <bean id="mySqlDataSource" class="org.springframework.jdbc.
            datasource.DriverManagerDataSource">
        <property name="driverClassName">
            <value>com.mysql.jdbc.Driver</value>
```

```xml
        </property>
        <property name="url">
            <value>jdbc:mysql://localhost:3306/test</value>
        </property>
        <property name="username">
            <value>root</value>
        </property>
        <property name="password">
            <value>mysql</value>
        </property>
    </bean>

    <bean id="jdbcTemplate" class="org.springframework.jdbc.core.
                            JdbcTemplate">
        <property name="dataSource">
            <ref bean="mySqlDataSource"/>
        </property>
    </bean>

    <bean id="userDAO" class="com.learning.spring.aop.dao.UserDAOImpl">
        <property name="jdbcTemplate" ref="jdbcTemplate"/>
    </bean>

    <!-- Enable the AspectJ support in Spring -->
    <aop:aspectj-autoproxy/>

    <!-- Aspect class wired as a spring bean -->
    <bean id="auditAspect" class="com.learning.spring.
                            aop.audit.AuditAspect">
        <property name="jdbcTemplate" ref="jdbcTemplate"/>
    </bean>
</beans>
```

Step 5: Create a main class to test the code.

Listing 7-1 provides the complete class code; run the following standalone class to view the output.

Listing 7-1: Standalone class used for testing

```java
// AopMain.java
package com.learning.spring.aop;

import org.springframework.context.support.
            ClassPathXmlApplicationContext;
import org.springframework.context.ApplicationContext;
import com.learning.spring.aop.dao.UserDAO;

public class AopMain {

    public static void main(String[] args) {
        ApplicationContext appContext =
            new ClassPathXmlApplicationContext(
                new String[]{"applicationContext-aop.xml"});

        UserDAO userDAO = (UserDAO) appContext.getBean("userDAO");
        userDAO.addUser();
    }
```

```
}
```

After (finally) Advice

The after advice is declared in an aspect using @After annotation. An example of this annotation's use is provided below. In this example, the @After-annotation intercepts the adduser()-method of a UserDAO interface. This advice runs after exiting the method execution.

```
@After("execution(* com.learning.spring.aop.dao.UserDAO.addUser(..)}")
public void addAfterAuditRecord(JoinPoint joinPoint) {
    ...
}
```

Example 2: How to use @After annotation

Add the following addAfterAuditRecord(...) method to the AuditAspect class. The addUser() method of a UserDAO interface is intercepted using @After annotation. The addAfterAuditRecord(...) method is invoked after exiting the addUser() method.

```
@After("execution(* com.learning.spring.aop.dao.UserDAO.addUser(..))")
public void addAfterAuditRecord(JoinPoint joinPoint) {
    String name = joinPoint.getSignature().getName();
    addAuditRecord(name);
}
```

Listing 7-1 provides the main method; run the following standalone class to view the output.

Listing 7-1: Standalone class used for testing

```
// AopMain.java
package com.learning.spring.aop;

import org.springframework.context.support.
            ClassPathXmlApplicationContext;
import org.springframework.context.ApplicationContext;
import com.learning.spring.aop.dao.UserDAO;

public class AopMain {

    public static void main(String[] args) {
        ApplicationContext appContext =
            new ClassPathXmlApplicationContext(
                new String[]{"applicationContext-aop.xml"});

        UserDAO userDAO = (UserDAO) appContext.getBean("userDAO");
        userDAO.addUser();
    }
}
```

AfterReturning Advice

The after returning advice is declared in an aspect using `@AfterReturning` annotation. An example of this annotation's use is provided below. In this example, the `@AfterReturning`-annotation intercepts the `getInsertedUserId()` method of a `UserDAO` interface. This advice runs after the method returns a result and can also intercept the returned result.

```
@AfterReturning(pointcut = "execution(* com.learning.spring.aop.dao.
            UserDAO.getInsertedUserId(..))", returning = "result")
public void auditAfterReturning(JoinPoint joinPoint, Object result) {
    ...
}
```

Example 3: How to Use @AfterReturning annotation

Add the following `auditAfterReturning(...)` method to the `AuditAspect` class. The `getInsertedUserId()` method of a `UserDAO` interface is intercepted using the `@AfterReturning` annotation. The `addAfterAuditRecord(...)` method is invoked after the method `getInsertedUserId()` returns a result. The returned result is intercepted in the advised method.

```
@AfterReturning(pointcut = "execution(* com.learning.spring.aop.
    dao.UserDAO.getInsertedUserId(..))", returning = "result")
public void auditAfterReturning(JoinPoint joinPoint, Object result) {
    String name = joinPoint.getSignature().getName();
    addAuditRecord("Name :" + name + " result is : " + result);
}
```

Listing 7-3 provides the main method; run the following standalone class to view the output.

Listing 7-3: Standalone class used for testing

```
// AopMain.java
package com.learning.spring.aop;

import org.springframework.context.support.
            ClassPathXmlApplicationContext;
import org.springframework.context.ApplicationContext;
import com.learning.spring.aop.dao.UserDAO;

public class AopMain {

    public static void main(String[] args) {
        ApplicationContext appContext =
            new ClassPathXmlApplicationContext(
                new String[]{"applicationContext-aop.xml"});

        UserDAO userDAO = (UserDAO) appContext.getBean("userDAO");
        userDAO.getInsertedUserId();
    }
}
```

AfterThrowing Advice

The after throwing advice is declared in an aspect using the `@AfterThrowing` annotation An example of this annotation's use is provided below. In this example, the `@AfterThrowing` annotation intercepts the `addUserThrowsException()` method of a `UserDAO` interface. This advice runs after the `addUserThrowsException()` method throws an exception.

```
@AfterThrowing(pointcut = "execution(* com.learning.spring.aop.dao.
        UserDAO.addUserThrowsException(..))",throwing = "error")
public void logAfterThrowing(JoinPoint joinPoint, Throwable error) {
    ...
}
```

Example 4: How to Use @AfterThrowing annotation

Add the following `auditAfterReturning(...)` method to the `AuditAspect` class. The `addUserThrowsException()` method of a `UserDAO` interface is intercepted using the `@AfterThrowing` annotation. The `auditAfterThrowing(...)` method is invoked after the `addUserThrowsException()` method throws an exception. The returned exception is intercepted in the advised method.

```
@AfterThrowing(pointcut = "execution(* com.learning.spring.aop.dao.
        UserDAO.addUserThrowsException(..))", throwing = "error")
public void auditAfterThrowing(JoinPoint joinPoint, Throwable error) {
    String name = joinPoint.getSignature().getName();
    addAuditRecord("Name :" + name + " Error is : " +
                        error.getLocalizedMessage());
}
```

Listing 7-4 provides the main method; run the following standalone class to view the output.

Listing 7-4: Standalone class used for testing

```
// AopMain.java
package com.learning.spring.aop;

import org.springframework.context.support.
            ClassPathXmlApplicationContext;
import org.springframework.context.ApplicationContext;
import com.learning.spring.aop.dao.UserDAO;

public class AopMain {

    public static void main(String[] args) {
        ApplicationContext appContext =
            new ClassPathXmlApplicationContext(
                new String[]{"applicationContext-aop.xml"});

        UserDAO userDAO = (UserDAO) appContext.getBean("userDAO");
        try {
            userDAO.addUserThrowsException();
        } catch (Exception ex) {
            ex.printStackTrace();
        }
```

```
        }
}
```

Around Advice

The around advice is declared in an aspect using the `@Around` annotation. An example of this annotation's use is provided below. In this example, the `@Around` annotation intercepts the `addUserAround()` method of a `UserDAO` interface. This advice runs around (before and after) the matched method.

```
@Around("execution(* com.learning.spring.aop.dao.
                UserDAO.addUserAround(..))")
public void auditAround(ProceedingJoinPoint joinPoint) throws Throwable {
    ...
}
```

Example 5: How to use @Around annotation

Add the following `auditAround(...)` method to the `AuditAspect` class. The `addUserAround()` method of a `UserDAO` interface is intercepted using the `@Around`-annotation. The `auditAround(...)` method is invoked before and after the `addUserAround()` method execution. The `joinPoint.proceed()` method is used to continue the execution of the intercepted method.

```
@Around("execution(* com.learning.spring.aop.dao.
                UserDAO.addUserAround(..))")
public void auditAround(ProceedingJoinPoint joinPoint) throws Throwable {
    String name = joinPoint.getSignature().getName();
    String arguments = Arrays.toString(joinPoint.getArgs());

    System.out.println("Around before is running!");
    // Continue on the intercepted method
    joinPoint.proceed();
    System.out.println("Around after is running!");

    // Insert a record in audit table
    addAuditRecord("Name :" + name + " arguments : " + arguments);
}
```

Listing 7-5 provides the main method; run the following standalone class to view the output.

Listing 7-5: Standalone class used for testing

```
// AopMain.java
package com.learning.spring.aop;

import org.springframework.context.support.
            ClassPathXmlApplicationContext;
import org.springframework.context.ApplicationContext;
import com.learning.spring.aop.dao.UserDAO;

public class AopMain {
```

```
    public static void main(String[] args) {
        ApplicationContext appContext =
            new ClassPathXmlApplicationContext(
                new String[]{"applicationContext-aop.xml"});

        UserDAO userDAO = (UserDAO) appContext.getBean("userDAO");
        userDAO.addUserAround("John", "McCoy");
    }
}
```

Example 6: How to Pass Parameters to Advice (Annotation-based)

This example illustrates how to access the method arguments in the body of the advice. The pointcut expression can use the `args()` method to receive the arguments of an intercepted method. An example method is provided below. Add the following `validateUser(...)` method to the `AuditAspect` class.

```
@Before("execution(* com.learning.spring.aop.dao.
            UserDAO.validateUser(..)) && args(user,..)")
public void validateUser(User user) {
    // Accessing the user data
    String description = "Id: " + user.getId() + "First Name: " +
        user.getFirstName() + " Last Name: " + user.getLastName();
    addAuditRecord(description);
}
```

Listing 7-6 provides the main method; run the following standalone class to view the output.

Listing 7-6: Standalone class used for testing

```
// AopMain.java
package com.learning.spring.aop;

import org.springframework.context.support.
            ClassPathXmlApplicationContext;
import org.springframework.context.ApplicationContext;
import com.learning.spring.aop.dao.UserDAO;

public class AopMain {

    public static void main(String[] args) {
        ApplicationContext appContext =
            new ClassPathXmlApplicationContext(
                new String[]{"applicationContext-aop.xml"});

        UserDAO userDAO = (UserDAO) appContext.getBean("userDAO");

        User user = new User();
        user.setId(10);
        user.setFirstName("John");
        user.setLastName("Smith");
        userDAO.validateUser(user);
    }
}
```

Demo Examples: XML-based Approach

Spring provides the `<xmlns:aop>` schema for configuring the aspects, pointcut expressions, and advices. The schema-based approach supports the AspectJ pointcut expressions and advices, as we saw in the previous section. This section illustrates the schema-based AOP framework configurations.

Before Advice - <aop:before>

The before advice is declared inside the `<aop:before>` element. This is equivalent to the `@Before` annotation. Let us review the following `@Before`-annotated method code.

```
@Before("execution(* com.learning.spring.aop.dao.UserDAO.addUser(..))")
public void addBeforeAuditRecord(JoinPoint joinPoint) {
    ...
}
```

The equivalent XML configuration for the preceding annotation-based code is given below.

```
<aop:config>
    <aop:aspect id="aspectAuditing" ref="auditAspect">
        <!-- Pointcut expression -->
        <aop:pointcut id="pointCutBefore"
            expression="execution(* com.learning.spring.aop.dao.
                    UserDAO.addUser(..))"/>
        <!-- @Before advice -->
        <aop:before pointcut-ref="pointCutBefore"
                    method="addBeforeAuditRecord"/>
    </aop:aspect>
</aop:config>
```

Example 7: How to Use <aop:before> Element

This example illustrates the use of `<xmls:aop>` schema for configuring the aspects. The steps required to implement this example are listed below.

1. Create a DAO interface and its implementation class.
2. Create a data value object (DVO) class.
3. Create an Aspect class to intercept the DAO methods.
4. Enable the AOP-based configurations in a spring application context file.
5. Create a main class to test the code.

The above-specified steps are described in the following sections.

Step 1: Create a DAO interface and its implementation class.

Here, reuse the `UserDAO` and `UserDAOImpl` classes created in Example-1.

Step 2: Create a data value object (DVO) class.

Here, reuse the `User` domain object class created in Example-1.

Step 3: Create an Aspect class to intercept the DAO methods.

In this example, the aspect class does not require any annotations. The complete class code is provided below.

```java
// SchemaAuditAspect.java
package com.learning.spring.aop.audit;

import org.springframework.jdbc.core.JdbcTemplate;
import org.aspectj.lang.JoinPoint;
import org.aspectj.lang.ProceedingJoinPoint;

import java.util.Arrays;
import com.learning.spring.aop.dao.User;

public class SchemaAuditAspect {

    private JdbcTemplate jdbcTemplate;

    // Used for <aop:before> advice.
    public void addBeforeAuditRecord(JoinPoint joinPoint) {
        String name = joinPoint.getSignature().getName();
        System.out.println("--- name ---" + name);
    addAuditRecord(name);
    }

    // Used for <aop:after> advice.
    public void addAfterAuditRecord(JoinPoint joinPoint) {
        String name = joinPoint.getSignature().getName();
        addAuditRecord(name);
    }

    // Used for <aop:afterReturning > advice.
    public void auditAfterReturning(JoinPoint joinPoint,Object result) {
        System.out.println("--- result ---" + result);
        String name = joinPoint.getSignature().getName();
        addAuditRecord("Name :" + name + " result is : " + result);
    }

    // Used for <aop:afterThrowing > advice.
    public void auditAfterThrowing(JoinPoint joinPoint,Throwable error){
        String name = joinPoint.getSignature().getName();
        addAuditRecord("Name :" + name + " error is : " +
                        error.getLocalizedMessage());
    }

    // Used for <aop:around > advice
    public void auditAround(ProceedingJoinPoint joinPoint)
                    throws Throwable {
        String name = joinPoint.getSignature().getName():
        String arguments = Arrays.toString(joinPoint.getArgs());

        System.out.println("Around before is running!");
        // Continue on the intercepted method
        joinPoint.proceed();
```

```java
        System.out.println("Around after is running!");

        // Insert a record in audit table
        addAuditRecord("Name :" + name + " arguments : " + arguments);
    }

    // Used for <aop:before> advice with arguments
    public void validateUser(User user) {
        String description = "Id: " + user.getId() + "First Name: " +
            user.getFirstName() + " Last Name: " + user.getLastName();
        addAuditRecord(description);
    }

    public void addAuditRecord(String description) {
        final String SQL_INSERT_QUERY =
                    "INSERT INTO AUDIT (description) VALUES (?)";
        jdbcTemplate.update(SQL_INSERT_QUERY, description);
    }

    public void setJdbcTemplate(JdbcTemplate jdbcTemplate) {
        this.jdbcTemplate = jdbcTemplate;
    }
}
```

Step 4: Enable the AOP-based configurations in a spring application context file.

The spring application context file is used to configure the aspect classes, pointcut expressions and advices. The complete application context XML file is provided below; named the "applicationContext-aop-xml.xml".

```xml
<?xml version="1.0" encoding="UTF-8"?>
<beans xmlns="http://www.springframework.org/schema/beans"
    xmlns:xsi="http://www.w3.org/2001/XMLSchema-instance"
    xmlns:aop="http://www.springframework.org/schema/aop"
    xsi:schemaLocation="http://www.springframework.org/schema/beans
    http://www.springframework.org/schema/beans/spring-beans-3.0.xsd
    http://www.springframework.org/schema/aop
    http://www.springframework.org/schema/aop/spring-aop-3.0.xsd">

    <bean id="mySqlDataSource" >
        <!-- Reuse the code provided in Example-1 -->
    </bean>

    <bean id="jdbcTemplate" class="org.springframework.jdbc.core.
                        JdbcTemplate">
        <property name="dataSource">
            <ref bean="mySqlDataSource"/>
        </property>
    </bean>

    <bean id="userDAO" class="com.learning.spring.aop.dao.UserDAOImpl">
        <property name="jdbcTemplate" ref="jdbcTemplate"/>
    </bean>

    <!-- Aspect wired as a spring bean -->
    <bean id="auditAspect"
```

```
            class="com.learning.spring.aop.audit.SchemaAuditAspect">
            <property name="jdbcTemplate" ref="jdbcTemplate"/>
        </bean>

        <aop:config>
            <aop:aspect id="aspectAuditing" ref="auditAspect">
                <!-- Pointcut expression -->
                <aop:pointcut id="pointCutBefore"
                    expression="execution(* com.learning.spring.aop.
                                dao.UserDAO.addUser(..))"/>

                <!-- @Before advice -->
                <aop:before pointcut-ref="pointCutBefore"
                            method="addBeforeAuditRecord"/>
            </aop:aspect>
        </aop:config>

</beans>
```

Step 5: Create a main class to test the code.

Listing 7-7 provides the main method; run the following standalone class to view the output.

Listing 7-7: Standalone class used for testing

```java
// SchemaAopMain.java
package com.learning.spring.aop;

import org.springframework.context.ApplicationContext;
import org.springframework.context.support.
            ClassPathXmlApplicationContext;
import com.learning.spring.aop.dao.UserDAO;

public class SchemaAopMain {

    public static void main(String[] args) {
        ApplicationContext appContext = new
            ClassPathXmlApplicationContext(new String[]
                    {"applicationContext-aop-xml.xml"});

        UserDAO userDAO = (UserDAO) appContext.getBean("userDAO");
        userDAO.addUser();
    }
}
```

After Advice - <aop:after>

The after advice is declared inside the `<aop:after>` element. This is equivalent to the `@After` annotation. Let us review the following `@After`-annotated method code.

```java
@After("execution(* com.learning.spring.aop.dao.UserDAO.addUser(..))")
public void addAfterAuditRecord(JoinPoint joinPoint) {
    ...
}
```

The equivalent XML configuration for the preceding annotation-based code is provided below.

```xml
<aop:config>
    <aop:aspect id="aspectAuditing" ref="auditAspect">
        <!-- After pointcut expression -->
        <aop:pointcut id="pointCutAfter"
                expression="execution(* com.learning.spring.aop.dao.
                            UserDAO.addUser(..))"/>
        <!-- After advice -->
        <aop:after pointcut-ref="pointCutAfter"
                    method="addAfterAuditRecord"/>
    </aop:aspect>
</aop:config>
```

Example 8: How to Use <aop:after> Element

Here, reuse the "applicationContext-aop-xml.xml" file created in Example-7. Add the following pointcut and advice elements to the `<aop:aspect>` element.

```xml
<aop:pointcut id="pointCutAfter"
    expression="execution(* com.learning.spring.aop.dao.
                        UserDAO.addUser(..))"/>

<aop:after pointcut-ref="pointCutAfter" method="addAfterAuditRecord"/>
```

Here, reuse the main class created in Example-7 to view the result.

AfterReturning Advice - <aop:after-returning>

The after returning advice is declared inside the `<aop:after-returning>` element. This is equivalent to the `@AfterReturning` annotation. Let us review the following `@AfterReturning`-annotated method code.

```java
@AfterReturning(pointcut = "execution(* com.learning.spring.aop.dao.
            UserDAO.getInsertedUserId(..))", returning = "result")
public void auditAfterReturning(JoinPoint joinPoint, Object result) {
    ...
}
```

The equivalent XML configuration for the preceding annotation-based code is provided below.

```xml
<aop:config>
    <aop:aspect id="aspectAuditing" ref="auditAspect">

        <!-- After returning pointcut expression -->
        <aop:pointcut id="pointCutAfterReturning"
                expression="execution(* com.learning.spring.aop.dao.
                        UserDAO.getInsertedUserId(..))"/>

        <!-- After returning advice -->
        <aop:after-returning returning="result"
                pointcut-ref="pointCutAfterReturning"
```

```
                    method="auditAfterReturning"/>
        </aop:aspect>
</aop:config>
```

Example 9: How to Use <aop:after-returning> Element

Here, reuse the "applicationContext-aop-xml.xml" file created in Example-7. Add the following pointcut and advice elements to the <aop:aspect> element.

```
<aop:pointcut id="pointCutAfterReturning"
        expression="execution(* com.learning.spring.aop.dao.UserDAO.
                getInsertedUserId(..))"/>

<aop:after-returning returning="result"
            pointcut-ref="pointCutAfterReturning"
            method="auditAfterReturning"/>
```

Listing 7-8 provides the main method; run the following standalone class to view the output

Listing 7-8: Standalone class used for testing

```
// SchemaAopMain.java
package com.learning.spring.aop;

import org.springframework.context.ApplicationContext;
import org.springframework.context.support.
            ClassPathXmlApplicationContext;
import com.learning.spring.aop.dao.UserDAO;

public class SchemaAopMain {

    public static void main(String[] args) {
        ApplicationContext appContext = new
            ClassPathXmlApplicationContext(new String[]
                    {"applicationContext-aop-xml.xml"});

        UserDAO userDAO = (UserDAO) appContext.getBean("userDAO");
        userDAO. getInsertedUserId();
    }
}
```

AfterThrowing Advice - <aop:after-throwing>

The after throwing advice is declared inside the <aop:after-throwing> element. This is equivalent to the @AfterThrowing annotation. Let us review the following @AfterThrowing-annotated method code.

```
@AfterThrowing(pointcut = "execution(* com.learning.spring.aop.dao.
        UserDAO.addUserThrowsException(..))", throwing="error")
public void logAfterThrowing(JoinPoint joinPoint, Throwable error) {
    ...
}
```

The equivalent XML configuration for the preceding annotation-based code is provided below.

```
<aop:config>
    <aop:aspect id="aspectAuditing" ref="auditAspect">

        <!-- After throwing pointcut expression -->
        <aop:pointcut id="pointCutAfterThrowing"
                expression="execution(* com.learning.spring.aop.dao.
                    UserDAO.addUserThrowsException(..))"/>

        <!-- After throwing advice -->
        <aop:after-throwing throwing="error"
                pointcut-ref="pointCutAfterThrowing"
                method="auditAfterThrowing"/>
    </aop:aspect>
</aop:config>
```

Example 10: How to Use <aop:after-throwing> Element

Here, reuse the "applicationContext-aop-xml.xml" file created in Example-7. Add the following pointcut and advice elements to the `<aop:aspect>` element.

```
<aop:pointcut id="pointCutAfterThrowing"
        expression="execution(* com.learning.spring.aop.dao.
            UserDAO.addUserThrowsException(..))"/>

<aop:after-throwing throwing="error"
        pointcut-ref="pointCutAfterThrowing"
        method="auditAfterThrowing"/>
```

Listing 7-9 provides the main method; run the following standalone class to view the output.

Listing 7-9: Standalone class used for testing

```
// SchemaAopMain.java
package com.learning.spring.aop;

import org.springframework.context.ApplicationContext;
import org.springframework.context.support.
            ClassPathXmlApplicationContext;
import com.learning.spring.aop.dao.UserDAO;

public class SchemaAopMain {

    public static void main(String[] args) {
        ApplicationContext appContext = new
            ClassPathXmlApplicationContext(new String[]
                    {"applicationContext-aop-xml.xml"});

        UserDAO userDAO = (UserDAO) appContext.getBean("userDAO");

        try {
            userDAO.addUserThrowsException();
        } catch (Exception ex) {
            ex.printStackTrace();
```

```
            }
        }
}
```

Around Advice - <aop:around>

The around advice is declared inside the `<aop:around>` element. This is equivalent to the `@Around` annotation. Let us review the following `@Around`-annotated method code.

```
@Around("execution(* com.learning.spring.aop.dao.
                UserDAO.addUserAround(..))")
public void auditAround(ProceedingJoinPoint joinPoint) throws Throwable {
    ...
}
```

The equivalent XML configuration for the preceding annotation-based code is provided below.

```
<aop:config>
    <aop:aspect id="aspectAuditing" ref="auditAspect">

        <!-- Around pointcut expression -->
        <aop:pointcut id="pointCutAround"
                expression="execution(* com.learning.spring.aop.dao.
                    UserDAO.addUserAround(..))"/>

        <!-- Around advice -->
        <aop:around pointcut-ref="pointCutAround"
                method="auditAround"/>
    </aop:aspect>
</aop:config>
```

Example 11: How to Use <aop:around> Element

Here, reuse the "applicationContext-aop-xml.xml" file created in Example-7. Add the following pointcut and advice elements to the `<aop:aspect>` element.

```
<aop:pointcut id="pointCutAround"
        expression="execution(* com.learning.spring.aop.dao.
            UserDAO.addUserAround(..))"/>

<aop:around pointcut-ref="pointCutAround" method="auditAround"/>
```

Listing 7-10 provides the main method; run the following standalone class to view the output.

Listing 7-10: Standalone class used for testing

```
// SchemaAopMain.java
package com.learning.spring.aop;

import org.springframework.context.ApplicationContext;
import org.springframework.context.support.
            ClassPathXmlApplicationContext;
```

```
import com.learning.spring.aop.dao.UserDAO;

public class SchemaAopMain {

    public static void main(String[] args) {
        ApplicationContext appContext = new
            ClassPathXmlApplicationContext(new String[]
                    {"applicationContext-aop-xml.xml"});

        UserDAO userDAO = (UserDAO) appContext.getBean("userDAO");
        userDAO.addUserAround("John", "Smith");
    }
}
```

The complete XML configuration is provided below.

```xml
<?xml version="1.0" encoding="UTF-8"?>
<beans xmlns="http://www.springframework.org/schema/beans"
    xmlns:xsi="http://www.w3.org/2001/XMLSchema-instance"
    xmlns:aop="http://www.springframework.org/schema/aop"
    xsi:schemaLocation="http://www.springframework.org/schema/beans
    http://www.springframework.org/schema/beans/spring-beans-3.0.xsd
    http://www.springframework.org/schema/aop
    http://www.springframework.org/schema/aop/spring-aop-3.0.xsd ">

    <bean id="userDAO" class="com.learning.spring.aop.dao.UserDAOImpl">
        <property name="jdbcTemplate" ref="jdbcTemplate"/>
    </bean>

    <!-- Aspect wired as a spring bean -->
    <bean id="auditAspect"
        class="com.learning.spring.aop.audit.SchemaAuditAspect">
        <property name="jdbcTemplate" ref="jdbcTemplate"/>
    </bean>

    <aop:config>
        <aop:aspect id="aspectAuditing" ref="auditAspect">
            <!-- Before pointcut expression -->
            <aop:pointcut id="pointCutBefore"
                expression="execution(* com.learning.spring.aop.
                        dao.UserDAO.addUser(..))"/>
            <!-- Before advice -->
            <aop:before pointcut-ref="pointCutBefore"
                        method="addBeforeAuditRecord"/>

            <!-- After pointcut expression -->
            <aop:pointcut id="pointCutAfter"
                        expression="execution(* com.learning.spring.aop.
                            dao.UserDAO.addUser(..))"/>
            <!-- After advice -->
            <aop:after pointcut-ref="pointCutAfter"
                        method="addAfterAuditRecord"/>

            <!-- After-returning pointcut expression -->
            <aop:pointcut id="pointCutAfterReturning"
                        expression="execution(* com.learning.spring.aop.
                            dao.UserDAO.getInsertedUserId(..))"/>
```

```
                   <!-- After-returning advice -->
                   <aop:after-returning returning="result"
                           pointcut-ref="pointCutAfterReturning"
                           method="auditAfterReturning"/>

                   <!-- After-throwing pointcut expression -->
                   <aop:pointcut id="pointCutAfterThrowing"
                           expression="execution(* com.learning.spring.aop.
                                dao.UserDAO.addUserThrowsException(..)"/>
                   <!-- After-throwing advice -->
                   <aop:after-throwing throwing="error"
                           pointcut-ref="pointCutAfterThrowing"
                           method="auditAfterThrowing"/>

                   <!-- Around pointcut expression -->
                   <aop:pointcut id="pointCutAround"
                           expression="execution(* com.learning.spring.aop.
                                dao.UserDAO.addUserAround(..))"/>
                   <!-- Around advice -->
                   <aop:around pointcut-ref="pointCutAround"
                                method="auditAround"/>

          </aop:aspect>
      </aop:config>
</beans>
```

Example 12: How to Pass Parameters to Advice (Schema-based)

The following example of an XML configuration illustrates how to access the method arguments in the advice body.

```
<aop:pointcut id="pointCutForArgs"
        expression="execution(* com.learning.spring.aop.dao.
            UserDAO.validateUser(..)) and args(user,..)"/>

<aop:before pointcut-ref="pointCutForArgs" method="validateUser"/>
```

Summary

This section summarizes the features provided in the Spring-AOP framework.

- In Spring-AOP, the @Aspect-annotated classes are called aspects.
- Spring-AOP supports only method execution join points.
- The <aop:aspectj-autoproxy/> element in application context files enables the @AspectJ support in spring. Using this configuration, spring automatically detects the @AspectJ-annotated classes.
- The @Before advice runs before the method execution.
- The @After advice runs after the method execution is exited.
- The @AfterReturning runs after the method returns a result and can also intercept the returned result.
- The @AfterThrowing advice runs after the method throws an exception.

- The @Around advice runs around (before and after) the matched method.

Figure 7-1 summarizes the most important points described in this chapter.

Figure 7-1 Spring AOP features

Chapter 8. Spring-Security

Spring security is an open-source framework that provides security services to Java EE-based applications. This framework provides authentication, authorization, and access control to the enterprise applications. Initially this project was started as "Acegi Security" under the Apache license. Later, Acegi security was incorporated into the spring framework as a sub-project and was named spring security version 2.0. This framework provides annotation, tag library, namespace, and aspect-based security services for enterprise applications. This chapter illustrates the features provided in the spring security framework.

This chapter will discuss the following topics:

- Form and HTTP-based authentication
- Spring security configurations for authentication, authorization, and access control
- Spring security annotations for authorization and access control
- Spring security namespace configuration support for authorization and access control
- Spring security tab library support for securing view layers.
- How to provide authorization and access control for objects and methods
- How to use spring expression language
- The purpose of a spring custom expression evaluator

Spring Security Terminology

This section explains the terminology commonly used in spring security.

Principal: This represents the user id required for authentication.

Credentials: This represents the password required to authenticate a principal (user).

Authorities: These represent the authorities (roles) that have been assigned to the principal. These roles are used for authorization.

SecurityContextHolder: This is the primary object used to hold the security context information. This object is used to obtain the user context information and encapsulates the principal, credentials, and authorities of a user.

Security Namespace <xmlns:security/>: The spring `<xmlns:security>` namespace provides a set of XML tags that can be used to configure spring security. This eliminates the complexity of declaring the multiple spring beans and the syntax looks cleaner in your application context files. To start using this namespace, the application requires the "spring-security-config.jar" file on your classpath. The schema declaration syntax in your application context is provided below.

```
<beans xmlns="http://www.springframework.org/schema/beans"
    xmlns:security="http://www.springframework.org/schema/security"
    xmlns:xsi="http://www.w3.org/2001/XMLSchema-instance"
    xsi:schemaLocation="http://www.springframework.org/schema/beans
    http://www.springframework.org/schema/beans/spring-beans-3.0.xsd
    http://www.springframework.org/schema/security
    http://www.springframework.org/schema/security/
```

```
                    spring-security-3.1.xsd">

        <security:debug/>

        ...

</beans>
```

Security Tag Library: The spring security-provided tag library can be used to access the user-specific security context information in JSP pages. To start using security tags in your JSP pages, declare the following tag library in your JSP.

```
<%@ taglib prefix="sec"
           uri="http://www.springframework.org/security/tags"%>
```

Spring Expression Language (SpEL): Expression language is the scripting language used to access the objects and their parameters. These expressions can be used with security annotations for access-control checks.

@PreAuthorize: This annotation is used for pre-authorization and access control checks. The spring-provided `@PreAuthorize` annotation can be used for method and class-level authorization. This is the annotation most commonly used to provide the access control to a method or class. Spring expression language can be used to validate the method parameters. The following example demonstrates the use of the `@PreAuthorize` annotation.

```
public interface MainService {

    @PreAuthorize("hasRole('ROLE_ADMIN')")
    public void deleteAccount();

    @PreAuthorize("hasRole(#user.role)")
    public String getAccountHolderName(User user);

    @PreAuthorize("hasPermission(#account, 'fullcontrol') and
                   #account.balance > #amount")
    public void createAccount(Account account, Long amount);
}
```

The following example demonstrates the use of the `@PreAuthorize` annotation with a spring controller. This checks the access control before invoking the controller class.

```
@Controller
@PreAuthorize("hasAnyRole('ROLE_ADMIN', 'ROLE_USER', 'ROLE_SU')")
public class MainController {
    ...
}
```

@PostAuthorize: This annotation is used for post-authorization checks and for access control checks after a method has been invoked. The following example demonstrates the use of the `@PostAuthorize` annotation.

```
@PostAuthorize("hasPermission(returnObject, 'read')")
Account getAccount(String accountNumber) {
    ...
}
```

The following XML configuration enables the pre-and-post authorization annotations.

```
<security:global-method-security  pre-post-annotations="enabled"/>
```

Prerequisites/Setting Up the Environment

- The JAR files required to develop the spring-security examples are provided along with the spring distribution. Download the *spring-security-3.1.3-dist.zip* file from the Spring website.
- The complete distribution is available in the form of JAR files, so no additional software is needed for development.
- Spring security version 3.1.3 is used to demonstrate the code examples. The following table provides the complete list of JAR files.

spring-security-acl-3.1.3.jar	spring-security-aspects-3.1.3.jar
spring-security-config-3.1.3.jar	spring-security-core-3.1.3.jar
spring-security-crypto-3.1.3.jar	spring-security-taglibs-3.1.3.jar
spring-security-web-3.1.3.jar	Aspectjrt.jar
cglib-nodep-2.2.2.jar	aspectjtools-1.5.4.jar

Advantages of Spring Security

This section illustrates the technical and non-technical benefits of the spring security framework.

- Spring security provides namespace support for configuring spring security. The namespace-provided XML elements are simpler and cleaner.
- Spring security provides a simplified syntax for securing service layer methods, domain objects, and controller classes.
- Spring security provides support for JSP tag libraries for securing view layer contents.
- Spring security provides support for security filters and custom expression evaluators to intercept the service class method parameters for access control.
- Spring security provides utilities for integrating various back-end systems for authorization and authentication such as LDAP, CAS, OPENID, and database.
- Spring security provides support for expression language for access control.

Demo Examples

Example 1: Form-based Authentication

The steps required to implement form-based authentication using spring security framework are listed below:

1. Configure spring security in web.xml
2. Create a spring application context file.
3. Configure a JSP view resolver in the "springweb-servlet.xml" file.

---

4. Develop a custom authentication provider class.
5. Develop the required JSP and controller classes.
6. Deploy the WAR file and test the authentication

The above-specified steps are described in the following sections:

Step 1: Configure spring security in web.xml

The following XML integrates spring security with your web application.

```
<filter>
    <filter-name>springSecurityFilterChain</filter-name>
    <filter-class>
        org.springframework.web.filter.DelegatingFilterProxy
    </filter-class>
</filter>

<filter-mapping>
    <filter-name>springSecurityFilterChain</filter-name>
    <url-pattern>/*</url-pattern>
</filter-mapping>
```

The complete "web.xml" file is provided below.

```
<?xml version="1.0" encoding="UTF-8"?>
<web-app version="2.4" xmlns="http://java.sun.com/xml/ns/j2ee"
    xmlns:xsi="http://www.w3.org/2001/XMLSchema-instance"
    xsi:schemaLocation="http://java.sun.com/xml/ns/j2ee
    http://java.sun.com/xml/ns/j2ee/web-app_2_4.xsd">

    <display-name>Spring Security Application</display-name>

    <servlet>
        <servlet-name>springweb</servlet-name>
        <servlet-class>
            org.springframework.web.servlet.DispatcherServlet
        </servlet-class>
        <load-on-startup>2</load-on-startup>
    </servlet>

    <servlet-mapping>
        <servlet-name>springweb</servlet-name>
        <url-pattern>*.action</url-pattern>
    </servlet-mapping>

    <listener>
        <listener-class>
            org.springframework.web.context.ContextLoaderListener
        </listener-class>
    </listener>

    <context-param>
        <param-name>contextConfigLocation</param-name>
        <param-value>
            /WEB-INF/applicationContext-security.xml
```

```
            </param-value>
    </context-param>

    <filter>
        <filter-name>springSecurityFilterChain</filter-name>
        <filter-class>
            org.springframework.web.filter.DelegatingFilterProxy
        </filter-class>
        <init-param>
            <param-name>logLevel</param-name>
            <param-value>INFO</param-value>
        </init-param>
    </filter>

    <filter-mapping>
        <filter-name>springSecurityFilterChain</filter-name>
        <url-pattern>/*</url-pattern>
    </filter-mapping>

</web-app>
```

Step 2: Create a spring application context file.

Configure the users, roles, credentials, type of authentication manager, URL patterns, and type of authentication information in a spring application context file.

The following XML configuration enables the debug information.

```
<security:debug/>
```

The following XML element enables the web application security.

```
<security:http auto-config='true'>
```

The `security` attribute of the following `<http>` element specifies the URL patterns that do not require authentication.

```
<security:http pattern="/css/**" security="none"/>
<security:http pattern="/login.jsp" security="none"/>
```

The following XML element configures the role required to access the specified URL pattern.

```
<security:intercept-url pattern="/**" access="ROLE_USER"/>
```

The following XML element is used for form-based authentication.

```
<security:form-login/>
```

The following XML configures the log-out page.

```
<security:logout logout-success-url="/j_spring_security_logout"
            delete-cookies="JSESSIONID"/>
```

The following XML configures the users, credentials, and roles.

```
<security:authentication-manager>
    <security:authentication-provider>
        ...
    </security:authentication-provider>
</security:authentication-manager>
```

The complete spring application context file is provided below and is named the "applicationContext-security.xml".

```
<beans xmlns="http://www.springframework.org/schema/beans"
    xmlns:security="http://www.springframework.org/schema/security"
    xmlns:xsi="http://www.w3.org/2001/XMLSchema-instance"
    xsi:schemaLocation="http://www.springframework.org/schema/beans
    http://www.springframework.org/schema/beans/spring-beans-3.0.xsd
    http://www.springframework.org/schema/security
    http://www.springframework.org/schema/security/
        spring-security-3.1.xsd">

    <security:debug/>

    <security:http pattern="/css/**" security="none"/>
    <security:http pattern="/login.jsp" security="none"/>

    <security:http auto-config='true'>
        <!-- Securing all urls of an application. User role required to
            access the application -->
        <security:intercept-url pattern="/**" access="ROLE_USER"/>

        <security:form-login/>
        <security:logout logout-success-url="/j_spring_security_logout"
                delete-cookies="JSESSIONID"/>
    </security:http>

    <!-- Configure user name, password and roles -->
    <security:authentication-manager alias="authenticationManager"
                            erase-credentials="false">
        <security:authentication-provider>
            <security:user-service>
                <security:user name="john" password="johnpass"
                    authorities="ROLE_SU, ROLE_USER, ROLE_ADMIN"/>
                <security:user name="suk" password="sukpass"
                    authorities="ROLE_USER, ROLE_ADMIN" />
                <security:user name="Will" password="Willpass"
                    authorities="ROLE_ADMIN" />
            </security:user-service>
        </security:authentication-provider>
    </security:authentication-manager>

</beans>
```

CASE 1: Hard-coded user roles and credentials.

The `<security:user>` element is used to configure the user credentials and roles. In this example the user information is hard coded in an application context file.

```
<security:authentication-manager alias="authenticationManager"
```

```
                        erase-credentials="false">
    <security:authentication-provider>
        <security:user-service>
            <security:user name="john" password="johnpass"
                    authorities="ROLE_SU, ROLE_USER, ROLE_ADMIN"/>
            <security:user name="suk" password="sukpass"
                    authorities="ROLE_USER, ROLE_ADMIN" />
            <security:user name="Will" password="Willpass"
                    authorities="ROLE_ADMIN" />
        </security:user-service>
    </security:authentication-provider>
</security:authentication-manager>
```

CASE 2: Using custom authentication provider implementation.

In this example, the `MyAuthenticationProvider` class encapsulates the user-specific details. Spring supports the configuration of multiple custom authentication provider implementations.

```
<security:authentication-manager alias="authenticationManager"
                erase-credentials="false">
    <security:authentication-provider ref='myAuthenticationProvider'/>
</security:authentication-manager>

<bean id="myAuthenticationProvider"
    class="com.learning.spring.security.MyAuthenticationProvider"/>
```

Step 3: Develop a custom authentication provider class.

The `MyAuthenticationProvider` class encapsulates the authentication information. This class must implement the spring-provided `AuthenticationProvider` class.

The following `authenticate(...)` method receives the user name and password from the login page.

```
public Authentication authenticate(Authentication authentication) {
    ...
}
```

The following `getUserData(...)` method provides user details such as username, password, and roles. In real world, you can obtain this user information from the database or LDAP.

```
private List<User> getUserData() {
    ...
}
```

Listing 8-1 provides the complete custom authentication provider implementation class code.

Listing 8-1: Custom authentication provider class.

```
// MyAuthenticationProvider.java
package com.learning.spring.security;

import org.springframework.security.authentication.
            AuthenticationProvider;
import org.springframework.security.authentication.
```

```java
                    UsernamePasswordAuthenticationToken;
import org.springframework.security.authentication.
            AuthenticationServiceException;
import org.springframework.security.authentication.
            BadCredentialsException;
import org.springframework.security.core.Authentication;
import org.springframework.security.core.GrantedAuthority;
import org.springframework.security.core.authority.
            SimpleGrantedAuthority;

import java.util.*;

public class MyAuthenticationProvider implements AuthenticationProvider {

    @Override
    public boolean supports(Class<? extends Object> authentication) {
        return authentication.equals(
            UsernamePasswordAuthenticationToken.class);
    }

    @Override
    public Authentication authenticate(Authentication authentication) {
        try {
            // User provided data from login page.
            String principal = (String) authentication.getPrincipal();
            String password = (String) authentication.getCredentials();
            List<User> userData = getUserData();

            System.out.println("--- principal ---" + principal);
            System.out.println("--- password ---" + password);

            for(User user : userData) {
                String userName = user.getUserName();
                String userPassword = user.getPassword();
                if(userName.equals(principal) &&
                    userPassword.equals(password)) {

                    // Adding authorities (roles)
                    List<String> roles = user.getRoles();
                    List<GrantedAuthority> authorities =
                                    new ArrayList<GrantedAuthority>();
                    for(String role : roles) {
                        authorities.add(new
                            SimpleGrantedAuthority(role));
                    }
                    return new UsernamePasswordAuthenticationToken(
                        userName, password, authorities);
                }
            }

            // throw exception if there is no match.
            throw new BadCredentialsException("Username/Password does
                not match for " + principal);
        } catch (Exception e) {
            throw new AuthenticationServiceException(
                e.getMessage(), e);
        }
```

```
        }

    private List<User> getUserData() {
        List<User> userDataList = new ArrayList<User>();
        User user = new User();
        List<String> roles = new ArrayList<String>();
        roles.add("ROLE_SU");
        roles.add("ROLE_ADMIN");
        roles.add("ROLE_USER");
        user.setUserName("john");
        user.setPassword("johnpass");
        user.setRoles(roles);
        userDataList.add(user);

        user = new User();
        roles = new ArrayList<String>();
        roles.add("ROLE_USER");
        user.setUserName("suk");
        user.setPassword("sukpass");
        user.setRoles(roles);
        userDataList.add(user);

        user = new User();
        roles = new ArrayList<String>();
        roles.add("ROLE_ADMIN");
        user.setUserName("Will");
        user.setPassword("willpass");
        user.setRoles(roles);
        userDataList.add(user);

        return userDataList;
    }
}
```

The following `User` class is used to hold the user data.

```
public class User {

    private String userName;
    private String password;
    private List<String> roles = new ArrayList<String>();

    // Add getters and setters
}
```

Step 4: Configure a JSP view resolver in the "springweb-servlet.xml" file.

The following XML is used to configure the JSP view resolver and is named the "springweb-servlet.xml". Refer to the chapter on spring-MVC for complete details.

```
<?xml version="1.0" encoding="UTF-8"?>
<beans xmlns="http://www.springframework.org/schema/beans"
    xmlns:xsi="http://www.w3.org/2001/XMLSchema-instance"
    xmlns:context="http://www.springframework.org/schema/context"

    ...
```

```
<bean id="viewResolver" class="org.springframework.web.servlet.
                        view.InternalResourceViewResolver">
    <property name="prefix" value=""/>
    <property name="suffix" value=".jsp"/>
    <property name="contentType">
        <value>text/html</value>
    </property>
</bean>

</beans>
```

Step 5: Develop the required JSP and controller classes.

Develop simple test JSP pages to validate the authentication. The spring security framework automatically creates an authentication login page. In this example, the spring security provided login page is used to test the authentication. The structure of the WAR file is shown in Figure 8-1.

Figure 8-1: War file structure.

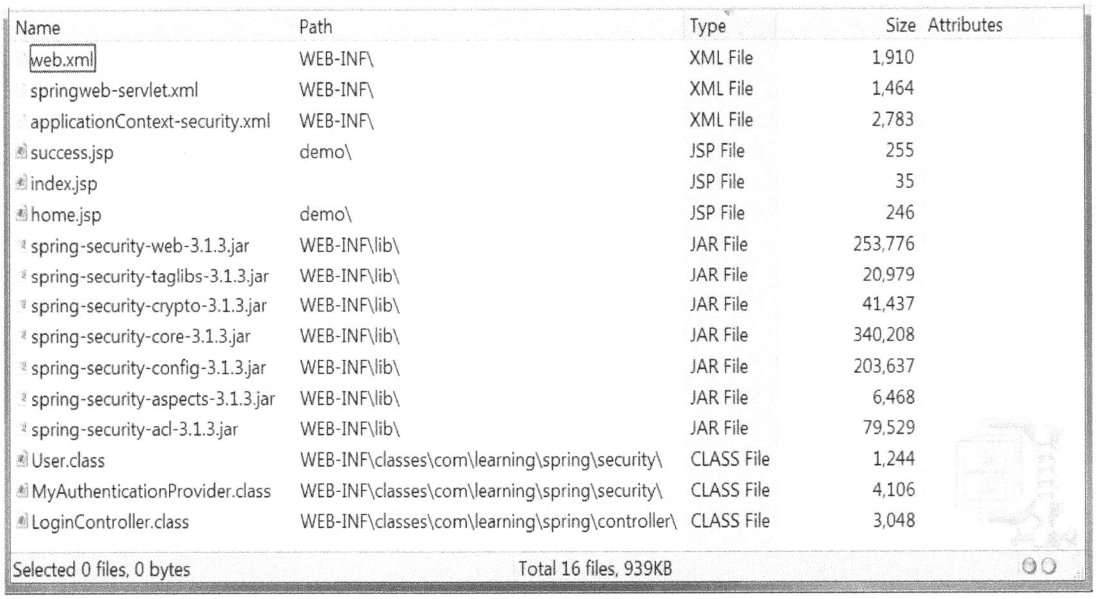

Name	Path	Type	Size	Attributes
web.xml	WEB-INF\	XML File	1,910	
springweb-servlet.xml	WEB-INF\	XML File	1,464	
applicationContext-security.xml	WEB-INF\	XML File	2,783	
success.jsp	demo\	JSP File	255	
index.jsp		JSP File	35	
home.jsp	demo\	JSP File	246	
spring-security-web-3.1.3.jar	WEB-INF\lib\	JAR File	253,776	
spring-security-taglibs-3.1.3.jar	WEB-INF\lib\	JAR File	20,979	
spring-security-crypto-3.1.3.jar	WEB-INF\lib\	JAR File	41,437	
spring-security-core-3.1.3.jar	WEB-INF\lib\	JAR File	340,208	
spring-security-config-3.1.3.jar	WEB-INF\lib\	JAR File	203,637	
spring-security-aspects-3.1.3.jar	WEB-INF\lib\	JAR File	6,468	
spring-security-acl-3.1.3.jar	WEB-INF\lib\	JAR File	79,529	
User.class	WEB-INF\classes\com\learning\spring\security\	CLASS File	1,244	
MyAuthenticationProvider.class	WEB-INF\classes\com\learning\spring\security\	CLASS File	4,106	
LoginController.class	WEB-INF\classes\com\learning\spring\controller\	CLASS File	3,048	
Selected 0 files, 0 bytes		Total 16 files, 939KB		

NOTE: Add the required spring JARs to the "WEB-INF/lib" directory. Figure-8.1 shows only a few JAR files.

Step 5: Deploy the WAR file and test the authentication

Follow these step-by-step instructions to test the authentication.

- Create a "springweb.war" file.
- Deploy the WAR file into Tomcat server → copy "springweb.war" into "webapps/" directory.
- Start the Tomcat server → run "/bin/startup.bat" from command line.

Input: Invoke the "home.jsp" from browser → http://localhost:8080/springweb/demo/home.jsp

Output: The spring provided login page will be displayed.

Provide correct and incorrect credentials to test the authentication functionality. The "home.jsp" page will be displayed after a successful login.

Example 2: HTTP Basic Authentication

The following XML configuration is used for HTTP basic authentication. Modify the spring application context "applicationContext-security.xml" file provided in Example-1 to test the basic authentication. In this scenario, the browser provides the login page dialog for authentication.

```
<security:http auto-config='true'>
    <security:intercept-url pattern="/**" access="ROLE_USER"/>
    <security:http-basic/>
</security:http>
```

How can one obtain the current user information?

The SecurityContextHolder is the primary object used to store the user context information. The following controller class can be used to obtain the security context information.

```
// LoginController.java
package com.learning.spring.controller;

import org.springframework.stereotype.Controller;
import org.springframework.web.bind.annotation.RequestMapping;
import org.springframework.web.bind.annotation.RequestMethod;
import org.springframework.ui.ModelMap;
import org.springframework.security.core.context.SecurityContextHolder;
import org.springframework.security.core.userdetails.UserDetails;
import org.springframework.security.core.Authentication;
import org.springframework.security.core.GrantedAuthority;

import javax.servlet.http.HttpServletRequest;

@Controller
public class LoginController {

    @RequestMapping(value = "/demo/login.action",
                    method = RequestMethod.POST)
        public String show(HttpServletRequest request, ModelMap model){

        String username = "";
        Object principal = SecurityContextHolder.getContext().
                getAuthentication().getPrincipal();
        if(principal instanceof UserDetails) {
            username = ((UserDetails) principal).getUsername();
        }
        System.out.println("<--- username --->" + username);

        Object credentials = SecurityContextHolder.getContext().
                getAuthentication().getCredentials();
```

```
        System.out.println("<--- password --->" + credentials);

        Authentication authentication =
            SecurityContextHolder.getContext().getAuthentication();
        for(GrantedAuthority auth : authentication.getAuthorities()) {
            System.out.println("<--- role --->" + auth.getAuthority());
        }

        request.setAttribute("Name", "LogIn");
        return "/demo/home";
    }
}
```

Example 3: Annotation-based Authorization for Classes and Methods

The spring-provided @PreAuthorize and @PostAuthorize annotations can be used for method and class-level authorization. This example illustrates the use of these annotations for providing authorization to classes and methods. The steps required to implement annotation-based authorization using the spring security framework are listed below:

1.   Configure spring security in web.xml
2.   Create a spring application context file.
3.   Configure spring security in a "springweb-servlet.xml" file.
4.   Develop service layer classes.
5.   Develop the required JSP and controller classes.
6.   Deploy the WAR file and test the authorization

The above-specified steps are described in the following sections:

Step 1: Configure spring security in web.xml

Here, reuse the web.xml provided in Example-1 with the following change.

```
<context-param>
    <param-name>contextConfigLocation</param-name>
    <param-value>
        /WEB-INF/applicationContext-auth-security.xml
    </param-value>
</context-param>
```

Step 2: Create a spring application context file.

The spring provided <security:global-method-security> XML element is used to enable the annotation-based authorization.

The following XML element enables the pre-and-post annotations.

```
<security:global-method-security pre-post-annotations="enabled"/>
```

The complete spring application context file is provided below and is named the "applicationContext-auth-security.xml"

```
<beans xmlns="http://www.springframework.org/schema/beans"
```

```
xmlns:security="http://www.springframework.org/schema/security"
xmlns:xsi="http://www.w3.org/2001/XMLSchema-instance"
xsi:schemaLocation="http://www.springframework.org/schema/beans
http://www.springframework.org/schema/beans/spring-beans-3.0.xsd
http://www.springframework.org/schema/security
http://www.springframework.org/schema/security/
        spring-security-3.1.xsd">

<security:debug/>

<security:http auto-config="true" use-expressions="true">
    <security:intercept-url pattern="/**"
                        access="isAuthenticated()"/>
    <security:form-login/>
</security:http>

<!-- Enable custom Spring-EL handling at the method level using an
     expression handler. -->
<security:global-method-security  pre-post-annotations="enabled"/>

<!-- Custom authentication -->
<security:authentication-manager alias="authenticationManager"
                        erase-credentials="false">
    <security:authentication-provider
                ref='myAuthenticationProvider'/>
</security:authentication-manager>
<bean id="myAuthenticationProvider" class="com.learning.spring.
                security.MyAuthenticationProvider"/>
```

```
</beans>
```

Step 3: Configure spring security in a "springweb-servlet.xml" file.

Here, reuse the "springweb-servlet.xml" file provided in Example-1. Add the following XML element to the "springweb-servlet.xml" file.

```
<security:global-method-security pre-post-annotations="enabled">
```

NOTE: Without this configuration, the pre-and-post annotations will not work. This element should be added to the spring servlet context file.

Step 4: Develop service layer classes.

In this example, the service layer methods require authorization. The following `MainService` interface has two methods. The ADMIN role is required to access the `deleteAccount()` method, and the USER role is required to access the `getAccountHolderName()` method.

The following `deleteAccount()` method can be invoked by clients with the ADMIN role. In this example, the `hasRole()` method has a hard-coded ADMIN role.

```
@PreAuthorize("hasRole('ROLE_ADMIN')")
public void deleteAccount();
```

The following `getAccountHolderName()` method can be invoked by clients with the USER role. In this example, the `hasRole()` method uses the spring expression-provided role. The spring expression language can be used to access the properties of the user object.

```
@PreAuthorize("hasRole(#user.role)")
public String getAccountHolderName(User user);
```

The complete interface code is provided below.

```java
// MainService.java
package com.learning.spring.service;

import org.springframework.security.access.prepost.PreAuthorize;
import com.learning.spring.security.User;

public interface MainService {

    @PreAuthorize("hasRole(#user.role)")
    public void deleteAccount(User user);

    @PreAuthorize("hasRole('ROLE_ADMIN')")
    public String getAccountHolderName();
}
```

The above-specified service interface methods are implemented in the implementation class. The complete class code is provided below.

```java
// MainServiceImpl.java
package com.learning.spring.service;

import org.springframework.stereotype.Component;
import com.learning.spring.security.User;
import com.learning.spring.security.Account;

@Component
public class MainServiceImpl implements MainService {

    public void deleteAccount(User user) {
        System.out.println("--- Deleted ---" + user.getUserName());
        //... implement your logic here
    }

    public String getAccountHolderName() {
        //... implement your logic here
        return " John Smith ";
    }
}
```

Step 5: Develop the required JSP and controller classes.

The following `MainController` class is annotated with `@PreAuthorize` annotation. An ADMIN, USER, or SU role is required to access this controller class.

```
@PreAuthorize("hasAnyRole('ROLE_ADMIN', 'ROLE_USER', 'ROLE_SU')")
public class MainController {
```

The complete spring controller class code is provided below.

```java
// MainController.java
package com.learning.spring.controller;

import org.springframework.web.bind.annotation.RequestMapping;
import org.springframework.web.bind.annotation.RequestMethod;
import org.springframework.ui.ModelMap;
import org.springframework.security.core.context.SecurityContextHolder;
import org.springframework.security.core.userdetails.UserDetails;
import org.springframework.security.core.Authentication;
import org.springframework.security.core.GrantedAuthority;
import org.springframework.security.access.prepost.PreAuthorize;
import org.springframework.stereotype.Controller;
import org.springframework.beans.factory.annotation.Autowired;

import javax.servlet.http.HttpServletRequest;
import com.learning.spring.service.MainService;
import com.learning.spring.security.User;

@Controller
@PreAuthorize("hasAnyRole('ROLE_ADMIN', 'ROLE_USER', 'ROLE_SU')")
public class MainController {

    @Autowired
    private MainService mainServiceImpl;

    @RequestMapping(value = "/demo/main.action",
                    method = RequestMethod.POST)
    public String show(HttpServletRequest request, ModelMap model) {

        String username = "";
        Object principal = SecurityContextHolder.getContext().
                           getAuthentication().getPrincipal();
        if(principal instanceof UserDetails) {
            username = ((UserDetails) principal).getUsername();
        }
        System.out.println("<--- username --->" + username);
        System.out.println("<--- principal --->" + principal);

        Object credentials = SecurityContextHolder.getContext().
                           getAuthentication().getCredentials();
        System.out.println("<--- password --->" + credentials);

        Authentication authentication = SecurityContextHolder.
                    getContext().getAuthentication();
        for(GrantedAuthority auth : authentication.getAuthorities()) {
            System.out.println("<--- Role --->" + auth.getAuthority());
        }

        // Calling service layer methods
        mainServiceImpl.deleteAccount();

        User user = new User();
        user.setUserName((String) principal);
        user.setPassword((String) credentials);
        user.setRole("ROLE_USER");
```

```
                mainServiceImpl.getAccountHolderName(user);

                return "/demo/testtaglibs";
        }
}
```

The following JSP is used for testing and is named the "main.jsp".

```
<html>
<head>
    <title> Main Page </title>
    <script type="text/javascript">
        function checkLogin() {
            document.forms[0].action = "/springweb/demo/main.action";
            document.forms[0].submit();
        }
    </script>
</head>
<body bgcolor="grey">
<form method="post">
    <table>
        <tr><td> <label><b>Page 1</b></label></td></tr>
        <tr><td> <label><b>Page 2</b></label></td></tr>
        <tr><td> <label><b>Page 3</b></label></td></tr>
        <tr>
            <td>
                <input type="button" name="Test"
                    value="Test" onclick="checkLogin()"/>
            </td>
        </tr>
    </table>
</form>
</body>
</html>
```

The spring controller class returns to the following JSP and is named the "testtaglibs.jsp".

```
<html>
<head>
    <title> Retuen Page </title>
</head>
<body>
<form method="post">
    <div> ... </div>

</form>
</body>
</html>
```

Step 6: Deploy the WAR file to test the authorization.

Follow these steps to test the annotation-based authorization.

- Create a "springweb.war" file.
- Deploy the WAR file into Tomcat server → copy "springweb.war" into "webapps/" directory.

- Start the Tomcat the server → run "/bin/startup.bat" from command line.

The structure of the WAR file is shown in Figure 8-2.

Figure 8-2: War file structure.

Name	Path	Type	Size	Attributes
MainController.class	WEB-INF\classes\com\learning\spring\controller\	CLASS File	4,026	
MainService.class	WEB-INF\classes\com\learning\spring\service\	CLASS File	704	
MainServiceImpl.class	WEB-INF\classes\com\learning\spring\service\	CLASS File	1,736	
MyAuthenticationProvider.class	WEB-INF\classes\com\learning\spring\security\	CLASS File	4,106	
User.class	WEB-INF\classes\com\learning\spring\security\	CLASS File	1,426	
spring-security-acl-3.1.3.jar	WEB-INF\lib\	JAR File	79,529	
spring-security-aspects-3.1.3.jar	WEB-INF\lib\	JAR File	6,468	
spring-security-config-3.1.3.jar	WEB-INF\lib\	JAR File	203,637	
spring-security-core-3.1.3.jar	WEB-INF\lib\	JAR File	340,208	
spring-security-crypto-3.1.3.jar	WEB-INF\lib\	JAR File	41,437	
spring-security-taglibs-3.1.3.jar	WEB-INF\lib\	JAR File	20,979	
spring-security-web-3.1.3.jar	WEB-INF\lib\	JAR File	253,776	
index.jsp		JSP File	444	
main.jsp	demo\	JSP File	1,208	
testtaglibs.jsp	demo\	JSP File	1,036	
MANIFEST.MF	META-INF\	MF File	102	
applicationContext-auth-security.xml	WEB-INF\	XML File	1,643	
springweb-servlet.xml	WEB-INF\	XML File	4,748	
web.xml	WEB-INF\	XML File	1,915	

Follow these step-by-step instructions.

- Invoke the "main.jsp" from the browser → http://localhost:8080/springweb/demo/home.jsp
- The spring provided user-id and login page will be displayed → Enter user-id = "john" and password = "johnpass"
- After a successful login, the "main.jsp" page will be displayed.
- Click on the Test button → "tagligs.jsp" page will be displayed.

Repeat the above tests for "suk" and "will" users to test the authorization functionality. Use the following user credentials.

- User name = "suk" and password = "sukpass"
- User name = "will" and password = "willpass"

NOTE: The user "will" does not have a USER role, so this user is not authorized to access the `getAccountHolderName()` service class method. Thus, this service class method will throw the "HTTP Status 403—Access is denied" exception. Also test the spring controller access with a user who does not have an ADMIN, USER, or SU role.

Example 4: View Layer Authorization Using JSP Tag Libraries

The spring provided security tag libraries can be used for role-based authorization with JSP pages. The complete user context is available in the JSP page, based on the user role; JSP provide access to the contents of the page.

Declare the following security tag in your JSP to start using the security tags.

```
<%@ taglib prefix="sec"
uri="http://www.springframework.org/security/tags" %>
```

The following `<sec:authorize>` tag can be used to provide access to the contents of a JSP page.

```
<sec:authorize access="hasRole('ROLE_SU')">
    ...
</sec:authorize>
```

Here, reuse the "main.jsp" provided in Example-3 with the following change. The complete JSP code is provided below.

```
<%@ page language="java" contentType="text/html; charset=UTF-8"
                      pageEncoding="UTF-8"%>
<%@ taglib prefix="sec" uri=
               "http://www.springframework.org/security/tags" %>
<%@ taglib uri="http://java.sun.com/jsp/jstl/core" prefix="c" %>

<html>
<head>
    <title> Main Page </title>
    <script type="text/javascript">
        function checkLogin() {
            document.forms[0].action = "/springweb/demo/main.action";
            document.forms[0].submit();
        }
    </script>
</head>
<body bgcolor="grey">
<form method="post">
    <table>
        <sec:authorize access="hasRole('ROLE_SU')">
            <tr><td> <label><b>Page 1</b></label> </td></tr>
        </sec:authorize>
        <tr><td> <label><b>Page 2</b></label></td></tr>
        <tr><td> <label><b>Page 3</b></label></td></tr>
        <tr>
            <td>
                <input type="button" name="Test"
                    value="Test" onclick="checkLogin()"/>
            </td>
        </tr>
    </table>
</form>
</body>
</html>
```

Example 5: Authorization Using Custom Expression Evaluators

Spring-provided built-in and custom expression evaluators can be used for providing method-level authorization. Spring security-provided expressions can be used with methods, classes, web URLs, and JSP tags. This example illustrates the use of custom expression evaluators for providing the authorization to service layer methods. The steps required to implement expression-based authorization using the spring security framework are listed below:

1. Configure spring security in web.xml
2. Create a spring application context file.
3. Develop a custom expression evaluator class.
4. Develop service layer classes.
5. Configure a custom expression evaluator in the "springweb-servlet.xml" file.
6. Develop the required JSP and controller classes.
7. Deploy the WAR file and test the authorization

The above-specified steps are described in the following sections:

Step 1: Configure spring security in web.xml

Here, reuse the "web.xml" created in Example-3

Step 2: Create a spring application context file.

Here, reuse the application context file created in Example-3

Step 3: Develop a custom expression evaluator class.

The custom expression evaluator class must extend the spring-provided `PermissionEvaluator` class. In this example, the custom expression evaluator class acts as a filter between the controller and service layer. This class intercepts the service class method parameters for proving the access-control. The complete user security context is available inside the `hasPermission(...)` method of the expression evaluator class.

The custom evaluator `hasPermission(...)` method signature is provided below.

```
public boolean hasPermission(Authentication authentication,
                Object targetDomainObject, Object permission) {
    ...
}
```

An example of a service interface method signature is provided below.

```
@PreAuthorize("hasPermission(#account, 'fullcontrol') and
                #account.balance > #amount")
public void createAccount(Account account, Long amount);
```

The mapping between the service interface method arguments and custom evaluator `hasPermission(...)` method arguments are provided below.

*   First Argument → Authentication → this object encapsulates the principal, credentials and authorities. This variable does not map to any service interface method variable.
*   Second Argument → targetDomainObject → maps to "#account" → Expression used for the "Account" method argument

- Third Argument → permission → maps to "fullcontrol" (hard-coded string value)

The complete custom evaluator class code is provided below.

```java
// SimplePermissionEvaluator.java
package com.learning.spring.security;

import org.springframework.security.access.PermissionEvaluator;
import org.springframework.security.core.Authentication;
import java.io.Serializable;

public class SimplePermissionEvaluator implements PermissionEvaluator {

    @Override
    public boolean hasPermission(Authentication authentication,
                    Object targetDomainObject, Object permission) {
        log("--- permission ---" + permission);

        // Service class method variable "account"
        Account account = (Account) targetDomainObject;
        log("--- Account holder name ---"+ account.getAccountNumber());

        String userName = (String) authentication.getPrincipal();
        log("--- user name ---" + userName);

        // ... Implement your logic here based on input received.

        if(permission.equals("fullcontrol")) {
            return true;
        } else if (permission.equals("readonly")) {
            return false;
        }
        return false;
    }

    @Override
    public boolean hasPermission(Authentication authentication,
                                Serializable targetId,
                                String targetType, Object permission) {
        //... This method is never called in this scenario.
        throw new UnsupportedOperationException();
    }

    private void log(String sop) {
        System.out.println(sop);
    }
}
```

Step 4: Develop service layer classes.

The following `hasPermission(...)` method determines the access to the `createAccount(...)` method. In this example, the custom expression evaluator is used to determine the authorization to the `createAccount(...)` method.

```java
@PreAuthorize("hasPermission(#account, 'fullcontrol') and
```

```
                              #account.balance > #amount")
public void createAccount(Account account, Long amount);
```

Here, reuse the `MainService` interface provided in Example-3 with the following change. The newly added `createAccount(...)` method is provided below.

```
// MainService.java
package com.learning.spring.service;

import org.springframework.security.access.prepost.PreAuthorize;
import com.learning.spring.security.Account;

public interface MainService {

    ...

    @PreAuthorize("hasPermission(#account, 'fullcontrol') and
                            #account.balance > #amount")
    public void createAccount(Account account, Long amount);
}
```

The interface method implementation is provided below. Reuse the `MainServiceImpl` class provided in Example-3.

```
// MainServiceImpl.java
package com.learning.spring.service;

import org.springframework.stereotype.Component;
import com.learning.spring.security.User;
import com.learning.spring.security.Account;

@Component
public class MainServiceImpl implements MainService {

    public void createAccount(Account account, Long amount) {
        System.out.println("--- create account ---" +
                        account.getAccountNumber());
        //... Implement your logic here
    }
}
```

The following `Account` object is used for data transfer.

```
public class Account {

    private String accountNumber;
    private String accountHolderName;
    private Long balance;

    // Add getters and setters
}
```

Step 5: Configure a custom expression evaluator in the "springweb-servlet.xml" file.

Here, reuse the "springweb-servlet.xml" xml file created in Example-3. Add the following expression evaluator-related configurations to the "springweb-servlet.xml" file.

```
<security:global-method-security  pre-post-annotations="enabled">
    <security:expression-handler ref="expressionHandler"/>
</security:global-method-security>

<!-- Custom expression handler implementation to check user permissions
    against an Object such as a method parameter. -->
<bean id="expressionHandler" class="org.springframework.security.access.
          expression.method.DefaultMethodSecurityExpressionHandler">
    <property name="permissionEvaluator" ref="permissionEvaluator"/>
</bean>

<bean id="permissionEvaluator" class="com.learning.spring.security.
                          SimplePermissionEvaluator"/>
```

NOTE: Without this configuration the expression evaluators will not work. These elements should be added to the "springweb-servlet.xml" file.

Step 6: Develop the required JSP and controller classes.

Reuse the JSP and controller class provided in Example-3. Invoke the `createAccount(...)` service method from the spring controller.

```
// MainController.java
public class MainController {

    @Autowired
    private MainService mainServiceImpl;

    @RequestMapping(value = "/demo/main.action",
                method = RequestMethod.POST)
    public String show(HttpServletRequest request, ModelMap model) {

        ...

        Account account = new Account();
        account.setAccountNumber("121332424");
        account.setBalance(5000L);
        mainServiceImpl.createAccount(account, 500L);

        return "/demo/testtaglibs";
    }
}
```

Step 7: Deploy the WAR file and test the authorization

Refer to the WAR file structure provided in Example-3. Follow the steps provided in Example-3 to test this expression evaluator's functionality.

ACL for Domain Objects

The previous examples demonstrated the authentication and various types of authorization techniques. The following example illustrates the spring Access Control List (ACL)-based security using a custom expression evaluator.

Business scenario:

- The USER role has only READ permission for the Account object
- The ADMIN role has only READ and WRITE permission for the Account object
- The SU role has only READ, WRITE, and DELETE permission for the Account object

Example 6: Providing ACL for Domain Objects

The steps required to implement the above business scenario are listed below.

1. Develop service layer classes.
2. Develop a custom expression evaluator class.
3. Configure the roles and objects in the "springweb-servelet.xml" file.
4. Develop the required JSP and controller classes.

Step 1: Develop service layer classes.

The following `hasPermission(...)` method determines the access to the `deleteAccount(...)` method. In this example, the custom expression evaluator is used to determine the authorization to the `deleteAccount(...)` method.

```
@PreAuthorize("hasPermission(#account, 'WRITE')")
public void deleteAccount(Account account);
```

Here, reuse the `MainService` interface provided in Example-3 with the following change. The newly added `deleteAccount(...)` method is provided below.

```
// MainService.java
package com.learning.spring.service;

import org.springframework.security.access.prepost.PreAuthorize;
import com.learning.spring.security.Account;

public interface MainService {

    ...

    @PreAuthorize("hasPermission(#account, 'WRITE')")
    public void deleteAccount(Account account);
}
```

The interface method implementation is provided below. Reuse the `MainServiceImpl` class provided in Example-3.

```
// MainServiceImpl.java
package com.learning.spring.service;
```

```
import org.springframework.stereotype.Component;
import com.learning.spring.security.User;
import com.learning.spring.security.Account;

@Component
public class MainServiceImpl implements MainService {

    public void deleteAccount(Account account) {
        System.out.println("--- delete account ---" +
            account.getAccountNumber());
        //... Implement your logic here
    }
}
```

Step 2: Develop a custom expression evaluator class.

The complete custom evaluator class code is provided below. The `hasPermission(...)`
method contains the implementation logic related to the authorization.

```
// ACLPermissionEvaluator.java
package com.learning.spring.security;

import org.springframework.security.core.Authentication;
import org.springframework.security.core.GrantedAuthority;
import org.springframework.security.access.PermissionEvaluator;
import org.springframework.security.access.
            hierarchicalroles.RoleHierarchy;

import javax.annotation.Resource;
import java.io.Serializable;
import java.util.Map;
import java.util.Collection;

public class ACLPermissionEvaluator implements PermissionEvaluator {

    @Resource(name = "permissionsMap")
    private Map permissionsMap;

    @Resource(name = "roleHierarchy")
    private RoleHierarchy roleHierarchy;

    @Override
    public boolean hasPermission(Authentication auth, Serializable
                targetId, String targetType, Object permission) {
        return false;
    }

    private String getRole(Authentication authentication) {
        String highestRole = null;
        try {
            Collection<GrantedAuthority> auths =
                            (Collection<GrantedAuthority>)
                roleHierarchy.getReachableGrantedAuthorities(
                            authentication.getAuthorities());
            for (GrantedAuthority auth : auths) {
```

```java
                highestRole = auth.getAuthority();
                break;
            }
            log("Highest role hiearchy: " +
                roleHierarchy.getReachableGrantedAuthorities(
                    authentication.getAuthorities()));
        } catch (Exception e) {
            log("No roles assigned");
        }
        return highestRole;
    }

    public boolean hasPermission(Authentication authentication, Object
                    targetDomainObject, Object permission) {
        log("targetDomainObject: " + targetDomainObject);
        log("permission: " + permission);
        String role = getRole(authentication);
        log("role: " + role);
        return hasPermission(role, permission, targetDomainObject);
    }

    private boolean hasPermission(String role, Object permission,
                        Object domain) {
        log("Check if role exists in map: " + role);
        if (permissionsMap.containsKey(role)) {
            log("Role exists in map: " + role);
            Permission userPermission = (Permission)
                            permissionsMap.get(role);
            log("Check if domain object exists: " +
                            domain.getClass().getName());
            if (userPermission.getObjects().containsKey(
                domain.getClass().getName())) {
                log("Domain object exists: "
                        +domain.getClass().getName());
                log("Check if permission exists: " + permission);
                for (String action : userPermission.getObjects().get(
                        domain.getClass().getName())) {
                    if (action.equals(permission)) {
                        log("Permission exists: " + action +
                                        "Permission Granted!");
                        return true;
                    }
                }
            }
        }
        log("Permission Denied!");
        return false;
    }

    private void log(String sop) {
        System.out.println(sop);
    }
}
```

Step 3: Configure the roles and objects in the "springweb-servelet.xml" file.

Here, reuse the "springweb-servlet.xml" xml file created in Example-3. Add the following XML configurations to the "springweb-servlet.xml" file.

```xml
<!-- Enable the annotations -->
<security:global-method-security  pre-post-annotations="enabled">
    <security:expression-handler ref="expressionHandler"/>
</security:global-method-security>

<!-- Custom expression eveluator implementation -->
<bean id="expressionHandler"
        class="org.springframework.security.access.
            expression.method.DefaultMethodSecurityExpressionHandler">
        <property name="permissionEvaluator"
                ref="permissionEvaluator"/>
        <property name="roleHierarchy" ref="roleHierarchy"/>
</bean>

<bean id="permissionEvaluator"
    class="com.learning.spring.security.ACLPermissionEvaluator"/>

<!-- Define the list of permissions -->
<util:map id="permissionsMap">
    <entry key="ROLE_ADMIN" value-ref="admin"/>
    <entry key="ROLE_USER" value-ref="user"/>
    <entry key="ROLE_SU" value-ref="su"/>
</util:map>

<!-- Account object has READ, WRITE permissions for admin -->
<bean id="admin" class="com.learning.spring.security.Permission">
    <property name="objects">
        <map>
            <entry key="com.learning.spring.security.Account">
                <list>
                    <value>READ</value>
                    <value>WRITE</value>
                </list>
            </entry>
            </map>
    </property>
</bean>

<!-- Account object has READ only permission for user role -->
<bean id="user" class="com.learning.spring.security.Permission">
    <property name="objects">
        <map>
            <entry key="com.learning.spring.security.Account">
                <list>
                    <value>READ</value>
                </list>
            </entry>
        </map>
    </property>
</bean>

<!-- Account object has READ, WRITE, DELETE permission for su role -->
<bean id="su" class="com.learning.spring.security.Permission">
    <property name="objects">
```

```xml
            <map>
                <entry key="com.learning.spring.security.Account">
                    <list>
                        <value>READ</value>
                        <value>WRITE</value>
                        <value>DELETE</value>
                    </list>
                </entry>
            </map>
        </property>
</bean>

<!-- Define the role hierarchy -->
<bean id="roleHierarchy" class="org.springframework.security.access.
                  hierarchicalroles.RoleHierarchyImpl">
    <property name="hierarchy">
        <value>
            ROLE_SU > ROLE_ADMIN
            ROLE_ADMIN > ROLE_USER
        </value>
    </property>
</bean>
```

Step 4: Develop the required JSP and controller classes.

Reuse the JSP and controller class provided in Example-3. Invoke the deleteAccount(...) service method from the spring controller.

```java
// MainController.java
public class MainController {

    @Autowired
    private MainService mainServiceImpl;

    @RequestMapping(value = "/demo/main.action",
                method = RequestMethod.POST)
    public String show(HttpServletRequest request, ModelMap model) {

        ...

        Account account = new Account();
        account.setAccountNumber("121332424");
        account.setBalance(5000L);
        mainServiceImpl.deleteAccount(account);

        return "/demo/testtaglibs";
    }
}
```

Refer to the WAR file structure provided in Example-3. Follow the steps provided in Example-3 to test this ACL functionality.

Summary

This section summarizes the features provided in the spring security framework.

- Spring provides the `@PreAuthorize` and `@PostAuthorize` annotations for pre and post authorization and access control checks.
- The spring-provided security filters and the built-in and custom expression evaluators can be used to intercept the service class method parameters to implement the access control functionality.
- The spring-provided `SecurityContextHolder` object holds the security context information. This object is used to obtain the user context information and encapsulates the user principal, credentials, and authorities of a user.
- The spring-provided `<xmlns:security>` namespace can be used to configure spring security. This namespace provides a set of xml tags for spring security configuration.
- Spring-provides a JSP tag library for securing the JSP contents.
- The spring-provided `<security:global-method-security/>` XML element configuration is used to enable the use of pre and post annotations.

Figure 8-3 summarizes the most important points described in this chapter.

Figure 8-3 Spring security summary

Chapter 9. Spring Batch

The spring batch framework is used for batch processing of large volumes of data. It provides the abstractions for scheduling and asynchronous task execution as well as an integration framework for Quartz batch scheduler and JDK timer scheduler, and it supports POJO-based development methodology. The operations of a plain Java class can be scheduled periodically using the spring batch framework. This chapter illustrates the Spring batch and task execution framework.

This chapter will discuss the following topics:

- Features of the spring batch scheduler
- Features of the spring task executer
- Spring annotations for scheduling and task execution
- Spring integration with the Quartz batch scheduler
- Spring integration with the JDK timer batch scheduler
- Features of the spring batch integration framework

Spring Batch Terminology

This section explains the terminology commonly used in spring batch scheduling and task execution. The spring batch terminology is defined below.

TaskScheduler: The `TaskScheduler` interface abstracts the spring batch scheduling functionality. This interface has various methods to schedule operations at specified time intervals.

TaskExecutor: The `TaskExecutor` interface abstracts the spring task executor functionality. This interface abstracts the Java multithreading functionality.

<xml:task> namespace: The spring-provided `<xml:task>` namespace can be used to configure batch scheduling and task execution. This namespace provides support for fixed-time and Cron-based configurations for batch scheduling and task execution.

The following XML element creates a `ThreadPoolTaskScheduler` instance with a specified thread pool size.

```
<task:scheduler id="taskScheduler" pool-size="4"/>
```

The following XML element is used to execute the `run(...)` method of a specified class.

```
<task:executor id="taskExecutor" pool-size="5-25"
               queue-capacity="100"/>
```

Refer to Examples-1 and 2 for complete details.

@Scheduled: The spring-provided `@Scheduled`-annotation can be used to schedule an operation periodically with the specified time interval. This annotation is used along with the trigger metadata at method level, and it also supports the Cron-based timer expressions. An example use of the `@Scheduled`-annotation is given below.

```
@Scheduled(fixedDelay = 5000)
public void generateMenu() throws Exception {
    ...
}

@Scheduled(fixedRate = 3000)
public void generateMenu() throws Exception {
    ...
}

@Scheduled(cron="*/5 * * * * MON-FRI")
public void generateMenu() throws Exception {
    ...
}
```

The @Scheduled-annotation metadata terminology is defined below.

- fixedDelay → time difference between the completion of the previous task and the starting of the next task
- fixedRate → time difference between the starting of the previous task and the starting of the next task.
- cron="*/5 * * * * MON-FRI" → runs for every five minutes Monday through Friday.

@Async: The spring-provided @Async-annotation can be used for asynchronous task execution. This annotation is used at method level. An example use of @Async annotation is given below.

```
@Async
public void generateMenu() throws Exception {
    ...
}
```

The following XML element is used to enable the @Service and @Async annotations.

```
<task:annotation-driven/>
```


Prerequisites/Setting Up the Environment

The following list of JAR files is required to run the examples provided in this chapter.

- All JAR files in the spring distribution → org.springframework.*.jar
- commons-logging.jar
- aopalliance-1.0.jar
- cglib-nodep-2.1_3.jar
- com.springsource.org.quartz-1.6.2.jar

Add the above-specified JAR files to the classpath to run the examples provided in this chapter.

Advantages of Spring Batch

This section illustrates the technical and non-technical benefits of the Spring batch framework.

- Spring batch provides support for the annotation-based programming model for batch scheduling and task execution.
- Spring batch provides XML namespace support for configuring the trigger metadata.
- Spring batch supports the POJO-based programming model for batch scheduling and task execution.
- With spring batch, it is easy to schedule an existing method operation to run periodically at the specified time interval.
- Spring batch can be combined with other batch scheduling frameworks. Spring batch provides an abstraction layer for various batch scheduling frameworks, such as, Quartz and JDK timer scheduler.
- The spring task executor framework provides an abstraction layer for Java thread programming.
- The spring batch integration framework provides utilities for reading, transforming, and writing large volumes of data. This framework supports several integration formats such as, file, database, XML, JSON, and so on.

Demo Examples

Example 1: Spring Batch Scheduler

The steps required to schedule-and-run a Java operation using the spring batch scheduler are listed below:

1. Create a spring application context file.
2. Create a Java operation to be scheduled.
3. Create a Java class to run the scheduled operation.

The above-specified steps are described in the following sections:

Step 1: Create a spring application context file.

Spring provides an XML namespace for configuring the task scheduler. The following XML element is used to schedule the `generateMenu(...)` method every five seconds.

```
<task:scheduled-tasks scheduler="taskScheduler">
    <task:scheduled ref="menuGenerator"
                  method="generateMenu" fixed-delay="5000"/>
</task:scheduled-tasks>
```

The significance of each attribute is listed below.

- ref → refers to the POJO component.
- method → method to be scheduled to run.
- fixed-delay → time interval between the runs.

The following XML element is used to schedule the `generateMenu(...)` method using a Cron expression.

```xml
<task:scheduled-tasks scheduler="taskScheduler">
    <task:scheduled ref="menuGenerator"
                method="generateMenu" cron="*/5 * * * * ?"/>
</task:scheduled-tasks>
```

The following XML element creates a `ThreadPoolTaskScheduler` instance with a specified thread pool size.

```xml
<task:scheduler id="taskScheduler" pool-size="4"/>
```

The complete XML file is provided below and is named the "spring-batch-scheduler.xml".

```xml
<?xml version="1.0" encoding="UTF-8"?>
<beans xmlns="http://www.springframework.org/schema/beans"
    xmlns:xsi="http://www.w3.org/2001/XMLSchema-instance"
    xmlns:context="http://www.springframework.org/schema/context"
    xmlns:task="http://www.springframework.org/schema/task"
    xsi:schemaLocation="http://www.springframework.org/schema/beans
        http://www.springframework.org/schema/beans/
        spring-beans-3.0.xsd
        http://www.springframework.org/schema/context
        http://www.springframework.org/schema/context/
        spring-context-3.0.xsd
        http://www.springframework.org/schema/task
        http://www.springframework.org/schema/task/
        spring-task-3.0.xsd">

    <context:component-scan base-package="com.learning.spring.batch"/>

    <task:scheduled-tasks scheduler="taskScheduler">
        <task:scheduled ref="menuGenerator"
                    method="generateMenu" fixed-delay="5000"/>
        <!--<task:scheduled ref="menuGenerator"
                    method="generateMenu" cron="*/5 * * * * ?"/>-->
    </task:scheduled-tasks>

    <task:scheduler id="taskScheduler" pool-size="4"/>

</beans>
```

Step 2: Create a Java operation to be scheduled

The following data value object is used to hold the data.

```java
// FoodItemDVO.java
package com.learning.spring.batch;

public class FoodItemDVO {

    private String country;
    private String id;
    private String name;
```

```
        private String description;
        private String category;
        private String price;

        // Add getters and setters
}
```

The following method is scheduled to run every five seconds. This method generates one menu text file for each run.

```
public void generateMenu() throws Exception {
        ...
}
```

The following private method writes data into a text file.

```
private void writeToTextFile(List<FoodItemDVO> menuCategoryList)
            throws Exception {
        ...
}
```

Listing 9-1 provides the complete class code.

Listing 9-1: Generates a menu for each run.

```
// MenuGenerator.java
package com.learning.spring.batch;

import org.springframework.scheduling.annotation.Scheduled;
import org.springframework.stereotype.Component;

import java.io.BufferedWriter;
import java.io.FileWriter;
import java.util.*;

@Component
public class MenuGenerator {

    private static int i = 0;

    public void generateMenu() throws Exception {
        List<FoodItemDVO> menuCategoryList =
                        new ArrayList<FoodItemDVO>();

        FoodItemDVO foodItemDVO = new FoodItemDVO();
        foodItemDVO.setCountry("GB");
        foodItemDVO.setId("100");
        foodItemDVO.setName("Traditional English Breakfast");
        foodItemDVO.setPrice("6.99");
        foodItemDVO.setCategory("Breakfast");
        foodItemDVO.setDescription("2 Fried eggs, 1 English pork
        sausage, 1 Back Bacon");
        menuCategoryList.add(foodItemDVO);

        foodItemDVO = new FoodItemDVO();
        foodItemDVO.setCountry("USA");
```

```java
            foodItemDVO.setId("101");
            foodItemDVO.setName("Jelly Doughnut");
            foodItemDVO.setPrice("0.85");
            foodItemDVO.setCategory("Appetizer");
            foodItemDVO.setDescription("Deep fried pastry covered in suger,
                    and filled with strawberry jelly.");
            menuCategoryList.add(foodItemDVO);

            writeToTextFile(menuCategoryList);
            System.out.println("--- Completed ---");
    }

    private void writeToTextFile(List<FoodItemDVO> menuCategoryList)
            throws Exception {
        i = i + 1;
        String fileName = "foodItemMenu"+ i +".txt";
        BufferedWriter bufferedWriter = new BufferedWriter(new
                    FileWriter("C:/files/" + fileName));

        for(FoodItemDVO foodItemDVO : menuCategoryList) {
            bufferedWriter.write("Category:" +
                        foodItemDVO.getCategory());
            bufferedWriter.newLine();
            bufferedWriter.write("Name:" + foodItemDVO.getName() + " -
            Price: " + foodItemDVO.getPrice() + "  -Currency: " +
            foodItemDVO.getCountry());
            bufferedWriter.newLine();
            bufferedWriter.write("Description: " +
                        foodItemDVO.getDescription());
            bufferedWriter.newLine();
            bufferedWriter.write("----------------------");
            bufferedWriter.newLine();
        }

        bufferedWriter.flush();
        bufferedWriter.close();
    }
}
```

Step 3: Create a Java class to run the scheduled operation

The following `TestBatchScheduler` class runs the scheduled operation with the specified time interval. Listing 9-2 provides the complete class code.

Listing 9-2: Test class used to run the scheduled operation

```java
// TestBatchScheduler.java
package com.learning.spring.batch;

import org.springframework.context.support.
            ClassPathXmlApplicationContext;

public class TestBatchScheduler {

    public static void main(String args[]) {
        try {
            ClassPathXmlApplicationContext context =
```

```
                new ClassPathXmlApplicationContext
                        ("spring-batch-scheduler.xml");
        } catch (Exception ex) {
            ex.printStackTrace();
        }
    }
}
```

Example 2: Spring Task Executor

The steps required to schedule-and-run a Java operation using spring task executer are listed below:

1. Create an operation to be executed.
2. Create a spring application context file.
3. Create a Java class to run the scheduled operation.

The above-specified steps are described in the following sections:

Step 1: Create an operation to be executed.

The `run()` method of the `MenuTask` class executes automatically using the spring task executor. The syntax of `MenuTask` class is similar to the Java thread operation.

```
// MenuTask.java
package com.learning.spring.batch;

public class MenuTask implements Runnable {

    public void run() {
        try {
            MenuGenerator menuGenerator = new MenuGenerator();
            menuGenerator.generateMenu();
        } catch (Exception ex){
            ex.printStackTrace();
        }
    }
}
```

Here, reuse the `MenuGenerator` class created in Example-1

Step 2: Create a spring application context file

There are two ways a task executor can be configured in a spring application context file.

CASE 1: Using the spring `<bean>` tag

The following XML element is used to execute the `run(...)` method of the `MenuTask` class.

```
<bean id="taskExecutor" class="org.springframework.scheduling.concurrent.
                            ThreadPoolTaskExecutor">
    <property name="corePoolSize" value="5"/>
    <property name="maxPoolSize" value="10"/>
```

```
        <property name="queueCapacity" value="15"/>
        <property name="waitForTasksToCompleteOnShutdown" value="true"/>
</bean>
```

CASE 2: Using the spring-provided `<xmlns:task>` namespace

The following XML element is used to execute the `run(...)` method of the `MenuTask` class.

```
<task:executor id="taskExecutor1" pool-size="5-25"
                queue-capacity="100"/>
```

The complete XML is provided below and is named the "spring-task-executor.xml"

```
<?xml version="1.0" encoding="UTF-8"?>
<beans xmlns="http://www.springframework.org/schema/beans"
    xmlns:xsi="http://www.w3.org/2001/XMLSchema-instance"
    xmlns:context="http://www.springframework.org/schema/context"
    xmlns:task="http://www.springframework.org/schema/task"
    xsi:schemaLocation="http://www.springframework.org/schema/beans
    http://www.springframework.org/schema/beans/spring-beans-3.0.xsd
    http://www.springframework.org/schema/context
    http://www.springframework.org/schema/context/spring-context-3.0.xsd
    http://www.springframework.org/schema/task
    http://www.springframework.org/schema/task/spring-task-3.0.xsd">

    <context:component-scan base-package="com.learning.spring.batch"/>

    <bean id="taskExecutor" class=
            "org.springframework.scheduling.concurrent.
                ThreadPoolTaskExecutor">
        <property name="corePoolSize" value="5"/>
        <property name="maxPoolSize" value="10"/>
        <property name="queueCapacity" value="15"/>
        <property name="waitForTasksToCompleteOnShutdown"
                value="true"/>
    </bean>

    <!-- OR use the below given namespace configuration -->
    <task:executor id="taskExecutor1" pool-size="5-25"
                queue-capacity="100"/>

</beans>
```

Step 3: Write a Java class to run the scheduled operation.

The following `TestTaskExecutor` class can be used to execute the `run()` method of the `MenuTask` class. Listing 9-3 provides the complete class code.

Listing 9-3: Test class used to execute the task

```
// TestTaskExecutor.java
package com.learning.spring.batch;

import org.springframework.context.support.
        ClassPathXmlApplicationContext;
```

```
import org.springframework.core.task.TaskExecutor;

public class TestTaskExecutor {

    public static void main(String[] args) {
        ClassPathXmlApplicationContext context =
            new ClassPathXmlApplicationContext("spring-task-
                          executor.xml");

        TaskExecutor te = (TaskExecutor)
                          context.getBean("taskExecutor1");
        te.execute(new DisplayTime());
    }
}
```

Example 3: Spring Annotations for Batch Scheduling

The steps required to schedule-and-run a Java operation using spring-batch annotations are listed below:

1. Create a spring application context file.
2. Write a Java operation task to be scheduled.
3. Write a Java class to run the scheduled operation.

The above-specified steps are described in the following sections:

Step 1: Create a spring application context file

There are two ways the spring batch annotations can be enabled in the spring application context. The complete application context XML file is provided below and is named the "spring-batch-annotations.xml"

The following XML element is used to enable the @Service and @Async annotations.

```
<task:annotation-driven/>
```

CASE 1: Using the `<task:annotation-driven/>` element

```
<?xml version="1.0" encoding="UTF-8"?>
<beans xmlns="http://www.springframework.org/schema/beans"
    xmlns:xsi="http://www.w3.org/2001/XMLSchema-instance"
    xmlns:context="http://www.springframework.org/schema/context"
    xmlns:task="http://www.springframework.org/schema/task"
    xsi:schemaLocation="http://www.springframework.org/schema/beans
    http://www.springframework.org/schema/beans/spring-beans-3.0.xsd
    http://www.springframework.org/schema/context
    http://www.springframework.org/schema/context/spring-context-3.0.xsd
    http://www.springframework.org/schema/task
    http://www.springframework.org/schema/task/spring-task-3.0.xsd">

    <!-- CASE 1 -->
    <context:component-scan base-package="com.learning.spring.batch"/>

    <!-- Activates @Scheduled and @Async annotations for scheduling -->
```

```
<task:annotation-driven/>

<!-Don't initialize the bean here; method will be executed twice -->
<!--<bean id="batchScheduler"
        class = "com.learning.spring.batch.MenuGenerator"/>-->

</beans>
```

CASE 2: Using the `<task:executor>` and `<task:scheduler>` elements

```
<?xml version="1.0" encoding="UTF-8"?>
<beans xmlns="http://www.springframework.org/schema/beans"
    xmlns:xsi="http://www.w3.org/2001/XMLSchema-instance"
    xmlns:context="http://www.springframework.org/schema/context"
    xmlns:task="http://www.springframework.org/schema/task"
    xsi:schemaLocation="http://www.springframework.org/schema/beans
    http://www.springframework.org/schema/beans/spring-beans-3.0.xsd
    http://www.springframework.org/schema/context
    http://www.springframework.org/schema/context/spring-context-3.0.xsd
    http://www.springframework.org/schema/task
    http://www.springframework.org/schema/task/spring-task-3.0.xsd">

    <!-- CASE 2 -->
    <context:component-scan base-package="com.learning.spring.batch"/>

    <task:annotation-driven executor="taskExecutor"
                            scheduler="batchScheduler"/>

    <task:executor id="taskExecutor"
                pool-size="5"
                queue-capacity="100"/>

    <task:scheduler id="batchScheduler" pool-size="5"/>

</beans>
```

Step 2: Write a Java operation-task to be executed

In this example, the class operations are annotated with the `@Service` and `@Async` annotations. The spring executor executes the tasks annotated with the `@Async` annotation; the scheduler reference executes the operations annotated with the `@Service` annotation.

The `AsyncMenuService` class is used to execute the task operation asynchronously, as seen below.

```
// AsyncMenuService.java
package com.learning.spring.batch;

import org.springframework.stereotype.Service;
import org.springframework.beans.factory.annotation.Autowired;

@Service
public class AsyncMenuService {

    @Autowired
```

```
        private AsyncMenuGenerator asyncMenuGenerator;

        public void generateMenu() throws Exception {
            System.out.println("--- Menu generation started ---");
            asyncMenuGenerator.generateMenu();
            System.out.println("--- Menu generation will complete after 20
                                seconds ---");
        }
}
```

The following method is scheduled to execute periodically with the specified time interval.

```
public void printTodaysDate() throws Exception {
    ...
}
```

The following task is executed using @Async annotation.

```
public void generateMenu() throws Exception {
    ...
}
```

Listing 9-4 provides the complete class code. The printTodaysDate() method is annotated with the @Schedule annotation and the generateMenu() method is annotated with the @Async annotation.

Listing 9-4: Operations using spring batch annotations.

```
// AsyncMenuGenerator.java
package com.learning.spring.batch;

import org.springframework.scheduling.annotation.Async;
import org.springframework.scheduling.annotation.Scheduled;
import org.springframework.stereotype.Component;

import java.util.*;
import java.io.*;

@Component
public class AsyncMenuGenerator {

    private static int i = 0;

    public AsyncMenuGenerator() {
    }

    @Scheduled(fixedRate = 3000)
    public void printTodaysDate() throws Exception {
        System.out.println("--- Inside Schedule ---" + new Date());
    }

    @Async
    public void generateMenu() throws Exception {
        System.out.println("--- Inside Async ---");
        List<FoodItemDVO> menuCategoryList =  new
                        ArrayList<FoodItemDVO>();
```

```java
        FoodItemDVO foodItemDVO = new FoodItemDVO();
        foodItemDVO.setCountry("GB");
        foodItemDVO.setId("100");
        foodItemDVO.setName("Traditional English Breakfast");
        foodItemDVO.setPrice("6.99");
        foodItemDVO.setCategory("Breakfast");
        foodItemDVO.setDescription("2 Fried eggs, 1 English pork
                    sausage, 1 Back Bacon");
        menuCategoryList.add(foodItemDVO);

        foodItemDVO = new FoodItemDVO();
        foodItemDVO.setCountry("USA");
        foodItemDVO.setId("101");
        foodItemDVO.setName("Jelly Doughnut");
        foodItemDVO.setPrice("0.85");
        foodItemDVO.setCategory("Appetizer");
        foodItemDVO.setDescription("Deep fried pastry covered in suger,
                and filled with strawberry jelly.");
        menuCategoryList.add(foodItemDVO);

        writeToTextFile(menuCategoryList);
        System.out.println("--------- Completed --------");
    }

    private void writeToTextFile(List<FoodItemDVO> menuCategoryList)
        throws Exception {
        // Sleep for 20 seconds; to test asynchronous scenario.
        Thread.sleep(20000);
        i = i + 1;
        String fileName = "foodItemMenu"+ i +".txt";
        BufferedWriter bufferedWriter = new BufferedWriter(new
                java.io.FileWriter("C:/files/" + fileName));

        for(FoodItemDVO foodItemDVO : menuCategoryList) {
            bufferedWriter.write("Category:" +
                                    foodItemDVO.getCategory());
            bufferedWriter.newLine();
            bufferedWriter.write("Name:" + foodItemDVO.getName() + " -
                                    Price: " +
            foodItemDVO.getPrice() + " -Currency: " +
                                    foodItemDVO.getCountry());
            bufferedWriter.newLine();
            bufferedWriter.write("Description: " +
                                    foodItemDVO.getDescription());
            bufferedWriter.newLine();
            bufferedWriter.write("-------------------------");
            bufferedWriter.newLine();
        }

        bufferedWriter.flush();
        bufferedWriter.close();
    }
}
```

Step 3: Write a Java class to run the scheduled operation.

The following `TestAnnotationsBatchScheduler` class runs the schedulec operation with the specified time interval. This class also executes the `generateMenu()` operation asynchronously.

Listing 9-5 provides the complete class code to test the spring batch operations.

Listing 9-5: Test class used to run the scheduled operation and task.

```java
// TestAnnotationsBatchScheduler.java
package com.learning.spring.batch;

import org.springframework.context.support.
            ClassPathXmlApplicationContext;

public class TestAnnotationsBatchScheduler {

    public static void main(String args[]) {
        try {
            ClassPathXmlApplicationContext context =
                new ClassPathXmlApplicationContext("spring-batch-
                                    annotations.xml");

            AsyncMenuService asyncMenuService = (AsyncMenuService)
                context.getBean("asyncMenuService");
            asyncMenuService.generateMenu();

        } catch (Exception ex) {
            ex.printStackTrace();
        }
    }
}
```

Example 4: Spring Integration with Quartz Scheduler

This example illustrates spring integration with the Quartz batch scheduler. The steps required to schedule a Java operation using this approach are listed below.

1. Create a spring application context file.
2. Write a Java operation to be scheduled periodically
3. Write a Java class to test the scheduled operation.

The above-specified steps are described in the following sections:

Step 1: Create a spring application context file

The following two approaches can be used to integrate spring with Quartz. The complete spring application context XML file is provided below and is named the "spring-quartz-scheduler.xml"

CASE 1: Schedule an operation using the `SchedulerFactoryBean` class.

```xml
<?xml version="1.0" encoding="UTF-8"?>
<beans xmlns="http://www.springframework.org/schema/beans"
    xmlns:xsi="http://www.w3.org/2001/XMLSchema-instance"
    xmlns:context="http://www.springframework.org/schema/context"
    xmlns:task="http://www.springframework.org/schema/task"
```

```xml
xsi:schemaLocation="http://www.springframework.org/schema/beans
http://www.springframework.org/schema/beans/spring-beans-3.0.xsd
http://www.springframework.org/schema/context
http://www.springframework.org/schema/context/spring-context-3.0.xsd
http://www.springframework.org/schema/task
http://www.springframework.org/schema/task/spring-task-3.0.xsd">

    <context:component-scan base-package="com.learning.spring.batch"/>

    <!-- CASE 1 -->
    <bean name="quartzBatchJob" class="org.springframework.scheduling.
                          quartz.JobDetailBean">
        <property name="jobClass"
                value="com.learning.spring.batch.QuartzBatchJob"/>
            <property name="jobDataAsMap">
                <map>
                    <entry key="timeout" value="5"/>
                    <entry key="menuGenerator"
                            value-ref="menuGenerator"/>
                </map>
        </property>
    </bean>

    <bean id="cronTrigger" class="org.springframework.scheduling.
                          quartz.CronTriggerBean">
        <property name="jobDetail" ref="quartzBatchJob"/>
        <!-- run this job every 5 seconds -->
        <property name="cronExpression" value="*/5 * * * * ?"/>
    </bean>

    <bean class="org.springframework.scheduling.
                      quartz.SchedulerFactoryBean">
        <property name="triggers">
            <list>
                <ref bean="cronTrigger"/>
            </list>
        </property>
    </bean>
</beans>
```

CASE 2: Schedule an operation using the `MethodInvokingJobDetailFactoryBean` class.

```xml
<?xml version="1.0" encoding="UTF-8"?>
<beans xmlns="http://www.springframework.org/schema/beans"
    xmlns:xsi="http://www.w3.org/2001/XMLSchema-instance"
    xmlns:context="http://www.springframework.org/schema/context"
    xmlns:task="http://www.springframework.org/schema/task"
    xsi:schemaLocation="http://www.springframework.org/schema/beans
    http://www.springframework.org/schema/beans/spring-beans-3.0.xsd
    http://www.springframework.org/schema/context
    http://www.springframework.org/schema/context/spring-context-3.0.xsd
    http://www.springframework.org/schema/task
    http://www.springframework.org/schema/task/spring-task-3.0.xsd">

    <context:component-scan base-package="com.learning.spring.batch"/>
```

```
<!-- CASE 2 -->
<bean id="menuGenerator"
    class="com.learning.spring.batch.MenuGenerator"/>
<bean id="quartzBatchJob" class="org.springframework.scheduling.
                quartz.MethodInvokingJobDetailFactoryBean">
    <property name="targetObject" ref="menuGenerator"/>
    <property name="targetMethod" value="generateMenu"/>
    <property name="concurrent" value="false"/>
</bean>

<bean id="simpleTrigger" class="org.springframework.scheduling.
                    quartz.SimpleTriggerBean">
    <property name="jobDetail" ref="quartzBatchJob"/>
    <property name="startDelay" value="5000"/>
    <property name="repeatInterval" value="10000" />
</bean>

<bean class="org.springframework.scheduling.
                quartz.SchedulerFactoryBean">
    <property name="triggers">
        <list>
            <ref bean="simpleTrigger"/>
        </list>
    </property>
</bean>
</beans>
```

The following XML configuration can be used to configure the multiple trigger operations.

```
<bean class="org.springframework.scheduling.quartz.SchedulerFactoryBean">
    <property name="triggers">
        <list>
            <ref bean="cronTrigger"/>
            <ref bean="simpleTrigger"/>
        </list>
    </property>
</bean>
```

Step 2: Write a Java operation to be scheduled periodically.

Here, reuse the `MenuGenerator` class created in Example-1

```
@Component
public class MenuGenerator {
    ...
}
```

Step 3: Write a Java class to test the scheduled operation.

The following `TestQuartzScheduler` class runs the scheduled operation with the specified time interval. Listing 9-6 provides the complete class code to test the scheduled operation.

Listing 9-6: Test class used to run the scheduled operation.

```
// TestQuartzScheduler.java
package com.learning.spring.batch;
```

```
import org.springframework.context.support.
            ClassPathXmlApplicationContext;

public class TestQuartzScheduler {

    public static void main(String args[]) {
        try {
            ClassPathXmlApplicationContext context =
                new ClassPathXmlApplicationContext(
                    "spring-quartz-scheduler.xml");
        } catch (Exception ex) {
            ex.printStackTrace();
        }
    }
}
```

Example 5: Spring Integration with JDK Timer Scheduler

This example illustrates spring integration with the JDK timer batch scheduler. The steps required to schedule a Java operation using this approach are listed below.

1. Create a spring application context file.
2. Write a Java operation to be scheduled periodically
3. Write a Java class to test the scheduled operation.

The above-specified steps are described in the following sections:

Step 1: Create a spring application context file.

The complete application context xml file is provided below and is named the "spring-quartz-scheduler.xml"

```
<?xml version="1.0" encoding="UTF-8"?>
<beans xmlns="http://www.springframework.org/schema/beans"
    xmlns:xsi="http://www.w3.org/2001/XMLSchema-instance"
    xmlns:context="http://www.springframework.org/schema/context"
    xmlns:task="http://www.springframework.org/schema/task"
    xsi:schemaLocation="http://www.springframework.org/schema/beans
    http://www.springframework.org/schema/beans/spring-beans-3.0.xsd
    http://www.springframework.org/schema/context
    http://www.springframework.org/schema/context/spring-context-3.0.xsd
    http://www.springframework.org/schema/task
    http://www.springframework.org/schema/task/spring-task-3.0.xsd">

    <context:component-scan base-package="com.learning.spring.batch"/>

    <bean id="jdkMenuGenerator"
        class="com.learning.spring.batch.JDKMenuGenerator"/>

    <bean id="scheduledTask" class="org.springframework.scheduling.
                    timer.ScheduledTimerTask">
        <property name="delay" value="5000"/>
        <property name="period" value="12000"/>
        <!-- Executed only once -->
```

```
            <!--<property name="period" value="0"/>-->
            <property name="timerTask" ref="jdkMenuGenerator"/>
        </bean>

        <bean id="timerFactory" class="org.springframework.scheduling.
                              timer.TimerFactoryBean">
            <property name="scheduledTimerTasks">
                <list>
                    <ref bean="scheduledTask"/>
                </list>
            </property>
        </bean>
</beans>
```

Step 2: Write a Java operation to be scheduled periodically.

Here, reuse the `MenuGenerator` class created in Example-1. The `JDKMenuGenerator` class must extend the `java.util.TimerTask` class. Listing 9-7 provides the complete class code.

Listing 9-7: Schedule an operation using JDK timer scheduler.

```java
// JDKMenuGenerator.java
package com.learning.spring.batch;

import org.springframework.stereotype.Component;
import org.springframework.beans.factory.annotation.Autowired;

import java.util.TimerTask;

@Component
public class JDKMenuGenerator extends TimerTask {

    @Autowired
    private MenuGenerator menuGenerator;

    public void run() {
        try {
            menuGenerator.generateMenu();
        } catch (Exception ex) {
            ex.printStackTrace();
        }
    }

    public void setMenuGenerator(MenuGenerator menuGenerator) {
        this.menuGenerator = menuGenerator;
    }
}
```

Step 3: Write a Java class to test the scheduled operation.

The following `TestJDKTimerScheduler` class runs the scheduled operation with the specified time interval. Listing 9-8 provides the complete class code.

Listing 9-8: Test class used to run the scheduled operation.

```java
// TestJDKTimerScheduler.java
```

```
package com.learning.spring.batch;

import org.springframework.context.support.
            ClassPathXmlApplicationContext;

public class TestJDKTimerScheduler {

    public static void main(String args[]) {
        try {
            ClassPathXmlApplicationContext context =
                    new ClassPathXmlApplicationContext(
                        "spring-jdk-scheduler.xml");
        } catch (Exception ex) {
            ex.printStackTrace();
        }
    }
}
```

Spring Batch Integration Framework

The spring batch integration framework can be used for application-to-application data integration. This framework provides utilities for reading, transforming and writing large volumes of data. This framework is suitable for implementing the data batch processing. Spring batch integration supports several input-and-output data formats, such as, flat files, XML files, JSON data, databases, and so forth. The steps required for data integration are listed below.

- Read the data from the source file.
- Apply transformation-and-filtering logic.
- Write data to an output file.

The following list of JAR files is required to run the spring batch integration demo examples.

- org.springframework.batch.core-2.0.0.RELEASE.jar
- org.springframework.batch.infrastructure-2.0.0.RELEASE.jar
- org.springframework.batch.test-2.0.0.RELEASE.jar
- spring-batch-test-2.1.7.RELEASE.jar
- commons-lang.jar

Demo Examples

Example 6: Reading Data from Text Files

The spring batch integration framework can be used to read data from text files. The steps required to read data from files are given below.

1. Identify the input file.
2. Create a spring application context file.
3. Write a Java class to read the data.

The above-specified steps are described in the following sections:

Step 1: Identify the input file.

The following input file is used for reading and is named the "inputdatafeed.txt'

```
ACCT....1234562012,3.625,100000,William Wen,687,Approved
ACCT....1234562011,5.500,200000,John Smith,700,Approved
ACCT....1234562010,3.625,100000,John Sims,626,Approved
ACCT....2121562012,3.625,300000,Wong Lee,777,pending
ACCT....2114562012,3.625,100000,Fung Suk,762,Approved
ACCT....1234562015,2.625,400000,Kristina patridge,800,Approved
ACCT....1234562016,2.625,600000,Jessika Adams,762,pending
```

Create a suitable Java object to hold the above-specified account information. This domain object represents the data for each record.

```java
// Account.java
package com.learning.spring.batch.core;

public class Account {

    private String accountNumber;
    private float rate;
    private String principal;
    private String name;
    private Integer ceditScore;
    private String status;

    // Add getters and setters
}
```

Step 2: Create a spring application context file

The following XML element reads the data from the input file.

```xml
<bean id="fileItemReader" class="org.springframework.batch.item.
                                 file.FlatFileItemReader">
    ...
</bean>
```

The following XML element reads the data from each record. This is used for reading the delimiter separated column data.

```xml
<bean id="accountLineTokenizer"
    class="org.springframework.batch.item.file.
            transform.DelimitedLineTokenizer">
    ...
</bean>
```

The following XML configuration maps the data retrieved from each record to the domain object.

```xml
<bean id="account" class="com.learning.spring.batch.core.Account"
                    scope="prototype"/>
```

```
<bean id="accountFieldSetMapper"
        class="org.springframework.batch.item.file.
                mapping.BeanWrapperFieldSetMapper">
    ...
</bean>
```

The complete application context XML file is provided below and is named the "spring-batch-data-reader.xml"

```
<?xml version="1.0" encoding="UTF-8"?>
<beans xmlns="http://www.springframework.org/schema/beans"
    xmlns:xsi="http://www.w3.org/2001/XMLSchema-instance"
    xmlns:context="http://www.springframework.org/schema/context"
    xsi:schemaLocation="http://www.springframework.org/schema/beans
    http://www.springframework.org/schema/beans/spring-beans-3.0.xsd
    http://www.springframework.org/schema/context
    http://www.springframework.org/schema/context/spring-context-
                3.0.xsd">

    <context:component-scan base-package=
                "com.learning.spring.batch.core"/>

    <bean id="fileItemReader" class="org.springframework.batch.item.
                                file.FlatFileItemReader">
        <property name="resource" value="classpath:inputdatafeed.txt"/>
        <property name="recordSeparatorPolicy"
                ref="recordSeparatorPolicy"/>
        <property name="lineMapper" ref="accountLineMapper"/>
    </bean>

    <bean id="recordSeparatorPolicy"
        class="org.springframework.batch.item.file.
                separator.DefaultRecordSeparatorPolicy"/>

    <bean id="accountLineMapper" class="org.springframework.batch.item.
                                file.mapping.DefaultLineMapper">
        <property name="lineTokenizer" ref="accountLineTokenizer"/>
        <property name="fieldSetMapper" ref="accountFieldSetMapper"/>
    </bean>

    <bean id="accountLineTokenizer"
        class="org.springframework.batch.item.
                    file.transform.DelimitedLineTokenizer">
        <property name="delimiter" value=","/>
        <property name="names" value=
            "accountNumber,rate,principal,name,ceditScore,status"/>
    </bean>

    <bean id="account" class="com.learning.spring.batch.core.Account"
                    scope="prototype"/>

    <bean id="accountFieldSetMapper"
        class="org.springframework.batch.item.file.
                mapping.BeanWrapperFieldSetMapper">
        <property name="prototypeBeanName" value="account"/>
    </bean>
```

```
</beans>
```

Step 3: Write a Java class to read the data

The following `TestSpringBatchDataReader` class reads the data from the "inputdatafeed.txt" file. Listing 9-9 provides the complete class code.

Listing 9-9: Reading data from text file

```java
// TestSpringBatchDataReader.java
package com.learning.spring.batch.core;

import org.springframework.context.support.
            ClassPathXmlApplicationContext;
import org.springframework.batch.item.file.FlatFileItemReader;
import org.springframework.batch.item.ExecutionContext;
import com.learning.spring.batch.Product;

public class TestSpringBatchDataReader {

    public static void main(String args[]) {
        try {
            ClassPathXmlApplicationContext context =
                    new ClassPathXmlApplicationContext
                    ("spring-batch-data-reader.xml");
            FlatFileItemReader reader = (FlatFileItemReader)
                        context.getBean("fileItemReader");

            reader.open(new ExecutionContext());
            for (int i = 0; i < 7; i++) {
                i = i++;
                Account account = (Account) reader.read();
                System.out.println("---- Acct Num ----" +
                        account.getAccountNumber() +
                        "--- name ---" + account.getName());
            }
            reader.close();

        } catch (Exception ex) {
            ex.printStackTrace();
        }
    }
}
```

The output of the above program is given below.

```
---- Acct Num ----ACCT....1234562012--- name ---William Wen
---- Acct Num ----ACCT....1234562011--- name ---John Smith
---- Acct Num ----ACCT....1234562010--- name ---John Sims
---- Acct Num ----ACCT....2121562012--- name ---Wong Lee
---- Acct Num ----ACCT....2114562012--- name ---Fung Suk
---- Acct Num ----ACCT....1234562015--- name ---Kristina patridge
---- Acct Num ----ACCT....1234562016--- name ---Jessika Adams
```

Example 7: Writing Data into Text Files

The spring batch integration framework can be used for data writing operations. The steps required to write data to a flat file are given below.

1. Create a spring application context file.
2. Write a Java class to write the data.

The above-specified steps are described in the following sections:

Step 1: Create a spring application context file.

The following XML element is used for data writing operations.

```
<bean id="fileItemWriter" class=
            "org.springframework.batch.item.file.FlatFileItemWriter">
    ...
</bean>
```

The complete application context XML file is provided below and is named the "spring-batch-write-data.xml"

```
<?xml version="1.0" encoding="UTF-8"?>
<beans xmlns="http://www.springframework.org/schema/beans"
    xmlns:xsi="http://www.w3.org/2001/XMLSchema-instance"
    xmlns:context="http://www.springframework.org/schema/context"
    xmlns:task="http://www.springframework.org/schema/task"
    xsi:schemaLocation="http://www.springframework.org/schema/beans
    http://www.springframework.org/schema/beans/spring-beans-3.0.xsd
    http://www.springframework.org/schema/context
    http://www.springframework.org/schema/context/spring-context-3.0.xsd
    http://www.springframework.org/schema/task
    http://www.springframework.org/schema/task/spring-task-3.0.xsd">

    <context:component-scan
            base-package="com.learning.spring.batch.core"/>

    <bean id="fileItemWriter" class=
            "org.springframework.batch.item.file.FlatFileItemWriter">
        <property name="resource" value=
                "file:c:/files/outputdata.txt"/>
        <property name="lineAggregator">
            <bean class="org.springframework.batch.item.file.
                            transform.DelimitedLineAggregator">
                <property name="delimiter" value="|"/>
                <property name="fieldExtractor">
                    <bean class="com.learning.spring.batch.
                            core.AccountFieldExtractor"/>
                </property>
            </bean>
        </property>
    </bean>
</beans>
```

Step 2: Write a Java class to write the data.

The following `AccountFieldExtractor` class transforms the data before saving it into a file. In this example, a new rate has been added to each record.

```java
// AccountFieldExtractor.java
package com.learning.spring.batch.core;

import org.springframework.batch.item.file.transform.FieldExtractor;
import java.text.DecimalFormat;

public class AccountFieldExtractor implements FieldExtractor<Account> {
    public Object[] extract(Account account) {
        return new Object[] {
            "START",
            account.getAccountNumber(),
            account.getRate(),
            new DecimalFormat("#.###").format(
                        (account.getRate() + 0.125)),
            account.getPrincipal(),
            account.getName(),
            account.getCeditScore(),
            account.getStatus(),
            "END"};
    }
}
```

The following `TestSpringBatchDataWriter` class writes data to a file. Listing 9-10 provides the complete class code.

Listing 9-10: Writing data to a text

```java
// TestSpringBatchDataWriter.java
package com.learning.spring.batch.core;

import org.springframework.context.support.
            ClassPathXmlApplicationContext;
import org.springframework.batch.item.file.FlatFileItemWriter;
import org.springframework.batch.item.ExecutionContext;

import java.util.*;

public class TestSpringBatchDataWriter {

    public static void main(String args[]) {
        try {
            ClassPathXmlApplicationContext context =
                new ClassPathXmlApplicationContext(
                        "spring-batch-data-writer.xml");
            FlatFileItemWriter writer = (FlatFileItemWriter)
                context.getBean("fileItemWriter");
            writer.open(new ExecutionContext());

            List<Account> accountList = new ArrayList<Account>();
            Account account = new Account();
            account.setAccountNumber("12344451998");
            account.setRate(3.625f);
            account.setPrincipal("100000");
            account.setName("Krisan");
```

```
            account.setCeditScore(785);
            account.setStatus("Approve");
            accountList.add(account);

            account = new Account();
            account.setAccountNumber("112133212001");
            account.setRate(6.625f);
            account.setPrincipal("800000");
            account.setName("Philips");
            account.setCeditScore(785);
            account.setStatus("Decline");
            accountList.add(account);

            // Writing data to a file
            writer.write(accountList);

        } catch (Exception ex) {
            ex.printStackTrace();
        }
    }
}
```

The output of the above program is provided below.

```
START|12344451998|3.625|3.75|100000|Krisan|785|Approve|END
START|112133212001|6.625|6.75|800000|Philips|785|Decline|END
```

Example 8: Spring Batch File Integration — Reading, Transforming, and Writing

This example illustrates batch file integration. The following three components are used for reading, transforming and writing.

- `FlatFileItemReader` → reads data from input file.
- `ItemProcessor` → used for transformation and filtering.
- `FlatFileItemWriter` → writes data to an output file.

Business Scenario:

Read the data from the input file; filter out accounts that have the "pending" account status before writing the data to an output file.

Input data: Here, reuse the input data provided in Example-6.

Output data: The output is provided below; it has no "pending" accounts.

```
START|ACCT....1234562012|3.625|3.75|100000|William Wen|687|Approved|END
START|ACCT....1234562011|5.5|5.625|200000|John Smith|700|Approved|END
START|ACCT....1234562010|3.625|3.75|100000|John Sims|626|Approved|END
START|ACCT....2114562012|3.625|3.75|100000|Fung Suk|762|Approved|END
START|ACCT....1234562015|2.625|2.75|400000|Kristina
patridge|800|Approved|END
```

The above-specified business scenario is illustrated in this example. The implementation steps are provided below.

1. Create a spring application context file.
2. Write a test java class.

Step 1: Create a spring application context file.

The following XML element is the entry point for the job execution.

```
<batch:job id="readWriteJob" job-repository="jobRepository">
    ...
</batch:job>
```

The following `jobLauncher` element is used to run the batch job.

```
<bean id="jobLauncher" class="org.springframework.batch.core.
                            launch.support.SimpleJobLauncher">
    ...
</bean>
```

The following `FilterAccountsItemProcessor` class applies the filtering-and-transformation logic.

```
<bean id="processor" class="com.learning.spring.batch.core.
                        FilterAccountsItemProcessor"/>
```

The complete application context XML file is provided below and is named the "spring-batch-data-integrator.xml"

```
<?xml version="1.0" encoding="UTF-8"?>
<beans xmlns="http://www.springframework.org/schema/beans"
    xmlns:xsi="http://www.w3.org/2001/XMLSchema-instance"
    xmlns:context="http://www.springframework.org/schema/context"
    xmlns:batch="http://www.springframework.org/schema/batch"
    xsi:schemaLocation="http://www.springframework.org/schema/beans
    http://www.springframework.org/schema/beans/spring-beans-3.0.xsd
    http://www.springframework.org/schema/context
    http://www.springframework.org/schema/context/spring-context-3.0.xsd
    http://www.springframework.org/schema/batch
    http://www.springframework.org/schema/batch/spring-batch-2.0.xsd">

    <context:component-scan base-package=
                        "com.learning.spring.batch.core"/>

    <!-- Job entry point-->
    <batch:job id="readWriteJob" job-repository="jobRepository">
        <batch:step id="readWriteStep">
            <batch:tasklet>
                <batch:chunk reader="fileItemReader"
                            processor="processor"
                            writer="fileItemWriter"
                            commit-interval="10"/>
            </batch:tasklet>
```

```xml
            </batch:step>
    </batch:job>

    <!-- Using in memory repositoy -->
    <bean id="jobRepository" class="org.springframework.batch.core.
                repository.support.MapJobRepositoryFactoryBean">
        <property name="transactionManager" ref="transactionManager" />
    </bean>

    <bean id="transactionManager" class="org.springframework.batch.
                support.transaction.ResourcelessTransactionManager">
    </bean>

    <!-- Launches a batch process -->
    <bean id="jobLauncher" class="org.springframework.batch.core.
                            launch.support.SimpleJobLauncher">
        <property name="jobRepository" ref="jobRepository" />
    </bean>

    <!-- Peocessor used to apply the filtering logic -->
    <bean id="processor" class="com.learning.spring.batch.core.
                        FilterAccountsItemProcessor"/>

    <!-- Writes the data to the output file -->
    <bean id="fileItemWriter" class="org.springframework.batch.item.
                    file.FlatFileItemWriter">
        <property name="resource"
                value="file:c:/jars/files/outputdata.txt"/>
        <property name="lineAggregator">
            <bean class="org.springframework.batch.item.file.
                        transform.DelimitedLineAggregator">
                <property name="delimiter" value="|"/>
                <property name="fieldExtractor">
                    <bean class="com.learning.spring.batch.core.
                                AccountFieldExtractor"/>
                </property>
            </bean>
        </property>
    </bean>

    <!-- Reads data from the input file -->
    <bean id="fileItemReader" class="org.springframework.batch.item.
                        file.FlatFileItemReader">
        <property name="resource" value="classpath:inputdatafeed.txt"/>
        <property name="recordSeparatorPolicy"
                ref="recordSeparatorPolicy"/>
        <property name="lineMapper" ref="accountLineMapper"/>
    </bean>

    <bean id="recordSeparatorPolicy" class="org.springframework.
            batch.item.file.separator.DefaultRecordSeparatorPolicy"/>

    <bean id="accountLineMapper" class="org.springframework.batch.
                    item.file.mapping.DefaultLineMapper">
        <property name="lineTokenizer" ref="accountLineTokenizer"/>
        <property name="fieldSetMapper" ref="accountFieldSetMapper"/>
    </bean>
```

```xml
<bean id="accountLineTokenizer" class="org.springframework.batch.
                          item.file.transform.DelimitedLineTokenizer">
    <property name="delimiter" value=","/>
    <property name="names" value="accountNumber,rate,
            principal,name,ceditScore,status"/>
</bean>

<bean id="account" class="com.learning.spring.batch.core.Account"
                  scope="prototype"/>

<bean id="accountFieldSetMapper" class="org.springframework.batch.
            item.file.mapping.BeanWrapperFieldSetMapper">
    <property name="prototypeBeanName" value="account"/>
</bean>

</beans>
```

The `FilterAccountsItemProcessor` class applies the filtering criteria. The "pending" status accounts are not included in output file.

```java
// FilterAccountsItemProcessor.java
package com.learning.spring.batch.core;

import org.springframework.batch.item.ItemProcessor;
public class FilterAccountsItemProcessor implements
                    ItemProcessor<Account, Account> {
    @Override
    public Account process(Account account) throws Exception {
        String status = account.getStatus();
        if(status != null && "pending".equalsIgnoreCase(status)) {
            return null;
        }
        return account;
    }
}
```

Step 2: Write a test Java class.

The following `TestSpringBatchDataIntegrator` class runs the configured batch job. This program reads the data from the "inputdatafeed.txt" file, filters out the pending status records, and writes data to an output file. Listing 9-11 provides the complete class code.

Listing 9-11: Reading-filtering-writing to an output file.

```java
// TestSpringBatchDataIntegrator.java
package com.learning.spring.batch.core;

import org.springframework.context.support.
            ClassPathXmlApplicationContext;
import org.springframework.batch.core.launch.support.SimpleJobLauncher;
import org.springframework.batch.core.Job;
import org.springframework.batch.core.JobParameters;
import org.springframework.util.StopWatch;

public class TestSpringBatchDataIntegrator {
```

```
public static void main(String args[]) {
    try {
        ClassPathXmlApplicationContext context =
            new ClassPathXmlApplicationContext(
                "spring-batch-data-integrator.xml");
        SimpleJobLauncher jobLauncher = (SimpleJobLauncher)
                    context.getBean("jobLauncher");
        Job readWriteJob = (Job) context.getBean("readWriteJob");
        JobParameters jobParameters = new JobParameters();

        StopWatch sw = new StopWatch();
        sw.start();
        jobLauncher.run(readWriteJob, jobParameters);
        sw.stop();
        System.out.println("--- Time taken---" + sw.prettyPrint());

    } catch (Exception ex) {
        ex.printStackTrace();
    }
}
}
```

Note: Spring batch integration supports several input-and-output data formats, such as, flat files, xml files, JSON data, databases, and so forth. Only flat file integration is discussed in this chapter.

Summary

Figure 9-1 Spring batch summary

Figure 9-1 summarizes the most important points described in this chapter.

This section summarizes the features provided in the spring batch framework.

- The spring-provided `<xml:task>` namespace can be used for configuring batch scheduling and task execution.
- The spring-provided `@Scheduled` annotation can be used to schedule an operation periodically with the specified time interval.
- The spring-provided `@Async` annotation can be used for asynchronous task execution
- The `<task:annotation-driven/>` XML element is used to enable the `@Service` and `@Async` annotations.
- Spring batch can be used with other batch scheduling frameworks, such as, Quartz and JDK timer scheduler.
- The spring batch integration framework provides utilities for reading, transforming, and writing large volumes of data.

Chapter 10. Spring-Remoting

There are several open-source frameworks available for sharing business functionality across applications in an enterprise. These frameworks expose the existing business data to remote access. One application exposes the business functionality as a service; another application consumes the service to obtain the business data. Each of these frameworks has its own architecture. The exposed service could be a plain Java class, servlet, soap-based web service, or EJB component. These frameworks provide RMI, EJB, SOAP, and HTTP-based services for application-to-application integration. The commonly used open-source Java frameworks currently available in the market for remote communication are listed below.

- Remote Method Invocation (RMI)
- Enterprise Java Beans (EJB)
- Hessian web services
- Burlap web services
- Spring-provided HTTP invoker services

Spring remoting is a framework used for developing, integrating, and accessing remote applications using the above-listed frameworks. The spring remoting framework encapsulates the details of these frameworks and provides a high-level API for remote communication. Spring remoting simplifies the application-to-application integration. There is no hard and fast rule regarding which framework should be used in your application; it totally depends on the application's requirement, the developer's comfort, and their prior experience with it. It is mandatory that the user understand the above-listed frameworks before attempting implementation.

Figure 10-1: Overview of the spring remoting architecture

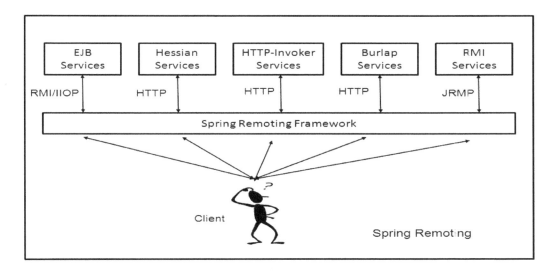

Figure 10-1 shows a high-level view of the spring remoting framework. Spring remoting provides an abstraction layer for integrating with various remoting technologies.

This chapter will discuss the following topics:

- The purpose of spring remoting
- The architecture details of Hessian, EJB3, and RMI
- How to develop and access RMI services using Spring
- How to develop and access Hessian services using Spring
- How to develop HTTP-based services using spring-provided HTTP invokers
- How to develop, integrate, and access EJB components using Spring

Prerequisites/Setting Up the Environment

Spring remoting does not require environment specific configurations. Include the respective framework JARS to your "/lib" directory.

Advantages of Spring Remoting

This section illustrates the technical and non-technical benefits of the spring remoting framework.

- The spring remoting framework provides an abstraction layer for various integration technologies. The client can transparently switch from one to another without any difficulty.
- Spring remoting eliminates the duplication of the boiler plate code inside your application. The framework-specific configurations can be reused from the spring context files.
- Spring remoting provides support for multiple protocols such as JRMP, HTTP, IIOP, SOAP, and so forth.
- Spring remoting provides a simplified approach to expose the existing application code for remote access to other applications.

RMI Architecture

Figure 10-2: RMI architecture

RMI Architecture

The popular Java-based technologies used to enable the distributed architectures are RMI and EJB. RMI uses JRMP as its underlying protocol, and it is used for communication between two Java applications. In the case of distributed architecture, the applications communicate through a common computer network. The applications must share a common computer network to share information.

The client and server communicate with each other through a remote proxy. RMI architecture is shown in Figure 10-2.

Advantages

- RMI is a good solution if both the internal and external systems use the same distributed technology.
- It is easy to implement and maintain. High-level APIs are available for development.
- Spring provides a high-level API and hides the low level details of the RMI API. The spring provided `RmiServiceExporter` class can be used to expose a specified Java class as an RMI service endpoint.

Hessian Architecture

Hessian web services are another popular web services technology used for remote communication. Hessian uses servlet-based technology to expose Java objects as a Hessian service endpoint. Hessian clients use the HTTP protocol to communicate with the service endpoints. The Hessian web services architecture is shown in Figure 10-3.

Figure 10-3: Hessian web services architecture

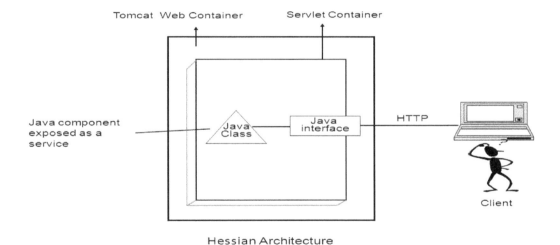

Advantages

- Hessian is a good solution if you decide to use a servlet-based web service endpoint.
- It is easy to implement and configure a Hessian service endpoint using any servlet container. Support is available from all servlet containers.
- Spring provides a high-level API and hides the low level details of the Hessian web services API. The spring-provided `HessianServiceExporter` class can be used to expose a specified Java class as a servlet-based Hessian web service endpoint.

EJB3 Architecture

Enterprise Java Bean (EJB) is a popular Java-based server side component model used for encapsulating the business functionality. To deploy and run the EJB's application server is needed. The EJB's resides inside the EJB container, and the EJB container resides inside the application server. The latest and most simplified version of the EJB is 3.0. EJB specification is part of Java EE. EJB architecture is shown in Figure 10-4.

Figure 10-4: EJB3 architecture

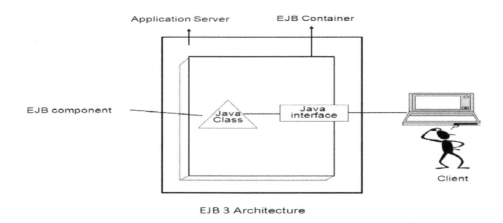

Advantages

- EJB is a very popular server side component model used for implementing the business functionality. The deployed EJB component can utilize services provided by the EJB container such as, transactions, concurrency, security, caching, and bean pooling.
- EJB3 is a simplified, annotation-based programming model; it is primarily geared toward junior and mid-level developers.
- Spring provides a high-level API to integrate the deployed EJB's into your application code. Example-4 provides the implementation details.

The following section illustrates each remoting framework with a code example.

Demo Examples

Example 1: Developing RMI Services Using Spring

Spring provides a high-level API for developing and accessing RMI-based services. The Spring-provided `RmiServiceExporter` class can be used to expose a Java class as an RMI service with a specified name. The client will use this name to invoke the service endpoint.

The steps required to implement a RMI service using Spring-API is listed below:

1. Create a service endpoint interface and its implementation class.
2. Create a server class.

---

3. Create a spring configuration file.
4. Create a client class to invoke the service endpoint methods.

The above-specified steps are described in the following sections:

Step 1: Create a service endpoint interface and its implementation class

The following StudentServiceImpl class is exposed as an RMI service.

```java
// Student.java
package com.learning.spring.rmi;

import java.io.Serializable;

public class Student implements Serializable {

    private String id;
    private String firstName;
    private String lastName;

    // Add getters and setters
}
```

The service endpoint interface definition is provided below. This interface has two methods. The method getStudentDetails() provides the student address details, and the getStudents() method provides the list of students.

```java
// StudentService.java
package com.learning.spring.rmi;

import java.rmi.Remote;
import java.rmi.RemoteException;
import java.util.List;

public interface StudentService {

    public String getStudentDetails(int id);

    public List<Student> getStudents();
}
```

The above-declared interface methods are implemented in the following service endpoint implementation class.

```java
// StudentServiceImpl.java
package com.learning.spring.rmi;

import java.util.List;
import java.util.ArrayList;

public class StudentServiceImpl implements StudentService {

    public String getStudentDetails(int id) {
        return "3943 W.McClintock Dr, Chandler, AZ";
    }
```

```
    public List<Student> getStudents() {
        List<Student> stuList = new ArrayList<Student>();
        Student stu = new Student();
        stu.setId("1");
        stu.setFirstName("John");
        stu.setLastName("Smith");
        stuList.add(stu);

        stu = new Student();
        stu.setId("2");
        stu.setFirstName("John");
        stu.setLastName("Sims");
        stuList.add(stu);

        System.out.println("Student List....." + stuList.size());
        return stuList;
    }
}
```

Step 2: Create a server class

Listing 10-1 provides an RMI server class. This class registers the objects specified in the spring "applicationContext-rmi.xml" file with spring runtime. This server class is a standalone Java program used to service the invoking client applications. Run the following RMI server class, which is ready to accept the client requests.

Listing 10-1: RMI Server class.

```
// RMIServer.java
package com.learning.spring.rmi;

import org.springframework.context.ApplicationContext;
import org.springframework.context.support.
        ClassPathXmlApplicationContext;

public class RMIServer {

    public static void main(String args[]) {

        String[] paths = {"applicationContext-rmi.xml"};
        ApplicationContext appContext =
                    new ClassPathXmlApplicationContext(paths);

        System.out.println("------ Server started ------");
    }
}
```

Step 3: Create a spring configuration file

The required client-and-server configurations are provided below. The following XML configuration is used to configure the RMI server.

```
<bean class="org.springframework.remoting.rmi.RmiServiceExporter">
    ...
</bean>
```

The following XML configuration is used to configure RMI client.

```
<bean id="studentService"
      class="org.springframework.remoting.rmi.RmiProxyFactoryBean">
    ...
</bean>
```

The complete XML configuration file is provided below and is named the "applicationContext-rmi.xml"

```xml
<?xml version="1.0" encoding="UTF-8"?>
<beans xmlns="http://www.springframework.org/schema/beans"
    xmlns:xsi="http://www.w3.org/2001/XMLSchema-instance"
    xmlns:context="http://www.springframework.org/schema/context"
    xsi:schemaLocation="http://www.springframework.org/schema/beans
    http://www.springframework.org/schema/beans/spring-beans-3.0.xsd
    http://www.springframework.org/schema/context
    http://www.springframework.org/schema/context/
                spring-context-3.0.xsd">

    <!-- Required server configurations -->
    <bean id="studentServiceImpl" class=
            "com.learning.spring.rmi.StudentServiceImpl"/>

    <bean class="org.springframework.remoting.rmi.RmiServiceExporter">
        <property name="serviceName" value="StudentService"/>
        <property name="service" ref="studentServiceImpl"/>
        <property name="serviceInterface" value=
                    "com.learning.spring.rmi.StudentService"/>
        <!-- defaults to 1099 -->
        <property name="registryPort" value="9990"/>
    </bean>

    <!-- Required client configurations -->
    <bean id="studentService" class=
            "org.springframework.remoting.rmi.RmiProxyFactoryBean">
        <property name="serviceUrl" value=
                    "rmi://localhost:9990/StudentService"/>
        <property name="serviceInterface" value=
                    "com.learning.spring.rmi.StudentService"/>
    </bean>

    <bean id="studentClient" class="com.learning.spring.rmi.RMIClient">
        <property name="studentService" ref="studentService"/>
    </bean>
</beans>
```

Step 4: Create a client class to invoke the service endpoint methods.

Listing 10-2 provides an RMI client class. This class invokes the service endpoint operations.

Listing 10-2: RMI client class

```
// RMIClient.java
package com.learning.spring.rmi;
```

```
import org.springframework.context.ApplicationContext;
import org.springframework.context.support.
        ClassPathXmlApplicationContext;
import java.util.List;

public class RMIClient {

    private StudentService studentService;

    public static void main(String args[]) {
        String[] paths = {"applicationContext-rmi.xml"};
        ApplicationContext appContext = new
                ClassPathXmlApplicationContext(paths);

        RMIClient studentClient = (RMIClient)
                    appContext.getBean("studentClient");
        String address =
                studentClient.studentService.getStudentDetails(10);
        List<Student> students =
                studentClient.studentService.getStudents();

        System.out.println("--- Address is ---" + address);
        for(Student student : students) {
            // print student data here
            System.out.println("--- student name ---"+student.getId());
        }
    }

    public void setStudentService(StudentService studentService) {
        this.studentService = studentService;
    }
}
```

Alternatively, the following method can also be used to invoke the service endpoint operations.

```
public static void main(String args[]) {
    String[] paths = {"applicationContext-rmi.xml"};
    ApplicationContext appContext = new
            ClassPathXmlApplicationContext(paths);

    StudentService studentService1 = (StudentService)
                appContext.getBean("studentService");
    String address = studentService1.getStudentDetails(10);
    List<Student> students = studentService1.getStudents();

    System.out.println("--- Address is ---" + address);
    for (Student student : students) {
        // Print student data here
        System.out.println("--- name ---" + student.getId());
    }
}
```

Example 2: Developing Hessian Services Using Spring

Hessian provides an HTTP-based protocol for accessing remote services. Spring provides a high-level API for developing and accessing the Hessian-based services. The spring-provided `HessianServiceExporter` class can be used to expose a specified Java class as a Hessian service. The spring-MVC-provided `DispatcherServlet` routes the requests to configured service endpoints.

CASE 1: Using a "remoting-servlet.xml" file.

The steps required to implement a Hessian service using this approach are listed below:

1. Create a service endpoint interface and its implementation class.
2. Create a spring configuration file.
3. Create a web.xml file
4. Create a WAR file and deploy the WAR file in the web container.
5. Create a client class to invoke the service endpoint methods.

The above-specified steps are described in the following sections:

Step 1: Create a service endpoint interface and its implementation class.

Here, re-use the `Student`, `StudentService`, and `StudentServiceImpl` classes we created in Example-1.

Step 2: Create a spring configuration file.

Set the service class and interface to the `HessianServiceExporter` class. The registered objects are exposed as Hessian services.

```
<bean name="/StudentService"
    class="org.springframework.remoting.caucho.HessianServiceExporter">
    ...
</bean>
```

The complete XML configuration file is provided below and is named the "remoting-servlet.xml".

```
<?xml version="1.0" encoding="UTF-8"?>
<beans xmlns="http://www.springframework.org/schema/beans"
    xmlns:xsi="http://www.w3.org/2001/XMLSchema-instance"
    xmlns:context="http://www.springframework.org/schema/context"
    xsi:schemaLocation="http://www.springframework.org/schema/beans
    http://www.springframework.org/schema/beans/spring-beans-3.0.xsd
    http://www.springframework.org/schema/context
    http://www.springframework.org/schema/context/
                spring-context-3.0.xsd">

    <context:annotation-config/>

    <context:component-scan base-package =
                "com.learning.spring.controller.rmi"/>

    <bean id="studentServiceImpl" class=
                "com.learning.spring.rmi.StudentServiceImpl"/>
```

```
<bean name="/StudentService" class=
      "org.springframework.remoting.caucho.HessianServiceExporter">
      <property name="service" ref="studentServiceImpl"/>
      <property name="serviceInterface"
               value="com.learning.spring.rmi.StudentService"/>
</bean>

</beans>
```

Step 3: Create a web.xml file.

The corresponding web.xml configurations are provided below. The spring `DispatcherServlet` class is configured in a web.xml file.

```
<?xml version="1.0" encoding="UTF-8"?>
<web-app version="2.4" xmlns="http://java.sun.com/xml/ns/j2ee"
    xmlns:xsi="http://www.w3.org/2001/XMLSchema-instance"
    xsi:schemaLocation="http://java.sun.com/xml/ns/j2ee
    http://java.sun.com/xml/ns/j2ee/web-app_2_4.xsd">

    <servlet>
        <servlet-name>remoting</servlet-name>
        <servlet-class>
            org.springframework.web.servlet.DispatcherServlet
        </servlet-class>
        <load-on-startup>1</load-on-startup>
    </servlet>

    <servlet-mapping>
        <servlet-name>remoting</servlet-name>
        <url-pattern>/remoting/*</url-pattern>
    </servlet-mapping>
</web-app>
```

Step 4: Create a WAR file and deploy the WAR file in the web container.

Figure 10-5: War file structure

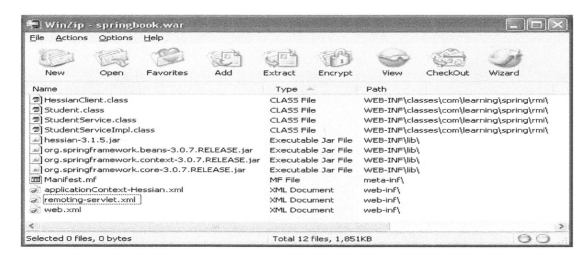

The structure of the generated WAR file is shown in Figure 10-5.

The XML file name follows the Spring-MVC-specific standard notation. The name of the xml file should be "remoting-servlet.xml". The prefix "remoting" should match the servlet-name specified in the web.xml file. The suffix must be "servlet". The prefix and suffix must be separated with a hyphen.

Step 5: Create a client class to invoke the service endpoint methods.

Listing 10-3 provides a Hessian client class. This client class invokes the service endpoint operations.

Listing 10-3: Hessian client class

```java
// HessianClient.java
package com.learning.spring.rmi;

import org.springframework.context.ApplicationContext;
import
org.springframework.context.support.ClassPathXmlApplicationContext;
import java.util.List;

public class HessianClient {

    private StudentService studentService;

    public static void main(String args[]) {
        String[] paths = {"applicationContext-Hessian.xml"};
        ApplicationContext appContext = new
            ClassPathXmlApplicationContext(paths);

        HessianClient studentClient = (HessianClient)
                appContext.getBean("hessianClient");

        // get the address
        String address =
            studentClient.studentService.getStudentDetails(10);

        // get list of students
        List<Student> students =
            studentClient.studentService.getStudents();

    }

    public void setStudentService(StudentService studentService) {
        this.studentService = studentService;
    }
}
```

The complete XML configuration file is provided below and is named the "applicationContext-Hessian.xml". The structure of the service endpoint URL is provided below.

- Host and Port → localhost:7001
- Web application context → springbook (war file name)
- URL mapping in web.xml → /remoting/*
- Bean name specified in "remoting-servlet.xml" → /StudentService

---

- The complete endpoint URL is → http://localhost:7001/springbook/remoting/StudentService

```xml
<?xml version="1.0" encoding="UTF-8"?>
<beans xmlns="http://www.springframework.org/schema/beans"
    xmlns:xsi="http://www.w3.org/2001/XMLSchema-instance"
    xmlns:context="http://www.springframework.org/schema/context"
    xsi:schemaLocation="http://www.springframework.org/schema/beans
    http://www.springframework.org/schema/beans/spring-beans-3.0.xsd
    http://www.springframework.org/schema/context
    http://www.springframework.org/schema/context/
                spring-context-3.0.xsd">

    <context:annotation-config/>
    <context:component-scan base-package="com.learning.spring.rmi"/>

    <!-- Client configurations -->
    <bean id="studentService" class=
        "org.springframework.remoting.caucho.HessianProxyFactoryBean">
        <property name="serviceUrl" value="http://localhost:7001/
                springbook/remoting/StudentService"/>
        <property name="serviceInterface" value=
                "com.learning.spring.rmi.StudentService"/>
    </bean>

    <bean id="hessianClient" class=
            "com.learning.spring.rmi.HessianClient">
        <property name="studentService" ref="studentService"/>
    </bean>
</beans>
```

CASE 2: Using an "applicationContext-Hessian.xml" file.

The following approach can also be used to develop a Hessian service. Configure the HessianServiceExporter in an "applicationContext-Hessian.xml" file. Load this xml in your root application context (/WEB-INF/applicationContext-Hessian.xml).

The complete "web.xml" configuration file is provided below.

```xml
<?xml version="1.0" encoding="UTF-8"?>
<web-app version="2.4" xmlns="http://java.sun.com/xml/ns/j2ee"
        xmlns:xsi="http://www.w3.org/2001/XMLSchema-instance"
        xsi:schemaLocation="http://java.sun.com/xml/ns/j2ee
        http://java.sun.com/xml/ns/j2ee/web-app_2_4.xsd">

    <display-name>Spring Web Application</display-name>

    <servlet>
        <servlet-name>studentExporter</servlet-name>
        <servlet-class>
            org.springframework.web.context.support.
                    HttpRequestHandlerServlet
        </servlet-class>
    </servlet>

    <servlet-mapping>
```

```xml
        <servlet-name>studentExporter</servlet-name>
        <url-pattern>/remoting/StudentService</url-pattern>
    </servlet-mapping>

    <listener>
        <listener-class>
            org.springframework.web.context.ContextLoaderListener
        </listener-class>
    </listener>

    <context-param>
        <param-name>contextConfigLocation</param-name>
        <param-value>
            /WEB-INF/applicationContext-Hessian.xml
        </param-value>
    </context-param>
</web-app>
```

The complete XML configuration file is provided below and is named the "applicationContext-Hessian.xml". This XML file contains the server-and-client specific configurations.

The <servlet-name> specified in the "web.xml" file must match the <bean> name specified in the "applicationContext-Hessian.xml" file.

```xml
<?xml version="1.0" encoding="UTF-8"?>
<beans xmlns="http://www.springframework.org/schema/beans"
    xmlns:xsi="http://www.w3.org/2001/XMLSchema-instance"
    xmlns:context="http://www.springframework.org/schema/context"
    xsi:schemaLocation="http://www.springframework.org/schema/beans
    http://www.springframework.org/schema/beans/spring-beans-3.0.xsd
    http://www.springframework.org/schema/context
    http://www.springframework.org/schema/context/
        spring-context-3.0.xsd">

    <context:annotation-config/>
    <context:component-scan base-package="com.learning.spring.rmi"/>

    <!-- Server configurations -->
    <bean id="studentServiceImpl"
        class="com.learning.spring.rmi.StudentServiceImpl"/>

    <bean name="studentExporter" class=
        "org.springframework.remoting.caucho.HessianServiceExporter">
        <property name="service" ref="studentServiceImpl"/>
        <property name="serviceInterface"
                value="com.learning.spring.rmi.StudentService"/>
    </bean>

    <!-- Client configurations -->
    <bean id="studentService" class=
        "org.springframework.remoting.caucho.HessianProxyFactoryBean">
        <property name="serviceUrl"
                value="http://localhost:7001/springbook/
                        remoting/StudentService"/>
        <property name="serviceInterface"
                value="com.learning.spring.rmi.StudentService"/>
```

```
    </bean>

    <bean id="hessianClient"
        class="com.learning.spring.rmi.HessianClient">
        <property name="studentService" ref="studentService"/>
    </bean>
</beans>
```

Follow, the steps specified in Example-2 to see the result.

Note: The Burlap services are same as the Hessian services. Replace Hessian with Burlap to implement the Burlap services.

Example 3: Developing HTTP-Invoker Services Using Spring

Spring provides HTTP-based invokers for accessing remote services and a high-level API for developing and accessing HTTP-based services. The spring-provided `HttpInvokerServiceExporter` class can be used to expose a specified Java class as an HTTP service.

The steps required to implement an HTTP-invoker service using this approach are listed below:

1. Create a service endpoint interface and its implementation class.
2. Create a spring configuration file.
3. Create a "web.xml" file
4. Create a WAR file; deploy the WAR file in the web container.
5. Create a client class to invoke the service endpoint methods.

The above-specified steps are described in the following sections:

Step 1: Create a service endpoint interface and its implementation class.

Here, re-use the `Student`, `StudentService`, and `StudentServiceImpl` classes we created in Example-1.

Step 2: Create a spring configuration file.

The complete XML configuration file is provided below and is named the "applicationContext-httpinvoker.xml". This XML file contains the server and client specific bean configurations.

The <servlet-name> specified in the "web.xml" file must match the <bean> name specified in the "applicationContext-httpinvoker.xml" file.

```
<?xml version="1.0" encoding="UTF-8"?>
<beans xmlns="http://www.springframework.org/schema/beans"
    xmlns:xsi="http://www.w3.org/2001/XMLSchema-instance"
    xmlns:context="http://www.springframework.org/schema/context"
    xsi:schemaLocation="http://www.springframework.org/schema/beans
    http://www.springframework.org/schema/beans/spring-beans-3.0.xsd
    http://www.springframework.org/schema/context
    http://www.springframework.org/schema/context/
```

```
                    spring-context-3.0.xsd">

    <context:annotation-config/>

    <context:component-scan base-package="com.learning.spring.rmi"/>

    <!-- Server configurations -->
    <bean id="studentServiceImplementation" class=
            "com.learning.spring.rmi.StudentServiceImpl"/>

    <bean name="studentExporter" class="org.springframework.remoting.
                    httpinvoker.HttpInvokerServiceExporter">
        <property name="service" ref="studentServiceImplementation"/>
        <property name="serviceInterface" value=
                            "com.learning.spring.rmi.StudentService"/>
    </bean>

    <!-- Client configurations -->
    <bean id="httpInvokerProxy" class="org.springframework.remoting.
                    httpinvoker.HttpInvokerProxyFactoryBean">
        <property name="serviceUrl" value="http://localhcst:7001/
                            springbook/remoting/StudentService"/>
        <property name="serviceInterface" value=
                            "com.learning.spring.rmi.StudentService"/>
    </bean>

    <bean id="httpInvokerClient"
        class="com.learning.spring.rmi.HttpInvokerClient">
        <property name="studentService" ref="httpInvokerProxy"/>
    </bean>
</beans>
```

Step 3: Create a web.xml file.

The required "web.xml" file configurations are provided below. This file is used to load the spring beans specified in "applicationContext-httpinvoker.xml" into a web application context.

```
<?xml version="1.0" encoding="UTF-8"?>
<web-app version="2.4" xmlns="http://java.sun.com/xml/ns/j2ee"
    xmlns:xsi="http://www.w3.org/2001/XMLSchema-instance"
    xsi:schemaLocation="http://java.sun.com/xml/ns/j2ee
        http://java.sun.com/xml/ns/j2ee/web-app_2_4.xsd">

    <servlet>
        <servlet-name>studentExporter</servlet-name>
        <servlet-class>
            org.springframework.web.context.support.
            HttpRequestHandlerServlet
        </servlet-class>
    </servlet>

    <servlet-mapping>
        <servlet-name>studentExporter</servlet-name>
        <url-pattern>/remoting/StudentService</url-pattern>
    </servlet-mapping>
```

```
        <listener>
            <listener-class>
                org.springframework.web.context.ContextLoaderListener
            </listener-class>
        </listener>

        <context-param>
            <param-name>contextConfigLocation</param-name>
            <param-value>
                /WEB-INF/applicationContext-httpinvoker.xml
            </param-value>
        </context-param>

</web-app>
```

Step 4: Create a WAR file; deploy the WAR file in the web container.

The structure of the generated WAR file is shown in Figure 10-6. Deploy the packaged WAR file.

Figure 10-6: War file structure

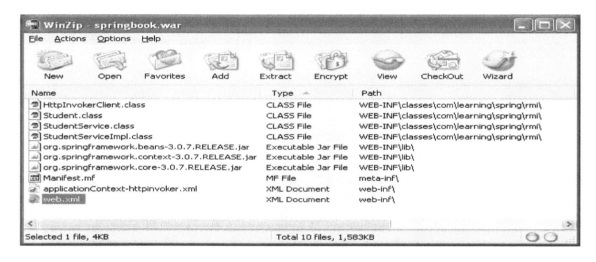

Step 5: Create a client class to invoke the service endpoint methods.

Listing 10-4 provides an HTTP invoker client class. This client class invokes the service endpoint operations.

Listing 10-4: HTTP invoker client class

```java
// HttpInvokerClient.java
package com.learning.spring.rmi;

import org.springframework.context.ApplicationContext;
import org.springframework.context.support.
        ClassPathXmlApplicationContext;
import org.springframework.remoting.httpinvoker.
        HttpInvokerProxyFactoryBean;
import java.util.List;
```

```java
public class HttpInvokerClient {

    private StudentService studentService;

    public static void main(String args[]) {
        String[] paths = {"applicationContext-httpinvoker.xml"};
        ApplicationContext appContext = new
                ClassPathXmlApplicationContext(paths);

        HttpInvokerClient httpInvokerClient = (HttpInvokerClient)
                    appContext.getBean("httpInvokerClient");
        String address =
            httpInvokerClient.studentService.getStudentDetails(10);
        List<Student> students =
            httpInvokerClient.studentService.getStudents();

        System.out.println("--- Address is ---" + address);
        System.out.println("--- students is ---" + students.size());

        for(Student student : students) {
            ... // print student data
        }
    }

    public void setStudentService(StudentService studentService) {
        this.studentService = studentService;
    }
}
```

Example 4: Developing-Integrating-Invoking EJB Components Using Spring

The steps required to develop, integrate and invoke an EJB component using Spring are listed below:

1. Create an EJB interface and its implementation class.
2. Create a spring configuration file.
3. Create a "web.xml" file
4. Create an "ear" file; deploy the "ear" file in an application server container.
5. Create a client class to invoke the service endpoint methods.

The above-specified steps are described in the following sections:

Step 1: Create an EJB interface and its implementation class.

This section illustrates the development of an EJB component. The following list provides the objects required to develop an EJB component.

- Local or Remote interface
- EJB implementation class
- Client class to invoke the deployed EJB

The following Student object is used for data transfer.

```
// Student.java
package com.learning.spring.rmi;

import java.io.Serializable;

public class Student implements Serializable {

    private String id;
    private String firstName;
    private String lastName;

    // Add getters and setters
}
```

The following `StudentServiceIF` interface specifies the EJB method operations. This interface can also be called the EJB remote interface.

```
// StudentServiceIF.java
package com.learning.spring.ejb;

import java.util.List;
import javax.ejb.Remote;

@Remote
public interface StudentServiceIF {

    public String getStudentDetails(int id);

    public List<Student> getStudents();
}
```

Listing 10-5 provides an EJB implementation class. This stateless EJB implements the methods specified in the `StudentServiceIF` interface.

Listing 10-5: Stateless EJB class

```
// StudentEJB.java
package com.learning.spring.ejb;

import javax.ejb.Stateless;
import javax.ejb.Remote;
import java.util.*;

@Stateless(mappedName="StudentServiceIF")
public class StudentEJB implements StudentServiceIF {

    public String getStudentDetails(int id) {
        return "3943 W.McClintock Dr, Chandler, AZ";
    }

    public List<Student> getStudents() {
        List<Student> stuList = new ArrayList<Student>();
        Student stu = new Student();
        stu.setId("1");
        stu.setFirstName("John");
        stu.setLastName("Smith");
```

```
            stuList.add(stu);

            stu = new Student();
            stu.setId("2");
            stu.setFirstName("John");
            stu.setLastName("Sims");
            stuList.add(stu);

            return stuList;
        }
}
```

Step 2: Create a spring configuration file

The complete XML configuration file is provided below and is named the "applicationContext-ejb.xml". This XML is used for accessing the deployed EJB using a standalone Java client.

CASE 1: Using the `JndiTemplate` class

```
<?xml version="1.0" encoding="UTF-8"?>
<beans xmlns="http://www.springframework.org/schema/beans"
    xmlns:xsi="http://www.w3.org/2001/XMLSchema-instance"
    xmlns:context="http://www.springframework.org/schema/context"
    xsi:schemaLocation="http://www.springframework.org/schema/beans
    http://www.springframework.org/schema/beans/spring-beans-3.0.xsd
    http://www.springframework.org/schema/context
    http://www.springframework.org/schema/context/
            spring-context-3.0.xsd">

    <bean id="jndiTemplate"
        class="org.springframework.jndi.JndiTemplate">
        <property name="environment">
            <props>
                <prop key="java.naming.factory.initial">
                    weblogic.jndi.WLInitialContextFactory
                </prop>
                <prop key="java.naming.provider.url">
                    t3://localhost:7001
                </prop>
            </props>
        </property>
    </bean>

    <bean id="studentEJBComponent"
        class="org.springframework.jndi.JndiObjectFactoryBean">
        <property name="jndiTemplate">
            <ref bean="jndiTemplate"/>
        </property>
        <property name="jndiName" value="StudentServiceIF#
                        com.learning.spring.ejb.StudentServiceIF"/>
        <property name="proxyInterface">
            <value>com.learning.spring.ejb.StudentServiceIF</value>
        </property>
    </bean>
</beans>
```

CASE 2: Using an application server-specific JNDI name

The complete XML configuration file is provided below and is named the "springbook-servlet.xml". The configurations provided in this XML are used for accessing the deployed EJB from your Spring-MVC controller. The prefix "springbook" maps to the `<servlet-name/>` specified in the "web.xml" file.

```xml
<?xml version="1.0" encoding="UTF-8"?>
<beans xmlns="http://www.springframework.org/schema/beans"
    xmlns:xsi="http://www.w3.org/2001/XMLSchema-instance"
    xmlns:context="http://www.springframework.org/schema/context"
    xmlns:p="http://www.springframework.org/schema/p"
    xmlns:jee="http://www.springframework.org/schema/jee"
    xsi:schemaLocation="http://www.springframework.org/schema/beans
    http://www.springframework.org/schema/beans/spring-beans-3.0.xsd
    http://www.springframework.org/schema/jee
    http://www.springframework.org/schema/jee/spring-jee-2.5.xsd
    http://www.springframework.org/schema/context
    http://www.springframework.org/schema/context/
                    spring-context-3.0.xsd">

    <context:annotation-config/>

    <context:component-scan base-package="com.learning.spring">
        <context:exclude-filter type="annotation" expression=
                "org.springframework.stereotype.Controller"/>
    </context:component-scan>

    <context:component-scan base-package=
                "com.learning.spring.controller"/>

    <bean class="org.springframework.web.servlet.mvc.
                SimpleControllerHandlerAdapter"/>
    <bean class="org.springframework.web.servlet.mvc.annotation.
                DefaultAnnotationHandlerMapping"/>
    <bean class="org.springframework.web.servlet.mvc.annotation.
                AnnotationMethodHandlerAdapter"/>

    <!-- EJB specific configurations -->
    <bean id="studentEJB" class="org.springframework.ejb.access.
                    LocalStatelessSessionProxyFactoryBean">
        <property name="jndiName" value="StudentServiceIF#
                    com.learning.spring.ejb.StudentServiceIF"/>
        <property name="businessInterface" value=
                    "com.learning.spring.ejb.StudentServiceIF"/>
    </bean>

</beans>
```

CASE 3: Using the `<xmlns:jee>` namespace

The following XML configurations are used to access an EJB component in the Spring-MVC controller. In this case, the spring-provided `<jee:local-slsb/>` namespace has been used to access the deployed EJB component.

```xml
<?xml version="1.0" encoding="UTF-8"?>
```

```
<beans>

        // Re-use the XML provided in CASE-2 with the following change.

        <!- EJB specific configurations -->
        <jee:local-slsb id="studentEJB"
                jndi-name="StudentServiceIF#
                        com.learning.spring.ejb.StudentServiceIF"
                business-interface="com.learning.spring.ejb.
                        StudentServiceIF"/>
</beans>
```

Step 3: Create a web.xml file

The complete "web.xml" configurations are provided below. The spring DispatcherServlet
class is configured in a "web.xml" file.

```
<?xml version="1.0" encoding="UTF-8"?>
<web-app version="2.4" xmlns="http://java.sun.com/xml/ns/j2ee"
    xmlns:xsi="http://www.w3.org/2001/XMLSchema-instance"
    xsi:schemaLocation="http://java.sun.com/xml/ns/j2ee
    http://java.sun.com/xml/ns/j2ee/web-app_2_4.xsd">

    <display-name>Spring Web Application</display-name>

    <servlet>
        <servlet-name>springbook</servlet-name>
        <servlet-class>
            org.springframework.web.servlet.DispatcherServlet
        </servlet-class>
        <load-on-startup>2</load-on-startup>
    </servlet>

    <servlet-mapping>
        <servlet-name>springbook</servlet-name>
        <url-pattern>*.action</url-pattern>
    </servlet-mapping>
</web-app>
```

Step 4: Create an EAR file; deploy the EAR file in application server container

Figure 10-7: War file structure

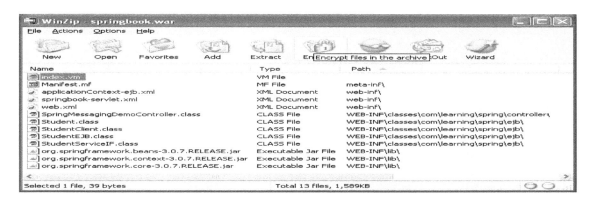

This section illustrates the packaging structure of "ear", "jar" and "war" files. The structure of the generated "war" file is shown in Figure 10-7. This "war" file contains Spring controllers, web layer dependent classes and web pages.

The structure of the generated "jar" file is shown in Figure 10-8. This "jar" file contains EJB's and their dependent classes.

Figure 10-8: Jar file structure

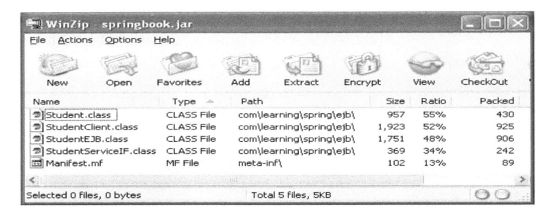

The structure of the generated "ear" file is shown in Figure 10-9. The "ear" file contains "jar" and "war" files.

Figure 10-9: Ear file structure

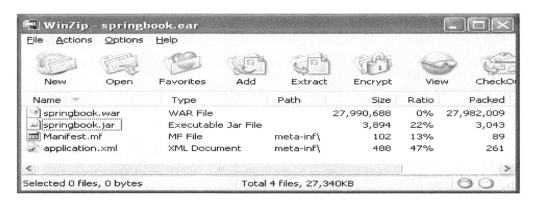

The contents of the "application.xml" file are provided below. This file contains entries of web and EJB modules.

```xml
<?xml version="1.0" encoding="UTF-8"?>
<!DOCTYPE application PUBLIC '-//Sun Microsystems, Inc.//DTD J2EE
Application 1.3//EN' 'http://java.sun.com/dtd/application_1_3.dtd'>
<application>
    <display-name>Spring EJB Application</display-name>
    <module>
        <ejb>springbook.jar</ejb>
    </module>

    <module>
```

```
        <web>
            <web-uri>springbook.war</web-uri>
            <context-root>springbook</context-root>
        </web>
    </module>
</application>
```

Step 5: Create a client class to invoke the service endpoint methods

There are several ways to invoke a deployed EJB component, as illustrated in this section

CASE 1: Invoking an EJB component using a standalone Java client without Spring

The following environment properties are specific to the Weblogic application server. Similarly, each application server vendor provides a proprietary API to create an initial context.

```
Hashtable<String, String> env = new Hashtable<String, String>();
env.put(Context.INITIAL_CONTEXT_FACTORY,
        "weblogic.jndi.WLInitialContextFactory");
env.put(Context.PROVIDER_URL, "t3://localhost:7001");
Context ctx = new InitialContext(env);
```

Listing 10-6 provides the complete class code.

Listing 10-6: Standalone EJB client using the Weblogic API.

```
// StudentClient.java
package com.learning.spring.ejb;

import javax.naming.InitialContext;
import java.util.Hashtable;
import java.util.List;
import javax.naming.Context;

import com.learning.spring.rmi.*;

public class StudentClient {
    public static void main(String args[]) {
        try {
            Hashtable<String, String> env =
                    new Hashtable<String, String>();
            env.put(Context.INITIAL_CONTEXT_FACTORY,
                    "weblogic.jndi.WLInitialContextFactory");
            env.put(Context.PROVIDER_URL, "t3://localhost:7001");
            Context ctx = new InitialContext(env);

            StudentServiceIF studentServiceIF = (StudentServiceIF)
                ctx.lookup("StudentServiceIF#com.learning.
                spring.ejb.StudentServiceIF");
            String result = studentServiceIF.getStudentDetails(121313);
            System.out.println("---- result ----" + result);

            List<Student> studentList = studentServiceIF.getStudents();

            // print your list here
```

```
            } catch (Exception ex) {
                ex.printStackTrace();
            }
        }
    }
}
```

CASE 2: Invoking an EJB component using a standalone Java client with Spring

Here, reuse the "applicationContext-ejb.xml" provided in this example. The spring-provided JndiObjectFactoryBean is used to configure the application server specific JNDI properties. Listing 10-7 provides the complete class code.

Listing 10-7: Standalone EJB client using Weblogic API and Spring

```
// StudentClient.java
package com.learning.spring.ejb;

import org.springframework.context.ApplicationContext;
import org.springframework.context.support.
        ClassPathXmlApplicationContext;

public class StudentClient {
    public static void main(String args[]) {
        String[] paths = {"applicationContext-ejb.xml"};
        ApplicationContext appContext = new
            ClassPathXmlApplicationContext(paths);
        StudentServiceIF studentServiceIF = (StudentServiceIF)
                    appContext.getBean("studentEJBComponent");
        String address = studentServiceIF.getStudentDetails(10);
        System.out.println("--- address ---" + address);

        List<Student> studentList = studentServiceIF.getStudents();
        System.out.println("--- studentList ---" + studentList.size());
    }
}
```

CASE 3: Invoking an EJB from the Spring-MVC controller class without Spring

Listing 10-8 demonstrates the EJB invocation from a spring controller class. The following code snippet obtains the handle of the remote interface, through which all business methods will be accessed.

```
StudentServiceIF studentServiceIF = (StudentServiceIF) ctx.lookup
        ("StudentServiceIF#com.learning.spring.ejb.StudentServiceIF");
```

The Listing 10-8 provides the complete controller class code.

Listing 10-8: Invoking an EJB from the Spring controller without using Spring

```
// SpringMessagingDemoController.java
package com.learning.spring.controller;

import org.springframework.stereotype.Controller;
import org.springframework.ui.ModelMap;
import org.springframework.web.bind.annotation.RequestMapping;
import org.springframework.web.bind.annotation.RequestMethod;
```

```java
import com.learning.spring.ejb.*;

import javax.servlet.http.HttpServletRequest;
import javax.naming.Context;
import javax.naming.InitialContext;
import java.util.List;

@Controller
public class SpringMessagingDemoController {

    @RequestMapping(value = "/demo/messageSender.action",
                    method = RequestMethod.POST)
    public String show(HttpServletRequest request, ModelMap model) {
        try {
            // Calling business methods
            Context ctx = new InitialContext();
            StudentServiceIF studentServiceIF =
            (StudentServiceIF) ctx.lookup("StudentServiceIF#com.
            learning.spring.ejb.StudentServiceIF");
            String result = studentServiceIF.getStudentDetails(121313);
            System.out.println("--- result ---" + result);

            List<Student> studentList = studentServiceIF.getStudents();

        } catch (Exception ex) {
            ex.printStackTrace();
        }

        request.setAttribute("name", "Success");
        return "demo/success";
    }
}
```

CASE 4: Invoking an EJB from the Spring-MVC controller class with Spring

Listing 10-9 demonstrates an EJB invocation from the spring controller class. In this example, the required JNDI-specific properties are configured using spring. The required configurations are provided in the "springbook-servlet.xml" file. Listing 10-9 provides the complete controller class code.

Listing 10-9: Invoking an EJB from the Spring controller using Spring

```java
// SpringMessagingDemoController.java
package com.learning.spring.controller;

import org.springframework.stereotype.Controller;
import org.springframework.beans.factory.annotation.Autowired;
import org.springframework.ui.ModelMap;
import org.springframework.web.bind.annotation.RequestMapping;
import org.springframework.web.bind.annotation.RequestMethod;
import com.learning.spring.ejb.*;

import javax.servlet.http.HttpServletRequest;
import java.util.List;

@Controller
public class SpringMessagingDemoController {
```

```
@Autowired
private StudentServiceIF studentEJB;

@RequestMapping(value = "/demo/messageSender.action",
            method = RequestMethod.POST)
public String show(HttpServletRequest request, ModelMap model) {
    try {
        // Calling business methods
        result = studentEJB.getStudentDetails(121313);
        System.out.println("--- result ---" + result);

        studentList = studentEJB.getStudents();

    } catch (Exception ex) {
        ex.printStackTrace();
    }

    request.setAttribute("name", "Success");
    return "demo/success";
}
}
```

Application Server Specific JNDI Naming Conventions for Spring-EJB Integration

This section illustrates the application server-specific naming conventions used to lookup an EJB component. The Weblogic and JOBSS application server default naming conventions are discussed below.

Weblogic

The Weblogic application server uses the following default naming convention to lookup the deployed EJB component. The structure of the lookup name is provided below:

- JNDI lookup name — StudentServiceIF#com.learning.spring.ejb.StudentServiceIF
- Name of the remote interface — StudentServiceIF
- The fully qualified interface name — com.learning.spring.ejb.StudentServiceIF
- The remote interface name and package name are separated by the hash (#) symbol.

JBOSS

The JBOSS application server uses the following default naming convention to lookup the deployed EJB component. The structure of the lookup name is provided below:

- JNDI lookup name — StudentEJB/Remote
- The name of the EJB — StudentEJB
- Interface type — the valid values are "Remote" or "Local"

It is possible to override this default behavior using the `@RemoteBinding` annotation. An example use of the `@RemoteBinding` annotation is provided below.

```
@RemoteBinding(jndiBinding="student/StudentEJB")
```

Summary

This section summarizes the features provided in the spring remoting framework.

- The spring-provided `RmiServiceExporter` class can be used to expose a specified Java class as an RMI service endpoint.
- The spring-provided `HessianServiceExporter` class can be used to expose a specified Java class as a servlet-based Hessian web service endpoint.
- The spring-provided `HttpInvokerServiceExporter` can be used to expose a specified Java class as a servlet-based web service endpoint.
- The spring-provided `BurlapServiceExporter` class can be used to expose a specified Java class as a servlet-based Burlap web service endpoint.
- The spring-provided `LocalStatelessSessionProxyFactoryBean` class can be used to expose a specified EJB component class as an EJB-based service endpoint.

Figure 10-10 summarizes the most important points described in this chapter.

Figure 10-10: Spring remoting summary.

Chapter 11. Spring-Messaging

Let us review a simple scenario before engaging in detailed discussion. How can two applications share data without knowing each other? One application sends the data to the destination, and the other application receives the data from the destination. The sender and receiver do not have direct communication and the receiver may not be available while the sender is sending the data to the destination. The receiver later retrieves the data from the destination for processing. The sender and receiver share only a common data type; the sender doesn't have knowledge about the receiver. The technique used in this type of situation is called "messaging"

Messaging is a method of loosely coupled communication between two applications or software components. The defined specification representing messaging is JMS, which stands for Java Message Service. The Java Message Service (JMS) is a message-oriented-middleware to create, send, and receive messages between two or more applications. The first JMS specification was published in 1998. The latest version of JMS is 2.0. JMS is part of Java EE.

There are several open-source and vendor-specific JMS implementations available for developing message-oriented applications. The JMS server is packaged with all Java EE-compliant application servers. If you use the application server in your application, your JMS provider (server) is your application server.

The messaging system provides support for both synchronous and asynchronous communications in a loosely coupled manner. The sender does not know anything about the receiver and the receiver does not have to know about the sender.

JMS can be integrated with the spring framework; thus, applications can take advantage of the spring framework for message processing. The spring messaging framework provides a simplified higher-level API for accessing JMS providers. This chapter illustrates the use of the spring framework to send-and-receive messages over the network.

This chapter will discuss the following topics:

- Messaging definitions and terminology
- The structure of a JMS message
- Spring framework support for messaging
- The primary spring-provided JMS classes and their use for message processing
- Spring framework support for message-driven POJOs
- The spring-provided message listener containers and their use
- The characteristics of point-to-point and publish-subscribe messaging models
- Spring framework support for synchronous and asynchronous message processing
- How to handle messaging transactions in message-driven POJOs
- The difference between a message-driven bean and a message-driven POJO.

JMS Architecture

Figure 11-1 illustrates JMS architecture. JMS provides an API similar to that of JDBC. The JDBC API is used for accessing the various relational databases. Similarly, the JMS-provided API is used for accessing the various messaging systems. The messaging provider implements the messaging server; JMS clients use the JMS API to connect to the messaging server. Spring messaging provides a high-level API to send-and-receive messages over the network.

Figure 11-1: JMS architecture

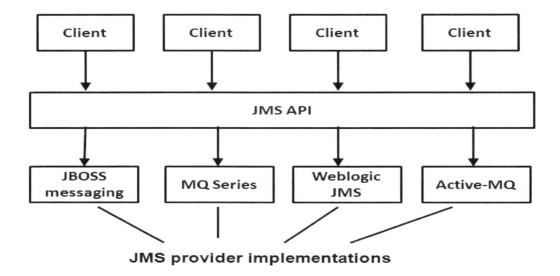

Messaging Terminology

This section explains the terminology commonly used in JMS while developing messaging-based applications. The messaging terminology is defined below.

Message: The message refers to information (data) that is passed between applications. This is a serialized message object that is sent from one application to another or from one program to another.

JMS Provider: The JMS provider is a messaging system that implements JMS specifications and interfaces. Almost all Java EE-compliant application servers include a JMS provider. If you use an application server in your application, your JMS provider is your application server.

Destination: The destination can be either "Queue" or "Topic". The destination is an object where the client specifies the target for messages and the consumer retrieves the messages. In the case of point-to-point messaging, the destinations are called "Queues"; in publish-subscribe messaging, the destinations are called "Topics"

Message Producer (Sender): A message producer is an object used for sending messages to a destination.

Message Consumer (Receiver): A message consumer is an object used for retrieving messages from the destination.

Point-to-Point Messaging Model:

The Point-to-point messaging model has the following characteristics.

- Commonly used terminology in the point-to-point messaging model: sender, receiver, and queue. The message producer is called the sender; the message consumer is called the receiver.

- The destination in point-to-point messaging is called "Queue"
- The messages in a queue are consumed in a First-In-First-Out (FIFO) order.
- The point-to-point messaging model ensures the delivery of a message to only one recipient. There is a one-to-one relationship between the sender and receiver.
- In some cases, multiple listeners may listen at one particular queue, but only one consumer will receive the message.
- The message sender sends a message to the queue; the message receiver retrieves the message from queue. After successful delivery of the message to the receiver, that message is removed from the queue.

The point-to-point messaging model is shown in Figure 11-2

Figure 11-2: Point-to-point messaging model

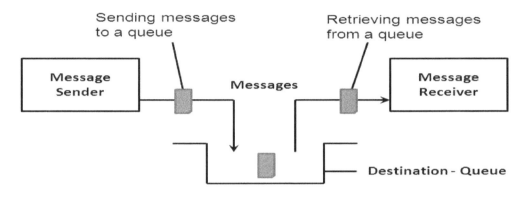

Point-to-Point messaging

Publish-Subscribe Messaging Model:

The publish-subscribe messaging model has the following characteristics.

- Commonly used terminology in the publish-subscribe messaging model: publisher, subscriber, and topic. The message producer is called the publisher; the message consumer is called the subscriber.
- The destination in publish-subscribe messaging is called "Topic"
- Messages sent to a topic can be generated by multiple publishers and consumed by multiple subscribers. Each message is delivered to multiple subscribers.
- The publisher publishes a message to the "Topic"; subscribers receive the messages from the "Topic". All subscribers receive the same message at the same time.
- The publish-subscribe messaging model is equivalent to an observer design pattern (GOF design pattern)

The publish-subscribe messaging model is shown in Figure 11-3

Figure 11-3: Publish-subscribe messaging model

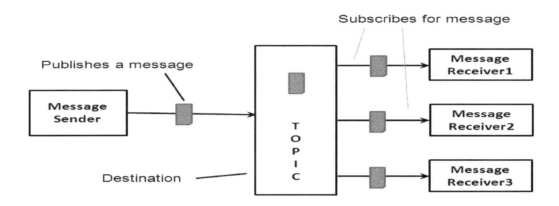

Publish-Subscribe messaging

Message Listeners: A message listener is an event handler used for asynchronous processing of messages. The message listener interface contains the `onMessage(...)` method. Whenever a message is delivered to the destination, the messaging-provider automatically invokes the `onMessage(...)` method of the message listener. This `onMessage(...)` method is used for implementing the business functionality.

Synchronous Messaging: The consumer retrieves the messages from the destination by calling the JMS-provided `receive(...)` method. The consumer will wait until the message arrives to the destination or reaches the specified timeout.

Asynchronous Messaging: The consumer's `onMessage(...)` method will be invoked automatically when the message arrives at the destination. The JMS provider delivers the message by calling the `onMessage(...)` method of the message listener. The complete message content is available in the `onMessage(...)` method. The asynchronous processing is used for requests that take a longer processing time. The client does not wait for response from the consumer.

Persistent Messages: The persistent messages are guaranteed to be delivered even in case of system failure. This type of message is physically stored in data files or in the database. After recovering from system failure, these messages can be recovered from the database.

Non-persistent Messages: The delivery of non-persistent messages is not assured in the case of system failure; rather, the messages will be lost. The messaging provider does not store these messages.

Message-Driven POJO (MDP): This is the technique used to receive JMS messages asynchronously using a plain java object as a message endpoint.

Message-Driven Bean (MDB): This is the technique used to receive messages asynchronously using an enterprise java bean (EJB) class. This is part of EJB specification.

JMS Connection Factory: This is an object used to establish a connection with the JMS provider. This object is used to create a `Connection`.

JMS Connection: This object establishes an active connection with the JMS provider.

JMS Session: This object is used for sending-and-receiving the messages.

Queue: The communication object between the programs is called a Queue. Queues are used to store messages in point-to-point messaging mode.

Topic: The communication object between the programs is called a Topic. Topic is used to store messages in publish-subscribe messaging mode.

The relation between connection factory, connection, session, message producer, message consumer, and destination is shown in Figure 11-4.

Figure 11-4: The relation between JMS components

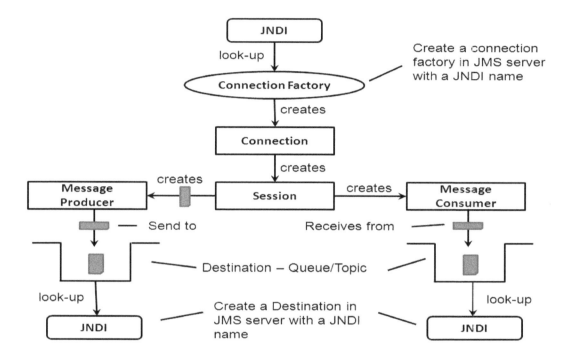

The message-sender puts a message into the Queue; the message-receiver retrieves the message from the Queue. A single queue configured between sender-and-receiver is shown in Figure 11-5

Figure 11-5: Single queue between sender-and-receiver

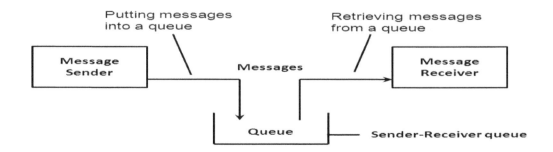

The message communication path between sender-and-receiver is shown in Figure 11-6. There are two queues configured between the message sender-and-receiver as shown in Figure 11-6. These two queues are connected though a message channel.

Figure 11-6: Two queues between sender-and-receiver

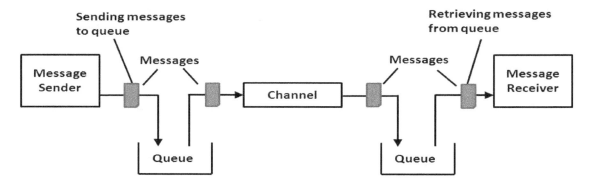

Message communication between sender-and-receiver

The Structure of a JMS Message

A JMS message contains three sections: Header, Properties and Body. The JMS message structure is shown in Figure 11-7.

Figure 11-7: JMS message structure

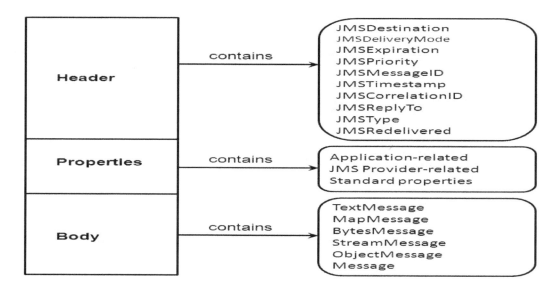

Header: The properties of the message header are shown in Figure 11-7. Some of these properties are set by the JMS provider and some are declared by the JMS client. The header is required and is created automatically for each message.

The following code example sets the correlation id to a message header.

```
message.setJMSCorrelationID("00001AA");
```

Properties: The three types of message properties are shown in Figure 11-7. These properties are optional.

Body: The body of the message contains actual payload. The supported data types of the message body are shown in Figure 11-7.

The following code example creates a text message. Example-1 provides the complete code.

```
TextMessage msg = session.createTextMessage();
msg.setText("--- Send your text message ---");
```

The following code example creates an object message. Example-1 provides the complete code.

```
ObjectMessage om = session.createObjectMessage();
MessageData message = new MessageData();
message.setProcessId(555);
message.setTaskId(5);
om.setObject(message);
```

Primary Spring-provided JMS Classes

Spring provides simplified JMS implementation framework. The spring framework encapsulates the lower-level messaging details and provides a high-level API to create, send, and receive the messages. It also provides support for both synchronous and asynchronous message processing. The spring-provided `JmsTemplate` helper class is used for synchronous message reception, while message-driven POJOs (MDP) are used for asynchronous message processing.

JmsTemplate

Spring provides a `JmsTemplate` helper class, similar to the spring `JdbcTemplate`, to send and receive messages synchronously. The methods `send(...)` and `convertAndSend(...)` are used to send messages. The methods `receive(...)` and `receiveAndConvert(...)` are used for synchronous message reception.

The following code is used to send messages to a Queue. Example-1 provides the complete code.

```
jmsTemplate.send(synchJMSQueue, new MessageCreator() {
    ...
}
```

The following code is used to send map messages to a Queue. Example-1 provides the complete code.

```
jmsTemplate.convertAndSend(jmsQueue, map, new MessagePostProcessor() {
    ...
}
```

The following code is used to receive messages from a Queue. Example-5 provides the complete code.

```
Object msg = jmsTemplate.receiveAndConvert(JMSQueue);
```

ConnectionFactory

The `ConnectionFactory` class is used to establish a connection with the JMS provider. This object encapsulates the JMS-provider's specific connection information. The spring-provided JMS containers use `ConnectionFactory` to obtain a connection with the JMS provider.

The following XML configuration is used to obtain a `ConnectionFactory` object reference.

```
<bean id="jmsConnectionFactory"
    class="org.springframework.jndi.JndiObjectFactoryBean">
    <property name="jndiTemplate">
        <ref bean="jndiTemplate"/>
    </property>
    <property name="jndiName">
        <value>pojo/jms/testjmsfactory</value>
    </property>
</bean>
```

JndiObjectFactoryBean

Spring provides a `JndiObjectFactoryBean` that is used for JNDI object look-ups. It exposes the object references found in JNDI look-ups such as, data source, EJB, queues, and queue connection factories.

The following XML configuration can be used to obtain a reference to the configured JMS queue from your JMS provider.

```
<bean id="jmsQueue"
    class="org.springframework.jndi.JndiObjectFactoryBean">
    <property name="jndiName">
        <value>pojo/jms/testjmsqueue</value>
    </property>
</bean>
```

MessageListener

A message listener is an event handler used for asynchronous processing of messages. The message listener interface contains the `onMessage(...)` method. This method will be invoked automatically whenever a message arrives to the destination.

```
public class ProcessMonitorMDB implements MessageListener {
    public void onMessage(javax.jms.Message message) throws
                RuntimeException {
        ...
    }
}
```

JmsTransactionManager

Spring provides a `JmsTransactionManager` class that manages transactions for a single JMS `ConnectionFactory`.

```
<bean id="jmsTransactionManager" class="org.springframework.jms.
                    connection.JmsTransactionManager">
    <property name="connectionFactory" ref="jmsConnectionFactory" />
</bean>
```

Prerequisites/Setting Up the Environment

Figure 11-8: JMS server, module, connection factory and queue configurations.

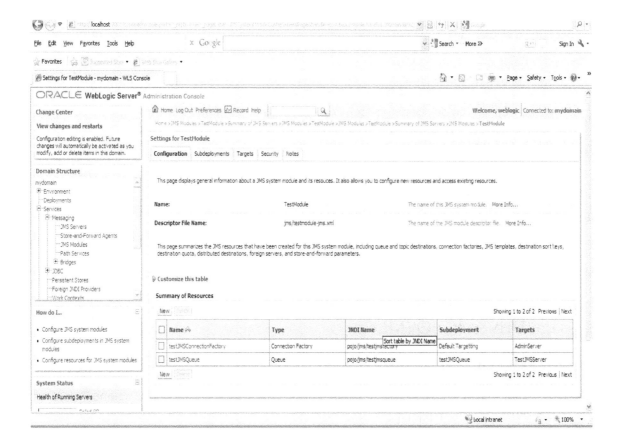

Before starting on application development, get familiar with your messaging server; all application servers have messaging support. In general, the following configurations are needed for developing message oriented middleware applications. I have used the Weblogic application server for developing these examples. The following configurations are specific to the Weblogic application server. However, these configurations are very similar in any messaging product. Figure 11-8 shows the JMS server, JMS Module, connection factory, and queue configurations.

The step-by-step instructions are provided below.

- Open your Weblogic console — http://localhost:7001/console
- Log in to the Weblogic domain — enter your Weblogic domain's user-id and password.
- Navigate to Services → Messaging → JMS Servers
- Create a new JMS Server; target this to "AdminServer".
- Navigate to Services → Messaging → JMS Modules
- Create a new JMS module — contains JMS connection factory and JMS queue information.
- Create a new JMS connection factory with your JMS provider — create a JMS connection factory with parameters such as, JNDI name, time-to-live, delivery mode, and so forth. The JNDI name is a required parameter; you can use default values for the others.
- Create a new queue/topic with your JMS provider — create a JMS destination (queue/topic) with required parameters such as, JNDI name, expiration policy, and so forth. The JNDI name is a required parameter; you can use default values for the others.

Advantages of Spring Messaging

This section illustrates the technical and non-technical features of spring messaging framework.

- Spring provides support for both synchronous and asynchronous message processing models.
- Spring provides a higher-level API to send and receive messages over the network. It also provides a `JmsTemplate` helper class, which encapsulates the JMS boiler plate code and allows the application developer to focus on message content and business-specific details.
- The spring `JmsTemplate` can be used for sending messages and for synchronous message reception. The message-driven POJOs are used for asynchronous message reception.
- The existing Java classes can be used for message reception without major modifications. The spring framework provides listener containers to make the Java class a message-driven POJO.
- Spring provides support for local and externally managed transactions.
- Spring provides support for Java EE and vendor-specific JMS providers.
- Spring provides support for various versions of JMS, such as, 1.0, 1.1, 1.2, and 2.0.
- The spring framework provides a simplified messaging framework that targets junior and mid-level developers.
- Spring provides an annotation-based programming model to send and receive messages.

Message-Driven POJO (MDP)

The spring framework provides several message listener containers to implement message-driven POJOs. Message listener containers receive messages from the JMS destination and invoke the message listener that is injected to the container. The spring-provided message listener container classes are listed below.

- SimpleMessageListenerContainer
- DefaultMessageListenerContainer

SimpleMessageListenerContainer

The simple message listener container creates a fixed number of JMS sessions and registers the listener using a JMS API-provided `MessageConsumer.setMessageListener()` method.

DefaultMessageListenerContainer

The default message listener container is commonly used for receiving messages from the destination. It invokes the injected message listener for message processing. This type of listener container can participate in externally managed transactions.

The default message listener container XML configuration is provided below.

```xml
<bean id="jmsContainer" class="org.springframework.jms.listener.
                            DefaultMessageListenerContainer">
    <property name="connectionFactory" ref="jmsConnectionFactory"/>
    <property name="destination" ref="jmsQueue"/>
    <property name="messageListener" ref="messageListener"/>
    <property name="sessionTransacted" value="true"/>
</bean>
```

The following XML configuration is used to participate in locally managed transactions.

```xml
<property name="sessionTransacted" value="true"/>
```

The following XML configuration is used to participate in externally managed transactions.

```xml
<property name="transactionManager" ref="transactionManager"/>
```

The steps generally required to send and receive messages are listed below.

1. Create a connection factory with the JMS provider.
2. Create a message destination (queue/topic) with the JMS provider.
3. Get the configured JMS connection factory using JNDI lookup.
4. Get the configured JMS queue using JNDI lookup
5. Configure the spring-provided message listener container.
6. Create a `JmsTemplate` class.
7. Create message sender and receiver classes to send and receive messages.

The following examples illustrate the above-specified steps in greater detail.

Demo Examples

Example 1: Spring-MDP using MessageListenerAdapter

The spring-provided `MessageListenerAdapter` class can be used for asynchronous message processing. This class is specially designed to make any Java class a MDP. The message receivers do not have to implement the JMS-provided `javax.jms.MessageListener` class to receive messages from the destination.

The steps required to implement an MDP using the spring-provided `MessageListenerAdapter` class are listed below:

1. Create a message sender class.
2. Implement a message receiver class.
3. Create an applicationContext-pojo.xml file.
4. Create a servlet controller class to invoke the MDP.

5. Create a web.xml file.
6. Create a WAR file, and deploy it in the Weblogic server.
7. Test the deployed message-driven POJO.

The above-specified steps are described in the following sections:

Step 1: Create a message sender class

The following `POJOMessageSender` class is used for sending messages to the JMS queue. The message receiver later retrieves the message from the JMS queue. The `POJOMessageSender` class has the following three methods.

- void sendMessage()—This method is used for sending String messages.
- void sendWithConversion()—This method is used for sending Map messages.
- void sendMessageData(MessageData message)—This method is used for sending serialized Object messages.

The complete message sender class code is provided in Listing 11-1.

Listing 11-1: Message Sender class used to send messages.

```java
// POJOMessageSender.java
package com.learning.spring.messaging;

import org.springframework.beans.factory.annotation.Autowired;
import org.springframework.jms.core.JmsTemplate;
import org.springframework.jms.core.MessageCreator;
import org.springframework.jms.core.MessagePostProcessor;
import org.springframework.stereotype.Component;

import javax.annotation.Resource;
import javax.jms.*;
import java.util.Map;
import java.util.HashMap;

@Component
public class POJOMessageSender {

    @Autowired
    private JmsTemplate jmsTemplate;

    @Resource(name = "jmsQueue")
    private Queue jmsQueue;

    public void sendMessage() {
        jmsTemplate.send(jmsQueue, new MessageCreator() {
            public javax.jms.Message createMessage(Session session)
                throws JMSException {
                TextMessage msg = session.createTextMessage();
                msg.setText("--- Send your text message ---");
                return msg;
            }
        });
    }
```

```java
    public void sendWithConversion() {
        Map map = new HashMap();
        map.put("Name", "John Smith");
        map.put("Age", new Integer(39));
        jmsTemplate.convertAndSend(jmsQueue, map,
                new MessagePostProcessor() {
            public javax.jms.Message postProcessMessage(
                javax.jms.Message message) throws JMSException {
                message.setIntProperty("AccountID", 1234);
                message.setJMSCorrelationID("00001AA");
                return message;
            }
        });
    }

    public void sendMessageData(final MessageData message) {
        jmsTemplate.send(jmsQueue, new MessageCreator() {
            public javax.jms.Message createMessage(Session
                session) throws JMSException {
                ObjectMessage om = session.createObjectMessage();
                message.setProcessId(555);
                message.setTaskId(5);
                om.setObject(message);
                return om;
            }
        });
    }

    public void setJmsTemplate(JmsTemplate jmsTemplate) {
        this.jmsTemplate = jmsTemplate;
    }

    public void setJmsQueue(Queue jmsQueue) {
        this.jmsQueue = jmsQueue;
    }
}
```

Step 2: Create a message receiver class

The following data value object can be used to hold the message data. This class holds the business data of a message to be sent from sender to receiver.

```java
// MessageData.java
package com.learning.spring.messaging;

import java.io.Serializable;

public class MessageData implements Serializable {

    private static final long serialVersionUID = 1234455L;
    private Integer processId;
    private Integer taskId;
    private String message;

    // Add getters and setters
}
```

The following interface contains various methods to process Text, Map and Object type messages.

```java
// MessageDelegate.java
package com.learning.spring.messaging;

import java.util.Map;

public interface MessageDelegate {

    // Method used to receive text message
    public void handleMessage(String message);

    // Method used to receive MAP message
    public void handleMessage(Map message);

    // Method used to receive Object message
    public void handleMessage(MessageData message);

}
```

Listing 11-2 provides a `POJOMessageDelegate` message receiver class. Generally, the message receiver implements the `javax.jms.MessageListener` class to retrieve the messages from the destination. But, the spring-provided `MessageListenerAdapter` class does not have to implement the JMS-provided `javax.jms.MessageListener` class to receive messages from the destination. The complete message-receiver class code is provided in Listing 11-2.

Listing 11-2: Message-receiver to process incoming messages.

```java
// POJOMessageDelegate.java
package com.learning.spring.messaging;

import org.springframework.stereotype.Component;
import java.util.Map;

@Component
public class POJOMessageDelegate implements MessageDelegate {

    public void handleMessage(String message) {
        System.out.println("--- Text Message Received ---" + message);
        //... Implement your logic here
    }

    public void handleMessage(Map mapMessage) {
        System.out.println("-- Map Message Received --" + mapMessage);
        String name = (String) mapMessage.get("Name");
        Integer age = (Integer) mapMessage.get("Age");
        System.out.println("-- Name --" + name + "-- Age --" + age);
        //... Implement your logic here
    }

    public void handleMessage(MessageData message) {
        Integer processId = message.getProcessId();
        Integer taskId = message.getTaskId();
        System.out.println("--- processId ---" + processId +
                           "--- taskId ---" + taskId);
```

```
            //... Implement your logic here
    }
}
```

Step 3: Create an applicationContext-pojo.xml file.

The spring-messaging framework provides XML-based tags to configure the message listeners.

The following XML tag is used to obtain the provider-specific message context.

```
<bean id="jndiTemplate"
    class="org.springframework.jndi.JndiTemplate">
    // ...
</bean>
```

The following XML tag is used to obtain the reference to the JMSConnectionFactory.

```
<bean id="jmsConnectionFactory"
    class="org.springframework.jndi.JndiObjectFactoryBean">
    <property name="jndiName">
        <value>pojo/jms/testjmsfactory</value>
    </property>

    // ...
</bean>
```

The following XML tag is used to obtain the reference to the message destination. The destination can be either "Queue" or "Topic".

```
<bean id="jmsQueue"
    class="org.springframework.jndi.JndiObjectFactoryBean">
    <property name="jndiName">
        <value>pojo/jms/testjmsqueue</value>
    </property>

    // ...
</bean>
```

The following XML tag is used to configure the message listener adapter, which is then used to configure message-driven POJO.

```
<bean id="messageListener"
     class="org.springframework.jms.listener.adapter.
                MessageListenerAdapter">
    // ...
</bean>
```

The following XML tag is used to obtain the reference to the Spring-specific JMSTemplate. This template class encapsulates the JMS send-receive functionality.

```
<bean id="jmsTemplate"
    class="org.springframework.jms.core.JmsTemplate">
    // ...
</bean>
```

The complete XML file is provided below and is named the "applicationContext-pojo.xml".

```xml
<?xml version="1.0" encoding="UTF-8"?>
<beans xmlns="http://www.springframework.org/schema/beans"
    xmlns:xsi="http://www.w3.org/2001/XMLSchema-instance"
    xmlns:context="http://www.springframework.org/schema/context"
    xsi:schemaLocation="http://www.springframework.org/schema/beans
    http://www.springframework.org/schema/beans/spring-beans-3.0.xsd
    http://www.springframework.org/schema/context
    http://www.springframework.org/schema/context/
                spring-context-3.0.xsd">

    <context:annotation-config/>

    <context:component-scan
            base-package="com.learning.spring.messaging"/>

    <!-- Getting the JNDI template reference -->
    <bean id="jndiTemplate"
        class="org.springframework.jndi.JndiTemplate">
        <property name="environment">
            <props>
                <prop key="java.naming.factory.initial">
                    weblogic.jndi.WLInitialContextFactory
                </prop>
                <prop key="java.naming.provider.url">
                    t3://localhost:7001
                </prop>
            </props>
        </property>
    </bean>

    <!-- Getting the JMS connection factory reference -->
    <bean id="jmsConnectionFactory"
        class="org.springframework.jndi.JndiObjectFactoryBean">
        <property name="jndiTemplate">
            <ref bean="jndiTemplate"/>
        </property>
        <property name="jndiName">
            <value>pojo/jms/testjmsfactory</value>
        </property>
    </bean>

    <!-- Getting the message destination reference -->
    <bean id="jmsQueue"
        class="org.springframework.jndi.JndiObjectFactoryBean">
        <property name="jndiTemplate">
            <ref bean="jndiTemplate"/>
        </property>
        <property name="jndiName">
            <value>pojo/jms/testjmsqueue</value>
        </property>
    </bean>

    <!-- This is the Message-Driven POJO (MDP) -->
    <bean id="messageListener"
        class="org.springframework.jms.listener.adapter.
```

```
                    MessageListenerAdapter">
        <constructor-arg>
            <bean class=
                "com.learning.spring.messaging.POJOMessageDelegate"/>
        </constructor-arg>
    </bean>

    <!-- This is the message listener container -->
    <bean id="jmsContainer"
        class="org.springframework.jms.listener.
                  DefaultMessageListenerContainer">
        <property name="connectionFactory" ref="jmsConnectionFactory"/>
        <property name="destination" ref="jmsQueue"/>
        <property name="messageListener" ref="messageListener"/>
    </bean>

    <!-- Getting the reference of a JMS Template -->
    <bean id="jmsTemplate"
        class="org.springframework.jms.core.JmsTemplate">
        <property name="connectionFactory">
            <ref bean="jmsConnectionFactory"/>
        </property>

        <!-- This is used for internal XA transactions -->
        <!--<property name="sessionTransacted" value="true"/>-->
    </bean>
</beans>
```

Step 4: Create a servlet controller class to invoke the MDP.

Listing 11-3 provides a spring controller class that invokes the message-sender class and passes the message data to message consumer. The complete spring controller class code is provided in Listing 11-3.

Listing 11-3: Spring controller to invoke the message sender.

```java
// SpringMessagingDemoController.java
package com.learning.spring.controller;

import org.springframework.stereotype.Controller;
import org.springframework.beans.factory.annotation.Autowired;
import org.springframework.ui.ModelMap;
import org.springframework.web.bind.annotation.RequestMapping;
import org.springframework.web.bind.annotation.RequestMethod;
import com.learning.spring.messaging.*;
import javax.servlet.http.HttpServletRequest;

@Controller
public class SpringMessagingDemoController {

    @Autowired
    private POJOMessageSender pojoMessageSender;

    @RequestMapping(value = "/demo/messageSender.action",
                      method = RequestMethod.POST)
    public String show(HttpServletRequest request, ModelMap model) {
        try {
```

```
                    MessageData message = new MessageData();
                    // Invoking the String message
                    pojoMessageSender.sendMessage();

                    // Invoking the MAP message
                    pojoMessageSender.sendWithConversion();

                    // Invoking the Object message
                    pojoMessageSender.sendMessageData(message);

            } catch (Exception ex) {
                    ex.printStackTrace();
            }
            return "demo/success";
        }
}
```

Step 5: Create a web.xml file.

The required "web.xml" file configurations are provided below.

```
<?xml version="1.0" encoding="UTF-8"?>
<web-app version="2.4" xmlns="http://java.sun.com/xml/ns/j2ee"
    xmlns:xsi="http://www.w3.org/2001/XMLSchema-instance"
    xsi:schemaLocation="http://java.sun.com/xml/ns/j2ee
    http://java.sun.com/xml/ns/j2ee/web-app_2_4.xsd">

    <servlet>
        <servlet-name>springbook</servlet-name>
        <servlet-class>
            org.springframework.web.servlet.DispatcherServlet
        </servlet-class>
        <load-on-startup>2</load-on-startup>
    </servlet>

    <servlet-mapping>
        <servlet-name>springbook</servlet-name>
        <url-pattern>*.action</url-pattern>
    </servlet-mapping>

    <listener>
        <listener-class>
            org.springframework.web.context.ContextLoaderListener
        </listener-class>
    </listener>

    <context-param>
        <param-name>contextConfigLocation</param-name>
        <param-value>/WEB-INF/applicationContext-pojo.xml</param-value>
    </context-param>
</web-app>
```

Step 6: Create a WAR File and deploy it in the Weblogic server.

1. Build a WAR file using Ant or any other build tool. Make sure the following files are packaged correctly in the WAR file.

a. Package the required classes into the "WEB-INF/classes" directory.
b. Package the "web.xml" file into the "WEB-INF/" directory.
c. Package the "springbook-servlet.xml" configuration file into the "WEB-INF/" directory.
d. Package all dependent JAR files into the "WEB-INF/lib" directory.

2. Deploy the WAR file in any JMS-compliant application server. The Weblogic deployment instructions are provided below.
   a. Deploy the packaged WAR file in Weblogic using the Weblogic console.
   b. Start the Weblogic server by running the "startWebLogic.cmd" batch file available in the "mydomain/bin" directory.
   c. View the server console output/logs; make sure the WAR file is deployed without any errors.

The structure of the generated WAR file is shown in Figure 11-9:

Figure 11-9: War file structure

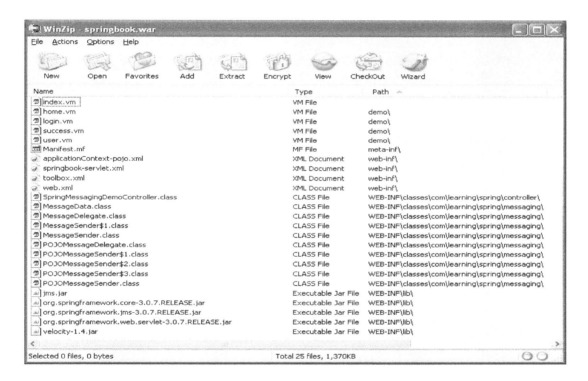

Step 7: Test the deployed Message-Driven POJO

The following web page can be used to invoke the `SpringMessagingDemoController` class.

CASE 1: Test the message-driven POJO using web page.

```html
<html>
    <head>
        <title> Welcome to Login Page </title>
        <script type="text/javascript">
            function checkLogin(base) {
                document.forms[0].action =
                    "/springbook/demo/messageSender.action";
```

```
                    document.forms[0].submit();
            }
        </script>
    </head>
    <body>
        <form method="post">
            <table>
                <tr>
                <td>
                    <input type="button" name="LogIn" value="LogIn"
                            onclick="checkLogin()"/>
                </td>
                </tr>
            </table>
        </form>
    </body>
</html>
```

CASE 2: Test the message-driven POJO using a simple URL

The following URL can be used to invoke the spring controller class. Make sure you use the GET-request in this scenario.

```
http://localhost:7001/springbook/demo/messageSender.action
```

CASE 3: Standalone Java client to test the message-driven POJO.

Add the following XML to the "applicationContext-pojo.xml" file.

```
<bean id="pojoMessageSender"
    class="com.learning.spring.messaging.POJOMessageSender">
</bean>
```

Listing 11-4 provides a standalone Java client to send messages to the destination.

Listing 11-4: Standalone java client to send messages.

```
// TestClient.java
package com.learning.spring.messaging;

import org.springframework.context.ApplicationContext;
import org.springframework.context.support.
        ClassPathXmlApplicationContext;

public class TestClient {

    public static void main(String args[]) {
        String[] paths = {"applicationContext-pojo.xml"};
        ApplicationContext appContext = new
                ClassPathXmlApplicationContext(paths);
        POJOMessageSender messageSender = (POJOMessageSender)
                    appContext.getBean("pojoMessageSender");

        // Sending messages to a queue
        messageSender.sendMessage();
        messageSender.sendWithConversion();
```

```
                messageSender.sendMessageData(new MessageData());
    }
}
```

Example 2: Spring-MDP using DefaultMessageListenerContainer

The use and capabilities of `DefaultMessageListenerContainer` are provided below:

- The spring-provided `DefaultMessageListenerContainer` can be used to process messages asynchronously.
- This is the most commonly used spring-based message listener container
- This container will support the externally managed transactions.

The steps required to implement an MDP using this approach are listed below:

1. Create a message sender class.
2. Implement a message receiver class.
3. Create an "applicationContext-pojo.xml" file.
4. Create a servlet controller class to invoke the MDP.
5. Create a WAR file, and deploy it in the Weblogic server.
6. Test the deployed message-driven POJO.

The above-specified steps are described in the following sections:

Step 1: Create a Message Sender class.

The following `SimpleMessageSender` class can be used for sending the messages to the JMS queue. The complete message sender class code is provided in Listing 11-5.

Listing 11-5: Message sender class used to send messages.

```
// SimpleMessageSender.java
package com.learning.spring.messaging;

import org.springframework.stereotype.Component;
import org.springframework.beans.factory.annotation.Autowired;
import org.springframework.jms.core.JmsTemplate;
import org.springframework.jms.core.MessageCreator;
import javax.annotation.Resource;
import javax.jms.*;

@Component
public class SimpleMessageSender {

    @Autowired
    private JmsTemplate jmsTemplate;

    @Resource(name="jmsQueue")
    private Queue jmsQueue;

    public void sendMessage(final MessageData message) {
        jmsTemplate.send(jmsQueue, new MessageCreator() {
            public javax.jms.Message createMessage(Session session)
```

```
                  throws JMSException {
                      ObjectMessage om = session.createObjectMessage();
                      message.setProcessId(111);
                      message.setTaskId(11);
                      om.setObject(message);
                      return om;
                  }
              });
          }

          public void setJmsTemplate(JmsTemplate jmsTemplate) {
              this.jmsTemplate = jmsTemplate;
          }

          public void setJmsQueue(Queue jmsQueue) {
              this.jmsQueue = jmsQueue;
          }
}
```

Step 2: Implement a message receiver class.

The following rules are applied to a message receiver class.

- The message receiver class must implement the JMS-provided `javax.jms.MessageListener` interface.
- The message receiver class must implement the `onMessage(...)` method. This is the default method to be invoked while receiving the messages from the message destination.
- The `onMessage(...)` method does not throw any exceptions to the calling client.

The complete message-receiver class code is provided in Listing 11-6.

Listing 11-6: Message-receiver to process incoming messages

```
// MessageReceiver.java
package com.learning.spring.messaging;

import org.springframework.stereotype.Component;
import javax.jms.MessageListener;
import javax.jms.ObjectMessage;

@Component
public class MessageReceiver implements MessageListener {
    public void onMessage(javax.jms.Message message) {
        if (message instanceof ObjectMessage) {
            ObjectMessage om = (ObjectMessage) message;
            try {
                MessageData taskMessage =
                        (MessageData) om.getObject();
                Integer processId = taskMessage.getProcessId();
                Integer taskId = taskMessage.getTaskId();
                String messageId = taskMessage.getMessage();

                System.out.println("--- processId ---" + processId +
                    "--- taskId ---" + taskId +
                    "--- messageId ---" + messageId);
```

```
                        // ... Implement your logic here
            } catch (Exception ex) {
                ex.printStackTrace();
            }
        }
    }
}
```

Step 3: Create an applicationContext-pojo.xml file.

The spring-messaging framework provides XML-based tags to configure the message listeners.
The complete XML file is provided below and is named the "applicationContext-pojo.xml".

```xml
<?xml version="1.0" encoding="UTF-8"?>
<beans xmlns="http://www.springframework.org/schema/beans"
    xmlns:xsi="http://www.w3.org/2001/XMLSchema-instance"
    xmlns:context="http://www.springframework.org/schema/context"
    xsi:schemaLocation="http://www.springframework.org/schema/beans
    http://www.springframework.org/schema/beans/spring-beans-3.0.xsd
    http://www.springframework.org/schema/context
    http://www.springframework.org/schema/context/
                spring-context-3.0.xsd">

    <context:annotation-config/>

    <context:component-scan
        base-package="com.learning.spring.messaging"/>

    <bean id="jndiTemplate"
        class="org.springframework.jndi.JndiTemplate">
        <property name="environment">
            <props>
                <prop key="java.naming.factory.initial">
                    weblogic.jndi.WLInitialContextFactory
                </prop>
                <prop key="java.naming.provider.url">
                    t3://localhost:7001</prop>
                </props>
        </property>
    </bean>

    <bean id="jmsConnectionFactory"
        class="org.springframework.jndi.JndiObjectFactoryBean">
        <property name="jndiTemplate">
            <ref bean="jndiTemplate"/>
        </property>
        <property name="jndiName">
            <value>pojo/jms/testjmsfactory</value>
        </property>
    </bean>

    <bean id="jmsQueue"
        class="org.springframework.jndi.JndiObjectFactoryBean">
        <property name="jndiName">
            <value>pojo/jms/testjmsqueue</value>
```

```
            </property>
        </bean>

        <!-- This is the Message-Driven POJO (MDP) -->
        <bean id="messageListener"
            class="com.learning.spring.messaging.MessageReceiver"/>

        <!-- This is the message listener container -->
        <bean id="jmsContainer" class="org.springframework.jms.listener.
                DefaultMessageListenerContainer">
            <property name="connectionFactory" ref="jmsConnectionFactory"/>
            <property name="destination" ref="jmsQueue"/>
            <property name="messageListener" ref="messageListener"/>
        </bean>

        <!-- Getting the reference of a JMS Template -->
        <bean id="jmsTemplate" class=
            "org.springframework.jms.core.JmsTemplate">
            <property name="connectionFactory">
                <ref bean="jmsConnectionFactory"/>
            </property>
        </bean>
</beans>
```

Step 4: Create a servlet controller class to invoke the MDP.

Here, re-use the same controller class we created in Example-1. A snippet of the code is provided below.

```
@RequestMapping(value = "/demo/messageSender.action",
            method = RequestMethod.POST)
public String show(HttpServletRequest request, ModelMap model) {
    try {
        MessageData message = new MessageData();
        simpleMessageSender.sendMessage(message);
    } catch (Exception ex) {
        ex.printStackTrace();
    }
    request.setAttribute("name", "Success");
    return "demo/success";
}
```

Step 5: Create a WAR file and deploy it in the Weblogic server.

Follow the instructions as specified in Example-1.

Step 6: Test the deployed message-driven POJO.

Here, re-use the client we created in Example-1.

Example 3: Spring-MDP implementation using the <jms: listener> namespace

The steps required to implement a Java EE-compliant message-driven POJO using the Spring-provided <jms:> namespace is listed below:

1. Create a message sender class.
2. Implement a message receiver class.
3. Create an "applicationContext-mdp.xml" file.
4. Create a servlet controller class to invoke the MDP.
5. Create a "web.xml" file.
6. Create a WAR File, and deploy it in the Weblogic server.
7. Test the deployed message-driven POJO.

The above-specified steps are described in the following sections:

Step 1: Create a message sender class.

The following data value object is used to hold the message data. This class holds the business data of a message to be sent from sender-to-receiver.

```
// MessageData.java
package com.learning.spring.messaging;

import java.io.Serializable;

public class MessageData implements Serializable {

    private static final long serialVersionUID = 1234455L;
    private Integer processId;
    private Integer taskId;
    private String message;

    // Add getters and setters here
}
```

Listing 11-7 provides a MessageSender class, which is used for sending messages to the JMS-Queue. The message receiver gets the message from the JMS-Queue.

The following code is used to set the "message-type" property before sending the message into a Queue.

```
om.setStringProperty("MessageType", message.getMessage());
```

Its corresponding XML-configuration is provided below.

```
selector="MessageType IN ('DAILY_POLLER_MSG')"/>
```

The purpose of the message-selector is to filter the messages it receives. The message-consumers then receive only messages that have the specified message type, which is DAILY_POLLER_MSG. This message-selector is an optional property. Step-3 provides the complete message-selector XML configuration. The complete message-sender class code is provided in Listing 11-7.

Listing 11-7: Message sender class used to send messages.

```
// MessageSender.java
package com.learning.spring.messaging;

import javax.annotation.Resource;
```

```java
import javax.jms.Destination;
import javax.jms.JMSException;
import javax.jms.ObjectMessage;
import javax.jms.Session;
import org.springframework.beans.factory.annotation.Autowired;
import org.springframework.jms.core.JmsTemplate;
import org.springframework.jms.core.MessageCreator;
import org.springframework.stereotype.Component;

@Component
public class MessageSender {

    @Autowired
    private JmsTemplate jmsSpringTemplate;

    @Resource(name = "testJMSQueue")
    private Destination jmsQueue;

    public void sendMessage(final MessageData message)
                throws Exception {
        jmsSpringTemplate.send(jmsQueue, new MessageCreator() {
            public javax.jms.Message createMessage(Session session)
                throws JMSException {
                ObjectMessage om = session.createObjectMessage();
                om.setStringProperty("MessageType",
                                        message.getMessage());
                message.setProcessId(100);
                message.setTaskId(1);
                om.setObject(message);
                return om;
            }
        });
    }

    public void setJmsSpringTemplate(JmsTemplate jmsSpringTemplate) {
        this.jmsSpringTemplate = jmsSpringTemplate;
    }

    public void setJmsQueue(Destination jmsQueue) {
        this.jmsQueue = jmsQueue;
    }
}
```

Step 2: Implement a message receiver class.

Listing 11-8 provides a `ProcessMonitorMDP` class, which is used to receive the messages from the JMS-Queue. The message-receiver consumes only messages that have specified message type property, which is DAILY_POLLER_MSG. The complete message-receiver class code is provided in Listing 11-8.

Listing 11-8: Message receiver to process incoming messages

```java
// ProcessMonitorMDB.java
package com.learning.spring.messaging;

import org.springframework.stereotype.Component;
import org.springframework.beans.factory.annotation.Autowired;
```

```
import org.springframework.jms.core.JmsTemplate;
import javax.jms.MessageListener;
import javax.jms.ObjectMessage;

@Component
public class ProcessMonitorMDP implements MessageListener {
    public void onMessage(javax.jms.Message message) {
        if (message instanceof ObjectMessage) {
            ObjectMessage om = (ObjectMessage) message;
            try {
                MessageData taskMessage=(MessageData)om.getObject();
                Integer processId = taskMessage.getProcessId();
                Integer taskId = taskMessage.getTaskId();
                String messageId = taskMessage.getMessage();

                System.out.println("--- processId ---" + processId +
                        "--- taskId ---" + taskId +
                        "--- messageId ---" + messageId);

                // ... Impelement your logic here
            } catch (Exception ex) {
                ex.printStackTrace();
            }
        }
    }
}
```

Step 3: Create an applicationContext-mdp.xml file.

The spring-provided "jee" schema tags are used to deal with Java EE-related configurations, such as JNDI look-up for data sources, JNDI look-up for message queues, JNDI look-up for connection factories and JNDI look-up for EJB references.

The following XML tag is used to obtain the reference to the JMS connection factory, which is configured in your JMS provider.

```
<jee:jndi-lookup id="testJMSConnectionFactory"
                 jndi-name="pojo/jms/testjmsfactory"
                 lookup-on-startup="true"/>
```

The following XML tag is used to obtain the reference to the JMS destination, which is configured in your JMS-Provider.

```
<jee:jndi-lookup id="testJMSQueue"
                 jndi-name="pojo/jms/testjmsqueue"
                 lookup-on-startup="true"/>
```

The following XML tag is used to register the MDP with the message container The configured `ProcessMonitorMDP` class receives the messages from the JMS-Queue.

```
<jms:listener destination="testJMSQueue"
              ref="processMonitorMDP"
              selector="MessageType IN ('DAILY_POLLER_MSG')"/>
```

The above configuration is equivalent to the following bean definitions that we used in Example-1.

```xml
<bean id="messageListener" class="org.springframework.jms.listener.
                            adapter.MessageListenerAdapter">
    <constructor-arg>
        <bean class="com.learning.spring.messaging.ProcessMonitorMDB"/>
    </constructor-arg>
</bean>

<bean id="jmsContainer" class="org.springframework.jms.listener.
                            DefaultMessageListenerContainer">
    <property name="connectionFactory" ref="jmsConnectionFactory"/>
    <property name="destination" ref="jmsQueue"/>
    <property name="messageListener" ref="messageListener"/>
</bean>
```

The complete XML file is provided below and is named the "applicationContext-mdp.xml".

```xml
<?xml version="1.0" encoding="UTF-8"?>
<beans xmlns="http://www.springframework.org/schema/beans"
    xmlns:xsi="http://www.w3.org/2001/XMLSchema-instance"
    xmlns:context="http://www.springframework.org/schema/context"
    xmlns:jee="http://www.springframework.org/schema/jee"
    xmlns:jms="http://www.springframework.org/schema/jms"
    xsi:schemaLocation="http://www.springframework.org/schema/beans
    http://www.springframework.org/schema/beans/spring-beans-3.0.xsd
    http://www.springframework.org/schema/jee
    http://www.springframework.org/schema/jee/spring-jee-2.5.xsd
    http://www.springframework.org/schema/jms
    http://www.springframework.org/schema/jms/spring-jms-3.0.xsd
    http://www.springframework.org/schema/context
    http://www.springframework.org/schema/context/spring-
        context3.0.xsd">

    <context:annotation-config/>
    <context:component-scan base-package =
            "com.learning.spring.messaging"/>

    <!-- JMS Connection Factory -->
    <jee:jndi-lookup id="testJMSConnectionFactory"
            jndi-name="pojo/jms/testjmsfactory"
            lookup-on-startup="true"/>

    <!-- JMS Queue -->
    <jee:jndi-lookup id="testJMSQueue"
            jndi-name="pojo/jms/testjmsqueue"
            lookup-on-startup="true"/>

    <!-- Spring-specific JMS Template -->
    <bean id="jmsSpringTemplate"
        class="org.springframework.jms.core.JmsTemplate">
            <property name="connectionFactory">
                <ref bean="testJMSConnectionFactory"/>
            </property>
            <property name="pubSubDomain">
                <value>false</value>
            </property>
    </bean>
```

```xml
<!-- Destination resolver to look-up destinations configured
     as spring beans.-->
<bean id="destinationResolver"
      class="org.springframework.jms.support.destination.
                      BeanFactoryDestinationResolver"/>

<jms:listener-container
        connection-factory="testJMSConnectionFactory"
        destination-resolver="destinationResolver"
        concurrency="2-10">

      <!-- MDP to process incoming messages -->
      <jms:listener destination="testJMSQueue"
              ref="processMonitorMDP"
              selector="MessageType IN ('DAILY_POLLER_MSG')"/>

</jms:listener-container>

</beans>
```

Step 4: Create a servlet controller class to invoke the MDP.

Listing 11-9 provides a spring controller class. This class invokes the message-sender class and passes the message data to the consumer. The complete spring controller class code is provided in Listing 11-9.

Listing 11-9: Spring controller to invoke the message sender.

```java
// SpringMessagingDemoController.java
package com.learning.spring.controller;

import org.springframework.stereotype.Controller;
import org.springframework.beans.factory.annotation.Autowired;
import org.springframework.ui.ModelMap;
import org.springframework.web.bind.annotation.RequestMapping;
import org.springframework.web.bind.annotation.RequestMethod;
import com.learning.spring.messaging.MessageData;
import com.learning.spring.messaging.SimpleMessageSender;

import javax.servlet.http.HttpServletRequest;

@Controller
public class SpringMessagingDemoController {

    @Autowired
    private SimpleMessageSender simpleMessageSender;

    @RequestMapping(value = "/demo/messageSender.action",
                method = RequestMethod.POST)
    public String show(HttpServletRequest request, ModelMap model) {
        try {
            MessageData message = new MessageData();

            // Massage type is used for filtering the messages
            message.setMessage("DAILY_POLLER_MSG");
            messageSender.sendMessage(message);
        } catch (Exception ex) {
```

```
                    ex.printStackTrace();
            }

            request.setAttribute("name", "Success");
            return "demo/success";
    }
}
```

Step 5: Create a web.xml file.

The required "web.xml" file configurations are provided below.

```
<?xml version="1.0" encoding="UTF-8"?>
<web-app version="2.4" xmlns="http://java.sun.com/xml/ns/j2ee"
    xmlns:xsi="http://www.w3.org/2001/XMLSchema-instance"
    xsi:schemaLocation="http://java.sun.com/xml/ns/j2ee
    http://java.sun.com/xml/ns/j2ee/web-app_2_4.xsd">

    <servlet>
        <servlet-name>springbook</servlet-name>
        <servlet-class>
            org.springframework.web.servlet.DispatcherServlet
        </servlet-class>
        <load-on-startup>2</load-on-startup>
    </servlet>

    <servlet-mapping>
        <servlet-name>springbook</servlet-name>
        <url-pattern>*.action</url-pattern>
    </servlet-mapping>

    <listener>
        <listener-class>
            org.springframework.web.context.ContextLoaderListener
        </listener-class>
    </listener>

    <context-param>
        <param-name>contextConfigLocation</param-name>
        <param-value>/WEB-INF/applicationContext-mdp.xml</param-value>
    </context-param>

</web-app>
```

Step 6: Create a WAR File and deploy it in the Weblogic Server.

The structure of the generated WAR file is shown in Figure 11-10:

Step 7: Test the deployed message driven POJO.

Here, re-use the client we created in Example-1.

Figure 11-10: War file structure

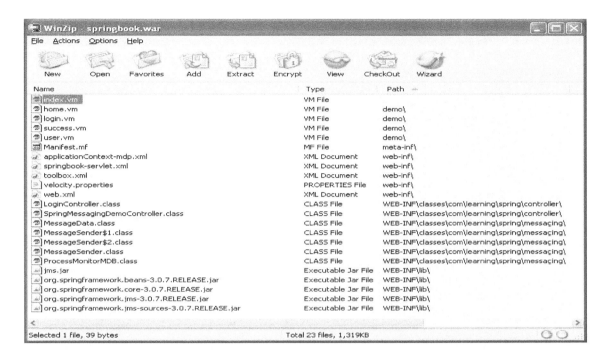

Example 4: How to Handle Messaging Transactions in MDP and MDB

The following scenarios illustrate spring support for processing messages within the transactions.

CASE 1: Working with local transactions

Local transactions can be activated by specifying the value of the `sessionTransacted` property of the message listener container as "true" The spring XML configuration for this type of transaction is provided below.

```
<!-- This is the Message Driven POJO (MDP) -->
<bean id="messageListener" class=
    "org.springframework.jms.listener.adapter.MessageListenerAdapter">
    <constructor-arg>
        <bean class=
            "com.learning.spring.messaging.POJOMessageDelegate"/>
    </constructor-arg>
</bean>

<!-- This is the message listener container -->
<bean id="jmsContainer" class="org.springframework.jms.listener.
                            DefaultMessageListenerContainer">
    <property name="connectionFactory" ref="jmsConnectionFactory"/>
    <property name="destination" ref="jmsQueue"/>
    <property name="messageListener" ref="messageListener"/>
    <property name="sessionTransacted" value="true"/>
</bean>
```

CASE 2: Working with external transactions

External transactions can be activated by specifying the value of the `transactionManager` property of the message listener container as the configured `JtaTransactionManager`. In this case, enable the XA transaction property of the configured JMS connection factory. The spring XML configuration for this type of transaction is provided below.

```xml
<!-- Tarnaction manager for XA transaction participation -->
<bean id="transactionManager" class =
        "org.springframework.transaction.jta.JtaTransactionManager"/>

<!-- This is the message listener container -->
<bean id="jmsContainer" class="org.springframework.jms.listener.
                        DefaultMessageListenerContainer">
    <property name="connectionFactory" ref="jmsConnectionFactory"/>
    <property name="destination" ref="jmsQueue"/>
    <property name="messageListener" ref="messageListener"/>
    <property name="transactionManager" ref="transactionManager"/>
</bean>
```

CASE 3: Working with external transactions using "<xmlns:jms>" namespace

The following configuration is the same as in CASE-2, but it uses the `<jms:>` namespace instead of `<bean>` tag to configure the transaction manager.

```xml
<!-- Destination resolver to look-up destinations configured as spring
beans. -->
<bean id="destinationResolver" class=
                "org.springframework.jms.support.destination.
                BeanFactoryDestinationResolver"/>

<!-- Tarnaction manager for XA transaction participation -->
<bean id="transactionManager" class=
        "org.springframework.transaction.jta.JtaTransactionManager"/>

<jms:listener-container connection-factory="testJMSConnectionFactory"
                destination-resolver="destinationResolver"
                transaction-manager="transactionManager"
                concurrency="2-10">

    <!-- MDP to process incoming messages -->
    <jms:listener destination="testJMSQueue"
                ref="processMonitorMDB"
                selector="MessageType IN ('DAILY_POLLER_MSG')"/>

</jms:listener-container>
```

Using Rollback in Message-Driven POJO

```java
@Component
public class ProcessMonitorMDB implements MessageListener {
    public void onMessage(Message message) throws RuntimeException {
        ...

        /* throw RuntimeException if there is
                any error in business logic */
```

```
        }
}

// getting the jms session
javax.jms.Session jmsSession = jmsTemplate.getConnectionFactory().
                    createConnection().createSession(true, 0);
boolean isTransacted = jmsSession.getTransacted();

// commits the tranaction
jmsSession.commit();

// rollback the tranaction
jmsSession.rollback();
```

Using Rollback in Message-Driven Bean (MDB)

```
public class ExampleMDB implements javax.ejb.MessageDrivenBean,
                            javax.jms.MessageListener {
    javax.ejb.MessageDrivenContext context;
    public void setMessageDrivenContext(javax.ejb.MessageDrivenContext
        aContext) {
            context = aContext;
    }

    public void onMessage(javax.jms.Message inMessage) {
        /* If there is any error in business logic, rollback the
            transaction */
        ...
        context.setRollbackOnly();
    }
}
```

What happens to the message if the transaction is rolled back due to an error?

- Discard the message if there are any exceptions. The message is lost.
- Write the message to an error queue.
- Redeliver the message after "n" seconds; then write the message to an error queue.
- Redeliver the message "n" number of times; then write the message to an error queue.

The application developer has to handle the above-specified scenarios based on the application requirements.

Example 5: Synchronous Message Processing with MDP

The following points demonstrate synchronous message processing.

- The message sender puts messages into a message queue.
- The message receiver retrieves the messages from the message queue.
- The message receiver class uses the `JMSTemplate.receiveAndConvert(...)` method to receive JMS messages synchronously. This `receiveAndConvert(...)` method retrieves messages from the message queue.
- In this example, a single message queue has been shared by the sender-and-receiver.

- After delivering the message into a message queue; run the message receiver to retrieve the message from the queue.

The sender-to-receiver message communication is shown in Figure 11-11:

Figure 11-11: Synchronous message processing example

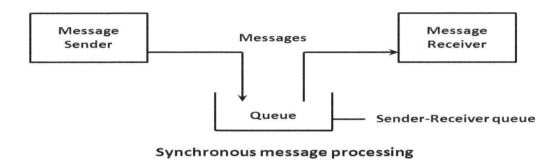

The steps required to implement a synchronous message-driven POJO are listed below:

1. Create a message-sender class.
2. Implement a message-receiver class.
3. Create an "applicationContext-synch.xml" file.
4. Create a servlet controller class to invoke the MDP.
5. Create a "web.xml" file.
6. Create a WAR File, and deploy it in the Weblogic server.
7. Test the deployed message-driven POJO.

The above-specified steps are described in the following sections:

Step 1: Create a message sender class.

Listing 11-10 provides a `SynchronousMessageSender` class, which is used for sending messages to the JMS-Queue. The complete message-sender class code is provided in Listing 11-10.

Listing 11-10: Message sender to send messages to a JMS queue

```
// SynchronousMessageSender.java
package com.learning.spring.messaging;

import org.springframework.jms.core.JmsTemplate;
import org.springframework.jms.core.MessageCreator;
import org.springframework.beans.factory.annotation.Autowired;
import javax.jms.*;
import javax.annotation.Resource;

public class SynchronousMessageSender {

    @Autowired
    private JmsTemplate jmsTemplate;
```

```
@Resource(name="synchJMSQueue")
private Queue synchJMSQueue;

public void sendMessage(final MessageData message) {
    jmsTemplate.send(synchJMSQueue, new MessageCreator() {
        public javax.jms.Message createMessage(Session session)
                throws JMSException {
            ObjectMessage om = session.createObjectMessage();
            message.setProcessId(111);
            message.setTaskId(11);
            om.setObject(message);
            return om;
        }
    });
}

public void setJmsTemplate(JmsTemplate jmsTemplate) {
    this.jmsTemplate = jmsTemplate;
}

public void setSynchJMSQueue(Queue synchJMSQueue) {
    this.synchJMSQueue = synchJMSQueue;
}
}
```

Step 2: Implement a message receiver class.

The message-receiver retrieves the messages from the JMS-Queue. The `JMSTemplate`-provided `receiveAndConvert(...)` method is used to retrieve the messages from the Queue. The complete message-receiver class code is provided in Listing 11-11.

Listing 11-11: Message receiver to retrieve messages.

```java
// SynchronousMessageReceiver.java
package com.learning.spring.messaging;

import org.springframework.beans.factory.annotation.Autowired;
import org.springframework.jms.core.JmsTemplate;
import javax.jms.*;
import javax.annotation.Resource;

public class SynchronousMessageReceiver {

    @Autowired
    private JmsTemplate jmsTemplate;

    @Resource(name = "synchJMSQueue")
    private Queue synchJMSQueue;

    public MessageData processMessage() {
        Object msg = jmsTemplate.receiveAndConvert(synchJMSQueue);
        MessageData objMessage = (MessageData) msg;
        if (msg != null) {
            System.out.println(" process id -->" +
                                objMessage.getProcessId());
            System.out.println(" Task id -->" +
                    objMessage.getTaskId());
```

```
        }

        //... Implement your logic here

        objMessage.setMessage("Responding back to caller ...");
        return objMessage;
    }

    public void setJmsTemplate(JmsTemplate jmsTemplate) {
        this.jmsTemplate = jmsTemplate;
    }

    public void setSynchJMSQueue(Queue synchJMSQueue) {
        this.synchJMSQueue = synchJMSQueue;
    }
}
```

Step 3: Create an applicationContext-synch.xml file.

Here, re-use the "applicationContext-pojo.xml" we created in Example-1 with the following change.

```
<bean id="jmsSender"
    class="com.learning.spring.messaging.SynchronousMessageSender">
        <property name="jmsTemplate">
            <ref bean="jmsTemplate"/>
        </property>
</bean>

<bean id="jmsReceiver"
    class="com.learning.spring.messaging.SynchronousMessageReceiver">
        <property name="jmsTemplate">
            <ref bean="jmsTemplate"/>
        </property>
</bean>
```

Step 4: Create a servlet controller class to invoke the MDP.

The following code sends the messages to a queue.

```
synchronousMessageSender.sendMessage(message);
```

After delivering the message into a message queue; run the message receiver to retrieve the message from the queue. The following code retrieves the messages from the JMS-Queue.

```
MessageData messageData = synchronousMessageReceiver.processMessage();
```

The complete Spring controller class code is provided in Listing 11-12.

Listing 11-12: Spring controller to call the message sender-and-receiver

```
// SpringMessagingDemoController.java
package com.learning.spring.controller;

import org.springframework.stereotype.Controller;
import org.springframework.beans.factory.annotation.Autowired;
```

```java
import org.springframework.ui.ModelMap;
import org.springframework.web.bind.annotation.RequestMapping;
import org.springframework.web.bind.annotation.RequestMethod;
import com.learning.spring.messaging.*;
import javax.servlet.http.HttpServletRequest;

@Controller
public class SpringMessagingDemoController {

    @Autowired
    private SynchronousMessageSender synchronousMessageSender;

    @Autowired
    private SynchronousMessageReceiver synchronousMessageReceiver;

    @RequestMapping(value = "/demo/messageSender.action",
            method = RequestMethod.POST)
    public String show(HttpServletRequest request, ModelMap model) {
        try {
            MessageData message = new MessageData();

            // Sending messages to a Queue
            synchronousMessageSender.sendMessage(message);

            // Retriving messages from a Queue
            MessageData messageData =
                synchronousMessageReceiver.processMessage();
            System.out.println(messageData.getMessage());

        } catch (Exception ex) {
            ex.printStackTrace();
        }

        request.setAttribute("name", "Success");
        return "demo/success";
    }
}
```

Step 5: Create a web.xml file.

Here, re-use the "web.xml" we created in Example-1 with the following change.

```xml
<context-param>
    <param-name>contextConfigLocation</param-name>
    <param-value>/WEB-INF/applicationContext-synch.xml</param-value>
</context-param>
```

Step 6: Create a WAR file and deploy it in the Weblogic server.

The structure of the generated WAR file is shown in Figure 11-12.

Step 7: Test the deployed message driven POJO.

Here, re-use the client we created in Example-1.

Figure 11-12: War file structure

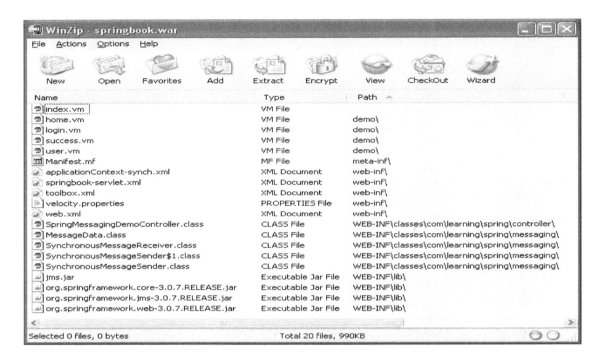

Comparison between MDP and MDB

The following table summarizes the comparison between the various technical features of message-driven POJO's and message-driven beans.

MDP	MDB
It's a plain Java class.	It's an enterprise java bean (EJB) class.
The message-driven POJO class implements JMS-provided `javax.jms.MessageListener` class	The message-driven bean class implements `javax.jms.MessageListener` and extends the `MessageDrivenBean`.
Not part of the EJB specification. MDP is a POJO class.	MDB is part of the EJB specification. The EJB container manages the bean life cycle.

Summary

This section summarizes the features provided in the spring messaging framework

- Spring provides a `JmsTemplate` helper class to send-and-receive messages synchronously. The methods `send(...)` and `convertAndSend(...)` are used to send messages. The methods `receive(...)` and `receiveAndConvert(...)` are used for synchronous message reception.

- Spring provides a `JmsTransactionManager` class that manages transactions for a single JMS `ConnectionFactory`.
- The spring-provided `DefaultMessageListenerContainer` can be used to process messages asynchronously.
- The spring-provided `<xmlns:jms>` namespace tags are used to deal with JMS-related message listeners and message listener containers.

Figure 11-13 summarizes the most important points described in this chapter.

Figure 11-13: Spring messaging summary

Chapter 12. Spring with REST (JAX-RS)

We see various types of URLs while browsing the Internet. Why are there various URL patterns? What are they used for? What are the most commonly used URL notations for developing Web applications? Let us review some examples.

Commonly used URL notations for MVC-based Web applications are provided below. Web application frameworks such as Struts, Spring MVC, and JSF follow this kind of notation for developing Web applications.

```
http://localhost:8080/wsbook/demo/getGrades.do
http://localhost:8080/wsbook/demo/getGrades.action
```

Similarly, a typical URL containing a query string is given below. This notation is used to pass the HTML form data query string parameters containing the name and values.

```
http://localhost:8080/wsbook/services/dataservice/student?name=john&id=5
```

The notation used to specify the matrix parameter key value pairs as part of a URI is given below.

```
http://localhost:8080/wsbook/services/bookservice/book/2012;author=john;c
ountry=usa
```

Now we have another set of URLs (below). The below provided URL's represent the grades, subjects, topics, and topic content. Let us examine each URL and its output.

```
http://localhost:8080/wsbook/services/gradeservice/grades
http://localhost:8080/wsbook/services/gradeservice/grade/1
http://localhost:8080/wsbook/services/gradeservice/grade/1/subject/Math
http://localhost:8080/wsbook/services/gradeservice/grade/1/subject/Math/t
opic/Mathematics and art
```

The URL is:

```
http://localhost:8080/wsbook/services/gradeservice/grades
```

Its output is:

```
<grades>
    <grade id="1"
    href="http://localhost:8080/wsbook/services/gradeservice/grade/1"/>
    <grade id="2"
    href="http://localhost:8080/wsbook/services/gradeservice/grade/2"/>
    <grade id="3"
    href="http://localhost:8080/wsbook/services/gradeservice/grade/3"/>
    <grade id="4"
    href="http://localhost:8080/wsbook/services/gradeservice/grade/4"/>
</grades>
```

Now take the URL from the above output to obtain further information about 1st grade.

The URL is:

```
http://localhost:8080/wsbook/services/gradeservice/grade/1
```

Its output is:

```xml
<?xml version="1.0" encoding="UTF-8" ?>
<subjects>

<subject id="Math"
    href="http://localhost:8080/wsbook/services/gradeservice/grade/1/sub
ject/Math"/>

<subject id="Art"
    href="http://localhost:8080/wsbook/services/gradeservice/grade/1/sub
ject/Art"/>

<subject id="Lit"
    href="http://localhost:8080/wsbook/services/gradeservice/grade/1/sub
ject/Lit"/>

</subjects>
```

Now take the URL from the above output to obtain further information about mathematics.

The URL is:

```
http://localhost:8080/wsbook/services/gradeservice/grade/1/subject/Math
```

Its output is:

```xml
<?xml version="1.0" encoding="UTF-8"?>
<topics>

<topic id="Mathematics and art"
href="http://localhost:8080/wsbook/services/gradeservice/grade/1/subject/
Math/topic/Mathematics and art"/>

<topic id="Algebra"
href="http://localhost:8080/wsbook/services/gradeservice/grade/1/subject/
Math/topic/Algebra"/>

<topic id="Calculus"
href="http://localhost:8080/wsbook/services/gradeservice/grade/1/subject/
Math/topic/Calculus"/>

</topics>
```

Now take the URL from the above output to obtain further information about mathematics and art.

The URL is:

```
http://localhost:8080/wsbook/services/gradeservice/grade/1/subject/Math/t
opic/Mathematics and art
```

Its output is:

```
<?xml version="1.0" encoding="UTF-8" ?>
<contents>
    <content id="content"
    href="http://localhost:8080/wsbook/services/gradeservice/grade/1/
    subject/Math/topic/Mathematics and art/content/
    Mathematics and art.pdf"/>
</contents>
```

Clicking on this link will open a PDF document to display the content. The pattern here is that each URL is used to navigate further (to next level) to obtain more information. Each parent resource is mapped to many other sub-resources to obtain next level information. This type of design is called REST. REST stands for representational state transfer.

Java API for Restful Web Services (also called JAX-RS) is a Java specification used for implementing Restful Web services. This specification defines guidelines to develop Web services conforming to REST principles. The JAX-RS is a specification used for developing non-SOAP-based Web services. JAX-RS is part of Java EE.

In this chapter will discuss the following topics:

- REST principles
- The meaning of representational state transfer
- Axiom principles of Web architecture
- REST fundamentals
- REST terminology
- REST advantages
- JAX-RS annotations and its usage
- REST using Spring Framework
- REST implementation examples using Spring, Apache-CXF framework
- REST client design scenarios
- REST service endpoint and URL design scenarios

REST Principles

The word "REST" stands for representational state transfer. *Roy Thomas Fielding* introduced it in his PhD dissertation in 2000. A Restful Web service is HTTP-based that conforms to the principles of REST. Roy's dissertation describes the following six constraints for the REST architecture.

Client-Server—Provide a uniform interface to separate the client and server so that the client and server can be developed independently without altering the interface.

Figure 12-1: Rest principles

Stateless—Communication must be stateless in nature; the server will not store a client-specific state. There is always stateless communication between a client and the server i.e., the output will be the same regardless of who the client is for a given input.

Figure 12-2: Rest principles

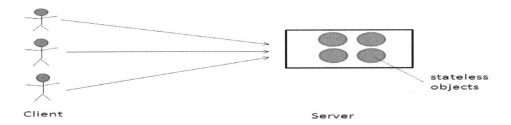

Cacheable—Clients can cache responses, but no client-specific state is stored on the server side. All server-side objects are identical.

Figure 12-3: Rest principles

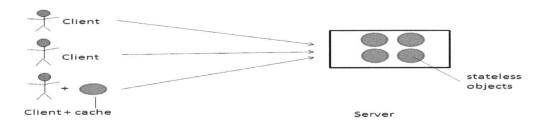

Uniform Interface—Provide a uniform interface between the client and server to decouple the client from a server. In this way, both can be developed independently; this allows the server to cache the data at interface point, this cache is shared across all invoking clients.

Figure 12-4: Rest principles

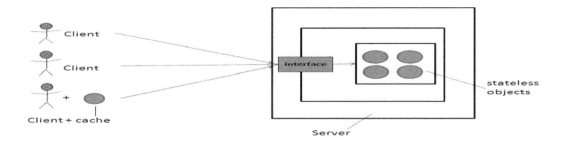

Layered System—This particular feature improves scalability through a load balancer. The load balancer routes the request to the available back-end servers. A client does not know which back-end server it is connected to. There are several ways to implement the layer server architecture that are not addressed here.

Figure 12-5: Rest principles

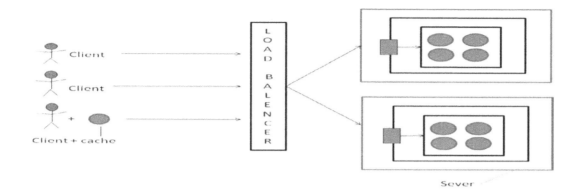

Code on Demand (Optional)—REST enables functionality by downloading and executing the code in the form of applets and Java scripts. This is an optional constraint within REST.

If a service violates any of the above six defined constraints, it cannot be strictly referred to as Restful.

The following terms best describes REST:

- REST is an architectural style
- REST is a design pattern
- REST is a certain approach for developing Web services
- REST is a guiding framework for designing Web services
- REST is not a standard, but it is a guiding framework for designing Web standards
- REST is not a tool, not a product, and not technology.

REST Terminology

The following table summarizes the terminology used in REST and their meaning:

Terminology	Meaning
Resource	Sources of specific information
Resource Identifier	URL or URI in HTTP
Representation	HTML document, image file, etc.
RESTful	Web service using HTTP that conforms to the principles of REST.
Resource class	Service endpoint implementation class that uses JAX-RS annotations to expose a Java class as a Web service
Root resource class	A class annotated with @Path. This is the entry point to the class and provides access to class methods
Resource method	Methods of a resource class
Provider	An implementation of JAX-RS extension interface

Why Is It Called Representational State Transfer?

Initially, the browser represents a state. If user performs an action on one hyperlink, the state of the client changes. With each user action, the state of the client changes; it is referred as state transfer of a client from one to another.

The client changes from one state to another when the user selects the available URLs in the response document. Here is an example of a REST-based Web service response document. The response document provides hyperlinks to connect to other sub-resources; the user should continue navigating through various logical URLs to find the final resource content.

<u>Example:</u>

```
<?xml version="1.0" encoding="UTF-8"?>
<subjects>
<subject id="Math"
href="http://localhost:8080/wsbook/services/gradeservice/grade/1/subject/
Math"/>

<subject id="Art"
href="http://localhost:8080/wsbook/services/gradeservice/grade/1/subject/
Art"/>

<subject id="Lit"
href="http://localhost:8080/wsbook/services/gradeservice/grade/1/subject/
Lit"/>

<subject id="Photograpy"
href="http://localhost:8080/wsbook/services/gradeservice/grade/1/subject/
Photograpy"/>
</subjects>
```

Figure 12-6: URL and a resource

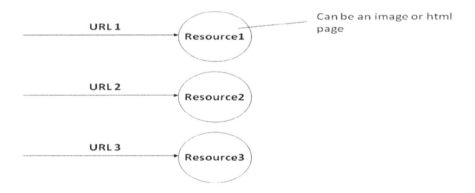

Each resource on the Web has an URI. The association between URL and Resource is shown in Figure 12-6.

REST Guidelines

The following points briefly explain the basic fundamentals of REST used to develop the REST-based Web services.

- Identify all resources you wish to present as Web services.
- Map service resources to sub-resources to obtain additional information.
- Create a URL for each resource. These resources should be nouns, not verbs.

Example:

Do not use this (Note the verb, getGrade)

```
- http://localhost:8080/wsbook/services/gradeservice/getGrade?grade=1
```

Instead, use a noun:

```
- http://localhost:8080/wsbook/services/gradeservice/grade/1
```

- Categorize resources based on mode of action (get/modify/add/delete etc.).
  - GET
  - POST
  - PUT
  - DELETE
- Provide a uniform interface between the client and server.
- All resources accessible via HTTP GET should be side-effect free; invoking a GET resource should not modify any other resource.
- Design to reveal data gradually. Don't display everything in a single response document; provide hyperlinks to obtain additional details.
- Use logical URLs instead of physical URLs. The logical URLs are constructed dynamically using the application data. They are not hard coded and they are not physical URLs; creating one thousand resources does not require one thousand physical URLs.
- Communicate statelessly. There will be no client-specific server side cache.
- The REST URLs do not follow the common ".do" or ".action" notation used for Web applications.

REST Advantages

- REST is consistent with Axiom principles of Web architecture.
- REST is Simple, easy to implement, manage, and maintain. No special tools or products are needed for development and deployment.
- REST provides lightweight services.
- REST provides simple and readable service endpoint designs.
- There are no additional testing frameworks/tools needed for testing REST services.
- It is easy to understand what each REST service does simply by examining the URL (i.e., it implements the principle of least surprise).
- There is no need to introduce rules. Rules and priorities are elevated at URL level. "What you see is what you get."
- It's easy to implement high priority—simply assign a faster processing machine to the premier member URL.

- The various URLs are discoverable by search engines and UDDI registries.
- REST architecture improves the scalability of your application.
- Client and server components can be developed independently without altering the interface.
- REST services are portable across the platforms; works well with all platforms (i.e., Windows, Mac, Unix, etc.).
- REST services are interoperable across various technology frameworks; does not matter whether it is Java or .Net.
- REST provides support for multiple content types; not limited to one XML; it can be HTML, SOAP, JSON, and many others.
- REST provides support for annotations; fewer lines to code in your application.
- Low development cost, no special skills or consulting needed for REST services development.

JAX-RS Annotations

JAX-RS provides several annotations for developing restful Web services. These annotations are defined in the "javax.ws.rs" package, and they conform to basic HTTP principles. They include query parameters, path parameters, and matrix parameters defined in the basic URI path. These annotations can be used at field level, method level, class level, and interface level, as well as with method parameters. The following section explains the commonly used annotations for implementing RESTful Web services. Each annotation is demonstrated using a code example.

- @GET
- @POST
- @DELETE
- @PUT
- @Path
- @Produces
- @Consumes
- @Context
- @PathParam
- @QueryParam
- @FormParam
- @MatrixParam
- @DefaultParam

@GET

The method annotated with @GET annotation is similar to HTTP GET request operation; GET requests should be used only for READ-ONLY resources. The get request should not add, modify, or delete any server-side resources. Get is a safe operation and has no side effects. "Safe" means that it should not modify any resource states on the server. An example of the use of the @GET annotation is given below.

```
public interface DocumentManager {
    @GET
    public String getDocument(String id);
}
```

@POST

The method annotated with @POST annotation is similar to HTTP POST request operation; the POST request is used for adding a new resource or to pass long parameters as a query string. The POST operation does have side effects; it will add a new resource. But in general, we use POST for things such as updates and for deleting and adding resources; because of this, the use of DELETE, PUT becomes minimal in Web applications. HTML forms support only GET and POST requests, so we have to improvise to identify DELETE and PUT requests using hidden fields in the HTML form. An example use of @POST annotation is given below.

```
public interface DocumentManager {
    @POST
    public void addDocument(String id);
}
```

@DELETE

The method annotated with @DELETE annotation is similar to HTTP DELETE operation; the DELETE operations are idempotent and used for deleting a resource. Whether you delete a resource at a specific URL once or ten times, the effect is the same. In general, we tunnel the DELETE and PUT requests through POST, because the HTML form supports only GET and POST. An example use of @DELETE annotation is given below.

```
public interface DocumentManager {
    @DELETE
    public void deleteDocument(String id);
}
```

@PUT

The method annotated with @PUT annotation is similar to HTTP PUT; the PUT operations are idempotent and are used for replacing a resource. Whether you replace a resource at a specific URL once or ten times, the effect is the same. An example use of @PUT annotation is given below.

```
public interface DocumentManager {
    @PUT
    public void replaceDocument(String id);
}
```

The use of GET, POST, DELETE, and PUT annotations are given below. Assume that we tunnel the DELETE and PUT requests through the POST operation.

```
public interface DocumentManager {

    @GET
    // This method is used for GET requests.
    public String getDocument(String id);

    @POST
    // This method is used for POST request.
    public void addDocument(String id) ;

    @POST
```

```
      /* This method is used to tunnel POST request for DELETE and PUT
         operations. */
      public void deleteOrReplaceDocument(String id);

      @DELETE
      // This method is used for deleting a resource.
      public void deleteDocument(String id);

      @PUT
      // This method is used for replacing a resource.
      public void replaceDocument(String id);

}
```

NOTE: Refer to Example-4 for complete working code.

@Path

The @Path annotation is used to identify the entry point of a service and its operation to be executed. This annotation can be used at class and method levels. This annotation looks for an URI path and searches for the exact match at the class and method levels to determine which method of the class should be executed. An example of the use of the @Path annotation is given below.

The URL provided below invokes the "getGrades()" method of "GradeManager" service.

```
http://localhost:8080/wsbook/services/gradeservice/grades
```

It looks for the matching URI path "/gradeservice" at the class level and "/grades" at the method level. The matching operation of a service class will be executed.

```
@Path("/gradeservice/")
public interface GradeManager {
    @GET
    @Path("/grades")
    public String getGrades();
}
```

Similarly, the URL provided below invokes the "getGradeSubjects()" method of "GradeManager" service.

```
http://localhost:8080/wsbook/services/gradeservice/grade/{grade}
```

The service class is given below.

```
@Path("/gradeservice/")
public interface GradeManager {
    @GET
    @Path("/grade/{grade}")
    public String getGradeSubjects(@PathParam("grade") Integer grade) ;
}
```

@Produces

This refers to the type of content a server delivers to the client. The @Produces annotation can be used at the class level and method level. It is allowed to declare more than one content type and is represented as @Produces("application/xml," "plain/text"). If it is declared at the method level and class level, the method-level annotation overrides that of the class level, and it produces the content type declared at the method level. An example of the use of a @Produces annotation is given below.

```
@Path("/gradeservice/")
@Produces("application/xml")
public interface GradeManager {
    @GET
    @Path("/grades")
    @Produces("plain/text")
    public String getGrades();
}
```

At the class level, it is declared to deliver the "application/xml" content type, and at the method level, it produces the "plain/text" content type. The method-level annotation overrides the class-level annotation and sends the "plain/text" content back to the client.

@Consumes

This refers to the type of content a server receives from the client. This annotation can be used at the class level and method level. It is represented as @Consumes("application/xml"), is allowed to declare more than one content type, and is represented as @Consumes("application/xml," "application/html"). An example of the use of the @Consumes annotation is given below.

```
@Path("/loginservice/")
@Consumes("application/x-www-form-urlencoded")
public class AccessManagerImpl {
    @POST
    @Path("/userName/{userName}/password/{password}")
    public void postUserData(MultivaluedMap<String,String> formParams) {
        // Implement your logic here, after getting the form data
        for (String key : formParams.keySet()) {
                System.out.println("-- value is --" +
            formParams.get(key) );
        }

        // (OR) use this
        for (Map.Entry<String, List<String>> entry :
                            formParams.entrySet()) {
            System.out.println("---- value ----" + entry.getValue());
        }
    }
}
```

@PathParam

The @PathParam annotation is used at the method level (parameter to method) to obtain the parameter values specified in the REST URL. The parameter name-values of a REST URL are shown in Figure 12-7.

Figure 12-7: PathParam URL notation

The example provided below obtains the parameter values of {grade} and {subject} specified in the REST URL.

```
@Path("/gradeservice/")
public interface GradeManager {
    @GET
    @Path("/grade/{grade}/subject/{subject}")
    public String getSubjectTopics(@PathParam("grade") Integer grade,
                                   @PathParam("subject") String subject);
    /* value of {grade} maps to Integer grade
        - parameter value "1" assigns to grade */

    /* value of {subject} maps String subject
        - parameter value "Drawing" assigns to subject. */
}
```

@QueryParam

Figure 12-8: QueryParam URL notation

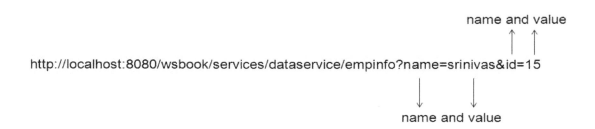

The @QueryParam annotation is used at the method level to obtain the query string values specified in the REST URL. An example use of query string parameter name and value is shown in Figure 12-8.

There are several options to get the query string parameter values. They are listed below.

1. How to get the query string parameters using @Context UriInfo class
2. How to get the query string parameters using @Context HttpServletRequest class
3. How to get the query string parameters using @QueryParam annotation

CASE 1:

How to get the query string parameters using @Context UriInfo

The JAX-RS-provided "UriInfo" class can be used to get the path and query parameters associated with any REST URL. The "getQueryParameters()" method of an "UriInfo" class is used to get the query string parameters of a REST URL. The example below gets the query parameter values specified in the REST URL.

```
@Path("/dataservice/")
@Produces("application/xml")
public class RestDataManagerImpl {
    @GET
    @Path("/restinfo")
    public void getCommmonInfo(@Context UriInfo uriInfo) {
        // Query Parameters
        MultivaluedMap<String, String> queryParams =
                        uriInfo.getQueryParameters();
        for(Map.Entry<String, List<String>> entry :
                        queryParams.entrySet()) {
            // prints [srinivas] and [15]
            System.out.println("-- param value --" + entry.getValue());
        }
    }
}
```

CASE 2:

How to get the query string parameters using @Context HttpServletRequest

The HTTP-provided "HttpServletRequest" class can be used to get the query parameters associated with any REST URL. This is an approach commonly used in Java servlet programming.

The example below gets the query parameter values specified in the REST URL.

```
@Path("/dataservice/")
@Produces("application/xml")
public class RestDataManagerImpl {
    @GET
    @Path("/restinfo")
    public void getCommonInfo(@Context HttpServletRequest req) {
        // Query Parameters
        String name = req.getParameter("name");
        String id = req.getParameter("id");
        System.out.println("-- name and id --" + name + "and" + id);
    }
}
```

CASE 3:

How to get the query string parameters using @QueryParam annotation

The JAX-RS–provided @QueryParam annotation can be used to get the query parameter values associated with any REST URL. The URL provided below specifies the stock symbol as a query string parameter; it invokes the service and returns the stock price.

```
http://localhost:8080/wsbook/services/stockservice/symbol?symbol=GOLD
```

The service code provided below gets the value specified in the above URL using @QueryParam annotation.

```
@Path("/stockservice/")
@Produces("text/plain")
public class StockServiceImpl {
    @GET
    @Path("/symbol")
    public String getStockPrice(@QueryParam("symbol") String symbol) {
        if(symbol.equalsIgnoreCase("GOLD")) {
            return "160.30";
        } else if(symbol.equalsIgnoreCase("XXX")) {
            return "10.0";
        }
        return symbol;
    }
}
```

@FormParam

The @FormParam annotation is used with content type "application/x-www-form-urlencoded" along with the HTTP POST operation. This is used to receive the HTML form data at service endpoint after the client submits the HTML form using the HTTP POST method. An example of the use of @FormParam annotation is given below.

The code provided below receives the individual field's data in method-level variables.

```
@POST
@Path("/userName/{userName}/password/{password}")
public void postUserData(@FormParam("userName") String userName,
                         @FormParam("password") String password) {
    System.out.println("-- userName --" + userName +
                        "--:--" + password);
    // Implement your logic here
}
```

The code provided below receives the entire HTML form data in a map. Iterate the map to get the required values.

```
@POST
@Path("/userName/{userName}/password/{password}")
public void postUserData(MultivaluedMap<String, String> formParams) {
    // Implement the logic here
    for(String key : formParams.keySet()) {
        System.out.println( "-- value is --" + formParams.get(key) );
    }

    // Implement your logic here
```

```
}
```

@MatrixParam

This annotation is used at the method level to extract the values of URI matrix parameter key value pairs. An example of the use of @MatrixParam annotation is given below.

```
@Path("/bookservice/")
@Produces("text/plain")
public interface BookService {
    @GET
    @Path("/book/{year}")
    String getBooks(@PathParam("year") String year,
                @MatrixParam("author") String author,
                @MatrixParam("country") String country);
}
```

The URL used to invoke the above service is given below.

```
http://localhost:8080/wsbook/services/bookservice/book/2012;author=sriniv
as;country=usa
```

NOTE: Refer to Example-5 for complete code.

@Context

This annotation is used at method level (as a method parameter). The @Context annotation is used to get a handle to the HttpHeaders, UriInfo, Request, HttpServletRequest, HttpServletResponse, SecurityContext, HttpServletConfig, and ServletContext classes. These objects can be used to manipulate the parameter values specified in the REST URL. An example of the use of @Context annotation is given below.

```
@Path("/dataservice/")
@Produces("application/xml")
public class RestDataManagerImpl {
    @GET
    @Path("/contextinfo")
    public void getCommmonInfo(@Context UriInfo uriInfo,
                        @Context HttpHeaders headers,
                        @Context HttpServletRequest req) {
        // Implement your logic here.
        // Refer to Example2 to for complete code.
    }
}
```

To summarize, the use of @PathParam, @QueryParam, @FormParam, and @MatrixParam annotations are explained with example URLs.

The @PathParam annotation is used to get the parameter values specified in the REST URL. An example URL of this type given below:

```
http://localhost:8080/wsbook/services/gradeservice/grade/1/subject/Art
```

The `@QueryParam` annotation is used to get the parameter values specified in the query string. An example URL of this type is given below:

```
http://localhost:8080/wsbook/services/dataservice/restinfo?name=john&id=5
```

The `@FormParam` annotation is used to get the entire HTML form data submitted through the HTTP POST method.

The `@MatrixParam` annotation is used to extract the values of URI matrix parameter key value pairs. An example URL of this type is given below.

```
http://localhost:8080/wsbook/services/bookservice/book/2012;author=john
```

@DefaultValue

The `@DefaultValue` annotation can be used at field level or method level to assign a default value to a variable if it does not find the key value.

Annotation Inheritance with REST

The JAX-RS specification supports the annotation inheritance. It is a very commonly used and is the most powerful feature; every REST developer needs to understand it. There are three ways REST annotations can be inherited.

1. Annotation inheritance by subclassing
2. Annotation inheritance by implementing annotated interfaces
3. Annotation inheritance by subclassing and implementing annotated interfaces

Annotation Rules:

- The annotations declared in the subclass will override the super-class annotations.
- The class will get the inherited annotations of the interface it implements.
- The subclass annotations can only override super-class annotations but cannot completely avoid them from a super class.
- Super class first and interface next - In annotation inheritance by subclassing and implementing annotated interfaces; annotations inherited from a super class will have the highest priority, followed by annotations declared in the interface.

The following example illustrates the use of annotation inheritance by subclassing. There are two scenarios associated with subclassing. The first scenario is that the subclass gets the inherited annotations from a super class; the second scenario is that the subclass will override the super class annotations.

CASE 1:

Let us now discuss the first scenario; the subclass gets the inherited annotations from its super class. The service "StockServiceImpl" class provided below produces the "text/plain" content type.

```
public class StockServiceImpl {
    @GET
    @Path("/symbol/{symbol}")
    @Produces("text/plain")
    public String getStockPrice(@PathParam("symbol") String symbol) {
        System.out.println("---- symbol ----" + symbol);
        if(symbol.equalsIgnoreCase("GLD")) {
            return "1800.30";
        } else if(symbol.equalsIgnoreCase("XXX")) {
            return "10.0";
        }
        return symbol;
    }
}
```

The annotation @Produces is not declared in its subclass "NewStockServiceImpl"; it inherits content type from its super class and produces the "text/plain" content type, provided below.

```
@Path("/stockservice/")
public class NewStockServiceImpl extends StockServiceImpl {
    @GET
    @Path("/symbol/{symbol}")
    public String getStockPrice(@PathParam("symbol") String symbol) {
        if(symbol.equalsIgnoreCase("SLV")) {
            return "32.30";
        } else if(symbol.equalsIgnoreCase("YYYY")) {
            return "10.0";
        }
        return symbol;
    }
}
```

CASE 2:

Let us now discuss the second scenario; the subclass overrides the annotations declared in its super class. The "StockServiceImpl" class produces the "text/plain" content type. The subclass "NewStockServiceImpl" provided below produces a different content type. The subclass annotation overrides the annotation declared in its super class and produces the new content type as "application/xml."

```
@Path("/stockservice/")
public class NewStockServiceImpl extends StockServiceImpl {
    @GET
    @Path("/symbol/{symbol}")
    @Produces("application/xml")
    public String getStockPrice(@PathParam("symbol") String symbol) {
        if(symbol.equalsIgnoreCase("SLV")) {
            return "<price>32.30</price>";
        } else if(symbol.equalsIgnoreCase("YYYY")) {
            return "<price>10.30</price>";
        }
        return symbol;
    }
}
```

CASE 3:

The following example illustrates the use of annotation inheritance by implementing annotated interfaces. The class "BookServiceImpl" implements the "BookService" interface; annotations are declared at the interface level, and the "getBooks()" method of the "BookServiceImpl" class declares all inherited annotations at the interface level and produces the "text/plain" content type.

```
@Path("/bookservice/")
@Produces("text/plain")
public interface BookService {
    @GET
    @Path("/book/{year}")
    String getBooks(@PathParam("year") String year,
                    @MatrixParam("author") String author,
                    @MatrixParam("country") String country);
}
```

The "BookServiceImpl" class implements the "BookService" interface and declares all inherited annotations at the interface level.

```
public class BookServiceImpl implements BookService {
    public String getBooks(String year, String author, String country) {
        return "year: " + year + " author: " + author + " country: " +
        country;
    }
}
```

CASE 4:

The following example illustrates annotation inheritance by subclassing and implementing annotated interfaces. The interface "StockService" produces the "application/xml" content type.

```
public interface StockService {
    @Produces("application/xml")
    public String getStockPrice(String symbol);
}
```

The super class "StockServiceImpl" provided below produces the "text/plain" content type.

```
public class StockServiceImpl {
    @Produces("text/plain")
    public String getStockPrice(String symbol) {
        if(symbol.equalsIgnoreCase("GLD")) {
            return "1800.30";
        } else if(symbol.equalsIgnoreCase("XXX")) {
            return "10.0";
        }
        return symbol;
    }
}
```

The subclass "NewStockServiceImpl" provided below extends the "StockServiceImpl" class and implements the "StockService" interface. It follows the super class first and interface next rule; it gets the inherited annotation from its super class and produces the "text/plain" content type.

```
@Path("/stockservice/")
public class NewStockServiceImpl extends StockServiceImpl implements
StockService {
    @GET
    @Path("/symbol/{symbol}")
    public String getStockPrice(@PathParam("symbol") String symbol) {
        if(symbol.equalsIgnoreCase("SLV")) {
            return "32.30";
        } else if(symbol.equalsIgnoreCase("YYYY")) {
            return "10.0";
        }
        return symbol;
    }
}
```

REST Code Examples

REST is part of Java specification request. This specification defines a set of guidelines for the development of Web services conforming to REST principles. There are several open-source REST implementation projects available for developing enterprise applications. All these frameworks provide similar features and support Spring framework integration. Some of the commonly used open-source REST implementations are listed below.

- Apache-CXF—Now part of Apache, which is a merger between Celtix and XFire
- Jersey—JAX-RS reference implementation from Sun
- RESTEasy—JBoss's JAX-RS project
- Restlet
- Spring

The following sections explain several REST implementation examples using Spring and Apache-CXF.

Example 1: REST using Apache-CXF framework

The Apache-CXF framework provides Java API for developing Restful Web services based on the REST architectural style. The steps required to develop a Web service of this type are given below.

1. Create a service endpoint interface.
2. Create a service implementation class.
3. Create dependent helper classes if any are required.
4. Create an Apache-CXF framework-specific configuration file.
5. Create a web.xml file.
6. Create a WAR file and deploy it in the Tomcat server.
7. Verify the deployment using the REST URL from a browser.
8. Write a client to invoke the deployed service.
9. Log the service request and response.

The above-specified steps are described in the following sections:

Step 1: Create a Service Endpoint Interface

The first step is to create a uniform interface between the client and server. This interface contains all required business methods. The interface provided below contains four business methods associated with corresponding REST URLs. These methods return the list of grades, subjects of each grade, and topics of each subject; finally, they display the content of each topic.

The REST URL paths specified for each method of a service are given below.

- `@Path("/gradeservice/")`—It represents the entry point of a service class or interface.
- `@Path("/grades")`—It represents the entry point for the "getGrades()" method of a service class.
- `@Path("/grade/{grade}")`—It represents the entry point for the "getGradeSubjects()" method of a service class.
- `@Path("/grade/{grade}/subject/{subject}")`—It represents the entry point for the "getSubjectTopics()" method of a service class.
- `@Path("/grade/{grade}/subject/{subject}/topic/{topic}")`—It represents the entry point for the "getTopicContent()" method of a service class.

The @PathParam annotation is used to obtain the values specified in the REST URL.

`@PathParam("grade") Integer grade`—Obtains the {grade} value specified in the REST URL.
`@PathParam("subject") String subject`—Obtains the {subject} value specified in the REST URL.
`@PathParam("topic") String topic`—Obtains the {topic} value specified in the REST URL

The "GradeManager" interface provided below contains all GET operations and produces an "application/xml" content type. Listing 12-1 provides the complete interface code.

Listing 12-1: Rest example using Apache-CXF

```java
// GradeManager.java
package com.learning.ws.rest;

import javax.ws.rs.Path;
import javax.ws.rs.Produces;
import javax.ws.rs.GET;
import javax.ws.rs.PathParam;

@Path("/gradeservice/")
@Produces("application/xml")
public interface GradeManager {
    @GET
    @Path("/grades")
    @Produces("application/xml")
    public String getGrades();

    @GET
    @Path("/grade/{grade}")
    public String getGradeSubjects(@PathParam("grade") Integer grade);

    @GET
    @Path("/grade/{grade}/subject/{subject}")
    public String getSubjectTopics(@PathParam("grade") Integer grade,
                          @PathParam("subject") String subject);
```

```
@GET
@Path("/grade/{grade}/subject/{subject}/topic/{topic}")
public String getTopicContent(@PathParam("grade") Integer grade,
                              @PathParam("subject") String subject,
                              @PathParam("topic") String topic);
}
```

Step 2: Create a Service Implementation Class

The implementations of the interface-defined methods are shown in Listing 12-2. A utility class "XMLBuilder" is used for building the response XML for each business method.

Listing 12-2: Service implementation class.

```
// GradeManagerImpl.java
package com.learning.ws.rest;

import com.learning.util.XMLBuilder;

public class GradeManagerImpl implements GradeManager {
    public String getGrades() {
        return XMLBuilder.getAllGrades();
    }

    public String getGradeSubjects(Integer grade) {
        return XMLBuilder.getAllSubjects(grade);
    }

    public String getSubjectTopics(Integer grade, String subject) {
        return XMLBuilder.getAllTopics(grade, subject);
    }

    public String getTopicContent(Integer grade,
                                  String subject, String topic) {
        return XMLBuilder.getTopicContent(grade, subject, topic);
    }
}
```

Step 3: Create any Dependent Helper, DAO Classes

The utility class provided below is used to generate the response XML. In the real world, this data comes from a database. The methods of this class are used to build the response XML using Dom4j API.

`public static String getAllGrades()`—Returns the list of grades.

`public static String getAllSubjects(Integer grade)`—Returns the subjects of a given a grade.

`public static String getAllTopics(Integer grade, String subject)`—Returns the topics of a given subject and grade.

`public static String getTopicContent(Integer grade, String subject, String topic)`—Returns the final content of the topic.

Listing 12-3 has the complete Java code used for creating the response XML.

Listing 12-3: Utility class used to create the response XML

```java
// XMLBuilder.java
package com.learning.util;

import java.util.List;
import java.util.ArrayList;
import org.dom4j.Document;
import org.dom4j.Element;
import org.dom4j.tree.DefaultDocument;

public class XMLBuilder {
    public static String getAllGrades() {
        Document doc = new DefaultDocument();
        doc.addElement("grades");
        Element rootElement = doc.getRootElement();

        List<String> grades = getGrades();
        for (String grade : grades) {
            Element gradeElement = rootElement.addElement("grade");
            gradeElement.addAttribute("id", grade);

            // Building logical url's
            gradeElement.addAttribute("href",
            "http://localhost:8080/wsbook/services/gradeservice/grade/"
            + grade);
        }
        return doc.asXML();
    }

    public static String getAllSubjects(Integer grade) {
        Document doc = new DefaultDocument();
        doc.addElement("subjects");
        Element rootElement = doc.getRootElement();

        // Building logical url's
        List<String> subjects = getSubjects(grade);
        for (String subject : subjects) {
            Element subjectElement = rootElement.addElement("subject");
            subjectElement.addAttribute("id", subject);
            subjectElement.addAttribute("href",
            "http://localhost:8080/wsbook/services/gradeservice/grade/"
            + grade + "/subject/" + subject);
        }
        return doc.asXML();
    }

    public static String getAllTopics(Integer grade, String subject) {
        Document doc = new DefaultDocument();
        doc.addElement("topics");
        Element rootElement = doc.getRootElement();

        // Building logical url's
        List<String> topics = getTopics(subject);
        for (String topic : topics) {
            Element topicElement = rootElement.addElement("topic");
            topicElement.addAttribute("id", topic);
```

```java
            topicElement.addAttribute("href",
            "http://localhost:8080/wsbook/services/gradeservice/grade/"
            + grade + "/subject/" + subject + "/topic/" + topic);
        }
        return doc.asXML();
    }

    public static String getTopicContent(Integer grade,
                                   String subject, String topic) {
        Document doc = new DefaultDocument();
        doc.addElement("content");
        Element rootElement = doc.getRootElement();

        Element contentElement = rootElement.addElement("content");
        contentElement.addAttribute("id", "content");
        contentElement.addAttribute("href",
        "http://localhost:8080/wsbook/services/gradeservice/grade/"
        + grade + "/subject/" + subject + "/topic/" + topic
        + "/content/" + topic + ".pdf");
        return doc.asXML();
    }

    private static List<String> getGrades() {
        List<String> gradesList = new ArrayList<String>();
        gradesList.add("1");
        gradesList.add("2");
        gradesList.add("3");
        gradesList.add("4");
        gradesList.add("5");
        gradesList.add("6");
        gradesList.add("10");
        return gradesList;
    }

    private static List<String> getSubjects(Integer grade) {
        List<String> subList = new ArrayList<String>();
        switch (grade) {
            case 10:
                subList.add("Math");
                subList.add("Reading");
                subList.add("Biology");
                return subList;
            case 1:
            case 2:
            case 3:
            case 4:
                subList.add("Math");
                subList.add("Art");
                subList.add("Lit");
                subList.add("Photograpy");
                return subList;
            default:
                subList.add("Java");
                subList.add(".Net");
                return subList;
        }
    }
}
```

```java
        private static List<String> getTopics(String subject) {
            List<String> topicList = new ArrayList<String>();
            if ("Java".equalsIgnoreCase(subject)) {
                topicList.add("An Overview of Java");
                topicList.add("Introduction to classes");
                topicList.add("Packages and Interfaces");
                topicList.add("Exception Handling");
                topicList.add("Mutithreading");
                topicList.add("String Handling");
                topicList.add("Collections Framework");
            }

            if ("Math".equalsIgnoreCase(subject)) {
                topicList.add("Mathematics and art");
                topicList.add("Philosophy of mathematics");
                topicList.add("Algebra");
                topicList.add("Trigonometry");
                topicList.add("Calculus");
            }
            return topicList;
        }
    }
```

Step 4: Create Apache-CXF Framework-Specific Configuration File

The Apache-CXF framework provides XML-based server-side tags to integrate REST services with the Spring application context. These XML tags seamlessly integrate the Apache-CXF with the Spring framework. The CXF-provided <jaxrs:serviceBeans/> tag is used to register the Java Beans with the Spring container. The complete XML configuration is given below. It is named the applicationContext-cxf.xml.

```xml
<?xml version="1.0" encoding="UTF-8"?>
<beans xmlns="http://www.springframework.org/schema/beans"
    xmlns:xsi="http://www.w3.org/2001/XMLSchema-instance"
    xmlns:jaxrs="http://cxf.apache.org/jaxrs"
    xmlns:cxf="http://cxf.apache.org/core"
    xsi:schemaLocation="http://www.springframework.org/schema/beans
    http://www.springframework.org/schema/beans/spring-beans.xsd
    http://cxf.apache.org/jaxrs
    http://cxf.apache.org/schemas/jaxrs.xsd
    http://cxf.apache.org/core
    http://cxf.apache.org/schemas/core.xsd ">

    <!-- Loads CXF modules from cxf.jar file -->
    <import resource="classpath:META-INF/cxf/cxf.xml"/>
    <import resource="classpath:META-INF/cxf/cxf-extension-soap.xml"/>
    <import resource="classpath:META-INF/cxf/cxf-servlet.xml"/>
    <import resource="classpath:META-INF/cxf/cxf-extension-jaxrs-
    binding.xml"/>

    <jaxrs:server id="gradeservice" address="/">
    <jaxrs:serviceBeans>
        <ref bean="gradeManagerImpl"/>
    </jaxrs:serviceBeans>
    <jaxrs:features>
```

```
            <cxf:logging/>
      </jaxrs:features>
      </jaxrs:server>

      <bean id="gradeManagerImpl"
            class="com.learning.ws.rest.GradeManagerImpl"/>
</beans>
```

The following XML is used to enable the user to log on to the server. It prints the request-and-response messages on the server console.

```
<jaxrs:features>
      <cxf:logging/>
</jaxrs:features>
```

Step 5: Create a web.xml File

The web.xml file is used for Java Web application-specific configurations. Configure the Apache-CXF–provided transport servlet for routing the request messages. The complete web.xml configurations are given below.

```
<?xml version="1.0" encoding="UTF-8"?>
<web-app version="2.4" xmlns="http://java.sun.com/xml/ns/j2ee"
            xmlns:xsi="http://www.w3.org/2001/XMLSchema-instance"
            xsi:schemaLocation="http://java.sun.com/xml/ns/j2ee
            http://java.sun.com/xml/ns/j2ee/web-app_2_4.xsd">

      <display-name>wsbook web application</display-name>
      <servlet>
            <servlet-name>wsbook</servlet-name>
            <servlet-class>
                  org.springframework.web.servlet.DispatcherServlet
            </servlet-class>
            <load-on-startup>2</load-on-startup>
      </servlet>
      <servlet-mapping>
            <servlet-name>wsbook</servlet-name>
            <url-pattern>*.action</url-pattern>
      </servlet-mapping>
      <listener>
            <listener-class>
                  org.springframework.web.context.ContextLoaderListener
            </listener-class>
      </listener>
      <context-param>
            <param-name>contextConfigLocation</param-name>
            <param-value>/WEB-INF/applicationContext-cxf.xml</param-value>
      </context-param>
      <servlet>
            <servlet-name>CXFServlet</servlet-name>
            <servlet-class>
                  org.apache.cxf.transport.servlet.CXFServlet
            </servlet-class>
      </servlet>
      <servlet-mapping>
            <servlet-name>CXFServlet</servlet-name>
```

```
            <url-pattern>/services/*</url-pattern>
    </servlet-mapping>
    <!-- Welcome Page -->
    <welcome-file-list>
    <welcome-file>index.vm</welcome-file>
    </welcome-file-list>
    <mime-mapping>
            <extension>wsdl</extension>
            <mime-type>text/xml</mime-type>
    </mime-mapping>
    <mime-mapping>
            <extension>xsd</extension>
            <mime-type>text/xml</mime-type>
    </mime-mapping>
</web-app>
```

Step 6: Create a WAR File and Deploy It in Tomcat Server

Figure 12-9: WAR file structure

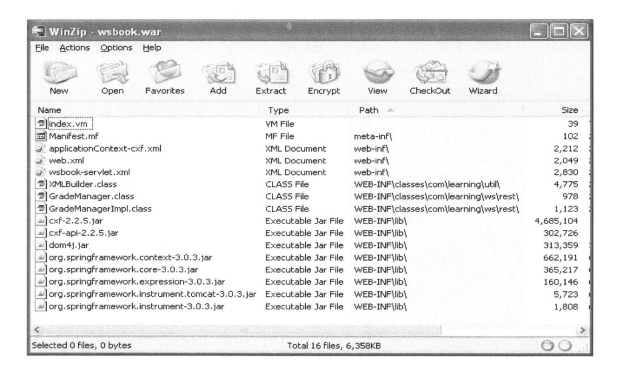

The structure of the generated war file is shown in Figure 12-9. Figure 12-9 shows only a few JAR files in "WEB-INF/lib" directory.

1. Build a WAR file using Ant or any other build tool. Make sure the following files are packaged correctly in a WAR file.

    a) Create a Service endpoint interface
    b) Create a Service endpoint implementation class and its dependent classes
    c) Create an Apache-CXF framework-specific configuration file. (applicationContext-cxf.xml)
    d) Create a web.xml configuration file

e) Create a Spring framework-specific configuration file. (wsbook-servlet.xml)
f) All required JAR files packaged in "WEB-INF/lib" directory.

2. Deploy the WAR file in any Java-compatible servlet container.
a) Copy the packed WAR into the "apache-tomcat/webapps" directory.
b) Start the tomcat server by running the startup.bat batch file available in the "apache-tomcat/bin" directory.
c) See the server console output and logs; make sure the WAR file is deployed without any errors.

Step 7: Verify the Service Deployment Using the REST URL from a Browser

Access the deployed service from a Web browser to make sure the service is deployed without any errors. The following URLs will show you the complete XML on the browser.

```
http://localhost:8080/wsbook/services/gradeservice/grades
http://localhost:8080/wsbook/services/gradeservice/grade/1
http://localhost:8080/wsbook/services/gradeservice/grade/1/subject/Math
http://localhost:8080/wsbook/services/gradeservice/grade/1/subject/Math/topic/Mathematics and art
```

These URLs are not physical URLs; they are logical URLs. After obtaining the list of grades, use the displayed content to navigate to other available sub-resources.

Step 8: Write a Client to Invoke the Deployed Service

There are several ways to consume the deployed REST service. JAX-RS specification does not define any standard for client invocation. Spring provides a "RestTemplate" class to invoke the deployed REST services. The following clients can be used to invoke the deployed REST service.

CASE 1:

Invoke the REST service using standard Java API. The "openConnection()" method of "java.net.URL" class is used to establish the connection and get the required output.

```
private static void invokeService() throws Exception {
    String url1 =
        "http://localhost:8080/wsbook/services/gradeservice/grades";
    URL url = new URL(url1);
    URLConnection conn = url.openConnection();
    conn.setDoOutput(true);

    InputStreamReader isr =
            new InputStreamReader(conn.getInputStream());
    BufferedReader br = new BufferedReader(isr);

    String response;
    while((response = br.readLine()) != null ) {
        System.out.println( response );
    }
    br.close();
}
```

CASE 2:

The Spring framework-provided "RestTemplate" class is used to access the deployed REST service. The use of the Spring framework-provided "RestTemplate" class is given below.

```
private static void invokeServiceUsingSpringAPI () throws Exception {
        RestTemplate restTemplate = new RestTemplate();
        String result = restTemplate.getForObject(
        "http://localhost:8080/wsbook/services/
                gradeservice/grade/{grade}",
                String.class, "1");
        System.out.println("result: " + result);

        Map<String, String> vars = new HashMap<String, String>();
        vars.put("grade", "1");
        vars.put("subject", "Java");

        String result1 = restTemplate.getForObject(
            "http://localhost:8080/wsbook/services/gradeservice/grade/
            {grade}/subject/{subject}",  String.class, vars);
        System.out.println("result1: " + result1);

        Map<String, String> topics = new HashMap<String, String>();
        vars.put("grade", "1");
        vars.put("subject", "Math");
        vars.put("topic", "Mathematics and art");

        String result2 = restTemplate.getForObject(
            "http://localhost:8080/wsbook/services
            /gradeservice/grade/1/subject/
            {subject}/topic/{topic}", String.class, vars);
    System.out.println("result2: " + result2);
}
```

Step 9: Log the Service Request-and-Response Message

Use the following configuration to log the inbound and outbound messages of a REST service. This information is useful for debugging the REST services.

```
<jaxrs:features>
     <cxf:logging/>
</jaxrs:features>
```

Example 2: How to get Context, Request Information in REST

The @Context annotation is used to get a handle to the HttpHeaders, UriInfo, Request, HttpServletRequest, HttpServletResponse, SecurityContext, HttpServletConfig, and ServletContext classes. The methods of these objects are used to obtain the data associated with URI and service requests. Data such as the host, post, request headers, parameter names, and parameter values can be obtained using these objects with the @Context annotation. The example provided below demonstrates how to obtain these values.

The steps required to develop a Web service to obtain the HTTP request data are given below.

1. Create a service endpoint interface.
2. Create a service implementation class.
3. Create any dependent helper classes.

4. Create an Apache-CXF framework-specific configuration file.
5. Create a web.xml file.
6. Create a WAR file and deploy it in the Tomcat server.
7. Verify the deployment using the REST URL from a browser.
8. Write a client to invoke the deployed service.

The above-specified steps are described in the following sections:

Step 1: Create a Service Endpoint Interface

The first step is to define an interface between the client and server. The complete interface code is given below.

@Context UriInfo—Used to obtain the URI-specific data such as host, port, and so forth
@Context HttpHeaders—Used to obtain the header information such as cookies, locale, and so forth
@Context HttpServletRequest—Used to obtain the HTTP request specific data such as parameter names, parameter values, and so forth.

Listing 12-4 demonstrates the use of the @Context annotation with the service endpoint interface.

Listing 12-4: service endpoint interface

```
// RestDataManager.java
package com.learning.ws.rest;

import javax.ws.rs.Path;
import javax.ws.rs.Produces;
import javax.ws.rs.GET;
import javax.ws.rs.core.Context;
import javax.ws.rs.core.UriInfo;
import javax.ws.rs.core.HttpHeaders;
import javax.servlet.http.HttpServletRequest;

@Path("/dataservice/")
@Produces("text/plain")
public interface RestDataManager {
    @GET
    @Path("/restinfo")
    public String getCommmonInfo(@Context UriInfo uriInfo,
                                 @Context HttpHeaders headers,
                                 @Context HttpServletRequest req);
}
```

Step 2: Create a Service Implementation Class

The implementation of the above-declared interface is shown in Listing 12-5. The output of each method is provided with inline comments along with the code.

Listing 12-5: service implementation class

```
// RestDataManagerImpl
package com.learning.ws.rest;

import javax.ws.rs.core.*;
import javax.servlet.http.HttpServletRequest;
```

```java
import java.net.URI;
import java.util.*;

public class RestDataManagerImpl implements RestDataManager {
    public String getCommmonInfo(UriInfo uriInfo,
                                 HttpHeaders headers,
                                 HttpServletRequest req) {

        /* Using @Context UriInfo uriInfo - To get the URI related info
           like, port, host, query parameters etc. */
        String path = uriInfo.getPath();
        System.out.println("---- path ----" + path);

        // Aboslute path
        URI uriPath = uriInfo.getAbsolutePath();
        System.out.println("--- uriPath ---" + uriPath);

        // host and port
        URI requestUri = uriInfo.getRequestUri();
        System.out.println("---- Host and Port ----" +
            requestUri.getHost() + ":" + requestUri.getPort());

        // Matched uri
        List<String> matchedUri = uriInfo.getMatchedURIs();
        System.out.println("---- matchedUri ----" + matchedUri);

        URI baseUri = uriInfo.getBaseUri();
        // http://localhost:8080/wsbook/services/
        System.out.println("---- baseUri ----" + baseUri);

        UriBuilder uriBuilder = uriInfo.getBaseUriBuilder();
        System.out.println("---- name -----" +
                    uriBuilder.queryParam("name"));

        // Query Parameters
        MultivaluedMap<String, String> queryParams =
                    uriInfo.getQueryParameters();
        System.out.println("--- queryParams ---" +
            queryParams);   //{name=[srinivas], id=[15]}

        for(Map.Entry<String, List<String>> entry :
                queryParams.entrySet()) {
            // Prints [srinivas] and [15]
            System.out.println("--- query param ---" +
            entry.getValue());
        }

        // Path Parameters
        MultivaluedMap<String, String> pathParams =
            uriInfo.getPathParameters();
        System.out.println("--- pathParams ---" + pathParams);

        /* Using HttpHeaders to obtain header information like cookies,
        locale etc. */
        MultivaluedMap<String, String> requestHeaders =
                                headers.getRequestHeaders();
        System.out.println("---- requestHeaders ---" + requestHeaders);
```

```
            // Obtaining the cookies related information.
            Map<String, Cookie> cookie = headers.getCookies();
            System.out.println("---- cookie ----" + cookie);

            // Obtaining the locale information.
            Locale locale = headers.getLanguage();
            System.out.println("---- locale ----" + locale);

            /* @Context HttpServletRequest req - Obtaining the http request
                parameters values */
            String paramName = req.getParameter("name");
            System.out.println("---- paramName ----" + paramName);
            return path;
        }
}
```

Step 4: Create Apache-CXF Framework-Specific Configuration File

Create an Apache-CXF framework-specific XML configuration file to register the REST Web service class. The complete XML configuration is given below.

```xml
<?xml version="1.0" encoding="UTF-8"?>
<beans xmlns="http://www.springframework.org/schema/beans"
    xmlns:xsi="http://www.w3.org/2001/XMLSchema-instance"
    xmlns:jaxrs="http://cxf.apache.org/jaxrs"
    xmlns:cxf="http://cxf.apache.org/core"
    xsi:schemaLocation="http://www.springframework.org/schema/beans
    http://www.springframework.org/schema/beans/spring-beans.xsd
    http://cxf.apache.org/jaxrs
    http://cxf.apache.org/schemas/jaxrs.xsd
    http://cxf.apache.org/core
    http://cxf.apache.org/schemas/core.xsd ">

    <!-- Loads CXF modules from cxf.jar file -->
    <import resource="classpath:META-INF/cxf/cxf.xml"/>
    <import resource="classpath:META-INF/cxf/cxf-extension-soap.xml"/>
    <import resource="classpath:META-INF/cxf/cxf-servlet.xml"/>
    <import resource="classpath:META-INF/cxf/cxf-extension-jaxrs-
                                        binding.xml"/>

    <jaxrs:server id="gradeservice" address="/">
    <jaxrs:serviceBeans>
        <ref bean="restDataManagerImpl"/>
    </jaxrs:serviceBeans>

    <jaxrs:features>
        <cxf:logging/>
    </jaxrs:features>
    </jaxrs:server>

    <bean id="restDataManagerImpl"
            class="com.learning.ws.rest.RestDataManagerImpl"/>
</beans>
```

Step 5: Create a Web.xml File

Reuse the web.xml file we created in Example-1.

Step 6: Create a War File and Deploy It in Tomcat Server

Figure 12-10: WAR file structure

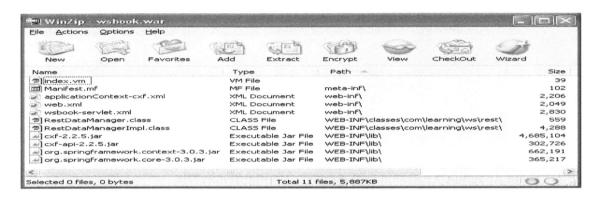

Follow the instructions specified in Example-1. The structure of the generated WAR file is shown in Figure 12-10.

Step 7: Verify the Deployment Using the REST URL from a Browser

Invoke the deployed REST service using the following URLs. It will print the data on the server console.

```
http://localhost:8080/wsbook/services/dataservice/restinfo
http://localhost:8080/wsbook/services/dataservice/restinfo?name=john&id=5
```

Example 3: How to Get the Entire HTML Form Data Using REST

This example demonstrates the use of HTML forms with the REST Web service. The client in this scenario is any Web page; it can be HTML, JSP, velocity template, or a Freemarker template. The service receives the user-entered data on the Web page, processes it, and sends the response back to the invoking client. The steps required to develop a Web service to get the HTTP POST request data are given below.

1. Create a service endpoint interface.
2. Create a service implementation class.
3. Create Apache-CXF framework specific configuration file.
4. Create a web.xml file.
5. Create a WAR file and deploy it in the Tomcat server.
6. Write a client to invoke the deployed service.

The above-specified steps are described in the following sections:

Step 1: Create a Service Endpoint Interface

This interface has defined two overloaded methods; which method to use totally depends on the application need. The first method is used to receive the individual field data from an HTML form.

```
@POST
@Path("/userName/{userName}/password/{password}")
```

```java
public void postUserData(@FormParam("userName")String userName,
                         @FormParam("password")String password);
```

The second method provided below is used to obtain all HTML form data in a key-value map.

```java
@POST
@Path("/userName/{userName}/password/{password}")
public void postUserData(MultivaluedMap<String, String> formParams);
```

The service must use the form URL of encoded content type at the service endpoint.

```java
@Consumes("application/x-www-form-urlencoded")
```

Listing 12-6 has the complete Java code that demonstrates the service interface.

Listing 12-6: service interface code

```java
// AccessManager.java
package com.learning.ws.rest;

import javax.ws.rs.POST;
import javax.ws.rs.Path;
import javax.ws.rs.FormParam;
import javax.ws.rs.Consumes;
import javax.ws.rs.core.MultivaluedMap;

@Path("/loginservice/")
@Consumes("application/x-www-form-urlencoded")
public interface AccessManager {
    @POST
    @Path("/userName/{userName}/password/{password}")
    public void postUserData(@FormParam("userName")String userName,
                             @FormParam("password")String password);

    // OR use the following method, based on the business need.
    @POST
    @Path("/userName/{userName}/password/{password}")
    public void postUserData(MultivaluedMap<String, String> formParams);
}
```

Step 2: Create a Service Implementation Class

The implementation of the above-declared interface is provided in Listing 12-7. It receives the HTML form data and prints it on the console.

Listing 12-7: service implementation class

```java
// AccessManagerImpl.java
package com.learning.ws.rest;

import javax.ws.rs.core.MultivaluedMap;
import java.util.Map;
import java.util.List;

public class AccessManagerImpl implements AccessManager {
    public void postUserData(String userName, String password) {
```

```java
            // Getting the HTML form data; implement your logic here.
            System.out.println("--- userName ---" + userName +
                        "--- password ---" + password);
        }

    public void postUserData(MultivaluedMap<String,String> formParams) {
        // Getting the HTML form data
        for(String key : formParams.keySet()) {
            System.out.println("-- value is --" + formParams.get(key));
        }
        //OR use this code for getting the form data.
        for(Map.Entry<String, List<String>> entry :
                            formParams.entrySet()) {
            System.out.println("-- value is ---" + entry.getValue());
        }
    }
}
```

Step 3: Create an Apache-CXF Framework-Specific Configuration File

Create an Apache-CXF framework-specific XML configuration file to register the REST Web service class with a Spring container. The complete XML configuration is given below.

```xml
<?xml version="1.0" encoding="UTF-8"?>
<beans xmlns="http://www.springframework.org/schema/beans"
        xmlns:xsi="http://www.w3.org/2001/XMLSchema-instance"
        xmlns:jaxrs="http://cxf.apache.org/jaxrs"
        xmlns:cxf="http://cxf.apache.org/core"
        xsi:schemaLocation="http://www.springframework.org/schema/beans
        http://www.springframework.org/schema/beans/spring-beans.xsd
        http://cxf.apache.org/jaxrs
        http://cxf.apache.org/schemas/jaxrs.xsd
        http://cxf.apache.org/core
        http://cxf.apache.org/schemas/core.xsd ">

    <!-- Loads CXF modules from cxf.jar file -->
    <import resource="classpath:META-INF/cxf/cxf.xml"/>
    <import resource="classpath:META-INF/cxf/cxf-extension-soap.xml"/>
    <import resource="classpath:META-INF/cxf/cxf-servlet.xml"/>
    <import resource="classpath:META-INF/cxf/cxf-extension-jaxrs-
            binding.xml"/>

    <jaxrs:server id="gradeservice" address="/">
        <jaxrs:serviceBeans>
            <ref bean="accessManagerImpl"/>
        </jaxrs:serviceBeans>
        <jaxrs:features>
            <cxf:logging/>
        </jaxrs:features>
    </jaxrs:server>

    <bean id="accessManagerImpl"
        class="com.learning.ws.rest.AccessManagerImpl"/>
</beans>
```

Step 4: Create a web.xml file

Reuse the web.xml file we created in Example-1.

Step 5: Create a War File and Deploy It in the Tomcat Server

Figure 12-11: WAR file structure

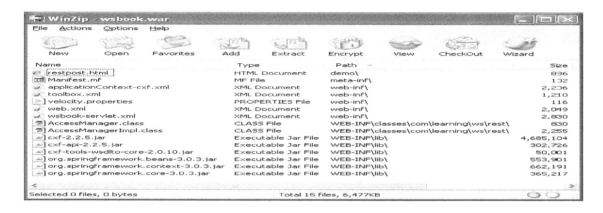

Follow the instructions specified in Example-1. The structure of the generated WAR file is shown in Figure 12-11.

Step 6: Write a Client to Invoke the Deployed Service

In this example, an HTML page is used to submit the request using the POST method. The user entered values in the text fields; "userName" and "password" are passed to the service endpoint class. The form provided below is submitted using a javascript function. The complete HTML form code is given below.

```html
<html>
<head>
    <title>WS REST DEMO</title>
    <script type="text/javascript">
        function submitUserForm() {
            document.forms[0].action = "/wsbook/services/loginservice
            /userName/XXXXX/password/XXXXXXX";
            document.forms[0].submit();
        }
    </script>
</head>
<body>
<form method="post">
    <table align="center">
        <tr>
            <td><label><b>User Id:</b></label></td>
            <td>
                <input type="text" name="userName"
                        id="userName" value="" size="40"/>
            </td>
        </tr>
        <tr>
            <td><label><b>Password:</b></label></td>
            <td>
                <input type="text" name="password"
                        id="password" value="" size="40"/>
```

```
                    </td>
                </tr>
                <tr>
                    <td>
                        <a href="javascript:submitUserForm()">1.Log In</a>
                    </td>
                </tr>
            </table>
</form>
</body>
</html>
```

Example 4: How to Use GET, POST, DELETE, and PUT

The example provided below demonstrates the use of GET, POST, DELETE, and PUT operations. The steps required to develop a Web service to get the HTTP request data are given below.

1. Create a service endpoint interface.
2. Create a service implementation class.
3. Create an Apache-CXF framework-specific configuration file.
4. Create a web.xml file.
5. Write a client to invoke the deployed service.
6. Create a WAR file and deploy it in the Tomcat server

The above-specified steps are described in the following sections.

Step 1: Create a Service Endpoint Interface

The interface provided uses four methods for GET, POST, DELETE, and PUT operations. The request for DELETE and PUT are routed through the HTTP POST operation. Listing 12-8 provides the complete Java code.

Listing 12-8: REST example using HTTP GET, POST, DELETE and PUT

```java
// DocumentManager.java
package com.learning.ws.rest;

import javax.ws.rs.*;
@Path("/document/")
@Produces("text/plain")
public interface DocumentManager {
    @GET
    @Path("/read/{id}")
    public String getDocument(@PathParam("id") String id);

    @POST
    @Path("/add/{id}")
    @Consumes("application/x-www-form-urlencoded")
    public void addDocument(@PathParam("id") String id);

    @POST
    @Path("/deleteReplace/{id}")
    @Consumes("application/x-www-form-urlencoded")
    public void deleteOrReplaceDocument(@PathParam("id") String id);

    @DELETE
```

```
        public void deleteDocument(String id);

        @PUT
        public void replaceDocument(String id);
}
```

Step 2: Create a Service Implementation Class

The implementation of the above-defined methods in an interface is shown in Listing 12-9. The GET operation is used for reading a document; the POST operation is used for adding a new document; the DELETE operation is used for deleting a document; and the PUT operation is used to replace one document with another.

Listing 12-9: REST service implementation class

```java
// DocumentManagerImpl.java
package com.learning.ws.rest;

public class DocumentManagerImpl implements DocumentManager {
    public String getDocument(String id) {
        // GET operation - implement your logic here to get a document
        System.out.println("---- GET ---" + id);
        return "your document content";
    }

    public void addDocument(String id) {
        /* POST operation - implement your logic here to add a new
             Document */
        System.out.println("---- POST ----" + id);
    }

    // Calling DELETE and PUT operations through POST.
    public void deleteOrReplaceDocument(String id) {
        /* DELETE and PUT operations
               -Implement your logic here to delete or replace document */
        deleteDocument(id);
        replaceDocument(id);
    }

    public void deleteDocument(String id) {
        // Implement your logic here to delete a document
        System.out.println("---- DELETE ----");
    }

    public void replaceDocument(String id) {
        // Implement your logic here to replace a document
        System.out.println("---- PUT ----");
    }
}
```

Step 3: Create Apache-CXF Framework-Specific Configuration File

Create an Apache-CXF framework-specific XML configuration file to register the REST Web service class with a Spring container. The complete XML configuration is given below.

```xml
<?xml version="1.0" encoding="UTF-8"?>
```

```xml
<beans xmlns="http://www.springframework.org/schema/beans"
       xmlns:xsi="http://www.w3.org/2001/XMLSchema-instance"
       xmlns:jaxrs="http://cxf.apache.org/jaxrs"
       xmlns:cxf="http://cxf.apache.org/core"
       xsi:schemaLocation="http://www.springframework.org/schema/beans
       http://www.springframework.org/schema/beans/spring-beans.xsd
       http://cxf.apache.org/jaxrs
       http://cxf.apache.org/schemas/jaxrs.xsd
       http://cxf.apache.org/core
       http://cxf.apache.org/schemas/core.xsd ">

    <!-- Loads CXF modules from cxf.jar file -->
    <import resource="classpath:META-INF/cxf/cxf.xml"/>
    <import resource="classpath:META-INF/cxf/cxf-extension-soap.xml"/>
    <import resource="classpath:META-INF/cxf/cxf-servlet.xml"/>
    <import resource="classpath:META-INF/cxf/cxf-extension-jaxrs-
                                        binding.xml"/>

    <jaxrs:server id="documentservice" address="/">
    <jaxrs:serviceBeans>
        <ref bean="documentManagerImpl"/>
    </jaxrs:serviceBeans>
    <jaxrs:features>
        <cxf:logging/>
    </jaxrs:features>
</jaxrs:server>

    <bean id="documentManagerImpl"
        class="com.learning.ws.rest.DocumentManagerImpl"/>
</beans>
```

Step 4: Create Web.xml File

Reuse the web.xml file we created in Example-1.

Step 5: Write a Client to Invoke the Deployed Service

The Web-based client provided below invokes the "deleteOrReplaceDocument()" method of a service endpoint.

The URL provided below invokes the "deleteOrReplaceDocument()" service operation.

```
document.forms[0].action = "/wsbook/services/document/deleteReplace/1";
```

The URL provided below invokes the "addDocument()" service operation.

```
document.forms[0].action = "/wsbook/services/document/add/1";
```

Submit the HTML form provided below and view the output on the server console.

```html
<html>
<head>
    <title>REST demo for GET, POST, DELETE and PUT</title>
    <script type="text/javascript">
        function submitUserForm() {
```

```
                 document.forms[0].action =
                     "/wsbook/services/document/deleteReplace/1";
                 document.forms[0].submit();
            }
      </script>
</head>
<body>
<form method="post">
      <table align="center">
            <tr>
                 <td><label><b>User Id:</b></label></td>
                 <td>
                     <input type="text" name="userName"
                              id=" documentId" value="" size="40"/>
                 </td>
            </tr>
            <tr>
                 <td>
                     <a href="javascript:submitUserForm()">1.Log In</a>
                 </td>
            </tr>
      </table>
</form>
</body>
</html>
```

Step 6: Create a WAR File and Deploy It in the Tomcat Server

Figure 12-12: WAR file structure

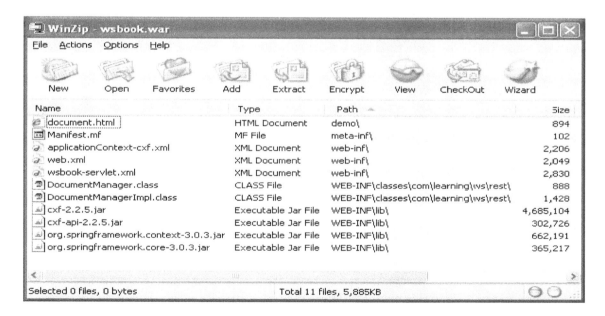

Follow the instructions specified in Example-1. The structure of the generated WAR file is shown in Figure 12-12.

Example 5: How to Use @MatrixParam

The example provided below demonstrates the use of the @MatrixParam annotation while developing REST-based Web services. The steps required to develop a REST Web service to obtain URL data using the @MatrixParam annotation is given below.

1. Create a service endpoint interface.
2. Create a service implementation class.
3. Create an Apache-CXF framework-specific configuration file.
4. Create a web.xml file.
5. Create a WAR file and deploy it in the Tomcat server.
6. Write a client to invoke the deployed service.

The above-specified steps are described in the following sections.

Step 1: Create a Service Endpoint Interface

The REST interface provided in Listing 12-10 has one service method; it obtains the URL metadata using the @PathParam and @MatrixParam annotations.

Listing 12-10: REST example using @MatrixParam annotation

```
// BookService.java
package com.learning.ws.rest;

import javax.ws.rs.*;

@Path("/bookservice/")
@Produces("text/plain")
public interface BookService {
    @GET
    @Path("/book/{year}")
    String getBooks(@PathParam("year") String year,
                @MatrixParam("author") String author,
                @MatrixParam("country") String country);
}
```

Step 2: Create a Service Implementation Class

The implementation code of the above-declared method in an interface is shown in Listing 12-11.

Listing 12-11: REST service implementation class

```
// BookServiceImpl.java
package com.learning.ws.rest;

import javax.ws.rs.MatrixParam;
public class BookServiceImpl implements BookService {
    public String getBooks(String year, String author, String country) {
        return "year: " + year + " author: "
                + author + " country: " + country;
    }
}
```

Step 3: Create Apache-CXF Framework-Specific Configuration File

Create an Apache-CXF framework-specific XML configuration file to register the REST Web service class with a Spring container. The complete XML configuration is given below.

```xml
<?xml version="1.0" encoding="UTF-8"?>
<beans xmlns="http://www.springframework.org/schema/beans"
        xmlns:xsi="http://www.w3.org/2001/XMLSchema-instance"
        xmlns:jaxrs="http://cxf.apache.org/jaxrs"
        xmlns:cxf="http://cxf.apache.org/core"
        xsi:schemaLocation="http://www.springframework.org/schema/beans
        http://www.springframework.org/schema/beans/spring-beans.xsd
        http://cxf.apache.org/jaxrs
        http://cxf.apache.org/schemas/jaxrs.xsd
        http://cxf.apache.org/core
        http://cxf.apache.org/schemas/core.xsd ">

        <!-- Loads CXF modules from cxf.jar file -->
        <import resource="classpath:META-INF/cxf/cxf.xml"/>
        <import resource="classpath:META-INF/cxf/cxf-extension-soap.xml"/>
        <import resource="classpath:META-INF/cxf/cxf-servlet.xml"/>
        <import resource="classpath:META-INF/cxf/cxf-extension-jaxrs-
                                        binding.xml"/>

        <jaxrs:server id="bookservice" address="/">
                <jaxrs:serviceBeans>
                        <ref bean="bookServiceImpl"/>
                </jaxrs:serviceBeans>
        </jaxrs:server>

        <bean id="bookServiceImpl"
                class="com.learning.ws.rest.BookServiceImpl"/>
</beans>
```

Step 4: Create a Web.xml File

Reuse the web.xml file we created in Example-1.

Step 5: Create a War File and Deploy It in the Tomcat Server

Figure 12-13: WAR file structure

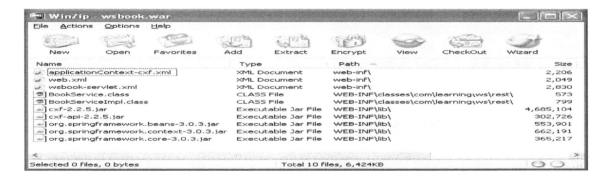

Follow the instructions specified in Example-1. The structure of the generated WAR file is shown in Figure 12-13.

Step 6: Invoke the Deployed Service from Your Browser

The deployed service is ready to invoke from a Web browser. Try the following set of REST URLs and view the output in the browser.

The URL is:

```
http://localhost:8080/wsbook/services/bookservice/book/2012
```

Its output is:

```
year: 2012 author: null country: null
```

The URL is:

```
http://localhost:8080/wsbook/services/bookservice/book/2012;author=john
```

Its output is:

```
year: 2012 author: srinivas country: null
```

The URL is:

```
http://localhost:8080/wsbook/services/bookservice/book/2012;author=john;c
ountry=usa
```

Its output is:

```
year: 2012 author: srinivas country: usa
```

REST Client Design Scenarios

There are several ways a REST client can invoke a deployed REST Web service. The JAX-RS specification does not define a standard for the client API. It is up to the developer to choose a suitable client for his service endpoint. The following client programs can be used to invoke a deployed Web service.

1.   How to invoke a REST service using standard Java API
2.   How to invoke a REST service using Spring `RestTemplate`
3.   How to invoke a REST service from a browser
4.   How to invoke a REST service from a Web page

The above-specified client design scenarios are explained in this section.

CASE 1: How to Invoke a REST Service Using Standard Java API

In this approach, the "openConnection()" method of the "java.net.URL" class is used to invoke the Web service endpoint. This approach is generally used for HTTP GET operations. The complete client code is given below.

```
private static void invokeService() throws Exception {
    // Service endpoint URL
```

```
String restURL =
    "http://localhost:8080/wsbook/services/gradeservice/grades";

URL url = new URL(restURL);
URLConnection conn = url.openConnection();
conn.setDoOutput(true);

InputStreamReader isr=new InputStreamReader(conn.getInputStream());
BufferedReader br = new BufferedReader(isr);

String response;
while((response = br.readLine()) != null) {
    System.out.println(response);
    // Implement your logic here to build the XML etc.
}
br.close();
}
```

CASE 2: How to Invoke a REST Service Using a Spring `RestTemplate`

In this approach, the Spring framework-provided `RestTemplate` class is used to invoke a deployed REST Web service. The client code provided below explains the use of the `RestTemplate` class.

```
private static void invokeServiceUsingSpringTemplate() throws Exception {

    /* Invoke the REST service using Spring framework provided
    RestTemplate class. */
    RestTemplate restTemplate = new RestTemplate();

    // Passing single input parameter from client
    String requestURL1 =
    "http://localhost:8080/wsbook/services/gradeservice/grade/{grade}";
    String result = restTemplate.getForObject(requestURL1,
        String.class, "1");
    System.out.println("result: " + result);

    // Passing multiple input parameters from the client
    Map<String, String> vars = new HashMap<String, String>();
    vars.put("grade", "1");
    vars.put("subject", "Java");

    String requestURL2 =
        "http://localhost:8080/wsbook/services/gradeservice/
        grade/{grade}/subject/{subject}";
    String result1 = restTemplate.getForObject(requestURL2,
            String.class, vars);
    System.out.println("result1: " + result1);

    // Passing multiple input parameters from the client
    Map<String, String> topics = new HashMap<String, String>();
    vars.put("grade", "1");
    vars.put("subject", "Math");
    vars.put("topic", "Mathematics and art");
```

```
    String requestURL3 =
        "http://localhost:8080/wsbook/services/gradeservice/
            grade/1/subject/{subject}/topic/{topic}";
    String result2 = restTemplate.getForObject(requestURL3,
            String.class, vars);
    System.out.println("result2: " + result2);
}
```

CASE 3: How to Invoke a REST Service from a Browser

In this scenario, use any Web browser to invoke a REST Web service. This approach is generally used for HTTP GET operations. Try the following URLs from your browser and view the results.

```
http://localhost:8080/wsbook/services/gradeservice/grade/1
http://localhost:8080/wsbook/services/gradeservice/grade/1/subject/Math
http://localhost:8080/wsbook/services/gradeservice/grade/1/subject/Math/t
opic/Algebra
http://localhost:8080/wsbook/services/stockservice/symbol?symbol=WFC
```

CASE 4: How to Invoke a REST Service from a Web Page

This approach is used to invoke a deployed REST service from a Web page. Submit the HTML form using the javascript function. This approach is generally used for the HTTP POST operations.

```html
<html>
<head>
<title>WS REST DEMO</title>
<script type="text/javascript">
    function submitUserForm() {
        document.forms[0].action=
            "/wsbook/services/loginservice/userName/XXXX/password/XXX";
        document.forms[0].submit();
    }
</script>
</head>
<body>
    <form method="post">
        <table align="center">
            <tr>
                <td> <label><b>User Id:</b></label></td>
                <td><input type="text" name="userName"
                        id="userName" size="40"/> </td>
            </tr>
            <tr>
                <td> <label><b>Password:</b></label></td>
                <td><input type="text" name="password"
                        id="password" size="40"/> </td>
            </tr>
            <tr>
                <td><b>
                    <a href="javascript:submitUserForm()">
                        1.Log In
                    </a>
                </td>
            </tr>
        </table>
```

```
        </form>
    </body>
</html>
```

REST Service Endpoint and URL Design Scenarios

The section will explain best practices for designing the service endpoint interface and REST URLs.

CASE 1: How to Design a REST URL

Don't display too much information on one page. Build the URLs logically, and provide links to other resources for additional information. Make sure the user understands the instructions when looking up the URL.

Do not use this, even though it is valid.

```
http://localhost:8080/wsbook/services/gradeservice/grade/GRADE_ID

http://localhost:8080/wsbook/services/gradeservice/grade/GRADE_ID/su
bject/SUB_ID
```

Instead use this, so it is easy for user to navigate from one page to other page. By looking into the URL, user knows the expected output.

```
http://localhost:8080/wsbook/services/gradeservice/grade/1
http://localhost:8080/wsbook/services/gradeservice/grade/1/subject/M
ath
```

Do not use this

```
http://localhost:8080/wsbook/services/gradeservice/getGrade?grade=1
```

Instead use this, use nouns rather than verbs.

```
http://localhost:8080/wsbook/services/gradeservice/grade/1
```

CASE 2: How to Design a Service Endpoint Interface

Provide a uniform interface between the client and service. This is the entry point between the client and service endpoint.

```
@Path("/gradeservice/")
@Produces("application/xml")
public interface GradeManager {
    @GET
    @Path("/grade/{grade}/subject/{subject}")
    public String getSubjectTopics(@PathParam("grade") Integer grade,
                                   @PathParam("subject") String subject);
}

public class GradeManagerImpl implements GradeManager {
```

```
        public String getSubjectTopics(Integer grade, String subject) {
            return XMLBuilder.getAllTopics(grade, subject);
        }
}
```

Do not use this, even though it is a valid service code.

```
@Path("/gradeservice/")
@Produces("application/xml")
public class GradeManagerImpl {
    @GET
    @Path("/grade/{grade}/subject/{subject}")
    public String getSubjectTopics(@PathParam("grade") Integer grade,
                                   @PathParam("subject") String subject) {
        return XMLBuilder.getAllTopics(grade, subject);
    }
}
```

Build and Deployment Instructions

This section explains the steps required to build, package, and deploy the code in any servlet container. The following software tools are used to develop and deploy the code examples.

- Apache-Tomcat—6.0.28
- JDK—1.6
- Ant
- Spring—3
- Apache-CXF—2.2.5
- IDE—Eclipse OR IntelliJ IDEA

Build a WAR file using Ant or any other build tool. Make sure the following files are packaged correctly in the WAR file.

- Service endpoint interface
- Service endpoint implementation class
- Any utility classes used for data access, etc.
- Web.xml file
- Spring, Apache-CXF specific configuration files
- Client code—can be a Web page, Java class, or simply a browser URL.

Deploy the WAR file in any servlet container.

- Copy the packaged WAR file into the "apache-tomcat/webapps" directory.
- Start the Tomcat server using the startup.bat batch file available in the "apache-tomcat/bin" directory.
- View the console output/logs; make sure WAR file is deployed without any errors.

Summary

This section summarizes the features provided in the Spring-REST framework.

- The CXF-provided `<jaxrs:serviceBeans/>` tag is used to register the Java Beans with the Spring container.
- Spring framework-provided `RestTemplate` class is used to invoke a deployed REST-based Web service endpoints.
- The `@PathParam` annotation is used to get the parameter values specified in the REST URL.
- The `@QueryParam` annotation is used to get the parameter values specified in the query string.
- The `@FormParam` annotation is used to get the entire HTML form data submitted through the HTTP POST method.
- The `@MatrixParam` annotation is used to extract the values of URI matrix parameter key value pairs
- The `@Path` annotation is used to identify the entry point of a service and its operation to be executed.

Figure 12-14 summarizes the most important points described in this chapter.

Figure 12-14 Spring REST summary

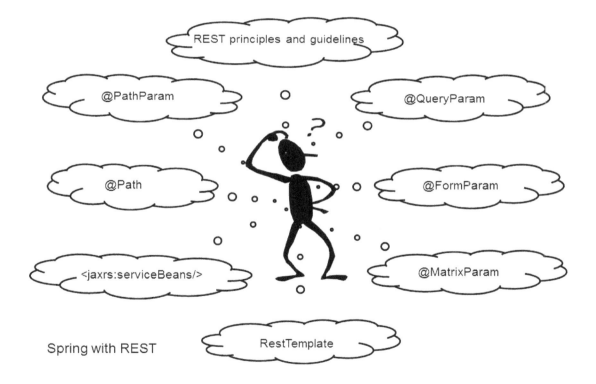

Chapter 13. Spring Web Services (SOAP-based)

A decade old open-source Spring framework can be used for developing enterprise applications. The Spring-provided IOC container is very popular since several years and it became the integral part of Java development for enterprise applications. In addition to the IOC container; Spring also provides many extensions to various application layers for Java-based application development. The Spring-provided MVC framework can be used for presentation layer framework, Spring JDBC API can be used for database layer framework; and similarly, Spring-based web service framework can be used for developing Java-based Web Services. The Spring Web Services (also called Spring-WS) is an open-source Web services framework used for developing SOAP-based Web services.

In general a Web Service can be developed in two different ways; the "contract-first" and "code-first". The Spring web services framework provide support for only "contract-first" type of web service development. The Spring-WS framework provides its own annotations and XML-based deployment descriptors for web services development. The Spring-WS can take the advantage of Spring IOC container and other core Spring framework provided features. The minimum requirement to develop Spring-based web services is JDK-1.5 and Spring-3.0.

In this chapter will discuss the following topics:

* The use of Spring-WS annotations and its deployment descriptors
* The advantages and disadvantages of Spring-WS.
* The Spring-WS supported web service development methodologies.
* Spring-WS service endpoint design scenarios
* Spring-WS client design scenarios
* How to configure SOAP message handlers using Spring-WS.

Prerequisites/Setting Up the Environment

* The required JAR files to develop Spring web services are provided along with the Spring web services distribution. Download Spring web services from the springsource.org website.
* Make sure the correct version of JAR files is used for development to avoid the class loader jar file version mismatch exceptions. The complete distribution is available in the form of JAR files; so no additional software needed for development.
* I tried Spring web services with several combinations, but only Spring-3.0.7 and Spring-WS-2.0.3 is working for complete end-to-end programs. I don't see any issues with other combinations while service deployment/development; but while invoking the service endpoints, the Spring web service template class is throwing exceptions. So this comment is valid only for web service client programs.
* The following JAR files are used for developing Spring-WS code examples. The Spring web services version-2.0.3 and Core Spring version-3.0.7 was used.

Spring-WS JAR files	Core Spring JAR files
spring-ws-2.0.3.RELEASE-all.jar	org.springframework.core-3.0.7.RELEASE.jar
spring-ws-2.0.3.RELEASE-sources.jar	org.springframework.core-sources-3.0.7.RELEASE.jar

spring-ws-core-2.0.3.RELEASE.jar	org.springframework.context-3.0.7.RELEASE.jar
spring-ws-security-2.0.3.RELEASE.jar	org.springframework.context.support-3.0.7.RELEASE.jar
spring-ws-support-2.0.3.RELEASE.jar	org.springframework.expression-3.0.7.RELEASE.jar
spring-xml-2.0.3.RELEASE.jar	org.springframework.beans-3.0.7.RELEASE.jar
	org.springframework.instrument-3.0.7.RELEASE.jar
	org.springframework.instrument.tomcat-3.0.7.RELEASE.jar
	org.springframework.oxm-3.0.7.RELEASE.jar
	org.springframework.oxm-sources-3.0.7.RELEASE.jar
	org.springframework.web-3.0.7.RELEASE.jar
	org.springframework.web.servlet-3.0.7.RELEASE.jar
	org.springframework.web-sources-3.0.7.RELEASE.jar
	org.springframework.test-3.0.7.RELEASE.jar
	org.springframework.context.support-sources-3.0.7.RELEASE.jar
	org.springframework.asm-3.0.7.RELEASE.jar
	org.springframework.asm-sources-3.0.7.RELEASE.jar

Spring-WS Architecture

Figure 13-1: Spring-WS Architecture using standard data types

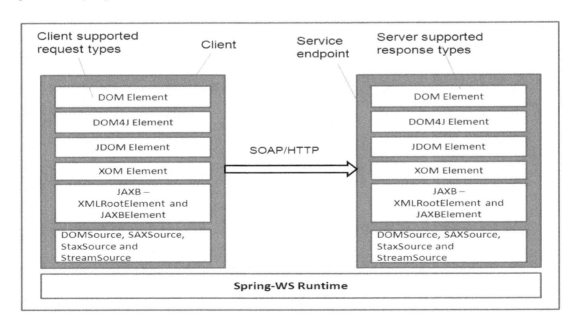

Spring web services architecture and its supported request-and-response types are shown in Figure 13-1. The client creates a request of the supported type to invoke the service endpoint. The service endpoint receives the client request; parse the XML to obtain the required input data. The service endpoint sends the response XML back to the client in the form of supported response types. We can use any suitable parsing technique to read/create the request-and-response XML. Spring web services provides XML-based and Java-based API support for configuring metadata related to client and service endpoint.

It is possible to use the custom data types for request-and-response messages, but it requires Spring adapters and some special configurations.

Spring-WS Advantages

- The Spring-WS can take advantage of the existing Spring IOC framework provided features.
- The Spring-WS provides support for various XML Java API's and marshaling techniques to handle request-and-response payloads. It supports Dom4j, JDOM, XOM, DOM, SAX, StAX, and JAXB annotated Java classes as parameters and return values.
- Using Spring-WS, easy to expose an existing XSD of an application as a Web service.
- A single framework can be used for developing enterprise applications in all layers. The Spring framework can be used in MVC layer, Database layer, Web services layer and application can take advantage of Spring IOC container.

Spring-WS Disadvantages

- Spring-WS provides support for only "contract-first" type of web services development.
- The development approach is not conforms to JAX-WS provided standards. It does not provide support for JSR-181 annotations.
- Less community support, poor documentation and availability of tutorials as compared with CXF and Axis-2 Web service frameworks.
- There are some issues reported, related to version mismatch of jar files used for Spring-WS, Spring-Core, Xalan, Xerces and SAAJ. The Spring Web services are working well with Spring-3.0.7 and Spring-WS-2.0.3 combination.

Spring-WS Annotations

Spring-WS provides annotations for developing Web Service endpoints. The list of annotations used to develop a Spring-based Web service is given below.

- @Endpoint
- @PayloadRoot
- @RequestPayload
- @ResponsePayload

@Endpoint

This annotation is used at class level to mark the class as a Web Service endpoint. The class annotated with the `@Endpoint` annotation is used to receive the inbound XML requests from the clients. The annotated class can have one or more methods to receive the request payloads; and sends the response back to the invoking clients. The Web service endpoint operations processes the incoming XML; and prepare the response XML based on the input received from the service client. The class annotated with `@Endpoint` is a special kind of Spring component suitable to handle the XML requests-and-responses. The `@Endpoint`-annotated classes are eligible for component scanning using Spring provided "<context: component-scan/>" xml tag.

The use of the `@Endpoint`-annotation is provided below.

```
@Endpoint
public class EmployeeEndPoint {
    // ...
}
```

@RequestPayload

This annotation is used with method parameters to receive the request XML messages. It maps the method parameter to the incoming message payload. The use of the `@RequestPayload`-annotation is given below. The payload of the message is passed as a DOM element to the endpoint method.

```
public Element getEmployee(@RequestPayload Element employeeRequest)
throws Exception {
}
```

The entire input request "<getEmployeeRequest/>" is wrapped inside the "<soap:body/>" element of the soap message. A sample request payload is given below:

```
<getEmployeeRequest xmlns="http://springws.ws.learning.com/emp/schemas">
    <employee>
        <employeeId>6666666</employeeId>
    </employee>
</getEmployeeRequest>
```

@PayloadRoot

This annotation is used at method-level to route the incoming request XML messages. It routes the incoming messages to the appropriate method of the service endpoint class. Based on the incoming message "namespace" and its "local name" it decides which method to execute. This annotation is used to identify which method of the service endpoint to be executed based on the message payload.

An example input request message is provided below. The local name is "getEmployeeRequest" and its namespace is "http://springws.ws.learning.com/emp/schemas"; so it will invoke the "getEmployee()" method of the web service endpoint.

```
<getEmployeeRequest xmlns="http://springws.ws.learning.com/emp/schemas">
    <employee>
```

```
            <employeeId>6666666</employeeId>
      </employee>
</getEmployeeRequest>
```

The corresponding web service method signature for the above-specified request payload is provided below.

```
@PayloadRoot(namespace = "http://springws.ws.learning.com/emp/schemas",
            localPart="getEmployeeRequest")
public Element getEmployee(@RequestPayload Element employeeRequest)
throws Exception {
}
```

What happens if the "local name" or "namespace" of endpoint class does not match?

Let us now review the below provided request payload message. The local rame of the below given payload is "<getEmployee>"; but the service endpoint expects "getEmployeeRequest" as local name; it does not know where to route the incoming request. The invoking client will throw an endpoint Not Found [404] exception.

Invalid request payload:

```
<getEmployee xmlns="http://springws.ws.learning.com/emp/schemas">
      <employee>
            <employeeId>6666666</employeeId>
      </employee>
</getEmployee>
```

@ResponsePayload

This annotation is used at method-level. It indicates the method return value should map to the response payload. The @ResponsePayload-annotation is used only if the method has any return value; and this is not applicable if the method has void return type.

The use of the @ResponsePayload-annotation is given below.

```
@PayloadRoot(namespace="http://springws.ws.learning.com/enp/schemas",
            localPart="getEmployeeRequest")
@ResponsePayload
public Element getEmployee(@RequestPayload Element emplcyeeRequest)
throws Exception {
    // ...
    return response;
}
```

The supported method parameter, return types of a payload message request-and-response are listed below:

* W3C DOM Element
* Dom4j Element
* JDOM Element
* XOM Element

- JAXB Type - Any type that is annotated with XMLRootElement and JAXBElement
- DOMSource, SAXSource, StaxSource and StreamSource
- Any type supported by Spring OXM Marsheller.

Spring-WS supports above-specified list of standard types as parameters and return values. It is possible to use other data types; but it requires Spring-provided custom adapter classes.

Development Methodologies

The Spring-WS supports only "contact-first" kind of Web service development methodology. The contract-first development for Spring-WS starts with WSDL or XSD. The web service developer can create a WSDL for service endpoint or create an XSD with request-response types. The Spring-WS provided tools take this XSD as input and generates the WSDL dynamically.

Example 1: Spring-WS Endpoint with Dom4j API

This Web service endpoint is developed with Dom4j *Element* type as request-and-response payload. The steps required to develop a Spring-based Web service using Dom4j API is given below.

1. Create a XSD document.
2. Create a service endpoint interface.
3. Create a "web.xml" file.
4. Create a "springws-servlet.xml" configuration file.
5. Create a WAR file and deploy it in Tomcat server.
6. Verify the generated WSDL document.
7. Write a client to invoke the deployed service endpoint.

The above-specified steps are described in the following sections:

This is an example of an employee web service; for a given employee id it provides the complete details about that employee. Let us now start with defining an XML schema for this service.

Step 1: Create a XSD Document

This is the first step to start with for developing a Spring-based web service.

- Convert the domain model to an XML type
- Create a XML request root element
- Create a XML response root element

The above defined XML types are used for request-and-response message payloads. The Spring runtime expects "Request" and "Response" suffix for data types.

The following XML element represents the request payload. This is the root element for the request payload message. The suffix "Request" is used to generate the WSDL message and part elements.

```
<xs:element name="getEmployeeRequest" type="emp:EmployeeRequest"/>
```

The following XML element represents the response payload. This is the root element for the response payload message. The suffix "Response" is used to generate the WSDL message and part elements

```xml
<xs:element name="getEmployeeResponse" type="emp:EmployeeResponse"/>
```

The following XML complex type represents the request payload type. It has only one input parameter employee id, of type string.

```xml
<xs:complexType name="EmployeeRequest">
    <xs:sequence>
    <xs:element minOccurs="0" name="employeeId" type="xs:string"/>
    </xs:sequence>
</xs:complexType>
```

The following XML complex type represents the response payload type. It wraps the complete employee details.

```xml
<xs:complexType name="EmployeeResponse">
    <xs:sequence>
        <xs:element minOccurs="0" name="return" type="emp:employee"/>
    </xs:sequence>
</xs:complexType>
```

The following XML complex type represents the details of an employee; it includes name, address, email, and phone number.

```xml
<xs:complexType name="employee">
    <xs:sequence>
        <xs:element minOccurs="0" name="nameInfo" type="emp:nameInfo"/>
        <xs:element minOccurs="0" name="homeAddress"
                type="emp:homeAddress"/>
        <xs:element minOccurs="0" name="emailAddress"
                type="emp:emailAddress"/>
        <xs:element minOccurs="0" name="phones" type="emp:phones"/>
    </xs:sequence>
</xs:complexType>
```

The complete XML schema document is provided below; named the "employee.xsd".

```xml
<?xml version="1.0" encoding="UTF-8"?>
<xs:schema xmlns:xs="http://www.w3.org/2001/XMLSchema"
        xmlns:emp="http://springws.ws.learning.com/emp/schemas"
        elementFormDefault="unqualified"
        targetNamespace="http://springws.ws.learning.com/emp/schemas">

    <!-- Root element for request -->
    <xs:element name="getEmployeeRequest" type="emp:EmployeeRequest"/>

    <!-- Root element for response -->
    <xs:element name="getEmployeeResponse" type="emp:EmployeeResponse"/>

    <xs:complexType name="EmployeeRequest">
        <xs:sequence>
            <xs:element minOccurs="0" name="employeeId"
```

```
                           type="xs:string"/>
        </xs:sequence>
</xs:complexType>

<xs:complexType name="EmployeeResponse">
        <xs:sequence>
              <xs:element minOccurs="0" name="return"
                         type="emp:employee"/>
        </xs:sequence>
</xs:complexType>

<xs:complexType name="employee">
        <xs:sequence>
              <xs:element minOccurs="0" name="nameInfo"
                         type="emp:nameInfo"/>
              <xs:element minOccurs="0" name="homeAddress"
                         type="emp:homeAddress"/>
              <xs:element minOccurs="0" name="emailAddress"
                         type="emp:emailAddress"/>
              <xs:element minOccurs="0" name="phones" type="emp:phones"/>
        </xs:sequence>
</xs:complexType>

<xs:complexType name="nameInfo">
        <xs:sequence>
              <xs:element minOccurs="0" name="id" type="xs:string"/>
              <xs:element minOccurs="0" name="firstName"
                            type="xs:string"/>
              <xs:element minOccurs="0" name="lastName"
                            type="xs:string"/>
        </xs:sequence>
</xs:complexType>

<xs:complexType name="homeAddress">
        <xs:sequence>
              <xs:element minOccurs="0" name="aptNumber"
                               type="xs:string"/>
              <xs:element minOccurs="0" name="streetName"
                               type="xs:string"/>
              <xs:element minOccurs="0" name="city" type="xs:string"/>
              <xs:element minOccurs="0" name="zipcode" type="xs:string"/>
              <xs:element minOccurs="0" name="state" type="xs:string"/>
              <xs:element minOccurs="0" name="country" type="xs:string"/>
        </xs:sequence>
</xs:complexType>

<xs:complexType name="emailAddress">
        <xs:sequence>
              <xs:element minOccurs="0" name="personal"
                         type="xs:string"/>
              <xs:element minOccurs="0" name="office" type="xs:string"/>
        </xs:sequence>
</xs:complexType>

<xs:complexType name="phones">
        <xs:sequence>
              <xs:element minOccurs="0" name="personal"
```

```
                            type="xs:string"/>
            <xs:element minOccurs="0" name="office" type="xs:string"/>
        </xs:sequence>
    </xs:complexType>
</xs:schema>
```

Step 2: Create a Service Endpoint Interface

Create a service endpoint class to receive the request-and-response payloads. The Spring-WS provided annotations are used for endpoint class. This endpoint class is annotated using `@Endpoint` annotation; so it marks as a special kind of Spring component that can handle XML request-and-response messages.

```
@Endpoint
public class EmployeeEndPoint {
}
```

The following code checks the "localPart" and "namespace" of the incoming request-payload and routes to the appropriate method.

```
@PayloadRoot(namespace = "http://springws.ws.learning.com/emp/schemas",
             localPart = "getEmployeeRequest")
```

The following code represents the method signature of the service endpoint used to process the incoming request payloads, and sends the response back to the invoking client. This method uses Dom4j *Element* as a request parameter and return value.

```
@ResponsePayload
public Element getEmployee(@RequestPayload Element employeeRequest)
throws Exception {
}
```

The complete method code is provided below:

```
@PayloadRoot(namespace = "http://springws.ws.learning.com/emp/schemas",
             localPart = "getEmployeeRequest")
@ResponsePayload
public Element getEmployee(@RequestPayload  Element  employeeRequest)
throws Exception {
    // private method used for parsing the request payload
    String employeeId =
    getEmployeeIdFromInputXML(employeeRequest.asXML());
    if (employeeId == null || employeeId == "") {
        employeeId = "99999999";
    }

    // private method used for creating the response payload
    Element response = createResponseXML(employeeId);
    System.out.println("-- response Message --" + response.asXML());
    return response;
}
```

The following private method is used for parsing the request payload. This method obtains the data from incoming XML to apply the business logic. The Dom4j API is used to create the request-and-response payloads.

```
String employeeId = getEmployeeIdFromInputXML(employeeRequest.asXML());
```

The following private method is used for creating the response payload. It creates the response payload. In real world we obtain the data from persistent store.

```
Element response = createResponseXML(employeeId);
```

The complete web service endpoint class code is provided in Listing 13-1.

Listing 13-1: Developing Spring-based endpoint using Dom4j

```java
// EmployeeEndPoint.java
package com.learning.springws;

import org.springframework.ws.server.endpoint.annotation.*;
import org.dom4j.*;
import org.dom4j.io.SAXReader;
import java.io.ByteArrayInputStream;
import java.util.Iterator;

@Endpoint
public class EmployeeEndPoint {

    @PayloadRoot(namespace=
            "http://springws.ws.learning.com/emp/schemas",
            localPart = "getEmployeeRequest")
    @ResponsePayload
    public Element getEmployee(@RequestPayload Element employeeRequest)
    throws Exception {
        // private method used for parsing the request payload
        String employeeId =
            getEmployeeIdFromInputXML(employeeRequest.asXML());
        if(employeeId == null || employeeId == "") {
            employeeId = "99999999";
        }

        // private method used for creating the response payload
        Element response = createResponseXML(employeeId);
        System.out.println("--response Message --" + response.asXML());
        return response;
    }

    // private method used for creating the response payload.
    private Element createResponseXML(String employeeId) {
        Document document = DocumentHelper.createDocument();
        Element responseElement =
                document.addElement("getEmployeeResponse");
        Element rootElement = responseElement.addElement("employee");
        Element nameElement = rootElement.addElement("nameinfo");
        nameElement.addElement("id").addText(employeeId);
        nameElement.addElement("firstName").addText("John");
        nameElement.addElement("lastName").addText("Smith");

        Element homeAddressElement =
                rootElement.addElement("homeAddress");
        homeAddressElement.addElement("aptNumber").addText("2340");
```

```java
            homeAddressElement.addElement("streetName").
                              addText("W.Roundabout Cir");
            homeAddressElement.addElement("city").addText("Chandler");
            homeAddressElement.addElement("zipcode").addText("85225");
            homeAddressElement.addElement("state").addText("AZ");
            homeAddressElement.addElement("country").addText("USA");

            Element emailElement = rootElement.addElement("emailAddress");
            emailElement.addElement("personal").
                            addText("wsbook@mymail.com");
            emailElement.addElement("office").addText("srinivas@abc.com");

            Element phoneElement = rootElement.addElement("phones");
            phoneElement.addElement("personal").addText("480-645-6753");
            phoneElement.addElement("office").addText("602-667-6782");
            return rootElement;
        }

        /* private method used for parsing the request payload to get the
        data*/
        public String getEmployeeIdFromInputXML(String inputXML) throws
        Exception {
            SAXReader reader = new SAXReader();
            Document document = reader.read(new
                        ByteArrayInputStream(inputXML.getBytes()));
            Element root = document.getRootElement();
            String employeeId = null;
            for (Iterator i = root.elementIterator(); i.hasNext();) {
                Element element = (Element) i.next();
                for (int j = 0,size = element.nodeCount(); j < size; j++) {
                    Node node = (Node) element.node(j);
                        if (node instanceof Element) {
                            if ("employeeId".
                                equalsIgnoreCase(node.getName())) {
                            employeeId = node.getText();
                            }
                        }
                }
            }
            System.out.println("--- employeeId: ---" + employeeId);
            return employeeId;
        }
    }
}
```

Step 3: Create a web.xml File

This is a standard Java EE container specific configuration which requires for any web services framework. The Spring provided servlet "MessageDispatcherServlet" class is used for HTTP transport. Configure this servlet in "web.xml" file. The servlet name and its mapping are given below.

```xml
<servlet>
    <servlet-name>springws</servlet-name>
    <servlet-class>
        org.springframework.ws.transport.http.MessageDispatcherServlet
    </servlet-class>
</servlet>
```

```
    <init-param>
        <param-name>transformWsdlLocations</param-name>
        <param-value>true</param-value>
    </init-param>
</servlet>

<servlet-mapping>
    <servlet-name>springws</servlet-name>
    <url-pattern>/services/*</url-pattern>
</servlet-mapping>
```

The endpoint URL which contains **"/services/"** URL pattern is routed through the Spring-WS configured message dispatcher servlet.

The following configuration is used for location transformation. So it allows us to access the WSDL without specifying the absolute path.

```
<init-param>
    <param-name>transformWsdlLocations</param-name>
    <param-value>true</param-value>
</init-param>
```

So we can specify locationUri="/services/employeeService/" where ever we use it in Spring configurations, instead of locationUri="http://localhost:8080/springws/services/employeeService/". This is further discussed in next section.

Step 4: Create a springws-servlet.xml Configuration File.

This file contains the Spring Web services related information such as endpoints, interceptors, etc. It loads all the defined Spring beans into the Spring IOC container. The name of the XML file follows the standard Spring syntax. The suffix should be "servlet"; and the prefix of the xml file should match the value of the "<servlet-name/>" tag specified in web.xml. The name used in web.xml is "springws"; so the file name "springws-servlet.xml" is used in this example. The prefix and suffix should be separated with a hyphen.

The file name syntax is: {prefix}-{suffix}.xml which is "springws-servlet.xml".

The complete XML file is given below. Let us now examine each element and its significance. The configurations specified in this XML are used for Spring IOC container.

```
<?xml version="1.0" encoding="UTF-8"?>
<beans xmlns="http://www.springframework.org/schema/beans"
    xmlns:xsi="http://www.w3.org/2001/XMLSchema-instance"
    xmlns:context="http://www.springframework.org/schema/context"
    xmlns:sws="http://www.springframework.org/schema/web-services"
    xsi:schemaLocation="http://www.springframework.org/schema/beans
    http://www.springframework.org/schema/beans/spring-beans-
        3.0.xsd
    http://www.springframework.org/schema/web-services
    http://www.springframework.org/schema/web-services/web-
    services-2.0.xsd
    http://www.springframework.org/schema/context
    http://www.springframework.org/schema/context/spring-context-
        3.0.xsd">

    <context:component-scan base-package="com.learning.springws"/>
```

```
<sws:annotation-driven/>

<sws:dynamic-wsdl id="employee"
    portTypeName="EmployeePortType"
    locationUri="/services/employeeService/"
    targetNamespace="http://springws.learning.com/emp/definitions">
    <sws:xsd location="/WEB-INF/employee.xsd"/>
</sws:dynamic-wsdl>

</beans>
```

The following code will detect the beans defined in the base package and loads them into the Spring IOC container without any overhead. So we can auto wire the required bean classes in our application code.

```
<context:component-scan base-package="com.learning.springws"/>
```

The following code is used to intimate the beans of Spring IOC container are annotation supported. So the service endpoint class can use Spring-WS provided annotations such as @Endpoint, @PayloadRoot, etc. This XML tag enables the use of annotations in web service endpoint classes.

```
<sws:annotation-driven/>
```

The Spring Web services can generate a WSDL from XSD schema. The elements of the schema which has suffix "Request" and "Response" is used for generating the WSDL *messages* and *part* elements. Spring runtime generates WSDL operations for all request-and-response elements.

```
<sws:dynamic-wsdl id="employee"
    portTypeName="EmployeePortType"
    locationUri="/services/employeeService/"
    targetNamespace="http://springws.learning.com/emp/definitions">
    <sws:xsd location="/WEB-INF/employee.xsd"/>
</sws:dynamic-wsdl>
```

The following XML tag is used to generate the WSDL for a given XML schema. The attribute "Id" is used to access the WSDL document.

```
<sws:dynamic-wsdl id="employee"
```

This attribute name "portTypeName" maps to the <wsdl:portType/> of the generated WSDL. The *port name* and generated WSDL is given below:

The port name is given below:

```
portTypeName="EmployeePortType"
```

The generated WSDL is given below:

```
<wsdl:portType name="EmployeePortType">
    <wsdl:operation name="getEmployee">
        <wsdl:input message="tns:getEmployeeRequest"
            name="getEmployeeRequest"/>
```

```
        <wsdl:output message="tns:getEmployeeResponse"
             name="getEmployeeResponse"/>
    </wsdl:operation>
</wsdl:portType>
```

The following attribute name "locationUri" represents the location of the Web service endpoint. The transform "transformWsdlLocations" enabled in web.xml so no need to specify the absolute URL.

```
locationUri="/services/employeeService/"
```

The following attribute name "targetNamespace" represents the target namespace used for generating the WSDL document.

```
targetNamespace="http://springws.learning.com/emp/definitions
```

The following XML element represents the location of the XML schema document used for generating the WSDL dynamically.

```
<sws:xsd location="/WEB-INF/employee.xsd"/>
```

Step 5: Create a WAR File, and deploy it in Tomcat Server.

The structure of the generated WAR file is shown in Figure 13-2:

Figure 13-2: WAR file structure

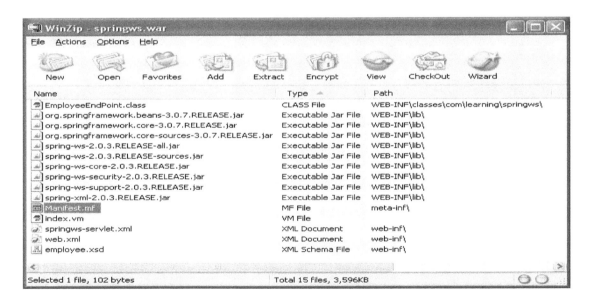

NOTE: The above provided Figure 13-2 shows only a few JAR files in "WEB-INF/lib" directory.

---

1. Build a war file using Ant or any other build tool. Make sure the following files are packaged correctly in WAR file.
    a. Service endpoint implementation class
    b. Any utility classes used for data access.

---

c. The "web.xml" file should be packaged into "WEB-INF/" directory.

d. The "springws-servlet.xml" configuration file should be packaged into "WEB-INF/" directory.

e. All dependent JAR files should be packaged into "WEB-INF/lib" directory.

2. Deploy the WAR file in any servlet container.
   a. Copy the packed WAR into "apache-tomcat/webapps" directory
   b. Start the tomcat server by running the "startup.bat" batch file available in "apache-tomcat/bin" directory
   c. View the server console output/logs; make sure WAR file is deployed without any errors.

Step 6: Verify the Generated WSDL Document.

Access the WSDL file from web browser to make sure the service is deployed properly without any errors. Use the following URL to view the complete WSDL.

```
http://localhost:8080/springws/services/employeeService/employee.wsdl
```

- The server name and port used = **localhost:8080**
- The web application context (default name is war file name) = **springws**
- The URL pattern defined in web.xml file is = **services**
- The name specified in location URI = **employeeService**
- The "id" attribute value of the "<sws:dynamic-wsdl>" tag = **employee**

Spring-WS framework uses "dot" notation to access the generated WSDL document. All other frameworks like CXF and Axis2 uses question mark (?) notation to access the generated WSDL documents.

Spring web service framework notation to access the WSDL is given below:

```
http://localhost:8080/springws/services/employeeService/employee.wsdl
```

Other web service frameworks notation to access the WSDL is given below:

```
http://localhost:8080/bookws/services/employeeService/employee?wsdl
```

Step 7: Write a Client to Invoke the Deployed Service Endpoint.

Spring web services framework provided "WebServiceTemplate" class can be used for accessing the deployed web service endpoint. There are two different ways a client can set the values of the metadata.

- Using Spring provided Java API.
- Using XML-based configuration.

The XML-based configuration is used for the below provided client.

The below given XML element is used for setting the message factory. This is the default setting used for Spring; so its use is optional.

```
<bean id="messageFactory"
    class="org.springframework.ws.soap.saaj.SaajSoapMessageFactory"/>
```

The following XML element is used for setting the protocol used for message transfer. By default Spring uses HTTP as a transfer protocol; so its use is optional.

```xml
<bean id="messageSender" class=
    "org.springframework.ws.transport.http.CommonsHttpMessageSender"/>
```

The "WebServiceTemplate" is the core template used for accessing the web service endpoint. The only mandatory required property for the web service template is "defaultUri"; it specifies the location of the deployed web service endpoint.

```xml
<bean id="webServiceTemplate"
    class="org.springframework.ws.client.core.WebServiceTemplate">
    <property name="defaultUri"
    value="http://localhost:8080/springws/services/employeeService/"/>
</bean>
```

The following "applicationContext-client.xml" file is used for client specific configurations.

```xml
<?xml version="1.0" encoding="UTF-8"?>
<beans xmlns="http://www.springframework.org/schema/beans"
    xmlns:xsi="http://www.w3.org/2001/XMLSchema-instance"
    xmlns:context="http://www.springframework.org/schema/context"
    xmlns:sws="http://www.springframework.org/schema/web-services"
    xsi:schemaLocation="http://www.springframework.org/schema/beans
    http://www.springframework.org/schema/beans/spring-beans-3.0.xsd
    http://www.springframework.org/schema/web-services
    http://www.springframework.org/schema/web-services/web-services-
    2.0.xsd
    http://www.springframework.org/schema/context
    http://www.springframework.org/schema/context/spring-context-
        3.0.xsd">

    <bean id="messageFactory" class=
        "org.springframework.ws.soap.saaj.SaajSoapMessageFactory"/>

    <bean id="messageSender" class=
    "org.springframework.ws.transport.http.CommonsHttpMessageSender"/>

    <bean id="webServiceTemplate"
        class="org.springframework.ws.client.core.WebServiceTemplate">
        <constructor-arg ref="messageFactory"/>
        <property name="messageSender" ref="messageSender"/>
        <property name="defaultUri" value=
        "http://localhost:8080/springws/services/employeeService/"/>
    </bean>
</beans>
```

Now let us review the client code to invoke the endpoint. The following code is used for getting the handle of the web service template which is configured in "applicationContext-client.xml" file.

```java
ClassPathXmlApplicationContext context
    = new ClassPathXmlApplicationContext(new
            String[]{"applicationContext-client.xml"});
WebServiceTemplate webServiceTemplate = (WebServiceTemplate)
                        context.getBean("webServiceTemplate");
```

This following private method is used for creating the input request payload. The Dom4j API is used for creating the request XML payload.

```
String requestXML = createInputXML(employeeId);
```

The created input request payload is provided below. The request payload must use the same local part name (getEmployeeRequest) and namespace (http://springws.ws.learning.com/emp/schemas) as specified in the web service endpoint using @PayloadRoot annotation. It matches these values to route the incoming request to an endpoint method. The Spring runtime constructs the SOAP envelope using this request payload.

The input request-message is provided below:

```
<getEmployeeRequest  xmlns="http://springws.ws.learning.com/emp/schemas">
    <employee>
        <employeeId>6666666</employeeId>
    </employee>
</getEmployeeRequest>
```

The Spring runtime generated SOAP request for this case is provided below:

```
<soapenv:Envelope
        xmlns:soapenv="http://schemas.xmlsoap.org/soap/envelope/">
    <soapenv:Body>
        <getEmployeeRequest
            xmlns="http://springws.ws.learning.com/emp/schemas">
            <employee>
                <employeeId>6666666</employeeId>
            </employee>
        </getEmployeeRequest>
    </soapenv:Body>
</soapenv:Envelope>
```

The "sendSourceAndReceiveToResult" method of the Spring web service template can be used for accessing the web service endpoint.

```
Source source = new StringSource(requestXML);
Result result = new StringResult();
webServiceTemplate.sendSourceAndReceiveToResult(source, result);
```

The service client can use any parsing technique to obtain the required data from response payload. Listing 13-2 provides the complete class code.

Listing 13-2: Client for accessing Spring-based endpoint.

```
// SpringWSClient.java
package com.learning.springws;

import org.springframework.ws.client.core.WebServiceTemplate;
import org.springframework.context.support.ClassPathXmlApplicationContext;
import org.springframework.xml.transform.StringSource;
import org.springframework.xml.transform.StringResult;
import org.dom4j.*;
import javax.xml.transform.Source;
```

```java
import javax.xml.transform.Result;

public class SpringWSClient {

    public static void main(String args[]) {
        try {
            SpringWSClient client = new SpringWSClient();
            client.invokeService("6666666");
        } catch (Exception ex) {
            ex.printStackTrace();
        }
    }

    private void invokeService(String employeeId) throws Exception {
        ClassPathXmlApplicationContext context
            = new ClassPathXmlApplicationContext(new
                String[]{"applicationContext-client.xml"});
        WebServiceTemplate webServiceTemplate = (WebServiceTemplate)
                        context.getBean("webServiceTemplate");

        String requestXML = createInputXML(employeeId);
        Source source = new StringSource(requestXML);
        Result result = new StringResult();
        webServiceTemplate.sendSourceAndReceiveToResult(source,result);

        // Parse the result using some parsing technique.
        System.out.println("-- result --" + result.toString());
    }

    // private method used for creating the request payload.
    private String createInputXML(String employeeId) throws Exception {
        Document document = DocumentHelper.createDocument();
        Element requestElement =
            document.addElement("getEmployeeRequest",
            "http://springws.ws.learning.com/emp/schemas");
        Element employeeElement=requestElement.addElement("employee");
        employeeElement.addElement("employeeId").addText(employeeId);
        // converting input XML to a String
        return document.asXML();
    }
}
```

The result of the web service endpoint is provided below. Use suitable parsing technique to obtain the employee information.

```xml
<?xml version="1.0" encoding="UTF-8"?>
<getEmployeeResponse>
    <employee>
        <nameinfo>
            <id>6666666</id>
            <firstName>John</firstName>
            <lastName>Smith</lastName>
        </nameinfo>

        <homeAddress>
            <aptNumber>2340</aptNumber>
```

```
                    <streetName>W.Roundabout Cir</streetName>
                    <city>Chandler</city>
                    <zipcode>85225</zipcode>
                    <state>AZ</state>
                    <country>USA</country>
            </homeAddress>

            <emailAddress>
                    <personal>wsbook@mymail.com</personal>
                    <office>srinivas@abc.com</office>
            </emailAddress>

            <phones>
                    <personal>480-645-6753</personal>
                    <office>602-667-6782</office>
            </phones>
        </employee>
</getEmployeeResponse>
```

Example 2: Spring-WS SOAP Message Handler Framework

The very common requirement while developing Web Services is to use the message handlers to intercept request-and-response soap messages. Spring web services provide a good support to configure the message interceptors with client and service endpoint to manipulate the request-and-response soap messages. This section illustrates the use of Spring interceptors with client and service endpoint.

Service Endpoint Side — Configuring SOAP Handler using Spring-WS

The endpoint handler class must implement the "org.springframework.ws.server.EndpointInterceptor" interface to configure the interceptor with service endpoint. This interface has four methods defined; the endpoint interceptor class must implement these four methods to process the request-and-response payloads. The four methods of this interface are listed below.

- boolean handleRequest() throws java.lang.Exception;
- boolean handleResponse() throws java.lang.Exception;
- boolean handleFault() throws java.lang.Exception;
- void afterCompletion() throws java.lang.Exception;

Now lets us write our own interceptor class to log the request-and-response payloads. Listing 13-3 has the complete class code can be used to log the soap messages with service endpoint.

Listing 13-3: Developing Spring-based SOAP message handlers

```java
// LogMessageHandler.java
package com.learning.springws;

import org.springframework.ws.server.EndpointInterceptor;
import org.springframework.ws.context.MessageContext;
import org.springframework.ws.WebServiceMessage;
import java.io.ByteArrayOutputStream;

public class LogMessageHandler implements EndpointInterceptor {
```

```
public boolean handleRequest(MessageContext messageContext,Object o)
throws Exception {
    WebServiceMessage requestMessage = messageContext.getRequest();
    if (requestMessage != null) {
        // Printing the request message on the console.
        ByteArrayOutputStream out = new ByteArrayOutputStream();
        requestMessage.writeTo(out);
        String request = new String(out.toByteArray());
        System.out.println("--- Endpoint request ---" + request);
    }
    return true;
}

public boolean handleResponse(MessageContext messageContext,
                Object o) throws Exception {
    WebServiceMessage responseMessage =
                messageContext.getResponse();
    if (responseMessage != null) {
        // Printing the response message on the console.
        ByteArrayOutputStream out = new ByteArrayOutputStream();
        responseMessage.writeTo(out);
        String response = new String(out.toByteArray());
        System.out.println("-- Endpoint response --" + response);
    }
    return true;
}

public boolean handleFault(MessageContext messageContext, Object o)
throws Exception {
    return true;
}

public void afterCompletion(MessageContext messageContext, Object o,
Exception e) throws Exception {
    }
}
```

The above class simply logs the request-and-response payload messages on the server console. Let us now examine code snippets and its significance.

The following endpoint class must implement Spring framework provided "EndpointInterceptor" interface.

```
public class LogMessageHandler implements EndpointInterceptor {
}
```

The following method is used to receive the complete request message.

```
public boolean handleRequest(MessageContext messageContext, Object o)
throws Exception
```

The following method is used to receive the complete response message.

```
public boolean handleResponse(MessageContext messageContext, Object o)
throws Exception
```

The following method is used to handle faults related soap messages.

```
public boolean handleFault(MessageContext messageContext, Object o)
throws Exception
```

The following method is used to perform required clean-up activities.

```
public void afterCompletion(MessageContext messageContext, Object o,
Exception e) throws Exception
```

The "hasResponse()" method of the "MessageContext" object can be used to know the direction of message; which is request or response. It returns "false" for the request messages, "true" for response messages.

```
Boolean hasResponse = messageContext.hasResponse();
```

How to integrate the above provided interceptor class with service endpoint.

The Spring framework provided "<sws:interceptors/>" tag can be used to integrate the interceptors with service endpoint.

```
<sws:interceptors>
    <sws:payloadRoot
        namespaceUri="http://springws.ws.learning.com/emp/schemas">
        <bean class="com.learning.springws.LogMessageHandler"/>
    </sws:payloadRoot>
</sws:interceptors>
```

Add the above provided XML to "springws-servlet.xml" file to log the request-and-response soap messages with service endpoint. The complete "springws-servlet.xml" file is provided below:

```
<?xml version="1.0" encoding="UTF-8"?>
<beans xmlns="http://www.springframework.org/schema/beans"
    xmlns:xsi="http://www.w3.org/2001/XMLSchema-instance"
    xmlns:context="http://www.springframework.org/schema/context"
    xmlns:sws="http://www.springframework.org/schema/web-services"
    xsi:schemaLocation="http://www.springframework.org/schema/beans
    http://www.springframework.org/schema/beans/spring-beans-3.0.xsd
    http://www.springframework.org/schema/web-services
    http://www.springframework.org/schema/web-services/web-services-
    2.0.xsd
    http://www.springframework.org/schema/context
    http://www.springframework.org/schema/context/spring-context-
    3.0.xsd">

    <context:component-scan base-package="com.learning.springws"/>

    <sws:annotation-driven/>

    <sws:dynamic-wsdl id="employee"
        portTypeName="EmployeePortType"
        locationUri="/services/employeeService/"
        targetNamespace="http://springws.learning.com/emp/definitions">
        <sws:xsd location="/WEB-INF/employee.xsd"/>
    </sws:dynamic-wsdl>
```

```
<sws:interceptors>
      <sws:payloadRoot namespaceUri=
          "http://springws.ws.learning.com/emp/schemas">
              <bean class="com.learning.springws.LogMessageHandler"/>
      </sws:payloadRoot>
</sws:interceptors>

</beans>
```

Client Side — Configuring SOAP Handler using Spring-WS

The client side handler class must implement the Spring framework provided interface
"org.springframework.ws.client.support.interceptor.ClientInterceptor" to configure the interceptor
with Web service client. This interface has three methods defined; the client side interceptor class
must implement these three methods to process the request-and-response payloads. The three
methods of this interface are listed below.

- boolean handleRequest() throws java.lang.Exception;
- boolean handleResponse() throws java.lang.Exception;
- boolean handleFault() throws java.lang.Exception;

Now lets us write our own interceptor class to log the request-and-response payloads. Listing 13-4
has the complete Java code that can be used to log the soap messages with web service client.

Listing 13-4: Using Spring-based SOAP message handlers

```java
// ClientLogMessageHandler.java
package com.learning.springws;

import
org.springframework.ws.client.support.interceptor.ClientInterceptor;
import org.springframework.ws.client.WebServiceClientException;
import org.springframework.ws.context.MessageContext;
import org.springframework.ws.WebServiceMessage;
import java.io.ByteArrayOutputStream;
import java.io.IOException;

public class ClientLogMessageHandler implements ClientInterceptor {

    public boolean handleRequest(MessageContext messageContext) throws
        WebServiceClientException {
    WebServiceMessage requestMessage = messageContext.getRequest();
        try {
                if (requestMessage != null) {
                // Printing the request message on console.
                ByteArrayOutputStream out = new
                    ByteArrayOutputStream();
                requestMessage.writeTo(out);
                String request = new String(out.toByteArray());
                System.out.println("--  Client Request --" + request);
                }
        } catch (IOException ex) {
            ex.printStackTrace();
        }
        return true;
```

```
    }

    public boolean handleResponse(MessageContext messageContext) throws
    WebServiceClientException {
        WebServiceMessage responseMessage=messageContext.getResponse();
        try {
            if (responseMessage != null) {
                // Printing the response message on console.
                ByteArrayOutputStream out = new
                            ByteArrayOutputStream();
                responseMessage.writeTo(out);
                String response = new String(out.toByteArray());
                System.out.println("--Service Response--" +response);
            }
        } catch (IOException ex) {
            ex.printStackTrace();
        }
        return true;
    }

    public boolean handleFault(MessageContext messageContext) throws
    WebServiceClientException {
        return true;
    }
}
```

How to configure the above provided interceptor class with web service client.

The "setInterceptors()" method of the "WebServiceTemplate" object can be used to configure the array of interceptors with web service client to process the request-and-response messages. The Spring-based interceptors can be added in two different ways.

- Non XML-based using Spring Java API
- Using XML-based configurations

CASE 1: Non XML-based Using Spring Java API

In this approach Spring-based Java API can be used to configure the interceptors with web service client. An example code is provided below.

```
ClientLogMessageHandler[] handler = new ClientLogMessageHandler[1];
handler[0] = new ClientLogMessageHandler();
WebServiceTemplate webServiceTemplate = new WebServiceTemplate();
webServiceTemplate.setDefaultUri("http://localhost:8080/springws/services
/employeeService/");
webServiceTemplate.setInterceptors(handler);
```

The below provided code can be used to configure the interceptors with web service client.

```
private void invokeService(String employeeId) throws Exception {
    ClientLogMessageHandler[] handler = new ClientLogMessageHandler[1];
    handler[0] = new ClientLogMessageHandler();
    WebServiceTemplate webServiceTemplate = new WebServiceTemplate();
    webServiceTemplate.setDefaultUri("http://localhost:8080/
                    springws/services/employeeService/");
```

```
webServiceTemplate.setInterceptors(handler);

// private method used to create a request payload.
String requestXML = createInputXML(employeeId);
Source source = new StringSource(requestXML);
Result result = new StringResult();
webServiceTemplate.sendSourceAndReceiveToResult(source, result);
System.out.println("--- result ---" + result.toString());
}
```

CASE 2: XML-based Configurations

The Spring also supports XML-based configuration to configure the interceptors with Web service client. The XML used to configure the interceptor bean with web service template is provided below:

```
<bean id="webServiceTemplate"
      class="org.springframework.ws.client.core.WebServiceTemplate">
    <constructor-arg ref="messageFactory"/>
<property name="defaultUri" value=
    "http://localhost:8080/springws/services/employeeService/"/>
    <property name="interceptors" ref="logMessages"/>
</bean>

<bean id="logMessages"
      class="com.learning.springws.ClientLogMessageHandler"/>
```

The below provided code can be used with web service client.

```
private void invokeService(String employeeId) throws Exception {
    ClassPathXmlApplicationContext context
        = new ClassPathXmlApplicationContext(new
                    String[]{"applicationContext-client.xml"});
    WebServiceTemplate webServiceTemplate = (WebServiceTemplate)
                            context.getBean("webServiceTemplate");

    String requestXML = createInputXML(employeeId);
    Source source = new StringSource(requestXML);
    Result result = new StringResult();
    webServiceTemplate.sendSourceAndReceiveToResult(source, result);
    System.out.println("--- result ---" + result.toString());
}
```

It is possible to configure any number of interceptors between client and service endpoint. Also Spring provides support to write log messages to Log4j configured log file.

Example 3: Spring-WS Endpoint with JDOM API

This type Web service endpoint is developed with JDOM Element type as request-and-response payload. JDOM is an open source XML parsing framework can be used for reading/writing XML documents. JDOM is an alternative to SAX and DOM. JDOM provides higher level API for parsing XML documents. The steps required to develop a Spring-based Web service using JDOM API is given below.

1. Create a XSD document.

2. Create a service endpoint interface.
3. Create the "springws-servlet.xml" configuration file.
4. Create a "web.xml" file
5. Create a WAR file and deploy it in Tomcat server.
6. Verify the generated WSDL document.
7. Write a client to invoke the deployed service endpoint.

The above-specified steps are described in the following sections:

This example demonstrates the use of holiday Web service; for a given year it provides the list of federal holidays. Let us now start defining the XML schema of the service.

Step 1: Create a XSD Document

The first step is to prepare a XSD of the web service endpoint. Convert the domain model to an XML types; and create a XML root element for request-response payloads. The complete XML schema document is provided below. Spring runtime uses this XSD for generating the WSDL.

```xml
<?xml version="1.0" encoding="UTF-8"?>
<xs:schema xmlns:xs="http://www.w3.org/2001/XMLSchema"
    xmlns:hol="http://springws.ws.learning.com/holidays/schemas"
    elementFormDefault="unqualified"
    targetNamespace="http://springws.ws.learning.com/holidays/schemas">

    <!-- Root element for request -->
    <xs:element name="getHolidayRequest" type="hol:HolidayRequest"/>

    <!-- Root element for response -->
    <xs:element name="getHolidayResponse" type="hol:HolidayResponse"/>

    <xs:complexType name="HolidayRequest">
        <xs:sequence>
            <xs:element minOccurs="0" name="year" type="xs:string"/>
        </xs:sequence>
    </xs:complexType>

    <xs:complexType name="HolidayResponse">
        <xs:sequence>
            <xs:element minOccurs="0" name="holidays"
                              type="hol:holidays"/>
        </xs:sequence>
    </xs:complexType>

    <xs:complexType name="holidays">
        <xs:sequence>
            <xs:element minOccurs="0" name="holiday" type="xs:string"/>
        </xs:sequence>
    </xs:complexType>
</xs:schema>
```

Step 2: Create a Service Endpoint Interface

Create a service endpoint class to receive the request-and-response payloads. The Spring-WS provided annotations are used for service endpoint class. The complete service endpoint code is provided in Listing 13-5.

Listing 13-5: Developing Spring-based web service using JDOM API

```java
// HolidayServiceEndpoint.java
package com.learning.springws;

import org.springframework.ws.server.endpoint.annotation.Endpoint;
import org.springframework.ws.server.endpoint.annotation.PayloadRoot;
import org.springframework.ws.server.endpoint.annotation.ResponsePayload;
import org.springframework.ws.server.endpoint.annotation.RequestPayload;
import org.jdom.Element;
import org.jdom.Document;
import org.jdom.input.SAXBuilder;
import org.jdom.output.XMLOutputter;
import java.io.InputStream;
import java.io.ByteArrayInputStream;
import java.util.List;
import java.util.Iterator;

@Endpoint
public class HolidayServiceEndpoint {
    @PayloadRoot(namespace =
            "http://springws.ws.learning.com/holidays/schemas",
            localPart = "getHolidayRequest")
    @ResponsePayload
    public Element getEmployee(@RequestPayload Element holidayRequest)
    throws Exception {
        // Converting the JDOM element to a Java String
        XMLOutputter outputter = new XMLOutputter();
        String inputRequest = outputter.outputString(holidayRequest);
        System.out.println("--- inputRequest ---- " + inputRequest);

        // Private method used to parse the XML to obtain the year
        String year = getYear(inputRequest);

        // Private method used to build the response XML
        Element holidayResponse = buildHolidaysResponse(year);

        return holidayResponse;
    }

    private String getYear(String inputRequest) throws Exception {
        InputStream is = new
                ByteArrayInputStream(inputRequest.getBytes("UTF-8"));
        SAXBuilder builder = new SAXBuilder();
        Document document = builder.build(is);
        Element root = document.getRootElement();
        List children = root.getChildren();
        Iterator iterator = children.iterator();
        String year = "";
        while (iterator.hasNext()) {
            Element child = (Element) iterator.next();
            year = child.getValue();
        }

        System.out.println("--- year --- " + year);
        return year;
    }
```

```
private Element buildHolidaysResponse(String year) throws Exception{
    Element responseElement = new Element("getHolidayResponse",
        "http://springws.ws.learning.com/holidays/schemas");
    Document myDocument = new Document(responseElement);
    Element holidaysElement = new
            Element("holidays").setAttribute("year", year);
    responseElement.addContent(holidaysElement);

    Element janElement1 = new Element("January").
                        setText("02-jan-2012");
    holidaysElement.addContent(janElement1);

    Element janElement2 = new Element("January").
                        setText("16-jan-2012");
    holidaysElement.addContent(janElement2);

    Element febElement = new Element("February").
                        setText("20-feb-2012");
    holidaysElement.addContent(febElement);

    Element mayElement = new Element("May").
                        setText("28-may-2012");
    holidaysElement.addContent(mayElement);

    Element julyElement = new Element("July").
                        setText("04-july-2012");
    holidaysElement.addContent(julyElement);

    Element septElement = new Element("September").
                        setText("03-sept-2012");
    holidaysElement.addContent(septElement);

    Element octElement = new Element("October").
                        setText("08-oct-2012");
    holidaysElement.addContent(octElement);

    Element novElement1 = new Element("November").
                        setText("12-nov-2012");
    holidaysElement.addContent(novElement1);

    Element novElement2 = new Element("November").
                        setText("22-nov-2012");
    holidaysElement.addContent(novElement2);

    Element decElement = new Element("December").
                        setText("25-dec-2012");
    holidaysElement.addContent(decElement);

    XMLOutputter outputter = new XMLOutputter();
    outputter.output(myDocument, System.out);

    return responseElement;
    }
}
```

The following private method is used to parse the XML to obtain the value of the year.

```
String year = getYear(inputRequest);
```

The following private method is used to prepare the response XML. It contains the list of federal holidays for year 2012.

```
Element holidayResponse = buildHolidaysResponse(year);
```

Step 3: Create a springws-servlet.xml Configuration File

This file contains the Spring web services related information such as endpoints, interceptors, and so forth. It loads the defined Spring beans into the Spring container. The WSDL is generated dynamically using Spring provided XML tag "<sws:dynamic-wsdl/>".

```
<?xml version="1.0" encoding="UTF-8"?>
<beans xmlns="http://www.springframework.org/schema/beans"
    xmlns:xsi="http://www.w3.org/2001/XMLSchema-instance"
    xmlns:context="http://www.springframework.org/schema/context"
    xmlns:sws="http://www.springframework.org/schema/web-services"
    xsi:schemaLocation="http://www.springframework.org/schema/beans
    http://www.springframework.org/schema/beans/spring-beans-3.0.xsd
    http://www.springframework.org/schema/web-services
    http://www.springframework.org/schema/web-services/web-services-
    2.0.xsd
    http://www.springframework.org/schema/context
    http://www.springframework.org/schema/context/spring-context-
    3.0.xsd">

    <context:component-scan base-package="com.learning.springws"/>

    <sws:annotation-driven/>

    <sws:dynamic-wsdl id="holidays"
                portTypeName="HolidayPortType"
                locationUri="/services/holidayService/"
                targetNamespace=
                "http://springws.learning.com/holidays/definitions">
        <sws:xsd location="/WEB-INF/holidays.xsd"/>
    </sws:dynamic-wsdl>
</beans>
```

Step 4: Create a web.xml File

Re-use the web.xml we created in Example-1

Step 5: Create a WAR file; and deploy it in Tomcat Server.

- Build a WAR file using Ant or any other build tool. Make sure files are packaged correctly in a war file.
- Deploy the WAR file in any servlet container.

The structure of the generated WAR file is shown in Figure 13-3:

Step 6: Verify the Generated WSDL Document

Access the WSDL file from web browser to make sure service is deployed without any errors. Use the below provided URL to view the complete WSDL.

```
http://localhost:8080/springws/services/employeeService/holidays.wsdl
```

Figure 13-3: war file structure

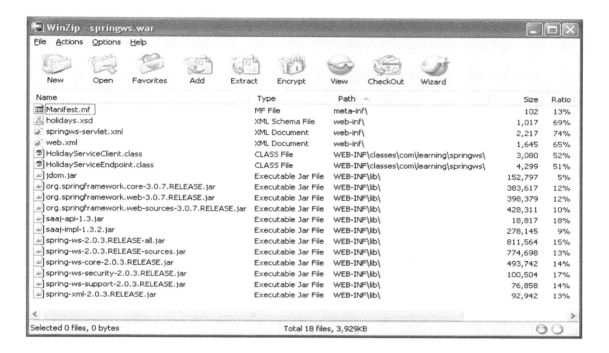

Step 7: Write a Client to Invoke the Deployed Service Endpoint

The Spring Web services framework provided "WebServiceTemplate" class can be used for accessing the deployed web service endpoint. This web service client can set the endpoint related metadata using Spring-based Java API or it can use XML-based configuration. The following web service client uses Spring-based Java API. The complete Web service client code is provided in Listing 13-6.

Listing 13-6: Spring-based web service client

```java
// HolidayServiceClient.java
package com.learning.springws;

import org.springframework.ws.client.core.WebServiceTemplate;
import org.springframework.xml.transform.StringSource;
import org.springframework.xml.transform.StringResult;
import org.jdom.Element;
import org.jdom.Document;
import org.jdom.output.XMLOutputter;
import javax.xml.transform.Source;
import javax.xml.transform.Result;

public class HolidayServiceClient {
    public static void main(String[] args) throws Exception {
        try {
```

```
                    HolidayServiceClient client = new HolidayServiceClient();
                    client.invokeService("2012");
            } catch (Exception ex) {
                ex.printStackTrace();
            }
        }

        private void invokeService(String year) throws Exception {
            ClientLogMessageHandler[] handler = new
                            ClientLogMessageHandler[1];
            handler[0] = new ClientLogMessageHandler();
            WebServiceTemplate webServiceTemplate = new
                            WebServiceTemplate();
            webServiceTemplate.setDefaultUri
            ("http://localhost:8080/springws/services/holidayService/");

            String requestXML = createRequestXML(year);
            Source source = new StringSource(requestXML);
            Result result = new StringResult();
            webServiceTemplate.sendSourceAndReceiveToResult(source,result);

            System.out.println("--- result ---" + result.toString());
        }

        private static String createRequestXML(String year)
        throws Exception {
            Element requestElement = new Element("getHolidayRequest",
                "http://springws.ws.learning.com/holidays/schemas");
            Document myDocument = new Document(requestElement);
            Element yearElement = new Element("year");
            yearElement.setText(year);
            requestElement.addContent(yearElement);

            XMLOutputter outputter = new XMLOutputter();
            String input = outputter.outputString(myDocument);
            System.out.println("--- input  --- " + input);

            return input;
        }
}
```

The following method is used to create the input request XML.

```
private static String createRequestXML(String year) throws Exception {
    // ...
}
```

The created request XML is provided below:

```
<?xml version="1.0" encoding="UTF-8"?>
<getHolidayRequest xmlns=
            "http://springws.ws.learning.com/holidays/schemas">
    <year xmlns="">2000</year>
</getHolidayRequest>
```

The following code invokes the service endpoint. The output is printed on the console; use suitable parsing technique to obtain the data.

```
webServiceTemplate.sendSourceAndReceiveToResult(source, result);
```

This Web service response XML is provided below:

```
<?xml version="1.0" encoding="UTF-8"?>
<getHolidayResponse
        xmlns="http://springws.ws.learning.com/holidays/schemas">
    <holidays xmlns="" year="2000">
        <January>02-jan-2012</January>
        <January>16-jan-2012</January>
        <February>20-feb-2012</February>
        <May>28-may-2012</May>
        <July>04-july-2012</July>
        <September>03-sept-2012</September>
        <October>08-oct-2012</October>
        <November>12-nov-2012</November>
        <November>22-nov-2012</November>
        <December>25-dec-2012</December>
    </holidays>
</getHolidayResponse>
```

Example 4: Spring-WS Endpoint with JAXB API

This Web service endpoint is developed with JAXB Object type as request-and-response payload. The request-response objects are annotated with JAXB annotations. The steps required to develop a Web service of this type are given below.

1. Create a XSD document.
2. Create a service endpoint interface.
3. Create a Request object using JAXB API.
4. Create a Response object using JAXB API.
5. Create a "springws-servlet.xml" configuration file.
6. Create a "web.xml" file
7. Create a WAR file and deploy it in Tomcat server.
8. Verify the generated WSDL document.
9. Write a client to invoke the deployed service endpoint.

The above-specified steps are described in the following sections:

This example demonstrates the use of stock change web service; for a given stock symbol it provides the current price and its price change. Let us now start defining the XML schema of the service.

Step 1: Create a XSD Document

The first step is to prepare a XSD of the Web Service endpoint. Convert the domain model to an XML types; and create a XML root element for request-response payloads. The complete XML schema document is provided below. Spring runtime use this schema document to generate the WSDL.

```
<?xml version="1.0" encoding="UTF-8"?>
```

```xml
<xs:schema xmlns:xs="http://www.w3.org/2001/XMLSchema"
           xmlns:stock="http://springws.ws.learning.com/stock/schemas"
           elementFormDefault="unqualified"
           targetNamespace=
               "http://springws.ws.learning.com/stock/schemas">

    <!-- Root element for request -->
    <xs:element name="getStockRequest" type="stock:StockRequest"/>

    <!-- Root element for response -->
    <xs:element name="getStockResponse" type="stock:StockResponse"/>

    <xs:complexType name="StockRequest">
        <xs:sequence>
            <xs:element minOccurs="0" name="symbol" type="xs:string"/>
        </xs:sequence>
    </xs:complexType>

    <xs:complexType name="StockResponse">
        <xs:sequence>
            <xs:element minOccurs="0" name="return"
                               type="stock:stockdata"/>
        </xs:sequence>
    </xs:complexType>

    <xs:complexType name="stockdata">
        <xs:sequence>
            <xs:element minOccurs="0" name="todayPrice"
                    type="xs:string"/>
            <xs:element minOccurs="0" name="change" type="xs:string"/>
        </xs:sequence>
    </xs:complexType>

</xs:schema>
```

Step 2: Create a Service Endpoint Class

Create a service endpoint class to receive the request-response payloads. This Web service endpoint is developed with JAXB annotated classes as request-response types. The Web service endpoint is expecting "StockRequest" as request type; and returning "StockResponse" as response type. The complete service endpoint class code is provided in Listing 13-7.

Listing 13-7: Developing Spring-based web service using JAXB API

```java
// StockServiceEndpoint.java
package com.learning.springws;

import org.springframework.ws.server.endpoint.annotation.Endpoint;
import org.springframework.ws.server.endpoint.annotation.PayloadRoot;
import org.springframework.ws.server.endpoint.annotation.ResponsePayload;
import org.springframework.ws.server.endpoint.annotation.RequestPayload;
import javax.xml.bind.JAXBContext;
import javax.xml.bind.Marshaller;
import java.io.StringWriter;

@Endpoint
public class StockServiceEndpoint {
```

Development Methodologies

```java
@PayloadRoot(namespace =
        "http://springws.ws.learning.com/stock/schemas",
        localPart = "getStockRequest")
@ResponsePayload
public StockResponse getStockInformaton(@RequestPayload
                StockRequest stockRequest) throws Exception {

    // Getting the input data from client request
    String symbol = stockRequest.getSymbol();

    // JAXB annotated response object
    StockResponse response = new StockResponse();

    // Apply the business logic based on input received.
    if (symbol != null && symbol.equalsIgnoreCase("GLD")) {
        response.setTodayPrice("32.15");
        response.setChange("1.13");
    } else {
        response.setTodayPrice("XXXX");
        response.setChange("XXXX");
    }

    // marshalling the Java object to a XML; to print the XML
    StringWriter writer = new StringWriter();
    JAXBContext context = JAXBContext.newInstance(
                        StockResponse.class);
    Marshaller m = context.createMarshaller();
    m.marshal(response, writer);
    System.out.println("-- Response --" + writer.toString());

    return response;
  }
}
```

Step 3: Create a Request Object Using JAXB API

The request object must conform to the following rules.

- The request-response types must be annotated with "@XmlRootElement' element
- The "@XmlRootElement" annotation member values "name", "namespace" must match the "localPart", "namespace" specified with "@PayloadRoot" annotation of the service endpoint

The complete Request object code is provided in Listing 13-8.

Listing 13-8: Request object used for the service endpoint

```java
// StockRequest.java
package com.learning.springws;

import javax.xml.bind.annotation.XmlRootElement;
import javax.xml.bind.annotation.XmlElement;
import javax.xml.bind.annotation.XmlType;

@XmlRootElement(name="getStockRequest",
            namespace="http://springws.ws.learning.com/stock/schemas")
```

```
@XmlType(name="StockRequest")
public class StockRequest {

    private static final long serialVersionUID = 1L;
    private String symbol;

    @XmlElement(name="symbol")
    public String getSymbol() {
        return symbol;
    }

    public void setSymbol(String symbol) {
        this.symbol = symbol;
    }
}
```

Step 4: Create a Response Object Using JAXB API

The following class is used for service method response. This class must use "@XmlRootElement" annotation.

The complete Response object code is provided in Listing 13-9

Listing 13-9: Response object used for the service endpoint

```
// StockResponse.java
package com.learning.springws;

import javax.xml.bind.annotation.XmlRootElement;
import javax.xml.bind.annotation.XmlElement;
import javax.xml.bind.annotation.XmlType;

@XmlRootElement(name = "getStockResponse",
        namespace = "http://springws.ws.learning.com/stock/schemas")
@XmlType(name="StockResponse",
        propOrder = {"todayPrice", "change"})
public class StockResponse {

    private static final long serialVersionUID = 1L;
    private String todayPrice;
    private String change;

    @XmlElement(name = "todayprice")
    public String getTodayPrice() {
        return todayPrice;
    }

    public void setTodayPrice(String todayPrice) {
        this.todayPrice = todayPrice;
    }

    @XmlElement(name = "change")
    public String getChange() {
        return change;
    }

    public void setChange(String change) {
```

```
                this.change = change;
        }
}
```

Step 5: Create a "springws-servlet.xml" Configuration File

This file contains the Spring web services related information such as endpoints, interceptors,
JAXB marshaller, and so forth. It loads the defined Spring beans into the Spring container. The
WSDL is generated dynamically using Spring provided XML tag "<sws:dynamic-wsdl/>".

```xml
<?xml version="1.0" encoding="UTF-8"?>
<beans xmlns="http://www.springframework.org/schema/beans"
    xmlns:xsi="http://www.w3.org/2001/XMLSchema-instance"
    xmlns:context="http://www.springframework.org/schema/context"
    xmlns:sws="http://www.springframework.org/schema/web-services"
    xsi:schemaLocation="http://www.springframework.org/schema/beans
    http://www.springframework.org/schema/beans/spring-beans-3.0.xsd
    http://www.springframework.org/schema/web-services
    http://www.springframework.org/schema/web-services/
                        web-services-2.0.xsd
    http://www.springframework.org/schema/context
    http://www.springframework.org/schema/context/
                        spring-context-3.0.xsd">

    <context:annotation-config/>
    <context:component-scan base-package="com.learning.springws"/>
    <sws:annotation-driven/>

    <sws:dynamic-wsdl id="stockchange"
                    portTypeName="StockChangePortType"
                    locationUri="/services/stockService/"
                    targetNamespace=
                "http://springws.ws.learning.com/stock/definitions">
        <sws:xsd location="/WEB-INF/stockchange.xsd"/>
    </sws:dynamic-wsdl>

    <bean id="jaxb2Marshaller"
        class="org.springframework.oxm.jaxb.Jaxb2Marshaller">
        <property name="classesToBeBound">
            <list>
                <value>com.learning.springws.StockRequest</value>
                <value>com.learning.springws.StockResponse</value>
            </list>
        </property>
            <property name="schema" value="/WEB-INF/stockchange.xsd"/>
    </bean>

    <bean id="marshallingPayloadMethodProcessor" class=
            "org.springframework.ws.server.endpoint.adapter.method.
            MarshallingPayloadMethodProcessor">
        <constructor-arg ref="jaxb2Marshaller"/>
        <constructor-arg ref="jaxb2Marshaller"/>
    </bean>

    <bean id="defaultMethodEndpointAdapter" class=
                    "org.springframework.ws.server.endpoint.adapter.
```

```
                    DefaultMethodEndpointAdapter">
        <property name="methodArgumentResolvers">
            <list>
                <ref bean="marshallingPayloadMethodProcessor"/>
            </list>
        </property>
        <property name="methodReturnValueHandlers">
        <list>
                <ref bean="marshallingPayloadMethodProcessor"/>
        </list>
        </property>
    </bean>
</beans>
```

Step 6: Create a "web.xml" Configuration File

Reuse the "web.xml" file we created in Example-1.

Step 7: Create a WAR File and deploy it in Tomcat Server

The structure of the generated WAR file is shown in Figure 13-4:

Figure 13-4: WAR file structure

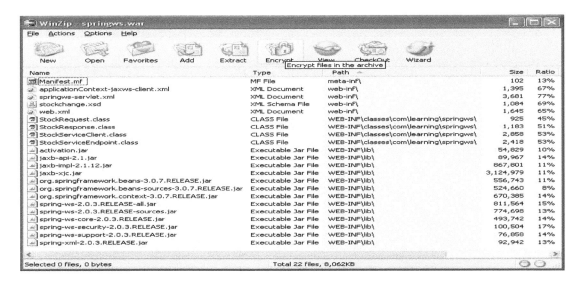

- Build a WAR file using Ant or any other build tool. Make sure files are packaged correctly in a WAR file.
- Deploy the WAR file in any servlet container.

Step 8: Verify the Generated WSDL Document

Invoke the deployed web service with below provided URL. You can view the complete WSDL.

`http://localhost:8080/springws/services/stockService/stockchange.wsdl`

Step 9: Write a Client to Invoke the Deployed Service Endpoint

Reuse the applicationContext-client.xml we created in Example1. Add the below provided XML to "applicationContext-client.xml" file.

```xml
<bean id="webServiceTemplate"
      class="org.springframework.ws.client.core.WebServiceTemplate">
    <constructor-arg ref="messageFactory"/>
    <property name="defaultUri" value=
            "http://localhost:8080/springws/services/stockService/"/>
    <property name="messageSender" ref="messageSender"/>
</bean>
```

The client used to invoke the web service endpoint is provided in Listing 13-10. Run this client to view the output.

Listing 13-10: Client to invoke the web service endpoint

```java
// StockServiceClient.java
package com.learning.springws;

import org.springframework.context.support.
            ClassPathXmlApplicationContext;
import org.springframework.ws.client.core.WebServiceTemplate;
import org.springframework.xml.transform.StringSource;
import org.springframework.xml.transform.StringResult;
import javax.xml.bind.JAXBContext;
import javax.xml.bind.Marshaller;
import javax.xml.transform.Source;
import javax.xml.transform.Result;
import java.io.StringWriter;

public class StockServiceClient {

    public static void main(String[] args) throws Exception {
        try {
            StockServiceClient client = new StockServiceClient();
            client.invokeService("GLD");
        } catch (Exception ex) {
            ex.printStackTrace();
        }
    }

    // Invoking the web service endpoint
    private void invokeService(String stockSymbol) throws Exception {
        ClassPathXmlApplicationContext context = new
                ClassPathXmlApplicationContext
            (new String[]{"applicationContext-jaxws-client.xml"});
        WebServiceTemplate webServiceTemplate = (WebServiceTemplate)
                context.getBean("webServiceTemplate");

        String requestXML = createInputXML(stockSymbol);
        Source source = new StringSource(requestXML);
        Result result = new StringResult();
        webServiceTemplate.sendSourceAndReceiveToResult(source, result);

        // Printing the response XML on the console.
        System.out.println("-- Response XML is --" +result.toString());
    }
```

```
        // private method used to create an input request
        private String createInputXML(String stockSymbol) throws Exception {
            // JAXB annotated request object
            StockRequest request = new StockRequest();
            request.setSymbol(stockSymbol);

            // Converting the Java objects into XML to see the request
            StringWriter writer = new StringWriter();
            JAXBContext context=
                    JAXBContext.newInstance(StockRequest.class);
            Marshaller m = context.createMarshaller();
            m.marshal(request, writer);
            System.out.println("-- Request XML is --" + writer.toString());

            return writer.toString();
        }
}
```

The "StockServiceClient" provides the following request payload to the service endpoint. The "createInputXML()" method of the "StockServiceClient" class is used to create the following request payload.

```
<?xml version="1.0" encoding="UTF-8" standalone="yes"?>
<ns2:getStockRequest
        xmlns:ns2 = "http://springws.ws.learning.com/stock/schemas">
    <symbol>GLD</symbol>
</ns2:getStockRequest>
```

The Web service response is provided below. Use suitable parsing technique to obtain the values from XML.

```
<?xml version="1.0" encoding="UTF-8"?>
<ns3:getStockResponse
        xmlns:ns3="http://springws.ws.learning.com/stock/schemas">
    <todayprice>32.15</todayprice>
    <change>1.13</change>
</ns3:getStockResponse>
```

Web Service Endpoint Design Scenarios

The Spring-based Web services supports only "contract-first" kind of web services. The web service provider starts the service development with XSD or WSDL. In general, the service endpoint method has one input parameter and one return value. Input parameters maps to the request-payload; and return value maps to the response-payload. The Web service endpoint supported request-and-response types are listed below:

- W3C DOM Element
- DOM4j Element (Refer to Example1)
- JDOM Element (Refer to Example3)
- XOM Element

- JAXB Type - Any type that is annotated with "XMLRootElement" and "JAXBElement" (Refer to Example4)
- DOMSource, SAXSource, StaxSource and StreamSource
- Any type supported by Spring OXM Marsheller

The following Web service endpoints are using "Dom4j", "JDOM" and "JAXB" data types. Similarly, other supported types can be used for designing the service endpoints.

The following endpoint uses Dom4j's "org.dom4j.Element" type for mapping the request-and-response payloads.

```
public org.dom4j.Element getEmployee(@RequestPayload org.dom4j.Element
employeeRequest) throws Exception {
}
```

The following endpoint uses JDOM's "org.jdom.Element" type for mapping the request-and-response payloads.

```
public org.jdom.Element getEmployee(@RequestPayload org.jdom.Element
employeeRequest) throws Exception {
}
```

The following endpoint uses JAXB annotated classes for mapping the request-and-response payloads.

```
public StockResponse getStockInformaton(@RequestPayload StockRequest
stockRequest) throws Exception {
}
```

Web Service Client Design Scenarios

The main class used for accessing the Spring-based Web service endpoint is "WebServiceTemplate". This class contains methods to send "Source" as request-payload, and receives response-payload as "Source" or "Result". The Web service client can also marshal request objects to XML and un-marshal the response XML to objects. The commonly used client methods of the Spring web service template class are listed below.

The following method sends the "Source" as input and receives "Result" as output.

```
webServiceTemplate.sendSourceAndReceiveToResult(source, result);
```

The following method sends the "Source" as input and receives "Object" as output.

```
Object result = webServiceTemplate.marshalSendAndReceive(source);
```

The Spring-WS can re-use your existing Spring expertise while developing web services. This book has covered the two (Apache-CXF and Spring-WS) open-source web service frameworks for developing enterprise applications. All these frameworks provide similar features; none is superior to the others. Which framework will you choose in your application? It is totally depends on the application requirement, developers comfort and their prior experience with it.

Summary

Figure 13-5 summarizes the most important points described in this chapter.

Figure 13-5 Spring web services summary

This section summarizes the features of Spring-WS framework.

- The class annotated with the @Endpoint is a special kind of Spring component suitable to handle the XML requests-and-responses. The @Endpoint-annotated classes are eligible for component scanning using Spring-provided <context:component-scan/> xml tag.
- The spring-provided @RequestPayload annotation is used with method parameters to receive the request XML messages
- The spring-provided @PayloadRoot annotation is used at method-level to route the incoming request XML messages.
- The spring-provided @ResponsePayload annotation maps the method return value to the response payload.
- The spring-provided <sws:interceptors/> xml tag can be used to integrate the interceptors with service endpoint.
- The spring-provided <sws:dynamic-wsdl/> xml tag generates the WSDL for a given XML schema.
- The WebServiceTemplate is the core class used for accessing the Spring-based web service endpoint

Chapter 14. Spring with Apache-CXF

Apache-CXF is a most popular open-source framework used for developing fully featured Web Services conforming to JAX-WS standards. This project is derived from combining the two open-source projects "**C**eltix" and "**XF**ire". The name CXF is derived from two projects "**C**eltix" and "**XF**ire". The combined project is now available with Apache Software Foundation. This chapter illustrates the Web Services development using Spring and Apache-CXF framework.

This chapter will discuss the following topics:

- The "code-first" and "contract-first" Web services development using Apache-CXF.
- The Provider-based web services development.
- The Web service client, endpoint design scenarios.
- The use of SOAP message handlers.
- How to configure a SOAP handler chain to a web service client and endpoint
- Build and Deployment instructions for Tomcat.
- The CXF framework tools and utilities.

There are several open-source Web Services frameworks available to implement JAX-WS conformant web services. The commonly used open-source Web service frameworks are listed below.

- JAX-WS (RI) – A reference implementation from Sun
- Spring Web Services (Spring-WS)
- Apache-CXF
- Apache-Axis2
- JBoss-WS

Prerequisites/Setting Up the Environment

- The JAR files required to develop the CXF-based Web Services are provided along with the CXF distribution. Download the CXF framework from apache website.
- The complete distribution is available in the form of JAR files. So no additional software needed for development.
- The below given table provides the primary list of JAR files used for developing CXF-based Web service endpoints.

cxf-2.2.5.jar	org.springframework.beans.jar
cxf-api-2.2.5.jar	org.springframework.context.jar
cxf-tools-wsdlto-core-2.0.10.jar	org.springframework.context.support.jar
org.springframework.aop.jar	org.springframework.core.jar
org.springframework.asm.jar	org.springframework.aspects.jar

Apache-CXF Advantages

- CXF provides good support for various Web Services standards like SOAP, WSDL and WS-I Basic profile.
- CXF provides support for various client side programming models to invoke the deployed service endpoint. It provides support for static and dynamic clients.
- CXF extensions available to configure the SOAP message handlers and interceptors.
- CXF provides a simple logging mechanism to log request-and-response SOAP messages.
- CXF provides support for both "code-first" and "contract-first" type of web service development models.
- CXF provides a seamless integration with Spring framework. The Spring and CXF XML tags can co-exist in the same application context configuration file. Both look similar.
- Using CXF, It is easy to expose existing business functionality as a Web service to other applications to meet the application-specific business need.
- CXF provided services are easy to plug into the already exiting application code.
- CXF follows simple syntax; so it is easy to learn.
- CXF provides wide range of annotations for Web services development.
- CXF provides support for JAX-RS and JAX-WS standards. It is possible to develop REST-based and SOAP-based Web service endpoint using CXF framework
- CXF provides support for various Java specification requests like JSR-181 (meta data annotations), JSR-224 (JSR-WS), JSR-311 (JAX-RS), and JSR-222 (JAXB)
- CXF provides support for multiple data formats like JSON, XML, and SOAP.

Development Methodologies

The following sections illustrate the web services development using CXF framework. There are two different ways we can develop Web Services using CXF.

- Write Java interface-first, and expose it as a Web Service
- Write WSDL document-first; generate Java classes using CXF-provided framework tools.

Example 1: Java First Development (Also Called Code First)

In this approach we start the development with Java interface and its implementation class by declaring @WebService annotation to mark it as a Web Service. The steps required to develop a Web Service of this type are provided below.

1. Create a service endpoint interface
2. Create a service implementation class
3. Create a CXF configuration file
4. Create a "web.xml" file
5. Create a WAR file and deploy into a Tomcat server
6. Verify the WSDL document
7. Write a client to invoke the deployed service

The above-specified steps are described in the following sections:

This is an employee web service; for a given employee id, it provides the employee details.

Step 1: Create a Service Endpoint Interface

The only required annotation at the service endpoint interface is "@WebService". All other annotations are optional; other annotations I used it here for sake of developers to get familiar with them. The following service endpoint interface "EmployeeService" has four methods. Listing 14-1 has a Java code that demonstrates the POJO-based web service implementation.

Listing 14-1: Developing POJO-based web service

```java
// EmployeeService.java
package com.learning.ws.jaxws;

import javax.jws.WebParam.Mode;
import javax.jws.*;

@WebService
public interface EmployeeService {
    @WebMethod(operationName="getEmployee")
    Employee getEmployee(@WebParam (name="employeeId")
                    String employeeId) throws EmployeeFault;

    @WebMethod(operationName="getEmployeeAddress")
    String getEmployeeAddressInfo(@WebParam(name="empId", mode= Mode.IN)
                    String employeeId) throws Exception;

    String getEmployerInformation(@WebParam(name="empId", mode= Mode.IN)
        String employeeId, @WebParam(name="state", mode= Mode.IN)
        String state) throws Exception;

    @WebMethod(operationName="deleteEmployee")
    void deleteEmployee(@WebParam (name="employeeId") String
                            employeeId);
}
```

The following "Employee" Java bean class is used for data population:

```java
// Employee.java
package com.learning.ws.jaxws;

public class Employee {

    private static final long serialVersionUID = 1L;
    private String employeeId;
    private String lastName;
    private String firstName;

    // Generate getters and setters for the above
}
```

Step 2: Create a Service Implementation Class

The service implementation class "EmployeeServiceImpl" is declared with "@WebService" annotation to mark it as a Web Service. The above interface-defined methods are implemented in its implementation class. They are provided in Listing 14-2.

Listing 14-2: POJO-based web service implementation class.

```java
// EmployeeServiceImpl.java
```

```java
package com.learning.ws.jaxws;

import javax.jws.*;
import javax.xml.ws.*;

@WebService(name="EmployeeService",
            serviceName="employeeService",
            endpointInterface="com.learning.ws.jaxws.EmployeeService")
public class EmployeeServiceImpl implements EmployeeService {

    public Employee getEmployee(String employeeId) throws EmployeeFault{

        if(employeeId == null) {
            throw new EmployeeFault("Invalid input received");
        }

        Employee emp = new Employee();
        emp.setEmployeeId(employeeId);
        emp.setFirstName("John");
        emp.setLastName("Smith");

        return emp;
    }

    public String getEmployeeAddressInfo(String employeeId)
    throws Exception {
        /* Implement your logic here to get the employee address,
        here the hard coded return value is used.*/
        String address = "3943 Roundabout CIR, Chandler,Arizona,85226";
        return address;
    }

    public void deleteEmployee(String employeeId) {
        System.out.println("--- Delete Employee ---" + employeeId);
        // Implement your logic here to delete an employee.
    }

    public String getEmployerInformation(String employeeId,
                String state) throws Exception {
        // Implement your logic here
        String employer = "Bank of Chandler, Chandler, Arizona, 85226";
        return employer;
    }
}
```

Step 3: Create a CXF Configuration File

Apache-CXF provides XML-based tags to configure the Web service endpoint with JAX-WS runtime. CXF tags look similar to Spring framework bean tags. Both Spring and CXF tags can co-exist in the same configuration file. Configure the Web service endpoint using "<jaxws:endpoint/>" tag. The use of CXF-provided "<jaxws:endpoint/>" tag is given below.

```xml
<jaxws:endpoint id="employee"
        implementor="com.learning.ws.jaxws.EmployeeServiceImpl"
        address="/employee">
</jaxws:endpoint>
```

This XML tag "<jaxws:endpoint/>" contains the details of web service implementation class and web service binding address. The complete XML file is provided below; named the "applicationContext-jaxws.xml".

```xml
<?xml version="1.0" encoding="UTF-8"?>
<beans xmlns="http://www.springframework.org/schema/beans"
        xmlns:xsi="http://www.w3.org/2001/XMLSchema-instance"
        xmlns:jaxws="http://cxf.apache.org/jaxws"
        xmlns:cxf="http://cxf.apache.org/core"
        xsi:schemaLocation="http://www.springframework.org/schema/beans
        http://www.springframework.org/schema/beans/spring-beans.xsd
        http://cxf.apache.org/jaxws
        http://cxf.apache.org/schemas/jaxws.xsd
        http://cxf.apache.org/core
        http://cxf.apache.org/schemas/core.xsd ">

    <!-- Loads CXF modules from cxf.jar file -->
    <import resource="classpath:META-INF/cxf/cxf.xml"/>
    <import resource="classpath:META-INF/cxf/cxf-extension-soap.xml"/>
    <import resource="classpath:META-INF/cxf/cxf-servlet.xml"/>
    <import resource="classpath:META-INF/cxf/cxf-extension-jaxrs-
    binding.xml"/>

    <!-- Configure the web service endpoint -->
    <jaxws:endpoint id="employee"
            implementor="com.learning.ws.jaxws.EmployeeServiceImpl"
            address="/employee">
    </jaxws:endpoint>
</beans>
```

Step 4: Create a web.xml File

Configure the spring context listener and CXF transport servlet in web.xml. The complete web.xml file is provided below.

```xml
<?xml version="1.0" encoding="UTF-8"?>
<web-app version="2.4" xmlns="http://java.sun.com/xml/ns/j2ee"
    xmlns:xsi="http://www.w3.org/2001/XMLSchema-instance"
    xsi:schemaLocation="http://java.sun.com/xml/ns/j2ee
    http://java.sun.com/xml/ns/j2ee/web-app_2_4.xsd">

<display-name>Web Services Application</display-name>
<listener>
    <listener-class>
        org.springframework.web.context.ContextLoaderListener
    </listener-class>
</listener>

<context-param>
    <param-name>contextConfigLocation</param-name>
    <param-value>/WEB-INF/applicationContext-jaxws.xml</param-value>
</context-param>

<servlet>
    <servlet-name>CXFServlet</servlet-name>
    <servlet-class>
```

```
            org.apache.cxf.transport.servlet.CXFServlet
     </servlet-class>
</servlet>

<servlet-mapping>
     <servlet-name>CXFServlet</servlet-name>
     <url-pattern>/services/*</url-pattern>
</servlet-mapping>

<mime-mapping>
     <extension>wsdl</extension>
     <mime-type>text/xml</mime-type>
</mime-mapping>
<mime-mapping>
     <extension>xsd</extension>
     <mime-type>text/xml</mime-type>
     </mime-mapping>
</web-app>
```

The following configurations initialize the root application context. This is the boot strap listener to start up the Spring root web application context and it loads all files specified in the <param-value/> into the context.

```
<listener>
     <listener-class>
            org.springframework.web.context.ContextLoaderListener
     </listener-class>
</listener>
<context-param>
     <param-name>contextConfigLocation</param-name>
     <param-value>/WEB-INF/applicationContext-jaxws.xml</param-value>
</context-param>
```

Configure the CXF transport servlet in web.xml. All Web Service requests routes through this transport servlet; it converts the HTTP request to SOAP request and vice versa.

```
<servlet>
     <servlet-name>CXFServlet</servlet-name>
     <servlet-class>
            org.apache.cxf.transport.servlet.CXFServlet
     </servlet-class>
</servlet>
<servlet-mapping>
     <servlet-name>CXFServlet</servlet-name>
     <url-pattern>/services/*</url-pattern>
</servlet-mapping>
```

Step 5: Create a WAR File and Deploy it in Tomcat Server.

1. Build a WAR file using Ant or any other build tool. Make sure the following files are packaged correctly in war file.

   a. Service endpoint interface
   b. Service endpoint implementation class
   c. Any utility classes used for data access.

d. web.xml file

e. CXF configuration file (applicationContext-jaxws.xml) file.

The structure of the WAR file is shown Figure 14-1.

Figure 14-1: Structure of a WAR file

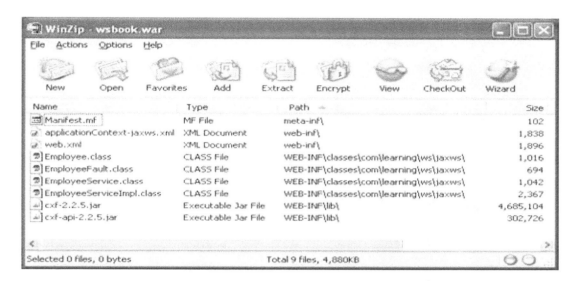

NOTE: Figure 14-1 shows only a few JAR files in "WEB-INF/lib" directory.

2. Deploy the WAR file in any servlet container.

a. Copy the packed WAR into "apache-tomcat/webapps" directory

b. Start the tomcat server by running the "startup.bat" batch file available in "apache-tomcat/bin" directory

c. See the server console output and logs; make sure WAR file is deployed without any errors.

Step 6: Verify the WSDL Document

Access the WSDL file from web browser to make sure service is deployed without any errors. Use the below given URL to view the complete WSDL.

```
http://localhost:8080/wsbook/services/employee?wsdl
```

Step 7: Write a Client to Invoke the Deployed Service

The following used to specify the location of the WSDL:

```
URL url = new URL("http://localhost:8080/wsbook/services/employee?wsdl");
```

The following "Service.create()" method is used to create an instance of "Service" object. It takes two parameters. The first parameter is service URI, second parameter is service name.

```
QName qname = new QName("http://jaxws.ws.learning.com/",
                        "employeeService");
Service service = Service.create(url, qname);
```

This is used to get the binding port to invoke the methods defined in the service endpoint interface.

```
EmployeeService employeeService = service.getPort(EmployeeService.class);
```

Listing 14-3 provides the Java code used to invoke the web service endpoint. Run this client to view the output.

Listing 14-3: Client to invoke the service endpoint

```java
// TestClient.java
package com.learning.ws.jaxws;

import java.net.URL;
import javax.xml.namespace.QName;
import javax.xml.ws.Service;

public class TestClient {
    public static void main(String args[]) throws Exception {
        try {
            TestClient client = new TestClient ();
            client.invokeEmployeeService();
        } catch(Exception ex) {
            ex.printStackTrace();
        }
    }

    private void invokeEmployeeService() throws Exception {
        // Location of the wsdl
        URL url = new URL("http://localhost:8080/
                wsbook/services/employee?wsdl");

        /* 1st argument is service URI - maps to targetNamespace in
         Wsdl, 2nd argument is service name - maps to <wsdl:service/>
         element's name attribute in wsdl */
        QName qname = new QName("http://jaxws.ws.learning.com/",
                "employeeService");
        Service service = Service.create(url, qname);

        // Get the service port - maps to <wsdl:portType/> in wsdl
        EmployeeService employeeService =
            service.getPort(EmployeeService.class);

        // Invoke the service endpoint methods.
        String address =
            employeeService.getEmployeeAddressInfo("823147");
        System.out.println("Address is: " + address);

        Employee emp = employeeService.getEmployee("133334");
        System.out.println("Employee Id:" + emp.getEmployeeId() +
        "-- First Name --" + emp.getFirstName() + "-- Last Name --"
            + emp.getLastName());
    }
```

}

Example 2: WSDL First Development (Also Called Contract First)

In this approach developer first creates a WSDL document, also called contract; this WSDL is used for generating the Java service endpoint interface and its dependent classes. The steps required to develop a Web Service of this type are given below.

1. Create a WSDL file
2. Generate service endpoint Java classes using WSDL2Java tool
3. Create a CXF configuration file
4. Create a web.xml file
5. Create a WAR file and deploy it in Tomcat server
6. Verify the WSDL document
7. Write a client to invoke the deployed service

The above-specified steps are described in the following sections:

Step 1: Create a WSDL File

Apache-CXF provides tools to generate the Java classes from WSDL. The following WSDL is used for generating the Java classes using "org.apache.cxf.tools.wsdlto.WSDL2Java" utility; available with CXF framework. The complete WSDL file is provided below.

```
<?xml version="1.0" encoding="UTF-8"?>
<wsdl:definitions name="employeeService"
        targetNamespace="http://jaxws.ws.learning.com/"
        xmlns:ns1="http://cxf.apache.org/bindings/xformat"
        xmlns:soap="http://schemas.xmlsoap.org/wsdl/soap/"
        xmlns:tns="http://jaxws.ws.learning.com/"
        xmlns:wsdl="http://schemas.xmlsoap.org/wsdl/"
        xmlns:xsd="http://www.w3.org/2001/XMLSchema">
    <wsdl:types>
        <xs:schema attributeFormDefault="unqualified"
            elementFormDefault="unqualified"
            targetNamespace="http://jaxws.ws.learning.com/"
            xmlns="http://jaxws.ws.learning.com/"
            xmlns:xs="http://www.w3.org/2001/XMLSchema">
        <xs:complexType name="employee">
            <xs:sequence>
                <xs:element minOccurs="0" name="employeeId"
                                    type="xs:string"/>
                <xs:element minOccurs="0" name="firstName"
                                    type="xs:string"/>
                <xs:element minOccurs="0" name="lastName"
                                    type="xs:string"/>
            </xs:sequence>
        </xs:complexType>
        <xs:element name="EmployeeFault" type="EmployeeFault" />
        <xs:complexType name="EmployeeFault">
            <xs:sequence />
        </xs:complexType>
        <xs:element name="getEmployeeAddress"
                type="getEmployeeAddress"/>
        <xs:complexType name="getEmployeeAddress">
```

```
        <xs:sequence>
            <xs:element minOccurs="0" name="empId"
                                    type="xs:string"/>
        </xs:sequence>
    </xs:complexType>
    <xs:element name="getEmployeeAddressResponse"
            type="getEmployeeAddressResponse"/>
        <xs:complexType name="getEmployeeAddressResponse">
            <xs:sequence>
                <xs:element minOccurs="0" name="return"
                                        type="xs:string"/>
            </xs:sequence>
        </xs:complexType>
    <xs:element name="getEmployee" type="getEmployee"/>
    <xs:complexType name="getEmployee">
        <xs:sequence>
            <xs:element minOccurs="0" name="employeeId"
                                    type="xs:string"/>
        </xs:sequence>
    </xs:complexType>
        <xs:element name="getEmployeeResponse"
                    type="getEmployeeResponse"/>
    <xs:complexType name="getEmployeeResponse">
        <xs:sequence>
            <xs:element minOccurs="0" name="return"
                                        type="employee"/>
        </xs:sequence>
    </xs:complexType>
    <xs:element name="getEmployerInformation"
                type="getEmployerInformation"/>
    <xs:complexType name="getEmployerInformation">
        <xs:sequence>
            <xs:element minOccurs="0" name="empId"
                                    type="xs:string"/>
            <xs:element minOccurs="0" name="state"
                                    type="xs:string"/>
        </xs:sequence>
    </xs:complexType>
    <xs:element name="getEmployerInformationResponse"
                type="getEmployerInformationResponse"/>
    <xs:complexType name="getEmployerInformationResponse">
        <xs:sequence>
            <xs:element minOccurs="0" name="return"
                                    type="xs:string"/>
        </xs:sequence>
    </xs:complexType>
    <xs:element name="deleteEmployee" type="deleteEmployee"/>
    <xs:complexType name="deleteEmployee">
        <xs:sequence>
            <xs:element minOccurs="0" name="employeeId"
                                    type="xs:string"/>
        </xs:sequence>
    </xs:complexType>
    <xs:element name="deleteEmployeeResponse"
            type="deleteEmployeeResponse"/>
    <xs:complexType name="deleteEmployeeResponse">
        <xs:sequence/>
```

```
            </xs:complexType>
    </xs:schema>
    </wsdl:types>

    <wsdl:message name="deleteEmployee">
        <wsdl:part element="tns:deleteEmployee" name="parameters"/>
    </wsdl:message>
    <wsdl:message name="EmployeeFault">
        <wsdl:part element="tns:EmployeeFault" name="EmployeeFault" />
    </wsdl:message>
    <wsdl:message name="getEmployee">
        <wsdl:part element="tns:getEmployee" name="parameters"/>
    </wsdl:message>
    <wsdl:message name="deleteEmployeeResponse">
        <wsdl:part element="tns:deleteEmployeeResponse"
                      name="parameters"/>
    </wsdl:message>
    <wsdl:message name="getEmployerInformationResponse">
    <wsdl:part element="tns:getEmployerInformationResponse"
            name="parameters"/>
    </wsdl:message>
    <wsdl:message name="getEmployeeAddress">
        <wsdl:part element="tns:getEmployeeAddress" name="parameters"/>
    </wsdl:message>
    <wsdl:message name="getEmployeeResponse">
        <wsdl:part element="tns:getEmployeeResponse"
                name="parameters"/>
    </wsdl:message>
        <wsdl:message name="getEmployerInformation">
        <wsdl:part element="tns:getEmployerInformation"
                name="parameters"/>
    </wsdl:message>
    <wsdl:message name="getEmployeeAddressResponse">
            <wsdl:part element="tns:getEmployeeAddressResponse"
                name="parameters"/>
    </wsdl:message>

    <wsdl:portType name="EmployeeService">
        <wsdl:operation name="getEmployeeAddress">
            <wsdl:input message="tns:getEmployeeAddress"
                        name="getEmployeeAddress"/>
            <wsdl:output message="tns:getEmployeeAddressResponse"
                        name="getEmployeeAddressResponse"/>
        </wsdl:operation>
        <wsdl:operation name="getEmployee">
            <wsdl:input message="tns:getEmployee" name="getEmployee"/>
            <wsdl:output message="tns:getEmployeeResponse"
                    name="getEmployeeResponse"/>
        </wsdl:operation>
        <wsdl:operation name="getEmployerInformation">
            <wsdl:input message="tns:getEmployerInformation"
                    name="getEmployerInformation"/>
            <wsdl:output message="tns:getEmployerInformationResponse"
                    name="getEmployerInformationResponse"/>
        </wsdl:operation>
        <wsdl:operation name="deleteEmployee">
            <wsdl:input message="tns:deleteEmployee"
```

```
                              name="deleteEmployee"/>
            <wsdl:output message="tns:deleteEmployeeResponse"
                         name="deleteEmployeeResponse"/>
            <wsdl:fault message="tns:EmployeeFault"
                             name="EmployeeFault" />
        </wsdl:operation>
</wsdl:portType>

<wsdl:binding name="employeeServiceSoapBinding"
              type="tns:EmployeeService">
    <soap:binding style="document"
              transport="http://schemas.xmlsoap.org/soap/http"/>
    <wsdl:operation name="getEmployee">
        <soap:operation soapAction="" style="document"/>
            <wsdl:input name="getEmployee">
                <soap:body use="literal"/>
            </wsdl:input>
            <wsdl:output name="getEmployeeResponse">
                <soap:body use="literal"/>
            </wsdl:output>
    </wsdl:operation>
    <wsdl:operation name="getEmployeeAddress">
        <soap:operation soapAction="" style="document"/>
            <wsdl:input name="getEmployeeAddress">
                <soap:body use="literal"/>
            </wsdl:input>
            <wsdl:output name="getEmployeeAddressResponse">
                <soap:body use="literal"/>
            </wsdl:output>
    </wsdl:operation>
    <wsdl:operation name="getEmployerInformation">
        <soap:operation soapAction="" style="document"/>
            <wsdl:input name="getEmployerInformation">
                <soap:body use="literal"/>
            </wsdl:input>
            <wsdl:output name="getEmployerInformationResponse">
                <soap:body use="literal"/>
            </wsdl:output>
    </wsdl:operation>
    <wsdl:operation name="deleteEmployee">
        <soap:operation soapAction="" style="document"/>
            <wsdl:input name="deleteEmployee">
                <soap:body use="literal"/>
            </wsdl:input>
            <wsdl:output name="deleteEmployeeResponse">
                <soap:body use="literal"/>
            </wsdl:output>
    </wsdl:operation>
</wsdl:binding>

<wsdl:service name="employeeService">
    <wsdl:port binding="tns:employeeServiceSoapBinding"
               name="EmployeeServicePort">
        <soap:address
        location="http://localhost:8080/wsbook/services/employee"/>
    </wsdl:port>
</wsdl:service>
```

```
</wsdl:definitions>
```

Step 2: Generate Service Endpoint Java Classes using WSDL2Java Utility

The "WSDL2Java" utility takes the WSDL input; and generates the fully annotated Java classes to implement the Web service. There are three different ways we can generate code using "WSDL2Java" utility.

- Using command line
- Using Ant build tool
- Using Maven CXF Maven plug-in.

Using command line:

Specify the physical location of WSDL file as input to generate the Java classes.

<u>Example:</u>

```
wsdl2java employee.wsdl
```

Specify the package for the generated classes

```
wsdl2java -p com.learning.ws.jaxws employee.wsdl
```

Using Ant Build Tool:

Add the below provided Ant target to your application build script. This Ant target generates and compiles the JAX-WS/JAXB code. This "build-wsdl2java" ant target takes many optional arguments; and only required argument for code generation is "wsdl-path".

```
<!-- Apache-CXF Ant target - To Generate and compile JAX-WS/JAXB code
     from WSDL -->
<target name="build-wsdl2java">
    <echo message="Running WSDL2Java task"/>
    <delete quiet="true" dir="${build-gen}"/>
    <mkdir dir="${build-gen}"/>
    <java classpathref="build.classpath" fork="true"
        classname="org.apache.cxf.tools.wsdlto.WSDLToJava">

        <!-- -d parameter sets the output root directory for
        generated files -->
        <arg value="-d"/>
        <arg value="${source.dir}"/>

        <!-- -p parameter specifies the complete package name of the
        generated code -->
        <arg value="-p"/>
        <arg value="${package-name}"/>

        <!-- -validate parameter used for WSDL validation before
        generation -->
        <arg value="-validate"/>

        <!-- actual input WSDL -->
```

```
            <arg value="${wsdl-path}"/>
        </java>

        <!-- Compile the generated code -->
        <mkdir dir="${build-gen}/bin"/>
        <javac srcdir="${source.dir}" destdir="${build-gen}/bin"
                                        debug="true">
            <classpath>
                <path refid="build.classpath"/>
            </classpath>
        </javac>
    </target>
</target>
```

The above provided Ant target generates the following list of Java files in the specified location. Make sure, all generated files use the correct package name before going for service endpoint implementation.

- DeleteEmployee.java
- DeleteEmployeeResponse.java
- Employee.java
- EmployeeFault.java
- EmployeeFault_Exception.java
- **EmployeeService.java**
- EmployeeService_Service.java
- GetEmployee.java
- GetEmployeeAddress.java
- GetEmployeeAddressResponse.java
- GetEmployeeResponse.java
- GetEmployerInformation.java
- GetEmployerInformationResponse.java
- ObjectFactory.java
- package-info.java

Now write your service endpoint implementation class to implement the application specific business logic; and make sure it implements the generated endpoint interface "EmployeeService.java". In this example "EmployeeServiceImpl.java" class is used to implement the business functionality; and this class implements the auto-generated methods defined in the interface "EmployeeService.java". Listing 14-4 has the complete service implementation class code.

Listing 14-4: Web service implementation class

```
// EmployeeServiceImpl.java
package com.learning.ws.jaxws.wsdl2java;

@WebService(name="EmployeeService",
            serviceName="employeeService",
            endpointInterface="
            com.learning.ws.jaxws.wsdl2java.EmployeeService")
public class EmployeeServiceImpl implements EmployeeService {

    public Employee getEmployee(String employeeId) throws EmployeeFault{
        System.out.println("--- employeeId ---" + employeeId);
        if(employeeId == null) {
            throw new EmployeeFault("Invalid input received");
```

```
        }

        Employee emp = new Employee();
        emp.setEmployeeId(employeeId);
        emp.setFirstName("John");
        emp.setLastName("Smith");

        return emp;
    }

    public String getEmployeeAddressInfo(String employeeId) throws
    Exception {
    /* Implement your logic here to get the employee address, here I
    have hard coded the value. */
        return "3943 Roundabout CIR, Chandler, Arizona, 85226";
    }

    public void deleteEmployee(String employeeId) {
        // Implement your logic here to delete an employee.
    }

    public String getEmployerInformation(String employeeId,
        String state) throws Exception {
        // Implement your logic here…
        return "Bank of Chandler, Chandler, Arizona, 85226";
    }
}
```

Step 3: Create a CXF Configuration File

Apache-CXF uses Spring framework to configure of Web Service endpoints. We can integrate the CXF-provided XML tags with Spring framework provided "<bean/>" tags. The complete XML used for this example is provided below. It is named the "applicationContext-jaxws.xml".

```xml
<?xml version="1.0" encoding="UTF-8"?>
<beans xmlns="http://www.springframework.org/schema/beans"
    xmlns:xsi="http://www.w3.org/2001/XMLSchema-instance"
    xmlns:jaxws="http://cxf.apache.org/jaxws"
    xmlns:cxf="http://cxf.apache.org/core"
    xsi:schemaLocation="http://www.springframework.org/schema/beans
    http://www.springframework.org/schema/beans/spring-beans.xsd
    ttp://cxf.apache.org/jaxws
    http://cxf.apache.org/schemas/jaxws.xsd
    http://cxf.apache.org/core
    http://cxf.apache.org/schemas/core.xsd ">

    <!-- Loads CXF modules from cxf.jar file -->
    <import resource="classpath:META-INF/cxf/cxf.xml"/>
    <import resource="classpath:META-INF/cxf/cxf-extension-soap.xml"/>
    <import resource="classpath:META-INF/cxf/cxf-servlet.xml"/>
    <import resource="classpath:META-INF/cxf/cxf-extension-jaxrs-
    binding.xml"/>

    <jaxws:endpoint id="EmployeeService" implementor=
                "com.learning.ws.jaxws.wsdl2java.EmployeeServiceImpl"
            wsdlLocation="WEB-INF/wsdl/employee.wsdl"
```

```
                    address="/employeeService"/>

</beans>
```

Now let us go through "<jaxws:endpoint/>" tag parameters to have the better understanding of the service endpoint.

```
<jaxws:endpoint id="EmployeeService"
            implementor=
            "com.learning.ws.jaxws.wsdl2java.EmployeeServiceImpl"
            wsdlLocation="WEB-INF/wsdl/employee.wsdl"
            address="/employeeService"/>
```

- id – Id used for this endpoint.
- implementor – It specifies the service endpoint implementation class
- wsdlLocation – It specifies the location of the WSDL file available at runtime
- address – It maps to "<wsdl:service name="employeeService">" of WSDL. It specifies the service endpoint name.

Step 4: Create a web.xml file

Configure the Spring context listener and CXF transport servlet in web.xml. Re-use the same web.xml file we created in Example1. The complete web.xml file is provided below.

```
<?xml version="1.0" encoding="UTF-8"?>
<web-app version="2.4" xmlns="http://java.sun.com/xml/ns/j2ee"
    xmlns:xsi="http://www.w3.org/2001/XMLSchema-instance"
    xsi:schemaLocation="http://java.sun.com/xml/ns/j2ee
    http://java.sun.com/xml/ns/j2ee/web-app_2_4.xsd">

<display-name>Web Services Application</display-name>
<listener>
<listener-class>
    org.springframework.web.context.ContextLoaderListener
    </listener-class>
</listener>
<context-param>
    <param-name>contextConfigLocation</param-name>
    <param-value>
        /WEB-INF/applicationContext-jaxws.xml
    </param-value>
</context-param>

<servlet>
    <servlet-name>CXFServlet</servlet-name>
        <servlet-class>
            org.apache.cxf.transport.servlet.CXFServlet
        </servlet-class>
</servlet>
<servlet-mapping>
    <servlet-name>CXFServlet</servlet-name>
        <url-pattern>/services/*</url-pattern>
    </servlet-mapping>
</web-app>
```

Step 5: Create a WAR file and deploy it in Tomcat server

1. Build a WAR file using Ant or any other build tool. Make sure the following files are packaged correctly in WAR file.
   a. All generated class files including endpoint interface
   b. Service endpoint implementation class
   c. Any utility classes used for data access etc.
   d. web.xml file
   e. CXF configuration file (applicationContext-jaxws.xml) file.
   f. WSDL file.

2. Deploy the WAR file in any servlet container.
   a. Copy the packed war into "apache-tomcat/webapps" directory
   b. Start the tomcat server by running the "startup.bat" batch file available in "apache-tomcat/bin" directory
   c. See the server console output and logs; make sure WAR file is deployed without any errors.

NOTE: Figure 14-2 shows only a few JAR files in "WEB-INF/lib" directory.

The structure of the WAR file is shown Figure 14-2.

Figure 14-2: Structure of a WAR file

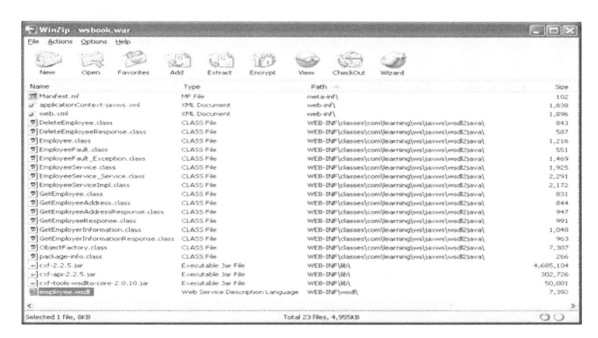

Step 6: Verify the WSDL Document

Access the WSDL file from web browser to make sure service is deployed without any errors. Use the below given URL to view the complete WSDL.

```
http://localhost:8080/wsbook/services/employeeService?WSDL
```

Step 7: Write a Client to Invoke the Deployed Web Service.

There are several ways we can invoke the deployed Web Service. In this example we use the "WSDL2Java" generated classes to invoke the web service endpoint methods. Listing 14-5 has the Web service client used to invoke deployed web service.

Listing 14-5: Web service client code

```java
// Client.java
package com.learning.ws.jaxws.wsdl2java;

import javax.xml.ws.BindingProvider;

public class Client {
    public static void main(String args[]) throws Exception {
        try {
            Client client = new Client();
            client.invokeService();
        } catch(Exception ex) {
            ex.printStackTrace();
        }
    }

    private void invokeService() throws Exception {
        // create the client stub using tool generated classes.
        EmployeeService_Service service = new
                        EmployeeService_Service();
        EmployeeService stub = service.getEmployeeServicePort();

        // Service endpoint URL
        String target =
            "http://localhost:8080/wsbook/services/employeeService";
        BindingProvider provider = (BindingProvider) stub;
        provider.getRequestContext().
            put(BindingProvider.ENDPOINT_ADDRESS_PROPERTY, target);

        // Invoking the endpoint method - getEmployeeAddress()
        String address = stub.getEmployeeAddress("823147");
        System.out.println("Address  is : " + address);

        // Invoking the endpoint method - getEmployee()
        Employee emp = stub.getEmployee("133334");
        System.out.println("Employee Id:" + emp.getEmployeeId() +
        "-- First Name --" + emp.getFirstName() + "-- Last Name --" +
            emp.getLastName());
    }
}
```

The generated "EmployeeService_Service" class for the above-specified WSDL is given below. The name attribute of the "<wsdl:service/>" element maps to the "name" attribute of the "@WebServiceClient" annotation. This web service client uses this information to invoke the Web Service endpoint.

```java
@WebServiceClient(name = "employeeService",
    wsdlLocation =
        "file:/C:/projects/Learning/book_ws/build/employee.wsdl",
    targetNamespace = "http://jaxws.ws.learning.com/")
```

```
public class EmployeeService_Service extends Service {

}
```

Let us now take the below provided code to understand it better. This gives the handle to the web service endpoint stub; this stub can be used to invoke the service endpoint operations.

```
EmployeeService_Service service = new EmployeeService_Service();
EmployeeService stub = service.getEmployeeServicePort();
```

After accessing the client stub; use "javax.xml.ws.BindingProvider" interface to get access to the protocol binding, associated context objects for request-and-response processing.

```
String target = "http://localhost:8080/wsbook/services/employeeService";
BindingProvider provider = (BindingProvider) stub;
provider.getRequestContext().put(BindingProvider.ENDPOINT_ADDRESS_PROPERTY, target);
```

NOTE: Web service client is used to invoke the deployed web service endpoint. In Example1 the "Service.create()" method is used to invoke the service endpoint; in this example "WSDL2Java" generated stub classes are used to invoke the service endpoint.

Example 3: An Alternative to Service Endpoint Interface (Using Provider interface)

The *Provider* interface provides an alternative to service endpoint interfaces (SEI) for implementing Web Services. In this case the developer needs to work with low level message API's like SOAP messages and DOM sources; so we have to learn the details of the structure of request-response messages; and API's used to manipulate these messages. The Provider-based service endpoint implementation class must satisfy the following conformance rules:

- The following valid object types the "javax.xml.ws.Provider" interface must support.
  - javax.xml.transform.Source
  - javax.xml.soap.SOAPMessage
  - javax.activation.DataSource
- The Provider interface must use concrete Java type parameter like Provider<Source>, and Provider<SOAPMessage>. It is not allowed to use generic type like Provider<T>
- The Provider-based service endpoint implementation class must have a default public constructor.
- The service endpoint implementation class must implement Provider interface of valid type.
- The service endpoint implementation class must use "@WebServiceProvider" annotation to mark it as a Web Service.
- The messaging mode of the Provider service is configured using "@ServiceMode" annotation. This is optional, by default it uses "PAYLOAD" service mode.

The steps required to develop-and-run the Web Service of this type are given below.

1. Create a Provider-based service implementation class
2. Create a web.xml file
3. Create a CXF configuration file
4. Create a WAR file and deploy it in Tomcat server

---

5. Verify the WSDL document
6. Create a *Dispatch* client to invoke the deployed service

The above-specified steps are described in the following sections:

Step 1: Create a "Provider" Based Service Implementation Class

Make sure the Provider-based web service endpoint implementation class follows the conformance rules listed above. In this example the Provider implementation class satisfies to the following conformance rules.

- The endpoint implementation class implements the "Provider<SOAPMessage>" interface.
- The endpoint implementation class has public default constructor.
- The annotation "@WebServiceProvider" is declared to mark it as Web Service.

```
@WebServiceProvider(serviceName="employeeServiceProvider")
@ServiceMode(value= Service.Mode.MESSAGE)
public class EmployeeServiceProvider implements Provider<SOAPMessage> {
    // Default public constructor
    public EmployeeServiceProvider() {}
}
```

For each client request "invoke()" method of the service endpoint is called; and this is the entry point to the web service endpoint. It receives the client request; processes it; sends the response back to the invoking client. Listing 14-6 demonstrates the Provider-based Web service implementation.

Listing 14-6: Provider-based web service implementation class

```
// EmployeeServiceProvider.java
package com.learning.ws.jaxws;

import org.w3c.dom.Element;
import org.w3c.dom.NodeList;
import javax.xml.soap.*;
import javax.xml.ws.Provider;
import javax.xml.ws.Service;
import javax.xml.ws.ServiceMode;
import javax.xml.ws.WebServiceProvider;
import java.util.*;
import java.io.ByteArrayOutputStream;

@WebServiceProvider(serviceName="employeeServiceProvider")
@ServiceMode(value= Service.Mode.MESSAGE)
public class EmployeeServiceProvider implements Provider<SOAPMessage> {

    // Default public constructor
    public EmployeeServiceProvider() {}

    // invoke method - this is called for each request
    public SOAPMessage invoke(SOAPMessage request) {
        SOAPMessage response = null;
        try {
            //Printing the input request message.
            ByteArrayOutputStream out = new ByteArrayOutputStream();
            request.writeTo(out);
```

```java
                String requestMessage = new String(out.toByteArray());
                System.out.println("--request Message--" + requestMessage);

                SOAPBody requestBody = request.getSOAPBody();
                Iterator iterator = requestBody.getChildElements();
                SOAPBodyElement bodyElement = (SOAPBodyElement)
                                iterator.next();
                String employeeId = null;
                if(requestBody.getElementName().
                        getLocalName().equals("Body")) {
                    for(Element result : getElements(bodyElement.
                    getElementsByTagName("employeeId"))) {
                        employeeId = getNamedElement(result,
                        "employeeId").getTextContent();
                        System.out.println(" employeeId -" + employeeId);
                    }
                }

                // Implement your logic here based on input data received.
                MessageFactory mf = MessageFactory.newInstance();
                SOAPFactory sf = SOAPFactory.newInstance();
                if(employeeId != null &&
                    employeeId.equalsIgnoreCase("12345678")) {
                    // Creating the response message
                    response = mf.createMessage();
                    SOAPBody respBody = response.getSOAPBody();
                    SOAPElement responseElement =
                        respBody.addChildElement("getEmployeeResponse");
                    SOAPElement firstNameContent =
                        responseElement.addChildElement("firstName");
                    firstNameContent.setValue("John");
                    SOAPElement lastNameContent =
                    responseElement.addChildElement("lastName");
                    lastNameContent.setValue("Smith");
                    response.saveChanges();
                }

                // Printing the output response message.
                ByteArrayOutputStream out1 = new ByteArrayOutputStream();
                response.writeTo(out1);
                String responseMessage = new String(out1.toByteArray());
                System.out.println("- Response Message -" +
                                responseMessage);
                return response;
        } catch(Exception ex) {
            ex.printStackTrace();
        }
        return response;
    }

    // Utility method used for SOAP message processing
    private static List<Element> getElements(NodeList nodes) {
    List<Element> result = new ArrayList<Element>(nodes.getLength());
    for(int i = 0; i < nodes.getLength(); i++) {
        Node node = (Node) nodes.item(i);
        if(node instanceof Element) {
                result.add((Element)node);
```

```
        }
    }
        return result;
}

    // Utility method used for SOAP message processing
    private static Element getNamedElement(Element element,
            String name) {
        if(!element.getNodeName().equals(name))
            throw new IllegalArgumentException("Expected " + name +
                ",but got " + element.getNodeName());
        return element;
    }
}
```

Step 2: Create a web.xml File

Re-use the previously created web.xml file.

Step 3: Create a CXF Configuration File

Re-use the previously created "applicationContext-jaxws.xml" file. Add the below provided endpoint configuration.

```
<jaxws:endpoint id="employeeServiceProvider"
        implementor="com.learning.ws.jaxws.EmployeeServiceProvider"
        address="/employeeServiceProvider"/>
```

Step 4: Create a WAR File and deploy it in Tomcat Server

The structure of the WAR file is shown in Figure 14-3.

Figure 14-3: Structure of a WAR file

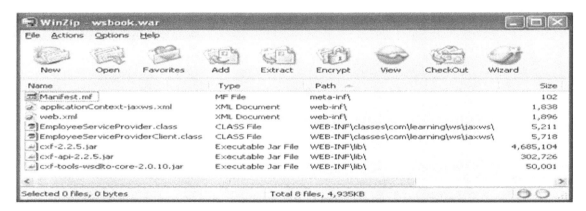

1. Build a WAR file using Ant or any other build tool. Make sure the following files are packaged correctly in WAR file.

   a. Service endpoint implementation class
   b. Any utility classes used for data access etc.
   c. web.xml file
   d. CXF configuration file (applicationContext-jaxws.xml) file.

2. Deploy the WAR file in any servlet container.

    a. Copy the packed WAR into "apache-tomcat/webapps" directory

    b. Start the tomcat server by running the "startup.bat" batch file available in "apache-tomcat/bin" directory

    c. See the server console output and logs; make sure WAR file is deployed without any errors.

Step 5: Verify the WSDL Document

Access the WSDL file from web browser to make sure service is deployed without any errors. Use the below provided URL to view the complete WSDL.

```
http://localhost:8080/wsbook/services/employeeServiceProvider?WSDL
```

Step 6: Create a "Dispatch" Client to Invoke the Deployed Service

The dynamic client API for JAX-WS is called the *Dispatch* client (javax.xml.ws.Dispatch). The higher level JAX-WS API's hides the message communication between client and service endpoint interfaces. The conversions between XML to Java classes are hidden to the developer; but in some scenarios it is essential to work with lower level messages. The Dispatch client is an XML-oriented messaging client used to work with lower messages. It works with two message modes.

- javax.xml.ws.Service.Mode.MESSAGE – In this mode the *Dispatch* client provides complete message including <soap:Envelope/>, <soap:Header/>, and <soap:Body/>
- javax.xml.ws.Service.Mode.PAYLOAD – In this mode the *Dispatch* client provides only <soap:Body/>. The JAX-WS runtime adds the <soap:Envelope/> and <soap:Header/> to the soap message.

The below provided *Dispatch* client is used to invoke the deployed web service endpoint. The Java code is provided in Listing 14-7.

Listing 14-7: Dispatch client

```java
// EmployeeServiceProviderClient.java
package com.learning.ws.jaxws;

import org.w3c.dom.Element;
import org.w3c.dom.NodeList;
import javax.xml.namespace.QName;
import javax.xml.ws.Service;
import javax.xml.ws.Dispatch;
import javax.xml.ws.BindingProvider;
import javax.xml.ws.soap.SOAPBinding;
import javax.xml.soap.*;
import java.net.URL;
import java.util.*;
import java.io.ByteArrayOutputStream;

public class EmployeeServiceProviderClient {

    public static void main(String args[]) throws Exception {
        try {
            EmployeeServiceProviderClient client = new
                            EmployeeServiceProviderClient();
            client.invokeProvider();
```

```java
        } catch(Exception ex) {
            ex.printStackTrace();
        }
    }

    private void invokeProvider() throws Exception {
        // Service endpoint URL used to create a service instance
        URL url = new URL("http://localhost:8080/wsbook/
            services/employeeServiceProvider?wsdl");
        QName qname = new QName("http://jaxws.ws.learning.com/",
                    "employeeServiceProvider");
        Service service = Service.create(url, qname);
        QName portName = new QName("http://jaxws.ws.learning.com/",
                    "EmployeeServiceProviderPort");

        // Create a dispatch instance
        Dispatch<SOAPMessage> dispatch = service.createDispatch(
            portName,SOAPMessage.class, Service.Mode.MESSAGE);
            System.out.println("-- dispatch --" + dispatch.toString());

        // Use Dispatch as BindingProvider
        BindingProvider bp = (BindingProvider) dispatch;

        // create a request message
        MessageFactory factory = ((SOAPBinding)
        bp.getBinding()).getMessageFactory();
        SOAPMessage request = factory.createMessage();

        // Request message Body
        SOAPBody body = request.getSOAPBody();

        // Compose the soap:Body payload
        QName payloadName = new QName("http://localhost:8080/wsbook/
                services/employeeServiceProvider", "invoke", "ns1");
        SOAPBodyElement payload = body.addBodyElement(payloadName);
        SOAPElement message = payload.addChildElement("employeeId");
        message.addTextNode("12345678");

        // invoke the service endpoint.
        SOAPMessage replyMessage = dispatch.invoke(request);

        // Printing the response message on the console.
        ByteArrayOutputStream out = new ByteArrayOutputStream();
        replyMessage.writeTo(out);
        String responseMessage = new String(out.toByteArray());
        System.out.println("-- reply Message --" + responseMessage);

        // process the response to obtain the data.
        SOAPBody responseBody = replyMessage.getSOAPBody();
        for(Element result : getElements(responseBody.
            getElementsByTagName("getEmployeeResponse")))  {
            List<Element> resultDataChildren =
                getElements(result.getChildNodes());
            String firstName = getNamedElement(
            resultDataChildren.get(0), "firstName").getTextContent();
            String lastName = getNamedElement(
            resultDataChildren.get(1), "lastName").getTextContent();
```

```
                System.out.println("-- firstName ---" + firstName + "--
                            lastName ---" + lastName);
            }
        }

    private static List<Element> getElements(NodeList nodes) {
        List<Element> result = new
                ArrayList<Element>(nodes.getLength());
        for(int i = 0; i < nodes.getLength(); i++) {
            Node node = (Node) nodes.item(i);
            if(node instanceof Element) {
                result.add((Element)node);
            }
        }
        return result;
    }

    private static Element getNamedElement(Element element,
    String name) {
        if(!element.getNodeName().equals(name))
            throw new IllegalArgumentException("Expected " + name
            + ",but got " + element.getNodeName());
        return element;
    }
}
```

Examine the following request-and-response messages while invoking the *Provider* service endpoint. The web service request message is provided below.

```
<SOAP-ENV:Envelope xmlns:SOAP-
ENV="http://schemas.xmlsoap.org/soap/envelope/">
  <SOAP-ENV:Header/>
  <SOAP-ENV:Body>
    <ns1:invoke xmlns:ns1=
     "http://localhost:8080/wsbook/services/employeeServiceProvider">
      <employeeId>12345678</employeeId>
    </ns1:invoke>
  </SOAP-ENV:Body>
</SOAP-ENV:Envelope>
```

The web service response message is provided below.

```
<SOAP-ENV:Envelope xmlns:SOAP-
ENV="http://schemas.xmlsoap.org/soap/envelope/">
  <SOAP-ENV:Header/>
  <SOAP-ENV:Body>
    <getEmployeeResponse>
       <firstName>John</firstName>
       <lastName>Smith</lastName>
    </getEmployeeResponse>
  </SOAP-ENV:Body>
</SOAP-ENV:Envelope>
```

Example 4: Composite Endpoints (Single Endpoint for JAX-RS and JAX-WS)

In this approach a single service endpoint can be used for both SOAP and REST-based endpoint. A single service class is supporting both REST and SOAP-based annotations at the same time using JAX-WS, JAX-RS runtimes.

Figure 14-4: Composite endpoint

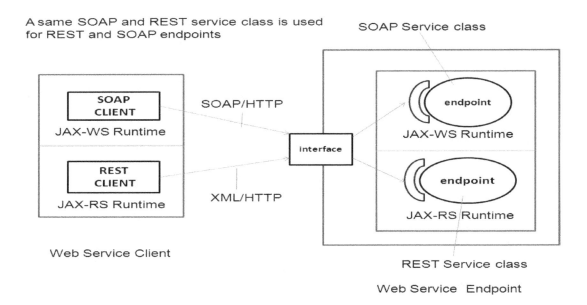

This endpoint implementation class uses the annotations declared with its service endpoint interface. An endpoint class is loaded into SOAP and REST runtime environments to service the clients. Apache-CXF supports the sharing of both REST and SOAP-based annotations for the same endpoint interface.

The steps required to develop a web service of this type are given below.

1. Create a service endpoint interface
2. Create a service implementation class
3. Create a CXF configuration file
4. Create a web.xml file
5. Create a WAR file and deploy into a Tomcat server
6. Verification of the deployment.
7. Write a client to invoke the deployed service

The above-specified steps are described in the following sections:

Step 1: Create a Service Endpoint Interface

Define a service endpoint interface. This interface is annotated with JAX-WS and JAX-RS-provided annotations. The "@Webservice" annotation is declared with the interface to mark it as a SOAP-based endpoint; and "@Path" annotation is declared with the class and method to identify the entry point for the REST-based endpoint.

Listing 14-8 has the service endpoint interface code.

Listing 14-8: Endpoint interface code

```java
// GradeManager.java
package com.learning.ws.jaxws.composite;

import javax.ws.rs.Path;
import javax.ws.rs.Produces;
import javax.ws.rs.GET;
import javax.ws.rs.PathParam;
import javax.jws.WebService;

@WebService
@Path("/compositegradeservice/")
@Produces("application/xml")
public interface GradeManager {
    @GET
    @Path("/grade/{grade}")
    public String getGradeSubjects(@PathParam("grade")Integer grade);
}
```

Step 2: Create a Service Implementation Class

This class implements the methods defined in the interface. This service endpoint class is annotated with "@Webservice" annotation.

The endpoint implementation class code is provided in Listing 14-9.

Listing 14-9: Endpoint implementation class

```java
// GradeManagerImpl.java
package com.learning.ws.jaxws.composite;

import com.learning.util.XMLBuilder;
import javax.jws.WebService;

@WebService(name = "GradeManagerService",
    endpointInterface="com.learning.ws.jaxws.composite.GradeManager")
public class GradeManagerImpl implements GradeManager {
    public String getGradeSubjects(Integer grade) {
        return XMLBuilder.getAllSubjects(grade);
    }
}
```

NOTE: Re-use the XMLBuilder utility class we created in Spring with REST chapter.

Step 3: Create a CXF Configuration File

Apache-CXF provides XML tags to configure the Web Service endpoint with JAX-WS and JAX-RS runtimes. Both Spring and CXF tags can co-exist in the same configuration file. Configure the SOAP-based web service endpoint using "<jaxws:endpoint/>" tag; and REST-based endpoint using "<jaxrs:serviceBeans>" tag. The Spring container loads the service implementation class into corresponding SOAP and REST runtime environments.

The use of CXF tags "<jaxws:endpoint/>", "<jaxrs:serviceBeans>" are provided below.

```xml
<?xml version="1.0" encoding="UTF-8"?>
<beans xmlns="http://www.springframework.org/schema/beans"
         xmlns:xsi="http://www.w3.org/2001/XMLSchema-instance"
         xmlns:jaxws="http://cxf.apache.org/jaxws"
         xmlns:jaxrs="http://cxf.apache.org/jaxrs"
         xmlns:cxf="http://cxf.apache.org/core"
         xsi:schemaLocation="http://www.springframework.org/schema/beans
         http://www.springframework.org/schema/beans/spring-beans.xsd
                  http://cxf.apache.org/jaxws
                  http://cxf.apache.org/schemas/jaxws.xsd
                  http://cxf.apache.org/jaxrs
                  http://cxf.apache.org/schemas/jaxrs.xsd
                  http://cxf.apache.org/core
                  http://cxf.apache.org/schemas/core.xsd ">

     <!-- Loads CXF modules from cxf.jar file -->
     <import resource="classpath:META-INF/cxf/cxf.xml"/>
     <import resource="classpath:META-INF/cxf/cxf-extension-soap.xml"/>
     <import resource="classpath:META-INF/cxf/cxf-servlet.xml"/>
     <import resource="classpath:META-INF/cxf/cxf-extension-jaxrs-
     binding.xml"/>

     <!-- Loading the JAX-RS endpoint -->
     <jaxrs:server id="restGradeService" address="/">
         <jaxrs:serviceBeans>
             <ref bean="gradeManagerImpl"/>
         </jaxrs:serviceBeans>

         <jaxrs:features>
             <cxf:logging/>
         </jaxrs:features>
     </jaxrs:server>

     <!-- Loading the JAX-WS endpoint -->
     <jaxws:endpoint id="jaxwsGradeService"
                  implementor="#gradeManagerImpl"
                  address="/jaxwsGradeService"/>

     <!-- Spring bean used as a service endpoint -->
     <bean id="gradeManagerImpl"
         class="com.learning.ws.jaxws.composite.GradeManagerImpl"/>

</beans>
```

The following configuration is used to load the service implementation class into JAX-RS runtime.

```xml
<jaxrs:server id="restGradeService" address="/">
    <jaxrs:serviceBeans>
        <ref bean="gradeManagerImpl"/>
    </jaxrs:serviceBeans>
</jaxrs:server>
```

The following configuration is used to load the service implementation class into JAX-WS runtime.

```xml
<jaxws:endpoint id="jaxwsGradeService"
             implementor="#gradeManagerImpl"
```

```
                    address="/jaxwsGradeService"/>
```

The service endpoint implementation class is loaded into the Spring container. The same class is used for both SOAP and REST runtimes.

```
<bean id="gradeManagerImpl"
      class="com.learning.ws.jaxws.composite.GradeManagerImpl"/>
```

Step 4: Create a web.xml File

Configure the spring context listener and CXF transport servlet in web.xml. The complete web.xml file is provided below.

```xml
<?xml version="1.0" encoding="UTF-8"?>
<web-app version="2.4" xmlns="http://java.sun.com/xml/ns/j2ee"
         xmlns:xsi="http://www.w3.org/2001/XMLSchema-instance"
         xsi:schemaLocation="http://java.sun.com/xml/ns/j2ee
         http://java.sun.com/xml/ns/j2ee/web-app_2_4.xsd">

    <display-name>wsbook Web Application</display-name>

    <listener>
        <listener-class>
            org.springframework.web.context.ContextLoaderListener
        </listener-class>
    </listener>

    <context-param>
        <param-name>contextConfigLocation</param-name>
        <param-value>
            /WEB-INF/applicationContext-composite.xml
        </param-value>
    </context-param>

    <servlet>
        <servlet-name>CXFServlet</servlet-name>
            <servlet-class>
                org.apache.cxf.transport.servlet.CXFServlet
        </servlet-class>
    </servlet>

    <servlet-mapping>
        <servlet-name>CXFServlet</servlet-name>
        <url-pattern>/services/*</url-pattern>
    </servlet-mapping>

</web-app>
```

Step 5: Create a WAR File and deploy it in Tomcat Server

1. Build a WAR file using Ant or any other build tool. Make sure the following files are packaged correctly in WAR file.

    a. Service endpoint interface
    b. Service endpoint implementation class

c. Any utility classes used for data access etc.
d. web.xml file
e. CXF configuration file (applicationContext-jaxws.xml) file.

2. Deploy the WAR file in any servlet container.

a. Copy the packed WAR into "apache-tomcat/webapps" directory
b. Start the tomcat server by running the "startup.bat" batch file available in "apache-tomcat/bin" directory
c. See the server console output and logs; make sure WAR file is deployed without any errors.

The structure of the generated WAR file is shown Figure 14-5.

Figure 14-5: Composite endpoint WAR file structure

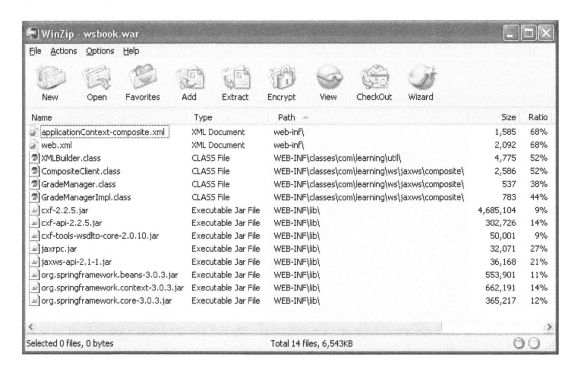

Step 6: Verification of the Deployment.

Verify the deployment to make sure the service is deployed without any errors.

The following URL can be used to test the SOAP service endpoint. It displays the complete WSDL.

```
http://localhost:8080/wsbook/services/jaxwsGradeService?wsdl
```

The following URL can be used to test the REST service endpoint. It displays the XML.

```
http://localhost:8080/wsbook/services/compositegradeservice/grade/1
```

Step 7: Write a Client to Invoke the Deployed Service

There are several ways a client can invoke the deployed service endpoint. This example uses the following clients.

- How to invoke the service endpoint using JAX-WS proxy client (for SOAP endpoint)
- How to invoke the service endpoint using REST client (for REST endpoint)

CASE 1: How to Invoke the Service Endpoint Using JAX-WS Proxy Client

The following JAX-WS proxy client cab be used to invoke the SOAP-based service endpoint.

```java
private void invokeSOAPEndpoint() throws Exception {
    URL url = new URL("http://localhost:8080/wsbook/services/
            jaxwsGradeService?wsdl");
    QName qname = new QName("http://composite.jaxws.ws.learning.com/",
                           "GradeManagerImplService");
    Service service = Service.create(url, qname);
    GradeManager gradeManager = service.getPort(GradeManager.class);

    String subjects = gradeManager.getGradeSubjects(1);
    System.out.println("--- subjects is --- " + subjects);
}
```

CASE 2: How to Invoke the Service Endpoint Using REST Client

The following JAX-RS client can be used to invoke the REST-based service endpoint.

```java
private void invokeRestEndpoint() throws Exception {
    RestTemplate restTemplate = new RestTemplate();
    String result = restTemplate.getForObject("http://localhost:8080/
            wsbook/services/compositegradeservice/grade/{grade}",
            String.class, "1");
    System.out.println("--- result is ---" + result);
}
```

The complete client code is provided below.

```java
// CompositeClient.java
package com.learning.ws.jaxws.composite;

import org.springframework.web.client.RestTemplate;
import javax.xml.namespace.QName;
import javax.xml.ws.Service;
import java.net.URL;

public class CompositeClient {

    public static void main(String args[]) throws Exception {
        try {
            CompositeClient client = new CompositeClient();
            client.invokeSOAPEndpoint();
            client.invokeRestEndpoint();
        } catch(Exception ex) {
            ex.printStackTrace();
        }
    }
```

```
    private void invokeSOAPEndpoint() throws Exception {
        URL url = new URL("http://localhost:8080/wsbook/services/
            jaxwsGradeService?wsdl");
        QName qname = new
            QName("http://composite.jaxws.ws.learning.com/",
                "GradeManagerImplService");
        Service service = Service.create(url, qname);
        GradeManager gradeManager =
                service.getPort(GradeManager.class);

        String subjects = gradeManager.getGradeSubjects(1);
        System.out.println("--- subjects is --- " + subjects);

    }

    private void invokeRestEndpoint() throws Exception {
        RestTemplate restTemplate = new RestTemplate();
        String result =
            restTemplate.getForObject("http://localhost:8080/
            wsbook/services/compositegradeservice/grade/{grade}",
            String.class, "1");
        System.out.println("---- result is ---- " + result);
    }
}
```

Web Service Endpoint Design Scenarios

There are two different ways we can mark the Java class or interface as a Web Service. The one way is using "@WebService" annotation and another way is Provider-based web service implementation using "@WebServiceProder" annotation. The `@WebService`, `@WebServiceProder` annotations are mutually exclusive; so both cannot be used for the same service endpoint. This section demonstrates the various Web service endpoint design options for implementing web services.

Implementing SEI with @WebService Annotation

The only mandatory annotation required to mark a class or interface as a web service is "@WebService"; all other annotations are optional. The metadata declared with the "@WebService" annotation is mapped to the "<wsdl:service/>" element of the generated WSDL.

The steps required to develop a Web Service of this type are given below.

1. Declare `@WebService` annotation with the SEI and its implementation class.
2. The annotation metadata values of "serviceName", "endpointInterface" are assigned while declaring the service implementation class.

The following code example explains the use of the "@WebService" annotation:

```
@WebService
public interface EmployeeService {
    String getEmployeeAddressInfo(String  employeeId) throws Exception;
```

```
}

@WebService(endpointInterface="com.learning.ws.jaxws.EmployeeService",
            serviceName="employeeService")
public class EmployeeServiceImpl  implements  EmployeeService {
    public EmployeeServiceImpl() {}

    public String getEmployeeAddress(String employeeId)
    throws Exception {
        // Implement your logic here to get the address.
        return "3943 W.Roundabout CIR, Chandler, Arizona, 85226";
    }
}
```

Implementing SEI of type RPC/LITERAL style

This type of web service endpoint is created by declaring the "@SOAPBinding" annotation with "style = Style.RPC" and "use = Use.LITERAL". It specifies the type of message formatting the web service endpoint is using during deployment. In case of "RPC/LITERAL" style each message part is a method parameter or return value. The parameter and return values maps to the corresponding standard Java types.

The following code example explains the use of the "RPC/LITERAL" messaging style.

```
@WebService
@SOAPBinding(style = Style.RPC, use = Use.LITERAL)
public interface EmployeeService {
    String getEmployerInformation(@WebParam(name="empId")
        String employeeId, @WebParam(name="state") String state)
        throws Exception;
}
```

And its implementation is provided below.

```
@WebService(name="EmployeeService",
            serviceName="employeeService",
            endpointInterface="com.learning.ws.jaxws.EmployeeService")
public class EmployeeServiceImpl implements EmployeeService {
    public  String  getEmployerInformation(String employeeId, String
        state) throws Exception {
        return "Bank of Chandler, Chandler, Arizona, 85226";
    }
}
```

The generated WSDL is provided below. The endpoint method input parameters "empId" and "state" mapped to "<wsdl:part/>" elements in WSDL.

```
<wsdl:message name="getEmployerInformation">
    <wsdl:part name="empId" type="xsd:string" />
    <wsdl:part name="state" type="xsd:string" />
</wsdl:message>
```

Implementing SEI of type DOCUMENT/LITERAL style

This type of web service endpoint is created by declaring the "@SOAPBinding" annotation with "style = Style.DOCUMENT" and "use = Use.LITERAL". If you don't annotate the service endpoint by default it uses "DOCUMENT/LITERAL" messaging style. In case of "DOCUMENT/LITERAL" style the input parameters and return values are wrapped in a single XML element.

The following code example explains the use of the "DOCUMENT/LITERAL" messaging style.

```
@WebService
@SOAPBinding(style = Style. DOCUMENT, use = Use.LITERAL)
public interface EmployeeService {
String getEmployerInformation(@WebParam(name="empId") String employeeId,
            @WebParam(name="state") String state) throws Exception;
}
```

And its implementation is provided below.

```
@WebService(name="EmployeeService",
        serviceName="employeeService",
        endpointInterface="com.learning.ws.jaxws.EmployeeService")
public class EmployeeServiceImpl implements EmployeeService {
    public String getEmployerInformation(String employeeId, String
    state) throws Exception {
        return "Bank of Chandler, Chandler, Arizona, 85226";
    }
}
```

The generated WSDL is provided below. The endpoint method input parameters "empId" and "state" are wrapped in a "<getEmployerInformation/>" element.

```
<xs:element name="getEmployerInformation"
        type="getEmployerInformation"/>
<xs:complexType name="getEmployerInformation">
    <xs:sequence>
        <xs:element minOccurs="0" name="empId" type="xs:string" />
        <xs:element minOccurs="0" name="state" type="xs:string" />
    </xs:sequence>
</xs:complexType>

<wsdl:message name="getEmployerInformation">
    <wsdl:part element="tns:getEmployerInformation" name="parameters"/>
</wsdl:message>
```

Implementing Provider-based Web Service Endpoint

The service endpoint implementation class is declared with "@WebServiceProvider" annotation and implements "javax.xml.ws.Provider" interface to mark it as a Web Service. This type of web service endpoint is used to operate with low level XML-oriented messages. The Dispatch type of binding provider is used to invoke this service endpoint.

The following code example explains the use of the "@WebServiceProvider" annotation and "javax.xml.ws.Provider" interface:

```
@WebServiceProvider(serviceName="employeeServiceProvider")
@ServiceMode(value= Service.Mode.MESSAGE)
public class EmployeeServiceProvider implements Provider<SOAPMessage> {
    // Default public constructor
    public EmployeeServiceProvider() {}

    // invoke method - this is called for each client request
    public SOAPMessage invoke(SOAPMessage request) {
        // Implement your logic here and send the response back
    }
}
```

Web Service Client Design Scenarios

There are several ways a client can access the deployed web service endpoint. This section illustrates the various client design scenarios to access a deployed web service endpoint. The JAX-WS provides two types of client programming models to access the web service endpoint.

- Static client programming model
- Dynamic client programming model

The *static client* programming model for JAX-WS is the called the *Proxy* client. The Proxy client invokes a Web Service based on a Service Endpoint Interface (SEI); which must be provided. The JAX-WS runtime hides the complexities of XML to Java class conversions.

The *dynamic client* programming model for JAX-WS is called the *Dispatch* client. The Dispatch client is an XML messaging oriented client, the data is sent in either "PAYLOAD" or "MESSAGE" mode. Dispatch client operates with low level messages using SAAJ and JAXP API's.

Figure 14-6: Proxy and Dispatch client

The Figure 14-6 is a class diagram shows the relationship between Proxy client, Dispatch client and Binding Provider.

Now let us see how various types of client API's are used to invoke a deployed Web Service endpoint. The following Web Service client types are covered in this section.

1. Creating a client using WSDL2Java Generated stub (stub clients)
2. Creating a client using JAX-WS Proxy
3. Creating a client using Apache-CXF provided "ProxyFactoryBean" class
4. Creating a client using JAX-WS Dispatch API

---

5. Creating a SOAP client to invoke the Web Service endpoint

Creating a Client using WSDL2Java Generated Stub

This type of Web Service client can also be called as static stub clients. The "WSDL2Java" utility generates client classes using WSDL files. It provides a strongly typed Java interface through which you can invoke the service endpoint operations. One major drawback with this approach is; the client classes have to be generated each and every time if there is a change in WSDL. Let us now see the following code example to demonstrate the use of stub clients. The "getPort()" methods of a service endpoint provides stub instance, by which we can invoke all service endpoint operations.

```
private static void invokeService() throws Exception {
    // Create the client stub
    EmployeeService_Service service = new EmployeeService_Service();
    EmployeeService stub = service.getEmployeeServicePort();

    // Invoking the endpoint method - getEmployeeAddress()
    String address = stub.getEmployeeAddress("823147");
}
```

Creating a Client using JAX-WS Proxy

The Proxy client can access the service endpoint interface operations during runtime without generating the static stub classes. The Proxy clients are not thread safe, thread synchronization techniques can be used to make it thread safe. Let us now see the following code example to demonstrate the use of Proxy clients. The "Service.create()" method is used to create the service instances. The "getPort()" method of a service class instance is used to get the handle of the service endpoint interface by which we can invoke the service endpoint operations.

```
private void invokeService () throws Exception {
    // Service endpoint URL
    URL url = new URL
            ("http://localhost:8080/wsbook/services/employee?wsdl");

    // 1st argument service URI; 2nd argument is service name
    QName qname = new QName("http://jaxws.ws.learning.com/",
                            "employeeService");
    Service service = Service.create(url, qname);

    EmployeeService  employeeService =
                        service.getPort(EmployeeService.class);
    String address = employeeService.getEmployeeAddress("823147");
}
```

Creating a Client using CXF-Provided "JaxWsProxyFactoryBean" Class

Apache-CXF frame work provides a simple client API to invoke the deployed web services using "JaxWsProxyFactoryBean" class. This is also a Proxy type client, does not need to generate the stub classes to invoke the service endpoint operations.

The following code example explains the use of "JaxWsProxyFactoryBean" class to invoke the service endpoint operations.

```
private void invokeService() throws Exception {
    JaxWsProxyFactoryBean factory = new JaxWsProxyFactoryBean();
    factory.setServiceClass(EmployeeService.class);
    factory.setAddress("http://localhost:8080/wsbook/services/employee")
    EmployeeService client = (EmployeeService) factory.create();
    String data = client. getEmployeeAddress("823147");
    System.out.println("---- Server said: ----" + data);
}
```

Creating a Client using JAX-WS Dispatch API

The dynamic client API (javax.xml.ws.Dispatch) for JAX-WS is called the *Dispatch* client. The Dispatch client creates the XML messages of types "SOAPMessage" or "Source" objects; and dispatches them to the service endpoint method. The data is sent in either PAYLOAD or MESSAGE mode. The service endpoint method processes the request; and sends the response back to the client.

Let us now examine following client code to demonstrate the use of Dispatch client. This client uses "invoke()" method of the dispatch object to invoke the service endpoint interface.

```
private void invokeProvider() throws Exception {
    // serice endpoint URL used to create a service instance
    URL url = new URL("http://localhost:8080/wsbook/services/
        employeeServiceProvider?wsdl");
    QName qname = new QName("http://jaxws.ws.learning.com/",
                "employeeServiceProvider");
    Service service = Service.create(url, qname);

    // Port name
    QName portName = new QName("http://jaxws.ws.learning.com/",
        "EmployeeServiceProviderPort");

    // Create a dispatch instance
    Dispatch<SOAPMessage> dispatch = service.createDispatch(portName,
                SOAPMessage.class, Service.Mode.MESSAGE);

    // Use Dispatch as BindingProvider
    BindingProvider bp = (BindingProvider) dispatch;

    // create a request message
    MessageFactory factory = ((SOAPBinding)
                    bp.getBinding()).getMessageFactory();
    SOAPMessage request = factory.createMessage();

    // Request message Body
    SOAPBody body = request.getSOAPBody();

    // Compose the soap:Body payload
    QName payloadName = new QName("http://localhost:8080/wsbook/
                services/employeeServiceProvider", "invoke", "ns1");
    SOAPBodyElement payload = body.addBodyElement(payloadName);
    SOAPElement message = payload.addChildElement("employeeId");
```

```
message.addTextNode("12345678");

// Invoke the service endpoint.
SOAPMessage replyMessage = dispatch.invoke(request);
}
```

Creating a SOAP Client to Invoke the Web Service Endpoint

A SOAP client can be used to invoke the deployed service endpoint. The SAAJ API is used to send messages over the network; and get the response back to the client. SAAJ provides an API to invoke the Web Service endpoint operations in a request-response messaging mode. An example implementation of the SOAP client is provided below.

The following XML is used for the input request (inputdata.xml).

```
<ns1:getEmployee xmlns:ns1="http://jaxws.ws.learning.com/">
    <employeeId>666666</employeeId>
</ns1:getEmployee>
```

The "call()" method of the "SOAPConnection" object can be used to send-and-receive a SOAP message from the deployed Web Service.

```
private void invokeService() throws Exception {
    SOAPConnectionFactory  soapConnectionFactory =
                SOAPConnectionFactory.newInstance();
    SOAPConnection  soapConnection =
                soapConnectionFactory.createConnection();

    // Web service endpoint URL
    URL endpoint = new URL("http://localhost:8080/wsbook/
                services/employee");

    // Creating a w3c DOM document.
    DocumentBuilderFactory factory =
                DocumentBuilderFactory.newInstance();
    factory.setNamespaceAware(true);
    DocumentBuilder builder = factory.newDocumentBuilder();
    Document w3cDocument = builder.parse("inputdata.xml");

    // Creating the request SOAP Message using SAAJ API.
    MessageFactory messageFactory = MessageFactory.newInstance(
            SOAPConstants.SOAP_1_1_PROTOCOL);
    SOAPMessage message = messageFactory.createMessage();
    SOAPBody soapBody = message.getSOAPBody();
    soapBody.addDocument(w3cDocument);

    // Calling the service endpoint to get the response.
    SOAPMessage response = soapConnection.call(message, endpoint);

    // Printing the response message on the console.
    ByteArrayOutputStream out = new ByteArrayOutputStream();
    response.writeTo(out);
    String responseMessage = new String(out.toByteArray());
    System.out.println("---  Message ---" + responseMessage);
```

```
        // Closing the connection
        soapConnection.close();
}
```

Logging SOAP Messages Using CXF

The very common requirement in web services development is, logging of the request-and-response messages. It is very essential that every web service developer should know how to debug and log SOAP messages. Apache-CXF provides several logging mechanisms to log incoming-and-outgoing messages with client and server. The "in", "out" and "fault" interceptors can be used to log the messages with client and server. "LoggingOutInterceptor" can be used to log the outbound soap messages and "LoggingInInterceptor" can be used to log the inbound soap messages.

Logging Messages at Client Side

The following code can be used log outbound-and-inbound log messages.

```
Client client = ClientProxy.getClient(employeeService);
client.getInInterceptors().add(new LoggingInInterceptor());
client.getOutInterceptors().add(new LoggingOutInterceptor());
```

The following example demonstrates the use of logging interceptors at client side.

```
private void invokeService() throws Exception {
    URL url = new URL("http://localhost:8080/
                    wsbook/services/employee?wsdl");
    QName qname = new QName("http://jaxws.ws.learning.com/",
                        "employeeService");
    Service service = Service.create(url, qname);
    EmployeeService employeeService =
                    service.getPort(EmployeeService.class);

    // logs the outbound and inbound soap messages.
    Client client = ClientProxy.getClient(employeeService);
    client.getInInterceptors().add(new LoggingInInterceptor());
    client.getOutInterceptors().add(new LoggingOutInterceptor());

    // Invoke your service endpoint operations
    String address = employeeService.
                getEmployeeAddressInfo("823147");
    System.out.println("Address is: " + address);
}
```

The following example demonstrates the use of logging interceptors at client side using "JaxWsProxyFactoryBean" class.

```
private void invokeService() throws Exception {
    JaxWsProxyFactoryBean factory = new JaxWsProxyFactoryBean();

    // logs the outbound and inbound soap messages.
```

```
factory.getInInterceptors().add(new LoggingInInterceptor());
factory.getOutInterceptors().add(new LoggingOutInterceptor());
factory.setServiceClass(EmployeeService.class);

factory.setAddress("http://localhost:8080/wsbook/
                    services/employee");
EmployeeService client = (EmployeeService) factory.create();

// Invoke your service endpoint operations
String data = client.getEmployeeAddressInfo("823147");
}
```

Logging Messages at Web Service Endpoint

Apache-CXF provides annotation based logging mechanism to log the inbound-and-outbound soap messages at the service endpoint interface. The following example demonstrates the use of logging interceptors at server side. The service endpoint implementation class is annotated to log soap messages on the server console.

```
@WebService(name="EmployeeService",
        serviceName="employeeService",
        endpointInterface="com.learning.ws.jaxws.EmployeeService")
@InInterceptors(interceptors =
"org.apache.cxf.interceptor.LoggingInInterceptor")
@OutInterceptors(interceptors =
"org.apache.cxf.interceptor.LoggingOutInterceptor")

public class EmployeeServiceImpl implements EmployeeService {
    // ...
}
```

JAX-WS Message Handler Framework

In this chapter we discussed Web service client and endpoint implementation scenarios. All the time we deal with soap messages of a client and service endpoint. Is it possible to process the outbound/inbound messages on its way from client to service endpoint? Certainly yes, the JAX-WS provides a flexible message handler framework for soap message processing. In general, handlers are used for various purposes such as logging messages, validating header information, validating the message content, and so forth.

There are two types of handlers defined in JAX-WS:

- Logical Handlers
- Protocol Handlers

Logical handlers are protocol independent; works only with message payloads and message context properties. Logical Handlers are the handlers that implements "javax.xml.ws.handler.LogicalHandler" interface. Logical Handlers cannot change the protocol specific information like <header/>. It can change only the actual payload (body) of the message.

Protocol handlers are specific to a particular protocol; and works with entire protocol message and message context properties. Protocol Handlers are the handlers that implement "javax.xml.ws.handler.Handler" interface or any protocol specific interface that is derived from "javax.xml.ws.handler.Handler" interface. Protocol handlers can alter full message including the <header/> element.

The Figure 14-7 shows the Handler class hierarchy. The handler interfaces "LogicalHandler" and "SOAPHandler" extends the "Handler" interface. These handlers has three life cycle methods "handleMessage()", "handleFault()" and "close()" which will be discussed in this section.

Figure 14-7: Handler class hierarchy

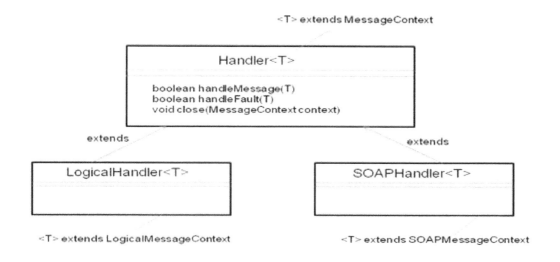

The below provided code explains the use of "SAOPHandler" interface using soap message context.

```
public class ValidationHandler implements SOAPHandler<SOAFMessageContext>
{
    // Life cycle methods to be added.
}
```

These message handlers can be attached to the client as well as the service endpoint. It is possible to add more than one message handler called as "handler chain". These handlers are executed for outbound-and-inbound messages in a specific order. The complete message context is available in handlers for processing. The Figure 14-8 shows the use of protocol handler chain between client and service endpoint.

Figure 14-8: Protocol handler chain

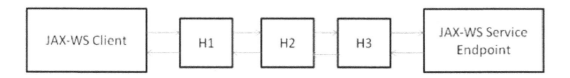

If the Logical handlers are included in a handler chain along with Protocol handlers, all logical handlers will be executed first followed by protocol handlers. The Figure 14-9 shows the use of logical handlers and protocol handlers in a handler chain between client and service endpoint.

Figure 14-9: Handler chain ordering – "L" and "H" are used for Logical and Protocol handlers.

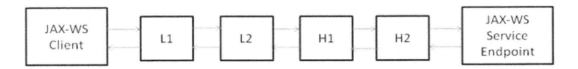

This handler chain can be configured programmatically or using deployment descriptors. JAX-WS provided "@HandlerChain" annotation can be used for configuring the handler chains. The below provided service endpoint interface is annotated using "@HandlerChain" annotation.

```
@HandlerChain(file="http://localhost:8080/wsbook/demo/handlerchain.xml")
public interface EmployeeService {
    Employee getEmployee(String employeeId) throws Exception;
}
```

Figure 14-10: JAX-WS Handler Architecture

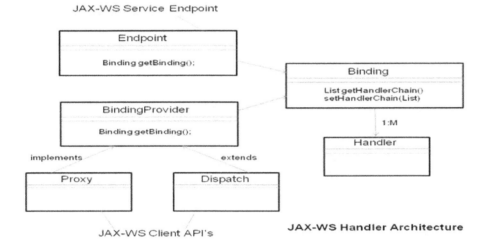

The inbound messages are processed by the handlers prior to the binding provider (Proxy or Dispatch) processing; and outbound messages are processed after the binding provider processing. The JAX-WS handler architecture is shown in Figure 14-10

SOAP Handler Life Cycle Management

The JAX-WS runtime is responsible for handler life cycle management. Also JAX-WS runtime is responsible for creation of the handler instances as specified in deployment descriptors, injecting any dependent resources, invocation of the container specific callback methods like "postConstruct()" and "postDestroy()". For each client request it invokes the life cycle methods of a handler class for outbound-and-inbound messages. There are three methods each protocol message handler class has to implement, they are "handleMessage()", "handleFault()" and "close()". The message context is passed to all the available handlers in a handler chain. The order of execution of the life cycle methods of a handler class is listed below.

- The life cycle of soap handler begins, when JAX-WS runtime start the creation of a handler instance. The default constructor of the handler class is first invoked.
- JAX-WS runtime injects any context specific resources using "javax.annotation.Resource".
- JAX-WS runtime invokes a method that is annotated with "@PostConstruct()" annotation, if exists any. This method is used to perform required initialization.
- The handler instance will be created and it is in ready state.
- The handler instance processes the inbound-and-outbound messages using "handleMessage()", "handleFault()" and "close()" methods. It ends the handler life cycle.
- JAX-WS runtime invokes a method that is annotated with "@PreDestroy()" annotation, if there is any. This method is used to perform cleanup activities like releasing the resources the process is holding.
- Finally the handler instance is available for garbage collection.

Figure 14-11: Handler life cycle

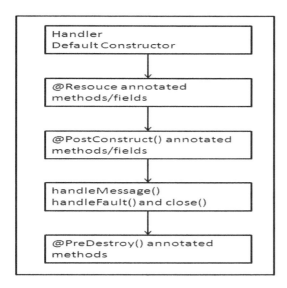

The order of execution of the handler life cycle methods are shown in Figure 14-11.

Let us now take the following example to demonstrate the above-specified steps.

```
public class ValidationHandler implements
SOAPHandler<SOAPMessageContext> {
    @Resource
    private WebServiceContext context;

    // Default constructor.
    public ValidationHandler() {
        System.out.println("--- Default Constructor ---");
    }

    // callback method - invoked by the container.
    @PostConstruct
    private void init() {
        System.out.println("--- PostConstruct - Perform required
        initialization ---");
    }
```

```
    // process outbound and inbound messages
    public boolean handleMessage(SOAPMessageContext context) {
        return true;
    }

    // handle faults
    public boolean handleFault(SOAPMessageContext context) {
        return true;
    }

    // close
    public void close(MessageContext context) {
        System.out.println("--- ValidationHandler : close() ---");
    }

    @PreDestroy
    private void doCleanUp() {
        System.out.println("-- ValidationHandler - PreDestroy -
        doCleanUp() ---");
    }

    @Override
    public Set<QName> getHeaders() {
        return null;
    }
}
```

The first step is to create a handler class by implementing "SOAPHandler" interface.

```
public class ValidationHandler implements
SOAPHandler<SOAPMessageContext> {
}
```

The following code injects any context specific resources using "javax.annotation.Resource" annotation.

```
@Resource
private WebServiceContext context;
```

The following code create a default public constructor of the handler class

```
public ValidationHandler() {
    System.out.println("--- Default Constructor ---");
}
```

The following "init()" method is annotated with "@PostConstruct" annotation. This method performs the required initializations if any.

```
@PostConstruct
private void init() {
    System.out.println("---- PostConstruct - Perform required
            initialization ----");
}
```

Implementing "handleMessage()" Method: This method is called for the normal processing of outbound-and-inbound messages. The entire soap message is available in this method to perform any application specific processing like validations, logging, encrypting data, decrypting the data, etc. After processing, this method can return any of the following:

- Return "true" indicates continue the processing with next available handler in a handler chain.
- Return "false" indicates stop further processing of available handlers in handler chain, so message not passed to the service endpoint.
- Throws a "RuntimeException"; indicates terminates the further processing of handler chain; start executing the "handleFault()" method of the current handler.

The method signature of the "handleMessage" is provided below:

```
public boolean handleMessage(SOAPMessageContext context) {
    return true;
}
```

Implementing "handleFault()" Method: This method is called for the fault message processing of outbound-and-inbound messages. The entire soap message is available in this method to capture the faults. After processing of the message this method can return any of the following:

- Return "true" indicates continue the processing with next available handler in a handler chain.
- Return "false" indicates stop further processing of available handler faults in a handler chain.
- Throws a "RuntimeException"; indicates terminates the further processing fault message in chain; and "close()" method of the each previously invoked handler in the chain is called.

The method signature of the "handleFault" is provided below:

```
public boolean handleFault(SOAPMessageContext context) {
    return true;
}
```

Implementing "close()" Method: This method concludes the message exchange between client and service endpoint. This method is called just before dispatching the final message to the service endpoint.

The method signature of the "close()" is provided below:

```
public void close(MessageContext context) {
    System.out.println("--- ValidationHandler : close() ---");
}
```

The below provided "doCleanUp()" method is used to perform cleanup activities if any. This callback method is invoked by the JAX-WS runtime.

```
@PreDestroy
private void doCleanUp() {
    System.out.println("---- ValidationHandler - PreDestroy -
                                doCleanUp() ----");
}
```

Example 5: SOAP Handler Example

The following example intercepts the inbound message; and validates the value of the employee id; if client sends any invalid input value of the employee id (example zero); handler class replaces the zero with default value before dispatching the message to the service endpoint. It validates only inbound messages to the web service endpoint; and outbound message are delivered to the client without any validations.

The "ValidationHandler" handler class implements "SOAPHandler" which intern extends "javax.xml.ws.handler.Handler" class. The "handleMessage()" method of the handler class receives the outbound-and-inbound messages; the SAAJ API is used for message processing.

The Web Service client sends the below provided inbound message to the service endpoint.

```
<soap:Envelope xmlns:soap="http://schemas.xmlsoap.org/soap/envelope/">
    <soap:Header/>
    <soap:Body>
        <ns1:getEmployee xmlns:ns1="http://jaxws.ws.learning.com/">
            <employeeId>000000</employeeId>
        </ns1:getEmployee>
    </soap:Body>
</soap:Envelope>
```

The "ValidationHandler" class intercepts the above message; reads the value of "<employeeId/>" element; If it has any invalid value of employee id; it replaces the employee id with default value before passing the message to the service endpoint.

The outbound message from the service endpoint is provided below:

```
<soap:Envelope xmlns:soap="http://schemas.xmlsoap.org/soap/envelope/">
    <soap:Body>
    <ns1:getEmployeeResponse xmlns:ns1="http://jaxws.ws.learning.com/">
        <return>
            <employeeId>99999</employeeId>
            <firstName>XXXXX</firstName>
            <lastName>XXXXX</lastName>
        </return>
    </ns1:getEmployeeResponse>
    </soap:Body>
</soap:Envelope>
```

Let us now examine the code example of the "ValideationHandler" class to have better understanding.

The "MESSAGE_OUTBOUND_PROPERTY" of the message context is used to determine the direction of the message at service endpoint. Its value is "true" for outbound messages, "false" for inbound messages. This flag is used to process only inbound messages.

```
Boolean isRequest = (Boolean)
context.get(MessageContext.MESSAGE_OUTBOUND_PROPERTY);
```

The following code receives the complete soap message from "SOAPMessageContext"; prints the message on the console.

```
SOAPMessage message = context.getMessage();
```

```
ByteArrayOutputStream out = new ByteArrayOutputStream();
message.writeTo(out);
String responseMessage = new String(out.toByteArray());
System.out.println("--- ValidationHandler entire message ---" +
responseMessage);
```

The following code extracts the message payload; iterates over the elements of the soap message body to obtain the value of employee id.

```
SOAPBody requestBody = message.getSOAPBody();
Iterator iterator = requestBody.getChildElements();
SOAPBodyElement bodyElement = (SOAPBodyElement) iterator.next();
```

The complete soap message handler code is shown in Listing 14-10. After completing the message processing the "handleMessage()" method returns "true"; so the handler will continue the message processing in a handler chain or dispatches the message to service endpoint.

Listing 14-10: SOAP message handler class

```
// ValidationHandler.java
package com.learning.ws.jaxws;

import org.w3c.dom.Element;
import org.w3c.dom.NodeList;
import javax.xml.ws.handler.soap.SOAPMessageContext;
import javax.xml.ws.handler.soap.SOAPHandler;
import javax.xml.ws.handler.MessageContext;
import javax.xml.soap.SOAPMessage;
import javax.xml.soap.SOAPBody;
import javax.xml.soap.SOAPBodyElement;
import javax.xml.soap.Node;
import javax.xml.namespace.QName;
import java.io.ByteArrayOutputStream;
import java.util.*;

public class ValidationHandler implements
                SOAPHandler<SOAPMessageContext> {

    public ValidationHandler() {}

    @Override
    public boolean handleMessage(SOAPMessageContext context) {
        /* message direction, true for outbound messages,
        false for inbound. */
        Boolean isRequest = (Boolean)
            context.get(MessageContext.MESSAGE_OUTBOUND_PROPERTY);

        if(!isRequest) {
            try {
            SOAPMessage message =  context.getMessage();
            // Printing the message on the console.
            ByteArrayOutputStream out = new
                    ByteArrayOutputStream();
            message.writeTo(out);
            String inboundMessage = new String(out.toByteArray());
            System.out.println("-- complete inbound message --" +
```

```java
                inboundMessage);

                // gets the SOAP body
                SOAPBody requestBody = message.getSOAPBody();
                Iterator iterator = requestBody.getChildElements();
                SOAPBodyElement bodyElement = (SOAPBodyElement)
                                        iterator.next();

                /* Iterates over the child elements to
                obtain the required value */
                String elementName = bodyElement.getNodeName();
                if(elementName != null &&
                    elementName.contains("ns1:getEmployee")) {
                    for(Element result : getElements(bodyElement.
                            getElementsByTagName("employeeId"))) {
                        //Obtain the employee id from inbound message
                        String employeeId =
                        getNamedElement(result,"employeeId").
                                        getTextContent();
                        Integer empId = new Integer(employeeId);

                        // Setting the default value
                        if(empId == 0) {
                            result.setTextContent("99999");
                        }
                    }
                }
            } catch(Exception ex) {
                ex.printStackTrace();
            }
        }

        // continue with handler chain
        return true;
        }

        @Override
        public boolean handleFault(SOAPMessageContext context) {
            return true;
        }

        @Override
        public void close(MessageContext context) {
        }

        @Override
        public Set<QName> getHeaders() {
            return null;
        }

        // Utility method used for message processing
        private static List<Element> getElements(NodeList nodes) {
            List<Element> result = new
                    ArrayList<Element>(nodes.getLength());
            for(int i = 0; i < nodes.getLength(); i++) {
                Node node = (Node) nodes.item(i);
                if(node instanceof Element) {
```

```
                    result.add((Element)node);
                }
            }
        return result;
    }

    // Utility method used for message processing
    private static Element getNamedElement(Element element,String name){
    if(!element.getNodeName().equals(name))
        throw new IllegalArgumentException("Expected " - name +  ",but
        received " + element.getNodeName());
        return element;
    }
}
```

Example 6: SOAP Handler Chain Example

The Figure 14-12 shows the use of "LogHandler" and "ValidationHandler" in a handler chain. The configured handlers in a handler chain intercept the soap messages between the client and service endpoint.

Figure 14-12: Message Handler Chain

The steps required to develop a Web service using handlers are given below:

1. Create a "ValidationHandler.java" class
2. Create a "LogHandler.java" class
3. Create Web service endpoint interface and its implementation class
4. Configure handlers with Web Service endpoint
5. Create a Web Service client

The above-specified steps are described in the following sections:

Step 1: Create a ValidationHandler.java Class

Reuse the validation handler class created in our previous example. It pre-validates the input data.

Step 2: Create a LogHandler.java Class

The below-provided "LogHandler" class logs the incoming-and-outgoing messages. We can redirect the generated log messages to a log file using standard logging framework like Log4j.

The complete "LogHandler" class code is provided in Listing 14-11

Listing 14-11: SOAP message handler class used to log messages

```
// LogHandler.java
package com.learning.ws.jaxws;
```

```java
import java.util.Set;
import java.io.ByteArrayOutputStream;
import javax.xml.namespace.QName;
import javax.xml.ws.handler.MessageContext;
import javax.xml.ws.handler.soap.SOAPHandler;
import javax.xml.ws.handler.soap.SOAPMessageContext;
import javax.xml.soap.SOAPMessage;

public class LogHandler implements SOAPHandler<SOAPMessageContext> {
    public LogHandler() {}

    @Override
    public boolean handleMessage(SOAPMessageContext context) {
        try {
            SOAPMessage message = context.getMessage();
            // Printing the message on the console.
            ByteArrayOutputStream out = new ByteArrayOutputStream();
            message.writeTo(out);
            String responseMessage = new String(out.toByteArray());
            System.out.println("--- LogHandler entire message
                    --" + responseMessage);
        } catch(Exception ex) {
            ex.printStackTrace();
        }
        // continue other handler chain
        return true;
    }

    @Override
    public boolean handleFault(SOAPMessageContext context) {
            return true;
    }

    @Override
    public void close(MessageContext context) {}

    @Override
    public Set<QName> getHeaders() {
        System.out.println("--- LogHandler : getHeaders() ---");
        return null;
    }
}
```

Step 3: Create Web Service Endpoint Interface and its Implementation Class

The web service endpoint interface and its implementation are provided in Listing 14-12.

Listing 14-12: Service endpoint interface and its implementation

```java
// EmployeeService.java
package com.learning.ws.jaxws;

@WebService
public interface EmployeeService {
    @WebMethod(operationName="getEmployee")
    Employee getEmployee(@WebParam (name="employeeId") String
    employeeId) throws EmployeeFault;
```

```
}
```

The "getEmployee()" method of the web service endpoint receives the input from the client; and sends the response back.

```
@WebService(name="EmployeeService",
          serviceName="employeeService",
          endpointInterface="com.learning.ws.jaxws.EmployeeService")
public class EmployeeServiceImpl implements EmployeeService {
    public Employee getEmployee(String employeeId) throws EmployeeFault{
        if(employeeId == null) {
            throw new EmployeeFault("Invalid input received");
        }
        Employee emp = new Employee();
        emp.setEmployeeId(employeeId);
        if("99999".equalsIgnoreCase(employeeId)) {
            emp.setFirstName("XXXXX");
            emp.setLastName("XXXXX");
        } else {
            /* Build your logic here to get the employee details. Using
            hard coded values */
            emp.setFirstName("John");
            emp.setLastName("Smith");
        }
        return emp;
    }
}
```

Step 4: Configure Handlers with Web Service Endpoint

There is no special server side configurations needed to attach message handlers to web service endpoint. Apache-CXF framework provides "<jaxws:handlers/>" tag; which can used to configure message handlers with any service endpoint. The complete handler configuration is provided below:

```
<jaxws:endpoint id="employee"
    implementor="com.learning.ws.jaxws.EmployeeServiceImpl"
    address="/employee">
    <jaxws:handlers>
        <bean class="com.learning.ws.jaxws.ValidationHandler"/>
        <bean class="com.learning.ws.jaxws.LogHandler"/>
    </jaxws:handlers>
</jaxws:endpoint>
```

Step 5: Create a Web Service Client

The following Proxy client can be used to invoke the web service endpoint. It invokes the service endpoint through configured intermediate message handlers. Listing 14-13 has a web service client code used to invoke the web service endpoint.

Listing 14-13: Web service client code.

```
// HandlerClient.java
package com.learning.ws.jaxws;

public class HandlerClient {
```

```
public static void main(String args[]) throws Exception {
    try {
    HandlerClient client = new HandlerClient();
        client.invokeService();
    } catch(Exception ex) {
        ex.printStackTrace();
    }
}

private void invokeService() throws Exception {
    URL url = new
        URL("http://localhost:8080/wsbook/services/employee?wsdl");
    QName qname = new QName("http://jaxws.ws.learning.com/",
            "employeeService");
    Service service = Service.create(url, qname);
    EmployeeService employeeService =
        service.getPort(EmployeeService.class);
    Employee emp = employeeService.getEmployee("000000");
    System.out.println("Employee Id:" + emp.getEmployeeId() +
                "-- First Name --" + emp.getFirstName() +
                "-- Last Name --" + emp.getLastName());
    }
}
```

Server Side - Configuring SOAP Handler Chain Using Apache-CXF

There are two types of handler's client and server. It is possible to configure a handler chain to the client as well as server. There is no limit on the number handlers that can be used in a handler chain. The Figure 14-13 explains the use of handlers at client and server (service endpoint). The terminology outbound-and-inbound is used with respect to the client and service endpoint. The notation used for client side handlers is "CH1", "CH2" and server side handlers is "SH1" and "SH2". The client side handlers "CH1" and "CH2" intercept the outbound messages from the client; inbound messages it receives as a service response. Similarly server side handlers "SH1" and "SH2" intercept the inbound messages received from the client; sends the outbound response from service endpoint. The message path between client and service endpoint is shown Figure 14-13.

Figure 14-13: Using Handler Chain with client and service endpoint

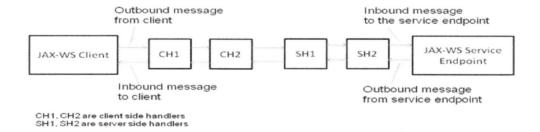

The below provided example demonstrates the use of server side handlers. Apache-CXF framework provided "<jaxws:handlers/>" tag can be used to configure message handlers to any service endpoint.

The complete configuration is provided below:

```xml
<?xml version="1.0" encoding="UTF-8"?>
<beans xmlns="http://www.springframework.org/schema/beans"
    xmlns:xsi="http://www.w3.org/2001/XMLSchema-instance"
    xmlns:jaxws="http://cxf.apache.org/jaxws"
    xmlns:cxf="http://cxf.apache.org/core"
    xsi:schemaLocation="http://www.springframework.org/schema/beans
    http://www.springframework.org/schema/beans/spring-beans.xsd
    http://cxf.apache.org/jaxws
    http://cxf.apache.org/schemas/jaxws.xsd
    http://cxf.apache.org/core
    http://cxf.apache.org/schemas/core.xsd ">

    <!-- Loads CXF modules from cxf.jar file -->
    <import resource="classpath:META-INF/cxf/cxf.xml"/>
    <import resource="classpath:META-INF/cxf/cxf-extension-soap.xml"/>
    <import resource="classpath:META-INF/cxf/cxf-servlet.xml"/>
    <import resource="classpath:META-INF/cxf/cxf-extension-jaxrs-
        binding.xml"/>

    <jaxws:endpoint id="employee"
            implementor="com.learning.ws.jaxws.EmployeeServiceImpl"
            address="/employee">
        <jaxws:handlers>
            <bean class="com.learning.ws.jaxws.ValidationHandler"/>
            <bean class="com.learning.ws.jaxws.LogHandler"/>
        </jaxws:handlers>
    </jaxws:endpoint>
</beans>
```

Client Side - Configuring SOAP Handler Chain Using Apache-CXF

Apache-CXF framework provides "<jaxws:handlers/>" tag; which can used to configure message handlers to any web service client. This is similar to the one used for service endpoint.

The complete configuration is provided below:

```xml
<?xml version="1.0" encoding="UTF-8"?>
<beans xmlns="http://www.springframework.org/schema/beans"
    xmlns:xsi="http://www.w3.org/2001/XMLSchema-instance"
    xmlns:jaxws="http://cxf.apache.org/jaxws"
    xmlns:cxf="http://cxf.apache.org/core"
    xsi:schemaLocation="http://www.springframework.org/schema/beans
    http://www.springframework.org/schema/beans/spring-beans.xsd
    http://cxf.apache.org/jaxws
    http://cxf.apache.org/schemas/jaxws.xsd
    http://cxf.apache.org/core
    http://cxf.apache.org/schemas/core.xsd ">

    <!-- Loads CXF modules from cxf.jar file -->
    <import resource="classpath:META-INF/cxf/cxf.xml"/>
    <import resource="classpath:META-INF/cxf/cxf-extension-soap.xml"/>
    <import resource="classpath:META-INF/cxf/cxf-servlet.xml"/>
    <import resource="classpath:META-INF/cxf/cxf-extension-jaxrs-
```

```
                binding.xml"/>

        <jaxws:client id="springHandlerClient"
                serviceClass="com.learning.ws.jaxws.EmployeeService"
                address="http://localhost:8080/wsbook/services/employee">
                <jaxws:handlers>
                        <bean class="com.learning.ws.jaxws.ValidationHandler"/>
                        <bean class="com.learning.ws.jaxws.LogHandler"/>
                </jaxws:handlers>
        </jaxws:client>
</beans>
```

Listing 14-14 has a web service client program which is used to invoke the service endpoint. View the output on console to track the message path between web service client and endpoint.

Listing 14-14: Web service client code.

```
public class CXFClientHandler {
    private CXFClientHandler() { }

    public static void main(String args[]) throws Exception {
        ClassPathXmlApplicationContext context
            = new ClassPathXmlApplicationContext(new String[]
                    {"applicationContext-client.xml"});

        EmployeeService employeeService = (EmployeeService)
                    context.getBean("springHandlerClient");

        Employee emp = employeeService.getEmployee("000000");
        System.out.println("Employee Id:" + emp.getEmployeeId() +
                "-- First Name --" + emp.getFirstName() +
                "-- Last Name --" + emp.getLastName());
        System.exit(0);
    }
}
```

Summary

This section summarizes the features provided in the Apache-CXF framework.

- CXF-provided `<jaxws:endpoint/>` tag is used for configuring the JAX-WS based service endpoints.
- CXF-provided `<jaxws:handlers/>` tag is used for configuring the SOAP message handlers.
- CXF-provided `<jaxrs:server/>` tag is used for configuring the JAX-RS based service endpoints.
- CXF-provides a seamless integration with Spring framework. The Spring and CXF tags can co-exist in the same application context configuration file. Both look similar.
- CXF-provides support for JAX-RS and JAX-WS standards.

Figure 14-14 summarizes the most important points described in this chapter.

Figure 14-14 CXF web services summary

Chapter 15. Spring with Drools Expert

Drools Expert is an open-source business rule engine. A business rule engine is a software component used to externalize the business rules from the application code. A business rule engine enables the enterprises to maintain business parameters outside the application code. The business vocabulary can be externalized from the application code, so that it can be reused across the applications in an enterprise. Business analysts can change the business parameters dynamically without affecting the application code. Applications use the rule engine-provided API to integrate with rule engine. Drools Expert is an open-source rule engine from JBOSS. This chapter illustrates the Drools Expert provided features and its integration with spring framework.

In this chapter will discuss the following topics:

- Drools rule engine terminology.
- Various available rule engines in the market.
- Drools architecture.
- Advantages of drools rule engine.
- Integrating Drools with Spring framework.
- The purpose and implementation details of the rule maintenance application (RMA).
- How to write rules in various drools supported formats.
- Converting rules from one form to another.
- The use and purpose of drools-specific change sets.

Drools Terminology

This section explains the terminology commonly used in Drools while developing business rules. The Drools terminology is defined below.

Drools Expert: Drools expert is a standalone business rule engine; used to run the rules defined in Drools Runtime Language (DRL). Drools expert is available in JAR files; which can be used for standalone rules development.

Drools Guvnor: Drools guvnor is a business rules manager (BRM). Guvnor provides a centralized rules repository for drools, rich web-based UI editors for rules development, and tools for the rules management. Drools guvnor is a web application; it can be deployed into any servlet container.

Rule: A rule contains condition-and-action. Each rule contains an if-and-else condition. The "if" block contains a condition, "else" block contains an action. Rules are executed by matching against the data.

Rule Set: A rule set contains a set of similar rules which are executed one-after-another. In drools, a rule file contains set of rules with ".drl" extension.

Generally, a business rule has "if-then-else" syntax as given below.

```
when
    <condition>
then
    <action>
```

Rule Flow: This is represented like a flowchart, which specifies the path of the rules that are executed.

Decision Table: Decision table is a form of rule representation. A decision table contains set of rules and conditions in the form of a table. The rules are represented as rows; conditions and actions are represented as columns. Drools decision tables are represented in excel spreadsheet format.

Salience: It specifies the rule order of execution. A large value of salience represents higher rule priority.

DRL: It stands for Drools Runtime Language. This language has its own syntax; used to write the rules in a file with ".drl" extension.

DSL: It stands for Domain Specific Language. This language is similar to English; used to write the rules in plain text format with a ".dsl" extension. This is designed for non-technical people; business users and domain consultant's uses this format to write the rules.

Change Set: The technique used to load a set of rule resources into the drools knowledge base.

Knowledge Base: This is a repository of all the application rule resources. This repository contains rules, decision tables, change sets, processes, and functions. Knowledge base can be obtained by calling the `newKnowledgeBase()` method of `KnowledgeBaseFactory` class.

```
KnowledgeBase kbase = KnowledgeBaseFactory.newKnowledgeBase();
```

Knowledge Session: The two types of knowledge sessions are stateless and stateful. The Drools knowledge session objects are used to execute the rules. The `execute(...)` method of `StatelessKnowledgeSession` object method can be used to start the rule execution. This is an interface point between rule engine and the application.

```
StatelessKnowledgeSession session = kbase.newStatelessKnowledgeSession();
session.execute(collection);
```

Drools Keywords

The following keywords are used while developing the rules using drools. A keyword cannot be used for a variable name.

package	function	exists
imports	salience	template
global	forall	extend
function	no-loop	declare
queries	init	date-effective
rule	action	date-expires
when	attributes	enabled
then	in	end, and

Various Available Rule Engines in the Market

The various available rule engines in the market are listed below. Some of they are open-source and some are vendor-specific. All these rules engines provide similar features. In this chapter Drools expert rule engine features are demonstrated in greater detail.

Open Source	Open Source	Licensed
Drools (JBOSS)	Prova Language	Blaze Advisor
Sweet Rules	Open Lexicon	JRules (IBM)
Open Rules	Zilonis	Quick Rules
Mandarax	Hammurapi Rules	Pega RULES
Take	OpenL Tables	Catalyst
TermWare	DTRules	Logic Engine
JRuleEngine	Roolie	irServer
JLisa		

Prerequisites/Setting Up the Environment

- The JAR files required to develop Drools examples are provided along with the Drools distribution. Download the *drools-distribution-5.3.0.zip* file from jboss.org website.
- Make sure you use the correct version of JAR files to avoid the class loader JAR file version mismatch related exceptions.
- The complete distribution is available in the form of JAR files. So no additional software needed for development.
- The eclipse plugins are available to develop rules using eclipse IDE. Download *drools-5.1.1-eclipse-all.zip* from internet. This zip file contains "features" and "plugins" folders. Copy these folders to the eclipse root directory. Make sure these files are copied to the eclipse "features" and "plugins" directories. Restart the eclipse.
- The following JAR files are used for developing Drools code examples. These JAR files are packaged with *drools-distribution-5.3.0.zip file*. The Drools version 5.3 is used to demonstrate code examples. The below provided table has the complete list of JAR files.

antlr-3.3.jar	drools-persistence-jpa-5.3.0-SNAPSHOT.jar
antlr-runtime-3.3.jar	drools-templates-5.3.0-SNAPSHOT.jar
bcmail-jdk14-138.jar	drools-verifier-5.3.0-SNAPSHOT.jar
bcprov-jdk14-138.jar	ecj-3.5.1.jar
commons-collections-3.1.jar	knowledge-api-5.3.0-20110518.143149-23.jar
dom4j-1.6.1.jar	mvel2-2.1-20110518.134219-28.jar
drools-clips-5.3.0-SNAPSHOT.jar	stringtemplate-3.2.1.jar
drools-compiler-5.3.0-SNAPSHOT.jar	xml-apis-2.0.2.jar
drools-core-5.3.0-SNAPSHOT.jar	xpp3_min-1.1.4c.jar
drools-decisiontables-5.3.0-SNAPSHOT.jar	xstream-1.3.1.jar
drools-jsr94-5.3.0-SNAPSHOT.jar	jxl-2.6.10
poi-2.5.1-final-20040804	

Advantages of Drools

This section illustrates the technical and non-technical features of a Drools rule engine.

- Drools provide a simple Java-based API to manage rules and decision tables.
- The language syntax is close to Java. It is easy to setup, learn, and debug.
- Drools expert is an open-source rule engine. No licensing costs.
- Provides support for various rule forms like "drl", "decision table", and "dsl".
- Various implementation solutions available for implementing the rule maintenance application (RMA) to maintain the business parameters.
- Provides support for spread sheet and CSV-based decision tables.
- Open source IDE Plugins are available for rules development.
- Provides support for multiple languages. Both Java and .Net-based rules engines are supported.

Drools Rule Execution

Drools rule execution steps are listed below.

- Drools knowledge base contains the repository of all rule resources.
- Drools runtime loads the rules from knowledge base into a knowledge session.
- The rules from knowledge session are executed, finds the possible rules to be executed.
- A rule is executed if the rule condition matches against the data. If data is not matched that particular rule will be skipped. The rule execution continues to the next rule in the rule set.

Figure 15-1 shows the rule execution sequence in Drools.

Figure 115-1: Drools rule execution sequence

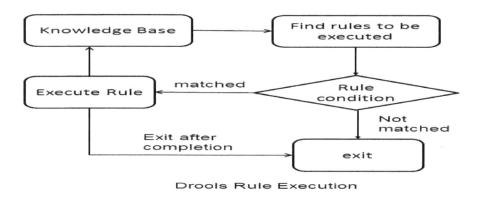

Drools Rule Execution

Various Forms of Rules

Rule developers can develop the rules in various forms. These are designed for different roles of personnel. Drools provide an API to convert rules from one form to another. The following list provides the various supported rule forms.

- DRL form — this is a file with ".drl" extension; designed for rules development.
- Decision Table form — Drools decision table is a excel spread sheet with ".xls" extension. This form is used to represent the rules in tabular (rows-and-columns) format.
- DSL form — this is a file with ".dsl" extension; specially designed for business consultants to represent the rules in English language with Drools syntax. Drools runtime translates the DSL into DRL form.

Demo Examples

Example 1: How to Write Rules in ".drl" Format

The following business scenario is implemented using Drools.

Business Scenario:

- A customer can have any one of the five plan statuses for his policy. They are Pending, Denied, Approved, Terminated, and Open.
- If the plan status is Pending (P) → set final action as POST_AND_SUSPEND_PLAN
- If the plan status is Denied (D) → set final action as DENIED_PLAN
- If the plan status is Approved (A) → set final action as ACTIVATE_PLAN
- If the plan status is Terminated (T) → set final action as TERMINATE_PLAN
- If the plan status is Open (O) → set final action as POST_PLAN

The steps required to implement the above-specified business scenario in "drl' form using drools are listed below:

1. Create a ".drl" file to write rules.
2. Write a Java class to test the rules.

The above-specified steps are described in the following sections:

Step 1: Create a ".drl" file to write rules.

The "drl" file contains five rules for the above-specified business conditions. Each rule has one condition and its corresponding action.

Rule 1:

The Java syntax for a rule implementation is provided below.

```java
// Condition for Pending status
if("P".equals(status.getStatus())) {
    status.setAction("POST_AND_SUSPEND_PLAN");
}
```

The corresponding rule implementation in Drools is provided below.

```
rule "BenefitStatus_1"
    salience 100
    when
```

```
        Status(status == "P")
        $status : Status()
    then
        $status.setAction("POST_AND_SUSPEND_PLAN");
end
```

The above-specified rule has the following syntax and characteristics.

- The rule must start with keyword "rule", followed by rule name.
- The salience specifies the rule order of execution. This is optional.
- The block "when" is used for declaring the condition. It is equivalent to Java "if" condition.
- The block "then" is used for taking the action.
- One rule can have one when-and-then block
- The rule must end with "end" keyword.

Similarly, other business rule scenarios are provided below.

Rule 2:

The Java syntax for 2nd rule is:

```
// Condition for Denied status
if("D".equals(planStatus)) {
    status.setAction("DENIED_PLAN");
}
```

The corresponding rule implementation in Drools is provided below.

```
rule "BenefitStatus_2"
    salience 90
    when
        Status(status == "D")
        $status : Status()
    then
        $status.setAction("DENIED_PLAN");
end
```

Rule 3:

The Java syntax for 3rd rule is:

```
// Condition for Activate status
if("A".equals(planStatus)) {
    status.setAction("ACIVATE_PLAN");
}
```

The corresponding rule implementation in Drools is provided below.

```
rule "BenefitStatus_3"
    salience 80
    when
        Status(status == "A")
        $status : Status()
    then
```

```
                    $status.setAction("ACIVATE_PLAN");
end
```

Rule 4:

The Java syntax for 4th rule is:

```
// Condition for Terminate status
if("T".equals(planStatus)) {
    status.setAction("TERMNATE_PLAN");
}
```

The corresponding rule implementation in Drools is provided below.

```
rule "BenefitStatus_4"
    salience 70
    when
        Status(status == "T")
        $status : Status()
    then
        $status.setAction("TERMNATE_PLAN");
end
```

Rule 5:

The Java syntax for 5th rule is:

```
// Condition for Open status
if("O".equals(planStatus)) {
    status.setAction("POST_PLAN");
}
```

The corresponding rule implementation in Drools is provided below.

```
rule "BenefitStatus_5"
    salience 60
    when
        Status(status == "O")
        $status : Status()
    then
        $status.setAction("POST_PLAN");
end
```

The complete ".drl" file is provided below; named the "planstatus.drl"

```
// starts with package name
package com.learning.spring.drools;

// import the required java classes
import com.learning.spring.drools.Status;

rule "BenefitStatus_1"
    salience 100
    when
        Status(status == "P")
```

```
        $status : Status()
    then
        $status.setAction("POST_AND_SUSPEND_PLAN");
end

rule "BenefitStatus_2"
    salience 90
    when
        Status(status == "D")
        $status : Status()
    then
        $status.setAction("DENIED_PLAN");
end

rule "BenefitStatus_3"
    salience 80
    when
        Status(status == "A")
        $status : Status()
    then
        $status.setAction("ACIVATE_PLAN");
end

rule "BenefitStatus_4"
    salience 70
    when
        Status(status == "T")
        $status : Status()
    then
        $status.setAction("TERMNATE_PLAN");
end

rule "BenefitStatus_5"
    salience 60
    when
        Status(status == "O")
        $status : Status()
    then
        $status.setAction("POST_PLAN");
end
```

Step 2: Write a Java class to test the rules.

The following Java bean class contains input-and-output data methods. The "status" attribute is used for passing the rule input and "action" attribute is used for setting the rule output.

```
package com.learning.spring.drools;

public class Status {

    private String status;
    private String action;

    // Add getters and setters
}
```

The following `execute(...)` method is used to execute the business rules. This is the interface point between the client and rule engine.

```
ksession.execute(Arrays.asList(new Object[] { status }));
```

The complete class code is provided in Listing 15-1. Listing 15-1 provides a Java class to test the above implemented rule conditions.

Listing 15-1: Main class used for testing

```java
// TestPlanStatus.java
package com.learning.spring.drools;

import java.util.Arrays;
import org.drools.KnowledgeBase;
import org.drools.KnowledgeBaseFactory;
import org.drools.builder.KnowledgeBuilder;
import org.drools.builder.KnowledgeBuilderFactory;
import org.drools.builder.ResourceType;
import org.drools.io.ResourceFactory;
import org.drools.runtime.StatelessKnowledgeSession;

public class TestPlanStatus {

    public static void main(String[] args) {
        try {
            // Specifies the location of the drl file
            String drlFileLocaton = "C:/drlfile/planstatus.drl";
            Status status = new Status();

            // Setting the input staus
            status.setStatus("O");
            invokeRuleEngine(status, drlFileLocaton);

            // Printing the return action on the console
            System.out.println("--- Final Action is ---" +
                                status.getAction());
        } catch (Exception ex) {
            ex.printStackTrace();
        }
    }

    /**
     * This method invokes the rule engine.
     *
     * @param status - The input bean with data
     * @param drlFile - The DRL rule file contains rules
     * @throws Exception - Throws exception if there is any error
     */
    private static void invokeRuleEngine(Status status, String drlFile)
        throws Exception {
        KnowledgeBuilder kbuilder =
                KnowledgeBuilderFactory.newKnowledgeBuilder();
        kbuilder.add(ResourceFactory.newFileResource(drlFile),
                                ResourceType.DRL);
        if (kbuilder.hasErrors()) {
            System.out.println(kbuilder.getErrors().toString());
```

```
        }
        KnowledgeBase kbase = KnowledgeBaseFactory.newKnowledgeBase();
        kbase.addKnowledgePackages(kbuilder.getKnowledgePackages());
        StatelessKnowledgeSession ksession = kbase
                .newStatelessKnowledgeSession();
        ksession.execute(Arrays.asList(new Object[] { status }));
    }
}
```

The following code is used for file resource.

```
kbuilder.add(ResourceFactory.newFileResource(drlFile),ResourceType.DRL);
```

The following code is used for classpath resource.

```
kbuilder.add(ResourceFactory.newClassPathResource("Applicant.drl"));
```

Example 2: How to Write Rules in "Decision Table" Format

Here, re-use the business scenario specified in Example-1. The steps required to implement the above-specified business scenario in "Decision Table" form using Drools are listed below.

1.   Create a Decision Table in excel format.
2.   Write a Java class to test the rules.

The above-specified steps are described in the following sections:

Step 1: Create a Decision Table in excel format

In Drools, the decision tables are represented in excel format. Figure 15-2 shows the decision table in excel format. This decision table is divided into two logical sections. The drools decision table has the following characteristics.

Section-1 is used to specify the package name, import the required classes and provide user readable comments. The details of Section-1 are provided below.

- The first row of the decision table must use "RuleSet" keyword. This keyword represents the package name.
- The second row of the decision table must use "import" keyword. This keyword is same as Java import statement. Import the required classes separated by commas.
- The third row of the decision table contains the "Notes" keyword. This is used to specify comments.

Section-2 contains conditions-and-actions. The details of Section-2 are provided below.

- The first row represents the "RuleTable". The RuleTable keyword must appear on top of the first condition column. All the columns to the left of this column will be ignored.
- Second row must have the CONDITION and ACTION keywords. The decision table can have any number of CONDITION columns followed by one ACTION column.
- The third row represents the class names.
- The fourth row represents the data conditions and final action.
- The fifth row is used to provide comments.

- Remaining all rows will have the rule-specific data.

An example decision table in excel form is shown in Figure 15-2 and it is named the "planstatus.xls".

Figure 115-2: Drools decision table

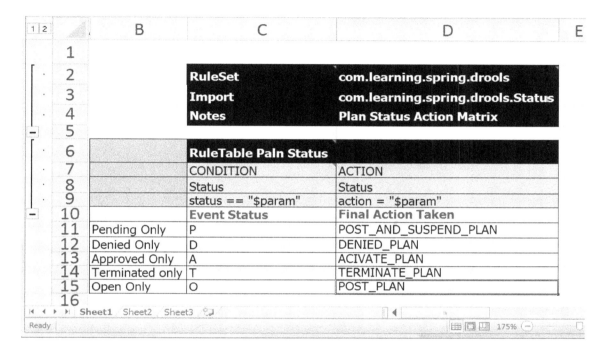

Step 2: Write a Java class to test the rules

The below given Java bean class contain input-and-output data methods. This class is used for data transfer between application and drools rule engine.

```java
// Status.java
package com.learning.spring.drools;

public class Status {

    public String status;
    public static String action = "No Data";

    // Add getters and setters
}
```

The following method obtains the knowledge session to execute rules. The code in this method uses Drools API.

```java
private StatelessKnowledgeSession getKnowledgeSessionForDrools() {
    ...
}
```

The following method is used for testing the rules specified in the decision table.

```
private void executeAllTests() throws Exception {
    ...
}
```

The following method calls the rule engine.

```
private String testPlanStatus() {
    ...
}
```

Listing 15-2 provides the complete class code.

Listing 15-2: Main class used for testing

```java
// PlanStatusTable.java
package com.learning.spring.drools;

import java.util.Arrays;

import org.drools.KnowledgeBase;
import org.drools.KnowledgeBaseFactory;
import org.drools.builder.DecisionTableConfiguration;
import org.drools.builder.DecisionTableInputType;
import org.drools.builder.KnowledgeBuilder;
import org.drools.builder.KnowledgeBuilderFactory;
import org.drools.builder.ResourceType;
import org.drools.io.ResourceFactory;
import org.drools.runtime.StatelessKnowledgeSession;

public class PlanStatusTable {

    public static void main(String[] args) {
        try {
            PlanStatusTable planStatusTable = new PlanStatusTable();
            planStatusTable.executeAllTests();
        } catch (Exception ex) {
            ex.printStackTrace();
        }
    }

    /**
     * Drools specific code to invoke the rule engine
     *
     * @return StatelessKnowledgeSession-session used to execute rules.
     * @throws Exception - if there are any errors.
     */
    private StatelessKnowledgeSession getKnowledgeSessionForDrools()
    throws Exception {
        DecisionTableConfiguration dtableconfiguration =
                KnowledgeBuilderFactory.newDecisionTableConfiguration();
        dtableconfiguration.setInputType(DecisionTableInputType.XLS);

        KnowledgeBuilder kbuilder =
                    KnowledgeBuilderFactory.newKnowledgeBuilder();
        kbuilder.add(ResourceFactory.
                    newFileResource("C:/conf/planstatus.xls"),
```

```java
                    ResourceType.DTABLE, dtableconfiguration);

        if (kbuilder.hasErrors()) {
            System.err.println(kbuilder.getErrors());
            return null;
        }

        KnowledgeBase kbase = KnowledgeBaseFactory.newKnowledgeBase();
        kbase.addKnowledgePackages(kbuilder.getKnowledgePackages());

        // Typical decision tables are used statelessly
        StatelessKnowledgeSession ksession =
            kbase.newStatelessKnowledgeSession();

        return ksession;
    }

    private void executeAllTests() throws Exception {
        StatelessKnowledgeSession ksession =
            getKnowledgeSessionForDrools();

        // Object used for Input/Output data
        Status status = new Status();

        // Plan status = "Pending"
        String finalAction = testPlanStatus("P", status, ksession);
        System.out.println( "Final Action Is: " + finalAction);

        // Plan status = "Denied"
        finalAction = testPlanStatus("D", status, ksession);
        System.out.println( "Final Action Is: " + finalAction);

        // Plan status = "Approved"
        finalAction = testPlanStatus("A", status, ksession);
        System.out.println( "Final Action Is: " + finalAction);

        // Plan status = "Terminated"
        finalAction = testPlanStatus("T", status, ksession);
        System.out.println( "Final Action Is: " + finalAction);

        // Plan status = "Open"
        finalAction = testPlanStatus("O", status, ksession);
        System.out.println( "Final Action Is: " + finalAction);

        // Plan status = "W" - To Test negative scenarios.
        status.setAction(null);
        finalAction = testPlanStatus("W", status, ksession);
        System.out.println( "Final Action Is: " + finalAction);
    }

    // Making a call to rule engine.
    private String testPlanStatus(String eventStatus, Status status,
        StatelessKnowledgeSession ksession) throws Exception {
        status.setStatus(eventStatus);
        ksession.execute( Arrays.asList(new Object[] {status}) );
        return status.getAction();
    }
```

```
}
```

Example 3: Converting Rules from one Form to another – Decision Table-to-DRL

Drools provide an API for converting rules from one form to another. Listing 15-3 provides a code example that converts rules from "Decision Table" form to "drl" form. The generated "drl" file is printed on the console.

Listing 15-3: Main class used for testing

```java
// DecisionTableToDRL.java
package com.learning.spring.drools;

import java.io.*;
import org.drools.builder.*;
import org.drools.compiler.DecisionTableFactory;

public class DecisionTableToDRL {

    public static final void main(String[] args) throws Exception {
        try {
            DecisionTableToDRL decisionTableToDRLTest = new
                    DecisionTableToDRL();
            decisionTableToDRLTest.convertDecisionTableToDRL();
        } catch(Exception ex) {
            ex.printStackTrace();
        }
    }

    private void convertDecisionTableToDRL() throws Exception {
        DecisionTableConfiguration dtableconfiguration =
            KnowledgeBuilderFactory.newDecisionTableConfiguration();
        dtableconfiguration.setInputType( DecisionTableInputType.XLS );

        // Converting Decision table to DRL
        String drlString = DecisionTableFactory.loadFromInputStream(
            getSpreadsheetStream(), dtableconfiguration);
        System.out.println(drlString);
    }

    private InputStream getSpreadsheetStream() throws Exception {
        return new FileInputStream(new File("C:/conf/planstatus.xls"));
    }
}
```

Example 4: Drools Using Java Collections

The following business scenario is implemented using Drools.

Business Scenario: This business scenario has set of rules. They are listed below.

- The value of the policy indicator does not contain valid value → report an alert → report an alert for all values except "II" ,"YI" ,"NI" ,"YE" ,"YY" ,"YN" ,"NE" ,"NY" and "NN".
- The value of phone flag = "4" and phone indicator = "Y" → report both update and correction.
- The value of appraisal type is null or blank → report an alert
- The value of bill mode = "9" and bill cycle value is "H01" or "H02" → report both update and correction.

The steps required to implement the above-specified business scenario in "drl" form using Drools are listed below:

1. Create a ".drl" file to write rules.
2. Write required Java classes to test the rules.

The above-specified steps are described in the following sections:

Step 1: Create a ".drl" file to write rules.

The `ReconciliationBean` holds the business data and final rule output. The alerts, updates, and corrections are populated for each business rule. An event map holds the complete data structure.

```java
// ReconciliationBean.java
package com.learning.spring.drools;

import java.util.*;

public class ReconciliationBean {

    private String policyIndicator;
    private String phoneFlag;
    private String phoneIndicator;
    private String appraisalType;
    private String billMode;
    private String billCycle;

    private List<RuleDVO> alertsList = new ArrayList<RuleDVO>();
    private List<RuleDVO> correctionsList = new ArrayList<RuleDVO>();
    private List<RuleDVO> updatesList = new ArrayList<RuleDVO>();
    private Map<String, List<RuleDVO>> eventMap =
        new HashMap<String,  List<RuleDVO>>();

    // Add getters and setters
}
```

The `RuleDVO` object holds the rule-specific data.

```java
// RuleDVO.java
package com.learning.spring.drools;

public class RuleDVO {
    private String exceptioncode;
    private String fieldOldValue;
    private String fieldNewValue;
    private String fieldName;
```

```
        // Add getters and setters
}
```

The "drl" file contains four rules for the above-specified business scenario. Each rule has one condition and its corresponding action. Each rule updates the list and map.

The complete "drl" file is provided below and it is named the "reconciliation.drl".

```
package com.learning.spring.drools;

#list any import classes here.
import   com.learning.spring.drools.ReconciliationBean;
import   com.learning.spring.drools.RuleDVO;

rule "Policy Indicators Rule"
    salience 100
    when
        $a : ReconciliationBean(policyIndicator != "II" && != "YI" &&
                        != "NI" && != "YE" && != "YY" &&
                        != "YN" && != "NE" && != "NY" && != "NN")
        $b : ReconciliationBean(eventMap : eventMap,
                        alertsList : alertsList)
        $ruleDVO : RuleDVO()
    then
        $ruleDVO = new RuleDVO();
        $ruleDVO.setExceptioncode("100");
        $ruleDVO.setFieldOldValue($a.getPolicyIndicator());
        $ruleDVO.setFieldName("POLICY_INDICATOR");
        alertsList.add($ruleDVO);
        eventMap.put("alerts", alertsList);
end

rule "Phone Flag Rule"
    salience 90
    when
        $a : ReconciliationBean(phoneFlag == "4" &&
                        phoneIndicator == "Y")
        $b : ReconciliationBean(eventMap : eventMap,
                        correctionsList : correctionsList,
                        updatesList : updatesList)
        $ruleDVO : RuleDVO()
    then
        $ruleDVO = new RuleDVO();
        $ruleDVO.setExceptioncode("101");
        $ruleDVO.setFieldOldValue($a.getPhoneFlag());
        $ruleDVO.setFieldNewValue("2");
        $ruleDVO.setFieldName("PHONE_INDICATOR");

        correctionsList.add($ruleDVO);
        updatesList.add($ruleDVO);
        eventMap.put("corrections", correctionsList);
        eventMap.put("updates", updatesList);
end

rule "Appraisal Type Rule"
    salience 70
```

```
    when
        $a : ReconciliationBean(appraisalType == "" ||
                                appraisalType == null)
        $b : ReconciliationBean(eventMap : eventMap,
                                alertsList : alertsList)
        $ruleDVO : RuleDVO()
    then
        $ruleDVO = new RuleDVO();
        $ruleDVO.setExceptioncode("102");
        $ruleDVO.setFieldOldValue($a.getAppraisalType());
        $ruleDVO.setFieldNewValue("XXX");
        $ruleDVO.setFieldName("APPRAISAL_TYPE");
        alertsList.add($ruleDVO);
        eventMap.put("alerts", alertsList);
end

rule "Bill Mode Rule"
    salience 50
    when
        $a : ReconciliationBean((billMode == "9") &&
                                (billCycle == "H01" || == "H20"))
        $c : ReconciliationBean(eventMap : eventMap, correctionsList :
correctionsList, updatesList : updatesList)
        $ruleDVO : RuleDVO()
    then
        $ruleDVO = new RuleDVO();
        $ruleDVO.setExceptioncode("104");
        $ruleDVO.setFieldOldValue($a.getBillMode());
        $ruleDVO.setFieldNewValue("7");
        $ruleDVO.setFieldName("BILL_MODE");

        updatesList.add($ruleDVO);
        correctionsList.add($ruleDVO);
        eventMap.put("corrections", correctionsList);
        eventMap.put("updates", updatesList);
end
```

Step 2: Write required Java classes to test the rules.

Listing 15-4 provides the complete Java class code. Run the `ReconciliationRuleManager`
class to view the output on the console.

Listing 15-4: Main class used for testing

```
// ReconciliationRuleManager.java
package com.learning.spring.drools;

import java.util.*;
import org.drools.KnowledgeBase;
import org.drools.KnowledgeBaseFactory;
import org.drools.builder.*;
import org.drools.io.ResourceFactory;
import org.drools.runtime.StatelessKnowledgeSession;

public class ReconciliationRuleManager {

    public static void main(String[] args) {
```

```
        try {
            executeRules();
        } catch (Exception ex) {
            ex.printStackTrace();
        }
    }

    private static void executeRules() throws Exception {
        // Location of the drl file
        String drlFile = "C:/conf/reconciliation.drl";

        // Input data to execute the rules
        ReconciliationBean reconBean = new ReconciliationBean();
        reconBean.setPolicyIndicator("YY");
        reconBean.setPhoneFlag("4");
        reconBean.setPhoneIndicator("Y");
        reconBean.setAppraisalType("");
        reconBean.setBillMode("9");
        reconBean.setBillCycle("H01");

        // Invoking the rule engine
        invokeRuleEngine(reconBean, drlFile);

        // Printing the data on the console
        Map<String, List<RuleDVO>> eventMap = reconBean.getEventMap();
        List<RuleDVO> alerts = eventMap.get("alerts");
        List<RuleDVO> updates = eventMap.get("updates");
        List<RuleDVO> corrections = eventMap.get("corrections");

        System.out.println("--- alerts ---" + alerts.size() +
                "--- updates ---" + updates.size() +
                "--- corrections ---" + corrections.size() );
        printListData(alerts);
        printListData(updates);
        printListData(corrections);
    }

    /**
     * This method invokes the rule engine.
     *
     * @param reconBean - The input bean with data
     * @param drlFile - The DRL file contains rules
     * @throws Exception - Throws exception if there is any error
     */
    private static void invokeRuleEngine(ReconciliationBean reconBean,
            String drlFile) throws Exception {
        KnowledgeBuilder kbuilder = KnowledgeBuilderFactory.
                newKnowledgeBuilder();
        kbuilder.add(ResourceFactory.newFileResource(drlFile),
                    ResourceType.DRL );
        if(kbuilder.hasErrors()){
            System.out.println(kbuilder.getErrors().toString());
        }
        KnowledgeBase kbase = KnowledgeBaseFactory.newKnowledgeBase();
        kbase.addKnowledgePackages(kbuilder.getKnowledgePackages());
        StatelessKnowledgeSession ksession = kbase.
                newStatelessKnowledgeSession();
```

```
        ksession.execute(Arrays.asList(new Object[]
                          {reconBean, new RuleDVO()}));
    }

    private static void printListData(List<RuleDVO> dataList)  {
        if(dataList != null) {
            for(RuleDVO ruleDVO : dataList) {
                System.out.println( "--- code ---" +
                        ruleDVO.getExceptioncode() );
                System.out.println( "--- field Name  ---" +
                        ruleDVO.getFieldName());
                System.out.println( "--- old Value ---" +
                        ruleDVO.getFieldOldValue());
                System.out.println( "--- New Value ---" +
                        ruleDVO.getFieldNewValue());
            }
        }
    }
}
```

Example 5: The Use of Change Sets while Developing Rules

In previous examples, a single "drl" or "decision table" was loaded into the drocls runtime environment using Drools API. Additionally, it is possible to load set of rule resources into the Drools knowledge base using Drools "changeset" feature. Drools-provided "changeset.xml" file can be used to configure the supported resource types.

In this example, the "changeset.xml" file contains three rule resources we created in previous examples; they are "planstatus.drl", "reconciliation.drl", and "planstatus.xls"

The complete XML configuration is provided below and it is named the "changeset.xml".

```
<change-set xmlns='http://drools.org/drools-5.0/change-set'
    xmlns:xs='http://www.w3.org/2001/XMLSchema-instance'
    xs:schemaLocation='http://drools.org/drools-5.0/changeset.xsd
    http://anonsvn.jboss.org/repos/labs/labs/jbossrules/trunk/
            drools-api/src/main/resources/change-set-1.0.0.xsd'>
    <add>
        <resource source='file:///C:/conf/reconciliation.drl'
                type='DRL'/>

        <resource source='file:///C:/conf/planstatus.drl' type='DRL'/>

        <resource source='file:///C:/conf/planstatus.xls'
                                    type="DTABLE">
            <decisiontable-conf input-type="XLS"
                        worksheet-name="Sheet1"/>
        </resource>
    </add>
</change-set>
```

The specified rule resources in "chageset.xml" file will be loaded into Drools runtime. So the rules are fired automatically based on the matching criteria.

The following Java code fires the rules specified in "planstatus.drl" file.

```java
// Case 1 : Fires planstatus.drl rules
Status status = new Status();
status.setStatus("O");
ksession.execute(Arrays.asList(new Object[] { status }));
System.err.println("--- fianl action ---" + status.getAction());
```

The following Java code fires the rules specified in "reconciliation.drl" file.

```java
// Case 2 : Fires reconciliation.drl rules
ReconciliationBean reconBean = new ReconciliationBean();
reconBean.setPolicyIndicator("YY");
reconBean.setPhoneFlag("4");
reconBean.setPhoneIndicator("Y");
reconBean.setAppraisalType("");
reconBean.setBillMode("9");
reconBean.setBillCycle("H01");
ksession.execute(Arrays.asList(new Object[] {reconBean, new RuleDVO()}));
```

The following Java code fires the rules specified in "planstatus.xls" file.

```java
// Case 3 : Fires planstatus.xls rules
Status status = new Status();
status.setStatus("P");
ksession.execute( Arrays.asList(new Object[] {status}) );
System.err.println("--- Decision Table Output ---"+ status.getAction());
```

In this scenario, add the change set resource type to the knowledge builder. An example code is provided below.

```java
kbuilder.add(ResourceFactory.newFileResource("C:/conf/changeset.xml"),
                    ResourceType.CHANGE_SET);
```

Listing 15-5 provides the complete Java code to fire the rules specified in the three rule resources.

Listing 15-5: Main class used for testing

```java
// TestChangeSet.java
package com.learning.spring.drools;

import java.util.*;

import org.drools.KnowledgeBase;
import org.drools.KnowledgeBaseFactory;
import org.drools.agent.*;
import org.drools.builder.*;
import org.drools.io.ResourceFactory;
import org.drools.runtime.StatelessKnowledgeSession;

public class TestChangeSet {

    public static final void main(String[] args) throws Exception {
        try {
```

```java
            TestChangeSet changeSetTest = new TestChangeSet();
            changeSetTest.executeRules();
        } catch (Exception ex) {
            ex.printStackTrace();
        }
    }


public void executeRules() throws Exception {

    StatelessKnowledgeSession ksession = getKnowledgeSession();

    // Case 1 : Fires planstatus.drl rules
    Status status = new Status();
    status.setStatus("O");
    ksession.execute(Arrays.asList(new Object[] { status }));
    System.out.println("--- fianl action ---"+status.getAction());

    // Case 2 : Fires reconciliation.drl rules
    ReconciliationBean reconBean = new ReconciliationBean();
    reconBean.setPolicyIndicator("YY");
    reconBean.setPhoneFlag("4");
    reconBean.setPhoneIndicator("Y");
    reconBean.setAppraisalType("");
    reconBean.setBillMode("9");
    reconBean.setBillCycle("H01");
    ksession.execute(Arrays.asList(new Object[] {reconBean,
                            new RuleDVO()}));

    // Printing the data on the console
    Map<String, List<RuleDVO>> eventMap = reconBean.getEventMap();
    List<RuleDVO> alerts = eventMap.get("alerts");
    List<RuleDVO> updates = eventMap.get("updates");
    List<RuleDVO> corrections = eventMap.get("corrections");

    System.out.println("--- alerts ---" + alerts.size()
            + "--- updates ---" + updates.size()
            + "--- corrections ---" + corrections.size());

    // Case 3 : Fires planstatus.xls rules
    status = new Status();
    status.setStatus("P");
    ksession.execute( Arrays.asList(new Object[] {status}) );
    System.out.println("--- Decision Table Output ---" +
                    status.getAction());
}

private static StatelessKnowledgeSession getKnowledgeSession()
        throws Exception {
    KnowledgeBuilder kbuilder =
    KnowledgeBuilderFactory.newKnowledgeBuilder();
    kbuilder.add(ResourceFactory.newFileResource(
            "C:/conf/changeset.xml"), ResourceType.CHANGE_SET);
    if( kbuilder.hasErrors() ) {
        System.out.println( kbuilder.getErrors().toString() );
    }
    KnowledgeBase kbase = KnowledgeBaseFactory.newKnowledgeBase();
    kbase.addKnowledgePackages(kbuilder.getKnowledgePackages());
```

```
        StatelessKnowledgeSession ksession =
                        kbase.newStatelessKnowledgeSession();
        return ksession;
    }
}
```

Example 6: Maintaining Rule-specific Business Data Using RMA

This example demonstrates the implementation details of the Rule Maintenance Application (RMA) to update business data. The purpose of RMA is to dynamically update rule-specific business data as per the changes in business requirements. The possible scenarios are listed below.

CASE 1: RMA Implementation for drl-based rules

In this approach, use suitable persistence store such as database to maintain the rule specific business parameters. Application reads the data from database, passes it to the rule engine while executing the rules. Applications provide web pages to update the rule-specific business data.

CASE 2: RMA Implementation for decision table-based rules

In this approach, use suitable Java API to add-modify-delete the excel rows-and-columns. There are several Java API's available to manipulate excel spread sheet content. In this example, the "Apache-poi" API is used to demonstrate the code examples.

The following method adds a new row to the "planstatus.xls" decision table.

```
private static void addingRuleToTheDecisionTable() throws Exception {
    FileInputStream fileInputStream = new FileInputStream(new
                File("C:/conf/planstatus.xls"));
    HSSFWorkbook workbook = new HSSFWorkbook(fileInputStream);
    HSSFSheet worksheet = workbook.getSheet("Sheet1");

    // Getting the last row
    int rowNum = worksheet.getLastRowNum();
    System.out.println("rowNum: " + rowNum);

    // Adding cell data to the last row
    HSSFRow newRow = worksheet.createRow((short) ++rowNum);
    newRow.createCell((short) 1).setCellValue("Suspended");
    newRow.createCell((short) 2).setCellValue("S");
    newRow.createCell((short) 3).setCellValue("SUSPENDED");

    // Data writing to a new file
    FileOutputStream fos = new FileOutputStream
                ("C:/conf/planstatus_rma1.xls", true);
    workbook.write(fos);
    fos.flush();
    fos.close();
}
```

Similarly, the following method updates the decision table cell data.

```
private static void updateDecisionTableRuleData() throws Exception {
    FileInputStream fis = new FileInputStream
```

```
        ("C:/conf/planstatus_rma1.xls");
HSSFWorkbook workbook = new HSSFWorkbook(fis);
HSSFSheet worksheet = workbook.getSheet("Sheet1");

int rowNum = worksheet.getLastRowNum();
System.out.println("rowNum: " + rowNum);

// Reading the last row
HSSFRow row = worksheet.getRow(rowNum);

// Getting the 1st cell
HSSFCell cell1 = row.getCell((short) 1);
String cel1Value = cell1.getStringCellValue();

// Getting the 2nd cell
HSSFCell cell2 = row.getCell((short) 2);
String cel2Value = cell2.getStringCellValue();

// Getting the 3rd cell- Setting the new value
HSSFCell cell3 = row.getCell((short) 3);
cell3.setCellValue("POST_SUSPENDED");

// Updated data writing to a new file.
FileOutputStream fos = new FileOutputStream
        ("C:/conf/planstatus_rma2.xls", true);
workbook.write(fos);
fos.flush();
fos.close();
}
```

Spring Integration with Drools Expert

Drools provided `<xmlns:drools>` namespace can be used to integrate the Drools with spring framework. The Drools provided XML tags are similar to spring tags, and they can use along with spring tags in application context XML files.

The following XML tag is used to define a rule resource in spring.

```
<drools:resource id="planStatusDRL" type="DRL"
            source="classpath:planstatus.drl"/>
```

The following XML tag is used to define the Drools knowledge base.

```
<drools:kbase id="knowledgeBase">
    ...
</drools:kbase>
```

The following XML tag is used to define the Drools knowledge session. Application uses this session to execute the rules.

```
<drools:ksession id="knowledgeSession" type="stateless"
                kbase="knowledgeBase"/>
```

Example 7: Spring Integration with Drools Expert

This example illustrates the Drools integration with spring framework. Here, reuse the previously created "drl" and "xls" files to test the rules.

Add the following list of JAR files to the application classpath to run this example.

- drools-grid-impl-5.2.0.Final.jar
- commons-logging.jar and
- Core spring framework provided JARs.

The steps required to integrate Drools with Spring are listed below.

1. Create a spring application context file.
2. Reuse the created "drl" and "xls" files.
3. Write a Java class to test the rules.

The above-specified steps are described in the following sections:

Step 1: Create a spring application context file

The complete spring application context XML file is provided below; named the "drools-spring.xml".

```xml
<?xml version="1.0" encoding="UTF-8"?>
<beans xmlns="http://www.springframework.org/schema/beans"
    xmlns:xsi="http://www.w3.org/2001/XMLSchema-instance"
    xmlns:drools="http://drools.org/schema/drools-spring"
    xsi:schemaLocation="http://www.springframework.org/schema/beans
    http://www.springframework.org/schema/beans/spring-beans-3.0.xsd
    http://drools.org/schema/drools-spring
    http://drools.org/schema/drools-spring.xsd">

    <drools:resource id="planStatusDRL" type="DRL"
                     source="classpath:planstatus.drl"/>

    <drools:resource id="reconciliationDRL" type="DRL"
                     source="classpath:reconciliation.drl"/>

    <drools:resource id="planStatusXLS" type="DTABLE"
                source="classpath:planstatus.xls">
        <drools:decisiontable-conf input-type="XLS"
                                   worksheet-name="Sheet1"/>
    </drools:resource>

    <drools:kbase id="knowledgeBase">
        <drools:resources>
            <drools:resource ref="planStatusDRL" />
            <drools:resource ref="reconciliationDRL" />
            <drools:resource ref="planStatusXLS" />
        </drools:resources>
        <drools:configuration>
            <drools:mbeans enabled="true" />
            <drools:event-processing-mode mode="STREAM" />
        </drools:configuration>
    </drools:kbase>
```

```
        <drools:ksession id="knowledgeSession" type="stateless"
                        kbase="knowledgeBase"/>
</beans>
```

Step 2: Reuse the created "drl" and "xls" file.

Here, reuse the rule resources created in previous examples. The following list of the rule resources are configured in spring.

- planstatus.drl
- reconciliation.drl
- planstatus.xls

Step 3: Write a Java class to test the rules.

Listing 15-6 provides the complete class code. Run the following Java class to view the output on the console. This class invokes the rules defined in the corresponding rule resources.

Listing 15-6: Main class used for testing

```java
// TestSpringIntegraton.java
package com.learning.spring.drools;

import java.util.*;
import org.drools.runtime.StatelessKnowledgeSession;
import org.springframework.context.support.
                ClassPathXmlApplicationContext;

public class TestSpringIntegraton {

    public static void main(String[] args) {
        try {
            test();
        } catch (Exception ex) {
            ex.printStackTrace();
        }
    }

    private static void test() throws Exception {
        ClassPathXmlApplicationContext context = new
            ClassPathXmlApplicationContext("drools-spring.xml");
        StatelessKnowledgeSession ksession =
                (StatelessKnowledgeSession)
                    context.getBean("knowledgeSession");

        // Case 1 : Fires planstatus.drl rules
        Status status = new Status();
        status.setStatus("T");
        ksession.execute(Arrays.asList(new Object[] { status }));
        System.out.println("--- Final Action is ---" +
            status.getAction());

        // Case 2 : Fires reconciliation.drl rules
        ReconciliationBean reconBean = new ReconciliationBean();
        reconBean.setPolicyIndicator("YY");
```

```
reconBean.setPhoneFlag("4");
reconBean.setPhoneIndicator("Y");
reconBean.setAppraisalType("");
reconBean.setBillMode("9");
reconBean.setBillCycle("H01");
ksession.execute(Arrays.asList(new Object[]
            {reconBean, new RuleDVO()}));

// Printing the data on the console
Map<String, List<RuleDVO>> eventMap = reconBean.getEventMap();
List<RuleDVO> alerts = eventMap.get("alerts");
List<RuleDVO> updates = eventMap.get("updates");
List<RuleDVO> corrections = eventMap.get("corrections");

System.out.println("--- alerts ---" + alerts.size()
        + "--- updates ---" + updates.size()
        + "--- corrections ---" + corrections.size());

// Case 3 : Fires planstatus.xls rules
status = new Status();
status.setStatus("P");
ksession.execute( Arrays.asList(new Object[] {status}) );
System.err.println("--- Decision Table Output ---" +
        status.getAction());
    }
}
```

Summary

Figure 15-3 summarizes the most important points described in this chapter.

Figure 15-3: Drools Expert summary

This section summarizes the Drools rule engine features and Spring support for Drools integration.

- Drools-provided `<xmlns:drools>` namespace can be used to integrate the Drools with spring framework.
- Drools rule engine provides support for writing rules in various forms; they are DRL, Decision Tables, and DSL.
- Drools-provided "changeset" feature can be used to load set of rule resources into the Drools knowledge. The "changeset.xml" file can be used to configure the resource types.

Chapter 16. Spring-Mail

Java-Mail is a Java API used to send-and-receive email messages. Application developers can enable the email functionality using Java mail API. Java mail is part of Java EE. Spring provides a high level API, which hides the low level details of the Java mail API and provides utility classes to enable email functionality within your application.

This chapter will discuss the following topics:

- The primary spring-provided API classes and their use.
- Configuring mail session with application server.
- Spring configurations for sending email messages.
- Spring support for sending email messages with attachments.
- Spring support for sending email messages using velocity templates.

Primary Spring-provided Mail Classes

- `SimpleMailMessage`—models a simple mail message with data such as from, to, cc, bcc, sent date, subject, and text.
- `MailSender`—this interface is used for sending simple email messages that does not have any advanced features.
- `JavaMailSender`—models a mail message with advanced features such as, attachments and MIME type messages.
- `JavaMailSenderImpl`—this class implements `MailSender` and `JavaMailSender` interfaces. This class encapsulates the properties such as, container-specific mail session, host, port, protocol, username, and password.
- `MimeMessagePreparator`—this is a callback interface used for preparing MIME messages.
- `MimeMessageHelper`—helper class used to send MIME messages. This class provides support for HTML messages, velocity and Freemarler templates, images, and attachments.

The examples provided in this chapter illustrate the use of above-specified classes and interfaces.

Prerequisites/Setting Up the Environment

The following instructions are valid only for the Weblogic application server. But, these configurations are similar for any Java EE-specific application server.

The step-by-step instructions are provided below.

- Open your weblogic console — http://localhost:7001/console
- Login-in to the weblogic domain — enter your weblogic domain's user-id and password.
- Navigate to Services → Mail Sessions
- Create a new Mail Session; target this to "AdminServer"
- Enter mail session name, JNDI Name and mail server properties.

An example mail session configuration properties are provided below:

- Name → MyMailSession
- JNDI Name → mail/maildemo
- Mail server properties → mail.host=spo.mymail.com (mail server name)

Advantages of Spring Mail

This section illustrates the technical and non-technical features of spring mail messaging framework.

- Spring provides support for both standalone and Java EE-specific mail sessions.
- Spring provides a simplified high level API, hides the low level details of the Java mail API.

Demo Examples

Example 1: Sending Mail using Standalone Client

The steps required to create a standalone mail client for sending simple mail messages are listed below. This example sends a simple text message without any attachments.

1. Create an "applicationContext-mail.xml" file.
2. Create a standalone mail client class.

The above-specified steps are described in the following sections:

Step 1: Create an "applicationContext-mail.xml" file.

Configure the mail server-related configurations in spring application context XML file. The complete application context file is provided below and it is named the "applicationContext-mail.xml".

```
<?xml version="1.0" encoding="UTF-8"?>
<beans xmlns="http://www.springframework.org/schema/beans"
    xmlns:xsi="http://www.w3.org/2001/XMLSchema-instance"
    xmlns:context="http://www.springframework.org/schema/context"
    xsi:schemaLocation="http://www.springframework.org/schema/beans
    http://www.springframework.org/schema/beans/spring-beans-3.0.xsd
    http://www.springframework.org/schema/context
    http://www.springframework.org/schema/context/
        spring-context-3.0.xsd">

    <context:annotation-config/>

    <context:component-scan base-package="com.learning.spring.mail"/>

    <bean id="mailSender" class=
            "org.springframework.mail.javamail.JavaMailSenderImpl">
        <property name="host" value="spo.mymail.com"/>
```

```
        </bean>

        <!-- This is a template message with default properties -->
        <bean id="templateMessage" class=
                    "org.springframework.mail.SimpleMailMessage">
            <property name="from" value="mudunuri@mymail.com"/>
            <property name="subject" value="This is a test message "/>
        </bean>

        <bean id="mailMan" class="com.learning.spring.mail.MailMan">
            <property name="mailSender" ref="mailSender"/>
            <property name="templateMessage" ref="templateMessage"/>
        </bean>
</beans>
```

NOTE: Make sure you have the access to your mail server in your network.

Step 2: Create a standalone mail client class.

The following standalone client can be used to send mail messages. The complete standalone class code is provided in Listing 16-1.

Listing 16-1: Standalone client code.

```java
// MailMan.java
package com.learning.spring.mail;

import org.springframework.mail.SimpleMailMessage;
import org.springframework.mail.MailSender;
import org.springframework.context.ApplicationContext;
import org.springframework.context.support.
        ClassPathXmlApplicationContext;
import org.springframework.stereotype.Component;

@Component
public class MailMan {

    private MailSender mailSender;
    private SimpleMailMessage templateMessage;

    public static void main(String args[]) {
        String[] paths = {"applicationContext-mail.xml"};
        ApplicationContext appContext = new
                ClassPathXmlApplicationContext(paths);
        MailMan mailMan = (MailMan) appContext.getBean("mailMan");
        mailMan.sendMail();
    }

    public void sendMail() {
        SimpleMailMessage msg = new
                SimpleMailMessage(this.templateMessage);
        msg.setTo("achyutha.s.mudunuri@wellsfargo.com");
        msg.setText(" This is a test message ");
```

```
        mailSender.send(msg);
    }

    public void setMailSender(MailSender mailSender) {
        this.mailSender = mailSender;
    }

    public void setTemplateMessage(SimpleMailMessage templateMessage) {
        this.templateMessage = templateMessage;
    }
}
```

Example 2: Sending Mail using Java EE Mail Session

The steps required to create a standalone mail client are listed below:

1. Configure a mail session with your application server
2. Create an "applicationContext-mail.xml" file.
3. Create a standalone mail client class.

The above-specified steps are described in the following sections:

Step 1: Configure a mail session with your application server

Here, follow the instructions provided in pre-requisite and setting-up the environment section.

Step 2: Create an applicationContext-mail.xml file.

Here, reuse the XML file provided in Example-1 with the following modifications.

```
<bean id="mailSession" class="org.springframework.jndi.
                             JndiObjectFactoryBean">
    <property name="jndiName" value="mail/maildemo"/>
    <property name="resourceRef" value="true"/>
</bean>

<bean id="mailSender" class= "org.springframework.mail.javamail.
                             JavaMailSenderImpl">
    <property name="session" ref="mailSession"/>
</bean>
```

Step 3: Create a Client class

Here, reuse the MailMan class provided in Example-1. Alternatively, you can auto-wire the mail man component into a spring controller class. An example spring controller class is provided below.

```
@Controller
public class SpringMessagingDemoController {

    @Autowired
    private MailMan mailMan;

    @RequestMapping(value="/demo/messageSender.action",
                    method=RequestMethod.POST)
```

```java
    public String show(HttpServletRequest request, ModelMap model) {
        try {
            mailMan.sendMail();
        } catch (Exception ex) {
            ex.printStackTrace();
        }

        request.setAttribute("name", "Success");
        return "demo/success";
    }
}
```

NOTE: In this scenario, make sure "applicationContext-mail.xml" file is loaded in "web.xml"

Example 3: Sending Mail with Attachments

The following example illustrates how to send mail messages with attachments. The steps required to create a standalone mail client are listed below.

1. Create an "applicationContext-mail-attchment.xml" file.
2. Create a standalone mail client class.

The above-specified steps are described in the following sections:

Step 1: Create an applicationContext-mail-attchment.xml file.

The complete application context file is provided below and it is named the "applicationContext-mail-attchment.xml"

```xml
<?xml version="1.0" encoding="UTF-8"?>
<beans xmlns="http://www.springframework.org/schema/beans"
    xmlns:xsi="http://www.w3.org/2001/XMLSchema-instance"
    xmlns:context="http://www.springframework.org/schema/context"
    xsi:schemaLocation="http://www.springframework.org/schema/beans
    http://www.springframework.org/schema/beans/spring-beans-3.0.xsd
    http://www.springframework.org/schema/context
    http://www.springframework.org/schema/context/
        spring-context-3.0.xsd">

    <bean id="mailSender" class=
        "org.springframework.mail.javamail.JavaMailSenderImpl">
        <property name="host" value="spo.wellsfargo.com"/>
    </bean>

    <bean id="attachmentMailMan"
            class="com.learning.spring.mail.AttachmentMailMan">
        <property name="mailSender" ref="mailSender"/>
    </bean>

</beans>
```

Step 2: Create a standalone mail client class.

The following standalone client can be used to send mail messages with attachments. The complete standalone class code is provided in Listing 16-2.

Listing 16-2: Mail with attachments

```java
// AttachmentMailMan.java
package com.learning.spring.mail;

import org.springframework.mail.javamail.JavaMailSenderImpl;
import org.springframework.mail.javamail.MimeMessageHelper;
import org.springframework.context.ApplicationContext;
import org.springframework.context.support.ClassPathXmlApplicationContext;
import org.springframework.core.io.FileSystemResource;
import javax.mail.internet.MimeMessage;
import java.io.File;

public class AttachmentMailMan {

    private JavaMailSenderImpl mailSender;

    public static void main(String args[]) {
        try {
            String[] paths = {"applicationContext-mail-
                                    attachments.xml"};
            ApplicationContext appContext = new
                ClassPathXmlApplicationContext(paths);
            AttachmentMailMan mailMan = (AttachmentMailMan)
                appContext.getBean("attachmentMailMan");

            mailMan.sendMail();
        } catch (Exception ex) {
            ex.printStackTrace();
        }
    }

    public void sendMail() throws Exception {
        MimeMessage message = mailSender.createMimeMessage();

        MimeMessageHelper helper =
                new MimeMessageHelper(message, true);
        helper.setTo("mudunuri@cox.com");
        helper.setText("Sending an image ....");

        FileSystemResource file = new FileSystemResource(new
                                    File("c:/myphoto.jpg"));
        helper.addAttachment("myphoto.jpg", file);

        mailSender.send(message);
    }

    public void setMailSender(JavaMailSenderImpl mailSender) {
        this.mailSender = mailSender;
    }
}
```

Example 4: Sending Mail using Velocity Mail Templates

The following example illustrates how to send mail messages using velocity templates. The steps required to create a standalone mail client are listed below.

1. Create an "applicationContext-mail-velocity.xml" file.
2. Create a standalone mail client class.

The above-specified steps are described in the following sections:

Step 1: Create an applicationContext-mail-velocity.xml file.

The complete application context file is provided below and it is named the "applicationContext-mail-velocity.xml"

```xml
<?xml version="1.0" encoding="UTF-8"?>
<beans xmlns="http://www.springframework.org/schema/beans"
    xmlns:xsi="http://www.w3.org/2001/XMLSchema-instance"
    xmlns:context="http://www.springframework.org/schema/context"
    xsi:schemaLocation="http://www.springframework.org/schema/beans
    http://www.springframework.org/schema/beans/spring-beans-3.0.xsd
    http://www.springframework.org/schema/context
    http://www.springframework.org/schema/context/
             spring-context-3.0.xsd">

    <bean id="mailSender" class=
            "org.springframework.mail.javamail.JavaMailSenderImpl">
        <property name="host" value="spo.wellsfargo.com"/>
    </bean>

    <bean id="velocityMailMan" class="com.learning.spring.mail.
                                    VelocityMailMan">
        <property name="mailSender" ref="mailSender"/>
        <property name="velocityEngine" ref="velocityEngine"/>
    </bean>

    <bean id="velocityEngine" class=
        "org.springframework.ui.velocity.VelocityEngineFactoryBean">
        <property name="velocityProperties">
            <value>
                resource.loader=class
                class.resource.loader.class=
                    org.apache.velocity.runtime.resource.loader.
                    ClasspathResourceLoader
            </value>
        </property>
    </bean>

    <bean id="velocityConfig" class="org.springframework.web.servlet.
                view.velocity.VelocityConfigurer">
        <property name="resourceLoaderPath" value="C:/vmtest"/>
    </bean>
</beans>
```

The velocity template (customer.vm) code is provided below. This template has customer name and email address.

```
<html>
    <body>
        <div>
            Customer name is: $customer.firstName$customer.lastName
            Email address is: $customer.emailAddress
        </div>
    </body>
</html>
```

NOTE: Make sure "C:/vmtest" directory is added to your classpath. The "customer.vm" file should be placed inside the "C:/vmtest" directory.

Step 2: Create a standalone mail client class.

The following standalone client can be used to send mail messages using velocity templates. The velocity template engine applies the business data to the velocity template. Velocity-provided utilities can be used to convert velocity template into a plain text. The complete standalone class code is provided in Listing 16-3.

Listing 16-3: Mail with velocity templates

```java
// VelocityMailMan.java
package com.learning.spring.mail;

import org.apache.velocity.app.VelocityEngine;
import org.springframework.context.ApplicationContext;
import
org.springframework.context.support.ClassPathXmlApplicationContext;
import org.springframework.mail.javamail.*;
import javax.mail.internet.MimeMessage;
import org.springframework.ui.velocity.VelocityEngineUtils;
import java.util.*;

public class VelocityMailMan {
    private VelocityEngine velocityEngine;
    private JavaMailSenderImpl mailSender;

    public static void main(String args[]) {
        String[] paths = {"applicationContext-mail-velocity.xml"};
        ApplicationContext appContext = new
            ClassPathXmlApplicationContext(paths);
        VelocityMailMan velocityMailMan = (VelocityMailMan)
            appContext.getBean("velocityMailMan");

        Customer customer = new Customer();
        customer.setFirstName("Srinivas");
        customer.setLastName("Mudunuri");
        customer.setEmailAddress("Achyutha.S.Mudunuri@cox.com");
        velocityMailMan.sendConfirmationEmail(customer);
    }

    private void sendConfirmationEmail(final Customer customer) {
        MimeMessagePreparator preparator=
            new MimeMessagePreparator() {
```

```java
        public void prepare(MimeMessage mimeMessage) throws
                                        Exception {
            MimeMessageHelper message = new
            MimeMessageHelper(mimeMessage);
            message.setTo(customer.getEmailAddress());
            message.setFrom("achyutha.s.mudunuri@cox.com");

            // map contains data
            Map model = new HashMap();
            model.put("customer", customer);

            String text = VelocityEngineUtils.
                    mergeTemplateIntoString(velocityEngine,
                        "customer.vm", model);
            System.out.println("- print your content here --"
                                + text);
            message.setText(text, true);
          }
      };
    mailSender.send(preparator);
  }

  public void setMailSender(JavaMailSenderImpl mailSencer) {
      this.mailSender = mailSender;
  }

  public void setVelocityEngine(VelocityEngine velocityEngine) {
      this.velocityEngine = velocityEngine;
  }
}
```

Summary

Figure 16-1: Spring mail summary

Figure 16-1 summarizes the most important points described in this chapter.

This section summarizes the provided features of the Spring-Mail framework.

- How to configure a mail session with applications server.
- Sending email messages with and without attachments.
- Sending email messages using velocity templates.

Chapter 17. Annotations, Namespaces and Templates

This chapter illustrates the commonly used Spring annotations, namespaces and template classes. The purpose of this chapter is to provide a quick reference to the complete spring framework. Refer to the corresponding chapters for complete details.

This chapter will discuss the following topics:

- The Spring-provided annotations and their use
- The Spring-provided namespaces and their use
- The Spring-provided templates and their use

Spring-Core Annotations

This section illustrates the commonly used spring core annotations.

@Required

This annotation is used with the bean property setter methods. It forces you to inject the object references using setter methods during the configuration time to avoid the runtime exceptions. The following example demonstrates the use of the `@Required` annotation. In this example, the `@Required`-annotation is applied to the setter method of a bean class.

```
public class StockQuoteService {
    private StockQuoteDAO stockQuoteDAO;

    @Required
    public void setStockQuoteDAO(StockQuoteDAO stockQuoteDAO) {
        this.stockQuoteDAO = stockQuoteDAO;
    }
}
```

The corresponding application context XML configuration is provided below.

```
<bean id="stockQuoteService" class="com.learning.spring.core.
                                    StockQuoteService">
    <property name="stockQuoteDAO" ref="stockQuoteDAO" />
</bean>

<bean id="stockQuoteDAO" class="com.learning.spring.core.StockQuoteDAO"/>
```

@Autowired

This annotation can be applied to setter methods, constructors, and fields of a bean class to inject the object references. The following example demonstrates the use of the `@Autowired` annotation. In this example, the `@Autowired` annotation is applied to the setter method of a bean class. The spring container creates a `StockQuoteDAO` object reference and injects this object into `StockQuoteService` using the setter method.

```
public class StockQuoteService {

    @Autowired
    private StockQuoteDAO stockQuoteDAO;

    @Required
    public void setStockQuoteDAO(StockQuoteDAO stockQuoteDAO) {
        this.stockQuoteDAO = stockQuoteDAO;
    }
}
```

@Qualifier

This annotation can be applied to classes, methods, fields, constructors, and parameters of a bean class to allow for greater control in using the correct reference types. The following example demonstrates the use of the `@Qualifier` annotation. In this example, the `@Qualifier` annotation is applied to the member of a class.

```
public class StockQuoteService {

    @Autowired
    @Qualifier("stockDAO")
    private StockQuoteDAO stockQuoteDAO;

    public void setStockQuoteDAO(StockQuoteDAO stockQuoteDAO) {
        this.stockQuoteDAO = stockQuoteDAO;
    }
}
```

The corresponding `StockQuoteDAO` class definition is provided below.

```
@Qualifier("stockDAO")
public class StockQuoteDAO {
    ...
}
```

@Component

This annotation applies to classes and indicates that the annotated class is a component. Spring provides specialized component-annotated classes such as `@Controller`, `@Service`, `@Repository`, and `@Endpoint`. These component-annotated classes are eligible for component scanning using the spring-provided `<context:component-scan/>` XML tag. The component-annotated classes can be auto-detected using annotation-based configurations. The following example demonstrates the use of the `@Component`-annotation.

```
@Component
public class StockQuoteService {
    ...
```

```
}
```

Similarly, the following example demonstrates the use of the `@Controller`-annotation for a web controller class.

```
@Controller
public class LoginController {

    @RequestMapping(value = "/demo/login.action",
                    method = RequestMethod.POST)
    public String show(HttpServletRequest request, ModelMap model) {
        ...
    }
}
```

@Bean

This annotation is used at the method level. The `@Bean`-annotated method represents a spring-managed bean that can be used for injection. An example of this annotation's use is provided below. The `@Bean`-annotated method is equivalent to the `<bean/>` element in XML-based configuration.

```
public class ApplicationConfig {

    @Bean
    public StockQuoteDAO stockQuoteDAO() {
        return new StockQuoteDAO();
    }
}
```

@Configuration

This annotation is used at the class level. The `@Configuration`-annotated class can be used as a container to configure other spring-managed bean classes. An example of this annotation's use is provided below. The `@Configuration`-annotated class is equivalent to the `<beans/>` element in XML-based configuration.

```
@Configuration
public class ApplicationConfig {

    @Bean
    public StockQuoteDAO stockQuoteDAO() {
        return new StockQuoteDAO();
    }

    @Bean
    public StockQuoteService stockQuoteService() {
        return new StockQuoteService(stockQuoteDAO());
    }
}
```

@Service

This annotation is used at the class level. Spring container automatically detects the @Service-annotated classes and registers them with the application context. The @Service-annotated classes are eligible for auto-scanning using <context:component-scan/> XML configuration. An example use of this annotation is provided below.

```
@Service
public class StockQuoteService {

    @Autowired
    private StockQuoteDAO stockQuoteDAO;

    public void setStockQuoteDAO(StockQuoteDAO stockQuoteDAO) {
        this.stockQuoteDAO = stockQuoteDAO;
    }
}
```

@Value

The @Value annotation can be used with bean methods, fields, and constructor and method parameters to set a specified value. In this example, SpEL is used to set the data.

The following code is used to set the bean object.

```
@Value("#{subjects}")
private Subjects subjects
```

The following code is used to set the bean property value.

```
@Value("#{subjects.primary}")
private String primarySubject;
```

The complete Grade bean class code is provided below.

```
public class Grade {

    @Value("#{subjects}")
    private Subjects subjects;

    @Value("#{subjects.primary}")
    private String primarySubject;
}
```

@Import

This annotation is used at the class level to load the bean definitions from some other class. An example use of this annotation is provided below.

```
@Configuration
public class MyBeanOne {
```

```
    public @Bean MyBeanOne myBeanOne() {
        return new MyBeanOne();
    }
}
```

The below provided bean class imports the `MyBeanOne` class.

```
@Configuration
@Import(MyBeanOne.class)
public class MyBeanTwo {
    public @Bean MyBeanTwo myBeanTwo() {
        return new MyBeanTwo();
    }
}
```

@ImportResource

The `@ImporResource`-annotation is used at the class level to load the resources. An example use of this annotation is provided below.

```
@Configuration
@ImportResource("classpath:database-properties.xml")
public class StockQuoteDAO {
    private @Value("${jdbc.url}") String url;
    private @Value("${jdbc.username}") String username;
    private @Value("${jdbc.password}") String password;

    ...
}
```

An example "database-properties.xml" file is provided below.

```
<beans ...>
    <context:component-scan
            base-package="com.learning.spring.core.java"/>

    <context:property-placeholder
            location="classpath:database.properties"/>
</beans>
```

The equivalent XML configuration is provided below.

```
<context:property-placeholder location="classpath:database.properties"/>

<bean id="driverManager" class="org.springframework.jdbc.
                    datasource.DriverManagerDataSource">
    <property name="url" value="${jdbc.url}"/>
    <property name="username" value="${jdbc.username}"/>
    <property name="password" value="${jdbc.password}"/>
</bean>
```

@DependsOn

This annotation is used to specify the bean metadata. The `@DependsOn`-annotation of a bean can be used to initialize the all dependent beans. An example use of this annotation is provided below.

```
@Configuration
public class AppConfig {

    @Bean
    @DependsOn("myBeanOne")
    public StockQuoteDAO stockQuoteDAO() {
        return new StockQuoteDAO();
    }

    @Bean
    public MyBeanOne myBeanOne() {
        return new MyBeanOne();
    }
}
```

The equivalent XML configuration is provided below.

```
<bean id="stockQuoteDAO" class="com.learning.spring.core.StockQuoteDAO"
    depends-on="myBeanOne">
    ...
</bean>

<bean id="myBeanOne" class="com.learning.spring.core.MyBeanOne"/>
```

@Scope

This annotation is used to specify the bean metadata. The valid scope values are "singleton", "prototype", "request", "session" and "global session". An example use of this annotation is provided below.

```
@Component
@Scope("prototype")
public class StockQuoteService {
    ...
}
```

The equivalent XML configuration is provided below.

```
<bean id="stockData"
    class="com.learning.spring.core.StockQuoteService "
    scope="protoype">
```

@Lazy

This annotation is used to specify the bean metadata. This option enables the beans to be created when it is requested. An example use of this annotation is provided below.

```
@Bean
@Lazy(false)
public MyBeanOne myBeanOne() {
    return new MyBeanOne();
}
```

JSR-250 Annotations

JSR 250: The annotations defined in this JSR (provided below) are used for resource injection and bean life cycle management.

- javax.annotation.PostConstruct
- javax.annotation.PreDestroy
- javax.annotation.Resource

@PostConstruct

This annotation is used at the method level to perform the required initialization. The method annotated using the @PostConstruct is called after the default constructor. The following example demonstrates the @PostConstruct annotation's use. In this example, the @PostConstruct annotation is applied to the "init()" method of an EmployeeServiceImpl class to perform the required initialization.

```
public class EmployeeServiceImpl {

    public EmployeeServiceImpl() {
        System.out.println("--- Constructor called ---");
    }

    @PostConstruct
    private void init() {
        System.out.println("--- Perform required initialization ---");
    }
}
```

@PreDestroy

This annotation is used at method level to perform cleanup activities such as releasing the resources the process is holding. The method annotated with @PreDestroy is a callback method managed by the container. The following example demonstrates the @PreDestroy annotation's use. In this example, the @PreDestroy annotation is applied to the "doCleanUp()" method of a bean class to perform the required cleanup activity.

```
public class EmployeeServiceImpl {

    @PreDestroy
    private void doCleanUp() {
        System.out.println("-- Perform clean-up after you are done with
        it -");
    }
```

```
}
```

@Resource

This annotation can be applied to setter methods or fields of a spring-managed bean class. This is an annotation commonly used in Java-EE to obtain the information related to the web services context, message context, JNDI names, user principle, and role. This annotation can be used with spring-managed beans. The following example demonstrates the use of the `@Resource` annotation. In this example, the `@Resource` annotation is applied to the setter method of a spring managed bean.

```
// EmployeeServiceImpl.java
package com.learning.spring.core.java;

import javax.annotation.Resource;

public class EmployeeServiceImpl {

    private EmployeeDAO employeeDAO;

    @Resource
    public void setEmployeeDAO(EmployeeDAO employeeDAO) {
        this.employeeDAO = employeeDAO;
    }

    public void printData() {
        System.out.println(employeeDAO.getData());
    }
}
```

Spring-MVC Annotations

This section illustrates the commonly used Spring-MVC annotations and they are listed below.

- @Controller
- @RequestMapping
- @ModelAttribute
- @RequestParam

@Controller

The `@Controller` annotation is used at the class level. The class annotated with `@Controller` is a web application controller. The `@Controller`-annotated classes are eligible for component scanning using the spring-provided "<context: component-scan/>" XML tag. This annotation is used with `@RequestMapping` annotation to handle the web requests. An example of a `@Controller` annotation's use is provided below.

```
@Controller
public class JSPDemoController {
```

```
        public ModelAndView view() {
            ...
        }
}
```

@RequestMapping

The @RequestMapping annotation can be used at the class level and method level. This annotation maps the http-requests to specific controller classes and controller class methods. @RequestMapping-annotated methods may have various supported method parameters and return values. The supported method parameters are HttpServletRequest, HttpSession, @RequestParam, @ModelAttribute, ModelMap, BindingResult, and so forth. The supported return values are String, ModelAndView, Model, and so on.

The following updatePricing(...) method is annotated with @RequestMapping annotation. An example of the use of a @RequestMapping-annotation is given below.

```
@RequestMapping(value = "/main/updateData.action",
            method = RequestMethod.POST)
public String updatePricing(
    @ModelAttribute("custProfile") CustomerProfile custProfile,
    @ModelAttribute("loan") Loan loan,
    @ModelAttribute("line") Line line,
    BindingResult result, ModelMap model) {

    ...

    return "main/layout_main";
}
```

Another example of @RequestMapping annotated method signature is provided below.

```
@RequestMapping(value = "/main/showTestPage.action",
            method = RequestMethod.POST)
public String show(HttpServletRequest request, ModelMap model) {

    ...

    return "main/layout_main";
}
```

@ModelAttribute

The @ModelAttribute annotation can be used for method parameters and return values. This annotation binds the method parameter and return value to a model object. An example of the use of a @ModelAttribute-annotation is given below.

```
public String updatePricing(
    @ModelAttribute("custProfile") CustomerProfile custProfile,
    @ModelAttribute("loan") Loan loan,
    @ModelAttribute("line") Line line,
    BindingResult result, ModelMap model) {
```

```
...

        return "main/layout_main";
}
```

@RequestParam

The @RequestParam annotation is used with method parameters. This annotation binds the HTTP-request parameter values to annotated method parameters. An example of the use of a @RequestParam-annotation is given below.

```
@Controller
public class SimpleDemoController {

    @RequestMapping(value = "/demo/validLogin.action",
                    method = RequestMethod.POST)
    public String show(@RequestParam("userName") String userId,
                       @RequestParam("passCode") String passCode,
                       ModelMap model) {
            ...

        return "demo/success";
    }
}
```

Spring-JDBC and Transaction Annotations

This section illustrates the commonly used Spring-JDBC annotations and they are listed below.

- @Repository
- @Transactional

@Repository

The @Repository annotated class is a special type of component class used for data access components. The @Repository-annotated classes are eligible for auto-scanning using the spring-provided <context:component-scan> configuration. An example use of this annotation is provided below.

```
@Repository
public class PetDAOImpl implements PetDAO {

    @Autowired
    private HibernateTemplate hibernateTemplate;

    public PetDVO getPeyByName(final String name) {
        final String HQL_GET_PET_DATA_BY_NAME =
                "from PetDVO p where p.name = '" + name + "'";
        List<PetDVO> petList = hibernateTemplate.
```

```
                        find(HQL_GET_PET_DATA_BY_NAME);
        return petList.get(0);
    }
}
```

@Transactional

The `@Transactional` annotation with `<tx:annotation-driven>` XML configuration provides the transactional behavior to the annotated methods. The `@Transactional` annotation is used to specify the metadata required for the runtime infrastructure in managing transactions. This annotation can be used with interfaces, methods of an interface, classes, and methods of a class. The `<tx:annotation-driven>` element enables the annotation-based transactional behavior, and this tag looks for only `@Transactional`-annotated methods or classes.

The following XML element enables the annotation-based transaction behavior.

```
<tx:annotation-driven transaction-manager="txManager"/>
```

The default `@Transactional`-annotation properties are listed below.

- Transaction Propagation = REQUIRED
- Isolation level = DEFAULT
- Rollback-for = Any runtime exception triggers a transaction rollback

The following code demonstrates the use of `@Transactional`-annotation.

```
@Transactional(readOnly = false)
public void doInsertAndUpdateInTx() {

    // Insert a record
    insertPet(petDVO);

    // Update a record
    updatePetData("Steven Sun", "Buffy");
}
```

Spring-Web Services Annotations

This section illustrates the commonly used spring web services annotations and they are listed below.

- @Endpoint
- @PayloadRoot
- @RequestPayload
- @ResponsePayload

@Endpoint

This annotation is used at class level to mark the class as a Web Service endpoint. The class annotated with `@Endpoint` annotation is used to receive the inbound XML requests from the clients. The annotated class can have one or more methods to receive the request payloads; and sends the response back to the invoking clients. The Web service endpoint operations processes the incoming XML; and prepare the response XML based on the input received from the service client. The class annotated with `@Endpoint` is a special kind of Spring component suitable to handle the XML requests-and-responses. The `@Endpoint`-annotated classes are eligible for component scanning using spring-provided "<context: component-scan/>" xml tag.

The use of the `@Endpoint`-annotation is provided below.

```
@Endpoint
public class EmployeeEndPoint {
    // ...
}
```

@RequestPayload

This annotation is used with method parameters to receive the request XML messages. It maps the method parameter to the incoming message payload. The use of the `@RequestPayload` annotation is given below.

```
public Element getEmployee(@RequestPayload Element employeeRequest)
throws Exception {
    ...
}
```

The entire input request "<getEmployeeRequest/>" is wrapped inside the "<soap:body/>" element of the soap message. A sample request payload is given below:

```
<getEmployeeRequest xmlns="http://springws.ws.learning.com/emp/schemas">
    <employee>
        <employeeId>6666666</employeeId>
    </employee>
</getEmployeeRequest>
```

@PayloadRoot

This annotation is used at method-level to route the incoming request XML messages. It routes the incoming messages to the appropriate method of the service endpoint class. Based on the incoming message "namespace" and its "local name" it decides which method to execute. This annotation is used to identify which method of the service endpoint to be executed based on the message payload.

An example input request message is provided below. The local name is "getEmployeeRequest" and its namespace is "http://springws.ws.learning.com/emp/schemas"; so it will invoke the "getEmployee()" method of the web service endpoint.

```
<getEmployeeRequest xmlns="http://springws.ws.learning.com/emp/schemas">
    <employee>
```

```
        <employeeId>6666666</employeeId>
    </employee>
</getEmployeeRequest>
```

The corresponding web service method signature for the above-specified request payload is provided below.

```
@PayloadRoot(namespace = "http://springws.ws.learning.com/emp/schemas",
             localPart="getEmployeeRequest")
public Element getEmployee(@RequestPayload Element employeeRequest)
throws Exception {
}
```

@ResponsePayload

This annotation is used at method-level. It indicates the method return value should map to the response payload. The `@ResponsePayload` annotation is used only if the method has any return value; and it is not applicable if the method has void return type.

The use of the `@ResponsePayload`-annotation is given below.

```
@PayloadRoot(namespace="http://springws.ws.learning.com/emp/schemas",
             localPart="getEmployeeRequest")
@ResponsePayload
public Element getEmployee(@RequestPayload Element employeeRequest)
throws Exception {
    // ...
    return response;
}
```

REST Annotations

This section illustrates the commonly used REST annotations.

@GET

The method annotated with `@GET` annotation is similar to HTTP GET request operation; GET requests should be used only for READ-ONLY resources. The get request should not add, modify, or delete any server-side resources. Get is a safe operation and has no side effects. "Safe" means that it should not modify any resource states on the server.

An example of the use of the `@GET`-annotation is given below.

```
public interface DocumentManager {
    @GET
    public String getDocument(String id);
}
```

@POST

The method annotated with @POST annotation is similar to HTTP POST request operation; the POST request is used for adding a new resource or to pass long parameters as a query string. The POST operation does have side effects; it will add a new resource. But in general, we use POST for things such as updates and for deleting and adding resources; because of this, the use of DELETE, PUT becomes minimal in Web applications. HTML forms support only GET and POST requests, so we have to improvise to identify DELETE and PUT requests using hidden fields in the HTML form. An example use of @POST-annotation is given below.

```
public interface DocumentManager {
    @POST
    public void addDocument(String id);
}
```

@DELETE

The method annotated with @DELETE annotation is similar to HTTP DELETE operation; the DELETE operations are idempotent and used for deleting a resource. Whether you delete a resource at a specific URL once or ten times, the effect is the same. In general, we tunnel the DELETE and PUT requests through POST, because the HTML form supports only GET and POST. An example use of @DELETE annotation is given below.

```
public interface DocumentManager {
    @DELETE
    public void deleteDocument(String id);
}
```

@PUT

The method annotated with @PUT annotation is similar to HTTP PUT; the PUT operations are idempotent and are used for replacing a resource. Whether you replace a resource at a specific URL once or ten times, the effect is the same. An example use of @PUT annotation is given below.

```
public interface DocumentManager {
    @PUT
    public void replaceDocument(String id);
}
```

@Path

The @Path annotation is used to identify the entry point of a service and its operation to be executed. This annotation can be used at class and method levels. This annotation looks for an URI path and searches for the exact match at the class and method levels to determine which method of the class should be executed. An example of the use of the @Path annotation is given below.

The URL provided below invokes the "getGrades()" method of "GradeManager" service.

```
http://localhost:8080/wsbook/services/gradeservice/grades
```

It looks for the matching URI path "/gradeservice" at the class level and "/grades" at the method level. The matching operation of a service class will be executed.

```
@Path("/gradeservice/")
public interface GradeManager {
    @GET
    @Path("/grades")
    public String getGrades();
}
```

Similarly, the URL provided below invokes the "getGradeSubjects()" method of "GradeManager" service.

```
http://localhost:8080/wsbook/services/gradeservice/grade/{grade}
```

The service class is given below.

```
@Path("/gradeservice/")
public interface GradeManager {
    @GET
    @Path("/grade/{grade}")
    public String getGradeSubjects(@PathParam("grade") Integer grade) ;
}
```

@Produces

This refers to the type of content a server delivers to the client. The @Produces annotation can be used at the class level and method level. It is allowed to declare more than one content type and is represented as @Produces("application/xml," "plain/text"). If it is declared at the method level and class level, the method-level annotation overrides that of the class level, and it produces the content type declared at the method level. An example of the use of a @Produces annotation is given below.

```
@Path("/gradeservice/")
@Produces("application/xml")
public interface GradeManager {
    @GET
    @Path("/grades")
    @Produces("plain/text")
    public String getGrades();
}
```

At the class level, it is declared to deliver the "application/xml" content type, and at the method level, it produces the "plain/text" content type. The method-level annotation overrides the class-level annotation and sends the "plain/text" content back to the client.

@Consumes

This refers to the type of content a server receives from the client. This annotation can be used at the class level and method level. It is represented as @Consumes("application/xml"), is allowed to declare more than one content type, and is represented as

`@Consumes("application/xml," "application/html")`. An example of the use of the `@Consumes`-annotation is given below.

```
@Path("/loginservice/")
@Consumes("application/x-www-form-urlencoded")
public class AccessManagerImpl {
    @POST
    @Path("/userName/{userName}/password/{password}")
    public void postUserData(MultivaluedMap<String,String> formParams) {
        ...
    }
}
```

@PathParam

The `@PathParam` annotation is used at the method level (parameter to method) to obtain the parameter values specified in the REST URL. The following example obtains the parameter values of {grade} and {subject} specified in the REST URL.

```
@Path("/gradeservice/")
public interface GradeManager {
    @GET
    @Path("/grade/{grade}/subject/{subject}")
    public String getSubjectTopics(@PathParam("grade") Integer grade,
                                   @PathParam("subject") String subject);
    ...
}
```

@QueryParam

The `@QueryParam` annotation is used at the method level to obtain the query string values specified in the REST URL. An example of the use of the `@QueryParam`-annotation is given below.

```
public class StockServiceImpl {
    @Path("/symbol")
    public String getStockPrice(@QueryParam("symbol") String symbol) {
        if(symbol.equalsIgnoreCase("GOLD")) {
            return "160.30";
        } else if(symbol.equalsIgnoreCase("XXX")) {
            return "10.0";
        }
        return symbol;
    }
}
```

@FormParam

The `@FormParam` annotation is used with content type "application/x-www-form-urlencoded" along with the HTTP-POST operation. This is used to receive the HTML form data at service endpoint after the client submits the HTML form using the HTTP POST method. An example of the use of `@FormParam`-annotation is given below.

The following code receives the individual field's data in method-level variables.

```
@POST
@Path("/userName/{userName}/password/{password}")
public void postUserData(@FormParam("userName") String userName,
                         @FormParam("password") String password) {
    ...
}
```

The following code receives the entire HTML form data in a map. Iterate the map to get the required values.

```
@POST
@Path("/userName/{userName}/password/{password}")
public void postUserData(MultivaluedMap<String, String> formParams) {
    for(String key : formParams.keySet()) {
        ...
    }
}
```

@MatrixParam

This annotation is used at the method level to extract the values of URI matrix parameter key value pairs. An example of the use of @MatrixParam-annotation is given below.

```
@Path("/bookservice/")
@Produces("text/plain")
public interface BookService {
    @GET
    @Path("/book/{year}")
    String getBooks(@PathParam("year") String year,
                @MatrixParam("author") String author,
                @MatrixParam("country") String country);
}
```

The URL used to invoke the above service is given below.

```
http://localhost:8080/wsbook/services/bookservice/book/2012;author=sriniv
as;country=usa
```

@Context

This annotation is used at method level (as a method parameter). The @Context annotation is used to get a handle to the HttpHeaders, UriInfo, Request, HttpServletRequest, HttpServletResponse, SecurityContext, HttpServletConfig, and ServletContext classes. These objects can be used to manipulate the parameter values specified in the REST URL. An example of the use of @Context annotation is given below.

```
@Path("/dataservice/")
@Produces("application/xml")
public class RestDataManagerImpl {
    @GET
```

```
@Path("/contextinfo")
public void getCommmonInfo(@Context UriInfo uriInfo,
                           @Context HttpHeaders headers,
                           @Context HttpServletRequest req) {
    ...
    }
}
```

@DefaultValue

The `@DefaultValue` annotation can be used at field level or method level to assign a default value to a variable if it does not find the key value.

Spring-AOP Annotations

This section illustrates the commonly used Spring-AOP annotations and they are listed below.

- @Aspect
- @Before
- @After
- @AfterReturning
- @AfterThrowing
- @Around

@Aspect

In Spring-AOP, the `@Aspect`-annotated classes are called aspects. The `@Aspect`-annotated class can be configured in like a regular Java bean. An example `@Aspect`-annotated class is provided below.

```
@Aspect
public class AuditAspect {
    ...
    }
```

The corresponding application context configuration of the aspect bean is provided below.

```
<bean id="auditAspect" class="com.learning.spring.aop.audit.AuditAspect">
    ...
</bean>
```


@Before

The before advice is declared in an aspect using `@Before` annotation. This advice runs before the method execution. An example of the use of such annotation is provided below. In this example, the `@Before`-annotation intercepts the `adduser()` method of a `UserDAO` class.

```
@Before("execution(* com.learning.spring.aop.dao.UserDAO.addUser(..))")
```

```
public void addBeforeAuditRecord(JoinPoint joinPoint) {
    ...
}
```

@After

The after advice is declared in an aspect using `@After` annotation. An example of this annotation's use is provided below. In this example, the `@After`-annotation intercepts the `adduser()`-method of a `UserDAO` interface. This advice runs after exiting the method execution.

```
@After("execution(* com.learning.spring.aop.dao.UserDAO.addUser(..))")
public void addAfterAuditRecord(JoinPoint joinPoint) {
    ...
}
```

@AfterReturning

The after returning advice is declared in an aspect using `@AfterReturning` annotation. An example of this annotation's use is provided below. In this example, the `@AfterReturning`-annotation intercepts the `getInsertedUserId()` method of a `UserDAO` interface. This advice runs after the method returns a result and can also intercept the returned result.

```
@AfterReturning(pointcut = "execution(* com.learning.spring.aop.dao.
            UserDAO.getInsertedUserId(..))", returning = "result")
public void auditAfterReturning(JoinPoint joinPoint, Object result) {
    ...
}
```

@AfterThrowing

The after throwing advice is declared in an aspect using the `@AfterThrowing` annotation. An example of this annotation's use is provided below. In this example, the `@AfterThrowing`-annotation intercepts the `addUserThrowsException()` method of a `UserDAO` interface. This advice runs after the `addUserThrowsException()` method throws an exception.

```
@AfterThrowing(pointcut = "execution(* com.learning.spring.aop.dao.
        UserDAO.addUserThrowsException(..))",throwing = "error")
public void logAfterThrowing(JoinPoint joinPoint, Throwable error) {
    ...
}
```

@Around

The around advice is declared in an aspect using the `@Around` annotation. An example of this annotation's use is provided below. In this example, the `@Around` annotation intercepts the `addUserAround()` method of a `UserDAO` interface. This advice runs around (before and after) the matched method.

```
@Around("execution(* com.learning.spring.aop.dao.
                    UserDAO.addUserAround(..))")
public void auditAround(ProceedingJoinPoint joinPoint) throws Throwable {
    ...
}
```

Spring-Batch Annotations

This section illustrates the commonly used Spring-Batch annotations and they are listed below.

- @Scheduled
- @Async

@Scheduled

The spring-provided @Scheduled-annotation can be used to schedule an operation periodically with the specified time interval. This annotation is used along with the trigger metadata at method level, and it also supports the Cron-based timer expressions. An example use of the @Scheduled-annotation is given below.

```
@Scheduled(fixedDelay = 5000)
public void generateMenu() throws Exception {
    ...
}

@Scheduled(fixedRate = 3000)
public void generateMenu() throws Exception {
    ...
}
```

The following example uses a Cron expression.

```
@Scheduled(cron="*/5 * * * * MON-FRI")
public void generateMenu() throws Exception {
    ...
}
```

The @Scheduled-annotation metadata terminology is defined below.

- fixedDelay → Time difference between the competition of the previous task and starting of the next task
- fixedRate → Time difference between the starting of the previous task and starting of the next task.
- cron="*/5 * * * * MON-FRI" → runs for every five minutes Monday-to-Friday.

@Async

The spring-provided @Async-annotation can be used for asynchronous task execution. This annotation is used at method level. An example use of @Async annotation is given below.

```
```

```
@Async
public void generateMenu() throws Exception {
    ...
}
```

The following XML element is used to enable `@Service` and `@Async` annotations.

```
<task:annotation-driven/>
```

Spring-Security Annotations

This section illustrates the commonly used Spring-Security annotations and they are listed below.

- @PreAuthorize
- @PostAuthorize

@PreAuthorize

This annotation is used for pre-authorization and access control checks. The spring-provided `@PreAuthorize` annotation can be used for method and class-level authorization. This is the annotation most commonly used to provide the access control to a method or class. Spring expression language can be used to validate the method parameters. The following example demonstrates the use of the `@PreAuthorize` annotation.

```
public interface MainService {

    @PreAuthorize("hasRole('ROLE_ADMIN')")
    public void deleteAccount();

    @PreAuthorize("hasRole(#user.role)")
    public String getAccountHolderName(User user);

    @PreAuthorize("hasPermission(#account, 'fullcontrol') and
                    #account.balance > #amount")
    public void createAccount(Account account, Long amount);
}
```

The following example demonstrates the use of `@PreAuthorize`-annotation with spring controller. This checks the access-control before invoking the controller class.

```
@Controller
@PreAuthorize("hasAnyRole('ROLE_ADMIN', 'ROLE_USER', 'ROLE_SU')")
public class MainController {
    ...
}
```

@PostAuthorize

This annotation is used for post-authorization checks and for access control checks after a method has been invoked. The following example demonstrates the use of the `@PostAuthorize` annotation.

```
@PostAuthorize("hasPermission(returnObject, 'read')")
Account getAccount(String accountNumber) {
    ...
}
```

The following XML configuration enables the use of pre-post authorization annotations.

```
<security:global-method-security  pre-post-annotations="enabled"/>
```

Spring-JMX Annotations

This section illustrates the commonly used Spring-JMX annotations and they are listed below.

- @ManagedResource
- @ManagedOperation
- @ManagedAttribute
- @ManagedOperationParameters
- @ManagedOperationParameter

@ManagedResource

The `@ManagedResource` annotation is used at class level. This annotation marks the class as a JMX-managed bean and registers the instance of a class with JMX server. The following example demonstrates the use of `@ManagedResource`-annotation.

```
@ManagedResource(objectName = "bean:name=annotationEmployeeImpl",
        description = "JMX Managed Bean",
        currencyTimeLimit = 15,
        persistPolicy = "OnUpdate", persistPeriod = 200,
        persistLocation = "employeeImpl", persistName = "employeeImpl")
public class AnnotationEmployeeImpl implements EmployeeMBean {
    ...
}
```

@ManagedOperation

The `@ManagedOperation` annotation is used at method level. This annotation exposes the Java bean method as a JMX-managed bean operation. The following example demonstrates the use of `@ManagedOperation`-annotation.

```
@ManagedOperation(description = "Calculate Total Salary")
public int calculateTotalSalary(int base, int bonus) {
    return base + bonus;
```

```
}
```

@ManagedAttribute

The `@ManagedAttribute` annotation is used only for getter-and-setter methods. This annotation exposes the Java bean properties as a JMX-managed bean attributes. The following example demonstrates the use of `@ManagedAttribute`-annotation.

```
@ManagedAttribute(description = "The Name Attribute",
                    persistPolicy = "OnUpdate")
public void setName(String name) {
    this.name = name;
}
```

@ManagedOperationParameters and @ManagedOperationParameter

These annotations are used at method level for method parameters to define their descriptions. The following example demonstrates the use of these annotations.

```
@ManagedOperationParameters({
    @ManagedOperationParameter(name = "base",
                              description = "Base Amount"),
    @ManagedOperationParameter(name = "bonus",
                              description = "Bonus Amount")})
public int calculateTotalSalary(int base, int bonus) {
    return base + bonus;
}
```

Spring Namespaces

This section illustrates the various spring-supported XML namespaces.

<xmlns:beans>

The Spring-provided `<xmlns:beans>` namespace tags are used to configure the spring beans and bean metadata. An example use is provided below.

```
<?xml version="1.0" encoding="UTF-8"?>
<beans xmlns="http://www.springframework.org/schema/beans"
    xmlns:xsi="http://www.w3.org/2001/XMLSchema-instance"
    xsi:schemaLocation="http://www.springframework.org/schema/beans
    http://www.springframework.org/schema/beans/spring-beans-3.0.xsd">

    <!-- Employee class configured in Spring -->
    <bean id="employee" class="com.learning.spring.core.Employee"/>

    <!-- Department class configured in Spring -->
    <bean> id="dept" class="com.learning.spring.core.Department"
```

```
                scope="protoype">
        ...
    </bean>
</beans>
```

<xmlns:context>

The Spring-provided `<xmlns:context>` namespace tags are used to deal with
`ApplicationContext`-related configurations. Spring container uses this information to do the
required ground work.

The following XML tag used to auto-scan the `@Component`-annotated classes.

```
<context:component-scan base-package="com.learning.spring.controller"/>
```

The following XML tag enables the use of annotations in spring bean classes.

```
<context:annotation-config/>
```

The following XML tag imports the properties from a supplied properties file.

```
<context:property-placeholder location="classpath:database.properties"/>

<bean id="driverManagerDataSource" class="org.springframework.jdbc.
        datasource.DriverManagerDataSource">
    <property name="url" value="${jdbc.url}"/>
    <property name="username" value="${jdbc.username}"/>
    <property name="password" value="${jdbc.password}"/>
</bean>
```

<xmlns:jee>

The Spring-provided `<xmlns:jee>` namespace tags are used to deal with Java EE-related
configurations, such as JNDI look-up for data sources, JNDI look-up for message queues, JNDI
look-up for connection factories, and JNDI look-up for enterprise java bean references.

The following XML tag is used to obtain the reference to the datasource which is configured with
your Tomcat server.

```
<?xml version="1.0" encoding="UTF-8"?>
<beans ...>
    <!-- Using JNDI look-up for datasource -->
    <jee:jndi-lookup id="mySQLDataSource" jndi-name="mysqltestdb"/>

    <!-- JDBC access to the datasource -->
    <bean id=" springJdbcTemplate"
        class="org.springframework.jdbc.core.JdbcTemplate">
        <constructor-arg>
            <ref bean="mySQLDataSource"/>
        </constructor-arg>
    </bean>
</beans>
```

The following XML tag is used to obtain the reference to the JMS connection factory, which is configured with your JMS-Provider.

```
<jee:jndi-lookup id="testJMSConnectionFactory"
                 jndi-name="pojo/jms/testjmsfactory"
                 lookup-on-startup="true"/>
```

The following XML tag is used to obtain the reference to the JMS destination, which is configured with your JMS-Provider.

```
<jee:jndi-lookup id="testJMSQueue"
                 jndi-name="pojo/jms/testjmsqueue"
                 lookup-on-startup="true"/>
```

The following XML tag is used to register the MDP with the message container. The configured ProcessMonitorMDP class receives the messages from JMS-Queue.

```
<jms:listener destination="testJMSQueue"
              ref="processMonitorMDP"
              selector="MessageType IN ('DAILY_POLLER_MSG')"/>
```

The following `<jee:local-slsb/>` XML tag is used for accessing the deployed EJB component.

```
<jee:local-slsb id="studentEJB"
     jndi-name="StudentServiceIF#
                       com.learning.spring.ejb.StudentServiceIF"
     business-interface="com.learning.spring.ejb.StudentServiceIF"/>
```

<xmlns:jms>

The Spring-provided `<xmlns:jms>` namespace tags are used to deal with JMS-related message listeners and message listener containers. The following XML tag is used to register the MDP with the message container. The configured ProcessMonitorMDP class receives the messages from JMS-Queue.

```
<jms:listener-container connection-factory="testJMSConnectionFactory"
        destination-resolver="destinationResolver"
        concurrency="2-10">

    <!-- MDP to process incoming messages -->
    <jms:listener destination="testJMSQueue"
                  ref="processMonitorMDP"
                  selector="MessageType IN ('DAILY_POLLER_MSG')"/>

</jms:listener-container>
```

<xmlns:util>

The Spring-provided `<xmlns:util>` namespace tags are commonly used for Java EE-collection configurations, configuring constant values, and referencing constant values.

The following XML tag creates a `java.util.Map` from the supplied key-values.

```xml
<util:map id="permissionsMap">
    <entry key="ROLE_ADMIN" value-ref="admin"/>
    <entry key="ROLE_USER" value-ref="user"/>
    <entry key="ROLE_SU" value-ref="su"/>
</util:map>
```

The following XML tag creates a `java.util.List` from the supplied list of values.

```xml
<util:list id="permissions">
    <value>READ</value>
    <value>WRITE</value>
    <value>ALL</value>
</util:list>
```

The following XML tag creates a `java.util.Set` from the supplied list of values.

```xml
<util:set id="subjects">
    <value>Math</value>
    <value>Reading</value>
    <value>History</value>
</util:set>
```

The following XML tag creates a `java.util.Properties` from the "database.properties" file.

```xml
<util:properties id="databaseConfiguration"
                location="classpath:database.properties"/>
```

< xmlns :aop>

The Spring-provided `<xmlns:aop>` namespace tags are used for configuring the aspects, pointcut expressions and advices. The following element in application context file enables the @AspectJ-support in spring. Using this configuration spring automatically detects the @AspectJ-annotated classes.

```xml
<aop:aspectj-autoproxy/>
```

An example use of "before" advice configuration is provided below.

```xml
<aop:config>
    <aop:aspect id="aspectAuditing" ref="auditAspect">
        <!-- Pointcut expression -->
        <aop:pointcut id="pointCutBefore"
            expression="execution(* com.learning.spring.aop.dao.
                    UserDAO.addUser(..))"/>
        <!-- @Before advice -->
        <aop:before pointcut-ref="pointCutBefore"
                    method="addBeforeAuditRecord"/>
    </aop:aspect>
</aop:config>
```

An example use of "after" advice configuration is provided below.

```
<aop:after pointcut-ref="pointCutAfter" method="addAfterAuditRecord"/>
```

An example use of "after-returning" advice configuration is provided below.

```
<aop:after-returning returning="result"
        pointcut-ref="pointCutAfterReturning"
        method="auditAfterReturning"/>
```

An example use of "after-throwing" advice configuration is provided below.

```
<aop:after-throwing throwing="error"
        pointcut-ref="pointCutAfterThrowing"
        method="auditAfterThrowing"/>
```

An example use of "around" the advice configuration is provided below.

```
<aop:around pointcut-ref="pointCutAround" method="auditAround"/>
```

< xmlns:tx/>

The Spring-provided `<xmlns:tx>` namespace tags are used for spring transaction management. The following XML tag is used to configure the advice for interface methods.

```
<tx:advice id="txAdvice" transaction-manager="txManager">
    <tx:attributes>
        <tx:method name="get*" read-only="true"/>
        <tx:method name="*"/>
    </tx:attributes>
</tx:advice>
```

The following XML element enable the annotation-based transaction behavior.

```
<tx:annotation-driven transaction-manager="txManager"/>
```

<xmlns:lang>

The spring-provided `<xmlns:lang>` namespace tags are used to integrate spring with other languages such as JRbuy or Groovy. Spring-provided `<xmlns:lang/>` tags are used to expose the objects written in other languages such as JRuby or Groovy as spring beans in Spring container.

<xmlns:cxf>

The Apache-CXF provides XML tags to configure the Web Service endpoint with JAX-WS and JAX-RS runtimes. Both Spring and CXF tags can co-exist in the same configuration file. Configure the SOAP-based web service endpoint using "<jaxws:endpoint/>" tag; and REST-based endpoint using "<jaxrs:serviceBeans>" tag. The Spring container loads the service implementation class into corresponding SOAP and REST runtime environments.

The use of CXF tags "<jaxws:endpoint/>" and "<jaxrs:serviceBeans>" are provided below. The following XML configures the JAX-WS endpoint.

```
<jaxws:endpoint id="jaxwsGradeService"
            implementor="#gradeManagerImpl"
            address="/jaxwsGradeService"/>
```

The following XML configures the JAX-RS endpoint.

```
<jaxrs:server id="restGradeService" address="/">
    <jaxrs:serviceBeans>
        <ref bean="gradeManagerImpl"/>
    </jaxrs:serviceBeans>
</jaxrs:server>
```

<xmlns:mvc>

Spring-provided `<mvc:annotation-driven/>` tag can be used dispatch the web requests to the controllers. This tag will configure two beans; `DefaultAnnotationHandlerMapping` and `AnnotationMethodHandlerAdapter`. The required configuration is provided below.

```
<mvc:annotation-driven/>
```

<xmlns:drools>

The Drools-provided `<xmlns:drools>` namespace can be used to integrate the Drools with spring framework. The drools provided XML tags are similar to spring tags, and they can be used along with spring tags in application context XML files.

The following XML tag is used to define a rule resource in spring.

```
<drools:resource id="planStatusDRL" type="DRL"
            source="classpath:planstatus.drl"/>
```

The following XML tag is used to define the drools knowledge base.

```
<drools:kbase id="knowledgeBase">
    ...
</drools:kbase>
```

The following XML tag is used to define the drools knowledge session. Application uses this session to execute the rules.

```
<drools:ksession id="knowledgeSession" type="stateless"
            kbase="knowledgeBase"/>
```

\<xmlns:task\>

The spring-provided `<xml:task>` namespace can be used to configure batch scheduling and task execution. This namespace provides support for fixed-time and Cron-based configurations for batch scheduling and task execution.

The following XML element creates a `ThreadPoolTaskScheduler` instance with specified thread pool size.

```
<task:scheduler id="taskScheduler" pool-size="4"/>
```

The following XML element is used to execute the `run(...)` method of a specified class.

```
<task:executor id="taskExecutor" pool-size="5-25"
               queue-capacity="100"/>
```

\<xmlns:batch\>

Spring batch integration framework provides utilities for reading, transforming and writing large volumes of data. The spring-provided `<xmlns:batch>` namespace can be used to configure and execute the batch jobs. An example use of this namespace is given below.

```
<batch:job id="readWriteJob" job-repository="jobRepository">
    <batch:step id="readWriteStep">
        <batch:tasklet>
            <batch:chunk reader="fileItemReader"
                         processor="processor"
                         writer="fileItemWriter"
                         commit-interval="10"/>
        </batch:tasklet>
    </batch:step>
</batch:job>
```

\<xmlns:security/\>

The spring `<xmlns:security>` namespace provides a set of XML tags that can be used to configure spring security. This eliminates the complexity of declaring the multiple spring beans and the syntax looks cleaner in your application context files. To start using this namespace, the application requires the "spring-security-config.jar" file on your classpath. The schema declaration syntax in your application context is provided below.

```
<beans xmlns="http://www.springframework.org/schema/beans"
    xmlns:security="http://www.springframework.org/schema/security"
    xmlns:xsi="http://www.w3.org/2001/XMLSchema-instance"
    xsi:schemaLocation="http://www.springframework.org/schema/beans
    http://www.springframework.org/schema/beans/spring-beans-3.0.xsd
    http://www.springframework.org/schema/security
    http://www.springframework.org/schema/security/
                spring-security-3.1.xsd">

    <security:debug/>
```

```
      . . .
</beans>
```

The following XML configuration enables the debug information.

```
<security:debug/>
```

The following XML element enable the web application security.

```
<security:http auto-config='true'>
```

The `security` attribute of the below provided `<http>` element specifies the URL patterns that does not require authentication.

```
<security:http pattern="/css/**" security="none"/>
<security:http pattern="/login.jsp" security="none"/>
```

The following XML element configures the role required to access the specified url pattern.

```
<security:intercept-url pattern="/**" access="ROLE_USER"/>
```

The following XML configures the users, credentials and roles.

```
<security:authentication-manager>
     <security:authentication-provider>
          . . .
     </security:authentication-provider>
</security:authentication-manager>
```

The following XML configures the expression evaluator class.

```
<security:global-method-security  pre-post-annotations="enabled">
     <security:expression-handler ref="expressionHandler"/>
</security:global-method-security>
```

<xmlns:sws/>

The spring-provided `<xmlns:sws>` namespace tags can be used to configure web service endpoints with spring runtime. The following XML tag enables the use of spring web service annotations in web service endpoint classes.

```
<sws:annotation-driven/>
```

The following XML generates a WSDL from XSD schema. Spring runtime generates WSDL operations for all request-and-response elements.

```
<sws:dynamic-wsdl id="employee" portTypeName="EmployeePortType"
     locationUri="/services/employeeService/"
     targetNamespace="http://springws.learning.com/emp/definitions">
     <sws:xsd location="/WEB-INF/employee.xsd"/>
</sws:dynamic-wsdl>
```

Spring Templates

This section illustrates the various spring-provided template classes.

JdbcTemplate

This is the core class used in Spring-JDBC to execute SQL statements such as select, inserts, delete, and update, as well as stored procedures and functions. This `JdbcTemplate` class encapsulates database-specific information such as datasource, connection, statement, resultset creation, and cleanup. The `JdbcTemplate` class is obtained by injecting a `DataSource` reference. The following XML element provides the required XML configuration in the spring application context file.

```xml
<bean id="springJdbcTemplate"
    class="org.springframework.jdbc.core.JdbcTemplate">
    <property name="dataSource">
        <ref bean="mySqlDataSource"/>
    </property>
</bean>
```

Alternatively, configure the `DataSource` as spring bean; use this datasource reference to create a `JdbcTemplate` instance. An example code is provided below.

```java
JdbcTemplate jdbcTemplate = new JdbcTemplate(dataSource);
```

HibernateTemplate

This is the core class used in spring-based hibernate to execute SQL statements such as select, insert, delete, and update, as well as stored procedures and functions. The `HibernateTemplate` class is obtained by injecting a `SessionFactory` reference. An example `HibernateTemplate` configuration is provided below.

```xml
<bean id="hibernateTemplate"
    class="org.springframework.orm.hibernate3.HibernateTemplate">
    <property name="sessionFactory">
        <ref bean="sessionFactory"/>
    </property>
</bean>
```

SqlSessionTemplate

This is the core class used in spring-based MyBatis for executing SQL statements such as select, insert, delete, and update as well as stored procedures and functions. The `SqlSessionTemplate` class is obtained by injecting the `SqlSessionFactory` reference. An example of a `SqlSessionTemplate` configuration is provided below.

```xml
<bean id="sqlSessionTemplate" class="org.mybatis.spring.
                SqlSessionTemplate">
    <constructor-arg index="0" ref="sqlSessionFactory"/>
```

```
</bean>
```

TransactionTemplate

Spring provides the `TransactionTemplate` class to execute the methods in a transaction. The `status.setRollbackOnly()` method rolls back the transaction if any exception occurs within the scope of a transaction. An example use of `TransactionTemplate` class is provided below.

```
public void doInsertAndUpdateUsingTxTemplate() {

    transactionTemplate.execute(new TransactionCallbackWithoutResult() {
        protected void doInTransactionWithoutResult(
                        TransactionStatus status) {
            try {
                // Insert a record
                insertPet(petDVO);

                // Create an error to get the exception
                int i = 0;
                int j = 100 / i;

                // Update a record
                updatePetData("Steven Sun", "Buffy");

            } catch (Exception ex) {
                // Printing the transaction status
                System.out.println(" is Completed " +
                        status.isCompleted());
                status.setRollbackOnly();
            }
        }
    });
}
```

JmsTemplate

Spring provides a `JmsTemplate` helper class to send-and-receive messages asynchronously. The methods `send(...)` and `convertAndSend(...)` are used to send messages. The methods `receive(...)` and `receiveAndConvert(...)` are used for synchronous message reception.

The following code is used to send messages to a Queue. Refer to Spring-messaging chapter for complete details.

```
jmsTemplate.send(synchJMSQueue, new MessageCreator() {
    ...
}
```

The following code is used to send map messages to a Queue. Refer to Spring-messaging chapter for complete details.

```
jmsTemplate.convertAndSend(jmsQueue, map, new MessagePostProcessor() {
    ...
```

```
}
```

The following code is used to receive messages from a Queue. Refer to Spring-messaging chapter for complete details.

```
Object msg = jmsTemplate.receiveAndConvert(JMSQueue);
```

WebServiceTemplate

The `WebServiceTemplate` class is used for accessing the Spring-based web service endpoints. This class contains methods to send "Source" as request-payload, and receives response-payload as "Source" or "Result". The Web service client can also marshal request objects to XML and un-marshal the response XML to objects. The commonly used client methods of the Spring web service template class are listed below.

The following method sends the "Source" as input and receives "Result" as output.

```
webServiceTemplate.sendSourceAndReceiveToResult(source, result);
```

The following method sends the "Source" as input and receives "Object" as output.

```
Object result = webServiceTemplate.marshalSendAndReceive(source);
```

RESTTemplate

The Spring-provided `RestTemplate` class is used to invoke REST-based Web service endpoints. The client code provided below illustrates the use of the `RestTemplate` class.

The following example, client is passing a single parameter to invoke the REST service.

```
RestTemplate restTemplate = new RestTemplate();
String requestURL1 = "http://localhost:8080/wsbook/
                     services/gradeservice/grade/{grade}";
String result = restTemplate.getForObject(
               requestURL1, String.class, "1");
```

The following example, client is passing multiple parameters to invoke the REST service.

```
Map<String, String> vars = new HashMap<String, String>();
vars.put("grade", "1");
vars.put("subject", "Java");

String requestURL2 = "http://localhost:8080/wsbook/services/gradeservice/
                     grade/{grade}/subject/{subject}";
String result1 = restTemplate.getForObject(requestURL2,
                 String.class, vars);
```

The below provided example, client is passing multiple parameters to invoke the REST service.

```
Map<String, String> topics = new HashMap<String, String>();
```

```
vars.put("grade", "1");
vars.put("subject", "Math");
vars.put("topic", "Mathematics and art");

String requestURL3 = "http://localhost:8080/wsbook/services/gradeservice/
                     grade/1/subject/{subject}/topic/{topic}";
String result2 = restTemplate.getForObject(requestURL3,
                                     String.class, vars);
```

JndiTemplate

The `JndiTemplate` is a utility class used for JNDI lookup operations. This template class used to deal with Java EE-related configurations, such as JNDI look-up for data sources, JNDI look-up for message queues, JNDI look-up for connection factories, and JNDI look-up for enterprise java bean references. An example configuration is provided below.

The following XML configuration is used for getting the provider-specific initial context.

```xml
<bean id="jndiTemplate" class="org.springframework.jndi.JndiTemplate">
    <property name="environment">
        <props>
            <prop key="java.naming.factory.initial">
                weblogic.jndi.WLInitialContextFactory
            </prop>
            <prop key="java.naming.provider.url">
                t3://localhost:7001
            </prop>
        </props>
    </property>
</bean>
```

The following XML configuration is used to obtain a `ConnectionFactory` object reference.

```xml
<bean id="jmsConnectionFactory"
    class="org.springframework.jndi.JndiObjectFactoryBean">
    <property name="jndiTemplate">
        <ref bean="jndiTemplate"/>
    </property>
    <property name="jndiName">
        <value>pojo/jms/testjmsfactory</value>
    </property>
</bean>
```

References

The following documents and web links are referenced in this book.

Spring XML Schema configurations
http://static.springsource.org/spring/docs/2.5.3/reference/xsd-config.html

Spring projects - http://www.springsource.org/projects

Spring batch integration framework
http://static.springsource.org/spring-integration/reference/pdf/spring-integration-reference.pdf

Distributed transaction using Spring
http://www.javaworld.com/javaworld/jw-01-2009/jw-01-spring-transactions.html

MySQL installation for Windows7
http://www.landpro.com.au/Windows_7_Install_MySQL.php

MyBatis-Spring module
http://www.mybatis.org/spring/getting-started.html

MyBatis SQL maps with Spring
http://static.springsource.org/spring/docs/3.0.0.M4/reference/html/ch13s06.html

MyBatis with Spring
http://www.mybatis.org/spring/

Spring-JDBC
http://static.springsource.org/spring/docs/3.0.x/spring-framework-reference/html/jdbc.html

Hibernate - http://www.hibernate.org/

ORM Data Access with Spring - http://static.springsource.org/spring/docs/2.5.x/reference/orm.html

MySQL Database - http://www.mysql.com/

Drools business rule engine - http://www.jboss.org/drools/

Drools integration with Spring framework
http://docs.jboss.org/drools/release/5.2.0.M2/droolsjbpm-integration-docs/html/ch02.html

Constructing objects for better modularity - http://www.eclipse.org/aspectj/

AOP with Spring - http://static.springsource.org/spring/docs/2.0.8/reference/aop.html

JMX Technology
http://www.oracle.com/technetwork/java/javase/tech/javamanagement-140525.html

Spring JMX - http://www.springbyexample.org/examples/spring-jmx.html

Spring Mail - http://static.springsource.org/spring/docs/2.0.8/reference/mail.html

EJB Specification - http://download.oracle.com/otndocs/jcp/ejb-3.1-pfd-oth-JSpec/

Remote Method Invocation - http://docs.oracle.com/javase/1.4.2/docs/guide/rmi/spec/rmiTOC.html

Spring Expression Language
http://static.springsource.org/spring/docs/3.0.x/reference/expressions.html

Spring Transaction Management
http://static.springsource.org/spring/docs/2.0.x/reference/transaction.html

Message Driven POJOS - http://blog.springsource.org/2006/08/11/message-driven-pojos/

Spring Security - http://static.springsource.org/spring-security/site/

Architectural Styles and the Design of Network-based Software Architectures
http://www.ics.uci.edu/~fielding/pubs/dissertation/top.htm

Making Right Architecture Decision – Restful Services vs. "BIG" Services
http://www.jopera.org/files/www2008-restws-pautasso-zimmermann-leymann.pdf

JAX-RS Specifications - http://download.oracle.com/otndocs/jcp/jaxrs-1.0-fr-eval-oth-JSpec/

Processing XML with Java - http://www.jdom.org/downloads/docs.html

DOM4j - http://dom4j.sourceforge.net/

JDOM - http://www.jdom.org/

XML programming with JDOM - http://www.ibm.com/developerworks/java/library/j-jdom/

Universal Resource Identifiers - Axioms of Web Architecture
http://www.w3.org/DesignIssues/Axioms.html

Apache CXF - http://cxf.apache.org/

Basic Profile Version 1.1 - http://www.ws-i.org/profiles/basicprofile-1.1-2004-08-24.html

SOAP Version 1.2 - http://www.w3.org/TR/soap/

SOAP Version 1.2 Primer - http://www.w3.org/TR/2007/REC-soap12-part0-20070427/

SOAP with Attachments API for Java (SAAJ) Specification 1.1
http://download.oracle.com/otndocs/jcp/7752-saaj-1.1-spec-oth-JSpec/

The SOAP with Attachments API for Java (SAAJ) Specification 1.1
http://java.sun.com/webservices/saaj/downloads/saajarchive.html

Basic Profile Version 1.1 - http://www.ws-i.org/Profiles/BasicProfile-1.1.html

Java API for XML Web Services Annotations
http://jax-ws.java.net/jax-ws-ea3/docs/annotations.html

Java Platform, Standard Edition 6 API Specification
http://docs.oracle.com/javase/6/docs/api/javax/xml/bind/annotation/XmlType.html

Creating and Using SOAP Message Handlers
http://docs.oracle.com/cd/E12840_01/wls/docs103/webserv_adv/handlers.html

WSDL Specification - http://www.w3.org/TR/wsdl

WSDL Version 2.0 Adjuncts - http://www.w3.org/TR/wsdl20-adjuncts/wsdl20-adjuncts.pdf

WSDL Version 2.0 Primer - http://www.w3.org/TR/wsdl20-primer/wsdl20-primer.pdf

WSDL Version 2.0 Part 2: Predefined Extensions - http://www.w3.org/TR/2004/WD-wsdl20-extensions-20040803/

WSDL SOAP Binding Styles - http://www.ibm.com/developerworks/webservices/library/ws-whichwsdl/

Spring Web Services - http://www.springsource.org/spring-web-services#documentation

TOGAF Open Group Standard - http://pubs.opengroup.org/architecture/togaf9-doc/arch/

Index